£9·95

KV-045-885

PERGAMON INTERNA
of Science, Technology, Enginee ... ...u Social Studies
*The 1000-volume original paperback library in aid of education,
industrial training and the enjoyment of leisure*
Publisher: Robert Maxwell, M.C.

The Psychology of
Social Situations

Selected Readings

THE PERGAMON TEXTBOOK
INSPECTION COPY SERVICE

An inspection copy of any book published in the Pergamon International Library will
gladly be sent to academic staff without obligation for their consideration for course
adoption or recommendation. Copies may be retained for a period of 60 days from
receipt and returned if not suitable. When a particular title is adopted or recommended
for adoption for class use and the recommendation results in a sale of 12 or more copies,
the inspection copy may be retained with our compliments. The Publishers will be
pleased to receive suggestions for revised editions and new titles to be published in this
important International Library.

Other Pergamon Titles of Interest

H. GILES, P. ROBINSON & P. SMITH
Language: Social Psychological Perspectives

H. GILES & B. SAINT-JACQUES
Language and Ethnic Relations

L. KRASNER
Environmental Design and Human Behavior

M. MORRIS
Saying and Meaning in Puerto Rico

M. SHERMAN
Personality: Inquiry and Application

T. TAYLOR
Linguistic Theory and Structural Stylistics

A Journal of Related Interest

PERSONALITY AND INDIVIDUAL DIFFERENCES

An international journal of research into the structure and development of personality, and the causation of individual differences

Editor: H. J. Eysenck, Institute of Psychiatry, London

This journal publishes articles which aim either to integrate major factors of personality, with empirical paradigms from experimental, physiological, animal or clinical psychology, or seek an explanation for the causes and major determinants of individual differences in concepts derived from these disciplines.

Free specimen copies available on request

The Psychology of
Social Situations
Selected Readings

U.K.	Pergamon Press Ltd., Headington Hill Hall, Oxford OX3 OBW, England
U.S.A.	Pergamon Press Inc., Maxwell House, Fairview Park, Elmsford, New York 10523, U.S.A.
CANADA	Pergamon Press Canada Ltd., Suite 104, 150 Consumers Road, Willowdale, Ontario M2J 1P9, Canada
AUSTRALIA	Pergamon Press (Aust.) Pty. Ltd., P.O. Box 544, Potts Point, N.S.W. 2011, Australia
FRANCE	Pergamon Press SARL, 24 rue des Ecoles, 75240 Paris, Cedex 05, France
FEDERAL REPUBLIC OF GERMANY	Pergamon Press GmbH, 6242 Kronberg-Taunus, Hammerweg 6, Federal Republic of Germany

First Edition 1981

British Library Cataloguing in Publication Data

The psychology of social situations, selected readings.
1. Social psychology—Addresses, essays, lectures
2. Human behavior—Addresses, essays, lectures
I. Furnham, Adrian
II. Argyle, Michael
302   HM251   80-41189

ISBN 0-08-024319-3 (Hardcover)
ISBN 0-08-023719-3 (Flexicover)

Printed in the United States of America

Preface

Our own research into personality and social behaviour has led us to an interest in the person-situation debate, or what is now known as Interactional Psychology, and the issues that arose serendipitously from it. Some of these issues are, like the person-situation debate itself, perennially debated in the journals. These issues include the measurement of personality, the consistency or stability of behaviour across time and situations, and the 'fit' between personality and environment. However, other issues arose which were relatively new and previously neglected in the social sciences. The most important of these seemed to be the analysis of social situations—which is a natural segment of social life defined by the *people involved,* the *place of action,* and the *nature of the activities* or action occurring. It soon became apparent that we do not have a satisfactory method for analysing social situations, creating a useful taxonomy, or explaining how the social situations people find themselves in affect aspects of their social behaviour.

Consistent, slightly obsessional, collecting of relevant articles over a three year period produced a bibliography of over 1,000 articles, papers and books that dealt with the psychology of social situations. These papers were written by researchers in widely varying fields and published in diverse journals ranging from those covering architecture to anthropology, and marketing to microsociology. It became apparent to us that there was a need for a book of readings, which included a comprehensive bibliography, and that would be of use to a wide range of social scientists interested in the psychology of social situations from a broad perspective. This book is a response to that perceived need.

The book has four sections. The first section is an introduction written by the editors, which explores the reasons for the current interest in social situations and why we should consider the social situation as a new unit of psychological research. It also covers the methods of analysis and the relevance or application of a psychology of social situations.

The second section contains five widely diverse papers written by historians, educationalists, sociologists and psychologists who approach very differently the nature of the social environment. The third section, which represents the approach of social psychology to the analysis of social situations, is divided into four sub-sections representing the major trends in social psychology. The final section, which represents the way other disciplines in the social sciences have investigated social situations, also has four sections. These are studies from environmental psychologists, sociologists, socio- and psycho-linguistics and clinical psychologists.

This book is designed for advanced undergraduates and graduates in many disciplines within the social sciences and related fields. The book may usefully serve as a companion volume, or supplementary text for studies in personality theory, social psychology and micro-sociology. Each section includes a bibliography of related papers that the reader might consult to add to his/her understanding of the issues.

We would like to thank our colleagues in the Department of Experimental Psychology at the University of Oxford for their encouragement, help and constructive criticism. We would also like to thank the library staff for their assistance in tracing obscure papers, and Ann McKendry for her immeasurable assistance in preparing the text.

Adrian Furnham
Michael Argyle

March 1980

Contents

"Thus, the persisting pattern which permeates everyday life of interpreting individual behavior in the light of personal factors (Traits) rather than in the light of situational factors must be considered one of the fundamental sources of misunderstanding personality in our time. It is both the cause and the symptom of the crisis of our society."

Ichheiser, 1943

"For the social psychology of this century reveals a major lesson: often, it is not so much the kind of person a man is as the kind of situation in which he finds himself determines how he will act."

Milgram, 1974.

Introduction

This book is concerned with the situations in which social behaviour occurs, and the effects of those situations on various forms of social behaviour. Psychologists and other social scientists have long studied various forms of social behaviour in laboratories or other controlled settings far removed from the everyday situations in which those behaviours occur. More recently, however, there has been an attempt to 'recontextualize' the study of social behaviour, in order to better understand the nature of numerous situational determinants of behavior.

The interest in situational determinants of behaviour is neither new, nor exclusive to the social sciences. While fighting in the trenches of the First World War, Lewin (1917) first wrote about psychological zones and fields which he later developed into his field theory (Lewin, 1936). It was Lewin (1935) who proposed the famous equation $B = f(P,S)$. In a celebrated study, Hartshorne and May (1928) found that the honesty of children varied quite considerably from one temptation situation to the next and concluded that children's behaviour was less an outcome of their personality than of the particular situations in which they found themselves. During the 1930's there was a lively debate in American Sociology journals regarding the concept of the situation and the joint role of personality and situation in determining social behaviour (Allport, 1937; Bruno, 1931; Queen, 1931; Reinhardt, 1937; Thomas, 1928; Wirth, 1939).

Not only social scientists but philosophers, theologians and lawyers have been interested in the effects of social situations on various forms of behaviour. Popper (1957) introduced the concept of situational logic which explains human behaviour as various attempts to achieve goals or aims within limited means (Jarvie, 1972). Harré (1979) too, has paid particular attention to the analysis and structure of social episodes in understanding human action. The theologian Fletcher (1966) caused a great stir with his book *Situation Ethics* in which he argued that goodness and badness are not inherent, essential, unchangeable human qualities, but are rather descriptions of actions in different situations— they are properties, not predicates. Thus, for situation ethicists, what is good or bad, right or wrong is dependent on specific situational factors (Barclay, 1971). Lawyers too are concerned with different aspects of situational behavioural determinants—not only how the circumstances in which crimes are tried and examined affect the testimony but also how situational factors contribute to the crime committed (Anastasi, 1964).

SUMMARY OF INTRODUCTION CONTENTS

(1) The definition and use of the term situation

(2) Recent Research

    A. Developments and changes within various fields of psychology
       1. The personality-situation debate and Interactional Psychology
       2. Social skills training, anxiety research and self-monitoring therapies
       3. Ecological and environmental psychology
       4. Socio- and psycho-linguistics
       5. Social psychology
       6. Applied psychology

    B. The social psychology of the psychology experiment
       1. Psychological reactions and artifacts
       2. Ethical problems
       3. The unrepresentativeness of the laboratory
       4. Test anxiety, situational stress of measurement
       5. Neglect of wider social processes
       6. The definition of the experiment and situated identity

    C. The development and use of psychological techniques
       1. Psychological techniques
       2. Electrical and photographic equipment
       3. Statistical methods

    D. The tradition of microsociology
       1. Symbolic interactionism
       2. Ethnomethodology
       3. Ethogenics and the dramaturgical model

(3) The Analysis of Social Situations
       1. Dimensional or perceptual
       2. Componential or structural
       3. Process or applied
       4. Environmental
       5. Ecological
       6. Ethogenics or role-rules

(4) The Uses of Situational Analysis
       1. The modification or control of social behaviour
       2. The selection of people for situations and vice versa
       3. Teaching self-monitoring and training in situational skills
       4. The descriptions of situations and the construction of taxonomies

5. The invention or construction of new situations
6. Predicting social behaviour

(1) THE DEFINITION AND USE OF THE TERM SITUATION

Every aspect of experimental social psychology deals with the influence of the situation on social behaviour in the general sense. For nearly fifty years researchers have been combining situational and environmental effects in models of social behaviour (Kantor, 1926; Koffka, 1935; Lewin, 1936; Murray, 1938). As a result there are a number of widely different definitions, classifications and conceptualizations, and though there have been attempts to arrive at an agreed, unambiguous definition, none exists. Pervin (1978) has stated that "distinctions among the concepts of stimulus' situation and environment would appear to relate to the kinds of variables and relationships among variables which one considers to be critical to understanding the phenomenon of interest (p. 79)." Pervin argues in his review paper, that a stimulus may be an organism, place or thing, whereas a situation always includes an organism, a place and an action. An environment, on the other hand, includes an organization of discrete situations and characteristics that may be continuous across situations but relevant to each of them.

The psychological situation may be described or conceptualized at different levels ranging from the micro to the macro (Bronfenbrenner, 1977; Moos, 1973; Magnusson, 1978; Pervin, 1978). Magnusson (1978) has suggested five levels of definition of the psychological situation though he labels them somewhat ambiguously. The five levels are essentially the following:

A. Stimuli. Stimuli are single identifiable objects or acts. The concept of stimulus with its numerous definitional and conceptual problems, has a long history in psychology (Gibson, 1960). Pervin (1978) has outlined three major problems with the concept of stimulus. They are first, whether a stimulus can be defined independently of the perceiver; second, whether one should distinguish between actual or potential stimuli; and third, whether stimuli motivate the organism broadly or trigger specific responses only.

B. Episodes. Episodes are specific meaningful events which can be delimited as separate units of observation in terms of cause and effect, according to Argyle (1979). Watson and Potter (1972) were probably the first to use the concept of episode to describe the different things that happened at parties. Harré and Secord (1972), on the other hand, define an episode as "any sequence of happenings . . . which has some principle of unity (p. 154)." The sequence in which these episodes occur has been of particular interest to applied social psychologists (Argyle, 1978; Rausch, 1965). Forgas (1976) has argued that people from different cultures, groups and milieus have different experiences of social episodes, and hence have different cognitive representations of them.

C. Situations. Situations are physical, temporal and psychological frames of reference, determined by the external conditions on a specific occasion. Magnusson (1978) argues that stimuli and episodes are given meaning in the frame of reference, which is the situation as it is perceived and interpreted by the actors in the situation. An important distinction in the analysis of situations exists between the subjective situation as defined and perceived by participants and the objective situation as defined by the physical and social characteristics of observers' reports.

D. Settings. Settings are generalized frames of reference determined by types of situations, but without the specifications of a certain occasion. Settings function as homeostatic systems and thereby regulate and control behaviour (Pervin, 1978). Barker (1968), who uses the term *behaviour setting,* views settings as having defined boundaries and physical properties that lead them to be associated with ongoing patterns of extra-individual behaviour.

E. Environments. Environments consist of the physical and social variables that people encounter in the outer world, and which act upon people in their daily lives. This concept has been made popular by environmental psychologists, though no clear definition exists in their literature. Pervin (1978) notes that "regardless of whether the environment is defined in actual or perceived terms few definitions do much to limit or focus attention upon specific variables." (p.78).

Magnusson (1978) has reviewed and criticized seven definitions of situation in the psychological literature, yet many others exist. For our purposes we shall concentrate on two, which in combination present the most salient features of situations. Pervin (1977) defined a situation as having four major components. "A situation is described as involving a specific place, in most cases involving specific people, a specific time and specific activities." (p. 376). A situation, then, is a gestalt defined by the organization of various components consisting of who is involved, what is going on, and where the action is taking place. Furthermore, people have shared cognitive representations of typical, regularly occurring situations that they have experienced in their subculture. Forgas (1978) used the following definition: "a cognitive representation of recurring, stereotyp- ical sequences of social interaction, within a cultural environment, with consensually defined boundaries and with a set of subcultural-specific rules and norms relating to appropriate and inappropriate behaviours." (p. 435).

The reason for selecting these two definitions is that they clearly indicate the level at which the term *situation* is used, and some of its salient components which form a gestalt as well as drawing attention to the fact that all individuals have a cognitive representation of familiar situations and the social behaviours associated with them. Much of the more recent experimentation in social psychology has been based on the fact that individuals in different groups have clear representations of situations that they can imagine and respond to easily. Pervin's definition suggests that there are four major components—place, people, time, and action. Argyle's (1979) games model of the situation includes these in a list of seven elements or components that combine to form a gestalt: the elements of behaviour used, the goals or motivations of the participants, the rules of behaviour, the social or formal roles, the physical setting and equipment, salient cognitive concepts and relevant skills (Argyle, Furnham and Graham, 1981).

Magnusson (1978) has made a number of distinctions in the theoretical and empirical analysis of situations. He suggests theoretically that the structural properties of situations may be distinguished from the content characteristics. Structural properties include the extent to which the situation promotes or restrains certain behaviour, the ambiguity of situations in terms of which behaviours are appropriate and the physical aspect of the situation. Content characteristics include those listed by Argyle (1979) in his games analogy of social situations (goals, rules, roles, concepts, pieces, themes), as well as motivational variables such as needs, motives, desires, etc., anticipated outcomes or expectations, perceived control over the effective and satisfactory handling of situations and the affective tone of situations. Empirically Magnusson suggests that there are three possible approaches to the analysis of situations. They are: situation perception, which includes the perception of situational expectations, perceived control, ambiguities, interpersonal relationships, etc.; mediating motivational variables, which include needs, motives, etc.; and responses to situations, which may be somatic and affective or planned and purposive.

(2) RECENT RESEARCH

The current interest in situational determinants of social behaviour in many of the social sciences has a number of different origins independent of one another. We shall consider four different areas:

A. Developments and Changes within Various Fields of Psychology

1. The Personality-Situation Debate and Interactional Psychology. Like philosophy, psychology has a number of central questions that become fashionable to discuss and debate at certain times. One of the perennially debated questions in psychology is the extent to which stable internal (personality) or

external (situational) factors determine behaviour. This has received a great deal of attention during the last 15 years in personality and social psychology literature (Ekehammar, 1974; Sarason, Smith and Diener, 1975). The recent interest was stimulated independently by the work of Endler, Hunt and Rosenstein (1962) who demonstrated statistically that the quality and quantity of anxiety reactions is largely dependent on situational factors and the interaction of personality factors and situational differences; and that of Mischel (1968) who, after reviewing the whole field of personality research and measurement, concluded that a person's social behaviour was not directly related to his/her personality, and that personality tests are poor predictors (.25 or less) of social behaviour. These two reports, particularly the latter, led to the beginning of what was to become the person-situation debate—a debate centering upon whether social behaviour is primarily determined by the enduring personality traits of individuals or the situational pressures, rewards, and constraints within which people find themselves. Bowers (1973) pointed out that two camps existed:

1. The traitists who by using mainly correlational techniques and individuals of various salient extremes, revealed consistency of behaviour across social situations.
2. The situationalists who by using mainly experimental techniques and average or normal individuals revealed inconsistency of behaviour across social situations.

This is something of an oversimplification however and may even be considered misleading. Firstly because trait theorists have consistently used situational variables in their equations (Cattell, 1966) and do not always consider 'extreme individuals', and secondly because situational theorists do not always average over normal individuals, avoiding correlational techniques (Mischel et al., 1972). In fact the debate has been characterized by a number of pseudo issues and attempts to erect and knock down straw men. For a period the debate centred around proportions of variance accounted for by various factors (person, mode of response, situation) in 2 or 3 way ANOVA's and 'how much' questions predominated over 'how' questions i.e., how do personality and situation interact? (Endler, 1973). A number of researchers have pointed out the problems in early attempts to resolve this debate by use of S (situation)—R (response) questionnaires and ANOVA designs (Argyle, 1976; Cartwright, 1975; Golding, 1975; Jaspars and Furnham, 1979; Olweus, 1977).

However, a phoenix was to arise out of this work called Interactional Psychology according to Ekehammar (1974) the 'current zeitgeist' of modern personality psychology. The basic assumptions of the person by situation interaction model are:

1. Actual behaviour is a function of a continuous process of two directional interactions between the individual and the situations he or she encounters.
2. The individual is an intentional active agent in this interaction process.
3. On the person side of the interaction, cognitive and motivational factors are essential determinants of behaviour.

4. On the situation side, the psychological meaning of situations for the individual is the important determining factor. (Endler and Magnusson, 1976; Magnusson and Endler, 1977).

However, despite these assumptions, they are not demonstrably obvious in the studies of many interactional psychologists. The concept of interaction is, however, not without its problems as reviewers have pointed out, primarily because it has been borrowed from statistical literature and used inappropriately and inconsistently in a psychological sense (Buss, 1977; Howard, 1979; Olweus, 1977; Krauskopf, 1978). Because of the implications of the findings of interactional psychologists a number of other issues related to person-situation interactions have been discussed. These include the consistency or stability of behaviour over time and across situations (Alker, 1972; Argyle, 1976; Bem, 1972; Bem and Allen, 1974; Block, 1971; Epstein, 1979), the assessment of certain institutional psychosocial environments (Craik, 1970; Kasmar, 1970; Moos, 1974), the relationship between perception and behaviour in specific situations (Magnusson and Ekehammar, 1975, 1978) and the nature of stressful situations (Bryant and Trower, 1974; Endler and Hunt, 1969; Hodges and Felling, 1970).

Most importantly the debate has directed the attention of psychologists to analyzing the structure and function of everyday social situations in which the behaviour in which they are interested occurs. As a result many personality theorists, cognitive psychologists and social psychologists have turned their attention to the psychology of social situations (Mischel, 1979).

2. Social Skills Training, Anxiety Research, and Self-Monitoring Therapies.

The extensive theoretical and practical work on social skills training and assessment has led investigators to develop a situation specific concept of social skill and competence (Gambrill, 1977; Hersen and Bellack, 1976; Trower, Bryant and Argyle, 1978). Eisler (1978) has written: "The general application of specific behavioural skill measures to all populations in varying social situations seems doubtful. It may be that some identified behavioural measures will reflect social competence in a variety of interactive situations while others will apply to relatively few situations." (p. 393). As Argyle (1979) has pointed out, part of the recent development in the analysis of social skills has been to concentrate on social episodes and the social rules operating in social situations. Furthermore the extensive research on assertiveness has shown that not only are there different types of assertiveness but that situational rather than personal factors are primary determinants of assertiveness (Eisler et al., 1975; Furnham, 1979; Skillings et al., 1978; Zeicher et al., 1977).

Anxiety research also has begun to concentrate on situational factors that elicit anxiety forms rather than on personality differences. Endler and Hunt (1968, 1969) and Magnusson and Ekehammer (1975) have demonstrated (and replicated) certain underlying dimensions of stressful situations such as threat of punishment, anticipation, fear, and inanimate threat. Spielberger (1966, 1978) has distinguished between trait anxiety, which consists of relatively stable individual differences in the tendency to perceive as threatening and to respond with anxiety to a wide range of situations, and state anxiety, which is characterized by subjective, consciously perceived feelings of tension, apprehension, etc. in a specific situation. Spielberger has demonstrated the existence of situation-specific anxiety traits and advocates an interactionist approach to the study of anxiety.

Finally clinical psychologists interested in the control of various forms of maladaptive or addictive behaviour have developed strategies based on situational appraisal and management. Best and Hakstian (1978) developed a situation-specific model for smoking behaviour which was concerned with describing and analyzing the situations that provoke people to smoke, and, hence, modifying the smoking behaviour. Similarly, Sanchez-Craig (1976) described a therapy whereby problem drinkers could control their drinking by analyzing various aspects of alcohol-related situations. Weight loss programmes have also been developed based on situational management (monitoring salient aspects of situations that provoked food intake) (Chapman and Jeffrey, 1979). Snyder (1979) has extensively studied self-monitoring processes and describes stereotypic high and low self monitors, the former changing many aspects of their social behaviour to conform to their perceived requirements of the social situation.

Thus recent work in the area of clinical and counselling psychology has begun to look at the psychological properties of everyday social situations which elicit or extinguish various forms of normal and abnormal behaviour.

3. Ecological and Environmental Psychology. The comparatively recent development of ecological and environmental psychology has made researchers much more aware of the effect of the physical environment on various forms of behaviour. Altman (1976) suggested that people × place units may act as a potentially important unit of enquiry for social and environmental psychologists. He suggested that this approach would have three advantages: it would encourage the study of the interrelationship of various behaviour modalities, it would necessitate the analysis of patterns of simultaneously occurring behaviours, and it would stress the dynamic nature of behaviour which changes over time and circumstances.

The pioneering work of Barker (1961, 1963) on behaviour settings as natural units of behaviour commonly found in communities, institutions, etc., and his emphasis on thorough observation of naturally occurring behaviour sequences made an important contribution to the psychology of social situations. Barker (1977) maintains that behaviour within the setting where people live is influenced by three classes of variables: the physical properties (amount and arrangement of space); the number, location and properties of entrances and exits; the illumination, temperature and decoration, etc.; the number and character of their programs (the sequence of events). The methodology developed by Barker has been used by his associates to study a wide range of behaviour settings (Gump, 1965; Wicker, 1969; Willems, 1967).

Environmental psychology has been responsible for developing numerous methodologies for the investigation of social situations, such as the use of unobtrusive measures; time, space, and event sampling techniques; and the application of facet analysis (Canter, 1976; Lee, 1976). Further, many concepts used by environmental psychology, particularly those associated with space-territoriality, privacy, proxemics (Ittelson et al., 1974), place-appropriateness, differentiation (Canter, 1977), stressors-overloading, enrichment (Wicker, 1966) have proved very useful in the analysis of social situations.

As Stokols (1978) has indicated, the field of environmental psychology has expanded to include cognitive and behavioural variables as well as active and reactive transactions between a person and his physical environment. The study of particular environments such as offices (Joiner, 1970), hospital wards (Trites et al., 1970), classrooms (Sommer, 1967), etc., has done a great deal to make planners and researchers more aware of the importance of situational determinants of behaviour.

4. Socio and Psycho-Linguistics. The comparatively new disciplines of socio-linguistics (Trudgill, 1977), psycho-linguistics and the social psychology of language (Giles and St. Clair, 1979; Robinson, 1972) have shown that certain aspects of language vary as a function of situational or contextual factors. Brown and Fraser (1979) have argued that there are three important situational speech markers—the setting of the interaction and its associated norms, rules, etc.; the purpose of the interaction such as the goals, tasks, topics involved; and the relationship between the participants such as their role, group membership, etc. They argue that a situational analysis of language is particularly valuable as it encourages researchers to look both at the individuals interacting in the situation and at the structure of the society that encloses the interaction. Similarly Halliday (1979) has argued that one needs to know three things about the context of the situation in order to predict linguistic features that are likely to be associated with it. They are: the field of discourse (the institutional setting, the activity, the other participants), the style or tenor of discourse (the relationship between participants, the emotional tone) and the mode of discourse (the channel of communication).

Linguists have generally used concepts such as *context* or *text* rather than *situation;* however, the rise of interest in social psychological correlates of speech and language have broadened those original concepts to that of *social situation* and its associated synonyms. Social psychologists interested in language have been particularly interested in such phenomena as accent, vocabulary, slang, and linguistic codes varying as a function of different social situations.

5. Social Psychology. Apart from the results of the person-situation debate, which have overflowed into social psychological theorizing and experimentation, there has been a paucity of organized research into social situational determinants of behaviour. More importantly there exist no theoretical models suggesting how situations function and what their components are. Endler and Edwards (1978) reviewed person × situational interaction studies in anxiety, conformity and locus of control, and noted how the studies of these social psychological processes have been erratic and atheoretical.

Argyle, Furnham and Graham (1981) reviewed the effect of various situational aspects on eight different social psychological processes—aggression, altruism, assertiveness, attraction, gaze, conformity, leadership and self disclosure. This review revealed that whereas researchers in some areas had taken cognizance of numerous situational determinants such as social rules, roles, norms, and physical props, others had done much less to investigate the immediate physical and psychological situations in which these processes occur. It also seemed that where social situational variables had been considered, these were not selected or studied in any consistent, systematic or theoretical way.

However, as Backman (1979) has pointed out, one of the themes of the new approach to, or paradigm of, social psychology is situationism—the view that social behaviours is largely determined by situational factors. He maintaines that this movement from concentrating on intra-individual variables to looking at situational variables began with leadership and interpersonal attraction studies over two decades ago, and has spread through other areas, even shifting the focus of work on social motives such as aggression and altruism to situational rather than personality explanations. Other areas of research, still within the confines of social psychology, such as proxemics and spatial behaviour, have as their starting point the social situation.

With recent work on personality and social behaviour and the studies of specific situated interactions like doctor-patient communication, social psychologists are moving from a narrowly interpersonal conception of psychological processes to a person-situation conception. Hence in social psychology there is a renewed interest in the social situation—how it is structured, how it is perceived and cognized, how it affects behaviour, how it is defined, etc.

6. Applied Psychology. Unfortunately, applied psychologists have as a rule paid more attention to academic psychologists than the other way around. Because of their limited success with prediction and description, using an intrapersonal approach to measurement and description, psychologists from a wide range of different applied areas began to take more seriously the role of the social situation in explaining that behaviour. Four examples will be considered: consumer psychology, industrial psychology, legal psychology and educational psychology.

Recently a number of studies by consumer psychologists have demonstrated that knowledge of a consumer's personality traits, desires and attitudes is not enough to be able to predict with much accuracy a consumer's choices of products and services. Studies on the effects of consumption situations have highlighted the importance of situational effects on consumer processes and the need for developing product-specific taxonomies of consumption situations. These effects have been found for the following products and services: fast foods (Belk, 1975), soft drinks (Bearden and Woodside, 1976), snack products (Lutz and Kakkar, 1975), beer (Bearden and Woodside, 1977), meat products (Belk, 1974a), mouthwash (Srivastava and Shocker, 1977) and motion pictures (Belk, 1974b).

Similarly industrial psychologists have focussed on certain situational determinants of psychological processes at work. These have included leadership style (Csoka and Bons, 1978), the desire to work (Russell and Mehrabian, 1975), group performance (Mitchell, Larson and Green, 1977; Burke, 1978), sales force performance and satisfaction (Bagozzi, 1978), and job satisfaction (Mount and Muchinsky, 1978). Applied psychologists have also adopted strategies used in social psychology such as the interactionist approach to measuring anxiety at work (Payne, Fireman and Jackson, 1978).

Psychologists interested in the law have also turned their attention to social situational determinants of behaviour. These have included situational determinants of crime reporting (Bickman and Green, 1977), eye witness testimony (Clifford and Scott, 1978) and deviance (Orcutt, 1975). Two closely related areas that have taken particular notice of social situational determinants of behaviour are attributions of responsibility and moral reasoning (Leming, 1978).

Because educational psychologists are interested in phenomena in a particular setting, they have always been interested in situational factors effecting learning. However, recent studies in education have looked particularly at situational determinants and the interaction between personality and situational factors (Stebbins, 1975; Trickett and Moos, 1970; Bryant and Trower, 1974; Ellison and Trickett, 1978).

The reasons for the current interest in the psychology of social situations are partly historical and partly theoretical. Disillusionment and limited success with old theories and methods have led many psychologists to take a broader view of psychological processes. This has not only included wider social processes in society, but also the natural social situations in which behaviour occurs. It may well be that the social situation, rather than the individual, may develop into a new unit of psychological research. This would allow much more beneficial multidisciplinary cooperation in the study of human behaviour.

B. The Social Psychology of the Psychology Experiment

The interest in the study of social situations can be seen partially as a consequence of one of the most carefully studied social situations—the psychology experiment. Over the last twenty years different criticisms of the use of laboratory experiments for the scientific analysis of social behaviour have caused what Westland (1978) described as the 'laboratory crisis'. Paradoxically this self criticism has revealed a number of important processes which occur in many social situations. Many European psychologists have made extensive and sophisticated criticisms of the experimental method (Israel and Tajfel, 1972; Tajfel and Fraser, 1978). The criticisms of the laboratory-based psychological experiment are essentially sixfold.

1. Psychological Reactance and Artefacts. This criticism is based on the fact that because of the manipulations and actions of the experimenters, the unspoken assumptions and the nature of the contract between experimenter and subject, any results that may be obtained are likely to be artefactual, epiphenomenal or biased. More specifically these criticisms are related to experimenter effects—the changes or distortions produced by specific characteristics or behaviour of the experimenter (Rosenthal, 1966); demand characteristics—explicit or implicit norms or rules of how to behave in experimental situations (Orne, 1961); volunteering subjects—studies have shown that volunteers differ on a number of criteria from nonvolunteers, which could affect experimental results (Rosenthal and Rosnow, 1969); response sets—these include socially desirable response, faking bad, acquiescence, opposition or extreme responding (Couch and Keniston, 1960); and role-playing—subjects actually playing a role implicitly demanded or expected by the experimenter (Mixon, 1972).

2. Ethical Problems. There are at least four ethical problems which often result from the standard psychological experiment. The most important is probably deception and the possible resultant suspicion on the part of subjects (Miller, 1972). A second ethical objection is the invasion of privacy where people are observed or experimented on without their consent (Westland, 1978). A third problem is of consent, that is, the subject misinterpreting or not realizing the implications of their agreed willingness to participate in experiments. Finally there are possibilities of harmful consequence or personal risk which may be intrinsic or extrinsic (Wolfenberger, 1967).

3. The Unrepresentativeness of the Laboratory. A laboratory experiment is usually designed to observe the relationship of two or more psychological variables. To ensure that the precise nature of the relationship is understood, other possibly confusing, moderating or mediating variables are 'controlled' or held constant. This often leads to highly artificial conditions, far removed from the natural situations in which this behaviour occurs. Campbell and Stanley (1966) distinguished between an experiment's internal validity—the successful and accurate measurement and presentation of variables, and its external validity—the generalisability or applicability of the findings to other populations, settings, situations or times. Clearly if the nature of the laboratory situation is very different from naturally-occurring situations the results may be quite unrepresentative and hence not generalisable.

4. Test Anxiety, Situational Stress of Measurement. It has been demonstrated that there are individual and group differences in the way people respond to psychological testing situations. Katz (1967) has shown that the performance of black university students in standard testing and laboratory situations is influenced by such factors as the race of the experimenter, the race and presence of other testees, the nature of the task, the nature of the instructions, and the personality characteristics of the subjects. Further studies of test anxiety have shown that in situations that emphasize evaluation of the subject's performance, high-test anxious groups tend to perform more poorly on general ability tests, verbal learning, and other tasks than do low-test anxious groups (Sarason, 1972).

5. Neglect of Wider Social Processes. Of necessity the psychological experiment cannot take into consideration wider sociological variables that may effect behaviour in similar situations. Traditionally experimenters vary or control subject or task variables, ignoring others, and in so 'clarifying' the problem they simplify it (Westland, 1978). It is often the subtle nebulous variables operating in natural situations that make laboratory experiments so unnatural and unreal.

6. The Definition of the Experiment and Situated Identity. Because psychologists rarely check if their definition of the experimented situation is the same as that of their subjects, it is often difficult to understand why a subject behaves in the way he or she does. Alexander and his colleagues (Alexander and Knight, 1971; Alexander and Lauderdale, 1977; Alexander and Sagatur, 1973) in a series of studies on situated identity showed that both the subjects and the experimenter identify and act in accordance with the rules of self-presentation that appear to be relevant to their definition of the experimental situation.

C. The Development and Use of Psychological Techniques

A third reason for the interest in the psychology of social situations is the development of new techniques and strategies to record, describe, and analyze social situations. Some of these have been around for a very long time but have been more recently adapted to the study of behaviour in specific social situations. There appear to be three separate types of development: the adaptation of proven psychological techniques to explore perceptions of, and reactions to, specific social situations; the development and widespread use of electrical equipment such as the video camera; and the increased sophistication of statistical techniques for describing large amounts of data.

1. Psychological Techniques. Dissatisfaction with the laboratory experiment has led researchers to adopt new techniques or adapt old ones to current problems and issues. Apart from the use of self report questionnaires, repertory grids etc., there appear to be four techniques that are used in the analysis of social situations. Nearly all have been used for some time, for other purposes, but have been very usefully adapted to studying social situations.

(i) Account gathering. Harré and Secord (1972) have argued that we need to gather and analyze the accounts that people offer of their behaviour in social situations in order to understand the structure of everyday episodes. What they are advocating is, quite simply, unstructured interviewing, which is aimed at encouraging subjects to describe in their own words their perceptions and experiences in social situations. Marsh et al. (1978) has used this technique to investigate public behaviour at football matches.

(ii) Biographies and autobiographies. This technique has been used since the 1930's, particularly by phenomenological psychologists. Bannister (1975) has argued that the use of biographies gives us unique insights into the consistency and stability of behaviour across time and situations. It also provides an accurate description of the ecology of a person's life and his habitual pattern of choice and avoidance of social situations. De Waele and Harré (1979) have advocated the use of autobiographies as a means of discovering how individuals render events intelligible. One technique they have used in evaluating autobiographies is to expose people to conflict and problem situations, and then ask them to recall and describe life story descriptions that seem to pick out moments in their life that are 'formally isomorphic' to those crises.

(iii) Role playing. The use of role-playing as a technique to investigate processes in specific social situations has been widely and very successfully used for a long time (Ginsburg, 1979). It is particularly useful in simulating situations that are otherwise difficult to investigate and for revealing some of the implicit norms of behaviour. The dramatic findings of Zimbardo on institutional behaviour in prisons and of Rosenhan on behaviour in mental hospitals both resulted from role playing experiments. Mixon (1974) has pointed out some of the problems and strengths associated with role playing.

(iv) Unobtrusive measures. The development and use of a wide range of unobtrusive techniques has meant that psychologists are able to study numerous aspects of behaviour in social situations without causing psychological reactance

(Webb et al., 1966). These techniques may vary from archival research (McClelland, 1961) to dropping letters (Milgram, 1970) and may be particularly useful in the study of particular forms of private or public behaviour in institutions and public places.

2. Electrical and Photographic Equipment. The widespread use of videotapes and associated electrical equipment attests to the usefulness of this equipment. It allows the research to record accurately nearly all salient aspects of a social situation, and these can be analyzed later at various levels. Kendon (1979) has argued that film specimens show how complex interaction is and that it allows the researchers' attention to be directed to behavioural relationships between people in different situations. However, he points out that a technical innovation does not in itself bring about new discoveries as there must also be a theoretical viewpoint to provide a rationale for using the new innovation. Videotapes have proven to be of immeasurable use in collecting and storing data. They are also helpful in therapy by providing patients with useful video feedback (Trower, Bryant and Argyle, 1978). Used in conjunction with interviews, videorecording can provide valuable insights for a wide range of situated behaviours.

Video and audio tape recorders, etc., have also proved invaluable in recording certain forms of behaviour in specific social situations. Dakin (1960) developed a taxonomy of commonly occurring situations by an analysis of over 6,000 photographs. Others have used prepared videotapes of stressful situations to elicit perceptual responses in neurotic and nonneurotic subjects (Young, 1979).

3. Statistical Methods. The development of multivariate statistical methods now allows for large amounts of data to be gathered from a person and to be subjected to analyses which provide a sensitive, multidimensional representation of complex cognitions. The three types of multivariate analyses most widely used in this regard are multidimensional scaling, three-mode factor analysis and cluster analysis. Forgas (1976) and Jones and Young (1973) have demonstrated the usefulness of multidimensional scaling in revealing how people structure or cognize common social situations in their everyday lives. Three-mode factor analysis has been successfully used to describe the structure of leisure activities (London, Crandall and Fitzgibbons, 1977) and situations in which people will engage in self-disclosure (McCloskey, 1978). Cluster analysis is also extensively used to describe the relationship between the perception of rules in various situations (Argyle et al., 1979).

If used sensitively and appropriately these tools may prove invaluable to cognitively oriented social psychologists to uncover the cognitive maps that people have of social situations.

D. The Tradition of Microsociology

Unlike psychologists, who have not specifically concentrated on the role of social situations in determining behaviour, preferring rather to look for intra- and interpersonal differences, sociologists from various theoretical traditions have consistently emphasized situational determinants of social behaviour. They have not agreed on the elements or aspects of the situation important in determining behaviour however, and three different traditions can be discerned: symbolic interactionism, ethnomethodology and ethogenics.

1. Symbolic Interactionism. Since their seminal work in 1928, Thomas and Thomas's concept of the definition of the situation—a negotiated social process of appraising one's environment—has been fundamental to symbolic interactionists. For them, situational analysis is a means whereby we can observe the difference between socially imposed and governed schemes of behaviour and the individual's personal perception of those behavioural schemes. For symbolic interactionism the most important determinant of action, and hence the most important aspect of social order, is the situation and the individual's perception of it. To understand how people define situations is to understand the meaning that situation has for them and thereby to understand why they behave as they do. Symbolic interactionists put a heavy stress on language and meaning, using examples of how the very name or label attached to social situations effects the behaviour in those situations (Whorf, 1956). Their method of analysis is usually detailed observations or participation in specially selected social situations. Much of the work in symbolic interactionism, particularly that of Goffman, has had an impact on social psychology, not least of which is to redirect psychologists interests to the process of cognising and labelling social situations (Goffman, 1964; Lauer and Handel, 1977; Stone and Farberman, 1970).

2. Ethnomethodology. Ethnomethodologists study the cognitive methods used in everyday life to construct meaningful, coherent and consistent patterns of social interaction. They are not as interested in the cultural or subcultural definition of the situation as in how people realize or make situations intelligible. As Forgas (1980) has pointed they are extremely situational in their conception of social behaviour, being concerned with the achievement of communication within the limitations of situational conventions. Although, like symbolic interactionists, they are concerned primarily with the analysis of naturalistic social situations, they differ from other sociologists on two important grounds. First, there is the exclusive concentration on rules, rule-following and conventions in social situations to the point of neglect of other important issues such as the goals of the interaction, or the physical environment. Second, there is the methodology which is primarily concerned with rulebreaking 'games', which lead to confusion and attempts to repair, and so manifest the implicit rules and conventions underlying that situation. Another technique is the observation of individuals who change groups in some way, hence becoming aware of the conventions which regulate the two groups. The work of ethnomethodologists has made researchers particularly aware of certain ritualized behaviours in social situations (Garfinkel, 1967; Schegloff and Sacks, 1973).

3. Ethogenics and the Dramaturgical Model. Perhaps more than the work of symbolic interactionists and the ethnomethodologists, the work of the sociologist Goffman (1967) and the philosopher Harré (1979) has drawn attention to the situation in which behaviour occurs. Goffman uses the model of theatre with persons as actors and the situation as the stage which defines the actor. Actors are active self-monitors of their own behaviour and role and are assumed to seek out and negotiate the script, stage directions and theme of everyday episodes in the process of interaction. Goffman (1967) distinguished between a social occasion, a gathering and a social situation; the latter being defined as "the full spatial environment anywhere within which an entering person becomes a member of the gathering that is present" (p. 144). Goffman (1974) is not particularly interested in the way people create, interpret or define situations, but in how they react to them in terms of what he calls "face-work." Through observation he has managed to sympathetically describe stereotyped, subcultural, scripted interactions in a wide range of social situations. Harré and Secord (1972), in adopting the same outlook and model, have attempted to go further than Goffman in providing a theoretical model for the understanding of everyday social episodes and situations. They present a conceptual scheme for studying and analyzing the structures of social episodes, which they call ethogenics. Harré (1979) argues that episodes reveal different structures depending on the choice of units of analysis and of time-perspectives, and suggests an act-action approach to the analysis of everyday, yet highly complex, social situations. His work methodologically differs from Goffman's as he is primarily concerned with the analysis of behavioural accounts of social situations rather than with observation.

The numerous criticisms of empirical social psychology in the 60's and 70's have led many social psychologists to study the work of microsociologists, who in their different ways have all placed heavy emphasis on the situation in which behaviour occurs, for the interpretation and explanation of that behaviour.

(3) THE ANALYSIS OF SOCIAL SITUATIONS

Once the importance of social situational determinants of behaviour has been established, an adequate conceptualisation of a situation and its relationship to behaviour has to be found. Thereafter we require techniques and strategies to analyze social situations. The psychologist interested in this analysis is in a far better position than his predecessors of fifty years ago, who were about to embark on the study of a phenomenon just as nebulous and intangible—that of personality. This is because a number of established and sophisticated research strategies already exist that may be usefully adapted to the analysis of social situations. More recently we have seen the development of strategies and theories specifically developed to analyse social situations (Argyle, Furnham and Graham, 1981, Bem and Funder, 1979; Harré, 1979).

We shall consider six different strategies that are currently being used to analyze social situations. There are fundamental differences between these approaches however, as each stems from a different tradition and has been designed to answer a different question. Each technique clearly has certain advantages and strengths as well as certain weaknesses. These approaches are not the only ones which may profitably be used; however they do represent those most commonly employed at the present and which show most promise.

1. Dimensional or Perceptual. A dimensional or perceptual approach is similar to those used by personality theorists like Cattell (1965) who seek to find the underlying dimensions or traits of individuals. This approach has borrowed many techniques from social psychology and psychophysics. Essentially this approach seeks to describe the major dimensions along which people subjectively perceive or react to a wide range of social situations. This usually involves calculating how a number of variables (semantic differential scales, situation descriptors, etc.) load on a small number of emerging dimensions. There are a number of statistical techniques appropriate for this type of analysis, the most sophisticated being multi-dimensional scaling and factor analysis. The former is a more powerful and flexible technique, though the latter is more widely used.

There are a number of possible ways of collecting data for this type of analysis, though a standard questionnaire is most commonly used. Once the stimulus situations have been selected on theoretical or empirical grounds they may be compared in terms of similarity or dissimilarity or rated on a number of pre-selected and piloted scales. The way in which the stimulus and rating scales are described, piloted and presented of course has very important consequences for the dimensions that emerge.

This technique has been successfully used to describe the underlying perceived dimensions of everyday social episodes (Forgas, 1976), the dimensions of stressful situations (Magnusson and Ekehammar, 1973, 1975), the dimensions of communication situations (Wish and Kaplan, 1977), the dimensions of the social episodes in an academic group, (Forgas, 1978) and others. Many researchers have successfully replicated their results, and also found cultural or group differences among the perceived dimensions of situations (see Chapter 3).

A number of criticisms can be made of this method. First, the methodology itself may be problematic as a good deal of pilot work is necessary to ensure that the stimuli and rating scales are appropriate (Argyle, Furnham and Graham, 1981;

Pervin, 1976). Also, the factors have to be intuitively labelled. Second, this approach is at best descriptive of differences between situations and does not tell us much about the dynamics of social situations. Argyle (1976) has argued that to describe a situation as active, formal and pleasant does not give us much idea of the nature of that situation. Third, different dimensions might arise depending on whether one used situation perception or situation reaction results (Magnusson and Ekehammar, 1978). That is, the dimensions that arise from one set of questions may not be the same as those that arise from another.

Despite its drawbacks, this approach is able to deal with large amounts of data; ratings are fast and simple; and both individual and group data can be used. Behavioural and cognitive (perceptual) scores may be used. As a preliminary to investigating the cognitive maps of subjects, or to finding an emerging pattern in a large amount of data, the dimensional approach of social situational analysis is promising (Forgas, 1979).

2. Componential or Structural. Whereas the dimensional approach seeks to provide the various salient dimensions along which social situations are experienced, the componential approach seeks to uncover the structure of everyday situations. This necessitates deciding what the important elements are and then discovering their structure in relation to one another. This approach has its origins in linguistics and ethnology, though proponents quote chemistry as examples of the way in which we should proceed (Argyle, 1976.)

Argyle, Furnham and Graham (1981) adopted this strategy, suggesting the games model analogy (Avedon, 1971). They argue that if a person were to describe satisfactorily the salient features of a game so that another person could understand it and participate, he or she would adopt a componential approach. That is he or she would describe the goal or aim of each team player, the roles, the rules, the meaning of certain game-specific concepts, the use of certain props, the advantage of certain skills, etc. Although this analogy may not apply to all social situations (Brenner, 1980)—perhaps because it implies competition rather than cooperation, or because the goals in social situations, unlike those in games, might be vague and changeable (some situations being loosely structured, for example)—it has been found to be a very useful heuristic. An important consequence of using this analogy is the stress by Argyle, Furnham and Graham (1980) on the goal structure which is seen to be the central component of situations, and around which the other components are structured. They use the idea of a mobile, ever readjusting its internal dynamics in accordance with external pressures. Further it is suggested that a situation is a basic unit of social behaviour and that the components take their meaning and order from the episode which they are creating and should not be considered in isolation from it (Ginsburg, 1979).

No one methodological technique is used by proponents of the approach. However, as they are more interested in the internal structure of a situation rather than comparisons between situations, the methodology is primarily aimed at revealing the nature of certain components such as the social rules or the concepts. Cluster analysis is favoured for its categorical rather than dimensional representation of the relationship between elements (Argyle, 1976).

Numerous standard techniques such as rating scales, sorting tasks and parsing tasks are given to subjects familiar with the social situations in question. They are usually asked to judge the extent, importance or presence of some components of that situation.

This approach has been used successfully to show the goal structure of situations (Graham, Argyle and Furnham, chs. 1–6), the rules of different situations (Argyle et al., 1979), the sequences in social behaviour as a function of the situation (Argyle, 1979), and the salience, equivalence and sequential structure of behavioural elements in different social situations (Graham et al., in press).

There are a number of problems associated with this approach. First, the number and type of components selected for investigation is somewhat arbitrary. The use of the games analogy provides a good list, but it is not necessarily appropriate for all social situations. Second, the appoach so far has failed to explore the structure of more than one or two elements at a time. For a fully structured model it is important that the dynamics of the relationship between all the elements are known. Third, the reliance on the explicit knowledge of the participants in any social situation could obscure the structure of certain elements that only detailed observation in natural social situations would reveal. However this is an extremely promising approach which could provide a new insight into the workings of social situations.

3. Process or Applied. The process or applied approach grows out of concern with the workings of one particular type of situation, and seeks to find its underlying processes. This approach is characteristic of applied psychologists, who are given the job of training people to behave in particular situations, or showing why certain social situations lead to negative or undesirable outcomes. This approach is guided by no particular theoretical or methodological tradition. It is for the most part aimed at diagnosis and training. There are numerous examples of this approach but we shall consider three.

Cross-cultural contact is often difficult and leads to misunderstandings because people from different groups have different perceptions and expectations of similar social situations. That is, they are perplexed, anxious or behave inappropriately because they are unaware of the meanings of certain actions and their appropriate response (Furnham and Bochner, in press). Researchers have investigated some of these misunderstandings in particular situations and developed situational exercises in cross-cultural awareness (Nitsche and Green, 1977).

Similarly the doctor's surgery has been thoroughly investigated in order to understand how the behaviour patterns in this situation lead to effective communication or misunderstanding (Rachman & Philips, 1978). Pendleton and Furnham (1980) reported a number of observations and questionnaire studies in doctor's surgeries that assess the nature of the factors that account for communication difficulty. Pendleton (1981) also pointed out the highly rule-governed and goal-directed nature of doctor-patient interaction, and the result of clashing long-term and short-term goals.

Similarly, studies in classrooms (Stebbins, 1975) have shown how different definitions of the classroom situation lead to communication breakdowns. Flanders (1970) studied the turn-taking of questions and answers in classrooms and found that different consequences resulted from different cycles of teacher-pupil behaviour. Other situations that have been studied are interviews (Brenner, 1978), court rooms (Atkinson, 1979) and psychotherapy sessions.

Because this approach is designed to discover the behavioural processes in different types of situations, a wide variety of data collection techniques and analyses are used. These range from videotapes to questionnaires and from multivariate analyses to nonparametric analyses. As a rule all the participants in a setting are studied.

The major weaknesses of this approach are, first, because it is often atheoretical, researchers have no model to follow. Thus, they may focus on one aspect of the situation, such as the physical modifiers or the social rules, and neglect other equally important variables. Second, it is extremely important that the situations studied be representative of that particular type of situation, otherwise the generalizability of the findings is questionable. Third, the exclusive focus on one or two outcome variables may have unfortunate consequences in that other relevant variables are ignored.

A major strength of this approach however, is its careful observation of a particular situation and its attempts to uncover processes that relate directly to specific behaviour outcomes.

4. Environmental. Due to its diversity, it is difficult to present a coherent, unified picture of the environmental analysis of social situations. However, it is fair to say that environmental psychologists have focused primarily on the physical features of social situations in order to understand how various factors in the natural and built environment affect social behaviour. Environmental psychologists seem happier with such concepts as place (Canter, 1977) and space (Ittelson et al., 1974) rather than situation. That is, they are particularly interested in the physical environment and the norms and rules associated with it, rather than exclusively in some interaction occurring within it.

This approach, which is closely linked to evaluation research and planning, uses extremely diverse methodologies including surveys, field observations, questionnaires, laboratory experiments, diaries, etc. Similarly the data analysis is not restricted to any particular approach though descriptive techniques like factor analysis and facet theory are popular. Furthermore, there is a perceptible movement away from the simple, man-as-a-passive-reactor-to-the-environment approach, to one in which a person is seen as a modifier and monitor of his or her social and physical environment. This is best reflected in the work on mental maps (Gould and White, 1974) and on role differences in the experience of environment (Canter, 1977). However, this approach often involves a wider definition of the situation or the environment than that given by social psychologists. Whole institutions, neighbourhoods, even countries are studied by environmental psychologists, though a lot of work has been done on the layout or symbolic messages of rooms. Certainly this approach has done much to emphasise the importance of the physical environment on social behaviour.

A possible weakness of this approach is an over-emphasis on physical factors and neglect of important social and temporal factors. The concern with place and space rather than action structure may also lead to a rather static picture of social situations. Finally the participants' own definition of the situation—in terms of images, symbols, and feelings—has been neglected in favour of a controlled objective or 'average' view. However, when looking at social interaction in particular environments, this approach may prove particularly beneficial for an analysis of the geography of social situations.

5. Ecological. The ecological approach, which has its origin in the methods of anthropology and ethology, seeks to describe naturally occurring situations, called settings, which are natural units in the stream of behaviour. The aim of this approach is to develop a detailed taxonomy of the commonly occurring behavioural settings of an institution, a community, or the life of a particular person.

This approach was pioneered by Barker (1968) and his colleagues, who are concerned with developing an eco-behavioural science that accurately records the stream of behaviour as it naturally occurs. The approach is characterized by rigorous, detailed and time-consuming methodology which involves first establishing the range and extensiveness of the settings to be investigated, and then having trained observers record detailed notes on the behaviour of all the participants in that setting. These observations by different observers are collated over a period of time, and the patterns of behaviour in that setting are described. This description includes overt behaviour patterns as well as the inferred feelings and cognitions of the people in settings. Barker (1968) suggested that behaviour should be analyzed in terms of 5 mechanisms: affective behaviour, gross motor activity, manipulation, talking and thinking. Studies using this approach have concentrated on the behaviour settings of children (Fawl, 1963), hospitals (Willens and Halstead, 1978), schools (Gump, 1965) and churches (Wicker, 1969). Researchers have carefully documented the range of behaviour settings within these institutions and the commonly occurring patterns of behaviour. A number of concepts such as under- and over-manning which have proved very useful in the analysis of other situations have grown out of this work.

Both the strength and the weakness of this approach lies in its methodology. It is a strength because the observations are thorough, rich, comprehensive and insightful, and there is a minimal psychological reactance on the part of the subjects. However, it is limited in its exclusive concern with observation of overt behaviour and thus neglects both the affective and cognitive processes of the people in behaviour settings. Observation alone cannot reveal the subjects' personal definitions of the situation, their plans for action, their feelings, or reasons for coming to the setting. Secondly there seems to be no set way of integrating or selecting observations to build up the final picture, or of quantifying them. Finally it is not entirely clear what one is to do with the taxonomy of settings once it has been established.

However, the ecological approach did much to further the psychology of social situations by stressing the problems of laboratory studies and the advantage of natural observation, by emphasising a natural unit of behaviour, and stressing hitherto neglected temporal factors in interaction (the diachronic and synchronic perspective).

6. Ethogenic or Roles-Rules. The ethogenic, or roles-rules, approach draws heavily on two other branches of microsociology—ethnomethodology and symbolic interactionism. From the former comes the emphasis on rules and from the latter the emphasis on actors' roles and symbols. The ethogenic approach has a characteristic philosophical and theoretical stance developed by Harré (Harré and Secord, 1972; Harré, 1979) and a limited data-gathering method based on interviews. This approach has been particularly concerned with the analysis of social episodes, which are defined as structured groups of action-sequence clusters that are necessary for the performance of social acts which collectively constitute a continuing and unfolding social life. This approach is unique in that it has a sound theoretical base and a sophisticated conception of the nature and workings of social episodes. The most commonly quoted analogy for the episodes is the play or drama, and the work of Goffman is often quoted.

The method advocated by exponents of this approach is twofold, though there is more concentration on one method than the other. The primary method is the gathering of accounts—natural unstructured reports, in a participant's own words, of the happenings in a particular situation. The solicited, but uncensored testimonies or accounts are gathered from all the relevant actors and observers in the particular situation, and provide a rich data source of the different perspectives, explanations and rationalizations of the participants. However, advocates of this method also maintain that an accurate or objective recording of the episode, such as that provided by a videocamera or tape recorder, are necessary to provide a way of checking the system of social knowledge and belief. The method then is opposed in method to the ecological approach and in emphasis to the environmental approach.

A few studies have used this approach to investigate particular social situations: they include studies of football hooliganism (Marsh, Rosser and Harré, 1978), introductions (Harré and De Waele, 1976) and the study of violence in pubs.

Three major problems characterize this approach. First, people often will not or cannot produce an accurate description of their own observations, thoughts or behaviour because of memory or language deficits, social desirability factors, attribution errors, etc. Second, there seems to be no method whereby accounts are selected, integrated, or checked, and thus they could represent the bias or intuitions of the experimenter rather than the subjects' view. Third, this technique is retrospective and episode-specific—that is, it is concerned with revealing how a particular episode was structured. Unless the situations under review are typical of their type, and the personality and demographic variables associated with the participants known, the approach might be seen as a historical analysis, such as one sees in a courtroom, and thus might have limited generalizability.

However, this approach has done much to present the actor as an active, self-monitoring creator of situations, responding to and modifying particular situational areas as well as acting in accordance with his or her social knowledge. The emphasis on rules, roles and impression management, as well as on the necessity to tap the rich knowledge of everyday social situations of participants, has led psychologists from other research areas to become interested in the concept of situated action.

Table 1 represents a schematic comparison of the six approaches to the analysis of social situations. The major differences and similarities between the various approaches are apparent.

Argyle, Furnham and Graham (1981) have highlighted a number of methodological and conceptual problems in the study of social situations that are the causes of some of the major differences between approaches. They include:

1. *How should situations be defined and measured?* This problem concerns which definition of the situation should be used: that of the actor, that of the observer, a subcultural definition, or a full description of a unique situation. It also necessitates deciding whether actual or hypothetical situations should be studied.
2. *Should behavioural measures or self reports be used?* This problem concerns the type of data which is most applicable, given that each has certain advantages and disadvantages. It is also concerned with the integration of data of different types from different sources.
3. *What level of analysis and definition is most useful?* This concerns the level at which we choose to define such a situation as described at the beginning of this chapter (stimuli, episode, situation, setting, environment). It also relates as to whether ratings should be global and evaluative of the entire social situation, or specific to observable pieces of behaviour within that situation.
4. *Are situations comparable?* To some extent this problem is similar to the one above in that it concerns levels of analysis. A categorical approach holds that situations are discrete and not dimensionable, while a continuous approach holds that they are usefully compared on a

Table 1. Methods for Analysing Social Situations

	Academic Tradition	Descriptive vs. Hypothesis Testing	Subjects	Within/Between Situation Analysis	Methods of Data Collection	Type of Data	Treatment of Data	Level of Definition
Dimensional (Perceptual)	Psychophysics Social Psychology	Descriptive	Observers usually grouped according to some criterion	Between	Questionnaire Sorting Task	Rating Scales Similarity rating	M.D.S., Factor Analysis	Situations Episode
Componential (Structural)	Linguistics, Ethology	Descriptive testing and Hypothesis	Observers who have experienced these situations	Within (and between)	Questionnaire Sorting/Rating Tasks	Rating Scales Similarity ratings, 'Parsing' Data	Cluster Analysis, ANOVA, Appropriate Stats.	Situational Stimuli (objects, acts)
Process (Applied)	Applied Psychology	Hypothesis testing and Descriptive	All participants in a setting	Within and Between	Observation, Behavioural Measures, Interview	Rating Scales, Behavioural Counts, Self Reports	Varied	Total Actual Situations
Environmental	Evaluation Assessment Research, Architecture	Hypothesis testing and Descriptive	Users, planners, assessors of an environment	Within and Between	Questionnaire, Observation, Behavioural Measures	Varied	Varied	Situational events and Total Situation
Ecological	Anthropology Microsociology	Descriptive	Whole population of a setting	Between	Observation	Detailed Notes	Development of taxonomy	Situational Settings.
Ethogenic (Roles-Rules)	Microsociology Philosophy	Descriptive	Selected participants in a natural episode	Within	Interview, Observation	Accounts	Selection of 'representative' accounts	Situational episode

number of dimensions.
5. *What stimuli should be used?* This problem concerns what stimuli are used, who generates
   them and how they are presented. Each method has its associated strengths and weaknesses.
   Pervin (1978) has suggested four modes of presentation: direct contact, simulation,
   photographs, and drawings and written descriptions.
6. *What tasks should subjects be asked to do?* These might include rating scales, sorting tasks,
   keeping diaries, recollecting experiences, being observed, etc. The major distinction to be
   made in the measures of response is whether they are objective or subjective reports.
7. *Which analysis is appropriate?* Most statistical needs require that certain assumptions be
   met before an analysis is possible. Therefore, data might have to be collected in a manner
   applicable to a certain technique or else potentially-rich data may be unexplored.

Pervin (1978) has pointed to a number of problems associated with measurement. These include the sources of error and bias common to all reactive
measures, the confusion that exists between measurement of the concept *per se,*
and the measurement of its effects upon the responding organism. Problems also
exist concerning the lack of agreement among data obtained from different
modes of presentation (role playing, photographs, written descriptions) and
different modes of response (objective measures of behaviour, subjective
reports). "To the extent that there has been a limited sampling of the phenomena
of interest, with a mode of presentation variant from the natural engagement of
the organism with the variable of interest (e.g., written descriptions of situations
as opposed to real-life situations), and a reactive measure of response, the results
of a research effort may, in Brunswick's terms, have limited ecological
generalizability" (p. 100).

The analysis of social situations is not a simple task. However it is both
important and necessary to a full understanding of social behaviour in context.

(4) THE USES OF SITUATIONAL ANALYSIS

The analysis of social situations may be put to a number of uses. For the most
part psychologists have concentrated on changing, controlling, or training people
to behave as certain situational forces dictate, rather than modifying the
situational forces in accordance with the person's ability or needs. Once the
effect of social situations and persons on behaviour, and vice versa, is
understood, psychologists should be in a position to apply situational analysis to
useful ends. There are at least six ways of usefully applying a situational
analysis.

1. The Modification or Control of Social Behaviour. This includes both the
discouragement and prevention of illegal or maladaptive responses and the
reinforcement and shaping of coping, prosocial bahaviour. The two aspects of
'negative' behaviour that could be modified by situational analysis are those
associated with crime, delinquency and amoral acts, and those related to mental

illness, maladaptation and addiction. A number of studies have shown that cheating and stealing are dependent on situational factors (Burton, 1963; Hartshorne and May, 1928; Nelson, Grinder and Mutterer, 1969). Hence certain temptations may be removed while other constraints may be introduced. Various forms of vandalism and delinquency have also been associated with situational factors such as situated aggression rituals, or symbolic public places or facilities. Marsh, Rosser and Harré (1978) maintain that classroom and football violence may be controlled by better understanding the roles, the rules and the concepts associated with these situations. Other studies on male offenders (Spence, 1979; Spence and Marzillier, 1979; Fawcett, Ingham, McKeever and Williams, 1979) have shown how subjects with a deficit of situation-specific coping skills are more likely to become criminals. Studies have also shown that certain forms of aggression and criminal violence are the result of a lack of situation-specific skills (Rimm, et al., 1974; Rathus et al., 1979). More recently it has been shown that providing arsonists with socially appropriate methods of perceiving and coping with anger-provoking, interpersonal situations greatly reduced their fire-setting behaviour (Rice and Chaplin, 1979). Apart from the teaching of appropriate situation-specific skills to various groups of law breakers there are a number of changes that can be made to commonly occurring social situations to control and manage different forms of criminal behaviour. For example, to control shoplifting, these may include the introduction of obvious surveillance methods, the removal of certain symbolic objects, and a rearrangement of space.

Various forms of abnormal and maladaptive behaviour can be modified by a more thorough situational analysis. These include social inadequacy, phobias, and loneliness. Nearly all forms of social skills training for the socially inadequate involve training in the assessment of and training in appropriate behaviour in social situations (Capon, 1977; Trower, Bryant and Argyle, 1978). This is because it has been found that people who are socially inadequate are unable to read everyday situations and respond appropriately. They are unable to perform or interpret nonverbal signals, unaware of the rules of social behaviour, mystified by ritualized routines and conventions of self-presentation and self-disclosure, and are hence like foreigners in their own land. Indeed most of the assessment techniques used in assessing social skill deficits are based on situation-specific scales (Herson and Bellack, 1976). Phobias and obsessions can be treated by sensitive situational analysis and training (Melville, 1977). The treatment of social anxiety can be greatly facilitated by situational analysis. Indeed, a great deal of the interest in the psychology of social situations owes its origins to researchers who were eager to develop better ways of assessing and treating anxiety (Endler, Hunt and Rosenstein, 1962). More recently a number of studies have looked specifically at the nature of stressful situations in various groups of subjects (Spielberger, 1978; Zuckerman and Mellstrom, 1977). Further loneliness or lack of social interaction can be changed by quite simple forms of situational adjustment (Argyle, Furnham and Graham, 1981).

As well as modifying illegal and maladaptive behaviour, situational analysis can be used to encourage adaptive or prosocial behaviour. Two areas where this has been done are altruistic behaviour, and friendship formation. Situational factors that have been seen to effect altruism include the number of bystanders, the effects of models, the ambiguity or familarity of the situation, cultural rules and norms, and the characteristics of the victim (Argyle, Furnham and Graham, 1981). Thus where helping behaviour is to be encouraged, the number of bystanders could be reduced and helping models introduced. Furthermore, where there is any ambiguity in the situation regarding what type or amount of help is needed, the victim could be taught how to signal for help. Similarly, friendship formation can be encouraged by situational analysis and manipulation. It has often been demonstrated that proximity leads to attraction and friendship formation (Festinger, Schachter and Back, 1950; Nahemow and Lawtin, 1975; Zajonc, 1968). Similarly, the presence of certain environmental stressors such as harsh light or loud sounds can prevent attraction and friendship formation (Griffitt and Veitch, 1971). The formality and structure of common interaction rituals also may encourage or prevent friendship formation (Harré, 1977). Therefore friendship formation can be encouraged by arranging functions where similar and equal status people are likely to meet one another fairly regularly over time, in pleasant surroundings, in fairly unstructured episodes that favour rewarding activities and self disclosure. This is exactly what dating agencies and lonely hearts clubs aim to do.

Thus certain forms of social behaviour may be easily modified by changing situational characteristics. Not all are equally simple to modify—changing the lighting and the furnishings is easier than changing the rules, which in turn is easier than changing the role relationship or status hierarchy among the participants.

2. The Selection of People for Situations and Vice Versa. This includes both the selection of people for specific roles or to achieve specific tasks in social situations, and the selection of situations for people. The former involves mainly personnel selection for performance at a particular job and the validity and reliability of job interviews. The latter includes vocational guidance and the therapeutic or punitive relegation of people to certain social situations that will affect them in certain desired ways.

One of the most important aspects of personnel selection is to determine the range of situations in which a person is required to work, and then to decide which skills or attributes a person needs in order to successfully undertake the tasks of these situations. It is important for successful candidates to be competent in or matched to the entire range of situations in which they are required to perform. Pervin (1968), in a review of performance and satisfaction as a function of individual-environment fit, in both interpersonal and noninterpersonal situations, concluded that a match or best fit of individual to environment results in high performance and satisfaction and low stress, while lack of fit is viewed as resulting in decreased performance and satisfaction and high stress. Indeed, the whole area of careers, guidance and personnel selection is aimed at matching people's abilities and interests to the requirements or restraints of certain situations (Payne and Pugh, 1972).

Personnel selection and career guidance may be greatly improved by better situational analysis. This could take two forms: a job interview may be replaced by a longer observation of the candidate in the work situation as performance in interviews often does not relate to performance at work. Or the full range of situations in which the candidate is required to work could be assessed and the list of requisite skills compiled. These specific skills in the candidate could then be assessed by the interviewers. These skills will include both task and socio-emotional abilities (Bales, 1950). Sidney, Brown and Argyle (1973) have produced a list of the situationally based skills needed by managers, which vary from negotiation to committee chairmanship. Some jobs, such as that of a diplomat, require a great range of skills and hence special institutions are set up to train diplomatic staff by instruction, role-play, and culture assimilators, in the situation specific skills they are likely to need.

As well as personnel selection—that is the choosing of people with certain abilities, skills and needs for certain jobs—it is often necessary to have situational selection, i.e. the selection of certain jobs for people with given needs or disabilities. The people for whom certain jobs may be found include the physically disabled (blind, limbless), the mentally retarded, the aged, prisoners and criminals, and people from minority groups who are the targets of prejudice. In these cases the particular weaknesses or problems of the people are known and it is therefore important that work situations be found which do not require the performance of activities which are beyond their capabilities. In other words, jobs or activities can be found or designed for people with certain needs. This requires that a careful situational analysis be done to determine the range of skills and activities required by each situation. Similarly recidivists and delinquents are sent to specific institutions that will expose them to situations involving discipline, assertiveness, etc. in order that they learn relevant skills.

Thus the matching of people to situations is an important activity which has been handicapped in the past by too little attention to the analysis of situations and too much attention to the analysis of people. It is not until both are equally, thoroughly and comparably assessed that an ideal person-situation fit can be found.

3. Teaching Self-Monitoring and Training in Situational Skills. It is equally important to teach people to control their own behaviour by monitoring situations and their effect on people as it is to teach the skills appropriate to each situation. This is particularly the case with compulsive or addictive behaviours. It is well known that people respond to certain situations in characteristic ways that are the result of learning experiences and that one way to change these responses is to get them to monitor more carefully their responses to these particular situations. Hart (1978) demonstrated that the monitoring of situational goals had beneficial effects on various kinds of abnormal behaviour. These forms of situational therapy have been used successfully with overeating, smoking, drinking and drug-taking. Chapman and Jeffrey (1978) showed that situational management produced an average weight loss of 7 pounds after two months of weekly sessions with obese subjects. The management programme included the listing and elimination of situational cues that provoked each subject into overeating and a later elimination of cues closely associated with the preparation of food and the act of eating.

Similarly Best and Hakstian (1978) identified 63 situations that provoked people to smoke. A different factor structure emerged for the two sex groups. Situations characterized by nervous tension, frustration, discomfort and restlessness provoked the male sample to smoke, whereas in females it was situations characterized by nervous tension, self-image monitoring, frustration and relaxation. Heavy smokers had the urge to smoke in many social situations whereas lighter smokers showed greater situational variability. Best and Hakstian advocate a smoking modification programme that determines situations that provoke the need for smoking and the inculcation of satisfactory alternatives.

Sanchez-Craig (1979) developed a situationally-based alcoholism programme that required patients to identify the range of situations which lead them to drink too much, and an analysis of these situations. Thereafter the programme was designed to provide patients with coping strategies to prevent heavy drinking from reoccurring. These involved rehearsal of self-statements to inhibit drinking, rules for drinking, and a consideration of the consequences of drinking and skills of refusal. Zielinski (1978) and Van Hasselt, Hersen and Milliones (1978) used a similar technique to train assertiveness in depressed alcoholics and social skills for alcohol and drug addicts.

Recently work has also been done on drug abuse (Bearden and Woodside, 1978). Bearden, Woodside and Jones (1979) have demonstrated how belief patterns and situational variables together determine subjects' motivation to use marijuana. They believe that varying situations may independently influence drug-taking intentions, and hence behaviour, without affecting attitudes and well-formed beliefs about the expectation of others.

Teaching situational monitoring may also be useful to motivate certain behaviours. Cooperation rather than competition between groups of people may be encouraged by the introduction of certain rules. Chang (1978) developed a scale to measure the situational control of daily activities in an institutional setting. The aim of this technique is to help nursing staff to teach patients to recognize cues about their physical, mental, social and emotional states in daily institutionalized situations. Teaching people situational self-monitoring may also allow them to examine in a new light their own and others' behaviour in previously occurring situations and allow for new insights.

4. The Description of Situations and the Construction of Taxonomies.

Although it is doubtful whether it is possible or necessary to develop a comprehensive taxonomy of social situations, it may be very useful for specific purposes. Frederickson (1972) has indicated some of the problems involved and the possible ways forward. Certainly since the construct of situation must be able to be operationally specified and measured to be of any use, some sort of classification of situations or situational elements seems essential (Pervin, 1978; Magnusson, 1979). Pervin (1978) has suggested that concepts be defined in terms of objective characteristics while allowing for the study of the transactional relationship between organism and environment. He also notes that classifications may be hierarchical, which allows us to move from stimuli to situations to environments, in the way we can move from elements to compounds in chemistry.

Situations may be described in terms of many features—the demographic characteristics of the people present, the social rules, the behaviour manifested, etc.—the more limited and specific the criteria used, the less generalizable the description. There are two broad approaches to situational description. One is to formulate a model or analogue for a social situation and then describe the workings of situations in terms of the elements in the model. Models that have been suggested include sports and games (Argyle, 1976), the theatre (Harré and Secord, 1972), a mobile (Argyle, Furnham and Graham, 1981) and a land dispute (Price, 1979). A second approach is to attempt to classify all possible situations (Sells, 1963) or to classify in terms of situational variables affecting given domains of behaviour (Mehrabian and Russell, 1974).

There have been a number of attempts to develop situational taxonomies. Schiedt and Schaie (1978) developed a taxonomy of situations for an elderly population in a home, while Belk (1978) developed an idiographic taxonomy of clothing choices across different situations, and Pervin (1978) a taxonomy of social situations occurring in a student's life. Belk (1978) has illustrated a number of options for the development of a situational taxonomy. He has been concerned specifically with the developing of product-specific taxonomies of consumption situations. The options he considers are:

(1.) Attempting to classify all situations or all situations relevant to a given domain of behaviour.
(2.) Distinguishing between purchasing, communication or consumption situations which often occur at different times and different places.
(3.) Distinguishing between different products (or forms of behaviour) or looking at the same type of product.
(4.) Distinguishing between looking at the whole situation or specific features of it.

(5.) Offering a conceptual theoretical or an empirical classification.
(6.) Distinguishing between types of data to be used—descriptive, similarity, behavioural.
(7.) Distinguishing between actually occurring behavioural data and perceived appropriate measures of behaviour.

Figure 1 diagrammatically presents these decisions as well as the options Belk favours.

Figure 1.   Options for Situational Taxonomy

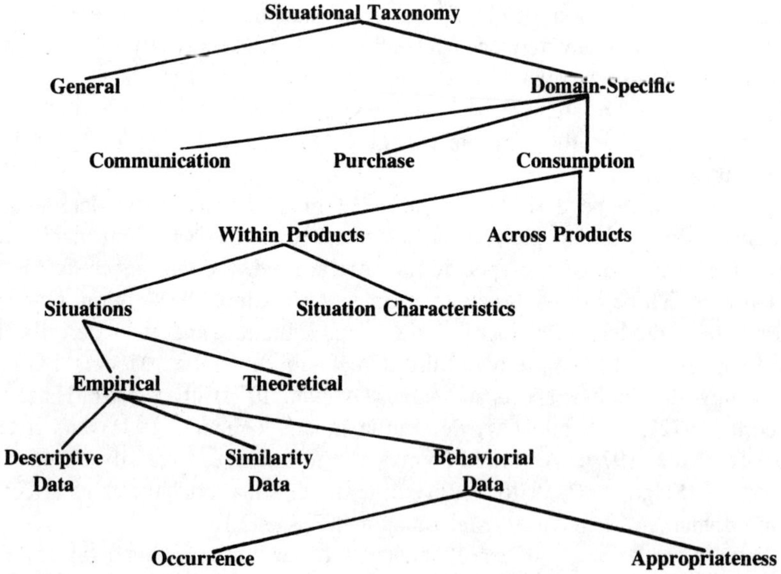

Careful situational analysis will provide psychologists with a better means of describing and categorising situations. It may also help the development of concepts and terms that are specific to situational analysis. Examples of this are Barker's over- and under-manning concept, and Goffman's back stage and front stage regions.

5. The Invention or Construction of New Situations. In their functional model of social situations Argyle, Furnham and Graham (1981) have argued that nearly all social situations fulfil a social function that is either explicit or implicit. Furthermore all social situations have a history, and it may happen that they no longer serve to function in the original way of fulfilling the same goals. An analysis of these situations may allow for the invention of new situations to fulfil new goals or needs. A useful analogy may be that of patenting a new game that must be carefully thought out and piloted. This also requires a thorough analysis of other related games and an understanding of their basic structure (Avedon, 1970).

Situations may be invented in many ways. More familiar situations may be modified in terms of their rules, or roles, or goals to create new situations. The traditional setting and props associated with a social situation may be changed and hence the situation will be defined differently. A new jargon or set of concepts could be used in a familiar situated behaviour sequence to produce a new set of situational definitions. Finally an entirely new situation may be created—on purpose or by accident—which becomes a regularly occurring and well understood feature of a subculture. We shall consider instances of each of these. The rules of T- and encounter groups are deliberately designed to break normal conventions of touching, politeness, discussing emotions, criticism, etc. (Kisker, 1964). Certain laws have to be introduced to prevent some situations from being abused. These mainly include the buying and selling of goods or services.

By changing the physical setting of a situation various consequences may occur. The use of open-planning in place of closed offices for instance can change the nature of interaction at work. Also the meaning and experience of specific emotional situations may vary as a function of environmental setting—a religious service in a church or a home, a play production in the street or in the theatre. A new jargon too can help redefine situations—a 'sit-in' is behaviourally similar to many other situations (religious meetings) but is seen to be a form of non-violent protest. A plenary session, a brain-storming group, and a buzz session, though very similar are different because they have different concepts associated with them.

Finally, in response to a perceived need, various situations may be invented for, and widely accepted in a subculture. Singles bars or gay clubs may be seen to be situations invented to fulfil various needs in the community. Similarly womens' groups and patients' organizations can invent of social situations to fulfil needs. Situational formats may be borrowed from other cultures to promote certain ends.

6. Predicting Social Behaviour. It has been consistently found that a person's attitudes are not a good predictor of his behaviour (Wicker, 1969), and there have been several attempts to explain this finding in terms of moderator variables (Snyder and Tanke, 1974). There has recently been a considerable number of attempts to improve prediction. Bem and Funder (1978) and Epstein (1979) both entitled radically different articles 'Predicting more of people more of the time'. Bem and Funder (1978) argued that we need a common language to describe both persons and situations and suggested that situations be characterized by a set of template-behaviour pairs, which are personality descriptions of the hypothetical "ideal" person, each associated with a particular behaviour. Having first characterized situations with templates couched in the language of personality, the next step could be to characterize people with templates couched in the language of situations which would describe a person in terms of how he or she behaves in a set of hypothetical ideal situations. Epstein (1979), on the other hand, concentrated on the stability of behaviour and demonstrated that, although it is not normally possible to predict single instances of behaviour, it is possible to predict behaviour averaged over a sample of situations. Thus, in order to predict for most of the people most of the time, we need to have an adequate sample of situation-specific behaviours to compute.

It has also been found in the study of consumer behaviour that an individual's attitude toward a product is a very poor indicator of his/her likelihood to purchase or use that product. Recently a number of studies have suggested that two situational criteria are important factors affecting the consumer choice process. These are the buying situation such as a shop or restaurant, and the anticipated consumption situation such as the home or picnic. Belk (1974a) argued that as situational effects and interactions provided nearly half of the explained variance in meat and snack preferences, consumer research has much to gain by the explicit recognition of purchase and consumption situations. Using a three mode factor analysis Belk found four consumption situations which affected snack product purchasing, which he labelled informal serving, nutritive, impulsive consumption and unplanned. This confirms the finding of Sandell (1968) that the probability of choosing certain drinks was more heavily influenced by situational than by attitudinal factors. Apart from food products, the evidence of consumption situation effects has also been demonstrated in studies on the preferences for mouthwash (Srivastava and Schocker, 1977), films (Belk, 1974), clothes (Belk, 1978) and cars (Berkowitz, Ginter and Talarzvk, 1977). Similarly, Belk (1975, 1978) noted that the involvement and effort that goes into a purchase is a function of certain situational characteristics.

Apart from consumer behaviour, it is quite possible that other choice behaviour such as voting and gambling is as much dependent on situational factors as on attitudes and beliefs. This has been experimentally demonstrated in studies on conformity, where conformist decisions that go against a subject's values and attitudes are occasioned by situational pressures such as group size (Kidd, 1958), and unanimity of judgement (Asch, 1956). Milgram's (1974) study of obedience to authority was an even more dramatic demonstration of this.

Thus situational analysis, in conjunction with an analysis of a person's personality and cognitive ability, would lead to much better predictions of certain forms of social behaviour.

THE PLAN OF THIS BOOK

Following the introductory chapter there are three sections containing theoretical and empirical papers.

The first section, which has conceptual papers from different fields, reveals some of the diversity in dealing with the topic. The papers have been written by sociologists and clinical community and social psychologists reflecting their different approaches to the psychology of social situations.

The second section reflects the approach of social psychology. This section is further subdivided into four sections containing papers that best reflect the work in this area. The papers reflect the work done on the perception of various social situations, the reactions to and in specific situations, the nature of stressful or difficult situations, and the work on person-situation interaction.

The third section reflects the approach of four other disciplines to the study of social situational determinants of behaviour. They are environmental psychology, microsociology, sociolinguistics and psycholinguistics, and clinical psychology.

In addition to a brief introduction to each section and subsection there is a list of suggested additional readings after each subsection. These have been collected with a view to providing a thorough and up-to-date bibliography on the subject.

REFERENCES

Alexander, C. & Knight, G. Situated identities and social psychological experimentation. *Sociometry,* 1971, *34,* 65-82.

Alexander, C. & Lauderdale, P. Situated identities and social influence. *Sociometry,* 1977, *40,* 225-233.

Alexander, C. & Sagatuin, I. An attributional analysis of experimental norms. *Sociometry,* 1973, *36,* 127-142.

Alker, H. Is personality situationally specific or intrapersonally consistent. *Journal of Personality,* 1972, *40,* 1-16.

Allport, G. *Personality: a psychological interpretation.* New York: Holt, 1937.

Altman, I. Environmental psychology and social psychology. *Personality and Social Psychology Bulletin,* 1976, *2,* 96-113.

Anastasi, A. *Psychological Testing.* New York: Macmillan, 1964.

Asch, S. Studies of independence and conformity. *Psychological Monographs,* 1956, *70,* 1-70.

Argyle, M. Personality and social behaviour. In R. Harré (ed.) *Personality.* Oxford: Blackwell, 1976.

Argyle, M. *The Psychology of Interpersonal Behaviour.* 3rd edition. Harmondsworth: Penguin 1978.

Argyle, M. Sequences in social behaviour as a function of the situation. In G. Ginsburg (ed.) *Emerging Strategies in Social Psychological Research*. Chichester: Wiley, 1979.

Argyle, M., Furnham, A. & Graham, J. *Social Situations*. Cambridge: Cambridge University Press, 1981.

Argyle, M., Graham, J., Campbell, A., and White, P. The rules of different situations. *New Zealand Psychologist*, 1979, *8*, 13-27.

Atkinson, M. *Order in Court*. London: Macmillan, 1979.

Avedon, E. The structural elements of games. In E. Avedon & B. Sutton Smith (Eds.) *The Study of Games*. New York: Wiley, 1971, pp. 419-426.

Backman, C. Epilogue: a new paradigm. In G. Ginsburg (Ed.) *Emerging Strategies in Social Psychological Research*, Chichester: Wiley, 1979.

Bagozzi, R. Salesforce performance and satisfaction as a function of individual difference, interpersonal and situational factors. *Journal of Marketing Research*, 1978, *15*, 517-531.

Bales, R. *Interaction Process Analysis*. Cambridge, Mass.: Addison-Wesley, 1950.

Bannister, D. Biographies as a source in psychology. Paper given at PPA Conference, 1975.

Barclay, W. *Ethics in a Permissive Society*. London: Fontana, 1971.

Barker, R. (Ed.) *The Stream of Behavior*. New York: Appleton-Century-Crofts, 1963.

Barker, R. *Ecological Psychology: Concepts and Methods of Studying the Environment of Human Behavior*. Stanford: Stanford University Press, 1968.

Barker, R. et al. *Habitats, Environments and Human Behavior*. San Francisco: Jossey-Bass, 1978.

Bearden, W. and Woodside, A. Interactions of consumption situations and brand attitudes. *Journal of Applied Psychology*, 1976, *6*, 764-769.

Bearden, W. and Woodside, A. Moderating influences of situations on consumer brand preferences. In J. Stoler and J. Conway (Eds.) *Proceedings of the American Institute for Decision Sciences*, 1977.

Bearden, W., Woodside, A. and Jones, J. Beliefs and anticipated situations influencing intentions to use drugs. *Perceptual and Motor Skills*, 1979, *48*, 743-751.

Belk, R. An exploratory assessment of situational effects in buyer behavior. *Journal of Marketing Research*, 1974a, *11*, 156-163.

Belk, R. Application and analysis of the behavioral differential inventory for assessing situational effects in consumer behavior. In S. Ward and P. Wright (Eds.) *Advances in Consumer Research*, Urbana: ACR, 1974b.

Belk, R. Situational variables and consumer behaviour. *Journal of Consumer Research*, 1975, *2*, 157-164.

Belk, R. Developing product-specific taxonomies of consumption situations. University of Illinois, unpublished paper, 1978.

Bem, D. Constructing cross-situational consistencies in behavior: some thoughts on Alker's critique of Mischel. *Journal of Personality*, 1972, *40*, 17-26.

Bem, D. and Allen, A. On predicting some of the people some of the time: the search for cross-situational consistency in behavior. *Psychological Review*, 1974, *81*, 506-520.

Bem, D. and Funder, D. Predicting more of the people more of the time: assessing the personality of situations. *Psychological Review*, 1978, *85*, 485-501.

Berkowitz, E., Ginter, G., and Talarzyk, W. An investigation of the effects of specific usages of situations on the prediction of consumer choice behavior. In B. Greenberg and D. Bellinger (Eds.) *Contemporary Thought in Marketing*. Chicago: AMA, 1977.

Best, J. and Hakstian, A. A situation-specific model for smoking behaviour. *Addictive Behaviors*, 1978, *3*, 79-92.

Bickman, L. and Green, S. Situational cues and crime reporting. *Journal of Applied Social Psychology*, 1977, *7*, 1-18.

Block, J. *Lives Through Time*. Berkeley: Bancroft, 1971.

Bowers, K. Situationalism in psychology: an analysis and a critique. *Psychological Review*, 1973, *80*, 307-336.

Brenner, M. Interviewing: the social phenomenology of a research instrument. In M. Brenner, P. Marsh, and M. Brenner (eds.) *The Social Contexts of Method*, London: Croom Helm, 1978.

Bronfenbrenner, U. Toward an experimental ecology of human development. *American Psychologist*, 1977, *32*, 513-531.

Brown, P. and Fraser, C. Speech as a marker of situations. In K. Scherer and H. Giles (Eds.) *Social Markers in Speech*, Cambridge: Cambridge University Press, 1979.

Bruno, F. The situational approach—reaction to individualism. *Social Forces*, 1931, *9*, 482-483.

Bryant, B. and Trower, P. Social difficulty in a student population. *British Journal of Educational Psychology*, 1974, *44*, 73-91.

Burke, W. Leadership behavior as a function of the leader, the follower, and the situation. *Journal of Personality*, 1978, *23*,60-81.

Burton, R. The generality of honesty reconsidered. *Psychological Review*, 1963, *70*, 481-499.

Buss, A. The trait-situation controversy and the concept of interaction. *Personality and Social Psychology Bulletin*, 1977, *3*, 196-201.

Campbell, D. and Stanley, J. *Experimental and Quasi-Experimental Designs for Research*. Chicago: Rand-McNally, 1966.

Canter, D. *The Psychology of Place*. London: The Architecture Press, 1977.

Capon, M. Basic course in social skills training. Unpublished manual, St. Crispin Hospital, Northampton, 1977.

Cartwright, D. Trait and other sources of variance in the S-R Inventory of Anxiousness. *Journal of Personality and Social Psychology*, 1975, *32*, 408-414.

Cattell, R. *The Scientific Analysis of Personality*. Harmondsworth: Penguin, 1965.

Chang, B. Perceived situational control of daily activities: a new tool. *Research in Nursing and Health*, 1978, *1*, 181-188.

Chapman, S. and Jeffrey, D. Situational management, standard setting and self-reward in a behavior modification weight loss program. *Journal of Consulting and Clinical Psychology*, 1980, *46*, 1588-1589.

Clifford, B. and Scott, J. Individual and situational factors in eyewitness testimony. *Journal of Applied Psychology*, 1978, *63*, 352-359.

Couch, A. and Keniston, K. Yea sayers and nay sayers: agreeing response set as a personality variable. *Journal of Abnormal and Social Psychology*, 1960, *60*, 151-174.

Craik, K. Environmental psychology. In K. Craik et al. (Eds.) *New Directions in Psychology, 4,* New York: Holt, Rinehart & Winston, 1970.

Csoka, L. and Bons, P. Manipulating the situation to fit the leader's style. *Journal of Applied Psychology*, 1978, *63*, 295-300.

Dakin, R. Cultural occasions and group structures: a photographic analysis of American social situations. *American Sociological Review*, 1960, *25*, 66-74.

De Waele, J-P, and Harré, R. Autobiography as a psychological research. In G. Ginsburg (Ed.) *Emerging Strategies in Social Psychological Research*, Chichester: Wiley, 1979.

Eisler, R. The behavioral assessment of social skills. In M. Hersen and A. Bellack (Eds.) *Behavioral Assessment: A Practical Handbook*, Oxford: Pergamon, 1978.

Eisler, R., Hersen, P., and Miller, P. Situational determinants of assertive behavior. *Journal of Consulting and Clinical Psychology*, 1975, *43*, 330-340.

Ekehammar, B. Interactionism in personality from an interactional perspective. *Psychological Bulletin*, 1974, *80*, 1026-1048.

Ellison, T. and Trickett, E. Environmental structure and the perceived similarity-satisfaction relationship: traditional and alternative schools. *Journal of Personality*, 1978, *46*, 57-71.

Endler, N. The person versus the situation—a pseudo issue? A response to Alker. *Journal of Personality*, 1973, *41*, 287-303.

Endler, N. and Edwards, J. Person by treatment interactions in personality research. In L. Pervin (Ed.) *Perspectives in Interactional Psychology*, New York: Plenum, 1978.

Endler, N. and Hunt, J. Sources of behavioral variance as measured by the S-R Inventory of Anxiousness. *Psychological Bulletin*, 1966, *65*, 336-346.

Endler, N. and Hunt, J. Inventories of hostility and comparisons of the proportions of variance from persons, responses and situations for hostility and anxiousness. *Journal of Personality and Social Psychology*, 1968, *9*, 309-315.

Endler, N. and Hunt, J. Generalizability of contributions from sources of variance in the S-R Inventory of Anxiousness. *Journal of Personality*, 1969, *37*, 1-24.

Endler, N. and Magnusson, D. *Interactional Psychology and Personality*. New York: Wiley, 1976.

Endler, N., Hunt, J., and Rosenstein, A. An S-R Inventory of Anxiousness. *Psychological Monographs*, 1962, *76*, 1-33.

Epstein, S. The stability of behaviour: I. On predicting most of the people most of the time. *Journal of Personality and Social Psychology*, 1979, *37*, 1097-1126.

Fawcett, B., Ingham, E., McKeever, M., and Williams, S. Social skills group for young prisoners. *Social Work Today*, 1979, *10*, 16-18.

Fawl, C. Disturbances experienced by children in their natural habitat. In R. Barker (Ed.) *The Stream of Behavior*, New York: Appleton-Century-Crofts, 1963.

Festinger, L., Schachter, S., and Back, K. *Social Pressures in Informal Groups*. New York: Harper, 1950.

Flanders, N. *Analysing Teaching Behavior*. Reading, Mass.: Addison-Wesley, 1970.

Fletcher, J. *Situation Ethics*. London: SCM Press, 1966.

Forgas, J. The perception of social episodes: categorical and dimensional representations in two different social milieus. *Journal of Personality and Social Psychology*, 1976, *32*, 199-209.

Forgas, J. Social episodes and social structures in an academic setting: the social environment of an intact group. *Journal of Experimental Social Psychology*, 1978, *14*, 434-448.

Forgas, J. *Social Episodes: The Study of Interaction Routines*. London: Academic Press, 1979.

Frederickson, N. Toward a taxonomy of situations. *American Psychologists*, 1972, *27*, 114-123.

Furnham, A. Assertiveness in three cultures: multidimensional and cultural differences. *Journal of Clinical Psychology*, 1979, *35*, 522-527.

Furnham, A. and Bochner, S. Social difficulty in a foreign culture: an empirical analysis of culture shock. In S. Bochner (Ed.) *Cross-Cultural Interaction*. Oxford: Pergamon 1981 (in press).

Gambrill, E. *Behavior Modification*. San Francisco: Jossey-Bass, 1977.

Garfinkel, H. *Studies in Ethnomethodology*. New York: Prentice Hall, 1967.

Gibson, J. The concept of the stimulus in psychology. *American Psychologist*, 1960, *15*, 694-703.

Giles, H. and St. Clair, R. *Language and social psychology*. Oxford: Blackwell, 1979.

Ginsburg, G. The effective use of role-playing in social psychological research. In G. Ginsburg (Ed.) *Emerging Strategies in Social Psychological Research*, Chichester: Wiley, 1979.

Goffman, E. The neglected situation. *American Anthropologist*, 1964, *66*, part 2.

Goffman. E. *Interaction ritual*. New York: Anchor Books, 1967.

Goffman, E. *Frame analysis*. New York: Colophon Books, 1974.

Golding, S. Flies in the ointment: methodological problems in the analysis of variance due to persons and situations. *Psychological Bulletin*, 1975, *82*, 278-288.

Gould, P. and White, R. *Mental maps*. Harmondsworth: Penguin, 1974.

Graham, J., Argyle, M., Clarke, D., and Maxwell, G. The salience, equivalence and sequential structure of behavioural elements in different social situations. *Semiotica* (in press.)

Gump, P. *Big School, Small School*. Moravia, New York: Chronical Guidance Publications, 1965.

Halliday, M. *Language as a Social Semiotic*. London: Edward Arnold, 1979.

Harré, R. *Social Being*. Oxford: Blackwell, 1979.

Harré, R. and De Waele, J-P. The ritual for incorporation of a stranger. In R. Harré (Ed.) *Life Sentences,* New York: Wiley, 1976.

Harré, R. and Secord, P. *The Explanation of Social Behaviour*. Oxford/Blackwell.

Hart, R. Therapeutic effectiveness of setting and monitoring goals. *Journal of Consulting and Clinical Psychology*, 1978, *46*, 1242-1245.

Hartshorne, H. and May, M. *Studies in the Nature of Character: Studies in Deceit*. New York: Macmillan, 1928.

Hersen, M. and Bellack, A. Assessment of social skills. In A. Ciminero, K. Calhoun, and H. Adams (Eds.) *Handbook of Behavioral Assessment,* New York: Wiley, 1976.

Hodges, W. and Felling, J. Types of stressful situations and their relation to trait anxiety and sex. *Journal of Consulting and Clinical Psychology*, 1970, *34*, 333-337.

Howard, J. Person-situation interaction models. *Personality and Social Psychology Bulletin*, 1979, *5*, 191-195.

Israel, J. and Tajfel, H. (Eds.) *The Context of Social Psychology: a critical assessment*. London: Academic Press, 1972.

Ittelson, W., Proshansky, H., Rivlin, L. and Winkel, G. *An Introduction to Environmental psychology*. New York: Holt, Rinehart & Winston, 1974.

Jarvie, I. *Concepts and Society*. London: Academic Press, 1972.

Jaspars, J. and Furnham, A. Interactionism in psychology or the person revisited: a cirtical review and a conceptual analysis. Unpublished paper, University of Oxford, 1979.

Joiner, D. Social ritual and architectural space. Architectural Psychology Conference, Kingston, 1970.

Jones, L. and Young, F. Structure of a social environment: longitudinal individual differences scaling of an intact group. *Journal of Personality and Social Psychology*, 1973, *24*, 108-121.

Kantor, J. *Principles of psychology*. Vol. 2., Bloomington: Principia Press, 1926.

Kasmar, J. The development of a usable lexicon of environmental descriptors. *Environment and Behavior*, 1970, *2*, 153-169.

Katz, I. Some motivational determinants or racial differences in intellectual achievement. *International Journal of Psychology*, 1967, *2*, 1-12.

Kendon, A. Some theoretical and methodological aspects of the use of film in the study of social interaction. In G. Ginsburg (Ed.) *Emerging Strategies in Social Psychological Research*, Chichester: Wiley, 1979.

Kidd, J. Social influence phenomenon in a task oriented group situation. *Journal of Abnormal and Social Psychology*, 1958, *56*, 13-17.

Kisker, G. *The Disorganized Personality*. New York: McGraw-Hill, 1964.

Koffka, K. *Principles of Gestalt Psychology*. New York: Harcourt Brace, 1935.

Krauskopf, C. Comments on Endler and Magnusson's attempt to redefine personality. *Psychological Bulletin*, 1978, *85*, 200-203.

Lee, T. *Psychology and the Environment*. London: Methuen, 1976.

Leming, J. Intrapersonal variations in stage of mental reasoning among adolescents as a function of situational context. *Journal of Youth and Adolescence*, 1978, *1*, 405-416.

Lewin, K. Krieglandschaft. *Zeitschrift fur Angewandte Psychologie*. 1917, *12*, 440-447.

Lewin, K. *A Dynamic Theory of Personality*. New York: McGraw-Hill, 1935.

Lauer, R. and Handel, W. *Social psychology: The Theory and Application of Symbolic Interactionism*. Boston: Houghton Mifflin, 1977.

Lewin, K. *Principles of Topological Psychology*. New York: McGraw-Hill, 1936.

London, M., Crandall, F., and Fitzgibbon, D. The psychological structure of leisure: activities, needs, people. *Journal of Leisure Research*, 1977, *9*, 252-263.

Lutz, R. and Kakkar, P. The psychological situation as a determinant of consumer behaviour. In M. Schlinger (Ed.) *Advances in Consumer Research, 2*. Urbana: ACR, 1975.

Magnusson, D. On the psychological situation. *University of Stockholm Reports*, 1978.

Magnusson, D. and Ekehammar, B. Anxiety profile based on both situational and response factors. *Multidimensional Behavioral Research*, 1975, *10*, 29-43.

Magnusson, D. and Ekehammar, B. Similar situations—similar behaviors? A study of intra-individual congruence between situation perception and situation reactions. *Journal of Research in Personality*, 1978, *12*, 41-48.

Magnusson, D. and Endler, N. *Personality at the Crossroads: Current Issues in Interactional Psychology*. Hillsdale, N.J.: Lawrence Erlbaum Associates, 1977.

Marsh, P., Rosser, E., and Harré, R. *The Rules of Disorder*. London: Routledge and Kegan Paul, 1978.

McClelland, D. *The Achieving Society*. Princeton, N.J.: Van Nostrand, 1961.

McCloskey, J. An interactional approach to self disclosure. Unpublished paper, University of Sheffield, 1978.

Melville, J. *Phobias and Obsessions*. London: Allen & Unwin, 1977.

Milgram, S. The experience of living in cities. *Science*, 1970, *167*, 1461-1468.

Milgram, S. *Obedience to Authority*. London: Tavistock, 1974.

Miller, A. *The Social Psychology of Psychological Research*. London: Collier-Macmillan, 1972.

Mischel, W. *Personality and Assessment*. New York: Wiley, 1968.

Mischel, W. On the interface of cognition and personality: beyond the person-situation debate *American Psychologist*, 1979, *34*, 740-754.

Mitchell, T., Larson, J., and Green, S. Leader behavior, situational moderators and group performance: an attributional analysis. *Organizational Behavior and Human Performance*, 1977, *18*, 254-268.

Mixon, D. Instead of deception. *Journal for the Theory of Social Behaviour*, 1972, *2*, 145-177.

Moos, R. Conceptualizations of human environments. *American Psychologist*, 1973, *28*, 652-665.

Moos, R. Determinants of physiological responses to symbolic stimuli: the role of the social environment. *International Journal of Psychiatry in Medicine*, 1974, *5*, 389-399.

Mount, M. and Muchinsky, P. Person-environment congruence and employee job satisfaction: a test of Holland's theory. *Journal of Vocational Behavior*, 1978, *13*, 84-100.

Murray, H. *Explorations in Personality*. New York: Oxford University Press, 1938.

Nahemow, L. and Lawtin, M. Similarity and propinquity in friendship formation. *Journal of Personality and Social Psychology*, 1975, *32*, 205-213.

Nelson, E., Grinder, R. and Mutter, M. Sources of variance in behavioral measures of honesty in temptation situations: methodological analyses. *Developmental Psychology*, 1969, *1*, 265-279.

Nitsche, R. and Green, A. *Situational Exercises in Cross-cultural Awareness*. Columbus: C. Merril, 1977.

Olweus, P. Longitudinal studies of aggressive reaction patterns in males: a review. University of Bergen, Institute of Psychology, Report 2, 1977.

Orcutt, J. Deviance as as situated phenomenon: variations in the social interpretation of marijuana and alcohol use. *Social Problems*, 1975, *16*, 346-356.

Orne, M. On the social psychology of the psychology experiment. *American Psychologist*, 1962, *17*, 776-783.

Payne, R. and Pugh, D. Organization structure and organization climate. In M. Dunnette (Ed.) *Handbook of Industrial and Organizational Psychology*, Chicago: Rand-McNally, 1976.

Payne, R., Fireman, S. and Jackson, P. An interactionist approach to measuring anxiety at work. University of Sheffield, unpublished paper, 1978.

Pendleton, D. Doctor-patient communication. In M. Argyle, A. Furnham and J. Graham. *Social Situations*, Cambridge: Cambridge Univeristy Press, 1981.

Pendleton, D. and Furnham, A. Skills: a paradigm for applied social psychological research. In W. Singleton, P. Spurgeon and R. Stammers (Eds.) *The Analysis of Social*

Skill, New York: Plenum, 1979.

Pervin, L. Performance and satisfaction as a function of individual-environment fit. *Psychological Bulletin*, 1968, *69*, 56-68.

Pervin, L. A free response description approach of person-situation interaction. *Journal of Personality and Social Psychology*, 1976, *34*, 465-474.

Pervin, L. Definitions, measurements and classifications of stimuli, situations and environments. *Human Ecology*, 1978, *6*. 71-105.

Popper, K. *The poverty of historicism*. London: Routledge and Kegan Paul, 1957.

Price, R. Situational theory and social practice, unpublished paper, 1979.

Queen, S. Some problems of the situational approach. *Social Forces*, 1931, *9*, 480-481.

Rachman, S., and Philips, C. *Psychology and medicine*. Harmondsworth: Penguin, 1978.

Rathus, S., Fox, J., and De Cristofaro, J. Perceived structure of aggressive and assertive behaviors. *Psychological Reports*, 1979, *44*, 695-698.

Rausch, H. Interaction sequences. *Journal of Personality and Social Psychology*, 1965, *2*, 487-499.

Reinhardt, J. Personality traits and the situation. *American Sociological Review*, 1937, *2*, 492-500.

Rice, M. and Chaplin, T. Social skills training for hospitalized male arsonists. *Journal of Behavior Therapy and Experimental Psychiatry*, 1979, *10*, 105-108.

Rimm, D., Hill, G., Brown, N., and Stuart, J. Group assertiveness training in the treatment of expressions of inappropriate anger. *Psycholgical Reports*, 1974, *34*, 791-798.

Robinson, W. *Language and Social Behaviour*. Harmondsworth: Penguin, 1972.

Rosenthal, R. *Experimenter effects in behavioral research*. New York: Appleton-Century-Crofts, 1966.

Rosenthal, R. and Rosnow, R. *Artifact in behavioral research*. New York: Academic Press, 1969.

Russell, J. and Mehrabian, A. Task setting and personality variables affecting the desire to work. *Journal of Applied Psychology*, 1975, *60*, 518-520.

Sanchez-Craig, B. Cognitive and behavioral coping strategies in the reappraisal of stressful social situations. *Journal of Counseling Psychology*, 1976, *23*, 7-12.

Sarason, I. Experimental approaches to test anxiety: attention and the uses of information. In C. Spielberger (Ed.) *Anxiety: Current Trends in Theory and Research*, Vol. 2. New York: Academic Press, 1972.

Sarason, I., Smith, R. and Diener, E. Personality research: components of variance attributable to the person and the situation. *Journal of Personality and Social Psychology*, 1975, *32*, 199-204.

Schegloff, E. and Sacks, H. Opening up closings. *Semiotica*, 1973, *8*, 289-327.

Schiedt, R. and Schaie, K. A taxonomy of situations for an elderly population: generating situational criteria. *Journal of Gerontology*, 1978, *33*, 848-857.

Sidney, E., Brown, M., and Argyle, M. *Skills with People*. London: Hutchinson, 1973.

Skillings, R., Hersen, M., Bellack, A., and Becker, M. Relationship of specific and global measures of assertion in college females. *Journal of Clinical Psychology*, 1978, *34*, 346-353.

Snyder, M. Self monitoring processes. In L. Berkowitz (Ed.) *Advances in Experimental Social Psychology*, Vol. 12. New York: Academic Press, 1979.

Snyder, M. and Tanke, E. Behavior and attitude: some people are more consistent than others. *Journal of Personality*, 1976, *44*, 510-517.

Sommer, R. Small group ecology. *Psychological Bulletin*, 1967, *67*, 145-152.

Spence, S. Social skills training with adolescent offenders: a review. *Behavioral Psychotherapy*, 1979, *7*, 49-56.

Spence, S. and Marzillier, J. Social skills training with adolescent male offenders. *Behaviour Research and Therapy*, 1979, *17*, 7-16.

Spielberger, C. Theory and Research on Anxiety. In C. Spielberger (ed.) *Anxiety and Behaviour*. New York: Academic Press, 1966.

Speilberger, C. (Ed.) *Anxiety: Current Trends in Theory and Research*. Vol. 2. New York: Academic Press, 1972.

Spielberger, C. *Stress and anxiety*. Vol. 5. New York: Wiley, 1978.

Srivastava, R. and Shocker, A. An exploratory study of usage situational influences on the composition of competitive product markets. Paper at the Association of Consumer Research Conference, 1977.

Stebbins, R. *Teachers and Meaning: Definitions of Classroom Situations*. Leiden: Brill, 1975.

Stokols, D. Environmental psychology. *Annual Review of Psychology*, 1978, *29*, 253-295.

Stone, G. and Farberman, H. *Social Psychology through Symbolic Interaction*. Waltham: Ginn-Blaisdell, 1970.

Tajfel, H. and Fraser, C. *Introducing Social Psychology*. Harmondsworth: Penguin, 1978.

Thomas, W. The behavior pattern and the situation. *Publications of American Sociological Society*, 1928, *22*, 1-13.

Thomas, W. and Thomas, D. *The Child in America*. New York: Alfred Knopf, 1928.

Trickett, E. and Moos, R. Generality and specificity of student reactions in high school classrooms. *Adolescence*, 1970, *5*, 373-390.

Trites, D., Galbraith, F., Sturdevant, M., and Leckwary, J. Influence of nursing unit design on the activities and subjective feelings of nursing personnel. *Environment and Behavior*, 1970, *11*, 303-334.

Trower, P., Bryant, B., and Argyle, M. *Social Skills and Mental Health*. London: Methuen, 1978.

Trudgel, P. *Sociolinguistics*. Harmondsworth: Penguin, 1977.

Van Hasselt, V., Hersen, M., and Milliones, J. Social skills training for alcoholics and drug addicts: a review. *Addictive Behaviors*, 1978, *3*, 221-233.

Watson, J. and Potter, R. Analytic unit for the study of interaction. *Human Relations*, *1962*, *15*, 245-263.

Webb, E., Campbell, D., Schwartz, R., and Sechrest, L. *Unobstrusive Measures: Nonreactive Research in the Social Sciences*. Chicago: Rand-McNally, 1966.

Westland, G. *Current Crises in Psychology*. London: Heinemann, 1978.

Whorf, B. *Language, Thought and Reality*, Cambridge, Mass.: M.I.T. Press, 1956.

Wicker, A. Undermanning, performances and students' subjective experiences in behavior settings of large and small high schools. *Journal of Personality and Social Psychology*, 1968, *10*, 255-261.

Wicker, A. Cognitive complexity, school size, and participation in school behavior settings: a test of the frequency of interaction hypothesis. *Journal of Educational Psychology,* 1969, *60,* 200-203.

Willems, E. Sense of obligation to high school activities as related to school size and marginality of student. *Child Development,* 1967, *38,* 1247-1260.

Willems, E. and Halstead, L. An eco-behavioral approach to health status and health care. In R. Barker et al. (Eds.) *Habitats, Environments and Human Behavior,* San Francisco: Jossey-Bass, 1978.

Wirth, L. Social interaction: the problem of the individual and the group. *American Journal of Sociology,* 1939, *44,* 979.

Wish, M. and Kaplan, S. Towards an implicit theory of interpersonal communication. *Sociometry,* 1977, *40,* 234-246.

Wolfensberger, W. Ethnical issues in research with human subjects. *Science,* 1967, *155,* 47-51

Young, G. Selective perception in neurotics. D. Phil thesis, University of Oxford, 1979.

Zajonc, R. Attitudinal effects of mere exposure. *Journal of Personality and Social Psychology. Monograph Supplement,* 1968, *9,* 1-27.

Zeicher, A., Wright, J. and Herman, S. Effects of situation on dating and assertiveness behavior. *Psychological Reports,* 1977, *40,* 375-381.

Zielinski, J. Situational determinants of assertive behavior in depressed alcoholics. *Journal of Behavior Therapy and Experimental Psychiatry,* 1978, *9,* 103-107.

Zuckerman, M. and Mellstrom, M. The contribution of persons, situations, modes of responses and their interactions in self reported reactions to hypothetical and real anxiety-inducing situations. In D. Magnusson and N. Endler (Eds.) *Personality at the Crossroads: Current Issues in Interactional Psychology,* Hillsdale, N.J.: Erlbaum, 1977.

Part I
The Structure of Social Situations

The Structure of Social Situations: Introduction

The papers in this section are all concerned with structural features of social situations. Thomas and Znaniecki were the authors of an early sociological classic *The Polish Peasant in Europe and America* (1918), which is often quoted for their observation that it is the individual's perception of the situation which is important:—"If men define situations as real, they are real in their consequences." However, as this excerpt shows, they were also well aware of some of the objective features of situations: in the example of a wife's infidelity, the objective situation includes the rules of marriage, the role-system of relatives and neighbours, and economic conditions. The situation also includes the particular event, i.e. infidelity, as well as the institutional arrangements. Thomas and Znaniecki look forward to a new technology whereby it will become possible to better deal with, and to modify, situations.

There are a number of ways in which games are similar to other social events, and for this reason games have often been used as models for social behaviour. There is the pursuit of definite, and inter-related goals, agreement to keep the rules, limitation to certain kinds of moves, and so on. Avedon (1971) has provided a valuable analysis of the structural features of games—the components which would be needed to describe a game, or to instruct someone in how to play. These include the purpose, method of play, rules, roles, physical setting, and so on. Argyle, Furnham and Graham (1981) have used a similar set of features for the analysis of social situations. However, it should be observed that social situations are unlike games in certain respects—they are not always so competitive, or rule-governed, and usually involve less physical action.

Symbolic interactionists have been very interested in the definition of the situation, and the way in which this is negotiated and shared by interactors. Bennett and Bennett (1970), who come from this tradition, discuss the meaning of the physical features of situations. Their emphasis is on furnishing, decoration, colour, etc., all of which affect the way the situation is perceived, and the

3

way in which people behave, symbolically rather than directly. They show how a room used for interrogation is decorated entirely differently from rooms used for pleasant social events. They also include temporal features—how long each kind of encounter will last, and the anticipated sequence of events. However, they do not deal with the objective aspects of physical situations—barriers, distances, visibility, heights, etc. which have direct effects on interaction quite apart from questions of meaning.

Price and Bouffard (1974) studied one of the main features of situations—the rules which constrain and permit only certain kinds of behaviour. Subjects were asked to judge the appropriateness of 15 kinds of behaviour in each of 15 situations. There was considerable agreement that in each situation only certain kinds of behaviour were appropriate, while some situations were more constraining than others, and some kinds of behaviour were more often disallowed. The inappropriate behaviours were also rated as embarrassing. The next step in the study of such rules would be to explain them in terms of other features of the situation; Argyle et al. (1979) attempted to do this by showing the functions of rules in relation to situational goals. It should be observed too that rules are not only restraining, they are part of the "social construction of reality" which makes situations possible, as is most obvious in the case of complex games and formal occasions.

Pervin (1976) studied the classification of situations by four individuals. Each person generated a list of the situations in his current life and then rated them on situation-traits, feelings and kinds of behaviour, which were also generated by the individual. Factor analyses were carried out and five situation factors appeared—home-family, friends-peers, relaxation-play, work, and college. This would vary with different kinds of people, but probably family-friends-play-work is an important grouping of situations. Pervin also found that situations were often described and grouped in terms of affect, which influenced behaviour in a complex way. He found that situations were now classified in terms of certain general dimensions: friendly-unfriendly, tense-calm, interesting-dull and constrained-free.

One of the most important features of situations is the set of goals which people pursue in them. Graham, Argyle and Furnham (1980) studied the main goals of each participant in a number of common situations. Factor analyses produced similar factors in each case—bodily needs, social needs, and task goals. They then elicited the "goal structures," i.e. the extent to which each goal was reported to be instrumental to or in conflict with other goals. This produced a kind of map of the situations studied. The main limitation to this approach is that it depends on verbal reports, and it is possible that some kinds of motivation are inaccessible to such reports. In addition the scales used perhaps underemphasized dominance, aggression or anti-social goals.

MAJOR BOOKS COVERING RELATED ISSUES

Argyle, M., Furnham, A. and Graham, J.A. (1981) *Social Situations*. Cambridge: Cambridge University Press.

Argyle, M., Graham, J.A., Campbell, A. and White, P. (1979) The rules of different situations. *New Zealand Psychologist, 8,* 13-22.

Backman, C. Epilogue: A new paradigm. In G. Ginsburg (Ed.) *Emerging Strategies in Social Psychological Research*. New York: Wiley, 1979.

Ball, D. *Microsociology: Social Situations and Intimate Space*. Indianapolis: Bobbs-Merrill, 1973.

Barker, R. *The Stream of Behavior*. New York: Appleton-Century-Crofts, 1966.

Blass, G. *Personality Variables in Social Behavior*. New York: Erlbaum, 1977.

Block, J. *Lives through time*. Berkeley: Bancroft, 1971.

Bromley, D. *Personality Description in Everyday Language*. London: Wiley, 1977.

Collett, P. (Ed.) *Social Rules and Social Behaviour*. Oxford: Blackwell, 1976.

Douglas, J. (Ed.) *Understanding Everyday Life*. Chicago: Aldine, 1970.

Duncan, S. and Fiske, D. *Face-to-face Communication*. Hillsdale: Erlbaum, 1977.

Endler, N. and Magnusson, D. *Interactional Psychology and Personality*. New York: Wiley, 1976.

Forgas, J. *Social episodes: The Study of Interaction Routines*. London: Academic Press, 1980.

Ginsburg, G. (Ed.) *Emerging Strategies in Social Psychological Research*. Chichester: Wiley, 1979.

Goffman, E. *Encounters*. Harmondsworth: Penguin, 1961.

Harré, R. *Social Being*. Oxford: Blackwell, 1979.

Hartshorne, H. and May M. *Studies in the Nature of Character: Studies in Deceit*. New York: Macmillan, 1928.

Laver, R. and Handel, W. *Social Psychology: the Theory and Application of Symbolic Interaction*. Boston: Houghton, Mifflin, 1977.

Lofland, J. *Analysing Social Settings*. California: Wadworth, 1971.

London, H. *Personality: A New Look at Metatheories*. Washington: Hemisphere, 1978.

Magnusson, D. and Endler, N. (Eds.) *Personality at the Crossroads*. Hillsdale: Erlbaum, 1977.

Mischel, W. *Personality and Assessment*. New York: Wiley, 1968.

Moos, R. *The Human Context: Environmental Determinants of Behavior*. New York: Wiley, 1975.

Moos, R. *Evaluating Correctional and Community Settings*. New York: Wiley, 1975.

Nitsche, R. and Green, A. *Situational Exercises in Cross-Cultural Awareness*. New York: Merrill, 1977.

Pervin. L. *Current Controversies and Issues in Personality*. New York: Wiley, 1978.

Pervin, L. and Lewis, M. (Eds.) *Perspectives in Interactional Psychology*. New York: Plenum, 1978 (in press).

Sells, S. *Stimulus Determinants of Behavior*. New York: Ronald, 1963.

Stone, G. and Farberman, H. *Social Psychology through Symbolic Interaction*. Waltham, Mass.: Ginn-Blaisdell, 1970.

SUGGESTED ADDITIONAL REFERENCES

Argyle, M., and Furnham, A., and Graham, J. A. *Social situations*. Cambridge: Cambridge University Press, 1981.

Arsenian, J. and Arsenian, J. Tough and easy cultures: a conceptual analysis. *Psychiatry*, 1948, *11*, 377-385.

Bowers, K. Situationism in psychology: an analysis and a critique. *Psychological Review*, 1973, *80*, 307-336.

Cochran, L. Conceptual relatedness and the comprehension of social situations. *Social Behavior and Personality*, 1976, *4*, 91-96.

Cochran, L. Construct systems and the definition of social situations. *Journal of Personality and Social Psychology*, 1978, *36*, 733-740.

Coska, L. and Bons, P. Manipulating the situation to fit the leader's style. *Journal of Applied Psychology*, 1978, *63*, 295-300.

Cottrell, L. The analysis of situational fields in social psychology. *American Sociological Review*, 1942, *7*, 370-376.

Graham, J., Argyle, M., Clarke, D., and Maxwell, G. The salience, equivalence and sequential structure of behaviour elements in different settings. *Semiotica*, (in press).

Harré, R. Architectonic man. In H. Brown and S. Lyman (Eds.) *Structures, Consciousness and History*, Los Angeles: Cambridge University Press, 1978.

Krause, M. Use of social situations for research purposes. *American Psychologist*, 1970, *25*, 748-753.

Lane, M. A reconsideration of context. *American Psychologist*, 1977, *32*, 1056-59.

Meyer, K. and Seider, J. The structure of gatherings. *Sociology and Social Research*, 1978, *63*, 131-153.

Moos, R. Conceptualisations of human environments. *American Psychologist*, 1973, *28*, 652-665.

Noesjirwan, J. A rule-based analysis of cultural differences in social behaviour: Indonesia and Australia. *International Journal of Psychology*, 1978, *13*, 305-316.

Pervin, L. Definition, measurements, and classification of stimuli, situations, and environments. *Human Ecology*, 1978, *6*, 71-105.

Price, R. and Bouffard, D. Behavioral appropriateness and situational constraints as a dimension of social behavior. *Journal of Personality and Social Psychology*, 1974, *30*, 519-586.

Queen, S. Some problems of the situational approach. *Social Forces*, 1931, *9*, 480-481.

Rausch, H. Interaction sequences. *Journal of Personality and Social Psychology*, 1965, *2*, 487-499.

Segal, E. and Stacy, E. Rule governed behaviour as a psychological process. *American Psychologist*, 1975, *30*, 541-552.

Sherif, M. Stimulus situations in psychology. In M. Sherif (Ed.) *Psychology of Social Norms*, New York: Harper, 1936.

Sherif, M. Analysis of a social situation. In G. Di Renzo (Ed.) *Concepts, Theory, and Explanation in the Behavioral Sciences*, New York: Random House, 1966.

Twining, W. and Miers, D. *How to do things with rules*, London: Wieherfeld, Nicholson, 1976.

1

The Polish Peasant in Europe and America*

W. Thomas and F. Znaniecki

We cannot enter here into detailed indications of what social technology should be, but we must take into account the chief point of its method—the general form which every concrete problem of social technique assumes. Whatever may be the aim of social practice—modification of individual attitudes or of social institutions—in trying to attain this aim we never find the elements which we want to use or to modify isolated and passively waiting for our activity, but always embodied in active practical *situations,* which have been formed independently of us and with which our activity has to comply.

The situation is the set of values and attitudes with which the individual or the group has to deal in a process of activity and with regard to which this activity is planned and its results appreciated. Every concrete activity is the solution of a situation. The situation involves three kinds of data: (1) The objective conditions under which the individual or society has to act, that is, the totality of values—economic, social, religious, intellectual, etc.—which at the given moment affect directly or indirectly the conscious status of the individual or the group. (2) The pre-existing attitudes of the individual or the group which at the given moment have an actual influence upon his behavior. (3) The definition of the situation, that is, the more or less clear conception of the conditions and consciousness of the attitudes. And the definition of the situation is a necessary preliminary to any act of the will, for in given conditions and with a given set of attitudes an indefinite plurality of actions is possible, and one definite action can appear only if these conditions are selected, interpreted, and combined in a determined way and if a certain systematization of these attitudes is reached, so that one of them becomes predominant and subordinates the others. It happens,

*W. Thomas and F. Znaniecki: The Polish Peasant in Europe and America, 1928, 67-74 (Alfred A. Knopf, Inc.)

indeed, that a certain value imposes itself immediately and unreflectively and leads at once to action, or that an attitude as soon as it appears excludes the others and expresses itself unhesitatingly in an active process. In these cases, whose most radical examples are found in reflex and instinctive actions, the definition is already given to the individual by external conditions or by his own tendencies. But usually there is a process of reflection, after which either a ready social definition is applied or a new personal definition worked out.

Let us take a typical example out of the fifth volume of the present work, concerning the family life of the immigrants in America. A husband, learning of his wife's infidelity, deserts her. The objective conditions were: (1) the social institution of marriage with all the rules involved; (2) the wife, the other man, the children, the neighbors, and in general all the individuals constituting the habitual environment of the husband and, in a sense, given to him as values; (3) certain economic conditions; (4) the fact of the wife's infidelity. Toward all these values the husband had certain attitudes, some of them traditional, others recently developed. Now, perhaps under the influence of the discovery of his wife's infidelity, perhaps after having developed some new attitude toward the sexual or economic side of marriage, perhaps simply influenced by the advice of a friend in the form of a rudimentary scheme of the situation helping him to "see the point," he defines the situation for himself. He takes certain conditions into account, ignores or neglects others, or gives them a certain interpretation in view of some chief value, which may be his wife's infidelity, or the economic burdens of family life of which this infidelity gives him the pretext to rid himself, or perhaps some other woman, or the half-ironical pity of his neighbors, etc. And in this definition some one attitude—sexual jealousy, or desire for economic freedom, or love for the other woman, or offended desire for recognition—or a complex of these attitudes, or a new attitude (hate, disgust) subordinates to itself the others and manifests itself chiefly in the subsequent action, which is evidently a solution of the situation, and fully determined both in its social and in its individual components by the whole set of values, attitudes, and reflective schemes which the situation included. When a situation is solved, the result of the activity becomes an element of a new situation, and this is most clearly evidenced in cases where the activity brings a change of a social institution whose unsatisfactory functioning was the chief element of the first situation.

Now, while the task of science is to analyze by a comparative study the whole process of activity into elementary facts, and it must therefore ignore the variety of concrete situations in order to be able to find laws of causal dependence of abstractly isolated attitudes or values on other attitudes and values, the task of technique is to provide the means of a rational control of concrete situations. The situation can evidently be controlled either by a change of conditions or by a change of attitudes, or by both, and in this respect the role of technique as application of science is easily characterized. By comparing situations of a certain type, the social technician must find what are the predominant values or the predominant attitudes which determine the situation more than others, and then the question is to modify these values or these attitudes in the desired way by using the knowledge of social causation given by social theory. Thus, we may find that some of the situations among the Polish immigrants in America resulting in the husband's desertion are chiefly determined by the wife's infidelity, others by her quarrelsomeness, others by bad economic conditions, still others by the husband's desire for freedom, etc. And, if in a given case we know what influences to apply in order to modify these dominating factors, we can modify the situation accordingly, and ideally we can provoke in the individual a behavior in conformity with any given scheme of attitudes and values.

To be sure, it may happen that, in spite of an adequate scientific knowledge of the social laws permitting the modification of those factors which we want to change, our efforts will fail to influence the situation or will produce a situation more undesirable than the one we wished to avoid. The fault is then with our technical knowledge. That is, either we have failed in determining the relative importance of the various factors, or we have failed to foresee the influence of other causes which, interfering with our activity, produce a quite unexpected and undesired effect. And since it is impossible to expect from every practitioner a complete scientific training and still more impossible to have him work out a scientifically justified and detailed plan of action for every concrete case in particular, the special task of the social technician is to prepare, with the help of both science and practical observation, thorough schemes and plans of action for all the various *types* of situations which may be found in a given line of social activity, and leave to the practitioner the subordination of the given concrete situation to its proper type. This is actually the rôle which all the organizers of social institutions have played, but the technique itself must become more conscious and methodically perfect, and every field of social activity should have its professional technicians. The evolution of social life makes necessary continual modifications and developments of social technique, and we can hope that the evolution of social theory will continually put new and useful scientific generalizations within the reach of the social technician; the latter must therefore remain in permanent touch with both social life and social theory, and this requires a more far-going specialization than we actually find.

But, however efficient this type of social technique may become, its application will always have certain limits beyond which a different type of technique will be more useful. Indeed, the form of social control outlined above presupposes that the individual—or the group—is treated as a passive object of our activity and that we change the situations for him, from case to case, in accordance with our plans and intentions. But the application of this method becomes more and more difficult as the situations grow more complex, more new and unexpected from case to case, and more influenced by the individual's own reflection. And, indeed, from both the moral and the hedonistic standpoints and also from the standpoint at the level of efficiency of the individual and of the group, it is desirable to develop in the individuals the ability to control spontaneously their own activities by conscious reflection. To use a biological comparison, the type of control where the practitioner prescribes for the individual a scheme of activity appropriate to every crisis as it arises corresponds to the tropic or reflex type of control in animal life, where the activity of the individual is controlled mechanically by stimulations from without, while the reflective and individualistic control corresponds to the type of activity characteristic of the higher conscious organism, where the control is exercised from within by the selective mechanism of the nervous system. While, in the early tribal, communal, kinship, and religious groups, and to a large extent in the historic state, the society itself provided a rigoristic and particularistic set of definitions in the form of "customs" or "mores," the tendency to advance is associated with the liberty of the individual to make his own definitions.

We have assumed throughout this argument that if an adequate technique is developed it is possible to produce any desirable attitudes and values, but this assumption is practically justified only if we find in the individual attitudes which cannot avoid response to the class of stimulations which society is able to apply to him. And apparently we do find this disposition. Every individual has a vast variety of wishes which can be satisfied only by his incorporation in a society. Among his general patterns of wishes we may enumerate : (1) the desire for new experience, for fresh stimulations; (2) the desire for recognition, including, for example, sexual response and general social appreciation, and secured by devices ranging from the display of ornament to the demonstration of worth through scientific attainment; (3) the desire for mastery, or the "will to power," exemplified by ownership, domestic tyranny, political despotism, based on the instinct of hate, but capable of being sublimated to laudable ambition; (4) the desire for security, based on the instinct of fear and exemplified negatively by the wretchedness of the individual in perpetual solitude or under social taboo. Society is, indeed, an agent for the repression of many of the wishes in the individual; it demands that he shall be moral by repressing at least the wishes which are irreconcilable with the welfare of the group, but nevertheless it provides the only medium within which any of his schemes or wishes can be gratified. And it would be superfluous to point out by examples the degree to which society has in the past been able to impose its schemes of attitudes and values on the individual. Professor Sumner's volume, *Folkways,* is practically a collection of such examples, and, far from discouraging us as they discourage Professor Sumner, they should be regarded as proofs of the ability of the individual to conform to any definition, to accept any attitude, provided it is an expression of the public will or represents the appreciation of even a limited group. To take a single example from the present, to be a bastard or the mother of a bastard has been regarded heretofore as anything but desirable, but we have at this moment reports that one of the warring European nations is officially impregnating its unmarried women and girls and even married women whose husbands are at the front. If this is true (which we do not assume) we have a new definition and a new evaluation of motherhood arising from the struggle of this society against death, and we may anticipate a new attitude—that the resulting children and their mothers will be the objects of extraordinary social appreciation. And even if we find that the attitudes are not so tractable as we have assumed, that it is not possible to provoke all the desirable ones, we shall still be in the same situation as, let us say, physics and mechanics: we shall have the problem of securing the highest degree of control possible in view of the nature of our materials.

2

The Structural Elements of Games*

E. M. Avedon

What are games? Are they things in the sense of artifacts? Are they behavioral models, or simulations of social situations? Are they vestiges of ancient rituals, or magical rites? It is difficult and even curious when one tries to answer the question "what are games," since it is assumed that games are many things and at the same time specific games are different from one another—but are they?

> . . . but we enjoyed playing games and were punished for them by men who played games themselves. However, grown-up games are known as 'business' and even though boys' games are much the same, they are punished for them by their elders. No one pities either the boys or the men, though surely we deserved pity, for I cannot believe that a good judge would approve of the beatings I received as a boy on the ground that my games delayed my progress in studying subjects which would enable me to play a less creditable game later in life. . . .[1]

---

*E. M. Avedon and Sutton-Smith: The Study of Games, 419-426. Reprinted by permission of John Wiley & Sons, Inc.

[1]Saint Augustine (A.D. 354-430), Confessions, Book 1:10.

Personnel in the field of recreation have avoided answering the question and have subsequently avoided the adoption of a universal taxonomy for games, since to do so would demand a theory. Thus, many are content with the taxonomies that have appeared in the literature for the past fifty years, *i.e.,* indoor games, outdoor games; games of low organization, games of high organization; equipment games, non-equipment games; paper and pencil games, board and table games; games for girls and women, games for boys and men; children's games, adult games. All of these classifications refer to an element of a game and thus different games are grouped together because they have one element in common. This leads one to ask: Are there certain structural elements that are common to all games, regardless of the differences in games or the purposes for which the games are used, or the culture in which they are used? Are there elements that are invariant under certain transformations? If the answer is in the affirmative, then these invariant elements would not only lend themselves to scrutiny, but would enable personnel to standardize game utilization for therapeutic purposes, as well as modify professional program planning practices.

The notion of invariant structural elements in games has been an interest of mathematicians for a number of years. Von Neumann and others have delimited a number of elements which they believe are present in all games, elements that are necessary and invariant, *i.e.,* number of players, rules of the game, results or "pay-off," and strategies that could be employed in play of the game. However, from the point of view of recreation, these elements are not sufficient to make a game. In addition, strategy is something that a player brings to the game; it is not an intrinsic part of a game. It is something that the player develops, based on his past experience, knowledge of the game, and the personality of the other players.

In addition to mathematicians, others have also been interested in the structural elements of games. A contemporary of Von Neumann's, George H. Mead, was primarily interested in the influences of various aspects of society on human growth and development. Mead taught that games were primarily a pattern or set of specific social situations which affect personality. As a by-product of his concerns, he delimited a number of structural elements of games, which he felt influenced behavior.

> The game has a logic, so that there is a definite end to be obtained; the actions of the different individuals are all related to each other with reference to that end . . . so that they further the purpose of the game itself. They are interrelated in a unitary, organic fashion. . . .[2]

Thus, one element—the logic of the game, the definite end—may be thought of as the *purpose* on raison d'etre. A second element would be the actions in

---

[2]George H. Mead, "Play, the Game, and the Generalized Other" *Mind, Self, and Society,* Chicago: University of Chicago Press, 1934, pp. 158-159.

reference to the purpose, or the *procedures for action*. A third element would be the interrelated actions. Mead indicates that games include social processes which influence or regulate interaction of the players, and thus this third element might be termed *interaction patterns*.

A fourth element Mead specifies is that of the *roles* which games require players to take. The fifth element he identified is the only one which Von Neumann also identified, *i.e.*, *rules governing action*.

Szasz[3] built directly upon Mead's theories. Although applied within a psychiatric frame of reference, he too indicates that games may be viewed as objects affecting personality. He strengthens Mead's delimination of game elements and stresses the factor of interaction patterns. In analyzing the structure of games, he delimits such elements as rules, roles, procedures, etc.

Goffman,[4] a contemporary of Szasz, in studying the sociology of interaction also strengthens Mead's delimitation of game elements. Goffman reports on different types of "focused interactions" and stresses the same game elements as others before him. However, Goffman introduces a new element, which he refers to as *fun* or euphoria. He indicates that this element must be present to ensure participation, and that players modify and manipulate various other elements in order to find *fun* in a game. Fun, like strategies, is subjective and is therefore not an intrinsic element in games. As Goffman rightly points out, often the other elements must be manipulated for a participant to have fun.

In addition to the elements Mead identifies, Goffman emphasizes some of the elements Von Neumann and his colleagues have identified. Unlike Szasz, Goffman's concerns are not with the game as a mode of behavior, but the game as a milieu for behavior.

Recently another psychiatrist, Eric Berne, published an exposition on behavior and games.[5] Berne concerned with interaction, uses the term "transaction," while Goffman uses the term "encounters." They both discuss a variety of interaction patterns subsumed under these labels, and indicate that games are only one type of interaction. Berne emphasizes the same elements as Mead, Szasz, and Goffman; however, he uses different labels. A striking aspect of Berne's approach is his identification of seemingly non-game interactions as games. He points out that games are differentiated from other types of interaction because of their intrinsic elements, and many social situations, although appearing not to be games, possess these elements, and are in reality, games, a notion similar to the one expressed by Saint Augustine. He also indicates that some playing is with conscious intent, and some is the result of unconscious

[3]Thomas S. Szasz, "Game Model Analysis of Behavior," Part V. *The Myth of Mental Illness*, New York: 889-7500 Medical Division, Harper and Row Publishers, 1961, pp. 223-293.

[4]Erving Goffman, "Fun in Games," *Encounters*, Indianapolis: Bobbs-Merrill Company, Inc., 1961, pp. 17-18.

[5]Eric Berne, *Games People Play*, New York: Grove Press, 1964.

conflict. Szasz and Berne identify certain qualities in games which have pathological significance.

By combining the work of the mathematicians and the behaviorists, we are able to identify seven elements in games. These are:

1. Purpose or raison d'être.
2. Procedures for action.
3. Rules governing action.
4. Number of required players.
5. Roles of participant.
6. Participant interaction patterns.
7. Results or pay-off.

In addition to these, personnel in the field of recreation have called attention to additional game elements which must be considered. A major element which recreation personnel have long been concerned with are the *abilities and skills required for participation*. Other elements which recreation personnel consider to be of imporance are the *environmental requirements* and necessary *physical setting,* and the required *equipment* needed for participation in a game.

From a syntactical point of view then, games are composed of ten elements; possibly, additional elements will be identified at some future date. Presently, the ten elements to consider are as follows:

Element	Example
1. *Purpose of the game;* aim or goal, intent, the raison d'etre.	Checkmate one's opponent (chess). Bid and make a contract (bridge). Complete the course in as few strokes as possible (golf).
2. *Procedure for action;* specific operations, required courses of action, method of play.	Roll dice, move counter in clockwise direction around board, the number of spaces indicated on dice. Act in manner indicated by last space on which counter lands, *i.e.,* take a chance, pay rent, go to jail, etc. (Monopoly). Stand in box, toss two successive shoes at far stake, travel to that stake with opponent, tally score, pitch back to first stake (horseshoes).
3. *Rules governing action;* fixed principles that determine conduct and standards for behavior.	Go back where you were, you didn't say, "May I?" (Giant Steps).
N.B. Some games have very few rules, others have such elaborate sets of rules as to require a non-participant to keep	Regulations regarding weight and types of blows which may be employed. Panel of judges and referee determine infringe-

Element	Example
track of infringement of the rules or to enforce the rules.	ment of rules, and have responsibility for enforcing rules (boxing).
4. *Number of required participants;* stated minimum or maximum number of persons needed for action to take place. N.B. Sometimes minimum and maximum are identical.	Minimum of two required, no stated maximum (hide-and-go-seek). Eleven men required for each team, minimum and maximum of twenty-two (football).
5. *Roles of participants;* indicated functions and status. N.B. Role and power function may differ for each participant or may be the same.	Goalkeeper, center, others. Each player has a different role (hockey). Each player has no more or less power than the others, and each functions in the same way (backgammon).
6. *Results or pay-off;* values assigned to the outcome of the action.	Money (black-jack). A kiss (spin-the-bottle). A gold medal (relay race).
7. *Abilities and skills required for action;* aspects of the three behavioral domains utilized in a given activity. (a) Cognitive domain includes—figural, symbolic, semantic, and behavioral informational content; and operational processes, such as cognition, memory, divergent and convergent production, and evaluation.	Remembering which cards have been played and from which suits, in order to play the best card (hearts).
(b) Sensory-motor domain includes—bodily movement, manipulative motor skills, coordination, sequences and patterns of movement, endurance factors, sight, hearing, etc.	Grasping the ball, walking to the foul line, releasing the ball, etc (bowling).
(c) Affective domain includes—semiotic factors which stimulate emotions, *i.e.,* anger, joy, affection, disgust, hate, etc. Offers opportunities for object-ties, transference, identification.	Having one's disc knocked off the court (extension of self) requires affective control to continue game (shuffleboard).
8. *Interaction patterns:* (a) Intra-individual—action taking place within the mind of a person or action involving the mind and a part of the body, but requiring no contact with another person or external object.	Pillow puzzles. Finger-flexion tricks.
(b) Extra-individual—action directed by a person toward an object in the environ-	Jigsaw puzzle. Solitaire.

Element	Example
ment, requiring no contact with another person.	
(c) Aggregate—action directed by a person toward an object in the environment while in the company of other persons who are also directing action toward objects in the environment. Action is not directed toward each other, no interaction between participants is required or necessary.	Bingo. Roulette.
(d) Inter-individual—action of a competitive nature directed by one person toward another.	Checkers. Tennis.
(e) Unilateral—action of a competitive nature among three or more persons, one of whom is an antagonist or "it." Interaction is in simultaneous competitive dyadic relationships.	Tag. Dodge ball.
(f) Multi-lateral—action of a competitive nature among three or more persons, no one person is an antagonist.	Scrabble. Poker.
(g) Intra-group—action of a cooperative nature by two or more persons intent upon reaching a mutual goal. Action requires positive verbal and non-verbal interaction.	Cat's cradle. Maori sticks.
(h) Inter-group—action of a competitive nature between two or more intra-groups.	Soccer. Basketball.
9. *Physical setting and environmental requirements:*	
(a) Physical setting—man-made or natural facility in which action takes places.	Four-walled court (squash). No special setting (charades).
(b) Environmental requirements—natural circumstances which are indispensable or obligatory.	Pool (water polo).
N.B. This element may not always be present.	No special environment (dominoes).
10. *Required equipment;* man-made or natural artifacts employed in the course of action.	Rackets, bird, net (badminton).
N.B. This element may not always be present.	No equipment necessary (20 questions).

A variety of interesting questions are presented when one examines this list of elements—questions that demand rigorous scholarly inquiry. The most important question to consider is the notion that these elements are present in all games. Subsequent questions might be asked about each of the elements. For example, can the interaction patterns be viewed in a developmental hierarchy? Does one pattern have to be mastered before a participant can function effectively in another pattern, or are the patterns mutually exclusive? Using Guilford's model for *The Structure of Intellect,* can one delimit cognitive process in the same way that we are able to delimit sensory-motor process in a game?[6] Are there other, more effective theoretical models regarding cognition which would lend themselves to this purpose. What of the affective domain—is a psychoanalytic frame of reference the most effective one to use in delimiting ability and skill in this area? Are setting and environment one interrelated element, or are they really two elements? Are there more than eight interaction patterns that can be identified?

Redl, Gump, and Sutton-Smith have indicated that there are a number of behavioral dimensions other than the ones cited which should be considered when examining games. Thus, this exposition must of necessity be considered a preliminary excursion into the structure of games, and until considerable effort has been spent beyond this theoretical attempt, it must remain just that. However, it is hoped that some of these thoughts will stimulate others in this direction.

---

[6]J. P. Guilford, "Intelligence: 1965 Model," *American Psychologist,* **21,** (1), January, 1966, pp. 20-26.

3
Making the Scene*
David J. Bennett and
Judith D. Bennett

All social interaction is affected by the physical container within which it occurs. The various elements of the container establish a world of meaning through the arrangement of non-verbal symbolism. For this reason, the common practice in the social sciences of focusing on behavior without reference to the physical setting would seem to ignore an important dimension of the total picture of interaction.

As in the case of spoken language and even gestural conduct, there must be a consensus upon meaning for this symbolism to play a relevant part in social situations. The container imposes both physical and symbolic limitations upon behavior. Its sheer physical dimension limits the range of possible movement. We do not neck in the back of churches; we do in movie theatres.

Recently, some work has been done in exploring the relation between the physical and interactional worlds of human beings. The more obvious effects of the physical setting as the background against which interaction takes place have been dealt with as "regions" by Erving Goffman[1]; the physical territory as a generator of behavior has been hypothesized by Robert Ardrey[2]; the physical container as a variable matrix of interaction within different cultural frameworks

---

*First published in G. Stone & H. Farberman: Social Psychology through Symbolic Interactionism, 1970, 190-196 (Waltham, Massachusetts: Ginn-Blaisdell)

[1]Erving Goffman, *The Presentation of Self in Everyday Life* (Garden City: Doubleday Anchor Books, 1959), and his *Behavior in Public Places* (New York: The Free Press, A Division of The Macmillan Company, 1963).

[2]Robert Ardrey, *The Territorial Imperative* (New York: Dell Publishing Co., 1969).

has been studied by Edward T. Hall[3]; others[4] have concerned themselves with
the variable effects of physical containers. However, with the possible exception
of Hall, this area has not been dealt with systematically.

While very few systematic studies exist, the practice of dealing with the
physical environment by deliberately manipulating it and its constituent parts and
dimensions to secure some desired social effect has long been a practice of those
professions concerned with environmental design: architects, planners, industrial
designers, interior decorators, stage managers, and others. These people,
however, have not developed quantitative techniques for analyzing physical
settings as symbolic frameworks within which social interaction proceeds.
Rather, their work is guided by tradition, "common sense," and accumulated,
but unsystematized, experience. They assume causal relationships between
certain physical arrangements and specific social "end results."[5] Whether these
assumed relationships are valid has yet to be determined. Yet, there are some
physical arrangements that have occurred with remarkable consistency around
the world throughout human history.

The physical building or space which forms the symbolic edifice of superhu-
man power, whether God, Hero, or State, seems to have the following universal
characteristics: (1) tremendous size in relation to other buildings, or, when
diminutive in actual size, as in the case of some shrines in both Oriental and
Occidental civilizations, a scale, i.e., a relation of the elements of the object to
the whole, which suggests tremendous size; (2) an expression of great stability,
durability, and immutability, often achieved by symmetry, and, when not, by a
highly stylized arrangement of objects or parts of the whole; (3) a carefully
organized progression of spaces (be it the entrance to an ancient Egyptian royal
tomb, the path through the Acropolis at Athens, the forecourt to a Shinto shrine,
the road to Versailles, or the monumental steps up to almost any seat of judgment
of any time or place in the Western world) arranged so that they are experienced
as a linear sequence of events invested with awesome meaning. Similarly, other
symbolic-physical arrangements seemingly have the same cross-cultural uniformity. Authority is usually physically elevated.

---

[3]Edward T. Hall, *The Hidden Dimension* (Garden City: Doubleday and Co., 1966).

[4]In searching the literature for studies and discussions of how the physical container affects social
behavior, we find two areas which are indirectly related to our problem. The first of these is the work
of the transactional psychologists concerned with the nature of perception. See, for example, Franklin
P. Kilpatrick (ed.), *Explorations in Transactional Psychology* (New York: New York University
Press, 1961). Many of the studies in this collection deal with the ways in which the perception of
objects occurs. In addition, there is an excellent bibliography in that volume. From the developmental
perspective, Piaget has dealt with the problem of how children learn to organize external reality. See
Jean Piaget, *The Construction of Reality in the Child* (New York: Basic Books, 1954).

[5]Note well that the process of assuming a causal relationship between physical form and meaning
may act to bring about that very relationship. Thus, the recurring use of great scale (monumental
buildings) to symbolize super-human authority finally dictates that, if one wishes to symbolize
super-human authority, he must use great scale.

COMPONENTS AND DIMENSIONS OF THE SCENE

In order to analyze the specific relationships which obtain between physical environment and social behavior, it is necessary to establish precisely which elements of the environment or scene may affect human conduct. Such elements may have isolated effects or may affect human conduct in interaction with one another. We have made a preliminary attempt to list such elements, and our attempt has generated the following six components or dimensions of any scene:

1. The *container*—the fixed external enclosure of human interaction.
2. The *props*—physical objects which adhere to persons in the enclosure or to the enclosure itself, including dress and furnishings.
3. The *actors*—persons involved in, peripheral to, or spectators to the transactions carried on in the enclosure.

These components have been dealt with, one way or another, in the works we have cited earlier. Taken together, they are what most social psychologists have considered when they have included aspects of the scene in their analysis of social interaction. The following three elements have seldom been considered in such analyses:

4. The *modifiers*—elements of light, sound, color, texture, odor, temperature, and humidity which serve to affect the emotional tone or mood of the interaction.
5. *Duration*—the objective time in measurable units (minutes, hours, etc.) during which the interaction occurs, as well as the anticipated time the interaction will require.
6. *Progression*—the order of events which precede and follow, or are expected to follow, the interaction and have some bearing upon it.

These latter three terms, as can be seen, do not deal with objects, but with action or modifiers of action. In most European grammars, as Whorf noted, these are verbs or adverbs in the object-action conception of reality demanded by the rules of syntax.[6] As such, they add a critical dimension to the enclosure within which interaction transpires, but, more important, they lend the interaction a certain affect or mood. We can understand such affects by imagining four situations occurring within enclosures, each of identical dimensions, with three constant props and the same number of actors.

BEHAVIORAL CONSEQUENCES OF SCENES

The scene is a room only large enough to accommodate one table with sufficient space to move around it. Two men are seated at opposite sides of the table.

---

[6]Benjamin Lee Whorf, *Language, Thought, and Reality* (New York: John Wiley and Sons, Inc., 1959), pp. 207-219, 233-245.

Without changing the arrangement of the men, the chairs, and the table, let us show how the entire context of interaction—its symbolic significance—can be altered by manipulating other components and dimensions of the scene.

Situation One: The walls, floor, and ceiling of the room are concrete and plaster, unpainted and bare of any decoration. There is a single bare, bright electric bulb suspended above the table as the only source of light. The table and chairs are wood, bare, hard, and smooth. The temperature is relatively low (say 60 degrees Fahrenheit), and the relative humidity is high, making the room chilly and damp. There is a slight odor of mildew. The predominant colors are gray and white.

Situation Two: Now the walls are hung with dark red drapes. The floor is thickly carpeted, and the ceiling painted a soft off-white. The light source is a light cone around the ceiling which gives off a soft, diffuse, dim light. The table is covered with a white cloth and the chairs are upholstered with a nappy material. The temperature and humidity are a little above the American Standard Engineering "Comfort Range" (68 degrees Fahrenheit and 45% relative humidity), making the room feel a little warm and humid. There is a slightly "stuffy" odor in the room. The predominant colors are dark red, off-white, and a muted gold.

Situation Three: The ceiling is a luminous fluorescent ceiling such as may be found in many contemporary office buildings. Three of the walls are smooth white plaster; the fourth, a chromatic blue. The floor is covered with a dark gray carpet. The table is very low, its top no more than sixteen inches above the floor. Its base is polished steel, its top is glass. The chairs are polished steel frames fitted with black leather cushions. The room is cool and dry and, for all intents and purposes, "odorless."

Situation Four: The ceiling is off-white plaster. The walls, also plaster, are painted beige. The floor is a vinyl asbestos tile of a light brown color with a green oval woven area rug. The light source is a floor-to-ceiling pole light with three shaded fixtures. The table is a dark grained wood, and the chairs are wood frame with green upholstered seats and backs. The temperature and relative humidity are within the "comfort range." There is no discernible odor.

What is significant about the four situations presented above is not that a precise description of their meaning can be made—it cannot—but they are presented in the expectation that the reader will respond to each one of them differently despite the fact that: (1) the dimensions of the enclosure, the arrangement of people and objects (although the appearance of chairs and tables are modified) remain unchanged; (2) the reader knows nothing specific about either the people or the nature of the interaction; (3) the description of the situations is incomplete, having not included the elements of sound (although the quality of sound is implied), duration, or progression. Also, the situations, each a carefully contrived ensemble of mutually reinforcing conventionalized elements in conventionalized combinations, probably will evoke grossly predictable responses from specific audiences, presuming cultural, age, and socio-economic homogeneity.

We may describe these four situations as settings for the following interactions. The reader, although he will be able to supply alternatives, will find it difficult to reject these possibilities.

Situation One—an interrogation
Situation Two—a social conversation
Situation Three–an interview
Situation Four–indeterminate (could be any one of the above)

All of these interpretations apply, remember, to the same enclosure, the same number of objects, and the same number of people. The fourth scene is indeterminate, we would assert, because of the relative neutrality, in symbolic terms, of the modifying elements which ordinarily enhance mood or affect. That the reader may be able to supply alternative interpretations of the interaction taking place in any of the situations we have presented is not an indication of the symbolic imprecision, in any absolute sense, of our descriptions. In fact, the situations are of a generalized type. Each can accommodate a number—but a *finite* number—of different interactions in the context of our culture. It is important to note that, whatever number of events may occur in each of these situations, that number could probably be counted or estimated while the number which could *not* occur is probably beyond measure or estimate. We have mentioned that, among other elements of the situation, we have ignored matters of duration and progression. These seem to us to be of seminal importance, and we wish now to speculate about their possible impact on these situated interactions.

Duration. The expected duration of an interrogation has no objective time unit. Instead, it is a function of the relative definitions of the situation formulated by the interrogated and the interrogator. Both may, for separate reasons, want it over "quickly" (a subjective time unit). However, if the interrogated's aim is resistance, he may wish to extend it indefinitely, while the interrogator's desire may be a rapid termination of the encounter. The opposite may also be the case. In any event, the interrogation is a situation in which the duration of the situation is highly significant for the actor's conception of its meaning, even without some prior established expectation about the objective time of duration. For the interrogated, this is part of the terror.

In contrast, a social conversation or an interview present situations in which actors usually have distinct and mutual expectations about how long the encounter will last, and they are prepared to engage one another for that length of time. The job interviewer who conducts an interview with, let us say, a potential secretary over a four-hour period will be violating a norm so flagrantly that the applicant may well redefine the situation as an interrogation.[7] In other words, time can affect the definition, including the mood of the situation.

We enter a situation with a learned expectation of its duration and are prepared to participate for that length of time. If that expectation is not met, our definition of the situation will be altered, and our ability to sustain the appropriate mood of the encounter will be seriously tested. As Hall observed, our expectations in this regard vary widely from one culture to the next. In the unitary linear treatment of time which characterizes the ''American Way of Life'' time units, in discrete segments and in highly conventionalized sequences, are a salient feature of the way we give form and meaning to the sensational chaos of experience.

Progression. Like duration, progression is another dimension of the meaning of a situation. Having acquired expectations about the sequence of events both in space (one expects the invisible part of a road around a curve to *be there,* if one can see the continuation of the road in the distance and, often, if one cannot) and in time, we extend the isolated scene into a sequential pattern in order to increase our understanding of its scope. Progression, as sequence, affects both the meaning of the scope of the interaction and the interaction itself. To descend into a shaft in the earth and then step through an opening into outer space constitutes a break in environmental sequence for which our original definitions of that situation have left us unprepared. Kafka's *The Trial* achieves its sense of strangeness and distortion in part from the deliberate deletion of key transitional scenes so that both the protagonist and the audience—the observers and vicarious actors—lose confidence in their ability to predict what will happen next. Here, the factor of continuity emphasizes the overriding importance progression has in establishing the meaning of a situation.[8] Progression, therefore, is an ordered sequence of events within an ordered sequence of scenes which is related to learned expectations, i.e., the taken-for-granted dimensions of everyday conduct.

Social interaction, then, takes place in a physical world full of objects, their modifiers, movement, and change—not in a vacuum. What is more, this physical world, differentially arranged and modified, is not so ambiguous in its relation to social interaction that its effects cannot be measured or estimated by analytical inquiry. Nor is this world so incidental that it can continue to be ignored.

---

[7]Edward T. Hall, *The Silent Language* (New York: Doubleday, Inc., 1959), has discussed at length cultural differences in the perception and meaning of time.

[8]One reason that a film like *Last Year at Marienbad* is so disorienting is that it violates our expectations of progression. By externalizing the random order of events which we have learned to accept as the unique characteristic of thought, memory, and imagination and making them appear to be happening ''out there,'' the hermetic seal between internal and external experience is broken and our ability to produce within our conventionalized framework is destroyed.

A PARADIGM FOR THE ANALYSIS OF THE COMPONENTS AND DIMENSIONS OF SCENES

Although this treatment of the subject has been necessarily brief and tentative, too exploratory to establish a comprehensive scheme which will embrace all alternative possibilities, we can propose the following paradigm as a point of departure for the initial investigation of those effects on social interaction perpetrated by the scene:

The Setting

Basic Physical Container as It Might Affect Social Interaction	Number and Arrangement of Props and Persons in the Encounter
1. Natural, man-made, or both	1. Physical objects which are not part of the space, but are in it and are taken into account in the interaction, e.g., furniture, automobiles, etc.
2. Interior, exterior, or both.	2. Number of people who act as participants and their measurable spatial relation to each other.
3. Meaningful size in relation to type of interaction (too large? too small? not culturally significant?).	3. Number of people who act as spectators and their spatial relation to the other participants and to each other.
4. Single or multiple spaces.	4. Number of people who are neither participants nor observers, but who occupy the same significant area and who, by being present, affect interaction.
5. Connected or disconnected.	
6. Relative proximity (measured in real time, subjective time, means of locomotion).	
7. Salient features, scale, size, multiple levels, etc.	

			Modifiers		
Light	*Sound*	*Color*	*Texture*	*Odor*	*Relative Temperature and Humidity*
Source(s)	Volume	Hues	Location	Source(s)	
Intensity	Pitch	Location	Mixture	Mixture	
Direction	Intensity	Mixture		Permanence	
Color	Duration	Chromatic			
	Source	intensities			
	Direction				

Duration
Objective time span measured against conventional and/or subjective expectations.

Progression
The actual sequence of events implied by the scene and considered significant by those persons encountering one another on the scene.

From this rough diagram a list of questions may be drawn which adds another dimension to the existing set of questions about the meaning of behavior. Obviously, as the questions are asked and a body of quantitative information is assembled, an assessment can be made of what is or is not significant about physical environment as it applies to social interaction, and a more comprehensive and sophisticated scheme will evolve. Until such time, this scheme, or one like it, can serve as a point of departure from which an initial investigation can be made into the unexplored dimensions of non-verbal, non-gestural, symbolic reality.

4

Behavioral Appropriateness and Situational Constraint as Dimensions of Social Behavior*

R. H. Price and D. L. Bouffard

In the first of two studies, 52 subjects were required to judge the appropriateness of 15 behaviors in each of 15 situations in a behavior-situation matrix. Differences among behaviors, situations, and their interaction contributed substantial proportions of the total variance in judgments. The concepts of behavioral appropriateness and situational constraint were offered to account for the differences obtained among behaviors and situations, respectively. A second study using a new sample of 42 subjects and different methods of measurement provided initial construct validity evidence for the concepts. Implications of these results for the construction of situational response hierarchies, the development of behavior and situation taxonomies, and causal attribution were discussed.

Recently there has been considerable renewed interest in what has come to be called the "person versus situation" or the "consistency-specificity issue" in personality research. Several reviews of personality research (Hunt, 1965;

*Journal of Personality and Social Psychology, 1974, 30, 579-586. Copyright 1974 by the American Psychological Association. Reprinted by permission.

Mischel, 1968, 1969[3]; Peterson, 1965) have made it clear that traditional assumptions concerning the transituational consistency of personality are in need of considerable revision.

At the same time, a number of empirical studies (Endler & Hunt, 1966, 1968, 1969; Endler, Hunt, & Rosenstein, 1962; Moos, 1968, 1969; Raush, Dittmann, & Taylor, 1959; Raush, Farbman, & Llewellyn, 1960) have shown that, in general, interactions between persons, situations, and behaviors account for at least as much or more of the total variation than any of these sources considered by itself. *However, the consistency-specificity issue continues* to be a source of conroversy (*e.g.,* Alker, 1972; Bem, 1972; Endler, 1973; Wallach & Leggett, 1972).

These studies have made it clear that (a) simple trait-oriented conceptions of personality must be replaced by much more *complex* conceptualizations and (b) *the scope of* these conceptualizations must be expanded from exclusively person-oriented conceptions to approaches which include the domains of situations, behavior, and their interactions.

Although considerable effort has been expended in attempting to generate typologies or dimensions to characterize persons, much less attention has been devoted to the characterization of social behaviors and social situations. The present study represents an effort in that direction.

In collecting information characterizing behaviors and situations, it is possible to take advantage of the fact that *most individuals can readily judge the social appropriateness of a particular behavior in a particular social context,* although they would be hard put to list all of the behaviors which are appropriate or inappropriate in any given situation. Furthermore, it is quite likely that properties of the behavior itself, the particular situation in which it occurs, or their unique combination may affect this judgment. It is therefore necessary to separate analytically the contribution of each component.

A systematic framework that meets these requirements would be one in which the unit to be judged (a) *would be a particular behavior in a particular situation,* (b) *would involve the sampling of a fixed number of behaviors and a fixed number of situations for judgment,* and (c) *would require that subjects judge the appropriateness of each of the behaviors in each of the situations.*

If these requirements are met, it is possible to form a behavior-situation matrix in which the appropriateness of each of the sampled behaviors is indexed for each of the situations. Once such a matrix has been constructed, one can analyze the contribution of the behaviors themselves to judgments of appropriateness independent of the situations in which they occur. Similarly, it is possible to obtain information concerning the effect of situations on judged appropriateness

---

[3]W. Mischel. Specificity theory and the construction of personality. Address of the Chairman, Section III (Development of Clinical Psychology as an Experimental-Behavioral Science), Division 12, American Psychological Association, Washington, D.C., September 1971.

independent of the behaviors sampled, since each situation has been used as a context for all the behaviors in the matrix.

The purpose of the present study was, first, to demonstrate the utility of the behavior situation matrix as a means of collecting normative information concerning the judged appropriateness of behaviors in social situations and, second, to assess the degree to which behaviors, situations, and their interaction each independently account for variance in judgments of social appropriateness. Finally, in a second study it is shown that the behavior-situation matrix provides data which suggest that behaviors can be arranged along a dimension of behavioral appropriateness and situations can be arranged along a dimension of situational constraint.

STUDY 1

Method

Subjects. Fifty-two subjects were drawn from introductory psychology classes at Indiana University. The subjects volunteered to participate in the experiment in order to fulfill a course requirement. Testing was conducted in small groups, and subjects typically completed the task in less than one hour.

Selection of Behaviors and Situations. In initial pilot work, a sample of 15 students was asked to keep detailed diaries for one entire day. They were asked to record each situation they found themselves in and what behavior they engaged in for each situation. The diaries were abstracted to obtain separate lists of behaviors and situations, and after eliminating synonyms, 15 behaviors and 15 situations were selected from the lists.

The 15 behaviors selected for the present study were: "run, talk, kiss, write, eat, sleep, mumble, read, fight, belch, argue, jump, cry, laugh, and shout." The 15 situations selected were: "in class, on a date, on a bus, at a family dinner, in the park, in church, at a job interview, on a downtown sidewalk, at the movies, in a bar, in an elevator, in a restroom, in one's own room, in a dormitory lounge, and at a football game."

Procedure. The stimulus items presented to subjects were generated by pairing each of the *15 behaviors with each of the 15 situations resulting in 225* behavior-situation pairs. Thus, each item consisted of a behavior occurring in a situation (e.g., "read in a bus," "sleep in class," "shout in an elevator"). The resulting 225 stimulus items were then arranged in a fixed random order for presentation to subjects.

Subjects were asked to rate each of the 225 stimuli on a 10-point scale and then given the following instructions:

> From various sources in our everyday life we have all developed a subjective "impression" or "feeling" for the appropriateness of any given behavior in a particular situation. For example, we know that even some very common behaviors are more "appropriate" in some situations than in others. These judgments about appropriateness may not always be "rational" or "logical," but they are a very real part of all of us. In this experiment, we are interested in *your* judgment of the appropriateness of some particular behaviors in some particular situations. For example, an item might consist of something like *"Ride in a car"* or perhaps *"Giggle at a funeral."* Your task in each case is simply to rate, on a scale from 0 through 9, the appropriateness of the particular behavior in the situation given. *The rating scale is weighted as follows: 0 = The behavior is* extremely inappropriate *in this situation.* 9 = The behavior is extremely appropriate *in this situation.*

Results and Discussion

Variance in Appropriateness Ratings Accounted for by Differences among Persons, Behaviors, Situations, and Their Interactions. The mean appropriateness ratings for each of the 15 behaviors judged in each of the 15 situations for the 52 subjects are shown in Table 4.1.

In order to assess the degree to which variance in appropriateness ratings was due to differences among persons, situations, behaviors, or their interaction, the data was analyzed by a three-way analysis of variance (Persons × Situations × Behaviors). Variance components and their percentages are shown in Table 4.2 below.[4]

The results of principal interest in Table 4.2 are the relatively large effects obtained from differences among situations, behaviors, and their interaction. Considerably smaller effects were obtained for differences among persons and for the interactions of persons with either situations or behaviors. *Thus, it can be tentatively concluded that differences among situations, behaviors, and certain unique combinations of behaviors and situations account for fairly large proportions of variance in judgments of behavioral appropriateness.*

---

[4]The calculations performed here are based on Endler's (1966) extension of the Gleser, Cronbach, and Rajaratnam (1965) method of obtaining variance components for a three-way model. In the present analysis persons are assumed to be a random factor, while behaviors and situations are held as fixed factors as in Endler's (1966) "Mixed Effects Model, Case II." The present application of this solution pools error variance and the variance associated with the triple interaction. Since it is doubtful that error variance is in fact zero in most cases, this should be considered only an approximate solution; and no interpretation of the triple interaction is offered here.

Table 4.1 Mean Appropriateness Ratings for Each of the 225 Behavior-Situation Combinations

Situation	Run	Talk	Kiss	Write	Eat	Sleep	Mumble	Read	Fight	Belch	Argue	Jump	Cry	Laugh	Shout
Class	2.52	6.21	2.10	8.17	4.23	3.60	3.62	7.27	1.21	1.77	5.33	1.79	2.21	6.23	1.94
Date	5.00	8.56	8.73	3.62	7.79	3.77	3.12	2.88	3.58	2.23	4.50	4.42	3.04	8.00	3.79
Bus	1.44	8.08	4.27	4.87	5.48	7.04	5.17	7.17	1.52	2.15	4.17	3.12	3.08	7.10	3.00
Family dinner	2.56	8.52	4.92	2.58	8.44	2.29	2.54	3.96	1.67	2.50	3.25	2.29	3.21	7.13	1.96
Park	7.94	8.42	7.71	7.00	8.13	5.63	5.40	7.77	3.06	5.00	5.06	7.42	5.21	8.10	6.92
Church	1.38	3.29	2.38	2.85	1.38	1.77	3.52	3.58	.62	1.42	1.92	1.71	3.13	2.60	1.33
Job Interview	1.94	8.46	1.08	4.85	1.73	.75	1.31	2.48	1.04	1.21	1.83	1.48	1.37	5.88	1.65
Sidewalk	5.58	8.19	4.75	3.38	4.83	1.46	4.96	4.81	1.46	2.81	4.08	3.54	3.71	7.40	4.88
Movies	2.46	4.98	6.21	2.73	7.48	4.08	4.13	1.73	1.37	2.58	1.71	2.31	7.15	7.94	2.42
Bar	1.96	8.25	5.17	5.38	7.67	2.90	6.21	4.71	1.90	5.04	4.31	3.75	3.44	8.23	4.13
Elevator	1.63	7.40	4.79	3.04	5.10	1.31	5.12	4.48	1.58	2.54	2.58	2.12	3.48	6.77	1.73
Restroom	2.83	7.25	2.81	3.46	2.35	2.83	5.04	4.75	1.77	5.12	3.48	3.65	4.79	5.90	3.52
Own room	6.15	8.58	8.52	8.29	7.94	8.85	7.67	8.58	4.25	6.81	7.52	6.73	8.00	8.17	6.44
Dorm lounge	4.40	7.88	6.54	7.73	7.19	6.08	5.50	8.56	2.40	4.00	4.88	4.58	3.88	7.75	3.60
Football game	4.12	8.08	5.08	4.56	8.04	2.98	5.23	3.69	2.04	3.85	4.98	7.12	4.31	7.90	7.94

Note. 0 = "The behavior is extremely inappropriate in this situation." 9 = "The behavior is extremely appropriate in this situation."

Table 4.2   Variance Components and Percentage of Variance Accounted For by Persons, Situations, Behaviors, and Their Interactions in Appropriateness Ratings

Source	Variance component	% variance
Persons (A)	.708	6.1
Situations (B)	1.941	16.8
Behaviors (C)	2.066	17.9
A × B	.664	5.8
A × C	.881	7.6
B × C	1.697	14.7
A × B × C	3.577	31.0

Behavioral Appropriateness and Situational Constraint. Table 4.3 shows the means and standard deviations of appropriateness ratings for behaviors collapsed across situations and the means and standard deviations of appropriateness ratings for situations collapsed across behaviors. Situations and behaviors have been arranged according to increasing values of mean appropriateness ratings.

Examination of Table 4.3 reveals some interesting properties of behaviors and situations. For a given behavior (e.g., ''fight'' or ''belch''), low values of judged appropriateness reflect the fact that there are few situations in the present sample in which the behavior is considered appropriate. High values, on the other hand,

Table 4.3   Means and Standard Deviations of Appropriateness Ratings for Behaviors Collapsed Across Situations and for Situations Collapsed Across Behaviors

Behavior	M	SD	Situation	M	SD
Fight	1.96	.95	Church	2.19	.90
Belch	3.27	1.57	Job interview	2.47	2.12
Run	3.46	1.91	Elevator	3.58	1.87
Shout	3.68	1.99	Family dinner	3.85	2.24
Sleep	3.69	2.23	Class	3.88	2.17
Jump	3.74	1.92	Movies	3.95	2.20
Argue	3.97	1.52	Restroom	3.97	1.42
Cry	4.00	1.67	Sidewalk	4.39	1.79
Mumble	4.56	1.51	Bus	4.51	2.07
Write	4.83	1.98	Date	4.87	2.16
Kiss	5.00	2.22	Bar	4.87	1.97
Read	5.09	2.16	Football game	5.33	1.93
Eat	5.85	2.40	Dorm lounge	5.66	1.82
Laugh	7.01	1.41	Park	6.58	1.53
Talk	7.48	1.48	Own room	7.50	1.19

Note. 0 = extremely inappropriate; 9 = extremely appropriate.

reflect the fact that the behavior (e.g., "talk" or "laugh") is considered highly appropriate in a large proportion of the situations sampled. These mean values of judged appropriateness can, of course, be considered independent of the situation in the sense that each of the behaviors has been judged across the same sample of situations. It is suggested that the mean appropriateness rating for a given behavior across a representative sample of situations provides an estimate of the overall judged appropriateness of that behavior and is an index of a more general dimension of *behavioral appropriateness*.

However, the mean appropriateness ratings for situations collapsed across behaviors provide a different and perhaps more interesting index for situations. For a given situation (e.g., "job interview" or "church"), a low-rating value reflects the fact that there are few behaviors sampled that are considered appropriate in that situation. High values for a given situation, on the other hand (e.g., "in the park" or "own room"), reflect the fact that a wide range of the behaviors sampled are considered relatively appropriate in that situation. *It is suggested that the mean appropriateness rating for a given situation across a sample of behaviors provides an estimate of the overall* situational constraint *displayed by that situation.*

Thus, it has been tentatively suggested that an important characteristic of social behaviors is their behavioral appropriateness which is reflected in the distribution of appropriateness ratings across a specified sample of situations. In addition, an important property of situations is their situational constraint which is measured in terms of the distribution of appropriateness ratings across a specified sample of behaviors.

A question that immediately arises is whether the concepts of behavioral appropriateness and situational constraint display construct validity in the sense that other methods of measuring these concepts correlate with the indexes derived from the behavior-situation matrix. It is possible, for example, that the ordering of behaviors and situations shown in Table 4.3 is due to the particular method of measurement employed in the behavior-situation matrix or does not necessarily reflect the dimensions proposed here. If, on the other hand, different methods of measuring behavioral appropriateness and situational constraint produce a similar ordering of behaviors and situations, then preliminary evidence for the construct validity of the concepts will have been established. In order to provide some initial information on this question, a second study was conducted in which independent samples of subjects rated the same sample of behaviors and situations on dimensions expected to be relevant to these constructs.

STUDY 2

Method

Subjects. A new sample of 42 subjects was drawn from introductory psychology courses at Indiana University. The subjects participated in the experiment in order to fulfill a course requirement. Testing was conducted in small groups, and subjects typically completed the task in less than half an hour.

Procedure. *All of the 15 behaviors and the 15 situations used in Study 1 served as the stimuli in Study 2.*

The behaviors were judged on a 9-point scale (1=very little, 9=very much) for each of the following four rating scales:

> *Rating 1.* The extent to which the *behaviors might elicit disapproval or embarrassment* when performed out of their proper context.
>
> *Rating 2.* The extent to which most people would want to *think twice before agreeing to engage* in the behaviors.
>
> *Rating 3.* The extent to which someone would say that *the behaviors are inappropriate regardless of the situation.*
>
> *Rating 4.* The extent to which the *judge himself would say the behaviors are inappropriate regardless of the situation.*

These ratings should be negatively correlated with the matrix-derived measure of behavioral appropriateness and should show positive intercorrelations among themselves.

The situations were also judged on a 9-point scale (1=very little, 9=very much) for each of the following rating scales:

> *Rating 5.* The extent to which the situations are *"loaded"* in terms of their potential for *producing embarrassment:*
>
> *Rating 6.* The extent to which the *situations require that people monitor their own behavior* or "watch what they do."
>
> *Rating 7.* The extent to which the *approval of other people makes a difference in what most people would do in the situations.*
>
> *Rating 8.* The extent to which the situations call for or demand certain behaviors and not others.
>
> These ratings should be negatively correlated with the matrix-derived measure of situational constraint (as indexed by low appropriateness ratings for situations in Table 4.3) and should produce positive intercorrelations among themselves.

The total sample was divided into four subgroups ($n = 10$, 10, 11, 11) and assigned to rate each of the 15 behaviors on one of the four questions relevant to behaviors and one of the four questions relevant to situations. Thus, no subject rated more than one of the dimensions relevant to situations, nor did any subject rate more than one dimension relevant to behaviors.

Results

In order to assess the construct validity of the concept of behavioral appropriateness, the mean rating for each behavior was obtained on each of the four rating scales relevant to behaviors. These ratings were then correlated with the index of behavioral appropriateness obtained from the behavior-situation matrix described in Study 1. Results of this analysis as well as the intercorrelations among rating scales used in Study 2 are shown in Table 4.4.

Table 4.4   Correlations Between the Matrix-Derived Measure of Behavioral Appropriateness and Other Independently Derived Ratings of Behaviors

Measure	BA	1	2	3	4
BA	—				
Rating 1	−.56	—			
Rating 2	−.57	.90	—		
Rating 3	−.57	.39	.42	—	
Rating 4	−.70	.63	.63	.88	—

Note. BA = behavioral appropriateness; Rating 1: elicits embarrassment;
Rating 2: hesitates to engage in it; Rating 3: judged inappropriate by others;
Rating 4: judged inappropriate by rater.

In a similar manner, the mean ratings for each situation were obtained on each of the four situation-relevant rating dimensions and correlated with the index of situational constraint obtained in Study 1. Results of these analyses are shown in Table 4.5 as well as the intercorrelations among the rating scales used in Study 2.

It can be seen that, as predicted, the matrix-derived *measure of behavioral appropriateness is negatively correlated with ratings of behaviors in terms of potential for eliciting embarrassment* (Rating 1), hesitation to engage in the behavior (Rating 2), judgments of inappropriateness by others (Rating 3), and judgments of inappropriateness by the judge himself (Rating 4). Furthermore, the intercorrelations of the four rating scales are substantial and in the predicted direction.

Table 4.5   Correlations Between the Matrix-Derived Measure of Situational Constraint and Other Independently Derived Rating of Situations

Measure	SC	5	6	7	8
SC	—				
Rating 5	−.57	—			
Rating 6	−.80	.67	—		
Rating 7	−.69	.60	.80	—	
Rating 8	−.78	.74	.87	.84	—

Note. SC = situational constraint; Rating 5: loaded for potential embarrassment; Rating 6: elicits increased self-monitoring; Rating 7: associated with approval-disapproval; Rating 8: demands certain behaviors.

In addition, as predicted, situations high in situational constraint (as indexed by low mean appropriateness ratings for situations in Table 3) are seen as loaded for potential embarrassment (Rating 5), eliciting increased self-monitoring of one's own behavior (Rating 6), more likely to be associated with approval-disapproval by others which affects behavior (Rating 7), and demanding certain behaviors rather than others (Rating 8). Intercorrelations among the four independently derived rating scales for situational constraint are also substantial and in the predicted direction.

Thus, the concepts of behavioral appropriateness and situational constraint display a substantial degree of construct validity when the measures derived from the behavior-situation matrix in Study 1 are compared with different measures obtained from a new sample of subjects.

DISCUSSION

Results of Study 1 indicated that behaviors, situations, and their interaction each constituted a substantial and independent source of variance in ratings when the appropriateness of particular acts was judged in particular situations. Thus, the judgment of the appropriateness of behaviors is due to characteristics of the situation, characteristics of the behavior, and their unique combination, each of which makes an independent contribution to the variance in ratings.

It was suggested in Study 1 that within the context of the present experimental paradigm, behaviors could be arranged on a dimension of *behavioral appropriateness* and *situations could be arranged on a dimension of situational constraint*. It was argued that these were, in fact, important underlying dimensions which might account for the differences among behaviors and situations observed. In order to demonstrate the construct validity of these dimensions, additional independent ratings of behaviors and situations were collected in Study 2. These ratings were shown to correlate with the indexes of behavioral appropriateness and situational constraint obtained from the behavior-situation matrix, thus providing construct validation for both proposed dimensions.

The concept of behavioral appropriateness is not new or particularly unusual as a way of characterizing social behaviors. However, the idea that situations can in fact play such a substantial role in the judgments of social appropriateness is a great deal more interesting. Goffman (1963) has anticipated the situational constraint dimension proposed here when he stated:

> It would seem, then, that there may be one overall continuum or axis along which the social life in situations varies, depending on how disciplined the individual is obliged to be in connection with the several ways in which respect for the gathering and its social occasion can be expressed. . . . The terms "tight" and "loose" might be more descriptive and give more equal weight to each of the several ways in which devotion to a social occasion may be exhibited [pp. 199-200].

More recently, in discussing the theoretical basis of self-regulation, McReynolds (1972) has suggested that "situations differ among themselves in the extent to which they typically—i.e., for most persons—determine the behavior of persons in those situations [p. 9]." Similar suggestions have been made by Wicker (1972) and Barker (1968).

The behavior-situation matrix and the concepts derived from it offer a number of possibilities for further experimentation. One advantage of the present method is that it provides an empirical basis for the construction of response hierarchies for each of the situations sampled. Hierarchies may be constructed for a given situation by simply listing the behaviors sampled in order of the mean appropriateness rating for that situation. Behaviors with high appropriateness ratings can be assumed to be much more likely to be part of the hierarchy for that situation and perhaps are those which receive positive reinforcement in that situation. Naturally, the hierarchy obtained is limited to the behaviors sampled, but with sufficiently large samples of behaviors and situations such hierarchies could be constructed on an empirical basis and their validity checked in real-life situations.

Another advantage of the experimental paradigm is that it requires subjects to judge the appropriateness of behaviors which may have very low probabilities of occurrence in the situation examined. If only the behaviors most likely to occur were examined, important aspects of the situational structure might not be revealed. In many cases it is the exceptions to the rules of conduct for a particular situation that are most revealing, since the reactions to these exceptions allow inferences about the underlying structure or "meaning" of the situation. For example, the most common behavior in the situations of "job interview" and "class" may be "talking" and "writing," but the differential ordering of low-probability behaviors may reveal latent properties or *"demand characteristics"* of the situation which otherwise would not be apparent.

The behavior-situation matrix also offers the possibility of generating taxonomies of situations and taxonomies of behaviors (Frederiksen, 1972). The correlation of appropriateness ratings across behaviors for any pair of situations provides an index of the behavioral similarity of those two situations. A similarity matrix for situations can then be constructed by correlating each situation with every other situation across behaviors. This similarity matrix can then be subjected to cluster analysis to obtain a typology of situations. It should be noted that the variance associated with Situation × Behavior interactions (see Table 4.2) can be accounted for in this way, since clusters of situations with similar "profiles" across behaviors are clustered together and distinguished from other clusters of situations with markedly different "profiles." An analogous procedure can be carried out for behaviors to generate a taxonomy of behaviors where the similarity of behaviors is indexed by their correlations across situations. A recent study (Price, 1974) using a cluster analysis methodology yielded meaningful clusters of behaviors and situations and indicated that particular behavior clusters were uniquely appropriate in particular situation clusters.

In addition, the present approach offers the possibility of examining the role of behavioral appropriateness and situational constraint in stimulus versus person attribution (Frieze & Weiner, 1971; Jones & Davis, 1965; Kelley, 1967; Kukla, 1972; McArthur, 1972; Weiner, Frieze, Kukla, Reed, Rest, & Rosenbaum, 1971; Weiner & Kukla, 1970). For example, in inferring the meaning or cause of a particular action, the perceiver may make an initial judgment as to whether the act was due to the particular motivations, dispositions, or traits of the actor or whether the actor was merely responding to some aspect of the stimulus situation. *It is suggested that the dimensions of behavioral appropriateness and situational constraint may differentially affect the perceiver's attribution of the cause of a particular social act or achievement to the person or to be the situation in which it occurs.* For example, a study by Price and Bouffard (1973) indicated that behaviors low in appropriateness and situations high in constraint are much more likely to elicit attributions to the person.

It is also possible that the strong dispositional statements inherent in psychiatric diagnoses or in the attribution of mental illness to persons are controlled by these variables (Price, 1972; Price & Denner, 1973). In a similar vein, Goffman (1963) has noted that in diagnosing mental disorder psychiatrists frequently cite aspects of the patient's behavior that are "inappropriate to the situation," while Scheff (1966) has described the violation of such implicit rules of social conduct as "residual rule breaking."

Thus, the behavior-situation matrix and the measures derived from it may provide useful information about characteristics of social behavior, the settings in which that behavior occurs, and the judgments made about stimulus persons on the basis of their behavior in various social contexts.

References

Alker, H. A. Is personality situationally specific or intrapsychically consistent? *Journal of Personality,* 1972, 40, 1-16.

Barker, R. G. *Ecological Psychology: Concepts and Methods for Studying the Environment of Human Behavior.* Stanford, Calif.: Stanford University Press, 1968.

Bem, D. J. Constructing cross-situational consistencies in behavior: Some thoughts on Alker's critique of Mischel. *Journal of Personality,* 1972, 40, 17-26.

Endler, N. S. Estimating variance components from mean squares for random and mixed effects analyses of variance models. *Perceptual and Motor Skills,* 1966, 22, 559-570.

Endler, N. S. The person versus the situation—A pseudo issues? A response to Alker. *Journal of Personality,* 1973, 41, 287-303.

Endler, N. S., & Hunt, J. McV. Sources of behavioral variance as measured by the S-R Inventory of Anxiousness. *Psychological Bulletin,* 1966, 65, 336-346.

Endler, N. S., & Hunt, J. McV. S-R Inventories of Hostility and comparisons of the proportions of variance from persons, responses, and situations for hostility and anxiousness. *Journal of Personality and Social Psychology,* 1968, 9, 309-315.

Endler, N. S., & Hunt, J. McV. Generalizability of contributions from sources of variance in the S-R Inventories of Anxiousness. *Journal of Personality,* 1969, 37, 1-24.

Endler, N. S., Hunt, J. McV., & Rosenstein, A. J. An S-R Inventory of Anxiousness. *Psychological Monographs,* 1962, 76 (17, Whole No. 536).

Frederiksen, N. Toward a taxonomy of situations. *American Psychologist,* 1972, 27, 114-123.

Frieze, I., & Weiner, B. Cue utilization and attributional judgments of success and failure. *Journal of Personality,* 1971, 39, 372-386.

Gleser, G. C., Cronbach, L. J., & Rajaratnam, N. Generalizability of scores influenced by multiple sources of variance. *Psychometrika,* 1965, 30, 395-418.

Goffman, E. *Behavior in Public Places: Notes on the Social Organization of Gatherings.* New York: Free Press of Glencoe, 1963.

Hunt, J. McV. Traditional personality theory in the light of recent evidence. *American Scientist,* 1965, 53, 80-96.

Jones, E. E., & David, K. E. From acts to dispositions. In L. Berkowitz (Ed.), *Advances in Experimental Social Psychology*. Vol. 2. New York: Academic Press, 1965.

Kelley, H. H. Attribution theory in social psychology. In D. Levine (Ed.), *Nebraska Symposium on Motivation: 1967*. Lincoln: University of Nebraska Press, 1967.

Kukla, A. Foundations of an attributional theory of performance. *Psychological Review*, 1972, 79, 454-470.

McArthur, L. A. The how and what of why: Some determinants and consequences of causal attribution. *Journal of Personality and Social Psychology*, 1972, 22, 171-193.

McReynolds, P. Theoretical bases of self regulation. Paper presented at the Conference on Developmental Aspects of Self-Regulation, LaJolla, California, February 1972.

Mischel, W. Continuity and change in personality. *American Psychologist*, 1969, 24, 1012-1018.

Mischel, W. *Personality and assessment*. New York: Wiley, 1968.

Moos, R. H. Situational analysis of a therapeutic community milieu. *Journal of Abnormal Psychology*, 1968, 73, 49-61.

Moos, R. H. Sources of variance in response to questionnaires and in behavior. *Journal of Abnormal Psychology*, 1969, 74, 405-412.

Peterson, D. R. Scope and generality of verbally defined personality factors. *Psychological Review*, 1965, 72, 48-59.

Price, R. H. *Abnormal Behavior: Perspectives in Conflict*. New York: Holt, Rinehart & Winston, 1972.

Price, R. H. The taxonomic classification of behaviors and situations and the problem of behavior-environment congruence. *Human Relations*, 1974, 27, 507-585.

Price, R. H., & Bouffard, D. Behavioral and situational determinants of causal attribution. Unpublished manuscript, Indiana University, 1973.

Price, R. H., & Denner, B. (Eds.) *The Making of a Mental Patient*. New York: Holt, Rinehart & Winston, 1973.

Raush, H. L., Dittmann, A. L., & Taylor, T. J. The interpersonal behavior of children in residential treatment. *Journal of Abnormal and Social Psychology*, 1959, 58, 9-26.

Raush, H. L., Farbman, I., & Llewellyn, L. G. Person, setting, and change in social interaction: II. A normal control study. *Human Relations*, 1960, 13, 305-332.

Scheff, T. J. *Being Mentally Ill: A Sociological Theory*. Chicago: Aldine, 1966.

Wallach, M. A., & Leggett, M. I. Testing the hypothesis that a person will be consistent: Stylistic consistency versus situational specificity in size of children's drawings. *Journal of Personality*, 1972, 40, 309-330.

Weiner, B., Frieze, I., Kukla, A., Reed, L., Rest, S., & Rosenbaum, R. M. Perceiving the Causes of Success and failure. In E. E. Jones, D. E. Kanouse, H. H. Kelly, R. E. Nisbett, & B. Weiner (Eds.), *Attributions: Perceiving the Causes of Behavior*. Morristown, N.J.: General Learning Press, 1972.

Weiner, B., & Kukla, A. An attributional analysis of achievement motivation. *Journal of Personality and Social Psychology*, 1970, 15, 1-20.

Wicker, A. W. Processes which mediate behavior-environment congruence. *Behavioral Science*, 1972, 17, 265-277.

5

A Free-Response Description Approach to the Analysis of Person-Situation Interaction*

Lawrence A. Pervin

This study is a report on the utilization of a free-response description approach to address the following question: In what ways does an individual remain stable and vary as a function of situational characteristics, and what are those characteristics? Each of four subjects generated a list of situations in his or her current life which he or she then rated on lists of situation traits, feelings, and behaviors, which were also generated by the individual subject. For each subject the data were factor analyzed to determine groups of situations which were distinctive in terms of the feelings and behaviors associated with them. It was suggested that the personality of each individual could be understood in terms of the pattern of stability and change in feelings and behaviors in relation to defined groups of situations. It was also suggested that the approach utilized might serve as the basis for the future development of a taxonomy of situations and behaviors in situations.

Cronbach (1957, 1975) has brought attention to the problem of the two disciplines of scientific psychology—the emphasis on variation due to situation (treatment) differences as opposed to the emphasis on variation due to person (individual) differences. Over the years there has been an increase in studies

---

*Journal of Personality and Social Psychology, 1976, 34, 465-474. Copyright 1976 by the American Psychological Association. Reprinted by permission.

involving both person and situation variables (Sarason, Smith, & Diener, 1975), though such studies have remained a small proportion of the total personality and social literature. Within the past few years there has been a noteworthy increase in emphasis on interaction research in personality (Bem & Allen, 1974; Bowers, 1973; Carlson, 1975; Endler, 1973; Mischel, 1973; Pervin, 1968) to the extent that one psychologist reviewing the literature concludes that "if interactionism is not the Zeitgeist of today's personality psychology, it will probably be that of tomorrow's" (Ekehammar, 1974, p. 1045).

Despite the increased attention being given to framing personality questions in interaction terms, serious methodological and conceptual problems remain. In particular, we know little about the dimensions people use to perceive and organize situations or about the process of person-situation interaction. The Endler studies (Endler & Hunt, 1968) have been important in calling attention to person-situation interaction effects. In these studies the subject is symbolically presented with a variety of potentially anxiety-arousing or hostility-arousing situations and indicates on a scale the likelihood of his or her responding in each of a number of different ways to each situation. The data are then analyzed across subjects to determine the proportion of the variance that can be accounted for by person differences, situation differences, and person-situation interactions. While emphasizing person-situation interactions, however, such studies have done little to help us understand the process of such interactions. Also, a problem with these and other efforts to assess person-situation interactions through the use of questionnaires (Ekehammar & Magnusson, 1973; Magnusson & Ekehammar, 1975) has been that the situations described and responses provided may have limited applicability from the standpoint of the individual responding to them. An analogy may be drawn here to the person perception literature where responses of subjects have been found to vary according to whether the persons judged are known to them and whether the traits used are familiar to them (Koltuv, 1962). If we are going to consider persons in their interactions with situations, then we need to look at situations and responses that are relevant to the subjects being studied.

The aim of the present research is the development of a conceptual scheme and methodology to answer the following question: In what ways, and why, do people remain stable (consistent) in their behavior and feelings, and in what ways do they vary according to which situational characteristics? In terms of conceptual approach, the goal is a more differentiated understanding of the interactions and transactions between people and situations as opposed to an emphasis purely on persons, purely on situations, or on a global Person × Situation interaction effect. The effort is to understand personality as the individual's pattern of stability and change in relation to defined situational characteristics. In terms of methodological approach, the effort is to adapt some of the techniques of personality research and person perception (implicit personality theory) research toward the specific goal of understanding person-situation interactions. In particular, emphasis is placed on the development of free-response methods, as opposed to checklists or questionnaires, to study an individual's perception of situations and his or her perceived pattern of behavior in relation to these situations. Such techniques permit one to study situations and responses that are meaningful for the individual and still provide for systematic data analysis.

METHOD

Procedure

The approach to data collection used in this study was an adaptation of Rosenberg's (Note 1) method of obtaining free-response descriptions of persons or "naturalistic personality descriptions." Each of four subjects was asked to perform the following five tasks:

List the situations in his or her current life. A situation was defined as involving a specific place, a specific time, and one or more individuals involved in specific activities. Current life was defined as including situations occurring during the past year. The subjects reviewed their daily lives and listed situations that occurred and were of some importance. For example, situations noted included such items as presenting one's ideas before a class, arguing with one's mother, studying alone, being at a big party, and being alone with a good friend. Each situation represented a concrete situation for that subject. Because the subjects generated their unique lists of situations, they were free to list situations that were relevant to them and to survey a broad range of situations over which their feelings and behaviors might remain stable or vary.

Describe (adjectives, traits, phrases) each situation. This generated a list of situation traits for each subject.

Describe how he or she feels in each situation. This generated a list of feelings which, again, were relevant for the individual.

Describe his/her behavior in each situation. This generated a list of behaviors in situations.

Indicate the applicability of each situation trait, feeling, and behavior to each situation. The result of the first four steps was the generation by each subject of four lists: situations, situation characteristics, feelings in situations, and behaviors in situations. In the fifth step, the subjects scored the applicability (2 = very applicable, 1 = somewhat applicable, 0 = not at all applicable) of the above items to each situation. In other words, data were obtained for all subjects on the situations in their lives, how they perceived these situations, and how they perceived feeling and behaving in the situations.

As noted, the data gathering procedure used was similar to that used by Rosenberg (Note 1) in his research on implicit personality theory. However, while Rosenberg asked subjects to list people, traits of people, and feelings elicited by people, the current research asked people to list situations, characteristics of situations, and feelings and behaviors in situations. Whereas Rosenberg asks questions concerning the co-occurrences of traits and feelings with people, the current research asks questions concerning the co-occurrences of feelings and behaviors in relation to situations with defined perceived characteristics. The procedure used also bears some similarity to the procedure used by Block and Bennett (1955) in their study of an individual's perception of his or her interactions in varying behavioral contexts. However, in the Block and Bennett study the subject was asked to sort prepared statements into a fixed distribution, and the behavioral contexts were limited to personally relevant interpersonal situations.

Subjects

The subjects in this study were four (two male, two female) Rutgers undergraduates. All subjects were told that the research involved the study of the ways in which they were the same and different according to different situations in their current life. Four factor analyses were run on the data for each subject: factor analyses of (a) situations based on situation trait ratings, (b) situations based on feelings ratings, (c) situations based on behavior ratings, and (d) situations based on all three sets of ratings.[1] In sum, for each subject the data were factor analyzed to determine those feelings and behaviors which were perceived to be associated with specific situations. These data were taken to be expressive of the ways in which one perceives oneself to be stable and varying in feelings and behaviors in situations in one's life.

RESULTS AND DISCUSSION

Because this study does not involve the testing of hypotheses, but rather involves an effort to develop a conceptual scheme and methodology for the study of personality, there will be a simultaneous presentation of the results and discussion of them in terms of the following four areas: interindividual comparisons, intraindividual analyses and patterns of stability and change across

---

[1]The BMD 08M factor analysis package was used, consisting of a varimax rotation, squared multiple correlations in the diagonal, and an eigenvalue greater than 1.0 as the cut off for selecting the number of factors to be rotated. The intercorrelations among situations were factored and factor scores were obtained for the traits rated. Thus, factors were defined by situations with common factor loadings, and the situation characteristics, feelings, and behaviors associated with these situations were identified from analysis of the factor scores.

situations, relation of affects (feelings) to the perception of situations and behavior in situations, and implications for future research.

Since space does not permit the presentation of the four factor analyses for each subject, only the factor analyses of situations based on all ratings are presented.[2] Tables 5.1—5.4 contain, for each of the four subjects, the results of the factor analysis of situations across all ratings given by the subject.

Interindividual Comparisons

It is possible to compare the subjects in terms of the number and content of situations, traits (situation traits, feelings, behaviors), and factors. In relation to situations, the number of situations listed by the subjects was not inordinately large, ranging from 23 to 29. In the Block and Bennett (1955) study the subject listed 23 individuals with whom she had personally relevant relationships. Since it would have been possible to be in more than one type of situation with each person, there appears to be some agreement between the two studies in relation to the number of situations individuals find necessary to list to capture the essence of their current lives.

There appears to be considerable diversity among subjects in the types of situations listed and in the number and content of the characteristics associated with these situations. Obviously, the effort here needs to be directed toward a useful taxonomy of situations (Frederiksen, 1972). It should be clear that the study of many more subjects will be required before it is possible to develop such a taxonomy. However, the factor analyses do suggest some groupings of situations, such as Home-Family, Friends-Peers, Relaxation-Recreation-Play, Work-School, and Alone. As Krause (1970) points out, there are in every culture certain traditional classes of social situatioins. The categories of situations listed would appear to have considerable generality across subjects and to involve distinguishable differences in effects on behavior. In other words, it seems likely that most of the situations encountered by individuals could be conveniently classified into one of a relatively small number of categories, with important differences found in the behaviors associated with the situations in the various categories.

While it is possible to categorize situations objectively, it is also clear that situations so classified in the same category will be perceived, experienced, and responded to quite differently by different subjects. In other words, the data from two subjects may each involve a Home factor and a Work factor, but the perceived characteristics associated with the situations grouped in these factors may differ (e.g., the Home and School-Work factors for Jennifer and Harry in

---

[2]Results of the factor analyses of situation characteristic ratings, feelings ratings, and behaviors ratings for the individual subjects are available on request to the author.

Table 5.1 Illustrative Results from the Factor Analysis of Jennifer's Ratings of Situation Characteristics ($n = 64$), Feelings ($n = 62$), and Behaviors ($n = 59$) for 23 Situations

Factor (% variance)	Illustrative situations	Situation traits	Feelings	Behaviors
Home-Volatile (35%)	mother blows up at me honest with parents about leaving mother refuses gift someone else comes home upset	emotional, angry, volatile, excitable	angry, pressured, involved, insecure, unhappy	sensitive, concerned, caring, suppressed, confused, not compulsive
School, Work—Pressure to Perform (18%)	have to participate in class have to perform at work do the job wrong at work in a strange place	demanding, threatening, pressuring, awkward, challenging, embarrassing, unconcerned	self-conscious, challenged, vulnerable, awkward, pressured, anxious	self-conscious, controlled, ambitious, determined, compulsive, cool, responsible, diligent, nonrebellious
Friends, Alone (6%)	with friend—no problem with friend—problem alone	emotional, gentle, friendly, generous	caring, concerned, comfortable, melancholy, sad	concerned, caring, emotional, involved, insightful, responsive
Uncertain (5%)	come home from Philadelphia in a crowd taking the bus to class want to leave to go to Philadelphia in a strange place	ambiguous, nondefined uncertain, unconcerned, ignoring	bottled-up, melancholy, sad, lonely, frustrated, confused	preoccupied, detached, quiet, self-conscious, controlled, cool, introverted

Tables 5.1 and 5.2). This involves the traditional distinction made between the alpha press, or environment as it is, and the beta press, or environment as perceived by the individual (Murray, 1938; Pervin, Note 2). In terms of the latter, one may ask whether there are common dimensions that individuals use to perceive situations; that is, subjects may differ in the way they perceive a particular situation but be similar in the dimensions used to perceive situations

Table 5.2 Illustrative Results from the Factor Analysis of Harry's Ratings of Situation Characteristics ($n = 89$), Feelings ($n = 63$), and Behaviors ($n = 58$) for 25 Situations

Factor (% variance)	Illustrative situations	Situation traits	Feelings	Behaviors
Home-Family (35%)	talking with parents eating dinner with wife visiting my in-laws talking with wife	warm, caring, friendly, relaxed, inviting	affectionate, warm, secure, caring	caring, warm, affectionate, easygoing, emotional, pleasant, warm, open
Work-School (18%)	talking with patients at the clinic having lunch with patients and staff tutoring kids with problems participating in staff seminar seminar at school	thought-provoking, interesting, challenging, stimulating	challenged, curious, actualizing, interested, fascinated	curious, extroverted, warm, friendly, questioning
Private Recreation (8%)	reading for pleasure going to museum in New York shopping in New York	diverse, stimulating, enjoyable, spontaneous, fun	excited, pleasure-seeking, without a care in the world, stimulated, uninhibited	relaxed, intelligent, elated, awed, curious
Tension (5%)	driving alone in bad weather arguing with my wife with patients who are acting out	frustrating, threatening, intense, tense, anxiety-producing	nervous, tense, anxious, under pressure, displeased, depressed	frustrated, anxious, angry, emotional
Friends and Public Reaction (3%)	drinking in Mike's Bar joking with friend Pete relaxing in Jack's apartment talking with friends in the snack bar at school drinking in a New York bar	innocuous, tolerant, permissive, pleasant	friendly, easygoing, exhibitionistic, bored	flashy, extroverted, friendly, sociable, exhibitionistic

generally. Analysis of the factor score data for the trait ratings suggests that there is a limited range of dimensions subjects use to perceive situations and that there may be considerable similarity in the nature of these dimensions. In the data presented, four or five factors were found in each case. If one considers all of the factor analyses run (i.e., four for each of the five subjects), the range of number of factors in any one analysis was from four to nine. The finding of a limited number of dimensions along which situations are perceived is of interest in relation to Miller's (1956) work on the limits of our capacity for processing information. What, then, might be the nature of the dimensions used by individuals to construe situations? Four dimensions appear to be most salient in the ratings of situations: friendly-unfriendly, tense-calm, interesting-dull, and constrained-free. These dimensions are similar to the dimensions of semantic meaning identified by Osgood, Suci, and Tannenbaum (1957) and to the emotion-eliciting qualities of environments defined by Mehrabian and Russell (1974). The dimensions also are similar to the three categories noted by Insel and Moos (1974) to characterize environments: relationship, personal development, and system maintenance and system change.

Intraindividual Analyses and Patterns of Stability and Change Across Situations

The data presented indicate considerable diversity across subjects in the situations listed and the feelings and behaviors associated with these situations. One important statement about the personality of the individual would appear to be the kinds of situations he or she encounters in daily life. We could undoubtedly gain some insight into a person from an analysis of the range of situations encountered, the frequency with which various kinds of situations are encountered, and the time spent in each. A second interesting aspect of the analysis of the data from any one subject is the linkage among situations. For example, in the case of Jennifer (see Table 5.1) the situation "mother blows up at me" loads on the same factor as "honest with parents about leaving," suggesting problems in the area of separation. In the case of Jan (see Table 5.4) "drinking alone" and "fighting with mother" load on the same factor, suggesting a possible relationship between the two.

What is particularly instructive about the data concerning personality and person-situation interaction is that each individual has a reported pattern of feeling and behavior which in some ways is constant across all situations, in some ways is generally present except for some situations, and in some ways is almost never present except for a few specific situations. For example, according to her reports, Jennifer is almost always sensitive, vulnerable, and insightful. She also is friendly, warm, and accepting most of the time except when she is in some volatile home situations, at which times she is uniquely irritable, angry, upset, depressed, uncontrolled, and rebellious. She also tends to be involved and

Table 5.3 Illustrative Results from the Factor Analysis of Ben's Ratings of Situation Characteristics ($n = 66$), Feelings ($n = 37$), and Behaviors ($n = 59$) for 28 Situations

Factor (% variance)	Illustrative situations	Situation traits	Feelings	Behaviors
Social-Friends (35%)	drinking with Joe talking with Paul harmony in the band with girl friend	uninhibited, comfortable, open, flexible, receptive, masculine, talkative, not demanding	humorous, participating, not guilty, happy	uninhibited, receptive, friendly, masculine, humorous, tolerant, attentive
Work-Nonstimulating Situations (18%)	in a nonstimulating classroom living with group in Edison loading cartons at work at a boring party	boring, unstimulating, masculine, independent, traditional, affected by mood	eager to leave, aloof, bored, withdrawn	loner, aloof, masculine, intolerant, adamant
Family (8%)	visit my parents talk with my mother visit sister and her family	affectionate, loving, traditional, caring	emotional, affectionate, guilty, not free, not relaxed	affectionate, loving, emotional, masculine, bright, sensitive, loyal, not uninhibited, compromising
Army (5%)	working at Army headquarters in Army drills short timer in Army	humorous, authoritarian, new, serious, tense, militaristic, traditional, structured	nervous, powerless, scared, learning	nervous, learning, growing, masculine, eager, not uninhibited, sleepy
Band-Conflict (3%)	conflict in the band new band performance	challenging, demanding, musically tight, exclusive, frustrating	together, interested, participating, not calm, not secure	responsible, contributing, serious, decisive, demanding, intolerant, controlling, loyal

caring, except when she is in uncertain situations where she is detached, preoccupied, introverted, controlled, and cool. For all subjects one can define ways in which they reportedly are stable in some of their behavior throughout all situations, varying in some of their behavior in relation to different groups of

Table 5.4 Illustrative Results from the Factor Analysis of Jan's Ratings of Situation Characteristics ($n = 139$), Feelings ($n = 104$), and Behaviors ($n = 99$) for 29 Situations

Factor (% variance)	Illustrative situations	Situation traits	Feelings	Behaviors
Peer-Male (33%)	sharing with a male friend on a date talk with a student at an old friend's party with older friend like a brother	easygoing, sociable, light, friendly, intellectual	fun, okay, mature, appreciation	mature, enjoying, laughing, interested, respectful, honest, healthy, extraverted
Work (10%)	at work in Washington doing research in Boston at a male's party in a large, new group	difficult, tiring, demanding, interesting, intimidating	shy, inadequate, overwhelmed, introverted, quiet	listening, not demanding, fearful, shy, polite, cool, aloof, introverted
Therapy-Support (7%)	in personal counseling session in an encounter group with a male therapist in a therapy group talking with mother	unique, special, personal, important	love, sadness, affectionate, gratitude, tenderness, closeness	loving, hopeful, questioning, feeling, grateful
Family (4%)	at home—general with my relatives fighting with mother with my brother drinking alone	defensive, unaware, closed, lonely, familiar	want attention, defensive, frustrated	demanding, exploding, feeling, sharing, questioning, expecting too much

situations, and either never or very rarely exhibit other behaviors.

While some individuals may be introverted in all situations and some individuals extraverted in all situations, many individuals are introverted in some situations and extraverted in others. Individuals may differ, then, in the behaviors on which they are stable or varying (Bem & Allen, 1974) or in the kinds of situations in relation to which their behavior varies. An illustration of the former would be an individual who shows cross-situational variability in being friendly but stability in being exhibitionistic as compared with another individual who is always friendly and sometimes exhibitionistic. An illustration of differences in the kinds of situations in relation to which behavior varies would be an individual who is exhibitionistic in public settings and nonexhibitionistic in private settings as compared with an individual who follows the reverse pattern. It would appear to make some sense to include both stability and change in our definition of the person, as well as the relationship of stable and varying behaviors to specific kinds of situations. In sum, the data suggest that all subjects are stable in some of their behavior across all situations and variable in some of their behavior in relation to different situations. Whether a person exhibits a specific behavior in a situation will depend on whether that behavior is part of one's repertoire, if so, whether it is stable or varies according to the situation and, if variable, its relationship to the particular situation under consideration. One's personality, then, can be defined as one's pattern of stability and change in relation to defined situational characteristics.

Accepting the view that all behavior reflects both person and situation, we may also accept the view that some behaviors are more person determined for some people and other behaviors more situation determined for other people. Instead of deciding whether behavior is more person determined or more situation determined, the task of research becomes that of understanding the person and situation forces that account for the *pattern* of stability and change in behavior. The Moos (1969) study has often been cited as evidence of the contribution of both person and situation factors to behavior; however, what has been less often cited is the finding that the relative proportions of variance accounted for by persons and situations varied according to the behavior considered. While relevant data were not presented, one would expect to find that the relative contributions varied not only across behaviors but also across individuals on the same behavior. What appears to be needed is the kind of analysis suggested by Tucker's (1965) three-mode (person, situation, response) factor analysis—that is, analyses that indicate how groups of individuals show different patterns of behaviors in relation to groups of situations.

Relation of Affects to the Perception of Situations and to Behavior in Situations

Within the context of this research, affects have emerged as an important basis for the organization of situations. What is striking is the extent to which situations are described in terms of affects (e.g., threatening, warm, interesting, dull, tense, calm, rejecting) and organized in terms of the similarity of affects aroused in them. In other words, we may organize situations not so much in terms of cognitively perceived similar attributes but in terms of bodily experiences associated with them. A somewhat similar view is expressed by Mehrabian and Russell (1974) who, as noted, emphasize the emotion-eliciting qualities of environments. The use of affects as the basis for categorization of phenomena has also been noted by Plutchik (Note 3) in relation to the perception of people and interpersonal behavior.

A second important role of affects that emerges from this research is that of a mediator between the initial contact with a situation and the expression of behavior in it. The data, particularly some of the separate factor analyses, indicated a very complex relationship between feelings and behaviors. This complex relationship can be illustrated in the results from the factor analysis of Jennifer's behavior ratings (see Table 5.5). In the first factor, Jennifer reports behaving the same way regardless of whether she is criticized for doing the job wrong or praised for doing the job well. In both situations she behaves in a determined, responsible, ambitious way. Yet, the feelings in the two situations, while similar in some ways, are different in important ways. Ratings on the two situations correlate .49 in the factor analysis of behavior ratings, but they correlate − .05 in the factor analysis of feelings ratings.

Whereas in the above case different feelings were associated with similar behaviors, we also have evidence of similar feelings being associated with different behaviors. For example, similar feelings are experienced in the situations described in the Home-Volatile factor (see Table 5.1). In fact, in the factor analysis of feelings, all of the following situations load high on the first factor (Upset-Tension): "home from school visibly upset," "mother blows up at me," "want to leave home to go to Philadelphia," "mother refuses father's gift," and "honest with parents about leaving." Although there are some common aspects to the behaviors in these situations, there are important differences as well. As the data in Table 5.5 indicate, in some of these situations Jennifer is sharp-witted and jocular, in some she is emotional and uncontrolled, and in some she is peaceable, suppressed, and loyal.

Thus, we have illustrations of the complex relationship between feelings and behaviors, wherein behaviors may be expressive of or mask feelings, depending on the meaning of the feelings for the person and the context within which they are experienced. This emphasis on the complex relationship between situation, affect, and behavior is similar to Ekman's (1971) emphasis on the situation as capable of eliciting different emotions in different people, with the behavioral consequences being governed by learned display rules. Situations may also trigger the same facial affect program for two individuals, indicating that the same emotions have been elicited, but because they have learned different display rules, the behavioral consequences will differ in the two cases. An understanding of the linkages between feelings and behaviors, as governed by perceptions of the situation and learned display rules, becomes another component of understanding person-situation interaction and another dimension of intraindividual analysis.

Table 5.5   Illustrative Results from the Factor Analysis of Jennifer's Ratings of Behaviors ($n = 59$) for 23 Situations

Factor (% variance)	Illustrative situations	Illustrative behaviors
Pressure to Perform (32%)	have to perform at work have to participate in class do job wrong at work praised for doing well at work in a strange place with friend with a problem	Self-conscious, ambitious, determined, responsible, involved
Uncertain—Potentially Moving (19%)	return to my old neighborhood come home from Philadelphia want to leave home to go to Phila. talking with Mel	sharp-witted, jocular, sensitive, moody, nostalgic, not diligent, not assertive
Uncertain (9%)	in a crowd taking the bus to class caught not working with friend, no problem[a] come home from school pleased[a] alone[a]	detached, cool, controlled, introverted, self-conscious
Involved (7%)	honest with parents about leaving with friend with a problem come home from school upset mother blows up at me	emotional, uncontrolled, involved, upset, confused, not jocular, not sharp-witted, not detached
Upset (4%)	mother refuses father's gift someone else comes home upset mother blows up at me come home from Philadelphia	peaceable, suppressed, insightful, loyal, not honest, not aggressive, not outgoing

[a]Negative loading on the factor.

Implications for Future Research

The research presented expresses an effort to develop an approach to the study of person-situation interaction that allows for representativeness of design (Brunswik, 1956; Pervin, Note 4) and that goes beyond description of person-situation interactions toward an understanding of the processes involved. At least three major avenues of future research emerge. First, there is the need for more free-response description studies with many individuals so that we can move toward a meaningful taxonomy of situations. This taxonomy should be allowed to emerge from considerable observation of the ways in which individuals perceive and respond to situations they encounter in their daily lives. It is suggested that a priori taxonomies and taxonomies based on laboratory research will not be useful in advancing understanding and prediction; rather, observations related to individuals in situations in the natural habitat are needed.

Second, there is the need for observations of actual behavior in situations to accompany the reports of behavior presented in the current research. To the extent that the reports presented are matched by independent observations, we are basing our work on a solid foundation. However, we know that this may not always be the case. In the Block and Bennett (1955) study it was found that the subject's descriptions of herself interacting with other individuals were matched by the descriptions of some individuals and not by the descriptions of others. In neither case, however, was there the objective analysis of behavior in the situation. Naturalistic observation of behavior in a representative sampling of situations is a difficult task, but the work of Barker and his associates, the ethologists, and behavior modificationists are suggestive of what can be done (Barker & Wright, 1955; Bijou, Peterson, Harris, Allen, & Johnston, 1969; Blurton-Jones, 1972).

Finally, the research presented suggests that it would be useful to consider the perception of situations and behavior in situations from a developmental perspective. The conceptualization of the flood of detail of experience at the more general level of situations, enabling the individual to integrate his or her own experience and to anticipate the behavior of others, represents an important though little understood development achievement (Freedle, 1975; Livesley & Bromley, 1973).

REFERENCE NOTES

Rosenberg, S. A. *A free-response description approach to implicit personality theory.* Unpublished manuscript, 1975. (Available from Department of Psychology, Livingston College, Rutgers University, New Brunswick, N.J. 08903.)

Pervin, L. A. *Definitions, measurements, and classifications of stimuli, situations, and environments.* Unpublished manuscript, 1975. (Available from Department of Psychology, Livingston College, Rutgers University, New Brunswick, N.J. 08903.)

Plutchik, R. *A structural model of emotions and personality.* Paper presented at the meeting of the American Psychological Association, New Orleans, August 1974.

Pervin, L. A. *The representative design of person-situation research.* Paper presented at the Conference on Interactional Psychology, Stockholm, Sweden, June 1975.

REFERENCES

Barker, R. G., & Wright, H. F. *Midwest and its children.* Evanston, Ill.: Row, Peterson, 1955.

Bem, D. J., & Allen A. On predicting some of the people some of the time: The search for cross-situational consistencies in behavior. *Psychological Review,* 1974, *81,* 506-520.

Bijou, S. W., Peterson, R. F., Harris, F. R., Allen, K. E., & Johnston, M. S. Methodology for experimental studies of young children in naturalistic settings. *Psychological Record,* 1969, *19,* 177-210.

Block, J., & Bennett, L. The assessment of communication. *Human Relations,* 1955, *8,* 317-325.

Blurton-Jones, N. G. (Ed.). *Ethological studies of child behaviour.* Cambridge, England: Cambridge University Press, 1972.

Bowers, K. S. Situationism in psychology: An analysis and a critique. *Psychological Review,* 1973, *80,* 307-336.

Brunswik, E. *Perception and the representative design of psychological experiments.* Berkeley: University of California Press, 1956.

Carlson, R. Personality. *Annual Review of Psychology,* 1975, *26,* 393-414.

Cronbach, L. J. The two disciplines of scientific psychology. *American Psychologist,* 1957, *12,* 671-684.

Cronbach, L. J. Beyond the two disciplines of scientific psychology. *American Psychologist,* 1975, *30,* 116-127.

Ekehammar, B. Interactionism in personality from a historical perspective. *Psychological Bulletin,* 1974, *81,* 1026-1048.

Ekehammar, B., & Magnusson, D. A method to study stressful situations. *Journal of Personality and Social Psychology,* 1973, *27,* 176-179.

Ekman, P. Universals and cultural differences in facial expressions of emotion. In J. K. Cole (Ed.), *Nebraska Symposium on Motivation* (Vol. 19). Lincoln: University of Nebraska Press, 1971.

Endler, N. S. The person versus the situation—a pseudo issue? A response to Alker. *Journal of Personality,* 1973, *41,* 287-303.

Endler, N. S., & Hunt, J. M. S-R inventories of hostility and comparisons of the proportions of variance from persons, responses, and situations for hostility and anxiousness. *Journal of Personality and Social Psychology,* 1968, *9,* 309-315.

Frederiksen, N. Toward a taxonomy of situations. *American Psychologist,* 1972, *27,* 114-123.

Freedle, R. Some ingredients for constructing developmental models. In K. Riegel & J. Meacham (Eds.), *The developing individual in a changing world.* The Hague: Mouton, 1975.

Insel, P. M., & Moos, R. H. Psychological environments: Expanding the scope of human ecology. *American Psychologist*, 1974, *29*, 179-188.

Koltuv, B. Some characteristics of intrajudge trait intercorrelations. *Psychological Monographs*, 1962, *76* (33, Whole No. 552).

Krause, M. S. Use of social situations for research purposes. *American Psychologist*, 1970, *25*, 748-753.

Livesley, W. J., & Bromley, D. B. *Person perception in childhood and adolescence*. New York: Wiley, 1973.

Magnusson, D., & Ekehammar, B. Anxiety profiles based on both situational and response factors. *Multivariate Behavioral Research*, 1975, *10*, 27-44.

Mehrabian, A., & Russell, J. A. *An approach to environmental psychology*. Cambridge, Mass.: MIT Press, 1974.

Miller, G. A. The magical number seven, plus or minus two: Some limits on our capacity for processing information. *Psychological Review*, 1956, *63*, 81-97.

Mischel, W. Toward a cognitive social learning reconceptualization of personality. *Psychological Review*, 1973, *80*, 252-283.

Moos, R. H. Sources of variance in responses to questionnaires and behavior. *Journal of Abnormal Psychology*, 1969, *74*, 405-412.

Murray, H. A. *Explorations in personality*. New York: Oxford University Press, 1938.

Osgood, C. E., Suci, G. J., & Tannenbaum, P. H. *The measurement of meaning*. Urbana: University of Illinois Press, 1957.

Pervin, L. A. Performance and satisfaction as a function of individual-environment fit. *Psychological Bulletin*, 1968, *69*, 56-68.

Sarason, I. G., Smith, R. E., & Diener, E. Personality research: Components of variance attributable to the person and the situation. *Journal of Personality and Social Psychology*, 1975, *32*, 199-204.

Tucker, L. R. Experiments in multi-mode factor analysis. *Proceedings of the 1964 invitational conference on testing problems*. Princeton, N.J.: Educational Testing Service, 1965.

6

The Goal Structure of Situations*

Jean Ann Graham, Michael Argyle and Adrian Furnham

An empirical method for analysing the goal structure within and between persons in different social situations is described. The method involves establishing the main goals of occupants of situational roles and then finding out how the different goals inter-relate in terms of degree and type/direction of conflict and compatibility.

Principal components analyses were carried out on ratings of importance of goals of those in different situational roles. Criteria of high factor loadings combined with high mean importance ratings were used to produce the main higher order goals for each of the roles. The goals for the six roles studied were, in each case except one: social acceptance and developing relationships, own well being and achieving a specific situational task goal. However, the precise nature of these goals is rather different in the different situations.

Inter-relationship of goals was studied using ratings of conflict or compatibility between pairs of goals within and across roles of each situation. The results were used to describe the goal structures of the different situations. The situation with the most conflict between goals was, as expected, the complaint. Ways were suggested in which knowledge of the goal structure, particularly the points of conflict, could help with skilful handling of potentially difficult social situations

*Reprinted by permission of John Wiley & Sons, Ltd: Graham, J., Argyle, M., & Furnham, A. The goal of structure of situations. *European Journal of Social Psychology,* 1980. *10,* 345-366.

INTRODUCTION

It may be assumed that people enter situations because they are motivated to do so, i.e. they expect to be able to attain certain goals, which in turn lead to the satisfaction of needs or other drives. Situations have presumably developed as cultural institutions because they satisfy needs in this way. A goal may be defined as a state of affairs, whether a bodily or mental state, behaviour of self or others, or condition of the physical world, which is consciously desired, or is pursued without awareness, and gives satisfaction when attained.

Often a person is motivated to pursue more than one goal, in which case the two motives may come into conflict, or they may be compatible with one another. When two or more people enter a social situation, they are attracted to it by their particular combination of motives. The combination of the important goals of each person, and the relations between them, intra-personal and interpersonal, we shall call the "goal structure" of the situation. The present paper reports a number of exploratory studies aimed to develop a method of analysing goal structures. In addition it will describe the goal structures of a number of common social situations, within a given subculture. (There are likely to be different conceptions of the goals of certain situations within different subcultures.)

Consider a number of social situations—a selection interview, a date, and sales. It may be obvious what some of the main goals of the different participants are. Sometimes they may be in conflict—e.g. at a selection interview, where the weaker candidates are keen to get the job; sometimes they are not in conflict, e.g. a date where both partners like one another equally; sometimes the goals are symmetrical, as in the date example; sometimes the goals are complementary, as in a sales situation—one wants to buy, the other wants to sell.

It should be noted that although we are dealing here with a relatively static conception of goals of a situation there are also goals which emerge during the course of an encounter, and there may also be negotiation of goals within an ongoing situation. In the experiments reported here the term 'goal' (which it was thought might present a conceptualisation problem to the subjects) was described as meaning the aim of a situation or what the participants would be likely to be trying to do/achieve in a particular situation, assuming, of course that there are often several goals or aims in any one situation.

It is important to consider the organisation of goal-directed action in human social behaviour (Von Cranach, 1979). Lewin (1935) analysed the goal structures of different kinds of conflict situations, where one person was in a state of conflict between different drives, or where the routes to goals were blocked by barriers. Social psychologists have analysed simple forms of conflict between two people, affected by one drive each, as in competition. The Prisoner's Dilemma game is more complicated; again there is one drive each, but there is a combination of cooperation and competition. However, other studies have shown that even very simple social situations involve at least two drives per person, i.e., social and task goals, as Bales (1950) and others have recognised. Research in the exchange theory tradition, has shown that each participant is providing certain rewards for the other, though again only one goal per person is generally considered (Chadwick-Jones, 1976).

We have developed elsewhere a conceptual scheme for the analysis and description of situations in terms of their basic features—their goals, rules, repertoire of elements, roles, environmental setting, concepts, and skills needed (Argyle, 1976). This makes use of an anology between social situations and games, which also can be analysed in terms of their goals, rules, moves (repertoire), environmental setting, etc. (Avedon, 1971). We consider that the most basic feature is the goal structure, and that the other features can be given a functional explanation in terms of how they help in the realisation of these goals.

Several writers have offered a functional analysis of rules; Marvin Harris (1974) suggested an explanation of Indian rules protecting cows in terms of the value of cow-dung as fuel and fertiliser, of oxen for pulling farm instruments, and so on. We have studied the different rules in a number of common situations, and offered a functional interpretation (Argyle, Graham, Campbell and White, 1979). We found that some rules are universal to nearly all situations (e.g. "be polite", "be friendly"); these prevent withdrawal or aggression. Some rules are clearly related to the goals of particular situations, e.g. "answer truthfully" (at the doctor's). "don't pretend to understand when you haven't" (at a tutorial). Some rules guard against temptation which may occur in a situation, e.g., "don't leave others to pay" (at a pub), some rules help with common difficulties, e.g., "introduce yourself" (at a sherry party). However these functional interpretations are rather weak without independent evidence of what the goals actually are in each situation. That is what the first two studies presented here to aim to find out.

A similar functional analysis can be given of other features of situations, e.g. the repertoire and the roles (Argyle, Furnham and Graham, 1981). Knowledge of the goals does not however enable us to predict other features of a situation in detail, because cultures and groups can develop more than one set of rules etc., to enable a given set of goals to be met. For example buying and selling can be achieved using the rules, repertoires and roles of an auction sale, barter, or fixed-price sale. There may also be a build-up of rules and other features, so that elaborate sections of social reality are constructed, as in the invention of games and ceremonies (Twining and Miers, 1976).

Different goals may be related in several different ways, and this applies equally to two goals for the same person, or for different people. The last two studies presented here (3a and 3b) are concerned with discovering how different pairs of goals (within and between roles) relate to one another.

Two goals may:

1. be independent
2. be compatible:
   (i)   one may be instrumental to (help) the other
   (ii) each may be instrumental to the other
   (iii) each may be a part of a larger goal
3. interfere (be in conflict):
   (i)   one may interfere with the other
   (ii) each may interfere with the other
   (iii) achieving both goals may be logically impossible

We made a number of predictions about certain kinds of situations:

Persuasion, assertiveness, complaints. It might be expected that each person would be influenced by social needs (to be accepted, liked, etc), and by the goal of changing the other's behaviour in some other way. This would be likely to generate intra-personal and inter-personal conflict. The 'complaining' situation, looked at in these studies, was expected to contain the most conflict between goals.

Leadership, supervision and related skills involving status/dominance type role differences. It was expected that at least two goals would be operative for each person, but here the goal of establishing good relationships would be likely to be instrumental to influencing the other's behaviour. For the 'nursing' situation, looked at in these studies, some inter-personal conflict seemed likely as both nurses and patients can sometimes be thought to be 'difficult,' e.g. unco-operative about taking medicine (patient) or about giving information about the illness (nurse).

Social events, making friends, etc. Here there is no real task, and it was expected that there would be very little conflict. The goal of the 'party' situation is, presumably, to engage in a pleasant occasion.

The methods we have used all consist of various kinds of self-report—first by eliciting open-ended responses to find the range of goals reported for the situations studied, then by using 3-category and 5-point rating scales on the importance of each goal for each situation. The subjects had no difficulty in answering these questions. Two, criteria were used to establish the importance of a goal in a situation: (1) the goal emerged as an important factor from principal components analysis of a longer list of goals, and (2) the goals in the factor were on average rated as being at least 'fairly important' by most members of the sample. The degree and type of conflict or compatibility between two goals was also obtained by procedures of two different kinds; a 5-point rating scale and a 9-category scale, these yielded largely consistent results.

This study was not designed to test hypotheses, apart from the expectations about the three examples of the kinds of situations given above. The primary aim was to develop methods of analysis, and examine the results of using these methods. It was hoped that this form of analysis would lead to a greater understanding of situations. This in turn should suggest where the difficulties in a situation lie, and the social skills which might be used to overcome them.

Analysis of assertiveness situations, for example, is likely to reveal that the main conflict of goals for the assertor is for him to get his way *and* to keep on good terms with the others, rather than merely getting his way. If this is the case perhaps use of a lot of inter-personal rewards and persuasive arguments which will offer advantages to the other would be important in the situation. Difficulties might be likely to arise if insufficient attention is paid to the goal of keeping on good terms with the others and too much attention given to the goal of getting one's own way regardless of how this is done.

STUDY 1. A PRELIMINARY STUDY OF THE MAIN GOALS OF SOCIAL SITUATIONS

Method

Derivation of goals. A list of eight common dyadic social situations was presented to 3 female students in their early twenties. Most of the situations involved different roles, e.g. the roles of doctor and patient in the situation 'visit to the doctor'. Subjects were asked to write down all the goals/aims they thought the person in each of the roles in each situation would usually have (i.e., what they were trying to do/achieve). Subjects were told that they could deal with the roles within situations and the situations themselves in any order they wished and that they could take as much time as they liked (up to one hour).

The goals listed by the subjects were collected together to form one list of goals. To this list were added some goals thought to be relevant by the authors, and some of the basic motivations of social behaviour as described by previous researchers e.g., Murray (1938) and Atkinson (1958). Thus, approximately 120 goals were collected from these different sources. These, mostly fairly specific goals, were reduced to a smaller number (18) of higher order categories, which were more general in nature e.g. 'appear physically attractive', 'appear interested', 'appear clever', 'appear witty', were all grouped together to form a higher order, more general goal category of 'make favourable impression, appear attractive, interested'. And, 'seek advice', 'seek reassurance', 'seek help' were all grouped together to form a more general category, etc.

Subjects. The subjects used in this study were 60 female students, in their early twenties, who attended a college for occupational therapy.

Procedure. Subjects were presented with lists of the 18 goals subsumed under each of the 8 situations used in the preliminary study. The goals and situations are listed in Table 6.1. Subjects were asked to indicate how important they considered that each of the goals was in one role for each situation (the role this subject sample was most likely to have experienced, e.g. interviewee rather than interviewer, patient rather than doctor, etc.). Three categories were available for rating how important the goals were: *1* for no, *2* for perhaps and *3* for yes. The order of presentation of situations and goals was varied and counterbalanced, so that different subjects were presented with the situations, and the goals within the situations, in different orders.

Results

Frequency counts were taken of the responses in each of the 3 categories (no, perhaps and yes) for the importance of each of the 18 goals. Those for which 60% or more of the subject sample agreed with respect to whether they were definitely (yes) important, or could be important (perhaps), were selected. These are listed in Table 6.1.

STUDY 2. THE MAIN GOALS FACTORS IN SEVEN SITUATIONAL ROLES

Method

Revision of goals list. The list of goals used in Study 1 was revised to incorporate goals relevant to the new set of situations used here. These new situations were ones which it was thought this group of subjects (student nurses) would have experienced. Also, both roles were considered in each situation—not just one role as in Study 1. The new list of goals was thus revised to take account of both roles where appropriate, e.g. the goal 'be looked after' was complementary with the goal 'look after other(s)'. Also, goals which looked as if they might correlate highly—on the basis of conceptual similarity and having similar patterns of ratings in Study 1 were collapsed, e.g. 'have fun, enjoy yourself' and 'pleasant social activity' were collapsed to form a new goal 'pleasant/enjoyable social activity.'

Subjects. The subjects used here were 37 female student nurses.

Procedure. The procedure was essentially similar to that used in Study 1 except that 21 goals were now used instead of 18, and 4 situations were used (3 of which involved 2 different roles and 1 of which involved the same role for different participants) instead of 8.

Table 6.1 Percentages (over 60%) of Subjects in Study 1 Rating Goals as Important or Perhaps Important in Different Situations

SITUATIONS

GOALS	friendly chat Yes	friendly chat Perhaps	interview Yes	interview Perhaps	doctor's Yes	doctor's Perhaps	date Yes	date Perhaps	wedding Yes	wedding Perhaps	complaining Yes	complaining Perhaps	hostess Yes	hostess Perhaps	class Yes	class Perhaps
1. be accepted by others	80*		78				81		85				93			
2. convey information to others			80		71						85			65	50	
3. help look after other person(s)													76			
4. dominate others, be in control of the situation																
5. have fun, enjoy yourself	92						100		92				97			
6. reduce own anxiety					80											
7. maintain a satisfactory level of self-esteem, self-respect	65		85				80				81		88			
8. financial prospects																
9. physical well-being					95				68				87			
10. eating, drinking		(58)						70								
11. sexual activity								(59)								
12. do well, answer questions correctly			97												77	
13. make favourable impression, appear attractive, interested			100		95		95		85				83			
14. seek help, advice, reassurance		63			95											
15. persuade the other to do something, influence his/her behaviour		80									90					
16. obtain information, learn something new, solve problems			70		88										92	
17. pleasant social activity	92						93		83				92			
18. make new friends, get to know people better	68						93		83				70			

*Values shown are Percentages (rounded off)

62

The instructions to subjects were as follows:

"Please indicate, by referring to the following scale, how important each of the following 21 goals is likely to be for each person in each situation. Alongside each goal give a score from 1 to 5 (inclusive) for how important you think that goal would be for that person in that situation. If you feel any goal may oppose or be in conflict with a goal you have already rated as important, it is alright to say they are both important. So, please consider each one independently.

1	2	3	4	5
Not at all important	of minor importance	fairly important	important	very important

The order of presentation of situations, roles and goals was varied and counterbalanced so that different subjects were presented with the situations, the roles within those situations and, within that, the goals to be rated—in different orders.

Results

Frequency counts were taken of the ratings of (3) fairly important, (4) important and (5) very important given to each goal in each situational role. These frequencies are shown in Table 6.2.

A substantial degree of correspondence was found between the goals which were most important here and those found to be important in the corresponding situational roles for Study 1, e.g., the role of complainer in the complaint situation.

Although we had collapsed a number of very similar goals to form broader ones, there was still a number of goals which were conceptually similar and had rather similar patterns of ratings across situations. A principal components analysis was, therefore, carried out for each role using the entire original data (including ratings of 1 and 2 on the 5-point scale). It was thought that the loading of individual goals on to factors, considered in addition to the mean importance rating of individual goals and the proportion of subjects' rating a goal as at least fairly important, would in turn indicate how the goals should be classified and labelled as higher order goals.

The following criteria were therefore used for inclusion of goals contributing to a factor and, in addition, contributing substantially to a higher order goal which could be considered important in the situational role: eigen values > 2.0, a factor loading > 0.4, a mean importance rating > 3.0, with more than 65% (a frequency of at least 23 out of 35) of the subjects rating the goal at least fairly

Table 6.2   Frequencies for Ratings of at Least 'Fairly Important,'
for Goals in each Situational Role

	Party		Complaining		Nursing		Chat
	hostess	guest	person complaining	being complained to	nurse	patient	friend
1. be accepted by other(s)	34	34	25	25	30	26	34
2. convey information to other(s)	34	28	32	25	32	26	33
3. look after other person(s)	35	24	13	15	32	5	26
4. take charge of the situation	34	7	36	29	32	7	14
5. pleasant/enjoyable social activity	33	32	7	13	20	18	32
6. reduce own anxiety	28	25	30	27	28	33	27
7. maintain satisfactory level of self esteem/ self respect	34	32	32	33	34	30	33
8. sustain social relationship(s)	34	35	26	27	28	25	36
9. be looked after	10	22	9	9	12	28	16
10. physical well-being of other(s)	29	19	14	13	33	12	26
11. eating/drinking	25	29	4	5	25	26	18
12. sexual activity	8	13	4	7	7	13	6
13. make favourable impression e.g. appear attractive, intelligent, interesting	34	34	20	23	27	20	32
14. seek help/advice/ reassurance	16	16	15	20	27	31	29
15. persuade the other to do something, influence his/her behaviour	12	14	31	29	29	16	17
16. obtain information/learn something new/solve problems	27	28	28	23	30	24	33
17. reduce other's anxiety	31	24	14	26	35	16	32
18. own physical well-being	24	24	25	24	27	33	21
19. let other take charge of the situation	9	14	6	12	14	30	8
20. be accepting/welcoming to other(s)	35	32	17	18	32	24	33
21. make new friends, get to know people better	34	35	15	13	25	16	31

Total possible frequency = 35

important (see Table 6.2). From the Varimax rotated factor matrix for each situational role no more than 3 of the possible factors had eigen values > 2. For all situational roles the 2 or 3 factors which had eigen values > 2.0 accounted for between 47 and 55% of the total variance. Those goals which met the above criteria for each situational role were listed and it was on the basis of these goals that the factors were labelled. This formed the new labelling for the goals, which were now of a higher order and which were also of substantial importance in their particular situational role. The details of the original goals (their factor loadings and mean importance ratings) which contributed to the higher order goals are shown for the role of hostess at the small party or gathering, in Table 6.3. (This

Table 6.3   Factor Loading and Importance Ratings for Seven Situational Roles

Situational role	Higher order goal	Goal	Factor loading	Mean importance rating
		Note. Details of the analysis for the first situational role.		
Hostess at small party or gathering	own physical well being	own physical well being	0.71	3.03
	looking after others	convey information	0.36	3.97
		physical well being of others	0.68	9.91
		obtain information	0.87	3.14
		reduce other's anxiety	0.73	3.82
	developing relationships	be accepted	0.85	4.6
		convey information	0.51	3.97
		look after other	0.67	4.62
		make favourable impression	0.75	4.32
		be accepting	0.53	4.77
		Summary of above situations		
Guest at small party	developing friendships	be accepted	0.79	4.49
	exchanging information (make favourable impression)	be accepting	0.52	3.74
	own well being	reduce own anxiety	0.77	3.11
Complainer	dominance-persuasion	persuade the other	0.73	4.51
	being accepted	be accepted	0.45	3.31
Complainee	dominance	take charge	—0.76	3.85
	own physical well being	own physical well being	0.50	3.17
	self-esteem and being accepted	self-esteem	0.71	4.37
Nurse	mutual acceptance and self-esteem	self-esteem	0.76	4.20
	taking care of other	reduce other's anxiety	0.89	4.83
	looking after self	obtaining information	0.62	4.05
Patient	mutual acceptance	be accepted	0.60	3.60
	obtaining information	obtaining information	0.47	3.22
	own well being	own physical well being	0.75	4.57
Friend	friendship exchange	make new friends	0.74	4.17
	social	sustain social relationships	0.44	4.48

table also summarises the findings for other situational roles by showing just the goal with the highest mean importance rating contributing to each higher order goal in each role). The higher order goals were the goals which were used in follow up studies on the inter-relationship between goals.

The relative importance of the main important goals in a situational role can also be considered. For the nursing situation the most important goal of the nurse is 'taking care of the other'—'look after self' and 'mutual acceptance and self-esteem' are less important—in that they are only really important in leading to the patient's being taken care of. Similarly, for the patient, 'own well being' has the highest mean importance ratings for the components making up the goal factors for this role. The fact that 'obtaining information' and 'mutual accept-ance' are given lower mean importance ratings for their components makes sense in that these are subgoals to the goal of patient's well being.

For the party situation it is less obvious how the goals should be expected to inter-relate in terms of relative importance. For the complaint situation it is clear that the most important goal would be 'persuasion' on the part of the complainer. This indeed is supported by the fact that the one component loading on to the positive pole, persuasion, was persuade the other to do something, influence his/her behaviour, and this had the highest mean importance rating (4.51) within that situation.

STUDY 3. THE INTER-RELATIONS BETWEEN GOALS: CONFLICT AND COMPATIBILITY

In this experiment the main goals of three of the situations derived from Study 2 were used to look at the inter-relations between the goals of each situational role. Pairs of goals were considered both within the same individual or role and across the two roles of each situation. Inter-relating was considered in terms of compatibility, conflict or independence of achieving goals within a pair. The degree of conflict/compatibility was investigated using procedure (a) and/or direction of compatibility or conflict was investigated using procedure (b).

Preliminary work

Situation D—'a friendly chat with a friend of the same sex in the evening' was excluded because it does not contain two different roles—as do situations A, B and C.

The higher order goals listed in the results of Study 2 (Table 6.3) were used here. The labels remained the same. Three main goals were used for each situational role. In the case of situational role 2—guest at a small party, one of the higher order goals was derived from a bipolar factor exchanging information/make favourable impression. The negative end was suppressed in this case (as only one goal loaded negatively on the factor) and the higher order goal was thus considered to be exchanging information. In the case of situational role 3—complainer, the two poles of the bipolar factor were used as separate higher order goals (dominance, and persuasion) because in addition to the fact that they both seemed to capture important aspects of the situation it seemed that this polarity might in itself contain the essence of the conflict inherent in this situation.

Method

Subjects. The subjects were females who were 3rd year occupational therapy students attending a course on social skills training. Seventeen subjects were used for procedure (a) and nineteen subjects were used for procedure (b). Different subjects were used for each procedure.

Procedure (a). The following 3 situations, with their respective roles of the two people in them, were used:

Situation	*Roles*
A small party or gathering	hostess, guest
Complaining to a neighbour about constant noisy disturbance	complainer, complainee
Nursing someone who is physically unwell (could be at home in bed)	nurse, patient

For each situation three main goals of each of the two persons in that situation were used. They were then presented in pairs for each situation, firstly the three possible paired combinations of the 3 main goals for role 1, followed by the three possible pairs for role 2, followed by the nine possible combinations for both roles combined.

Subjects were asked to rate each pair of goals listed for each situation according to how much they were compatible or in conflict with one another, using a five point category scale. The five categories were: likely to be compatible (1), could/might be compatible (2), do not relate/not much to do with each other (3), could/might interfere (4), could/might be in conflict (5).

Procedure (b). A different procedure was used to provide information about the type/directionality of help or interference between pairs of goals. Subjects were asked to rate the relation between each pair of goals using 9 categories. The nine possible categories are shown below with some examples of ways in which the achieving of goals (inter- or intra-personal) could be compatible with, or in conflict with, or independent of one another. These nine categories seemed to cover the types of inter-relationship between goals which could possibly occur.

Types of compatibility or conflict of goals

1. Achieving 1st goal could help with achieving 2nd goal ('obtaining information' could lead to 'helping someone').
2. Achieving 2nd goal could help with achieving 1st goal.
3. Achieving each goal could help with achieving the other ('being cheerful', 'being liked').
4. Both goals are part of a larger goal ('put on make up' and 'brush hair' are part of larger goal 'improve appearance').
5. Both goals are independent—do not have much to do with one another ('dominance' and 'eating').
6. Achieving 1st goal could interfere with achieving 2nd goal ('getting someone to go away' and 'keeping on good terms with him').
7. Achieving 2nd goal could interfere with achieving 1st goal.
8. Achieving each goal could interfere with achieving the other ('telling someone bad news, and 'not making someone unhappy').
9. Achieving both goals is impossible ('have cake' and 'eat cake').

The questionnaire which consisted of three pages and which was administered in the presence of the experimenter, took about twenty minutes to complete.

Results

Frequency counts were taken of the responses in each of the 5 categories (for Study a) of compatibility and conflict, for each pair of goals within and across situational roles. The mean and modal response for each pair of goals is shown below, along with the proportion of subjects selecting the modal response category.

Frequency counts were also taken of the responses in each of the nine categories (for (b)) for types of compatibility and conflict for each pair of goals within and across situational roles. The modal responses for the pairs of goals were again calculated along with the proportion of subjects selecting each of the modal response categories. It was found that the results for the two methods were largely in agreement. Those cases in which there was not complete agreement appeared to be cases where different possible interpretations of the more specific nature of the goals were likely.

The results for the ratings of goal pairs in the three situations are represented diagrammatically in Figures 6.1, 6.2, and 6.3.

In these figures the results of procedures (a) and (b) are combined, the values shown in this figure represent the mean values of the conflict scores across subjects (if the 5-point scale is conceived of as a unidimensional scale representing increasing degrees of conflict). Only those values at the extremes of the scale are shown (i.e. between points 1 and 2 and between points 4 and 5) in order to highlight the points of likely difficulty. In this figure the solid lines represent the compatibility end of the scale and the dotted lines represent the conflict end of the scale.

The type/direction of compatibility or conflict (procedure (b)) is also shown on the figures. The double lines represent those instances in which the conflict or compatibility works both ways, as indicated by the modal response category for type or direction of compatibility or conflict. Single lines represent those

Table 6.4 Mean and Modal Responses with Procedure (a)

Goals	A small party			Complaining			Nursing		
	mean	mode	Proportion of S's agreeing	mean	mode	Proportion of S's agreeing	mean	mode	Proportion of S's agreeing
A & B	3.42	4	8	2.63	2	8	1.58	1	12
A & C	2.11	2	8	4.26	4	9	1.79	2	10
B & C	1.63	1	14	2.0	1	9	3.42	4	7
D & E	1.42	1	14	2.32	1	7	2.11	2	8
D & F	2.32	2	9	3.11	4	9	1.74	1	11
E & F	2.36	3	8	1.95	1	8	2.05	2	8
A & D	2.95	4	6	4.89	5	18	1.26	1	16
B & E	2.26	2	8	3.37	4	7	2.58	2/4	6
C & F	2.79	2	8	2.84	2	7	4.16	4	14
A & E	3.05	3	8	4.0	4	8	2.84	2	8
A & F	3.58	5	9	4.58	5	12	2.37	2	9
B & D	1.42	1	13	4.05	4	9	1.58	2	11
B & F	2.0	1	9	2.79	4	7	1.89	1	11
C & D	1.21	1	15	3.84	4	8	3.26	4	8
C & E	1.89	2	9 (out of total of 19)	2.47	2	9	3.95	4	10

Response
Categories:

1 = likely to be compatible
2 = might be compatible
3 = do not relate
4 = might interfere
5 = might be in conflict

Key
for Goals:

A =	own physical well being		dominance		mutual acceptance & self esteem		
B =	looking after others	hostess	persuasion	complainer	take care of other	nurse	
C =	developing relationships		being accepted		looking after self		
D =	developing friendships		dominance		mutual acceptance		
E =	exchanging information	guest	own physical well being	complainee	obtaining information	patient	
F =	own well being		self esteem & being accepted		own well being		

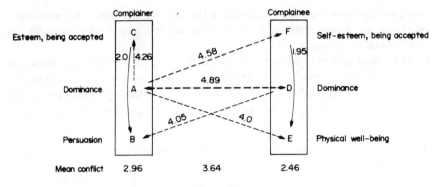

Figure 6.1

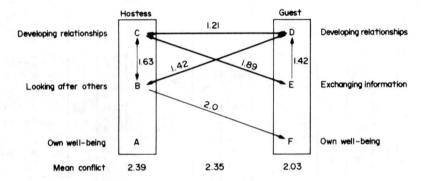

Figure 6.2

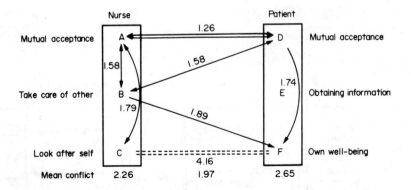

Figure 6.3

instances in which the conflict or compatibility works one way only—the arrow indicating which way. Lack of arrows represents independent goals (category 5). The mean conflict scores shown on the figures are the means of the mean conflict scores across goal pair combinations within each role separately and both roles combined.

DISCUSSION

In the experiments described we have developed an empirical method for discovering the main goals for different situational roles and the relations between goals. These methods may be applied to any situation which has fairly clearly defined goals.

A list of the main goals likely to be involved was elicited first by open-ended interviews. It was found that people were able to elicit goals without much difficulty—presumably this was partly facilitated by familiarity with the situations and roles depicted. The list of goals obtained was supplemented by reference to previous research on motivation. Principal components analyses were carried out on the ratings of the importance of each goal for each role: the main goals were those corresponding to the main factors whose labels were determined by the component goals which had high factor loadings and which were also rated as at least fairly important by most of the subjects for that situation. The relative importance of these main goals was also considered. For those situational roles where it was fairly clear which goal should be most important, the results were in keeping with these expectations.

The inter-relationships between pairs of important goals, within and across roles, was assessed using ratings/categorisations of degree and type/direction of compatibility and conflict.

One limitation of this approach is that subjects may not be consciously aware of all relevant goals, or they may be unwilling to reveal some of them. It is now familiar that people are often unable to provide accurate accounts of the causes of their behaviour (Nisbett and Wilson, 1977). However we obtained what seemed to be fairly comprehensive lists of goals in Study 1, and subjects in the later studies were evidently willing and able to rate the relevance of these goals in different situations. It would be possible to ask further questions like "What would make you particularly satisfied at (e.g.,) a party?", or "What would make you disappointed with (e.g.,) a party?", or "What do you enjoy most about (e.g.,) parties?".

It should be stressed that the goal structures studied in this work are those related to *roles* and situations rather than necessarily being the experienced goals of actors. The validity of these results for experienced actors' goal structures is therefore difficult to assess. The goal structures depicted here are likely to be the product of knowledge of the conventional character of situations—of social conventions, rules or norms related to the situations. These conventional social meanings may be known to the actor and thus influence his behaviour. The method of analysis of goal structure developed here may, therefore, also be useful for the assessment of social meaning of actions.

The value of the method used can be partly assessed by examining the results obtained. The fact that there is a substantial amount of agreement in the findings obtained using the different procedures, 1) for important goals and 2) for inter-relations between goals, provides some validation for the method.

Three main important goals were obtained for each situational role (in the way described above). These formed a fairly similar pattern for each situational role in five cases out of six: 1) social acceptance, developing relationships, 2) own well being, 3) achieving a specific situational task goal. In the case of the complainer in the complaint situation goals 1 and 3 were present and goal 2 was implicit, since the point of the complaint ('persuasion') was to remove an unwelcome noise. Dominance and persuasion were separate goals. There is however, considerable variation between situations in the more specific nature of the goals sought. In the first place the task goals are very different in each case. Secondly, the type of social relationship sought, apart from 'acceptance', is quite different, at a party, a complaint, and nursing.

'Dominance' emerged as an important goal factor for both sides of the complaint, but not in the other situations. From other studies it would be expected that two dimensions of social motivation might be commonly found— affiliation and dominance (e.g. Schutz, 1958; Foa, 1961). However we did not include many scales in the dominance area, which would therefore make such a factor less likely to appear. From the frequency data of Study 2, it can be seen that take charge was rated as important as a goal, by most subjects, for the hostess and nurse roles but not for guests or patients. We conclude that dominance is a goal which is relevant to some roles but not others.

From the results shown in Figures 6.1—6.3 it can be seen that in the case of the party situation, as expected, there is no conflict: there is mostly two-way interpersonal compatibility and 1-way and 2-way intra-personal compatibility. The hostess' goal 'looking after others' appears to be one of the most central goals in that it has three 2-way links with other goals—the goal of the guest 'developing relationships' also has 3 links. The goal of the hostess 'own well being' seems to be the most separate goal without strong inter-relations with the other goals.

The complaint is quite different from both of the other situations in that all of the interpersonal links are negative (av. 3.64)—this situation was expected to have the most conflict. The central goal appears to be dominance on the part of the complainer: it has 4 links. Note that it creates internal conflict by interfering with the goal of being accepted, whereas being accepted is internally instrumental in relation to persuasion, presumably because being accepted makes persuasion easier. If the goal of dominance on the part of the complainer was absent the situation would be greatly improved. The goal seems to have more conflicting relations with other goals than does the goal of persuasion which is the real point of this situation (and most important as assssed by the importance ratings in Study 2). This is more complex than the goal structure which we had predicted for assertiveness situations, and three goals, not two are involved on each side.

The nursing situation is rather different again. The key role appears to be the nurse looking after the patient ('taking care of other')—it has three links. The only conflict is between the nurse looking after herself and the well being of the patient. As predicted, there are clear instrumental links in which the nurse's taking care of the patient leads to mutual acceptance (acceptance by the patient, at least, would be expected) which in turn is instrumental to the patient's well-being. This is in keeping with the general expectation for situations involving a status/dominance difference, that establishing good relationships is instrumental to influencing the other's (person being dominated) behaviour.

In further studies it would be useful to include more dominance goals; no dominance factor appeared with the scales which we were using.

What use can be made of this kind of goal-structure analysis? It is likely that some of the situations which are found difficult have conflicts between goals though this has yet to be established; we now have a measuring instrument that will enable us to test this hypothesis. However, knowledge of the goal structure, especially of the main points of conflict within and between persons in different roles, would help in handling these situations. The goal structure can provide a map for steering through these conflicts. How could the difficulty of making a complaint be reduced, for example? From our results the most important step would be to abandon dominance as a goal: the remaining goals would be 'being accepted' and 'persuasion', and the first is instrumental to the second. Could the conflict in nurse-patient encounters be avoided? In terms of goal conflict one of the problems seems to lie in the nurse's concern for her own well being; the solution to this may lie in steps such as greater medical precautions to protect nurses, which would remove this source of anxiety.

As, overall, there is not a great deal of evidence of conflict between the goals themselves it seems likely that a larger source of conflict may lie in the way the goals are attained e.g., if there is insufficient regard for the consequences of the other people present, etc. Attempts at attaining a goal in this kind of way may produce non-goal outcomes such as negative feelings as well as, or instead of the main goal(s) of the situation. An awareness of this kind of consideration may be reflected in the goal structures as developed with the kind of method used here. As we have seen in the complaint situation, for example, the goal 'being accepted' is one of the main goals, although subordinate to the goal of 'persuasion' (both in intuitive terms and in terms of the mean importance ratings attained). In other situations goals such as 'being accepted' which are concerned with consideration for the feelings of others, etc. may be less obviously important and may not be elicited using the method described here. Nevertheless, in addition to knowing the goal structure, *how* the main goals of a situation are attained, and the minimising of negative non-goal outcomes would each seem to be important aspects of social skills training which should not be overlooked.

BIBLIOGRAPHY

Argyle, M. (1976) Personality and social behaviour. In R. Harré (Ed.) *Personality*, Oxford: Blackwell.

Argyle, M., Furnham, A. and Graham, J. A. (1981) *Social Situations*. Cambridge: Cambridge University Press.

Argyle, M., Graham, J. A., Campbell, A. and White, P. (1979) The rules of different situations. *New Zealand Psychologist, 8,* 13-22.

Atkinson, J. W. (1958) *Motives in Fantasy, Action and Society: a Method of Assessment and Study*. N.J.: Von Nostrand.

Avedon, E. M. (1971) The structure of elements of games. In E. M. Avedon and B. Sutton-Smith (eds.) *The Study of Games*. New York: Wiley. pp. 419-426.

Bales, R. F. (1950) *Interaction Process Analysis: A Method for the Study of Small Groups*. Reading, Mass.: Addison-Wesley.

Chadwick-Jones, J. K. (1976) *Social Exchange Theory*. London: Academic Press.

Foa, U. G. (1961) Convergences in the analysis of the structure of interpersonal behaviour. *Psychol. Rev., 68,* 341-353.

Harris, M. (1975) *Cows, Pigs, Wars and Witches*. London: Hutchinson.

Lewin, K. (1935) *A Dynamic Theory of Personality*. New York & London: McGraw Hill.

Murray, H. A. (1938) *Explorations in Personality*. New York: Science Editions.

Nisbett, R. E. and Wilson, D. (1977) Telling more than we know: verbal reports on mental processes. *Psychol. Rev., 84,* 231-259.

Schutz, (1958) *FIRO: A Three Dimensional Theory of Interpersonal Behavior*. New York: Holt, Rinehart and Winston.

Twining, W. and Miers, D. (1976) *How to Do Things with Rules*. London: Weidenfeld and Nicholson.

Von Cranach, M. (1979) Goal-directed action. Oxford University Seminar.

Part 2
The Social
Psychological Approach

The Perception of Social Situations: Introduction

These three studies are all concerned with the classification and dimensionality of situations as perceived by participants.

Magnusson (1971) was one of the first people to study such dimensions. He asked three subjects to rate the similarity of pairs of situations out of a set of 36 situations at a university, and carried out principal components analyses of these ratings—an early form of multi-dimensional scaling (MDS). Rather similar dimensions of situations appeared for each person—positive and rewarding, negative and unrewarding, passive (e.g., waiting), social, and working alone.

Forgas (1976) tackled this problem by the use of multi-dimensional scaling, based on the analysis of ratings of situations, as devised by Kruskal. He obtained samples of situations and used two samples of subjects. For a sample of housewives two dimensions appeared: 1. intimacy, involvement and friendliness, and 2. subjective self-confidence and competence. For a sample of students a third dimension was needed—evaluation as pleasant or unpleasant. He also analysed the data using hierarchical cluster analysis: for housewives the main divisions were of family, casual and social; for the students, they were friends, acquaintances, strangers, and people in an official capacity. He discusses the relative merits of classifying situations in terms of dimensions and of categories.

Wish, Deutsch and Kaplan (1976) extended earlier work by Wish and colleagues in which certain dimensions of situations had consistently appeared, by means of multidimensional scaling—cooperative and friendly v. competitive and hostile, equal v. unequal, intense v. superficial, and socio-emotional and informal v. task-oriented and formal. In some studies the first dimension divided into two correlated dimensions of cooperative-competitive, and friendly-hostile. The present study confirmed this set of dimensions, and found that the same dimensions described a set of 25 dyadic relationships which were rated on 25 scales. These dimensions are also consistent with a great deal of previous research in social psychology.

While these dimensional studies have produced valuable findings, it can be argued that they have their limitations. For example, there are a great variety of situations which are cooperative, unequal, intense and task-oriented, including psychoanalysis, the confessional, a tennis lesson, a serious talk with father, various kinds of interviews (though some are competitive), and so on. Knowing the scores on dimensions would not help someone who wanted to know how to cope with one of these situations any more than it would help a person to play squash by telling him or her that it is friendly, competitive, and formal. In each case it would be necessary to know the rules, roles, and other features discussed in the Introduction.

SUGGESTED ADDITIONAL REFERENCES

Bean, L. Effects of the social circumstances surrounding the rating situation on students' evaluations of faculty. *Teaching of Psychology*, 1978, *5*, 200-202.

Buckley, P. Some parameters involved in perceived similarities of situations. *Perceptual and Motor Skills*, 1978, *46*, 1295-1302.

Cattell, R. Personality, role, mood, and situation—perception: a unifying theory of modulators. *Psychological Bulletin*, 1963, *70*, 1-18.

Chelune, C. Disclosure flexibility and social situational perceptions. *Journal of Consulting and Clinical Psychology*, 1977, *45*, 1139-1143.

Clifford, B. and Scott, J. Individual and situational factors in eye witness testimony. *Journal of Applied Psychology*, 1978, *63*, 352-359.

Crandell, V. and Sinkeldam, C. Children's dependent and achievement behaviours in social situations and their perceptual field dependence. *Journal of Personality*, 1964, *32*, 1-22.

Edinger, J. and Engum, E. General utility and relative efficacy of methods for clustering situations in terms of situational expectancies. *Perceptual and Motor Skills*, 1979, *48*, 735-742.

Forgas, J. Social episodes and social structure in an academic setting: the social environment of an intact group. *Journal of Experimental Social Psychology*, 1978, *14*, 434-448.

Forgas, J. and Brown, L. Environmental and behavioral cues in the perception of social encounters: an exploratory study. *American Journal of Psychology*, 1977, *90*, 635-644.

Forsyth, D., Albritton, E., and Schlinker, B. The effects of social context and size of injury on perceptions of the harm doer and victim. *Bulletin of the Psychonomic Society*, 1977, *9*, 37-38.

Fridman, M. and Stone, S. Effect of training, stimulus context, and mode of stimulus presentation on empathy ratings. *Journal of Counseling Psychology*, 1978, *25*, 131-136.

Greene, L., Morrison, T., and Tischler, N. Participants perceptions in small and large group contexts. *Human Relations*, 1979, *32*, 357-365.

Holahan, C. Effects of urban size and heterogeneity on judged appropriateness of altruistic responses. *Sociometry*, 1977, *40*, 378-382.

Infante, D. and Berg, C. The impact of music modality on the perception of communication situations in video sequences. *Communication Monographs*, 1979, *46*, 135-141.

Levitt, L. and Leventhal, G. Effect of density and environmental noise on perception of time, the situation, oneself and others. *Perceptual and Motor Skills*, 1978, *47*, 999-1009.

McFee, A. The relation of students needs to their perception of a college environment. *Journal of Educational Psychology*, 1961, *52*, 25-29.

Miller, N., Doob, A., Butler, D., and Marlowe, D. The tendency to agree: situational determinants and social desirability. *Journal of Experimental Research in Personality*, 1965, *1*, 78-83.

O'Briant, M. and Wilbanks, W. The effect of context on the perception of music. *Bulletin of the Psychonomic Society*, 1978, *12*, 441-443.

Pancer, S. The effects of situational demands on judgements on freedom and responsibility. *Social Behaviour and Personality*, 1977, *5*, 41-47.

Ross, L., Amabile, T., and Steinmetz, J. Social roles, social control, and biases in social perception processes. *Journal of Personality and Social Psychology*, 1977, *35*, 485-494.

Sadd, S., Welkowitz, J., and Feldstein, S. Judgements of characteristics of speakers in a natural stress situation. *Perceptual and Motor Skills*, 1978, *47*, 47-54.

Schneewind, K. Personality and Perception. In R. Cattell and R. Dreger (Eds.) *Handbook of Modern Personality Theory*, Washington: Hemisphere, 1977.

Schwarzwald, J., and Goldenberg, J. Compliance and assistance to an authority figure in perceived equitable or nonequitable situations. *Human Relations*, 1979, *32*, 877-888.

Tessler, R. and Sushelsky, L. Effects of eye contact and social status on the perception of a job applicant in an employment interviewing situation. *Journal of Vocational Behavior*, 1978, *13*, 338-347.

Van Der Veen, F., and Fiske, O. Variability among self-ratings in different situations. *Education and Psychological Measurement*, 1960, *20*, 83-93.

Vikan, A. Attribution of responsibility in ambiguous moral judgement situations. *Journal of Psychology*, 1978, *99*, 179-185.

Wish, M. Comparison among multidimensional structures of interpersonal relations. *Multivariate Behavioural Research*, 1976, *11*, 297-324.

Wish, M., Deutsch, M., and Kaplan, S. Perceived dimensions of interpersonal relations. *Journal of Personality and Social Psychology*, 1976, *33*, 409-420.

Wish, M. and Kaplan, S. Toward an implicit theory of interpersonal communication. *Sociometry*, 1977, *40*, 234-246.

1

The Perception of Social Episodes: Categorical and Dimensional Representations in Two Different Social Milieus*

Joseph P. Forgas

A study of the perceptions of typical social episodes was carried out in two different subcultural groups, housewives and students. First, a sample of representative episodes was obtained using an open-ended questionnaire. A second sample of subjects from each group was required to perform a similarity-sorting task of the most frequently mentioned social episodes. A measure of psychological relatedness, based on the sorting task, was used as input to a multidimensional scaling and a hierarchical clustering analysis of the episode space. In the scaling solution, perceived intimacy and subjective self-confidence were the two most important attributes differentiating episodes; the clustering solutions also highlighted the nature of the relationship to the interaction partner. The results are discussed in terms of the differences between the objective social environments of the two subsamples and the relative adequacy of the dimensional and categorical solutions. The utility of analyzing subjective and consensual representations of social episodes as a basis for a taxonomic system is also discussed.

In recent years, dissatisfaction with atomistic and often irrelevant experimentation in social psychology (Argyle, 1969; Armistead, 1974; Harré & Secord, 1972) led to growing interest in "natural" units of social behavior, such as social

---

*Journal of Personality and Social Psychology, 1976, 34, 2, 199-209. Copyright 1976 by The American Psychological Association. Reprinted by permission.

episodes. Although the term *social episode* has been widely invoked in different descriptive and analytic works concerned with social behavior, it has not yet found its way into empirical research. This is probably due to the considerable conceptual ambiguity surrounding the term and the absence of an acceptable taxonomy which would enable investigators to classify interaction episodes on the basis of empirically quantifiable characteristics. Not surprisingly, calls for taxonomic studies of situational characteristics have intensified in recent years, both from personality theorists (Bowers, 1973; Mischel, 1973) and social psychologists (Argyle & Little, 1972; Frederiksen, 1972; Magnusson, 1971; Moos, 1973). The aim of the present study is to propose a definition of social episodes as cultural representations of recurring interaction sequences, and to explore an empirical method of classifying social episodes within a defined social and cultural milieu on the basis of individuals' perceptions of them.

Social episodes are interaction sequences which constitute natural units in the stream of behavior (Dickman, 1963; Harré & Secord, 1972) and are distinguishable on the basis of symbolic, temporal, and often physical boundaries. More importantly, however, there is a shared, consensual representation in the given culture about what constitutes an episode and which norms, rules, and expectations apply. This definition of episodes as cultural objects is rooted in the symbolic interactionist tradition (Stone & Farberman, 1970). It is also closely related to some other definitions of interaction units, such as Goffman's (1963) "focused interaction", Watson and Potter's (1962) "episode", Barker and Wright's (1955) "behavior units", Bjerg's (1968) "agons", and Scheflen's (1964) idea of a "presentation".

The present definition of social episodes implies that individual members of a given cultural background should have an internal representation of the social episodes practiced in their environment. The term *episode structure* will be used to describe the perceived patterned relationship between different kinds of social encounters within the cultural milieu. Our task in deriving a meaningful taxonomy of episodes is thus to explicate subjectively perceived differences between episodes composing the episode structure.

A perceptual taxonomy of episodes has important advantages when contrasted with some more traditional approaches (Ekehammar, 1974), such as a priori category systems (Sells, 1963; Sherif & Sherif, 1969), classification systems developed in terms of need concepts (Rotter, 1954) and in terms of single response variables, such as anxiety (Ekehammar, Magnusson, & Ricklander, 1974), or the three-dimensional individual-situation-behavior data matrices proposed by Frederiksen (1972). All these approaches are either too atomistic in their reliance on observable behavior as criteria or are unsuited to the explication of the cultural content of episodes as defined here.

A few studies in recent years have attempted the scaling of individuals' perceptions of social situations. Magnusson and his co-workers (Ekehammar & Magnusson, 1973; Magnusson, 1971; Magnusson & Ekehammar, 1973) used factor analysis to extract the dimensionality of perceptions of a range of ad hoc situations, both solitary and social. Magnusson (1971) argued that "individuals discriminate among situations along cognitive dimensions, and . . . situations can be regarded as related to each other in cognitive space" (p. 853). The problem of stimulus sampling is crucial in such studies, and Magnusson states that "no systematic attempt has been made to solve it in this study" (1971, p. 854). Further, the lack of external validity in these studies, due to the small number of subjects used and the intuitive interpretation of the factor analytic results, is a serious shortcoming if an empirical taxonomy is attempted.

A different line was taken by Pervin (Note 1), who scaled single individuals' perceptions of their significant encounters. Although the idiographic orientation of this study makes it inappropriate for a cultural taxonomy, its findings are highly interesting. In a series of studies, Wish (Note 2) used multidimensional scaling to study communication episodes, but the representative sampling of episodes was not attempted. It is the aim of the present study to show that the scaling of individual perceptions of social episodes can be accomplished in such a way that the resulting taxonomy reflects a degree of consensual agreement in a given subculture. A nonmetric multidimensional scaling (MDS) procedure appears most appropriate for such a task because it allows data collection methods that make the complex cognitive comparisons intrinsically meaningful, without the imposition of external constructs by the experimenter: "Each subject determines which aspect of the stimulus . . . he will judge" (Jones & Young, 1973, p. 109). The interpretation of the solution can also be accomplished empirically, by fitting separately scaled hypothesis dimensions to the multidimensional space (Rosenberg & Sedlak, 1972).

However, if subjects' perceptions of the episodes are in terms of a finite number of discrete categories rather than in terms of gradual changes along different continua, the MDS solution will at best only approximate the actual cognitive representation of the episode space (Torgerson, 1963). By applying an alternative procedure more sensitive to categorical structures, such as cluster analysis, to the same set of data (Jones & Ashmore, 1973), the adequacy of the two representations can be compared.

Finally, the culture specificity of episodes as defined here offers the possibility of some potentially interesting comparisons between subcultures. Are the cognitive maps of episodes structurally different in different subcultures? Do the same episodes occupy similar or different structural positions in different subgroups? If there are structural differences, could these be related to the objective circumstances of the different groups? In order to provide at least some initial insight into problems such as these, it was decided to carry out the present investigation on two substantially different subcultural samples simultaneously.

In summary, the present study had three objectives: (a) to explore the possibility of constructing an empirical taxonomy of social episodes based on individuals' perception of them, (b) to compare the effectiveness of dimensional and categorical representations of the same data using MDS and cluster analysis, and (c) to contrast differences between different subcultural groups in their representations of social episodes.

METHOD

Subjects

The first population group was defined as married, middle-class housewives living in the Oxford area, who were 20-30 years of age and had completed secondary school. These subjects were drawn from the subject pool of the Department of Experimental Psychology, University of Oxford. In Stage 1, 25 subjects drawn from this population were used, and 26 subjects participated in Stage 2 of the study.

The second population group was defined as undergraduate University of Oxford students of both sexes, who were 18-25 years of age. Subjects from this group were recruited either through the subject pool, as described above, or by way of notices displayed in public places in the department. Stages 1 and 2 of the study employed 23 and 25 students, respectively. All subjects were paid for their participation.

Stimulus Sampling

The selection of a representative range of episodes is crucial for the adequate representation of the respondent's cognitive structure (Pervin, Note 1). Past studies have tended to bypass this problem by using a selection of sundry ad hoc situations on an intuitive basis. Stage 1 of the present study was designed to overcome this difficulty.

Subjects from both samples were given a questionnaire that asked them to (a) give a detailed account of their interactions during the past 24 hours in the form of a diary, and (b) list their recurring activities which did not occur within this period. Subjects were also required to give at least two descriptive adjectives for each of the interactions they nominated. These adjectives were collected as sources for the hypothesis dimensions to be used in the interpretation of the MDS configurations. For the housewives subsample, a total of 75 social episodes were nominated by at least two respondents. The 23 most frequently nominated episodes were retained for further use. For the student subsample, a similar procedure was followed, and again the top 23 episodes were retained. In each case an additional 23 episodes were added which would not have qualified in terms of the consensus criterion but which appeared to be interesting in their own right, and were nominated by at least five people in the respective subsamples (see Table 1.1, Items 7 and 23 for housewives; Items 23 and 25 for students). These 25 stimulus episodes were used throughout the main study.

Procedure

A categorization task, giving a basic datum of element co-occurrence, was used. On arrival subjects were given an instruction sheet explaining the task as follows:

> You are asked to compare different situations with each other, and after careful consideration place them into categories on the basis of their similarity. You will be given an envelope with 25 labels in it, each of them having the name of a typical everyday situation written on it. Look at each of the labels carefully, and try to imagine the episode it describes. Then sort the labels into distinct groups on the table, on the basis of their similarity. You may consider any aspect of the episodes in deciding whether they are similar or not. You may create as many groups as you wish, although 5 to 7 groups would be preferable. If you have any labels left over which you feel you cannot assign to any of the existing groups, you can create a miscellaneous group, and put them there. When you have finished, go through all the groups again to make sure that they do not contain any episodes which in your opinion do not fit, and which you may want to re-assign. When you have finished, please record your choices on the record sheet provided by putting down the numbers of the episodes in each group in a separate column.

Index of Psychological Relatedness

The basic input datum required for both the MDS and the clustering analysis is an index of relatedness between each pair of stimuli. In the present study, the raw datum is the number of times a pair of episodes was put into the same category, a measure involving the aggregation of data over subjects. This measure, as Rosenberg, Nelson, and Vivekananthan (1968) pointed out, does not take into account mutual co-occurrence between pairs and third elements. An index of dissociation, taking both direct and indirect ties into account, was proposed by Rosenberg et al.:

$$\delta_{i,j} = \sum_{k=1}^{25} (S_{i,k} - S_{j,k})^2.$$

This index reflects the direct co-occurrence of the two elements, i and j, as well as a measure of indirect co-occurrence with third elements, k. This index, which contains useful new information and was shown to yield superior configurations with better interpretability (Rosenberg & Jones, 1972; Rosenberg et al., 1968; Rosenberg & Sedlak, 1972), was calculated for each possible pair of episodes for both subsamples and was used as the input datum for both MDS and clustering analyses.

Table 1.1   The 25 Most Frequently Mentioned Social Episodes
Used as Stimuli for Each Subsample

Housewives (*n* = 25)	Students (*n* = 23)
1. Having a short chat with the house delivery man (15)	1. Having morning coffee with people in the department (18)
2. Playing with your children (18)	2. Having a drink with some friends in a pub (15)
3. Your husband rings up from work to discuss something (7)	3. Discussing an essay during a tutorial (19)
4. Having a short chat with the shop assistant while shopping (16)	4. Meeting an acquaintance while checking your pigeonhole for mail in college (10)
5. Having dinner with your family (18)	5. Going out for a walk with a friend (13)
6. Shopping on Saturday morning with your husband at the supermarket (16)	6. Shopping on Saturday morning with a friend at the supermarket (14)
7. Attending a wedding ceremony (6)	7. Acting as a subject in a psychology experiment (15)
8. Having a drink with some friends in the pub (14)	8. Going to the pictures with some friends (17)
9. Washing up dishes after dinner with family help (16)	9. Having a short chat with the shop assistant while shopping (15)
10. Chatting over morning coffee with some friends (14)	10. Getting acquainted with a new person during dinner in hall (11)
11. Reading and talking in bed before going to sleep (17)	11. Going to JCR meetings (13)
12. Chatting with an acquaintance who unexpectedly gave you a lift (13)	12. Chatting with an acquaintance before a lecture begins (14)
13. Watching TV with your family after dinner (16)	13. Discussing psychology topics with friends (12)
14. Having a short chat with an acquaintance whom you unexpectedly met on the street (15)	14. Meeting new people at a sherry party in college (16)
15. Going to the pictures with some friends (16)	15. Visiting your doctor (11)
16. Discussing the events of the day with your husband in the evening (18)	16. Chatting with an acquaintance who unexpectedly gave you a lift (11)
17. Talking to other customers while queueing in a shop (17)	17. Visiting a friend in his college room (17)
18. Talking to a neighbor who called to borrow some household equipment (14)	18. Going to see a play at the theatre with friends (15)
19. Having guests for dinner (18)	19. Going to the bank (18)
20. Visiting a friend in hospital (11)	20. Having an intimate conversation with your boy/girl friend (17)
21. Chatting with others while waiting for your washing in the coin laundry (14)	21. Having a short chat with an acquaintance whom you unexpectedly met on the street (19)
22. Talking to a neighbor through the backyard fence (16)	22. Chatting with others while waiting for your washing in the coin laundry (14)
23. Playing chess (8)	23. Attending a wedding ceremony (6)
24. Going to the bank (18)	24. Watching TV with some friends (17)
25. Visiting your doctor (13)	25. Playing chess (9)

Note.   The numbers in parentheses after each episode indicate the frequency of nomination.

Undimensional Scales

The interpretation of MDS configuration can be accomplished by the fitting of undimensional hypothesis scales: These scales, on which the elements were independently rated, represent a priori hypotheses as to the identities of the dimensions of episode structure. These scales were derived from the analysis of free-response adjectives elicited in Stage 1 of the study in terms of three criteria: (a) salience, as indicated by overall frequency of usage across subjects and episodes, (b) productivity, or diversity of usage by individual subjects across episodes, and (c) independence, or lack of co-occurrence between any two adjectives to describe an episode. From a pool of 146 adjectives, 10 were identified as best conforming to these criteria; 4 of them formed natural antonyms (friendly-unfriendly; pleasant-unpleasant), while the remaining 6 were paired with appropriate antonyms to create the following dimensions: active-passive, involved-uninvolved, intimate-nonintimate, occasional-regular, organized-disorganized, simple-complex. In addition, some of the scales proposed in speculative taxonomies in the literature were also included: formal-informal, cooperative-competitive (Harré & Secord, 1972), very much at ease-very ill at ease (Argyle & Little, 1972), and I know exactly how to behave in this situation-I don't know how to behave in this situation (Bryant & Trower, 1974). These 12 undimensional scales, representing a priori assumptions about the identities of the dimensions underlying the episode structure, were used to independently rate each of the 25 episodes in both subsamples. The same subjects were used as for the episode categorization task, but ratings were taken at a separate session.

RESULTS

Multidimensional Scaling

This analysis was carried out using the TORSCA 9 nonmetric multidimensional scaling program, based on Kruskal's (1964) method.

One-, two-, three-, four-, and five-dimensional solutions were obtained for input data from both groups, using varimax rotation. In deciding the optimum number of dimensions, two main criteria can be used: (a) the minimum number of dimensions with a satisfactory level of fit can be selected, and (b) the interpretability of the different solutions can be taken into account. The TORSCA 9 program automatically calculates a goodness-of-fit measure, or stress, for each solution. In terms of the baseline values for stress suggested by Spence and Ogilvie (1973), the stress values for all solutions were considerably better than could be expected by chance (see Table 1.2). The degree of decrease in stress with increasing dimensionality is also an important indicator, and in terms of this criterion, the two-dimensional configuration for housewives and the three-dimensional configuration for students appear optimal.

The second criterion for deciding the optimum dimensional solution is interpretability. To gain some insight into the meaningfulness of the different solutions, a series of multiple regression analyses was carried out, using median ratings on the 12 hypothesis scales as dependent variables and the coordinates of the 25 episodes in different dimensional configurations as independent variables (Rosenberg & Jones, 1972). The number of significant multiple correlation coefficients is indicative of the potential interpretability of the different solutions. From Table 1.2 it seems that for housewives, optimal interpretability is achieved at the two-dimensional level, whereas for students, a noticeable further improvement at the three-dimensional level is apparent. In conclusion, the interpretation of the two-dimensional configuration for housewives and the three-dimensional configuration for students will be attempted before higher dimensionalities are considered.

Table 1.2 Multiple Correlation Coefficients Between Hypothesis Scales and Each of Five Multidimensional Configurations for Both Subsamples

	Housewives					Students				
Scale	1	2	3	4	5	1	2	3	4	5
Involved-uninvolved	.702*	.790*	.835*	.834*	.856*	.338	.395	.667*	.551	.789*
Simple-complex	.463	.586*	.609	.726*	.757*	.059	.488*	.575	.522	.708*
Active-passive	.600*	.604*	.624*	.632	.718*	.095	.252	.549	.393	.518
Pleasant-unpleasant	.272	.336	.607	.579	.538	.314	.682*	.761*	.764*	.791*
Intimate-nonintimate	.698*	.709*	.764*	.780*	.819*	.349	.623*	.801*	.803*	.829*
Very much at ease—very ill at ease	.449	.486	.597	.635	.618	.428	.747*	.725*	.867*	.879*
I know how to behave-don't know	.389	.682*	.709*	.743*	.813*	.394	.570*	.616*	.662*	.680*
Friendly-unfriendly	.554*	.621*	.658*	.738*	.737*	.540*	.760*	.864*	.873*	.880*
Occasional-regular	.597*	.664*	.685*	.700*	.693*	.094	.432	.446	.628	.641
Organized-disorganized	.569*	.629*	.805*	.825*	.830*	.238	.465	.562	.618	.620
Cooperative-competitive	.315	.371	.388	.614	.837*	.293	.550	.538	.596	.569
Formal-informal	.175	.179	.542	.617*	.789*	.364	.850*	.877*	.925*	.929*
Stress	13%	4.5%	2.8%	1.8%	1.5%	23%	10.5%	6.2%	3.8%	2.6%

* $p < .001$.

Interpretation of the Two-Dimensional Configuration—Housewives

This was accomplished by the fitting of the independently scaled univariate property dimensions to the multidimensional space, with significant and approximately orthogonal axes used as interpretative frameworks.

From Table 1.2 it can be seen that 8 of the 12 unidimensional scales are significantly related to the two dimensional configuration and are thus available for the interpretation of this space. These eight hypothesis dimensions were fitted to the two-dimensional space using the ratio of the regression weights as the slope of a line through the origin (Rosenberg & Jones, 1972). The two-dimensional configuration and six of the eight fitted unidimensional scales are shown in Figure 1.1. (Two scales, friendly-unfriendly and organized-disorganized, located between the involvement and intimacy scales, could not be shown in the space available). This episode space appears to be interpretable in terms of two general attribute clusters: the perceived intimacy, involvement and friendliness of episodes, and the subjective self-confidence or competence of the actors related to the regularity of the episodes. The exact relationship between property dimensions is shown in Figure 1.1.

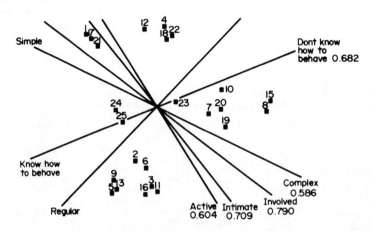

Figure 1.1   The two dimensional configuration of 25 episodes (see Table 1.1), with 6 significant hypothesis scales fitted (housewife sample).

Interpretation of the Three-Dimensional Configuration—Students

Seven hypothesis scales were found to be significantly related to the three-dimensional solution at the .001 level (see Table 1.2). A multiple regression analysis of the three MDS dimensions as predictor variables and the seven univariate scales as dependent variables was carried out, and the angles between the fitted hypothesis scales were calculated as before (see Table 1.3). Using the unidimensional scales as interpretative axes, a single approximately orthogonal framework is defined by three property dimensions: involvement, pleasantness, and know how to behave. The complete three-dimensional configuration, with these three hypothesis scales fitted, is presented in Figure 1.2. It is interesting to note that this framework is very similar to that derived for the housewives

Table 1.3   Angles Between Fitted Axes for Undimensional Scales
Significant at the .001 Level (Three-Dimensional Solution,
Students Sample)

Scale	1	2	3	4	5	6
1. Involved	—					
2. Pleasant	69	—				
3. Intimate	54	44	—			
4. At ease	95	54	61	—		
5. Know how	94	77	72	44	—	
6. Friendly	65	42	44	48	67	—
7. Informal	81	44	39	36	53	42

sample, except for the addition of an evaluative dimension, indicating perhaps the greater cognitive complexity of students in representing complex constructs.

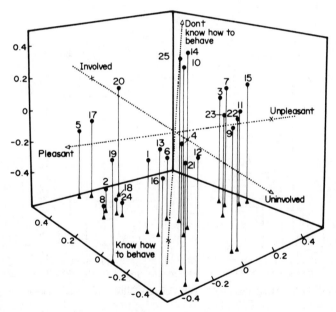

Figure 1.2   The three-dimensional configuration of 25 episodes (see Table 1.1), with 3 hypothesis scales fitted (student sample).

Cluster Analysis

This analysis was carried out using Andrew's (Note 3) CLUSTER program for the hierarchical clustering and a sequel program, DENDRO, which produces a dendrogram graph on the computer plotter. This program uses the distance between input elements as the criterion for partitioning the elements into increasingly heterogeneous, nonoverlapping clusters. The δ index of dissociation was used as input both for the housewife and the student samples (Jones & Ashmore, 1973). The dendrograms for both subsamples are shown in Figure 1.3.

The interpretation of hierarchical clustering configurations can be accomplished either by an intuitive analysis of the shared characteristics of elements within the same cluster or by a more accurate empirical procedure recently proposed by Rosenberg and Jones (1972), which is based on the fitting of unidimensional hypothesis scales to hierarchical clustering solutions using an analysis of variance technique. In principle, however, the intuitive interpretation is "acceptable when the underlying bases for partitioning are clear-cut and obvious" (Rosenberg & Sedlak, 1972, p. 270). As is apparent from Figure 1.3, the present solutions form clear and homogeneous clusters for both subsamples, which are easily interpretable and will be further discussed later. Accordingly, it was decided not to use Rosenberg and Jones' (1972) more sophisticated labeling technique for the present solution.

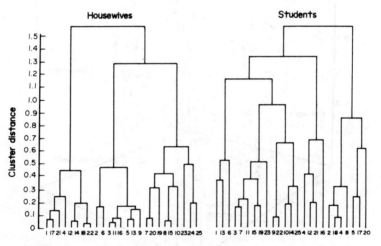

Figure 1.3.   Dendrogram of 25 episodes (see Table 1.1) for each subsample.

DISCUSSION

The overall results indicate that by using the present techniques, a psychologically meaningful and statistically satisfactory representation of the cognitive organization of different social episodes can be achieved. The main attributes of social episodes emerging from this study, *involvement or intimacy and subjective self-confidence,* are promising as criteria for a classificatory system: "It is possible to generate a classification of the situations themselves merely by taking all possible combinations of attributes" (Frederiksen, 1972, p. 118). Similar attributes were found to be relevant not only in person perception (Rosenberg et al., 1968) but also in some other studies of social situations (Pervin, Note 1; Wish, Note 2).

Beyond showing the feasibility of these techniques for the use suggested here, this study had two additional objectives: to compare categorical and dimensional representations of the stimulus space, and to compare the difference between the cognitive representations of the two subsamples.

The Dimensional Solutions

The structure of the 25 common episodes as perceived by Oxford housewives could be neatly represented in a two-dimensional space (see Figure 1.1). Episodes seen as nonintimate (e.g., Item 4: chatting with the shop assistant) are superficial, routine encounters with relative strangers in the course of performing daily chores. On the other hand, more intimate and involved episodes are clearly differentiated into regular interactions performed with confidence, mostly with family members (e.g., Item 5: having dinner with the family), and activities regarded with far less self-confidence, mostly social functions or entertainments (e.g., Items 8 and 15). It is remarkable that the alternative represented by self-confident but nonintimate interactions, so characteristic of institutionalized working environments, is almost completely absent. Clearly, the social environment of housewives provides few encounters of this type.

The dimensional representation of the episode structure of students was best accomplished in three-dimensional space (see Figure 1.2), with the addition of an evaluative dimension to the basic involvement—self-confidence framework. It seems an intriguing possibility to account for this either in terms of the greater cognitive complexity of students or in terms of their wider and more varied stimulus field.

The involvement dimension mainly differentiates encounters with friends and acquaintances on the basis of the duration and intimacy of the episode. The evaluative (pleasant-unpleasant) dimension seems to reflect the degree of situational constraint implied by different episodes (Price & Bouffard, 1974), with open and uncontrolled interactions seen as pleasant (e.g., Items 19, 16, and 5), and controlled and restrictive activities, such as tutorials, acting as a subject in an experiment, and attending formal meetings, being negatively evaluated.

The function of the self-confidence ("know how to behave") dimension in differentiating episodes is interesting because it relates to previous work on anxiety responses to different situations (Bryant & Trower, 1974; Ekehammer & Magnusson, 1973). Episodes involving prolonged interaction with strangers (i.e., the getting acquainted process) elicits the highest level of apprehension

(Items 10, 14, and 25), thus supporting Bryant & Trower's (1974) finding with a similar sample and showing that substantial numbers of students find episodes such as parties rather difficult to cope with.

Students seem to regard episodes involving entertainments and socializing with friends with great self-confidence (Items 2, 8, 18, and 24), in strong contrast to housewives, who viewed nearly identical episodes with a lack of self-confidence. The very different subjective definition of these interactions, involving nearly indistinguishable activities and objective characteristics, suggests that a classification of episodes in terms of objective factors may not tap the psychologically meaningful differences. While "socializing with friends" for students is a natural, self-selected entertainment, for housewives it may be a more formal, organized affair, with an element of self-presentation and potential loss of face (Goffman, 1955).

Thus, both dimensional representations provide a picture of the episode space which is (a) readily interpretable and meaningful, (b) appears to be sensitive to the cultural differences between the samples, and (c) tends to differentiate episodes primarily in terms of their perceived subjective, connotative rather than denotative, characteristics. It was surprising to note that the activities which make up an episode, the physical aspects of the environment, and other objective factors were of little consequence in determining this structure.

Categorical Representations

The two hierarchical clustering configurations shown in Figure 1.3 provide some important additional cues to the interpretation of the episode space.

For housewives, the three large primary categories, which could be labeled as "casual," "family," and "social," divide into subclusters in terms of the relationship to the interaction partner. Thus, family episodes can be differentiated by whether they involve the husband (Items 3, 11 and 16) or the whole family (Items 2, 5, 6, 9, and 13). Casual encounters can involve strangers (Items 1, 4, 17, and 21) and friends and neighbors (Items 12, 14, 18, and 22). It appears that the underlying dimensions of involvement—self-confidence closely match the relationship to the interaction partner.

For students, the primary division of episodes is in terms of the categories of people they involve: friends, acquaintances, strangers, people in their official capacity. When compared with the categorical structure of episodes for housewives, a reversal of the importance of differentiating criteria is apparent. Housewives differentiate their social episodes primarily in terms of which area of their lives they relate to (family, social, or casual), and the interaction partner is only a secondary criterion, whereas for students their relationship to people they encounter is of primary importance, and further subdivision is apparently in terms of intimacy, self-confidence, area of life, and so on.

In summary, the categorical representations are closely related to the MDS configurations and can be regarded as alternative ways of interpreting the same episode structure. Most of the characteristics mentioned in the interpretation of the cluster analysis were obviously overlapping and complementary to the basic involvement—self-confidence framework derived from MDS. It would be futile to regard either the categorical or the dimensional representations as "correct." In light of the complex nature of social episodes, it seems that the question of dimensional versus categorical representations is ill-conceived. Elements of both would have to be considered if crucial attributes of episodes are to be identified and understood.

The use of the present methods to explicate episode structure has potentially important implications for further interaction-oriented research. They can be used to test the relevance of the numerous speculative taxonomies in given cultural milieus. From the present data, it is clear that the often proposed distinctions between formal-informal and cooperative-competitive episodes (Harré & Secord, 1972) are of little relevance to the present sample in their construal of their social world. The present method is eminently applicable to the study of cross-cultural and subcultural differences in social perception. In our case, the structure of episodes strongly reflects the socialization experiences, lifestyles, and values of the two subsamples. It also provides a meaningful and quantified "map" of a sample of episodes, which can thus be incorporated into models concerned with the situational determination of behavior.

REFERENCE NOTES

Pervin, L. A. *A free-response description approach to the analysis of person-situation interaction* (ETS Bulletin No. 22). Princeton, N.J.: Educational Testing Service, 1975.

Wish, M. *Role and personal expectations about interpersonal communications*. Unpublished manuscript, 1975. (Available from Bell Laboratories, Murray Hill, New Jersey)

Andrew, I. A. *Clusteranalysis and dendrogram plotting programs*. Unpublished manuscript, Department of Forestry, University of Oxford, England, 1975.

REFERENCES

Argyle, M. *Social interaction*. London: Methuen, 1969.

Argyle, M., & Little, B. R. Do personality traits apply to social behaviour? *Journal for the Theory of Social Behaviour, 1972, 2,* 1-35.

Armistead, N. *Reconstructing social psychology*. Harmondsworth, Middlesex, England: Penguin, 1974.

Barker, R. F., & Wright, H. F. *Midwest and its children*. Evanston, Ill.: Row, Peterson, 1955.

Bjerg, K. Interplay analysis. *Acta Psychologica, 1968, 28,* 201-245.

Bowers, K. S. Situationism in psychology: An analysis and a critique. *Psychological Review*, 1973, *80*, 307-336.

Bryant, B. M. & Trower, P. Social difficulty in a student population. *British Journal of Educational Psychology*, 1974, *44*, 13-21.

Dickman, H. R. The perception of behavioural units. In R. G. Barker (Ed.), *The stream of behavior*. New York: Appleton-Century-Crofts, 1963.

Ekehammar, B. Interactionism in personality from a historical perspective. *Psychological Bulletin*, 1974, *81*, 1026-1048.

Ekehammar, B., & Magnusson, M. A method to study stressful situations. *Journal of Personality and Social Psychology*, 1973, *27*, 176-179.

Ekehammar, B., Magnusson, M., & Ricklander, R. An interactionist approach to the study of anxiety. *Scandinavian Journal of Psychology*, 1974, *15*, 4-14.

Frederiksen, N. Towards a taxonomy of situations. *American Psychologist*, 1972, *27*, 114-124.

Goffman, E. *On face-work: An Analysis of ritual elements in social interaction*. Indianapolis: Bobbs-Merril, 1963.

Harré, R., & Secord, P. *The Explanation of Social Behaviour*, Oxford, England: Blackwells, 1972.

Jones, L. E. & Young, F. W. Structure of a social environment: Longitudinal individual differences scaling of an intact group. *Journal of Personality and Social Psychology*, 1973, *24*, 108-121.

Jones, R. A., & Ashmore, R. D. The structure of intergroup perception: Categories and dimensions in views of ethnic groups and objectives used in stereotype research. *Journal of Personality and Social Psychology*, 1973, *25*, 428-438.

Kruskal, J. B. Nonmetric multidimensional scaling: I. *Psychometrica*, 1964, *29*, 1-27.

Magnusson, M. An analysis of situational dimensions. *Perceptual and Motor Skills*, 1971, *32*, 851-867.

Magnusson, M., & Ekehammar, B. An Analysis of situational dimensions: A replication. *Multivariate Behavioural Research*, 1973, *8*, 331-339.

Mischel, W. Toward a cognitive social learning reconceptualism of personality. *Psychological Review*, 1973, *80*, 252-283.

Moos, R. H. Conceptualizations of human environments. *American Psychologist*, 1973, *28*, 652-665.

Price, R. H., & Bouffard, D. L. Behavioral appropriateness and situational constraints as dimensions of social behavior. *Journal of Personality and Social Psychology*, 1974, *30*, 519-586.

Rosenberg, S., & Jones, R. A. A method for investigating and representing a person's implicit theory of personality: Theodore Dreiser's view of people. *Journal of Personality and Social Psychology*, 1972, *22*, 372-386.

Rosenberg, S., Nelson, C., & Vivekananthan, P. S. A multidimensional approach to the structure of personality impressions. *Journal of Personality and Social Psychology*, 1968, *9*, 283-294.

Rosenberg, S., & Sedlak, A. Structural representations of implicit personality theory. In L. Berkowitz (Ed.), *Advances in experimental social psychology* (Vol. 6). New York: Academic Press, 1972.

Rotter, J. B. *Social Learning and Clinical Psychology*. New York: Prentice-Hall, 1954.

Scheflen, A. E. The significance of posture in communication systems. *Psychiatry*, 1964, *27*, 316-331.

Sells, S. B. (Ed.). *Stimulus Determinants of Behavior*. New York: Ronald, 1963.

Sherif, M., & Sherif, C. W. *Social Psychology*. New York: Harper & Row, 1969.

Spence, I., Ogilvie, J. A table of expected stress values for random rankings in nonmetric multidimensional scaling. *Multivariable Behavioural Research*, 1973, *8*, 511-517.

Stone, G. P., & Farberman, H. A. *Social Psychology through Symbolic Interaction*. Waltham, Mass.: Ginn-Blaisdell, 1970.

Torgerson, W. S. Multidimensional scaling of Similarity. *Psychometrica*, 1965, *30*, 379-393.

Watson, J., & Potter, R. J. An analytic unit for the study of interaction. *Human Relations*, 1962, *15*, 245-263.

2
An Analysis of
Situational Dimensions*
David Magnusson

In order to study the dimensionality of 3 individuals' judgments of situations matrices for individual and group data consisting of similarity judgments of situations from a certain domain were factor analyzed. The results indicated: (a) judgments of perceived similarity between situations have a considerable degree of consistency over time, (b) the dimensionality of these judgments shows great agreement among individuals in a homogeneous group, and (c) dimensional analyses both of average and

*Reprinted with the permission of the author and the journal from: Perceptual and Motor Skills, 1971, 32, 851-867. Perceptual and Motor Skills 1971.

individual similarity matrices provide a clear and interpretable structure.
The potentials for further work with the methodology used were discussed.

This report presents an attempt to describe the dimensionality of individual judgments of situations. There is an extensive and well documented need for such an analysis.

The major conclusion from some recent experiments on the generality of behavioral data was that individuals differ not mainly with regard to certain stable aspects of behavior but particularly regarding their specific, characteristic ways of adjusting to the varying characteristics of different situations (Magnusson, Gerzén, & Nyman, 1968; Magnusson, Heffler, & Nyman, 1968; Magnusson & Heffler, 1969[3]). The results confirm the interactionistic views of psychological research advocated by researchers using different forms of approach (cf. e.g., Abelson, 1962; Brunswik, 1955; Carson, 1969; Cronbach, 1957; Endler & Hunt, 1966; Fiske, 1963; Helson, 1964; Hunt, 1965; Lewin, 1951; Meltzer, 1961; Miller, 1963; Mischel, 1968; Murphy, 1947; Sells, 1963b; Shibutani, 1961). Knowledge of the interaction between individual and situation is essential to an adequate description and understanding of behavior. Psychological research has to date almost exclusively studied one aspect of this interaction system, the *individual,* whereas systematic analyses of *situations* have been almost entirely lacking (cf. Miller, 1963, p. 700). "While work proceeds actively to extend the explorations of individual differences, however, the equally important frontier of situational dimensions is virtually ignored" (Sells, 1963b). It is urgent then that in the same way as we have for decades devoted our attention to systematic analysis of individual variations we now more systematically devote time and resources to a similar analysis of situations.

The task of determining psychologically relevant dimensions, which could be used for a description and classification of situations, is a difficult one. Only limited attempts have been made to develop a methodology suitable for this type of analysis (cf. e.g., Cattell, 1963; Sells, 1963a) and scarcely any empirical results are available. Concerning the study of situational variation, we find ourselves at the same stage as that concerning the study of individual differences at the initial development period of differential psychology. It is probable that the task of determining individual dimensions was at that time regarded as being as full of difficulties as we now regard the task of attacking the dimensionality of situations. During 50 to 60 yr. of systematic individual studies, we have, however, made conspicuous advances in research on dimensionality on the individual side. We may assume that the investigation of situations and the description of their relevant dimensions cannot be made without a considerable

---

[3]D. Magnusson & B. Heffler. The generality of behavioral data: IV. Cross-situational invariance in an objectively measured behavior. (Unpublished manuscript, Univer. of Stockholm: Applied Psychology Unit, 1968).

period for systematic, empirical studies and theoretical model construction, in the same way that it proved impossible to find immediate solutions and adequate methodology for the study of dimensions of individual differences.

Empirical studies of situation variables deal almost without exception with the effect on behavior of variation of one or several specific features within the framework of a given total situation, which is often laboratory-like. One of the weaknesses of this approach, as has been pointed out by Brunswik (1955) among others, is that the effect of variation of one or a few features of a situation while holding all others constant, does not correspond to the reality which we normally experience. There is a continuous interaction among all of the components in a real-life situation. Another deficiency is that the situations studied have a very limited range of variation.

A situation can be described in two different ways; by describing in objective terms the physical and social stimulus features, the situation as it actually is [cf. for example, Murray's "alpha press" (1938) and Koffka's "geographical environment" (1935)] or by describing in terms of different aspects of the psychological significance of the situation, how it is perceived and reacted to ("beta press," "behavioral environment," see above).

This report deals with the dimensionality of individuals' perception of situations. Empirical results from three individuals are presented as a basis for a cognitively oriented discussion of this matter. The data were collected and analyzed with the assumption that it is possible and fruitful to use situations as a whole as stimuli when studying the dimensionality of an individual's judgments of situations.

METHOD

A General Cognitive Model

Objects in the external world can, for every individual, be regarded as being represented in a cognitive space, defined by their internal cognitive relationships. The position of each object is then determined in relation to the cognitive dimensions used by the individual when he discriminates among objects. The psychological content of the objects is determined by their projections on these dimensions. The number and characteristics of cognitive dimensions for individuals has been the subject of extensive research (cf. e.g., Bieri, *et al.*, 1966).

The above description contains the basic elements of a general cognitive model which is used explicitly or implicitly not only for studying cognitive organization of objects and events, but also in other connections, e.g., by Osgood, Suci, and Tannenbaum (1957) for the study of the concepts of meaning, by Kelly (1955) in his theory of personal constructs, and by Sarbin, Taft, and Bailey (1960) for the study of the cognitive processes in person perception. The psychophysical, multidimensional scaling methods are based on the same basic model (cf. e.g., Ekman, 1970; Torgerson, 1958).

The present experiment was planned by assuming that the same general model can be used to study the structure of an individual's perception of situations. We assume, thus, that individuals discriminate among situations along cognitive dimensions and that situations can be regarded as related to each other in a cognitive space in the same way as objects, events, concepts, individuals, tones, colors, etc. Applying terms used by Sarbin, *et al.* (1960), we regard situations as modules in a modular organization. The psychological content of a situation is then determined by its projection on the cognitive dimensions applied by the individual in order to discriminate among situations. The task is to determine these dimensions.

The cognitive organization with respect to the number and nature of dimensions is not necessarily the same for different individuals. Individuals have varying degrees of cognitive complexity. An important task for research on the dimensionality of situation perception is, therefore, to analyze individual data (cf. Cronbach, 1958). Bearing in mind results from other areas, it is, however, reasonable to assume that if enough of the dimensionality is shared it would be meaningful to study also aggregates of individuals (cf. Bieri, *et al.*, 1966, pp. 191-193).

Cognitive Similarity

When the structure of the cognitive organization of objects, concepts, individuals, etc., is studied within the general model presented, it is assumed that distances in the cognitive space define the psychological relationships of the objects, concepts, individuals, etc., to each other. The more psychologically similar they are, the nearer they are assumed to be to each other in the cognitive organization. Different methods have been used to determine distances between objects in a cognitive space (cf. Attneave, 1950; Coombs, 1964; Ekman, 1970; Gulliksen & Messick, 1960; Kelly, 1955; Osgood, *et al.*, 1957; Shepard, 1962; Torgerson, 1958).

As an expression for the psychological similarity of situations, i.e., their proximity in the cognitive organization, similarity judgments were used. Similarity judgments as a basis for dimensional analyses have the advantage that it is not necessary to determine in advance the features of the situations to be measured.

Multidimensional Analysis

The analysis of the dimensionality of the similarity judgments was done using factor analysis. Previous studies have successfully used factor analysis of similarity judgments for the determination of the dimensionality of similarity ratings of colors (Ekman, 1954, 1961), odors (Ekman & Engen, 1962; Engen,

1962), emotions (Ekman, 1955; Ekman & Lindman, 1961), geometric figures (Kuennapas, Maelhammar, & Svenson, 1964), letters of the alphabet (Kuennapas, 1966, 1967, 1968), and words (Tolman, Jarret, & Bailey, 1959). Interesting in this connection is a study by Magnusson and Ekman (1970) in which factor analyses of a correlation matrix and a similarity rating matrix with respect to an array of behavior gave identical primary dimensions.

EXPERIMENTS

Situations

One problem common to the study of the dimensionality of individual perception and the dimensionality of other cognitive organizations is that of stimulus sampling. The problem is a difficult one and no systematic attempt has been made to solve it in this study.

Descriptions of 36 situations were formulated. These were chosen subjectively so as (a) to represent a definite domain of situations, namely, those which are common for students in connection with their academic studies, and (b) to cover different types of situations within this domain. Preliminary judgments showed that the situations ought to be defined as specifically and unequivocally as possible. Examples of situations are as follows. "You are sitting and listening carefully to a lecture but do not understand a thing."—"You are sitting at home alone preparing an oral report."

Judgmental Procedure

The degree of perceived similarity between situations was judged on a scale from 0 to 4, the different scale values being given the following general definitions: 0, Not at all similar; 1, Somewhat similar; 2, Rather similar; 3, Very similar; and 4, Identical.

The total matrix containing 36 × 36 situation descriptions was divided up into three submatrices. Each of them was judged without a break. Breaks of 30 min. were taken between the judgments of the submatrices.

The order of the situations in the matrix was determined using random tables and the order in which the submatrices were judged was also randomized among the judges.

The instructions called upon the judges to think very carefully about each situation and thereafter to judge the perceived similarity between the situations.

Subjects

Three students rated the similarity of the situations. Two of them gave judgments on more than one occasion, which gave a basis for the study of the constancy of the perception of situations.

RESULTS

Analysis of Group Data

Dimensionality Analysis. —The individual similarity ratings were transformed into a scale ranging from 0 (no similarity at all) to 1 (identity) by dividing by 4. Mean estimates of similarity of situations over subjects were computed from these transformed values. The similarity matrix was factor analyzed by the method of principal components and the obtained factor matrix was rotated to a varimax solution. After plotting the eigenvalues, the number of factors chosen to be rotated was five. The rotated factor matrix is shown in Table 2.1.

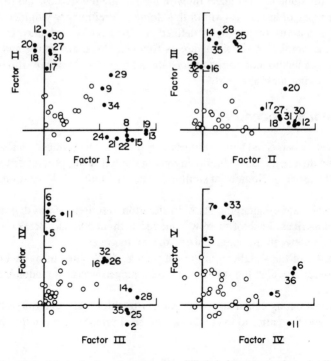

Figure 2.1. Plots of factor loadings for group data. Filled circles represent factor loadings higher than 0.50.

Even a cursory inspection of the values in Table 2.1 provides a picture of very clear structure. This is readily apparent from Fig. 2.1, where adjacent factor columns have been plotted against each other.

Table 2.1 Rotated Factor Matrix for Group Data

| Variable | Factor | | | | | b^2 |
	I	II	III	IV	V	
1	.371	.293	.147	.286	.191	.36
2	.011	.294	.742	−.162	.244	.72
3	.420	.384	.028	.032	.571	.65
4	.278	.174	.132	.181	.758	.73
5	.304	.170	.034	.609	.114	.50
6	.154	.110	.026	.811	.336	.80
7	.171	.081	.137	.109	.851	.79
8	.743	−.051	.028	.084	.309	.65
9	.515	.361	−.005	.169	.270	.49
10	.059	.200	.370	−.018	.427	.36
11	.135	.009	.164	.779	−.177	.68
12	.003	.848	.047	.013	.102	.73
13	.907	−.308	.059	.064	−.086	.84
14	.024	.046	.774	.137	−.062	.62
15	.794	−.077	.084	.108	−.081	.66
16	.191	.045	.538	.394	.034	.48
17	.021	.533	.184	.360	.011	.44
18	−.090	.688	.105	.025	.308	.58
19	.909	.000	.011	.161	.170	.88
20	−.097	.733	.353	.143	.123	.70
21	.664	−.070	.474	.181	.100	.71
22	.753	−.079	.068	.116	.289	.67
23	.421	.266	.246	.168	.233	.39
24	.557	−.063	.167	.472	.080	.57
25	−.004	.291	.753	−.055	.272	.72
26	.218	−.081	.574	.387	−.024	.53
27	.050	.691	.105	.064	.113	.50
28	.040	.155	.831	.066	.153	.74
29	.599	.486	−.032	.012	.282	.67
30	.043	.810	.043	.108	−.005	.67
31	.052	.760	.067	−.070	−.009	.59
32	.086	−.025	.538	.405	.053	.46
33	.212	.071	.150	.202	.866	.86
34	.541	.223	.004	.387	.249	.55
35	.098	.123	.743	−.042	.053	.58
36	.147	.138	.020	.796	.292	.76

Variables with factor loadings higher than 0.50 were chosen to describe the character of each factor. With that criterion the following variables represent Factor I:

13 Receive praise for a report during group work
19 Able to answer a difficult question during a lecture
15 Have passed an examination with top marks
22 A statistical problem becomes clear
 8 Get exactly the questions expected in an examination
21 Listen to a lecture about a subject which has been mastered
29 Undergo an oral examination
24 Listen to an interesting lecture
34 Sit together with fellow students and cross-examine before an examination
 9 Present a report during group work

The basic content of Factor I is very clear. The feature common to the situations which determine the dimension is their positive and rewarding character. None of the situations has a factor loading higher than 0.50 on any other dimension.

The following variables have factor loadings higher than 0.50 on Factor II:

12 Have just been returned a laboratory report with negative criticism
30 Cannot answer a simple question during a lecture
31 Have just failed an examination
20 Do not understand a thing about a lecture
18 Have unsuccessfully attempted to solve a numerical problem
27 Have forgotten to prepare a report
17 Unprepared for seminar and do not participate in the discussion

Factor II is also very pure and easy to interpret. All of the situations are of a negative nature. No loading on any other dimension is greater than 0.40 for these situations.

Factor III is characterized by the following variables:

28 Wait on laboratory subjects completing questionnaire
14 Rest during a break in lectures
25 Wait for the others before group work
35 Sit after an examination and wait for a fellow student
 2 Adjust to darkness prior to an experiment
26 Sit in the Student Union and read a paper
32 Listen to lectures during external study visit
16 Casual study before an examination knowing that there is plenty of time

The highest loadings suggest that Factor III should be interpreted as passiveness. It is interesting to note that lectures during external study visits are included in this group of situations. The highest loading on any other dimension for any of these situations is 0.41 (situation 32).

Four variables have factor loadings higher than 0.50 on Factor IV:

6   Carry out a joint group task together with fellow students
36 Plan a laboratory experiment together with some fellow students
11 Eat lunch with some fellow students
5   Discuss politics with fellow students

The common feature of the situations representing Factor IV appears to be the social interaction. Situations where one is together with others without this interaction (see, e.g., situations 8, 9, 17, 20, 21) belong to other factors than Factor IV.

Factor V can be characterized by the following four variables:

33 Sit alone at home and do homework
7   Sit alone at home and write a laboratory report
4   Sit alone at home and prepare an oral report
3   Undergo a written examination

The feature common to the four situations which determine Factor V is the activity of the individual, irrespective of whether he is together with others or not.

Three situations have no loadings which exceed 0.50. These are situation 1 (Interview a freshman student), 10 (Participate as a subject in an experiment), and 23 (Administer an intelligence test to a subject). It can be seen from Table 1 that these three situations have the lowest communalities. However, an analysis of the individual similarity matrices showed that the low communalities for group data is a result of the fact that these situations belong to different factors for individuals A, B, and C.

The interpretations given above of the factors are of course only very tentative and hold for the present only for the structure of these data.

Comments.—Analysis of group data shows a clear, concise, and easily interpreted structure. None of the situations has a loading higher than 0.50 on more than one dimension. It is clearly possible at the data level to assign the variation in similarity ratings of situations to a limited number of factors. One interpretation of this result is that it is possible to identify common cognitive dimensions used by individuals to discriminate between situations.

DIMENSIONALITY ANALYSIS OF INDIVIDUAL DATA

Factoring

A principal component analysis was carried out for each of the individual similarity matrices in exactly the same way as for group data. The rotations were also performed using the same program as for group data and rotating for five factors. As an example of an individual factor matrix the rotated matrix obtained for Judge A is shown in Table 2.2.

Table 2.2   Rotated Factor Matrix for Judge A

Variable	I	II	III	IV	V	b^2
1	.479	.106	−.006	.434	.136	.44
2	−.002	.111	.965	−.066	.005	.94
3	.328	−.025	−.065	.194	.650	.57
4	.241	−.034	.037	.115	.893	.87
5	.177	.018	.008	.775	.128	.64
6	.052	.063	.009	.876	.248	.83
7	−.042	.014	.038	.102	.833	.70
8	.595	−.056	−.011	.084	.664	.80
9	.590	.071	−.019	.428	.046	.53
10	.087	.122	−.055	.031	.045	.44
11	.029	.041	.149	.821	−.094	.70
12	.059	.975	−.053	−.112	.076	.97
13	.901	.015	.024	−.112	−.098	.83
14	−.009	.003	.920	−.042	−.024	.85
15	.837	−.007	−.000	−.045	−.190	.74
16	.147	.140	.386	.197	.423	.40
17	.008	.456	.173	.223	.017	.28
18	−.079	.807	−.020	−.135	.477	.90
19	.927	.133	.037	.105	.102	.90
20	−.103	.713	.276	.181	.104	.64
21	.575	−.080	.481	.235	.189	.66
22	.821	−.076	.108	.010	.432	.87
23	.466	−.011	.059	.368	.249	.41
24	.485	−.078	.258	.395	.376	.60
25	−.015	.049	.892	−.053	.008	.80
26	.125	−.103	.495	.317	.080	.37
27	.075	.550	.071	.082	−.062	.32
28	−.052	.065	.864	.105	−.054	.76
29	.677	.174	−.064	.406	.239	.71
30	.113	.809	−.039	.152	−.069	.69
31	.013	.536	−.039	−.035	−.027	.29
32	.031	−.005	.447	.281	.296	.36
33	.031	.035	.097	.070	.999	1.00
34	.663	.036	−.024	.535	.270	.80
35	.108	.154	.870	−.061	−.048	.79
36	.040	.229	.025	.841	.111	.77

Structure

An inspection of the three rotated factor matrices showed a clear structure for all the judges. This is indicated by the fact that it occurred only twice for Judge A that a situation had two factor loadings higher than 0.50. The same thing happened only twice for Judge B and three times for Judge C. A representative picture of the clearness of structure at the individual level is shown in Fig. 2.2, where adjacent columns of Judge A's factor matrix have been plotted against each other.

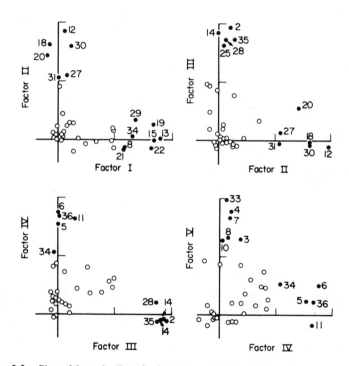

Figure 2.2.   Plots of factor loadings for Judge A on occasion 1. Filled circles represent factor loadings higher than 0.50.

Table 2.3 shows the individual factor loadings for the situations used previously to characterize the principal dimensions for individual data. The table shows that the five main dimensions can be given the same basic interpretations for each of the three judges as for the group data.

A rough estimate of the degree of agreement in structure among the judges was obtained by computing product-moment coefficients of correlation between

Table 2.3   Individual Factor Loadings for Situations at Group Level

Factor	Variable	Judge			Group
		A	B	C	
I. "Positive"	13	.90	.95	.87	.91
	19	.93	.99	.92	.91
	15	.84	.63	.88	.79
	22	.82	.67	.79	.75
	8	.60	.71	.94	.74
	21	.58	.79	.58	.66
	29	.68	.54	.43	.60
	24	.49	.55	.47	.56
	34	.66	.48	.45	.54
	9	.59	.41	.41	.52
II. "Negative"	12	.98	.87	.89	.85
	30	.81	.97	.70	.81
	31	.54	.82	.93	.76
	20	.71	.70	.76	.73
	18	.81	.65	.86	.69
	27	.55	.73	.65	.69
	17	.46	.63	.55	.53
III. "Passive"	28	.86	.73	.82	.83
	14	.92	.43	.83	.77
	25	.89	.87	.54	.75
	35	.87	.83	.58	.74
	2	.97	.49	.73	.74
	26	.50	.40	.61	.57
	32	.45	.62	.61	.54
	16	.39	.27	.82	.54
IV. "Social"	6	.88	.74	.76	.81
	36	.84	.66	.76	.80
	11	.82	.80	.75	.78
	5	.78	.42	.64	.61
V. "Active"	33	.99	.84	.51	.87
	7	.83	.74	.47	.85
	4	.89	.79	.52	.76
	3	.65	.56	.58	.57

factor loadings for the factors most nearly corresponding to each other. The obtained correlations are shown in Table 2.4. With few exceptions the values show a high level of agreement in structure among the individual factor matrices. This is another way of illustrating that all three judges have the same basic structure for their ratings as that obtained at group level.

An inspection of the individual factor matrices showed, however, differences that can be of some interest in judging the implications of this methodology for the study of individual ways of interpreting situations. For Judge A situations 1 (Interviewing a freshman student) and 23 (Administer an intelligence test to a subject) have high loadings on Factor I (tentatively interpreted as "positive") and on Factor IV ("social"). For Judges B and C the same situations have high factor loadings on Factor III ("passive"). Another example is situation 10 (Participate as a subject in an experiment) which has its highest loading on Factor V ("active") for Judge A but on Factor III ("passive") for B and C. Such differences among the judges may be interpreted in terms of the cognitive model; the judges differ with respect to the dimensions along which they discriminate certain situations.

Table 2.4   Correlation Coefficients Between Factor Loadings for Principal Factors for Individual Judges

Factor	τ_{AB}	τ_{AC}	τ_{BC}
I	0.90	0.83	0.86
II	0.82	0.87	0.86
III	0.65	0.81	0.59
IV	0.53	0.82	0.73
V	0.69	0.34	0.43

Comments

The fact that the main dimensions were the same for the three judges in this study cannot, of course, be used as the basis for the conclusion that the same main dimensions would be found for any group of individuals whatsoever. The judges were an extremely homogeneous group in certain important respects. All three had concrete experience of the situations and this experience was relatively recent. There is, in fact, reason to believe that the structure of situational perception differs between groups of individuals. This is in all probability a fruitful problem for further research.

Differences among individual factor matrices may be interpreted to reflect the well-known fact that a situation can have a different psychological relevance for different individuals. Previous findings mentioned in the introduction suggest that the important characteristics of an individual are to be found in his specific manner of adjusting to different situations. The method used here may provide a possibility to study this problem in a more systematic way than has hitherto been possible.

STABILITY OF JUDGMENTS

Analyses and Results

One of the requirements for the meaningful study of the structure of situational perception is that this structure has some degree of stability. Two of the three judges who participated on the first judgmental occasion were able to provide further judgments on a later occasion under varying conditions, and this has permitted the following analyses of the stability of the similarity judgments and their structure.

Judge B performed new similarity judgments for half of the situations a fortnight after the first rating. An estimate of the stability of the judgments was obtained by computing a product-moment correlation coefficient for the relationship between the judgments on the two occasions. Its value was 0.68. Still another week later he performed similarity ratings for the remaining situations. The correlation coefficient for the relationship between the judgments on the two occasions for this part of the similarity judgments was 0.62.

Judge A carried out new similarity judgments of the complete array of situations 3 wk. after the first judgment under experimental conditions similar to those on the first occasion. The correlation between judgments for the two occasions was 0.77.

Judge A thus provided a new complete judgment matrix with judgments given at a single setting. This matrix was factored in exactly the same way as the earlier matrices.

A study of the factor matrix shows the same clear structure as on the first judgment occasion. Plotting the factor loadings from the two factor matrices against each other for Judge A suggests a remarkably great stability in the structure from the one occasion to the other (see Fig. 2.3). The correlations

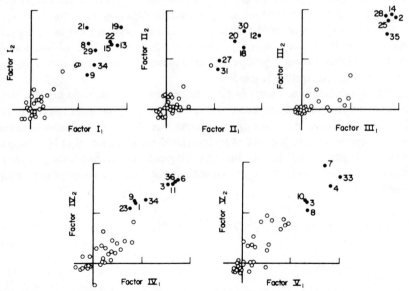

Figure 2.3.   Factor loadings from occasion 1 plotted against factor loadings from occasion 2 for Judge A. Filled circles represent factor loadings higher than 0.50 for both factors.

between the factor loadings for congruent principal factors from the two occasions expressed by product-moment correlations coefficients are 0.94 (I), 0.97 (II), 0.93 (III), 0.92 (IV), and 0.97 (V).

Comments

It is hard to believe that the constancy in structure between the judgment occasions is the result of memory from the first occasion. Although caution should be shown in drawing conclusions based on a single case, the outcome of the analysis supported the assumption that we are dealing with a cognitive structure with a considerable degree of stability over time.

CONCLUSIONS

The main findings were (a) that judgments of perceived similarity between situations have a considerable degree of consistency over time, (b) that the dimensionality of these judgments shows great agreement among individuals in a homogeneous group, and (c) that dimensional analysis both of average and individual similarity judgment matrices provides a clear and psychologically interpretable structure.

The results suggest that the methodology applied here can be used to study the structure of individual and group perception of situations and to express this structure in psychologically relevant dimensions. This result may be of importance for further research on the relationship between individual and environment, seen both from the interactionistic and transactionistic viewpoints (see Pervin, 1968). It should now, for example, be possible to relate changes in individual *behavior* from situation to situation to information about how the individual himself *perceives* these situations.

The individual's interpretation of different situations plays an essential part in his adjustment to reality, i.e., for his satisfaction and social relationships. There is in research and practice a need for systematic analyses of these interpretations *per se,* both for groups and for individuals. Some examples will be given of the possibilities of attacking these problems by means of individual and group analysis using the methodology outlined here.

With the methodology used here, it should be possible to obtain measures of the structure of the situational perception of different clinical groups and compare them with measures from relevant control groups. This type of comparisons might be useful both in construct validation studies and in clinical diagnostic work. One could, for example, test the prediction that individuals with specific symptoms, say claustrophobia, would discriminate situations in closed and narrow spaces along other dimensions than individuals in general.

As a rule, clinical treatment aims at producing greater adjustment to reality on the part of the patient. The effect of the treatment can be studied by means of the extent and nature of changes during treatment, both in the structure of situational perceptions, and in the perception of specific situations which may be of special interest in the individual case (cf. Kelly, 1955; Osgood & Luria, 1967).

At the group level, opportunities are opened for the study of social psychological problems. The method could, for example, be used to study differences between politically, religiously, socio-economically homogeneous groups with respect to attitudes to situation—specific questions such as problems of interpersonal relationships, conflict research, etc.

It is possible that the method can also be used within a further area, where suitable methodology has long been the subject of research, namely, that of job evaluation. It should be possible to use similarity judgments for job positions and work duties in order to empirically determine the relevant dimensions. The judgments could be performed by individuals at different levels of proximity to the duties and positions.

All research concerning the dimensionality of cognitive organization presents some form of sampling problem. Here the problem is, however, scarcely greater than or different from that involved when studying cognitive structure within other areas. Only one consideration on sampling situations will be mentioned in this connection. The total cognitive organization of an individual can be assumed to be flexible and elastic, so that the internal relationships of the objects are variable under varying circumstances. It is probable that the organization changes both over time according to a more general trend, as well as between situations as a result of the specific domain which is focused upon. It may be assumed, for example, that if the focus is changed, this will also change the internal relationships between the objects in the cognitive organization. This means that the sampling of situations ought to be limited to some specific domain of situations, e.g., interpersonal relationships, leisure activities, studies, work duties, job positions, etc., as was the case in this study.

REFERENCES

Abelson, R. P. Situational variables in personality research. In S. Messick & J. Ross (Eds.), *Measurement in Personality and Cognition*. New York: Wiley, 1962. Pp. 241-248.

Attneave, F. Dimensions of similarity. *American Journal of Psychology*, 1950, 63, 516-556.

Bieri, J., Atkins, A. L., Briar, S., Leaman, R. L., Miller, H., & Tripodi, T. *Clinical and Social Judgment: the Discrimination of Behavioral Information*. New York: Wiley, 1966.

Brunswik, E. Representative design and probabilistic theory in a functional psychology. *Psychological Review*, 1955, 62, 193-218.

Carson, R. C. *Interaction Concepts of Personality*. Chicago: Aldine, 1969.

Cattell, R. B. Formulating the environmental situation and its perception in behavior theory. In S. B. Sells (Ed.), *Stimulus Determinants of Behavior*. New York: Ronald, 1963. Pp. 46-75.

Coombs, C. A. *A Theory of Data*. New York: Wiley, 1964.

Cronbach, L. J. The two disciplines of scientific psychology. *American Psychologist*, 1957, 12, 671-684.

Cronbach, L. J. Proposals leading to analytic treatment of social perception scores. In R. Tagiuri & L. Petrullo (Eds.), *Person Perception and Interpersonal Behavior*. Stanford: Stanford Univer. Press, 1958. Pp. 353-380.

Ekman, G. Dimensions of color vision. *Journal of Psychology*, 1954, 38, 467-474.

Ekman, G. Dimensions of emotion. *Acta Psychologica*, 1955, 11, 279-288.

Ekman, G. Multidimensional ratio scaling applied to color vision. *Report Psychological Laboratories, Univer. of Stockholm*, 1961, No. 92.

Ekman, G. Comparative studies on multidimensional scaling and related techniques. *Report Psychological Laboratories, Univer. of Stockholm*, 1970, Supplement 3.

Ekman, G., & Engen, T. Multimensional ratio scaling and multidimensional similarity in olfactory perception. *Report Psychological Laboratories, Univer. of Stockholm*, 1962, No. 126.

Ekman, G., & Lindman, R. Multidimensional ratio scaling and multidimensional similarity. *Report Psychological Laboratories, Univer. of Stockholm*, 1961, No. 103.

Endler, N. S., & Hunt, J. McV. Sources of variance in reported anxiousness as measured by the S-R Inventory. *Psychological Bulletin*, 1966, 65, 336-346.

Engen, T. Psychophysical similarity of the odors of aliphatic alcohols. *Report Psychological Laboratories, Univer. of Stockholm*, 1962, No. 127.

Fiske, D. W. Problems in measuring personality. In J. W. Wepman & R. W. Heine (Eds.), *Concept of personality*. Chicago: Aldine, 1963. Pp. 449-473.

Gulliksen, H., & Messick, S. (Eds.) *Psychological scaling: theory and applications*. New York: Wiley, 1960.

Helson, H. *Adaptation-level theory: an experimental and systematic approach to behavior*. New York: Harper & Row, 1964.

Hunt, J. McV. Traditional personality theory in the light of recent evidence. *American Scientist*, 1965, 53, 80-96.

Kelly, G. A. *The psychology of personal constructs*. New York: Norton, 1955.

Koffka, K. *Principles of Gestalt psychology*. New York: Harcourt, 1935.

Kuennapas, T. Visual perception of capital letters: multidimensional ratio scaling and multidimensional similarity. *Scandinavian Journal of Psychology*, 1966, 7, 189-196.

Kuennapas, T. Visual memory of capital letters: multidimensional ratio scaling and multidimensional similarity. *Perceptual and Motor Skills*, 1967, 25, 345-350.

Kuennapas, T. Acoustic perception and acoustic memory of letters: multidimensional ratio scaling and multidimensional similarity. *Acta Psychologica*, 1968, 28, 161-170.

Kuennapas, T., Maelhammar, G., & Svenson, O. Multidimensional ratio scaling and multidimensional similarity of simple geometric figures. *Scandinavian Journal of Psychology*, 1964, 5, 249-256.

Lewin, K. *Field Theory in Social Science*. New York: Harper & Row, 1951.

Magnusson, D., & Ekman, G. A psychophysical approach to the study of personality traits. *Multivariate Behavioral Research*, 1970, 5, 255-274.

Magnusson, D., Gerzen, M., & Nyman, B. The generality of behavioral data: I. Generalization from observation on one occasion. *Multivariate Behavioral Research,* 1968, 3, 295-320.

Magnusson, D., Heffler, B. & Nyman, B. The generality of behavioral data: II. Replication of an experiment on generalization from observation on one occasion. *Multivariate Behavioral Research,* 1968, 3, 415-422.

Magnusson, D., Heffller, B, & Nyman, B. The generality of behavioral data: II. Replication of an experiment on generalization from observation on one occasion. *Multivariate Behavioral Research,* 1968, 3, 415-422.

Meltzer, L. The need for a dual orientation in social psychology. *Journal of Social Psychology,* 1961, 55, 43-47.

Miller, D. R. The study of social relationships: situation, identity, and social interaction. In S. Koch (Ed.), *Psychology: a Study of a Science.* New York: McGraw-Hill, 1963. Pp. 639-737.

Mischel, W. *Personality and Assessment.* New York: Wiley, 1968.

Murphy, G. *Personality: a biosocial interpretation.* New York: Harper, 1947.

Murray, H. A. *Explorations in Personality.* New York: Oxford, 1938.

Osgood, C. E., & Luria, Z. A blind analysis of a case of multiple personality using the semantic differential. In D. N. Jackson & S. Messick (Eds.), *Problems in Human Assessment.* New York: McGraw-Hill, 1967. Pp. 600-615.

Osgood, C. E., Suci, G. J., & Tannenbaum, P. H. *The Measurement of Meaning.* Urbana, Ill.: Univer. of Illinois Press, 1957.

Pervin, L. A. Performance and satisfaction as a function of individual-environment fit. *Psychological Bulletin,* 1968, 69, 56-68.

Sarbin, T. R., Taft, R., & Bailey, D. E. *Clinical Inference and Cognitive Theory.* New York: Holt, Rinehart & Winston, 1960.

Sells, S. B. Dimensions of stimulus situations which account for behavior variance. In S. B. Sells (Ed.), *Stimulus Determinants of Behavior.* New York: Ronald, 1963. Pp. 3-15. (a)

Sells, S. B. An interactionist looks at the environment. *American Psychologist,* 1963, 18, 696-702. (b)

Shepard, R. N. The analysis of proximities: multidimensional scaling with an unknown distance function: I and II. *Psychometrika,* 1962, 27, 125-140, 219, 246.

Shibutani, T. *Society and Personality: an interactional approach to social psychology.* Englewood Cliffs, N.J.: Prentice-Hall, 1961.

Tolman, E. G., Jarret, R. F., & Bailey, D. E. Degree of similarity and the ease of learning paired adjectives (1959). In T. R. Sarbin, R. Taft, & D. E. Bailey (Eds.), *Clinical Inference and Cognitive theory.* New York: Holt, Rinehart & Winston, 1960. Pp. 108-111.

Torgerson, W. S. *Theory and Methods of Scaling.* New York: Wiley, 1958.

3
Perceived Dimensions of
Interpersonal Relations*

Myron Wish
Morton Deutsch
Susan J. Kaplan

A questionnaire study was conducted to discover the fundamental dimensions underlying people's perceptions of interpersonal relations. In the sections of the questionnaire relevant to this report, 87 subjects rated 20 of their own interpersonal relations (e.g., between you and your spouse) and 25 typical, or role, relations (e.g., between husband and wife) on numerous bipolar scales. A multidimensional scaling analysis of the data revealed four dimensions, which were interpreted as cooperative and friendly versus competitive and hostile, equal versus unequal, intense versus superficial, and socioemotional and informal versus task-oriented and formal. The relative importance of these dimensions varied systematically across various subgroups based on biographical characteristics of the subjects. The four dimensions were compared to those from studies of personality, person perception, and individual behavior in interpersonal situations. The stability of the dimensions suggests that they should provide a valuable framework for future research on interpersonal relations and communication.

During a recent study that we were conducting on marital conflict, it became clear that it would be useful to have a method for characterizing how individuals thought of their own marital relationship and of the other kinds of interpersonal

*Journal of Personality and Social Psychology, 1976, 33, 4, 409-420. Copyright 1976 by the American Psychological Association. Reprinted by permission.

relationships in which they were involved. For example, does a particular man view his relationship with his wife as being like that of close friends, business partners, parent and child, master and servant, or what? How similar are the husband's and wife's conceptions of their marital relationship? And what kind of correspondence is there between a person's conceptions of his/her own relationships and the person's conceptions of various role relationships? Questions such as these underscored the need for a general framework for describing and comparing the variety of ways people relate to each other.

The present study was aimed at the following: (a) discovering the fundamental dimensions that characterize people's perceptions of typical as well as their own interpersonal relations; (b) assessing the degree and kinds of individual differences in perceptions of interpersonal relations and associating such differences to other characteristics of the subjects; and (c) investigating similarities and differences in multidimensional structures for interpersonal relations derived from different experimental tasks.

Underlying this research is the assumption that dyadic relations are meaningful perceptual-cognitive units that can be evaluated and compared with one another. Since some similarity would be expected between the ways people view dyads (i.e., dyadic relations) and single individuals, the large literature dealing with the dimensions of personality, person perception, and individual behavior in interpersonal situations is relevant to our concerns (see Foa, 1961; Rosenberg & Sedlak, 1972; Schutz, 1958, for summaries). However, it seems unreasonable to assume that there is a complete correspondence between the individual and dyadic levels.

The research most similar to ours are the studies or role relationships by Triandis and his colleagues (Triandis, 1972; Triandis, Vassiliou, & Nassiakou, 1968) and by Marwell and Hage (1970).[1] Triandis's research employed questionnaires in which American and Greek subjects rated the degree of appropriateness or likelihood of each of 120 different types of behavior for each of 100 different roles. The roles included a wide variety of dyadic relations, such as father to son, secretary to boss, tourist to native, prostitute to client, and negro to white. In the Marwell and Hage study, each of 100 role relations was rated on 16 general variables, which were generated by combining four elements of relationships (occupants, activities, locations, and occurrences) with four quantities of relationships (scope, intensity, integration, and independence). The data from both of these studies were analyzed by factor-analytic procedures.

---

[1] We were unaware of the research by either Triandis and his associates or of Marwell and Hage when we conducted this study. Since the methodological orientation of the present study and its objectives differ sufficiently from these prior studies, few changes in our experimental design would have occurred if we had been cognizant of these earlier investigations. However, results from the other studies might have influenced our selection of dyadic relations.

Our study differs from those by Triandis and by Marwell and Hage in terms of the kind of stimuli used, as well as in the data collection and analysis procedures employed. In addition to making judgments about typical relations of various kinds (e.g., between husband and wife), subjects evaluated some of their own interpersonal relations (e.g., between you and your spouse). The typical relations were evaluated by means of three judgmental methods: direct ratings of similarity between pairs of dyads; groupings, or clusterings, of the dyads; and ratings of the dyads on bipolar scales. The only method employed for subjects' own relations was the bipolar scale ratings. (This was the last task in the questionnaire.)

This report deals almost entirely with the ratings of typical and own relations on the bipolar scales. Results from this method are compared, however, with those based on the other data-collection procedures. A detailed exposition of the overall design and results is provided in a methodological article by Wish (in press).

METHOD

Subjects

Sixty-seven subjects were recruited for the study by means of posters placed at Columbia University and sign-up sheets distributed in classes at Teachers College. An approximately equal number of married males, married females, single males, and single females were selected. In addition, 20 marketing students from the Wharton School (University of Pennsylvania) participated in the study. The subjects, who were run in groups of 8 to 10, were paid $10 each for the 3 to 4 hours generally required to complete the questionnaire. Although most completed the questionnaire in a single session, some had to return to finish.

Selection of Bipolar Scales and Interpersonal Relations

The selection of rating scales and typical relations proceeded concurrently; the aim was to get a sample of dyadic relations that reflected the wide variety of ways people relate to each other, and a set of bipolar scales that represented the most important distinctions that could be made among different kinds of relations. After generating a long list of dyads, we used a procedure similar in principle to Kelly's (1955) repertory grid technique to choose a set of 25 bipolar scales on which these dyads could be rated. (These scales are listed in Table 3.1.) In other words, the process involved thinking of characteristics that certain relations have

Table 3.1 List of Stimuli Used in the Interpersonal Relations Study

I. Typical relations	II. Subjects' own relations
Between close friends	A. When you were a child
Between salesman and regular customer	
Between husband and wife	Between you and your mother
Between personal enemies	Between you and your father
Between parent and young child	Between you and your brothers and sisters
Between interviewer and job applicant	Between you and your close friends
Between business partners	Between you and people you disliked
Between professor and graduate student	Between you and your teachers
Between children in a family (siblings)	Between you and your classmates
Between opposing negotiators	Between your mother and father
Between nurse and invalid	
Between mother-in-law and son-in-law	B. Current relationships
Between political opponents	
Between parent and teenager	Between you and your mother
Between business rivals	Between you and your father
Between teacher and young pupil	Between you and your brothers and sisters
Between supervisor and employee	Between you and your close friends
Between second cousins	Between you and your casual acquaintances
Between psychotherapist and patient	Between you and people you dislike
Between fiancé and fiancée	Between you and your professors
Between master and servant	Between you and your supervisor
Between teammates (during a game)	Between you and your co-workers
Between casual acquaintances	Between you and your spouse
Between guard and prisoner	Between you and your spouse's parents
Between divorced husband and wife	Between you and your children
(formerly married to each other)	

in common and which distinguish them from other kinds (see also Osgood, 1970).

Twenty-five dyads were then selected from the original list which seemed sufficiently diverse to span the full range on each bipolar scale. These dyads (the typical relations) are listed in the left-hand column of Table 3.1. The representativeness of this sample was checked by having students generate lists of as many dyadic relations as they could think of. Among the approximately 100 lists obtained in this way, rarely did a dyad appear that was not some variant of one included in the stimulus sample.

In choosing a set of own relations we attempted to select ones which were likely to apply to most college students. As shown in the right-hand column of Table 3.1, the relations included 7 childhood and 12 current relationships. Due to a particular interest in marital relationships, we asked the subjects to evaluate the relationship between their mother and father when they (the subjects) were children. The relation, you and your children, was eliminated from all analyses since it applied to only eight subjects.

Rating the Dyads on Bipolar Scales

Every subject rated all the relations (typical and own) on 14 bipolar scales. Three of these scales were common to all questionnaire forms; each of the remaining 22 scales appeared in only half of the forms. All scales had 9 points; for example, one ranged from 1 for very cooperative relations to 9 for very competitive relations. In making their judgments, subjects were instructed to "take into account all aspects of the relationships—including the way the two individuals in each relationship typically think and feel about each other, how they act and react toward each other, how they talk and listen to each other, and any other characteristics of the relationships that occur to you." Different forms of the questionnaire were generated to balance the left and right poles of the scales, the stimulus ordering on the page, and the scale sequence in the response booklets.

A profile distance formula[2] was used to get the rating scale data in a form appropriate for multidimensional scaling. In this way a 44 × 44 matrix of dissimilarities among relations (25 typical and 19 own relations) was derived for each of the 25 bipolar scales. The entire set of dissimilarity matrices was used as input to the INDSCAL (Carroll & Chang, 1970) program for individual differences multidimensional scaling.

RESULTS

INDSCAL analyses of the rating scale data (25 dissimilarity matrices) in 6, 5, 4, and 3 dimensions accounted for 79%, 78%, 75%, and 67% of the variance, respectively. These results provide evidence that four dimensions are both necessary (8% more variance than three dimensions) and sufficient (only 3% less variance than five dimensions) to characterize the subjects' perceptions of the relations being studied.

Interpretation of Dimensions

Dimension weights for bipolar scales. In addition to stimulus coordinates on the dimensions, the computer output from the INDSCAL analyses included a set

---

[2]The dissimilarity, $\delta_{jk(s)}$, between relations j and k in the matrix for bipolar scale s was defined as follows:

$$\delta_{jk(s)} = \sqrt{\frac{1}{N} \sum_{i=1}^{N} (x_{ijs} - x_{iks})^2},$$

where x_{ijs} and x_{iks} are subject i's ratings of relations j and k on scale s, and N is the number of subjects who rated both relations j and k on scale s. The squared difference term $(x_{ijs} - x_{iks})^2$ was excluded from the summation if j or k was associated with an "own" relation that did not apply to subject i.

of dimension weights for each matrix of dissimilarities. Since each dissimilarity matrix used in these analyses was derived from all subjects' ratings of the relations on a single bipolar scale, the dimension weights are associated with rating scales instead of subjects. These weights provide statistical evidence for the interpretation of dimensions; that is, the higher the dimension weight for a bipolar scale, the more relevant the associated attribute is to the conceptualization of the dimension.

Weights for each bipolar scale from the four-dimensional INDSCAL solution are shown in Table 3.2. These dimension weights are analogous to partial correlations, while the R values in the last column are analogous to multiple correlations. Dimension weights and R values obtained directly from an INDSCAL analysis are lower, however, than regression weights and multiple

Table 3.2 Dimension Weights for Bipolar Scales from an INDSCAL
Analysis of 25 "Typical" and 19 "Own" Relations

| Bipolar scales | Dimension | | | | |
	1	2	3	4	R
1. Always harmonious vs always clashing	.89**	.04	−.01	−.10	.86
2. Very cooperative vs very competitive	.87**	.04	.04	−.06	.86
3. Very friendly vs very hostile	.87**	.04	.08	.12	.93
4. Compatible vs incompatible goals and desires	.87**	.06	.10	.01	.90
5. Very productive vs very destructive	.85**	.04	.16	−.06	.87
6. Easy vs difficult to resolve conflicts with each other	.84**	.05	.03	.04	.86
7. Very altruistic vs very selfish	.76**	.04	.07	.24	.89
8. Very fair vs very unfair	.75**	.22	.07	.13	.86
9. Very relaxed vs very tense	.73**	.07	.00	.29	.88
10. Exactly equal vs extremely unequal power	.02	.96**	.02	.03	.96
11. Very similar vs very different roles and behavior	.11	.91**	.09	.02	.92
12. Very active vs very inactive	.12	.07	.81**	−.06	.82
13. Intense vs superficial interaction with each other	.10	.10	.75**	.18	.86
14. Intense vs superficial feelings toward each other	−.03	.02	.73**	.22	.82
15. Very interesting vs very dull	.12	.12	.64*	.15	.75
16. Important vs unimportant to society	.16	.06	.53*	.01	.58
17. Pleasure-oriented vs work-oriented	−.03	.06	−.08	.95**	.93
18. Very informal vs very formal	.32	.05	.14	.70**	.92
19. Emotional vs intellectual	−.13	−.01	.22	.70**	.77
20. Very democratic vs very autocratic	.40*	.63*	.00	.27	.86
21. Important vs unimportant to the individuals involved	.42*	.02	.64*	.08	.85
22. Emotionally very close vs emotionally very distant	.47*	.04	.36	.42*	.90
23. Very sincere vs. very insincere	.55*	.10	.25	.40*	.87
24. Very flexible vs very rigid	.59*	.14	.00	.43*	.85
25. Difficult vs easy to break off contact with each other	.20	−.01	.53*	.43*	.86

Note. INDSCAL = individual differences multidimensional scaling.
*Weight between .40 and .70
**Weight greater than or equal to .70

correlations based on supplementary multiple regression analyses (see Wish & Carroll, 1974). The fact that almost all of the R values are very high shows that a wide variety of characteristics distinguishing among relations are predictable from these four dimensions.

The first dimension could have been broadly interpreted as an evaluative dimension. However, the more specific denotative interpretation, Cooperative and Friendly versus Competitive and Hostile was assigned since the scales with the highest weights deal with the degree of conflict in the relations. Dimension 2 has a very clear interpretation of Equal versus Unequal since the weights are very high for the scales *exactly equal versus extremely unequal power* and *very similar versus very different roles and behavior*. Based on the highest weights in the third and fourth columns of Table 3.2, dimension 3 was interpreted as Intense versus Superficial and dimension 4 was interpreted as Socioemotional and Informal versus Task Oriented and Formal.

Stimulus coordinates. The coordinate values, or projections, or stimuli on the *unrotated* dimensions from the INDSCAL analysis are plotted in Figures 3.1 and 3.2. (INDSCAL determines a statistically unique orientation of axes that maximize the proportion of variance accounted for by the multidimensional solution.)

Figure 3.1 shows that political opponents, personal enemies, and guard and prisoner are on the competitive-hostile side of the first dimension, while close friends, fiancé and fiancée, and husband and wife are at the cooperative-friendly extreme. The second dimension reflects the distribution of power between the two individuals in a relationship; the lower the coordinate value for a relation on this dimension, the more control one member of the dyad as over the other. Note that the subjects perceive the parent-teenager relationship to be less cooperative but more equal than the parent-child relationship and regard the relationship between their parents (when the subjects were children) as less cooperative and equal than their own or the typical husband-wife relationship. The relations are ordered along the third dimension (see Figure 3.2) according to degree of intensity, with superficial relations such as between second cousins or casual acquaintances on the left side and intense relations such as between parent and child or between psychotherapist and patient on the right side. Finally, the fourth dimension contrasts formal relations of a "strictly business" nature with socioemotional relations involving family members or close friends.

One can observe in Figures 3.1 and 3.2 that the typical relations tend to be at the extremes of the dimensions (the periphery of the space), while the own relations are closer to the center. In fact, the standard deviation of coordinate values is larger on each dimension for typical than for own relations. Although this effect is partially due to the broader sampling of the typical relations, it also reflects subjects' idealization of these relations. There is also a systematic difference between subjects' perceptions of their current and childhood relations;

that is, they tend to regard their current relations with the designated individuals as more equal and cooperative, but less intense.

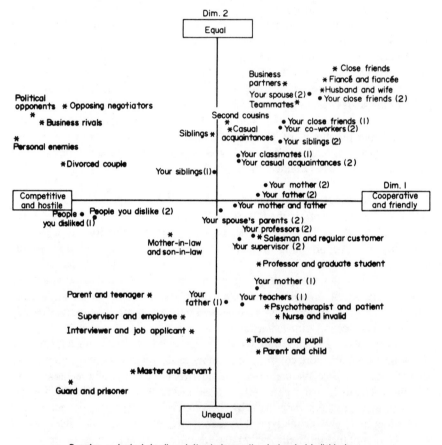

* Denotes a typical dyadic relation between the designated individuals
• Denotes a relation between the subject and the designated individual. The subject's childhood relations are indicated by a (1), while the subject's current relations are indicated by a (2)

Figure 3.1.   Dimensions 1 and 2 (unrotated) of the four-dimensional INDSCAL solution for 25 "typical" and 19 "own" relations. (Each dimension was normalized so that the mean of the coordinate values equals zero and the sum of squared coordinates equals 1.00. INDSCAL = individual differences multidimensional scaling.)

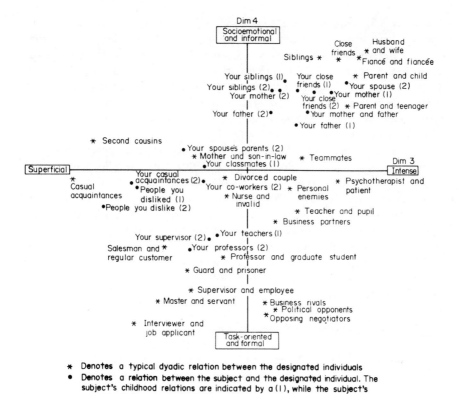

Figure 3.2. Dimensions 3 and 4 (unrotated) of the four-dimensional INDSCAL solution for 25 "typical" and 19 "own" relations. (Each dimension was normalized so that the mean of the coordinate values equals zero and the sum of squared coordinates equals 1.00. INDSCAL = individual differences multidimensional scaling.)

Variation in Ratings of Typical and Own Relations

While there is more variability in the coordinates for typical than for own relations on each dimension, there is greater variation among subjects in their ratings of any particular own relation than in their ratings of the associated typical relation. (In other words, there is greater between-relation variance for typical relations and greater within-relation variance for own relations.) For example, the average variance[3] in subjects' ratings of the typical parent and young child

---

[3]The variance of subjects' ratings of each relation was computed separately for each of the 25 bipolar scales. The average of the 25 such variances was then computed for each relation.

relation is 2.6, while the average variances for you and your father and you and your mother (when you were a child) are 4.6 and 5.8. Similarly, the average variance for typical close friends is 1.5, while the average variance for you and your close friends is 2.7 for current friends and 3.1 for childhood friends. Scale-by-scale comparisons of the variances in ratings of each typical and own relation show that differences are greater for scales having high weights on the first two dimensions (see Table 3.2) than for those associated with the third and fourth dimensions.

Other analyses show that there is much more subject agreement in ratings of relations judged to be friendly than those judged to be hostile, with neutral relations falling in between. For example, the average variance is 1.9 for between fiancé and fiancée and 4.7 for between divorced husband and wife. This reflects the large individual differences in evaluations of how hostile feelings are likely to be expressed. Some subjects' ratings suggest that they believe that people in hostile relationships avoid each other whenever possible and that their occasional interactions are marked by formality and superficiality. Others seem to believe that people in hostile relationships clash head-on and that their interactions are intense and emotional.

Subgroup Variation in Dimension Weights

As mentioned previously, the matrices used as input to the INDSCAL analysis were associated with the various bipolar scales rather than with different individuals or subgroups. In order to investigate differences in the relative importance of these dimensions, additional matrices were derived from the same bipolar scale ratings for 21 subgroups of the Columbia sample (see Tables 3.3 and 3.4). One set of matrices was derived for each subgroup from its members' ratings of the 19 own relations (between you and your children was excluded), and another set was determined from ratings of the 25 typical relations.[4] Matrices of dissimilarities among own and among typical relations were also derived for the Columbia sample as a whole and for the sample of Wharton marketing students.

---

[4]Two steps were involved in the computation of a matrix of dissimilarities among "own" or among "typical" relations for a particular subgroup or for the total group. The first step was to use the profile-distance formula to derive a matrix for each bipolar scale based only on ratings by individuals in that subgroup. The second step was to average (root mean square) the 25 dissimilarity matrices for the given subgroup (one for each bipolar scale) in order to get a composite matrix of "own" or of "typical" relations for that subgroup.

Table 3.3   Dimension Weights for Subgroups Based on Ratings of "Own" Relations

Subgroup	n	Dimension 1: "Cooperative vs Competitive"	Dimension 4: "Socio-emotional vs Task-oriented"	Dimension 2: "Equal vs Unequal"	Dimension 3: "Intense vs Superficial"
1. Age					
A. 24 or older	33	.39*	.13*	.27	.57
B. 23 or younger	34	.24*	.32*	.31	.53
2. Marital status					
A. Married	33	.39*	.10*	.30	.57
B. Single	34	.28*	.30*	.27	.55
3. Political orientation[a]					
A. Center-right (5 to 9)	15	.37*	.10*	.22*	.60*
B. Left-center (3 or 4)	33	.35*	.16*	.32*	.56*
C. Left (1 or 2)	18	.21*	.38*	.33*	.48*
4. Religion					
A. Jewish	24	.27	.27	.18*	.59*
B. Christian	20	.35	.17	.24*	.59*
C. Other or none	23	.32	.19	.48*	.29*
5. Gender					
A. Female	35	.34	.17	.24*	.61*
B. Male	32	.31	.28	.36*	.46*
6. Socioeconomic status (when growing up)					
A. Upper middle or above	30	.30	.16	.23	.63*
B. Lower middle or below	37	.35	.25	.32	.50*
7. Number of siblings					
A. None or one	36	.30	.23	.25	.58
B. Two or more	31	.36	.20	.33	.55
8. Birth order					
A. Oldest sibling	31	.38	.57	.31	.17
B. Middle or youngest	27	.31	.57	.28	.22
9. Field of study					
A. Psychology	27	.32	.24	.26	.55
B. Other arts & sciences	21	.36	.17	.33	.50
C. Education-related	19	.30	.20	.26	.59
Total Columbia sample	67	.34*	.22*	.29*	.57
Wharton marketing sample	20	.46*	.11*	.10*	.59

[a]Subjects indicated their political orientation by circling a number on a scale from 1, for political left, to 9, for political right. One subject did not give a response to this item.
*Statistically significant (at or below the .05 level) between the two or three subgroups in the set.

The INDSCAL program was used to compute dimension weights for each subgroup and for the total Columbia and Wharton groups.[5] The dimension weights derived from the matrices of dissimilarities among own relations are shown in Table 3.3, while the dimension weights associated with the typical relations are shown in Table 3.4.

Determination of statistically significant differences between subgroups involved a "Monte Carlo" procedure. Using the actual data from the subjects, subgroups of randomly selected individuals from the sample were formed. Weights were then determined for these random subgroups, and sampling distributions were derived. The .05 significance level was determined for each dimension by referring the weights for the subgroups listed in Tables 3.3 and 3.4 to these sampling distributions.

Dimension weights based on own relations. Table 3.3 indicates that in evaluating own relations the cooperative and friendly versus competitive and hostile dimension is more salient to the Wharton marketing students than to the Columbia students; this dimension is also more salient to older than to younger subjects, to married than to single subjects, and to subjects on the political right than to those on the political left. In contrast, weights on the socioemotional and informal versus task oriented and formal dimension are higher for the Columbia than for the Wharton students, and for the younger, single, and "leftist" subjects than for the older, married, and "rightist" subjects.

Weights on the equality versus inequality dimension are substantially higher for the Columbia sample as a whole than for the Wharton sample. In other words, the Columbia students perceive their relationships with peers to be very different from those with people to whom they are in some sense subordinate, while this power distinction is much less salient to the Wharton students. The second dimension is also more important to subjects with unconventional or no religious beliefs than to the Jewish and Christian subjects, to subjects on the left side of the political continuum than to those on the right, and to males than to females. Finally, the distinction between intense and superficial relations is more salient to Jews and Christians, political conservatives, females, and subjects from families of higher socioeconomic status than to subjects in the complementary subgroups.

Dimension weights based on typical relations. A comparison of Table 3.4 with Table 3.3 reveals that subgroup differences in dimension weights are

---

[5]INDSCAL is generally used to determine the stimulus coordinates as well as the dimension weights. In this case, however, we used an option provided in the INDSCAL program to keep the stimulus space fixed and to solve for the weights by a least-squares procedure. This involves reading in the stimulus coordinates of the space as the initial configuration and running the program for zero iterations.

generally consistent for typical and own relations. For example, the cooperative versus competitive dimension is more salient and the equal versus unequal dimension is less salient to the conservative than to the ''leftist'' Columbia

Table 3.4 Dimensions Weights for Subgroups Based on Ratings of ''Typical'' Relations

Subgroup	n	Dimension 1: ''Cooperative vs Competitive''	Dimension 4: ''Socio-emotional vs Task-oriented''	Dimension 2: ''Equal vs Unequal''	Dimension 3: ''Intense vs Superficial''
1. Age					
A. 24 or older	33	.66	.26*	.38	.26
B. 23 or younger	34	.58	.34*	.37	.28
2. Marital status					
A. Married	33	.60	.31	.38	.29
B. Single	34	.64	.28	.37	.26
3. Political orientation[a]					
A. Center-right (5 to 9)	15	.66*	.27	.31*	.25
B. Left-center (3 or 4)	33	.62*	.28	.37*	.30
C. Left (1 or 2)	18	.55*	.33	.44*	.26
4. Religion					
A. Jewish	24	.61	.32	.35	.28
B. Christian	20	.66	.23	.38	.28
C. Other or none	23	.58	.32	.40	.27
5. Gender					
A. Female	35	.63	.28	.37	.28
B. Male	32	.60	.31	.38	.26
6. Socioeconomic status (when growing up)					
A. Upper middle or above	30	.62	.30	.36	.28
A. Lower middle or below	37	.62	.29	.39	.28
7. Number of siblings					
A. None or one	36	.56*	.32	.40	.32*
B. Two or more	31	.66*	.27	.36	.23*
8. Birth of order					
A. Oldest sibling	31	.65	.27	.37	.26
B. Middle or youngest	27	.62	.25	.38	.31
9. Field of study					
A. Psychology	27	.62	.31	.33	.28
B. Other arts & sciences	21	.58	.28	.41	.32
C. Education-related	19	.63	.29	.40	.23
Total Columbia sample	67	.62*	.30*	.38*	.27
Wharton marketing sample	20	.74*	.18*	.26*	.26

[a]Subjects indicated their political orientation by circling a number on a scale from 1, for political left, to 9 for political right. One subject did not give a response to this item.
*Statistically significant (at or below the .05 level) between the two or three subgroups of the set.

subjects, and to the Wharton students than to the Columbia sample as a whole. The subgroup differences in dimension weights are generally smaller, however, for the typical than for the own relations. In other words, the subjects agree more in their evaluations of the cultural expectations concerning various relations than in the way they themselves relate to other people.

Perhaps the most striking difference between Tables 3.3 and 3.4 is in the magnitude of weights on the first and third dimensions. The intense versus superficial dimension is much more important for evaluations of own than of typical relations, while the reverse applies for the cooperative versus competitive dimension. Although these results are partially attributable to differences between the samples of own and typical relations (more family relations and fewer hostile relations in the own set), they do suggest that the degree of intensity of a relation is a more central characteristic when thinking about one's own relationships than when considering typical relations of various kinds.

DISCUSSION

Methodological Considerations

An important advantage of having used INDSCAL rather than another multi-dimensional scaling procedure or factor analysis was that the dimensions were both statistically unique and clearly interpretable. Other evidence for the uniqueness and stability of the dimensions was obtained by comparing the dimensions in Figures 3.1 and 3.2 with those from INDSCAL analyses of data from the pair-wise similarity ratings and groupings tasks (Wish, in press). The correlations between coordinates of the typical relations (perceptions of own relations were not investigated by the other methods) on dimensions 1 through 4 of this analysis with the coordinates of these relations on the corresponding dimensions for the other judgmental tasks were all very high. This concurrence of results, *without any rotation of axes,* demonstrates that the dimensions described here are not artifacts of our particular selection of bipolar scales. The agreement among methods also provides compelling evidence for the psychological uniqueness, meaningfulness, and importance of the four dimensions.

Another benefit of using INDSCAL was that it provided quantitative information about the salience of the four dimensions to different subgroups. Many of the obtained differences between subgroups seem intuitively reasonable, particularly those for own relations. All in all, INDSCAL provides an efficient and concise method for describing subjects' perceptions of interpersonal relations and for investigating personality and cultural differences in these perceptions.

Comparisons with Results from Other Studies

So far as we know, the only prior research dealing with the perceived dimensions of role relations was conducted by Triandis and his colleagues (Triandis, 1972; Triandis et al., 1968) and by Marwell and Hage (1970). Triandis's cross-cultural studies differ from ours in many ways; they studied many more dyadic relations, their relationships were unidirectional rather than bidirectional, they employed different data collection procedures, and they used factor analysis rather than INDSCAL to analyze their data. Nevertheless, Triandis (1972, p. 270) concludes that "association-dissociation, superordination-subordination, and intimacy are the fundamental dimensions of human social behavior and are obtained with different methods of investigation." Essentially, the three dimensions which they identify are the same as the ones we have labeled as cooperative and friendly versus competitive and hostile, equal versus unequal, and socioemotional and informal versus task oriented and formal. We have also identified a fourth dimension having to do with the intensity of the relationship. The correspondence between results from the two investigations provides additional assurance that fundamental dimensions of interpersonal relations have emerged from our data. Triandis's comparison of the results for Greek and American subjects does suggest a note of caution, however. Although the underlying dimensions appear to be the same in the two different cultures, the location within their dimensional space of specific role relations and specific social behaviors is different for the two cultures. Triandis et al. (1968, p. 31), for example, state the following:

> Greeks appear to define their ingroups in terms of family and friends, friends of one's friends, and people who are concerned; Americans define them as 'people like me' so that an unknown American from a different part of the country, having the same religion and set of values, would be perceived as belonging to the ingroup.

Thus, even though certain dimensions of interpersonal relations may be culturally invariant, the social meaning of particular role relations may vary from culture to culture.

Marwell and Hage (1970) identified three factors in their study of role relationships: (a) "intimacy," which is characterized by relations which have a high number of different activities, a high number of different locations, low distance between the partners, and high role-set overlap between occupants; (b) "visibility," which is primarily defined by public relationships that are open to intrusion as opposed to private relations that are not observable by the general public; and (c) "regulation" which distinguishes role relations in which the definition of activities, times, and locations are left to the members from those where there is a good deal of specification of what goes on (either through normative pressure or through integration into other ongoing social relationships). Two of the dimensions obtained by Marwell and Hage, "intimacy" and "regulation," appear to be included in our dimension of socioemotional and informal versus task-oriented and formal. In research subsequent to that reported in this article (Wish, 1974, 1975), this dimension appears as two dimensions— socioemotional versus task oriented and informal versus formal. Socioemotional versus task oriented corresponds to intimacy, and formal versus informal seeks akin to regulation, as defined in the Marwell and Hage study. No counterpart to the Marwell-Hage dimension of visibility was found, since our sample of relations contained practically none of the kinds that tend to be hidden from the general public.

An examination of the research literature dealing with personality, person perception, and individual behavior in interpersonal and group situations also shows a clear correspondence with three of the dimensions obtained in our study (see Bales, 1970; Foa, 1961; Leary, 1957; Rosenberg & Sedlak, 1972; Schutz, 1958). Repeatedly, one finds a dimension which is similar to our cooperative and friendly versus competitive and hostile dimension; it is labeled variously as "love-hate," "sociability," "affection," or "positive-negative interpersonal disposition." A second dimension which is comparable to our "equal-unequal" dimension is commonly characterized as "dominance-submission," "autonomy-control," or "power." A third dimension, like our "intense-superficial" dimension, is identified as "intensity" or "activity." The correspondence between these three dimensions and Osgood's (Osgood, Suci, & Tannenbaum, 1957) three dimensions of "evaluation," "potency," and "activity" is clear.

No exact parallel was found between our socioemotional and formal versus task oriented and formal dimension and well-established personality dimensions. However, Bales (1958) has made a related distinction between social-emotional and task leaders of groups; the former focuses on the solidarity relations among group members, and the latter focuses on the external task and problem-solving activities of the group.

Further Inquiry

Several lines of inquiry seem to be natural follow-ups to this study. One centers about the generalizability of the findings to different samples of subjects and stimuli. A second involves the utilization of a simplified version of the methodology of this study as a diagnostic procedure for (a) characterizing an individual's view of his/her varied interpersonal relations at different periods of life and for (b) comparing interrelated individuals (husband-wife, parent-child, etc.) in the way they view overlapping aspects of their lives. A third focuses on how the specific situational context combines with the interpersonal relation to affect the perceived and actual qualities of communication and interaction between the two individuals. Studies directed at this third line of inquiry are already in progress (see Wish, 1974, 1975).

REFERENCES

Bales, R. F. Task roles and social roles in problem-solving groups. In E. E. Maccoby, T. M. Newcomb, & E. L. Hartley (Eds.), *Readings in social psychology*. New York: Holt, 1958.

Bales, R. F. *Personality and interpersonal behavior*. New York: Holt, Rinehart & Winston, 1970.

Carroll, J. D., & Chang, J. J. Analysis of individual differences in multidimensional scaling via an N-way generalization of "Eckhart-Young" decomposition. *Psychometrika*, 1970, *35*, 283-319.

Foa, U. G. Convergences in the analysis of the structure of interpersonal behavior. *Psychological Review*, 1961, *68*, 341-353.

Kelly, G. A. *A theory of personality: The psychology of personal constructs*. New York: Norton, 1955.

Leary, T. F. *Interpersonal diagnosis of personality*. New York: Ronald Press, 1957.

Marwell, G., & Hage, J. The organization of role relationships: A systematic description. *American Sociological Review*, 1970, *35*, 884-900.

Osgood, C. E. Interpersonal verbs and interpersonal behavior. In J. L. Cowan (Ed.), *Studies in thought and language*. Tucson: University of Arizona Press, 1970.

Osgood, C. E., Suci, G. J., & Tannenbaum, P. H. *The measurement of meaning*. Urbana: University of Illinois Press, 1957.

Rosenberg, S., & Sedlak, A. Structural representations of implicit personality theory. In L. Berkowitz (Ed.), *Advances in experimental social psychology* (Vol. 6). New York: Academic Press, 1972.

Schutz, W. C. *Firo-B: A three-dimensional theory of interpersonal behavior*. New York: Holt, Rinehart & Winston, 1958.

Triandis, H. C. *The analysis of subjective culture*. New York: Wiley-Interscience, 1972.

Triandis, H. C., Vassiliou, V., & Nassiakou, M. Three cross-cultural studies of subjective culture. *Journal of Personality and Social Psychology, Monograph Supplement*, 1968, *8*, No. 4, Part 2, 1-42.

Wish, M. Dimensions of interpersonal communication. In *Proceedings of the 18th annual convention of the Human Factors Society*, 1974, 598-603.

Wish, M. Subjects' expectations about their own interpersonal communication: A multidimensional approach. *Personality and Social Psychology Bulletin*, 1975, *1*, 501-504.

Wish, M. Comparisons among multidimensional structures of interpersonal relations. *Multivariate Behavioral Research*, in press.

Wish, M., & Carroll, J. D. Applications of individual differences scaling to studies of human perception and judgment. In E. C. Carterette & M. P. Friedman (Eds.), *Handbook of perception* (Vol. 2). New York: Academic Press, 1974.

The Response to Social Situations: Introduction

Social situations affect every aspect of behaviour—anxiety, conformity, work performance, aggressiveness, and so on. These papers explore the ways in which three areas of response are affected by situations.

Kiritz and Moos (1974) review the literature concerning physiological and medical effects of situations. They show how positive social relations reduce stress responses, and suggest that this is due to increased hormonal activity. On the other hand, assuming responsibility for others leads to higher heart rates and other indices of physiological stress. Work pressures and "Type A" competitive behaviour result in higher rates of illness, particularly coronary disease. There are individual differences in susceptibility as a result of different perceptions of the situation, and the degree of social support at home. These are extremely important findings, though it is not yet clear exactly how the results are brought about by the situational variables in question.

Mehrabian and West (1977) studied some of the situational and personal factors that affect the desire to work. After subjects completed a number of rating scales it was found that reported desire to work was affected by the combined pleasantness and combined arousing quality of situation and task. These variables interacted, so that, for example there was less desire to work at a neutral or unpleasant task than there was at a task that was arousing. Subjects were compared who were high and low in "stimulus screening"; those high on this dimension were able to screen out unimportant stimuli, and thus reduced the rate of information received, and reduced arousal. Regression analyses showed that stimulus screeners had a greater desire to work, especially in unpleasant situations, while non-screeners' desire to work was increased more by task pleasantness. This study makes sophisticated use of regression equations, and of person variables theoretically linked with situational variables. Like many other studies, however, it relies on verbal reports, which are not wholly reliable in the field of work motivation.

Magnusson and Ekehammar (1978) tested the hypothesis which states that an individual behaves similarly in situations that he perceives as similar. Twelve stressful situations were used, and 10 kinds of anxious response. Perceived similarity of pairs of situations was obtained, which was compared with indices of profile similarity for the reported responses. Correlation between the two kinds of similarity were obtained for individuals, and most of the correlations were in the expected direction, though they were quite small, and for some subjects they were in the other direction. Although this study did not obtain very strong support for the hypothesis, it is of considerable methodological interest, especially in the use of profile similarity measures for responses and the study of individual subjects.

SUGGESTED ADDITIONAL REFERENCES

Abramovitch, R. and Daly, E. Inferring attributes of a situation from the facial expression of peers. *Child Development*, 1979, *50*, 586-589.

Alexander, C. and Knight, C. Situated identities and social psychological experimentation. *Sociometry*, 1971, 65-82.

Alexander, C. and Sagatun, I. An attributional analysis of experimental norms. *Sociometry*, 1973, *36*, 127-142.

Alexander, C. and Weil, H. Players, persons and purposes: situational meaning and the prisoner's dilemma game. *Sociometry*, 1969, *32*, 121-144.

Alexander, C., Zucker, L. and Brody, C. Experimental expectations and autokinetic experiences: consistency theories and judgmental convergence. *Sociometry*, 1970, *33*, 108-122.

Amir, Y. and Garti, C. Situational and personal influence on attitude change following ethnic contract. *International Journal of Intercultural Relations*, 1978, *21*, 58-75.

Bagozzi, R. Salesforce performance and satisfaction as a function of individual difference, interpersonal and situational factors. *Journal of Marketing Research*, 1978, *15*, 517-531.

Beach, B. and Beach, L. A note on judgments of situational favorableness and probability of success. *Organizational Behaviour and Human Performance*, 1978, *22*, 69-74.

Bearden, W. and Woodside, A. Situational and extended attitude models as predictors of marijuana intentions and reported behavior. *Journal of Social Psychology*, 1978, *106*, 57-67.

Bearden, W. and Woodside, A. Consumption occasion influence on a consumer brand choice. *Decision Sciences*, 1978, *9*, 273-283.

Beehr, R. Perceived situational moderators of the relationship between subjective role ambiguity and role strain. *Journal of Applied Psychology*, 1976, *61*, 35-40.

Belk, R. Situational variables and consumer behavior. *Journal of Consumer Research*, 1975, *2*, 157-167.

Belk, R. An exploratory assessment of situational effects in buyer behavior. *Journal of Marketing Research*, 1974, *11*, 156-163.

Belk, R. Situational mediation and consumer behavior: a reply to Russell and Mehrabian. *Journal of Consumer Research*, 1976, *3*, 175-177.

Best, J. and Hakstian, A. A situation-specific model for smoking behavior. *Addictive Behaviors*, 1978, *3*, 79-92.

Bickman, L. and Green, S. Situational cues and crime reporting. *Journal of Applied Social Psychology*, 1977, *7*, 1-18.

Burke, W. Leadership behavior as a function of the leader, the follower, and the situation. *Journal of Personality*, 19, *23*, 60-81.

Butter, E. and Seidenberg, B. Manifestations of moral development in concrete situations. *Social Behaviour and Personality*, 1973, *1*, 64-70.

Byrne, D., Allegeier, W. L., and Buckman, J. The situational facilitation of interpersonal attraction: a three factor hypothesis. *Journal of Applied Social Psychology*, 1975, *5*, 1-15.

Carney, R. The effect of situational variables on the measurement of achievement motivation. *Educational and Psychological Measurement*, 1966, *26*, 675-690.

Chell, E. A study of situational and personality factors on the role enactment of human relations problems. *Human Relations*, 1976, *29*, 1061-1081.

Clifford, B. and Scott, J. Individual and situational factors in eyewitness testimony. *Journal of Applied Psychology*, 1978, *63*, 352-359.

Cohen, J., Slade, B. and Bennett, B. The effects of situational variables on judgement of crowding. *Sociometry*, 1975, *38*, 273-281.

Cole, C. and Coyne, J. Situational specificity of laboratory-induced learned helplessness. *Journal of Abnormal Psychology*, 1977, *86*, 615-623.

DePaulo, B. Accuracy in predicting situational variations in help-seekers' responses. *Personality and Social Psychological Bulletin*, 1978, *4*, 330-333.

Fennell, G. Consumer's perceptions of the product use situation. *Journal of Marketing Research*, 1978, *42*, 38-47.

Frodi, A. Sexual arousal, situational restrictiveness, and aggressive behavior. *Journal of Research in Personality*, 1977, *11*, 48-58.

Gutek, B. and Stevens, D. Effects of sex of subject, sex of stimulus cue, and androgyny level on evaluations in work situations which evoke sex role stereotypes. *Journal of Vocational Behavior*. 1979, *14*, 23-32.

Goldstein, J. Outcome in professional team sports: chance skill and situational factors. In J. Goldstein (Ed.) *Sports, Games and Play*, Hillsdale, N.J.: Erlbaum, 1979.

Gutek, B. and Stevens, D. Effects of sex of subject, sex of stimulus cue, and androgyny level on evaluations in work situations which evoke sex role stereotypes. *Journal of Vocational Behavior*. 1979, *14*, 23-32.

Hatano, G. and Inagaki, K. Behavioural differences between extraverts and introverts in betting situations. *Japanese Psychological Review*, 1977, *19*, 174-183.

Herman, S. and Schild, E. Ethnic role conflict in a cross-cultural situation. *Human Relations*, 1960, *13*, 215-227.

Herzberger, S. and Clore, G. Actor and observer attributions in a multitrait-multimethod matrix. *Journal of Research into Personality*, 1979, *13*, 1-15.

Highlen, P. and Gillis, S. Effects of situational factors, sex, and attitude on affective self-disclosure and anxiety. *Journal of Consulting Psychology*, 1978, *25*, 270-276.

Holloway, W. and Ghulam, N. A study of leadership style, situation and favourableness, and the risk taking behavior of leaders. *The Journal of Educational Administration*, 1978, *16*, 160-168.

Holmes, T. Life situations, emotions and disease. *Psychosomatics*, 1978, *19*, 747-754.

Hunt, L., Cole, M. and Reis, E. Situational cues distinguishing anger, fear and sorrow. *American Journal of Psychology*, 1958, *71*, 136-151.

Iwata, O. Effects of bystander density upon altruistic behaviour. *Japanese Psychological Review*, 1977, *19*, 49-55.

Jones, F. and Lambert, W. Some situational influences on attitudes towards immigrants. *British Journal of Sociology*, 1976, 408-424.

Karabenick, S. and Srull, T. Effects of personality variation in locus of control and cheating: determinants of the "congruence effect." *Journal of Personality*, 1978, *46*, 72-95.

Kerr, N. and Gross, A. Situational and personality determinants of a victim's identification with a tormentor. *Journal of Research in Personality*, 1978, *12*, 450-468.

Leming, J. Cheating behavior, situational influence, and moral development. *Journal of Educational Research*, 1978, *71*, 214-217.

Leming, J. Intrapersonal variations in stage of moral reasoning among adolescents as a function of situational context. *Journal of Youth and Adolescence*, 1978, *1*, 405-416.

Leplat, J. Testing hypotheses in situations not designed by the experimenter. *Studia Psychologica*, 1976, *18*, 117-124.

Lorr, M., Suziedelis, R. and Kinnane, J. Characteristic reponse modes to interpersonal situations. *Multivariate Behaviour Research*, 1969, *4*, 445-458.

Masling, J. The influence of situational and interpersonal variables in projective testing. *Psychological Bulletin*, 1960, *57*, 65-85.

McGuire, W. Personality and susceptibility to social influence. Chap. 24. In E. Borgatta and W. Lambert (Eds.) *Handbook of Personality Theory and Research*, Chicago: Rand McNally, 1968.

Mehrabian, A. Characteristic individual reactions to preferred and unpreferred environments. *Journal of Personality*, 1978, *46*, 717-731.

Miller, K. and Ginter, J. An investigation of situational variation in brand choice behavior and attitude. *Journal of Marketing Research*, 1979, *16*, 111-123.

Mischel, W., Jeffrey, K. and Patterson, C. The layman's use of trait and behavioral information to predict behavior. *Journal of Research into Personality*, 1974, *8*, 231-242.

Mitchell, T., Larson, J. and Green, S. Leader behavior, situational moderators, and group performance: an attributional analysis. *Organizational Behavior and Human Performance*, 1977, *18*, 254-268.

Mount, M. and Muchinsky, P. Person-environment congruence and employee job satisfaction: a test of Holland's theory. *Journal of Vocational Behavior*, 1978, *13*, 84-100.

Murphy, G., Murphy, L. and Newcomb, T. Development of social behavior in a social context: age, levels, traits and the social situations. Chapt. 5. In *Experimental Psychology*, New York: Harper, 1937.

Page, R. and Moss, M. Environmental influences on aggression: the effects of darkness and the proximity of victim. *Journal of Applied Social Psychology*, 1976, *6*, 126-133.

Pellegrini, R., Hicks, R. and Meyers-Winton, S. Situational affective arousal, heterosexual attraction. *The Psychological Record*, 1979, *29*, 453-462.

Penner, L., Summers, L., Brookmire, D., and Dertke, M. The lost dollar: situational and personality determinants of a pro-and antisocial behaviour. *Journal of Personality*, 1976, *44*, 274-293.

Pervin, L. Performance and satisfaction as a function of the individual-environment fit. *Psychological Bulletin*, 1968, *69*, 56-68.

Rausch, H., Dittman, A., and Taylor, T. Person, setting, and change in social interaction. *Human Relations*, 1959, *12*, 361-378.

Richert, A. and Kettering, R. Psychological defense as a moderator variable. *Psychological Reports*, 1978, *42*, 291-294.

Rosenberg, M. A situational theory of attitude dynamics. *Public Opinion Quarterly*, 1960, *24*, 319-340.

Rotter, J. The role of the psychological situation in determining the direction of human behavior. *Nebraska Symposium on Motivation*, Vol. 3. 1955.

Russell, J. and Mehrabian, A. Task, setting, and personality variables affecting the desire to work. *Journal of Applied Psychology*, 1975, *60*, 518-520.

Sandell, R. Effects of attitudinal and situational factors on reported choice behavior. *Journal of Marketing Research*, 1968, *5*, 405-408.

Schmitt, N. and Saari, B. Behavior situation, and rater variance in descriptions of leader behaviours. *Multivariate Behavioral Research*, 1978, *13*, 483-496.

Shiomi, K. Differences in decision time between extraverts and introverts under the "task-oriented situation" and the "ego-oriented situation." *Psychological Reports*, 1978, *42*, 563-566.

Smith, R. and Hunt, S. Attributional processes and effects in promotional situations. *Journal of Consumer Research*, 1978, *5*, 149-158.

Soloman, S. Situational effects on the identification of emotions in children. *The Journal of Psychology*, 1977, *96*, 177-186.

Srull, T. and Karabenik, S. Effects of personality-situation locus of control congruence. *Journal of Personality and Social Psychology*, 1975, *32*, 617-628.

Sumprer, G. and Butter, E. Moral reasoning in hypothetical and actual situations. *Social Behaviour and Personality*, 1979, *6*, 205-209.

Snyder, C. and Clair, M. Does insecurity breed acceptance? Effects of trait and situational insecurity on acceptance of positive and negative diagnosis feedback. *Journal of Consulting and Clinical Psychology*, 1977, *48*, 843-850.

Snyder, M. and Monson, J. Persons, situations and control of social behavior. *Journal of Personality and Social Psychology*, 1975, *4*, 637-644.

Trickett, E. and Moos, R. Generality and specificity of student reactions in high school classrooms. *Adolescence*, 1970, *5*, 373-390.

Vanderkolk, C. Physiological reactions of black, Puerto-Rican, and white students in suggested ethnic encounters. *Journal of Social Psychology*, 1978, *104*, 107-114.

Vaughan, G. The trans-situational aspect of conforming behavior. *Journal of Personality*, 1964, *32*, 335-354.

Wicker, A. An examination of the 'other variables'. Explanation of attitude-behaviour inconsistency. *Journal of Personality and Social Psychology*, 1971, *19*, 18-30.

Wolk, S. and Bloom, D. The interactive effects of locus of control and situational stress upon performance accuracy and time. *Journal of Personality*, 1978, *46*, 279-298.

Woodside, A., and Bearden, W. Field theory applied to consumer behavior. *Research in Marketing*, 1978, *1* 303-330.

Woodside, A. and Fleck, R. The case approach to understanding brand choice. *Journal of Advertising Research*, 1979, 23-30.

Zuckerman, M. Development of a situation specific trait state test for the prediction and measurement of affective responses. *Journal of Consulting and Clinical Psychology,* 1977, *45,* 512-523.

1

Physiological Effects of Social Environments

Stewart Kiritz and Rudolf H. Moos*

The social environment has important effects on physiological processes. One can distinguish different dimensions of social environmental stimuli. These dimensions can have distinctive influences on physiological processes. The effects may differ from one individual to another. This review surveys some of the evidence supporting these assumptions, presents a model for conceptualizing social environment, and discusses implications for person-environment interaction.

INTRODUCTION

A physician advises a harried executive with high blood pressure to spend a week in the country. A pediatrician recommends that an underdeveloped, neglected child be sent to a foster home. A social worker encourages an asthmatic client to

---

*Psychosomatic Medicine, 1974, 36, 2, 96-114.

seek a job with more human contact. A cardiologist urges an administrator to delegate some of his responsibilities to others in his office. Each of these workers is, in part, responding to the belief that the social environment has important effects on physiological processes. In addition, their recommendations reflect the assumption that one can distinguish different types or dimensions of social environmental stimuli; that these dimensions can have distinctive influences on physiological processes; and that the effects may differ from one individual to another. We believe that these assumptions are valid. In this paper, we summarize some of the evidence supporting these assumptions, present a model for conceptualizing social environments, and discuss implications for person-environment interaction.

The measurement of the environment is a relatively recent development in psychology. Dissatisfaction with trait conceptualizations of personality is, in part, responsible for recent interest in environmental variables. This dissatisfaction stems from the low correlations obtained between measures of personality traits and validity criteria, and from growing evidence that substantial portions of the variance in response to questionnaires and in behavior may be accounted for by situational variables (1). Recent studies indicate that the variance accounted for by consistent differences among settings and by the interaction between setting characteristics and personal characteristics is generally as great or greater than the variance accounted for by consistent differences among persons (2, 3). In addition a number of studies have demonstrated that substantial differences may occur in the behavior of the same persons, when they are in different settings or milieus (4).

There are six major methods by which human environments have been assessed and characterized (5). 1) Ecological analyses, including geographical, meteorological, and architectural variables; 2) behavior settings, which are characterized as having both ecological and behavioral properties; 3) organizational structure, such as size/staffing ratios and average salary levels; 4) personal and behavioral characteristics of the individual members of a particular environment, e.g., average age, socioeconomic status; 5) functional analyses of environments in terms of social reinforcement contingencies; and 6) psychosocial characteristics and organizational climate, including, in particular, perceived social climate.

Measurement of the perceived social climate is a recent and particularly promising field for the systematic investigation of the general norms, values, and other psychosocial characteristics of diverse environments. Moos and his associates have studied nine types of environments extensively and have developed perceived climate scales for each of these environments: treatment environments such as 1) psychiatric wards (6) and 2) community-oriented treatment programs (7); "total" environments including 3) correctional institutions (8) and 4) military basic training companies (9); educational environments including 5) college dormitories (10) and 6) junior and senior high school classrooms (11); 7) primary work group environments (12); 8) therapeutic and task-oriented groups (13); and 9) families (14).

Each of the scales (which contain approximately ten dimensions) discriminates among environmental units, shows good profile stability, and has been or is in the process of being standardized on extensive normative samples.

The construction of the scales was inspired by the premise that environments, like people, have unique personalities. Just as some individuals are usually experienced by their associates as warm and supportive, some environments are felt to be supportive by their members. Some individuals are bossy and controlling; similarly, some environments are extremely controlling. Order and structure are important to many people; correspondingly, many environments emphasize regularity, system, and order.

An important aspect of this work is that similar dimensions are relevant to each of the nine types of environments and that these dimensions resemble those which have been found by other investigators. Moos conceptualizes three basic types of dimensions which characterize and discriminate among different subunits in each of the nine types of environments. (1) *Relationship* dimensions assess the extent to which individuals are involved in the environment and the extent to which they help and support each other. Examples are *involvement, affiliation, peer cohesion, staff support,* and *expressiveness.* (2) *Personal development* dimensions assess the basic directions along which personal development and self-enhancement tend to occur in the particular environment. Although an *autonomy* or *independence* dimension appears in all the environments, the exact nature of other personal development dimensions vary somewhat among the nine environments studied, depending on their functions. For example, on psychiatric wards and community-oriented treatment programs a dimension of *practical orientation* occurs which does not appear in military companies. *Responsibility* is also conceptualized as a personal development dimension. Finally, (3) *system maintenance* and *system change* dimensions are relatively similar across the nine environments. The basic dimensions are *order* and *organization, clarity* and *control.* An additional dimension in work environments is *work pressure,* and a dimension of *innovation* or *change* is identified in educational, work, and small group environments.

There is some initial evidence that these dimensions are related to important criteria such as morale and treatment outcome and that they may be applicable cross-culturally.

Finally, many of the dimensions found by Moos are strikingly similar to those found by other workers, (15-19), indicating that they may be salient characteristics in a wide variety of different social milieus.

In this review we shall survey some evidence concerning the physiological effects of selected dimensions of the social environment from each of the three categories as conceptualized above. Although the dimensions were derived from questionnaires concerning the perception of an environment by participants in the system, there is no inherent reason why information relevant to the identified dimensions could not be obtained by outside observers. The fact that the dimensions discriminate among environment subunits, and their apparent generality across environments and investigators make them promising candidates for the study of the relationship between environment and physiological responses. Their derivation from individuals' perceptions of environmental influences, rather than from "objective" stimulus factors is also important, especially in light of the evidence that individual differences in defenses and coping strategies can affect physiological responses to the same situation (20-22).

After summarizing evidence for the relationship of physiological changes and perceived social environmental dimensions, we discuss the interaction of environmental and individual variables and conclude with a discusson of the utility of measuring perceived social climate for the diagnosis and treatment of person and environment. In this paper we hope to offer and illustrate what we believe to be a useful framework by which social environments can be conceptualized and assessed.

RELATIONSHIP DIMENSIONS

Support

There is abundant evidence that *support* is a crucial dimension of the psychosocial environment, especially with regard to maturing organisms. Spitz' classic study of Foundling Home vs. Nursery (23, 24) related maternal and social deprivation to increased infant mortality, susceptibility to disease, retardation in growth, and failure to achieve developmental milestones. Spitz studied 130 infants in two institutions with comparable quality of food and levels of hygiene. In Foundling Home, the infants were cared for by nurses whereas in Nursery, the infants were cared for by their mothers. In contrast to Nursery children, Foundling Home children showed extreme susceptibility to disease. Almost all the children had histories of intestinal infection despite the fact the Foundling Home maintained excellent conditions of hygiene, including bottle sterilization. Contrary to what would be expected, older children—those who had been in Foundling Home longer—were more likely to die during a measles epidemic than younger children. In addition, growth levels, talking, and walking were severely retarded in the Foundling Home children.

MacCarthy and Booth (25) describe a syndrome which, in some respects, resembles Spitz' "hospitalism" but occurs in children living at home with their parents. The most prominent abnormalities are dwarfism and subnormal weight/height ratio, with evidence of little if any malnutrition. Other symptoms are skin changes suggestive of hypothyroidism, and such behavioral features as inability to play, bodily neglect, apathy, and subnormal intelligence levels. In a study of ten mothers of these children, seven were judged by a child psychiatrist to have rejecting attitudes towards their children. Two of the remaining mothers were judged "inadequate" by the authors, one because of subnormal intellience and the other because of neurotic depression. In most cases the symptoms, including the dwarfism, reversed themselves when the child was removed from home and placed in the hospital, where, presumably, the staff had at least a minimally supportive attitude.

Powell et al. (26, 27) studied 13 children initially believed to have idiopathic hypopituitarism. Interviews with parents revealed histories of emotional deprivation. About half the parents were divorced or separated and almost all the fathers spent little time at home. The children were all short for their ages and manifested polydipsia, polyphagia, and retardation of speech. Deficiencies in ACTH and growth hormone were found in a majority of cases. The physical symptoms and the hormonal deficiencies reversed themselves when the children were removed from home and placed in a convalescent hospital.

Reinhart and Drash (28) give a detailed account of a female fraternal twin who stopped growing normally between the ages of 6 and 12 months. During this time her mother was suffering from clinical depression and the child was forced to spend numerous weekends with relatives while her brother remained at home. Psychiatric interviews revealed that initial differences in activity levels had led to differential treatment of the twins and eventually hostility and deprivation directed toward the female. At age 7½ the girl was placed in special classes where she was given a great deal of attention by the teacher and a nurse. She began to grow rapidly during this period, both physically and intellectually, and by age 13½ she had reached approximately the same developmental level as her normal brother.

Some authors (29) criticize the assertion that it is deprivation of maternal love or support which is responsible for the physical, emotional and intellectual abnormalities in children such as those described above. Instead, they argue that a deficiency in the amount of stimulation, (visual, tactile, vestibular, or social) required for normal development is chiefly to blame. There is evidence from the animal literature that handling can increase developmental and growth rates (30), and much of the evidence cited above is amenable to the hypothesis of insufficient stimulation. However, we believe that the most reasonable interpretation of the available data is that both certain kinds and certain quantities of stimuli are required for normal development. Some of these kinds of stimuli, occurring predictably from the same persons and in sufficient quantity, are what is meant by a supportive psychosocial environment, particularly for infants and young children.

We have provided evidence that insufficient support is associated with retarded growth and other physical and behavioral abnormalities in the infant and young child. Lack of support also has varied physiological concomitants in maturity. Malmo et al. (31), for example, found that psychiatric patients experienced decreased muscular tension following praise, whereas sustained muscular tension followed criticism by an experimenter. Van Heijningen (32) observed that rejection by a loved one frequently preceded the clinical emergence of coronary disease.

The loss of a mate can represent a sudden severe loss of support. Parkes et al. (33) followed the death rates of 4,486 widowers of 55 years of age and older for nine years following the death of their wives in 1957. Of these, 213 died during the first six months of bereavement, 40% over the expected death rate for married men of the same ages. Death rate from degenerative heart disease was 67% above expected. The mortality rate dropped to that of married men after the first year. Since only 22.5% of the husbands' deaths were from the same cause as their wives' deaths, it is unlikely that a jointly unfavorable environment was the chief cause of the phenomenon. The authors argue that "the emotional effects of bereavement with the concomitant changes in psychoendocrine functions" accounted for the increased death rate.

An interesting study by Robertson and Suinn (34) demonstrated that mutual understanding, or empathy, on the part of stroke patients and their families is related to the patients' rate of rehabilitation. Both the patient and his family were administered 30-item Q-sorts including statements reflecting various positive and negative attitudes toward the illness. The family's ability to predict how the patient would sort the items correlated 0.43 with the patient's rate of progress, as judged by his physical therapist.

In a related investigation, Thoroughman et al. (35) studied two groups of patients with intractable duodenal ulcer and other intractable diseases—those who had good results in surgery and those who had poor results. The latter group scored higher on a scale of environmental deprivation which included such factors as emotional impoverishment within the family and in other social relations, providing further evidence that support is beneficial in recovery from serious illness.

Cohesion

Social environments may be distinguished on the basis of how close their members feel toward each other. Such a dimension can be called *cohesion* or *affiliation*. There is some evidence that cohesion or affiliation results in (a) physiological covariation between the members of an environment; (b) reduction of stress responses.

Physiological Covariation

A number of studies of individuals working closely together show a clustering on certain physiological indices. Mason and Brady (36) cite a study (37) in which three closely working crewmen on a long B-52 flight reached similar elevated 17 OHCS levels of 13 mg per day. They report another study in which clustering of 17 OHCS levels occurred in two all-girl groups in a volunteer ward of college age adults. A mixed-sex ward had no clustering, even after five weeks. This suggests that something more than simple exposure to a common physical environment was responsible for the clustering in the all-girl groups. In a third study (38) covariation of menstrual cycles occurred in best friends and roommates in a college dormitory. Randomly selected pairs of girls in the dorm did not show covariation.

Other findings support the conclusion that affiliation and not simply exposure to common environmental stimuli is responsible for physiological covariation. Kaplan, Burch, and Bloom (39) found that pairs of individuals who like each other were more likely to experience physiological involvement (GSR) when talking to each other in a group than were pairs of individuals with neutral attitudes towards each other. This was also true for pairs of individuals who disliked each other, however, suggesting that positive or negative involvement with others in one's psychosocial environment promotes physiological covariation (see below).

Several studies of the physiological responses of patient and therapist found significant covariation in their physiological responses, e.g., DiMascio et al. (40) found a positive correlation between patient and therapist heart rate responses. Coleman, Greenblatt, and Soloman (41) over a period of 44 interviews found that the patient's heart rate was highest during anxiety, lowest during depression and intermediate during hostility; the therapist manifested the same heart rate responses as the patient. DiMascio, Boyd, and Greenblatt (42) found that both patient and therapist manifested higher heart rates during interviews characterized by tension and lower rates during interviews characterized by tension release. Kaplan et al. (39) suggest that physiological covariation could provide an index of rapport in psychotherapy.

Reduction of Stress Responses

There is experimental evidence suggesting that *cohesion* or *affiliation* reduces susceptibility to physiological stress responses. Back and Bogdonoff (43) report a group experiment in which free fatty acid (FFA) levels were higher in subjects who were recruited individually than in subjects who were prior acquaintances. In another experiment, group agreement led to a decline in FFA level, when the groups were performing more difficult tasks. Gostell and Leiderman (44) monitored GSR during a Crutchfield type conformity experiment. There was some evidence that deviation from the group led to a rise in skin potential, and that when a previously deviant member conformed, his skin potential dropped. These experiments suggest that a cohesive group is less susceptible to stress, and also that a member may experience stress responses if he deviates from the norms of an otherwise cohesive group.

Involvement

Closely related to *affiliation* and *cohesion* is the notion of *involvement* in one's social environment. Involvement implies a strong affective relationship towards the members and goals of the environment in which one is participating. Clearly some environments are more involving for most of their members than other environments. Moos and his associates have shown that it is possible to distinguish among college dormitories (10) and psychiatric wards (6) in terms of the members' perceived levels of involvement. Involvement as conceived of in this manner has yet to be related to physiological variables. There is interesting data, however, concerning the physiological correlates of one individual's involvement with another person, or his involvement in a task or situation.

We have already cited the study by Kaplan, Burch, and Bloom (39) in which medical students who liked or disliked each other exhibited significantly more GSR response when interacting than those who had neutral attitudes, e.g., were uninvolved with each other. A study by Nowlin, Eisdorfer, Bogdonoff, and Nichols (45) found covariation in elevation of free fatty acid and heart rate in pairs of subjects, one of whom was listening passively while the other was answering personal questions. Postexperimental questionnaires and interviews revealed that the passive subjects felt involved in the responses of their partners. In this study, involvement in the emotion-arousing task of another person is associated with covariation of physiological responses.

Williams, Kimball, and Williard (46) had hypertensives and normals answer five personal questions displayed on cards by an interviewer. The questions were displayed two times and the interviewer was either warm and interactive or neutral and noninteractive. The subjects exhibited higher diastolic blood pressure in the high interaction than the low interaction interview, even though the content of the two interviews was found to be about the same. The authors concur with Singer (47) that it is the "transactional involvement with other people, rather than the sheer content of what people talk about in interviews . . ." that is the relevant variable for correlation with "concomitant physiologic behavior."

Mason and Brady believe that pituitary-adrenal cortical activity can be seen, in part, "as a general index of interaction or involvement of the animal with the physical and social environment" (36, p. 9). They present evidence that the mere presence of others with whom to interact leads to increases in 17 OHCS excretion. In one experiment, rhesus monkeys were housed in individual cages in the same room. When the cages were removed to separate rooms, 17 OHCS excretion dropped. In another study, a hospitalized patient experienced a drop in 17 OHCS excretion every weekend, when he was transferred from a bustling surgical ward to a quiet hospital across the street.

In an extensive review of psychoendocrine research Mason (20) concluded, in part, that elevation of 17 OHCS level is not related to a highly specific affective state, such as stress or anxiety, but "appears to reflect a relatively undifferentiated state of emotional arousal or involvement, perhaps in anticipation of activity or coping" (p. 596).

Back and Bogdonoff (43) manipulated the "importance" of an aircraft identification task by varying instructions. In the "important" condition, Naval ROTC cadets were told that the task was very relevant to their training and that the results would be given to their commanding officer. There was a significantly greater rise in free fatty acid during the important than the unimportant condition.

It is particularly necessary, in the case of the dimension of involvement, to consider the interaction of personal and environmental variables, to be discussed more fully below. This is examplified in a study of Friedman et al. (48). They studied the 17 OHCS excretion of parents of children hospitalized with leukemia and found that the steroid levels of the 43 subjects tended to remain within a relatively restricted range, even when the parents were exposed to severe acute stresses associated with the illnesses of their children. However, the subjects' rankings of mean daily 17 OHCS excretion were related to how emotionally vulnerable they were to their children's plight, as judged by the experimenters. The most vulnerable parents exhibited the most extreme elevations of 17 OHCS. Those parents who were judged to use denial defenses had the lowest 17 OHCS levels. These parents were, in a sense, insulated by their psychological defenses from involvement in the social environment which included their fatally ill children. Thus even extreme environmental press for involvement can be countermanded, at least temporarily, by the individual's defenses and other stable personality mechanisms.

To summarize, we believe that these findings support the general hypothesis that environments characterized by higher levels of involvement will be associated with increased hormonal activity in their members. It will be necessary to study more enduring environments, however, in order to determine the physiological effects of sustained participation in a highly involving environment, where physiological and psychological adaptation effects might be crucial. We suspect that the most extremely involving environments have a relatively short duration; little is known about the physiological effects of differences lower on the involvement continuum. Finally, individual personality differences must be taken into account, because of the evidence that some individuals can avoid becoming involved even in environments with extreme pressure for involvement.

PERSONAL DEVELOPMENT DIMENSIONS: RESPONSIBILITY

Within a given social environment, roles and duties may exert differential pressures on the members. Some individuals may have greater *responsibility* than others. Some environments may have greater press towards responsibility for all members than others, e.g., a disarmament conference vs a cookout. There is evidence that responsibility is a dimension of the social environment which is associated with physiological changes in its members. Miller (49) indicated that responsibility was one of the factors leading to increased blood or urine 17 OHCS in military aviators. Miller et al. (50) studied 17 OHCS secretion and self-reported anxiety in the 2-man crews of jet aircraft during practice carrier landings. The pilots who had exclusive control of the aircraft had greater corticosteroid responses than the passive radiomen. This was so even though the radiomen reported greater anxiety on the self-report measures than the pilots. Another study found 17-20% higher heart rates in active pilots manning aircraft than in the passive copilots at their sides; the difference reversed itself when pilot A became passenger and pilot B took charge of the aircraft (51). French and Caplan found that responsibility for other individuals was positively correlated with diastolic blood pressure in employees of the Goddard Space Flight Center (52). Morris (53) reports a greater incidence of coronary atherosclerosis in drivers than in fare collectors in London buses. Here differences in responsibility and differences in physical activity are confounded, however.

There is a considerable experimental literature supporting the claim that the active, responsible member of a pair of individuals subjected to the same threat experiences greater physiological stress. Brady showed that if a pair of monkeys is subjected to a noxious stimulus in an avoidance situation, the *executive* monkey (the one permitted to press a lever to avoid the noxious stimulus to both monkeys) develops gastrointestinal lesions, whereas the other animal does not (54). Davis and Berry (55) applied this experimental method to pairs of human subjects, one of whom was able to press a button to avoid a strong auditory stimulus to both, while the other was a passive control. The executive members of the pairs had significantly greater amplitude of gastric contractions than the control subjects.

On the other hand, Weiss found that being the "executive" rat that learns an avoidance task to avert a shock to itself and to a passive "yoked" animal reduces the amount of stomach lesions when the task is simple and clear-cut. When the task is difficult and produces conflict, however, "responsibility" greatly increases the amount of lesions (56).

Returning to observational studies, a number of workers find greater stress responses in those in positions of greater responsibility. Marchbanks (57) studying B-52 aircraft, found the highest level of 17 OHCS excretion in aircraft commanders. Bourne et al. (58) found that mean urine 17 OHCS excretion was considerably higher for two officers than for ten enlisted men in a team of soldiers during a time of anticipated attack by Viet Cong. They also found that on the day of the expected attack an officer and a radio operator showed a rise in 17 OHCS whereas the other men showed a drop. Bourne et al. suggest that leadership, responsibility, and response to the demands of the group are all involved in elevation of urinary 17 OHCS.

When key NASA personnel were suddenly given additional responsibility, for example, put in charge of a project or called upon to deliver a report at a high-level meeting, sharp increases in heart rate resulted. The medical director of the project concluded "something we simply call responsibility often results in extremely high cardiac rates and is probably a much larger factor in rate changes than was formerly thought" (51). Even top executives, men with long experiences in the handling of responsibility, almost invariably had marked ECG increases when given additional responsibility.

Responsibility is a complex social environmental dimension. The evidence demonstrates that responsibility for the avoidance of threat to oneself or others, as in the Brady paradigm, can produce physiological stress responses. The evidence further suggests that assuming responsibility for more symbolic outcomes, as in the NASA study, can also cause physiological changes. Thus, even that sort of responsibility which might be seen as ego-enhancing and positive by the individual may elicit increased activation of some physiological mechanisms. Such activation is not invariably aversive for the organism, however. More work is necessary to determine when, for example, heart rate or corticosteroid elevation becomes detrimental, and what aspects of responsibility are most conducive to aversive levels of activation.

SYSTEM MAINTENANCE AND SYSTEM CHANGE DIMENSIONS

Work Pressure

Rosenman and Friedman have identified a behavior pattern which they believe is associated with high risk of coronary artery disease (59). The coronary-prone behavior pattern, designated Type-A as distinguished from the low risk Type-B, is characterized by extreme aggressiveness, competitiveness, and ambition, along with feelings of restlessness and, in particular, a profound sense of time urgency. In one prospective study over 3,400 men free from coronary disease at intake were rated Type-A or Type-B without knowledge of any biological data. Two and one half years later, Type-A men aged 39 to 49 years had 6.5 times the incidence of coronary disease as Type-B men in the same age group (60).

Although their early work has been criticized on methodological grounds (61), Rosenman and Friedman's findings have, in general, received support in the critical literature (62).

Type-A persons are engaged in "a relatively chronic struggle to obtain an unlimited number of relatively poorly defined things from the environment in the shortest period of time" (59). Rosenman and Friedman believe that the contemporary Western environment encourages development of this pattern. They also believe that the pattern represents the interaction of environmental influences and individual susceptibilities and argue that it may not occur if a Type-A individual is removed to a Type-B setting.

Caffrey (63, 64) has shown that it is possible to rank environments according to the degree to which their "atmospheres" encourage Type-A behavior. He had three physicians rate 14 Benedictine and 11 Trappist monasteries using paired comparison methods. The individual monks were also rated by their Abbots and peers. Caffrey then showed that groups of monks having a higher proportion of Type-A's living in Type-A environments and taking a high fat diet had the highest prevalence rates of coronary disease.

Caffrey's work, in connection with that of Rosenman and Friedman, points to the existence of a dimension of the social environment associated with coronary artery disease, at least in predisposed individuals. We propose the term *work pressure* to include the sort of environmental influences which encourage the sense of time urgency experienced by the Type-A personality.

The association of work pressure and coronary disease gains support from elsewhere in the literature. Kritsikis (65) studied 150 men with angina pectoris in a population of over 4,000 industrial workers in Berlin. He found that work in the pressured environment of the conveyor-line system was associated with the disease. Sales (66) has reviewed the evidence and holds that work overload is implicated as a precursor of cardiovascular disease. French and Caplan studied 22 white collar males at NASA over a three day period. They telemetered heart rate, measured serum cholesterol and had observers rate behavior. "Quantitative work overload," as indexed by the observers' ratings, was positively correlated with serum cholesterol. Subjective indices of work overload were correlated with both physiological measures (52).

Other studies demonstrate relationships between work pressure and physiological changes. Mjasnikov (67) referred to the high prevalence of essential hypertension among telephone operators working in a large exchange, under pressure to complete a large number of transactions per unit time, with few rest periods. Froberg and his associates (68) studied twelve young female invoicing clerks during four consecutive days when performing their usual work in their usual environment. On the first experimental days, piece-wages were added to the subjects' salaries. Urine samples taken three times a day were assayed for adrenaline and noradrenaline. During the salaried control days, the work output was very close to normal. On the piece-work days, which the girls described as hurried and tiring, the mean adrenaline and noradrenaline excretion rose by 40% and 27%, respectively.

There is evidence that the dimension of work pressure can be distinguished in practice as well as in principle from the responsibility dimension discussed above. Type-A pattern and Responsibility emerged as distinct factors in a principal components factor analysis conducted on the monastery data (63). In addition, Rosenman reports that no correlation has been found between Type-A pattern and occupational position (59). It would seem reasonable, however, that when both responsibility and work pressure are high, coronary risk would be maximal. And in fact the monks with the highest incidence of coronary disease, the Benedictine priests, achieved the highest ratings of Type-A pattern and of responsibility.

Another finding supports the hypothesis that responsibility and work pressure have a cumulative, noxious effect. Air traffic controllers, who work under extreme time pressure and with the responsibility for hundreds of lives, have higher risk and earlier onset of hypertension and peptic ulcer than a control group of second class airmen (59).

The question of the relative contribution of work pressure and responsibility in the etiology of cardiovascular disease and peptic ulcers remains to be answered. But it is the possibility of conceptualizing distinct social environmental dimensions which allows us to frame this sort of question, with its implications for the differential diagnosis and treatment of persons and environments.

Clarity

Environments which are low in *clarity* seem to promote physiological changes. Ostfeld and Shekelle (70), in a review of the literature on pressor responses, found that uncertainty, along with the possibility of physical or psychological harm and the inability to flee until the situation was clarified, was associated with increased blood pressure.

Reiser et al. (71) manipulated the relative uncertainty as to the exact nature of an interview situation in an army subject population. Half of the subjects were immediately reassured as to the benign nature of the procedure and half were not given this information. The uninformed subjects experienced a greater rise in either blood pressure or cardiac output during the interview (depending on another experimental manipulation) than the informed subjects. In a number of experiments, differential GSR and heart rate responses occurred when temporal uncertainty concerning the receipt of a painful shock was manipulated. The data are complex, and reflect the subjects' extreme sensitivity to variations in experimental procedure (72).

French (73) uncovered a number of interesting relationships between "role ambiguity," physiological measures, and other social environmental factors in a study at Kennedy Space Center. For example, role ambiguity was positively correlated with serum cortisol, but only in those subjects reporting poor relationships with their work group subordinates. Those with good relations did not have elevated cortisol.

Mason and Brady distinguish between two stress response patterns. Elevated 17 OHCS and norepinephrine characterized rhesus monkeys' physiological behavior in a conditioned avoidance situation with a known noxious stimulus. In contrast, elevated epinephrine occurred in the ten minute intervals preceding experimental sessions characterized as "varied and unpredictable" (36).

Ruben et al. (74) in a study of naval underwater demolition training found that introduction of new equipment and procedures about the use of which the men were uncertain, produced elevations in serum cortisol. "The determination of transient increases in adrenal cortical activities . . . seemed to be the anticipation of an unknown situation more than the inherent difficulty or stress of the situation itself."

Change

Closely related to clarity is the dimension of *change*. There is considerable evidence that individuals experiencing change in their environment undergo physiological changes and are more susceptible to disease.

In his review paper, Mason (20) implicates change and novelty as influences leading to 17 OHCS elevation. Men being laid off their jobs experience elevated blood pressure until they are settled in their new jobs for a period of time (75). Syme et al. (76) found that independent of diet, cigarette smoking, parental longevity, etc., geographically and occupationally mobile men had incidences of coronary artery disease respectively two and three times that of stable men. Bruhn et al. (77) found that educational and occupational mobility distinguished coronary men and control subjects even when age, I.Q., and social class were equated.

Marlowe discovered a large increase in death rate among old people being relocated after the closing of Modesto State Hospital (California) in 1969. Of the 349 survivors, 45.6% had physically deteriorated, 24.9% had improved and 29.5% had remained unchanged (78). Other geriatric workers report similar findings (79).

Numerous studies by Holmes, Rahe, and others (80) relate increased incidence of disease to increases in frequency of life changes as measured by the Schedule of Recent Experiences (SRE). In one study, for example, tubercular patients were found to have experienced the greatest number of life changes in the final two years prior to onset of their illnesses. Another study (81) found a 0.648 correlation between number of life changes and seriousness of illness in a group of 232 patients.

Certainly some changes must reduce stress rather than increase it. An example might be the replacement of a hated boss by a well-liked one, or a reduction of working hours in an overworked staff. Examination of the Holmes data leaves some questions concerning the relative contribution of "positive" changes and negative changes or "stressors" to the correlations between change and illness in studies utilizing the SRE. It is Holmes' contention, however, that it is change *per se*, "by evoking adaptive efforts by the human organism that are faulty in kind and duration," that "lowers 'bodily resistance' and enhances the probability of disease occurrence" (82).

THE INTERACTION OF PERSONALITY AND SOCIAL ENVIRONMENTAL VARIABLES

We believe that the social environment can be seen as a system of interpersonal stimuli exerting influences on the individuals within that environment. These influences or *presses* can be categorized (see above) as relationship dimensions, personal development dimensions, and system maintenance and system change dimensions. Although individuals are sufficiently similar and environmental stimuli sufficiently potent that the individuals within a given environment can make reliable and consistent judgments about the magnitude of a given dimension, the social stimuli do not act directly on the individual. Rather, it is his *perception* of the social environment, as mediated by personality variables, role and status relationships, and his behavior within the environment, which affects him directly, and in turn affects his personality and behavior (see Fig. 1.1).

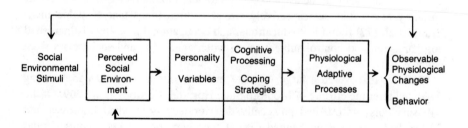

Figure 1.1.   Conceptual model for the relationship between social environmental stimuli and observable physiological changes.

There are two main ways in which individual and social environmental variables can interact, leading to differential physiological responses.

(1) Given the same social environmental presses, two individuals may perceive different levels of the same dimension. For example, a paranoid person might, because of his suspicious cognitive style, perceive little support in an office seen as very supportive by his less suspicious coworkers. In time, of

course, this individual might very well come to receive less support than his peers, thus confirming his perceptions.

(2) Given similar perceptions two individuals may still differ in their affective and adaptational responses to these perceptions. Person A and person B, for example, work in an office which both perceive as offering little support. Person A has a loving wife and children, many friends, and a history of interpersonal successes. Person B is recently divorced and has long regarded himself as an interpersonal failure. It is likely that A and B would differ in their emotional responses to the office environment, and in their resources for coping with or defending against the emotions aroused.

In practice it is often difficult or impossible to distinguish the operation of an individual's perceptions of a situation from his defenses or coping strategies. However, without attempting to differentiate perceptual from coping factors, it is possible to point to a number of studies which illustrate the interaction of personality and environmental variables.

Several studies demonstrate that certain psychological defenses, especially denial, are associated with reduced 17 OHCS secretion in what one would expect to be extremely stressful situations.

Katz et al. (83) assayed 17 OHCS in 30 women in hospitals with breast tumors, several days before biopsy was to be performed to determine if the patients had breast cancer. The subjects showed a broad range of 17 OHCS secretion, none of them remarkably high. In addition, the subjects were extensively interviewed to determine their patterns of coping and "adequacy of ego defenses." The three measures of adequacy of defenses were significantly correlated with 17 OHCS; those with the least effective defenses showed the greatest 17 OHCS elevations. Patients who used one of the three defensive patterns labeled "stoicism-fatalism," "prayer and faith," and "denial with rationalization" experienced considerably less disruption, as judged by the steroid hormone secretion rates and the psychiatric rating scores. These findings recall the study of leukemic children by Friedman et al. (48), in which those parents who utilized denial had low levels of 17 OHCS secretion. Summarizing much of this literature, Mason (20) points out that too much reliance has been placed "upon situational criteria of 'stress' and upon mean group values, with a relative lack of systematic evaluation of the important and often marked individual differences between subjects in their emotional and defensive reactions to a given situation" (p. 676).

Other studies underline the importance of the interaction of personality and social environmental variables. Kasl and Cobb's (75) study showed that men being laid off work experienced elevated blood pressure until they were settled in their new jobs. Men with higher ego resilience, lower irritation and higher self-esteem experienced a quicker drop in blood pressure after going on a new job. There is a small body of literature linking *status incongruence* with disease. Cobb (84), for example, showed that individuals who were equal on the two status dimensions of education (personality variable) and income (environmental variable) have a much lower incidence of rheumatoid arthritis than those whose education was higher than their income.

Several studies from Lazarus' laboratory (85, 86) suggest that a person's style of ego defenses can affect his response to an unpleasant film. Subjects with high scores on MMPI-derived scales of denial and represssion experienced greater GSR evaluations when shown a silent version of the film "Subincision," which displays painful native puberty rites. In addition, it seems that denial/reaction formation film commentary and introduction conditions were effective in reducing arousal with the high denial but ineffective with the low denial subjects.

Measurement of the perceived social climate could, we believe, provide an important bridge between "objective" environmental stimulus configurations and individual physiological responses, which are mediated by differences in perception, coping, and defense. The most efficient predictor of a person's physiological behavior in a given environment may consist of how he perceives that environment.

CONCLUSIONS

In conclusion, the evidence cited above supports the view that social environmental factors have pronounced effects on human physiological processes. It is difficult at this point to make conclusions about the specific kinds of effects associated with different psychosocial stimuli, given the diversity of the populations, variables, and settings considered. It does appear, however, that the social stimuli associated with the relationship dimensions of *support, cohesion,* and *affiliation* generally have positive effects—enhancing normal development and reducing recovery time from illness, for example. Personal Development and System Maintenance and System Change dimensions such as *responsibility, work pressure* and *change* can increase the likelihood of stress and disease.

One might argue that most of these physiological changes could be subsumed under the rubric of "stress" and that the evidence merely indicates that too little support and clarity or too much responsibility and change lead to stress responses. Individuals perform best within restricted ranges of levels of the social environmental variables. The physiological changes could represent the concomitants of adaptive efforts taking place when a perceived social environmental dimension is not of optimal magnitude. Rather than labeling the process by means of the global term stress, however, we feel that it is more fruitful to investigate the specific physiological effects of distinct social environmental dimensions.

For example, different dimensions may give rise to different affects. In a study of eight military basic training programs, Moos (unpublished data) found that low *officer support* is correlated with hostility, whereas low *peer cohesion* is correlated with depression. There is evidence that different affective states are associated with distinguishable psychophysiological responses (87, 88). Thus social milieu dimensions might relate differentially to different physiological effects. This would be in accord with the notion of stimulus specificity—that distinct stimuli (or situations) tend to evoke characteristic psychophysiological responses (89).

For these reasons we feel it would be more useful to study the complex relationships between environmental dimensions, personality characteristics, and physiological indices without imposing *a priori* conceptual closure. Social environmental measurement might enable us to predict which environments would be aversive or beneficial for particular groups of individuals, or to suggest specific and limited changes in environments in which a disproportionate number of individuals suffer from particular symptoms.

There is another important motivation for studying social environmental variables in connection with physiological processes. The social milieu may *moderate* or *mediate* the physiological effects of other ecological characteristics of an environment. Kellam et al. (90) found that schizophrenics treated with phenothiazines exhibited differential improvement rates depending on the environmental characteristics of their wards. Thus the milieu may moderate the effects of drugs. Moos (91) found that changes in size and staffing had differential effects on a number of perceived climate dimensions in hospital wards. Perhaps the physiological effects of such ecological variables as population density are mediated by changes in the social milieu. If this is the case, then it might be possible to effect important changes in an environment by manipulating the social milieu directly, when population density, size, or staffing ratios are fixed at aversive levels.

Finally, the measurement of perceived social climate has specific relevance for the issue of person-environment congruence. Social environmental profiles could enable the clinician, physician, or social worker familiar with the probable physiological effects of various configurations of dimensions to aid their clients in making prudent choices or in effecting beneficial changes in their social milieus. The systematic measurement of social climates could become an important aspect of the work of the diagnostician.

SUMMARY

Recent studies indicate the importance of settings or environmental variables in accounting for individual behavior. Measurement of the perceived social climate is a particularly promising way of investigating the psychosocial characteristics of diverse environments. Three types of dimensions characterize and discriminate among environmental subunits: relationship dimensions, personal development dimensions, and system maintenance and system change dimensions. There is evidence that dimensions within each of these three categories have important effects on physiological processes. Individual and social environmental variables can interact, leading to differential physiological responses. Measurement of perceived social climate could provide a bridge between "objective" environmental stimuli and individual physiological responses, which are mediated by differences in perception, coping, and defense. Measurement might enable us to make environments healthier in general, or improve person-environment fit for specific groups of individuals.

REFERENCES

1. Mischel, W: *Personality and Assessment,* New York, Wiley 1968
2. Endler, NS, Hunt, JMcV: S-R inventories of hostility and comparisons of the proportions of variance from persons, responses and situations for hostility and anxiousness. *J Pers Soc Psychol* 9:309-315, 1968
3. Moos, RH: Sources of variance in responses to questionnaires and in behavior. *J Abnorm Psychol* 74:405-412, 1969
4. Barker, RG, Gump, PV: *Big School Small School.* Stanford, Stanford Univ. Press, 1964
5. Moos, RH: *Systems for the assessment and classification of human environments: An overview,* in Issues in Social Ecology: Human Milieus. Palo Alto, National Press Books, 1974 (Edited by RH Moos, and PM Insel)
6. Moos, RH: *Ward Atmosphere Scale Manual.* Palo Alto, Consulting Psychologists Press, 1974
7. Moos, RH: *Community-Oriented Programs Environment Scale Manual.* Palo Alto, Consulting Psychologists Press, 1974
8. Moos, RH: *Correctional Institutions Environment Scale Manual.* Palo Alto Consulting Psychologists Press, 1974
9. Moos, RH: *Military Company Environment Inventory.* Palo Alto, Consulting Psychologists Press, 1974.
10. Moos, RH, Gerst, M: *University Residence Environment Scale Manual.* Palo Alto, Consulting Psychologists Press, 1974
11. Moos, RH, Trickett, E: *Classroom Environment Scale Manual.* Palo Alto, Consulting Psychologists Press, 1974
12. Insel, PM, Moos, RH: *Work Environment Scale.* Palo Alto, Social Ecology Laboratory. Department of Psychiatry, Stanford University, Stanford, California, 1972
13. Moos, RH, Humphrey, B: *Group Environment Scale Technical Report.* Palo Alto, Social Ecology Laboratory, Department of Psychiatry, Stanford University, Stanford, California, 1973
14. Moos, RH: *Family Environment Scale.* Palo Alto, Social Ecology Laboratory, Department of Psychiatry, Stanford University, Stanford, California, 1974
15. Stern, GG: *People in Context: Measuring Person Environment Congruence in Education and Industry.* New York, Wiley, 1970

16. Pace, CR: *College and University Environment Scales,* Technical Manual, Second ed. Princeton, Educational Testing Service, 1969
17. Peterson, R, Centra, J, Hartnett, R, Linn, R: *Institutional Functioning Inventory: Preliminary technical manual.* Princeton, Educational Testing Service, 1970
18. Halpin, AW, Croft, DB: *The organizational climate of schools.* Chicago, University of Chicago Midwest Administration Center, 1963
19. Walberg, HJ: *Social environment as a mediator of classroom learning.* J Educ Psychol 60:443-448, 1969
20. Mason, J: A review of psychoendocrine research on the pituary-adrenal cortical system. *Psychosom Med* 30:576-607, 1968
21. Mason, J: A review of psychoendocrine research on the sympathetic-adrenal medullary system. *Psychosom Med* 30:631-653, 1968
22. Mason, J: A review of psychoendocrine research on the pituitary-thyroid system. *Psychosom Med* 30:661-681, 1968
23. Spitz, RA: *Hospitalism, Psychoanalytic Study of the Child,* Volume 1. New York, International Universities Press, 1945
24. Spitz, RA: *Hospitalism: a follow-up report, Psychoanalytic Study of the Child,* Volume 2. New York, International Universities Press, 1947
25. MacCarthy, D, Booth, EM: Parental rejection and stunting of growth. *J Psychosom Res* 14:259-265, 1970
26. Powell, GF, Brasel, JA, Blizzard, RM: Emotional deprivation and growth retardation stimulating idiopathic hypopituitarism. I. Clinical evaluation of the syndrome. *New Eng J Med* 276:1271-1278, 1967
27. Powell, GF, Brasel, JA, Raiti, S, Blizzard, RM: Emotional deprivation and growth retardation stimulating idiopathic hypopituitarism. II. Endrocrinologic evaluation of the syndrome. *New Eng J Med* 276:1279-1283, 1967
28. Reinhart, J, Drash, A: Psychosocial dwarfism: environmental induced recovery. *Psychosom Med* 31:165-172, 1969
29. Casler, L: Maternal deprivation: a critical review of the literature. *Mon Soc Res Child Devel* 26:1-64, 1961
30. Levine, S: *Stimulation in Infancy, Frontiers of Psychological Research.* San Francisco, WH Freeman 1966 (Edited by S Coopersmith)
31. Malmo, RB, Boag, T, Smith, A: Physiological study of personal interaction. *Psychosom Med* 19:105-119, 1957
32. Van Heijningen, K: Psychodynamic factors in acute myocardial infarction. *Int J Psychoanal* 47:370-374, 1966
33. Parkes, CM, Benjamin, B, Fitzgerald, RG: Broken heart: a statistical study of increased mortality among widowers. *Brit Med J* 1:740-743, 1969
34. Robertson, EK, Suinn, RM: The determination of rate progress of stroke patients through empathy measures of patient and family. *J Psychosom Res* 12:189-191, 1968
35. Thoroughman, JC, Pascal, GR, Jarvis, JR, Crutcher, JR: A study of psychological factors in patients with surgically intractable duodenal ulcer and those with other intractable disorders. *Psychosom Med* 29:273-278, 1967
36. Mason, J, Brady, J: The sensitivity of psychoendocrine systems to social and physical environment, in *Psychobiological Approaches to Social Behavior.* Stanford, Stanford University Press, 1964 (Edited by PH Leiderman, D Shapiro)

37. Mason, J: Psychological influences on the pituitary adrenal-cortical system. *Rec Prog Horm Res* 15:345-389, 1959

38. McClintock, M: Menstrual synchrony and suppression. Nature 229:244-245, 1971

39. Kaplan, HB, Burch, NR, Bloom, SW: Physiological covariation and sociometric relationships in small peer groups, in *Psychobiological Approaches to Social Behavior*. Stanford, Stanford University Press 1964 (Edited by PH Leiderman, D Shapiro)

40. Dimascio, A, Boyd, R, Greenblatt, M, Solomon, HC: The psychiatric interview: a sociophysiologic study. *Dis Nerv Sys* 16:2-7, 1955

41. Coleman, R, Greenblatt, M, Solomon, HC: Physiological evidence of rapport during psychotherapeutic interviews. *Dis Nerv Sys* 17:2-8, 1956

42. Dimascio. A, Boyd, R, Greenblatt, M: Physiological correlates of tension and antagonism during psychotherapy: a study of "interpersonal physiology." *Psychosom Med* 19:99-104, 1957

43. Back, KW, Bogdonoff, M: Plasma lipid responses to leadership, conformity, and deviation, in *Psychobiological Approaches to Social Behavior*. Stanford, Stanford University Press 1964 (Edited by PH Leiderman, D Shapiro)

44. Costell, RM, Leiderman, PH: Physiological concomitants of social stress: the effects of conformity pressure. *Psychosom Med* 30:298-310, 1968

45. Nowlin, JB, Eisdorfer, C, Bogdonoff, MD, Nichols, CR: Physiological response to active and passive participation in a two person interaction. *Psychosom Med* 30:87-94, 1968

46. Williams, R, Kimball, C, Williard, H: The influence of interpersonal interaction on diagnostic blood pressure. *Psychosom Med* 34:194-198, 1972

47. Singer, MT: Enduring personality styles and responses to stress. Trans Assn Life Ins *Med Dir of Amer* 51:150-173, 1967

48. Friedman, S, Mason, J, Hamburg, D: Urinary 17-hydroxycortico-steroid levels in parents of children with neoplastic disease. *Psychosom Med* 25:364-376, 1963

49. Miller, R: Secretion of 17-hydroxycorticosteroids (17-OHCS) in military aviators as an index of response to stress: a review. *Aerospace Med* 39:498-501, 1968

50. Miller, R, Ruben, R, Clark, B, Crawford, W, Arthur, R: The stress of aircraft carrier landings. Part 1: cortical steroid responses in naval aviators. *Psychosom Med* 32:581-588, 1970

51. Responsibility brings jump in pulse. *JAMA* 201:23, 1967

52. French, J, Caplan, R: Organizational stress and individual strain, the *The Failure of Success*. New York, AMACOM, 1973 (Edited by A Marrow), pp 30-66

53. Morris, J: Occupation and coronary heart disease. *AMA Arch Int Med* 104:903-907, 1959

54. Brady, J, Porter, R, Conrad, D, Mason, J: Avoidance behavior and the development of gastroduodenal ulcers. *J Exp Anal Behav* 1:69-72, 1958

55. Davis, R, Berry, F: Gastrointestinal reaction during a noise avoidance task. *Psychol Rep* 12:135-137, 1963

56. Weiss, J: Effects of punishing the coping response (conflict) on stress pathology in rats. *J Comp Physiol Psychol* 77:14-22, 1971

57. Marchbanks, V: Flying stress and urinary 17-hydroxycorticosteroid levels during twenty-four hour missions. *Aerospace Med* 31:639-643, 1960

58. Bourne, P, Rose, R, Mason, J: 17-OHCS levels in combat: Special forces "A" team under threat of attack. *Arch Gen Psychia* 19:135-140, 1968

59. Friedman, M: *Pathogenesis of Coronary Artery Disease.* New York, McGraw-Hill 1969

60. Rosenman, R, Friedman, M, Straus, R, Wurm, M, Jenkins, D, Messinger, H: Coronary heart disease in the Western Collaborative Group study: a follow-up experience of two years. *JAMA* 195:86-92, 1966

61. Keith, R: Personality and coronary heart disease: a review. *J Chron Dis* 19:1231-1243, 1966

62. Jenkins, CD: Psychologic and social precursors of coronary disease. *New Eng J Med* 284:244-255, 307-317, 1971

63. Caffrey, B: Reliability and validity of personality and behavioral measures in a study of coronary heart disease. *J Chron Dis* 21:191-204, 1968

64. Caffrey, B: Behavior patterns and personality characteristics related to prevalence rates of coronary heart disease in American monks. *J Chron Dis*22:93-103, 1969

65. Kritsikis, S. Heinemann, A, Eitner, S: Die Angina pectoris im Aspekt ihrer Korrelation mit biologischer Disposition, psychologischen und soziologischen Einflussfaktoren. *Deutsch Gesundh* 23:1878-1885, 1968

66. Sales, S: Organizational role as a risk factor in coronary disease. *Admin Sci Quarter* 14:325-336, 1969

67. Majasnikov, A: Discussion, in *Proc Joint WHO-Czech Cardio Soc Symp Pathogen Essential Hypertension,* Prague, 1961

68. Froberg, J, Karlsson, C, Levi, L, Lidberg, L: Physiological and biochemical stress reactions induced by psychosocial stimuli, in *Society, Stress and Disease.* London, Oxford University Press, 1971 (Volume 1, edited by L Levi)

69. Cobb, S, Rose, R: Hypertension, peptic ulcer and diabetes in air traffic controllers, *JAMA* 224:489-492, 1973

70. Ostfeld, M, Shekelle, R: Psychological variables and blood pressure, *The Epidemiology of Hypertension,* Proceedings of an International Symposium. New York, Grune & Stratton, 1967 (Edited by J Stamler, R Stamler, T Pullman)

71. Reiser, M, Reeves, R, Armington, J: Effects of variations in laboratory procedure and experiments upon the ballistocardiogram, blood pressure, and heart rate in healthy young men. *Psychosom Med* 17:185-199, 1955

72. Bowers, K: The effects of UCS temporal uncertainty on heart rate and pain. *Psychophys* 8:382-389, 1971

73. French, J: Person role fit. *Occupat Ment Health* 3:13-20, 1973

74. Ruben, R, Rahe, R, Ransom, A, Clark, B: Adrenal cortical activity changes during underwater demolition team training. *Psychosom Med* 31:553-564, 1969

75. Kasl, S, Cobb, S: Blood pressure changes in men undergoing job loss: a preliminary report. *Psychosom Med* 32:19-38, 1970

76. Syme, S, Borhani, N, Buechley, R: Cultural mobility and coronary heart disease in an urban area. *Am J Epidem* 82:334-346, 1965

77. Bruhn, J, Chandler, B, Miller, M, Wolf, S, Lynn, T: Social aspects of coronary heart disease in two adjacent, ethnically different communities. *Am J Pub Health* 56:1493-1506, 1966

78. Marlowe, D: Personal communication with Stewart Kiritz, 1972

79. Blanker, M: Environmental change and the aging individual. *Gerontologist* 7:101-105, 1967

80. Rahe, R, Mahan, J, Arthur, R: Prediction of near future health changes from subjects' preceding life changes. *J Psychosom Res* 114:401-406, 1970

81. Wyler, A, Masuda, M, Holmes, J: Magnitude of life events and seriousness of illness. *Psychosom Med* 33:115-122, 1971

82. Holmes, T, Masuda, M: Life changes and illness susceptibility. Unpublished manuscript, 1970.

83. Katz, J, Weiner, H, Gallagher, T, Hellman, L: Stress, distress and ego defenses. *Arch Gen Psych* 23:131-142, 1970

84. Cobb, S, Kasl, S, Chen, E, Christenfeld, R: Some psychological and sociological characteristics of patients hospitalized for rheumatoid arthritis, hypertension and duodenal ulcer. *J Chron Dis* 18:1259-1278, 1965

85. Speisman, J, Lazarus, R, Mordkoff, A, Davison, L: Experimental reduction of stress based on ego-defense theory. *J Abnorm Soc Psychol* 68:367-380, 1964

86. Lazarus, R, Alfert, E: Short-circuiting of threat by experimentally altering cognitive appraisal. *J Abnorm Soc Psychol* 69:195-205, 1964

87. Ax, A: The physiological differentiation between fear and anger in humans. *Psychosom Med* 15:433-422, 1953

88. Ekman, P, Malmstrom, E, Friesen, W: Heart rate changes with facial displays of surprise and disgust. Unpublished manuscript, 1972

89. Engel, B, Moos, R: The generality of specificity. Arch Gen Psych 16: 574-581, 1967

90. Kellam, S, Goldberg, S, Schooler, N, Berman, A, Schmelzer, J: Ward atmosphere and outcome of treatment of acute schizophrenia. *J Psych Res* 5:145-163, 1967

91. Moos, RH: *Evaluating treatment environments: a social ecological approach.* New York, Wiley, 1974

2
Emotional Impact of a Task and its Setting on Work Performance of Screeners and Nonscreeners*
Albert Mehrabian and Suzanne West

This study explored desire to work at a task in a situation as a function of situational pleasantness, situational arousing quality, task pleasantness, and task arousing quality. The hypotheses which were based on a general theory of environmental psychology accounted for a major portion of the results. These showed that (1) the pleasantness of a task and/or situation is a direct correlate of desire to work, (2) the arousing quality of any situation-task combination is inversely related to the desire to work, and (3) desire to work is not affected by the arousing quality of a situation-task combination when that combination is pleasant, and decreases with arousing quality of a situation-task combination when that combination is either neutral (in terms of pleasantness) or unpleasant. An individual difference measure of stimulus screening was employed to assess characteristic differences in automatic screening of irrelevant stimuli and rapid habituation to distracting stimuli. Nonscreeners who are generally more arousable reported a lower desire to work than screeners. Further, as predicted, nonscreeners, compared with screeners, reported a greater desire to work at pleasant situation-task combinations. However, compared with screeners, they reported less desire to work at neutral (in terms of pleasantness) or unpleasant tasks.

Reprinted with persmission of the authors and publisher from: Perceptual and Motor Skills, 1977, 45, 895-909. ©Perceptual Motor Skills 1977.

Various theories of work performance have consistently emphasized the importance of the level of a worker's arousal on his task performance. (Duffy, 1962; Hebb, 1955; Malmo, 1959). A worker's arousal level may in turn be a function of the physical and social environment in which he performs the task, the complexity, novelty, or difficulty of the task itself (Schroder, Driver, & Steufert, 1967), and other internal factors associated with his personality, e.g., anxiety, or temporary emotional state, e.g., hunger, fatigue.

A general theory of work performance which employs the concept of arousal therefore requires one set of hypotheses relating situational and task characteristics to a worker's arousal levels and a second set of hypotheses relating arousal levels to task performance. In short, a framework is necessary in which arousal serves as a mediating variable.

Such a framework was proposed by Mehrabian (1976a) and Mehrabian and Russell (1974a, Chap. 6) in which environmental and task attributes were related to arousal using the concept of "information rate." This concept is based on information theory and serves to characterize the intensity, complexity, novelty, moving (versus static), and unpredictable quality of situational (or task) stimuli impinging on the worker. A measure of information rate has been proposed and shown to be reliable for characterizing any situation or stimulus, e.g., task, and furthermore, has been shown to be a direct correlate of arousal (Mehrabian & Russell, 1974b). In other words, according to the information rate-arousal hypothesis, a worker's arousal level is a direct function of the information rate in the situation where he performs a task plus the information rate of the task he performs. For instance, arousal levels are expected to be higher when (a) other workers are present compared to when the worker is alone, (b) the worker is required to move about and be physically active compared to when he is confined to the same position, the same location, or the same routine movement sequences, (c) the work setting is colorful and changeable compared to when it is monochromatic and static, (d) the task itself is novel, complex, difficult, or unpredictable compared to being familiar, simple, easy, or predictable. In short, the concept of information rate together with the information rate-arousal hypothesis allows one easily to conceptualize the effects of a myriad of situational and task variables on the worker's arousal level.

The second necessary link relating arousal level to performance historically has been provided by the Yerkes-Dodson (1908) hypothesis. According to this hypothesis, performance at a task is an inverted-U function of the worker's arousal level, such that performance is maximized at moderate levels of arousal and impaired at extremes of arousal. An examination of the literature which purportedly supports the Yerkes-Dodson hypothesis, however, indicates that experimental manipulations of arousal in the various studies almost invariably confounded task or situational arousing quality with its pleasantness-unpleasantness. Thus, for instance, in experiments which compared the effects of high versus low noise on performance (Bindra, 1959; Boggs & Simon, 1968;

Broadbent, 1954; Woodhead, 1966), the arousing high-noise condition that hindered performance was more unpleasant than the less arousing low-noise condition.

Based on available experimental findings, the present modification of the Yerkes-Dodson hypothesis includes the following propositions. First, pleasure-displeasure and level of arousal are orthogonal dimensions which can be used to describe a variety of specific emotional states, e.g., pleasure and high arousal = excitement, elation; pleasure and low arousal = relaxation, comfort; displeasure and high arousal = anxiety, fear; displeasure and low arousal = boredom, fatigue. Indeed, it has been shown that the three orthogonal dimensions of pleasure-displeasure, level of arousal, and dominance-submissiveness provide a comprehensive base for the description of all emotional states (Mehrabian & Russell, 1974a, Chap. 2; Russell & Mehrabian, 1977). Second, pleasure-displeasure is a direct correlate of work performance, irrespective of the source of pleasant or unpleasant feelings. For example, pleasure or displeasure may be due to task, setting in which it is performed, quality of interactions with coworkers, internal states induced by hunger, thirst, alcohol, drugs, illness, or fatigue, or due to a reward or punishment system that is contingent or noncontingent on work performance. Third, pleasure-displeasure and level of arousal interact in determining work performance: performance increases with level of arousal when the worker feels pleasure, but performance decreases with level of arousal when the worker feels displeasure. Preliminary evidence for these two hypotheses, i.e., the main effect of pleasure, and the interaction of Pleasure × Arousal, on performance, was reported by Russell and Mehrabian (1975). The present study was designed to incorporate a more comprehensive sample of tasks and settings so as to provide a more thorough evaluation of these two hypotheses.

Given the central importance of the concept of arousal in conceptualizing work performance, individual differences in stimulus screening (the converse of arousability) are useful in explaining characteristic differences in performance as a function of task or situational information rate. The dimension of stimulus screening characterizes individual differences in automatic, i.e., not conceptual or intentional, screening of irrelevant stimuli, and rapid habituation to distracting stimuli. The information rate-arousal hypothesis implies that screeners (those who by definition are more likely to impose a hierarchy of importance or pattern on the various components of a situation) in effect reduce the information rate of situations and are consequently less arousable than nonscreeners. In short, screeners, compared with nonscreeners, are more selective in information processing and are therefore generally less arousable. Mehrabian (1977) provided a questionnaire measure for this individual difference dimension and showed that level of stimulus screening is indeed a general information-processing characteristic of an individual that helps describe his consistent pattern of cognitive functioning in all sense modalities. As expected, Mehrabian (1976b) found that nonscreeners are more arousable than screeners and that nonscreening is directly correlated with other available individual difference measures, e.g., trait-anxiety or neuroticism, which are known to provide partial assessment of arousability.

To develop hypotheses for nonscreening-screening in relation to performance, one need only note the theoretically parallel function of (a) nonscreening (arousability) and (b) arousing quality (information rate) of the task or work situation. Both sets of variables have the result of increasing arousal state of the worker and should therefore exhibit similar patterns of relationships (alone or in combination with other independent effects) in determining level of performance.

Since there is no hypothesized main effect of arousing quality of task and/or situation on work performance, no main effect of stimulus screening on performance is predicted. However, pleasure and arousal levels are hypothesized to interact in determining performance. In parallel fashion, it is hypothesized that the pleasantness of a situation or task interacts with stimulus screening to determine performance, as follows: Performance increases with level of arousability (nonscreening) when workers feel pleasure, but performance decreases with arousability (nonscreening) when workers feel displeasure. Stated differently, nonscreeners are expected to perform better than screeners in pleasant tasks and/or situations, whereas nonscreenrs are expected to perform worse than screeners in unpleasant tasks and/or situations.

The following two studies were designed to prepare appropriately scaled tasks and work situations and to test the proposed hypotheses using subjects' reports of their desire to work at various tasks in different situations. Subjects in the first study rated verbal descriptions of various tasks and situations for pleasant-unpleasant and arousing-unarousing qualities. These ratings were employed to generate experimental conditions of three levels each of situational pleasantness, situation arousing quality, task pleasantness, and task-arousing quality. Subjects in the second study read descriptions of various situation-task combinations and reported the extent of their desire to work at each of these.

STUDY ONE: VERBAL RATINGS OF PLEASANTNESS AND AROUSING QUALITY OF VARIOUS WORK SITUATIONS AND TASKS

The tasks consisted of one-sentence written descriptions and included such things as reading a story to a small child, practicing a piece on a musical instrument, or planning and organizing a back-packing trip. Care was taken in writing these descriptions such that a wide range of pleasure-displeasure and levels of arousal would be induced by the tasks. Settings in which tasks might be performed also consisted of written descriptions about six sentences in length and included as great a diversity of settings as possible.

Method

Subjects. These were 270 University of California undergraduates who participated in the study as part of a course requirement.

Procedure. Each subject rated approximately six situations and nine tasks in a random order. Written instructions preceding each task or situation asked the subject to read the description and then to take a few minutes to imagine it clearly and to get into the mood of that task or situation. The subject then used a set of semantic differential type scales from Mehrabian and Russell (1974a, Appendix B) to rate the task or the setting. The six adjective pairs assessing pleasure-displeasure included happy-unhappy and pleased-annoyed. The six adjective pairs assessing level of arousal included stimulated-relaxed and wide awake-sleepy. These adjective pairs were randomly interspersed in a larger list. To rate a given task or situation, subjects checked any one of the nine spaces (-4 to $+4$ rating scale) between an adjective pair. A subject's report of pleasure-displeasure to a given task or a given situation was obtained by simply averaging his responses to the six pleasure items. A similar average arousal response was computed from the six arousal items.

Results

There was a total of 117 descriptions of tasks and 81 descriptions of situations and each of these was rated by 20 different subjects. Average ratings of pleasure and arousal across subjects were used to select 36 situations which fit the following conditions: Three levels of situational pleasantness (pleasant, neutral, unpleasant) × three levels of situation arousing quality (high, moderate, low) × four replications. Average pleasure and arousal ratings of the nine (3 × 3) situation conditions across four replications are given in Table 2.1.

Average pleasure and arousal ratings of tasks across subjects were used to select 36 tasks which fit the following conditions: three levels of task pleasantness (pleasant, neutral, unpleasant) × three levels of task arousing quality (high, moderate, low) × four replications. Average ratings of pleasure and arousal for the nine (3 × 3) task conditions across four replications are also given in Table 2.1. Examination of Table 2.1 shows that, for instance, the four situations assigned to the high-pleasure and high-arousal condition were rated as having an average pleasantness value of 2.02 and an average arousing quality of .78. It is seen that the pleasantness ratings of all high-pleasure situations were relatively constant across high, moderate, and low arousal conditions, and so on. In other words, situations were selected to combine orthogonally three levels of situational pleasantness with each of three levels of situation arousing quality. The same can be inferred from the ratings of pleasantness and arousing quality of tasks given in Table 2.1.

The results given in Table 2.1 confirm that a wide selection of tasks and situations had been devised to systematically tap all possible combinations of task (or situation) pleasatenss and arousing quality. That is, the sampling of situations and tasks in terms of their respective emotion-inducing qualities did not favor certain combinations of emotional qualities through disproportionate representation in the various cells.

Table 2.1 Mean Rated Pleasantness-Unpleasantness and Arousing Quality of Situations and Tasks

		Arousing Quality			
		High	Moderate	Low	Average
Mean Ratings of Situational Pleasantness for Each of Nine Cells					
Pleasantness	High	2.02	2.03	2.01	2.02
	Moderate	−.09	−.07	.03	−.04
	Low	−1.45	−1.53	−1.49	−1.49
Mean Ratings of Situational Arousing Quality for Each of Nine Cells					
Pleasantness	High	.78	−.01	−.99	
	Moderate	.68	−.05	−1.00	
	Low	.75	.00	−.95	
	Average	.74	−.02	−.98	
Mean Ratings of Task Pleasantness for Each of Nine Cells					
Pleasantness	High	1.12	1.11	1.04	1.09
	Moderate	.00	−.12	−.01	−.04
	Low	−1.09	−1.11	−1.10	−1.10
Mean Ratings of Task Arousing Quality for Each of Nine Cells					
Pleasantness	High	.99	.05	−.87	
	Moderate	.96	−.02	−.93	
	Low	.97	.03	−.93	
	Average	.97	.02	−.91	

Note.—Values entered in each cell are averages based on the four replications.

Computation of pleasantness and arousing-quality scores for situation-task combinations. Theoretically, the important variables affecting work performance (or desire to work in the present study) are the level of pleasantness of a particular situation-task combination and the level of arousing quality of that situation-task combination. Combined situation-task pleasantness is some function of situational pleasantness and task pleasantness, and, similarly, combined situation-task arousing quality is some function of situation arousing quality and task arousing quality. A sample of 80 subjects was used to assess these ''combined'' scores by having each subject read nine different situation-task descriptions and by asking him simply to note his emotional reaction to each combination using the pleasure and arousal scales (Mehrabian & Russell, 1974a, Appendix B) already noted. Eighty subjects × 9 combinations per subject produced 720 observations of combined scores as functions of emotion-inducing qualities of tasks and settings. A multiple regression analysis was used to assess pleasantness scores reported by subjects for various situation-task combinations as a function of situational pleasantness and task pleasantness of those combinations. The result is summarized below for independent variables measured on −4 to +4 scales of pleasantness—those used for calculating means in Table 2.1.

Situation-task pleasantness = 2.46 Situation pleasantness + 1.10 Task pleasantness

In terms of actual beta weights, i.e., coefficients calculated for standardized variables, the coefficient of situational pleasantness (.35) is 3.5 times the magnitude of the coefficient for task pleasantness (.10).

A second multiple regression analysis was used to assess arousing-quality scores reported by subjects for various situation-task combinations as a function of situation arousing quality and task arousing quality of each combination. The result is as follows:

Situation-task arousing quality = .27 Situation arousing quality
+ .08 Task arousing quality,

where the independent effects are measured on −4 to +4 scales of arousing quality—those used for calculating means in Table 2.1. In terms of actual beta weights, the coefficient of situational arousing quality (.072) is approximately 3.5 times the coefficient for task arousing quality (.023). It is seen, then, that the emotional impact of the situation was approximately 3.5 times that of the task with which it was combined. This finding may be due to the fact that task descriptions were generally shorter than situation descriptions. The preceding two regression equations were used to calculate a situation-task pleasantness score and a situation-task arousing quality score for each situation-task combination. The latter two scores were employed as well in the following regression analyses to test the theoretical predictions.

STUDY TWO: VERBAL REPORTS OF DESIRE TO WORK AT TASKS AND IN SITUATIONS SYSTEMATICALLY VARYING IN THEIR PLEASANTNESS AND AROUSING QUALITIES

This experiment was conducted entirely with verbal questionnaires. The various experimental conditions consisted of written descriptions of tasks and the situations in which they were to be performed. After reading the descriptions of a given task and its setting, subjects used a questionnaire to indicate their desire to work at that task in that situation. Desire to work, then, was the dependent measure.

Method

Subjects. A sample of 180 University of California undergraduates served as subjects as part of a course requirement.

Materials and procedures. Study Two provided descriptions of 36 situations which conformed to the following pattern: 3 levels of situational pleasantness × 3 levels of situation arousing quality × 4 replications. Study One also provided 36 descriptions of tasks which conformed to the following pattern: 3 levels of task pleasantness × 3 levels of task arousing quality × 4 replications. The various descriptions of tasks and situations were paired so as to yield a complete factorial design of the following conditions: 3 situational pleasantness × 3 situation arousing quality × 3 task pleasantness × 3 task arousing quality × 16 replications.

For example, one experimental condition which consisted of a combination of a situation plus a task, together with introductory instructions was as follows:

> On this page you will find descriptions of a *task* and of a *place*. Please read the descriptions very carefully and take a few minutes to get into the mood of really being in this place and doing this task. Try to imagine as best you can the details of the task and situation described below as if *you were really in this situation doing this task*. Then, answer the five questions on the next page according to the instructions.
>
> The room you are in has thick carpeting and a Moroccan tapestry of rich colors hung on the wall. Several pieces of heavy wood furniture are placed casually in the room and an excellent stereo system is playing soft, peaceful background music.
>
> You are helping a friend of yours who teaches elementary school to correct tests.

After reading the preceding instructions and situation and task descriptions, the subject read the following instruction: For each of the five questions below, please circle the number that best describes your preference.

> (+) 1. Would you like to do this task in this place?
> (−) 2. Would you avoid being in this place doing this task?
> (+) 3. Would you like to be in this place doing this task?
> (−) 4. Would you avoid doing this task in this place?
> (+) 5. How much time would you like to spend doing this task in this place? Circle one: none; a few minutes; half an hour; one hour; a few hours; a day; a few days; many days; many months.

Responses to Questions 1 and 3 were recorded on a scale ranging from −4 (absolutely not) to 0 (indifferent) to +4 (definitely so). Responses to Questions 2 and 4 were recorded on a scale ranging from −4 (absolutely no avoidance) to 0 (indifferent) to +4 (definitely avoid). For Question 5, "none" was scored as zero, "a few minutes" = 1, . . . to "many months" = 8. Thus, there were two negatively worded and three positively worded items, and of course subjects were not given the signs for direction of scoring which precede the questions above. As can be seen, the questions were worded so as to balance out the emphasis on task versus situation.

Each subject performed this sequence (of reading a task plus situational description and indicating his preference for it) a total of nine times for nine different task and situation combinations. The nine situational and task combinations administered to each subject contained all possible combinations of situation arousing quality and task arousing quality but were restricted to only a single level of task, and of situational, pleasantness. In other words, situation and task arousing quality were within-subjects factors, whereas situational and task pleasantness were between-subjects factors. As Table 2.1 indicates, the pleasantness conditions of situation and task were more distinctive than the situation and task arousing qualities. Since between-subjects factors generally yield weaker results than within-subjects factors, this assignment of factors was designed partially to counteract the differences in the magnitudes of the pleasantness and arousal factors.

The order of presentation of tasks and situations in the written descriptions was counterbalanced across subjects. Thus, each subject received four conditions in which descriptions of task preceded those of situation and five conditions in which descriptions of task followed those of situation, or he received five conditions in which tasks preceded situations and four in which tasks followed situations.

The order of presentation of the nine (3 situation arousing quality × 3 task arousing quality) conditions was counterbalanced across subjects. Sets of 20 subjects each received one of the nine (3 situational pleasantness × 3 task pleasantness) between-subjects conditions, thus necessitating the use of nine such groups.

After completing the nine pages consisting of each of nine conditions, subjects also responded to Mehrabian's (1976b) 40-item questionnaire measure of Stimulus Screening.

Results

Reliability of dependent measure. Five questions were used to assess a subject's desire to work at a particular task in a particular situation. Intercorrelations among these five questions across subjects and conditions (180 × 9 = 1,620 observations per correlation) ranged in absolute value from .57 to .84, with an average absolute value of .71, showing that these items may be summed algebraically to yield a single dependent measure.

Indeed, the Kuder-Richardson (1937) reliability coefficient for a scale composed of these five questions is .92 and is sufficiently high to justify the combination of these five into a single "desire to work" dependent measure. Since the standard deviations of responses to the five questions were comparable, the responses of each subject to the five questions for a given condition were simply algebraically summed to obtain his over-all "desire to work" score for that condition.

Regression analyses of the effects of the experimental conditions. A "desire to work" score was available for each subject from his responses to each situation-task combination. This constituted the dependent variable in the regression analyses. Three separate multiple regression analyses were used to assess the main and interactive effects of (a) situational pleasantness and situational arousing quality on desire to work, (b) task pleasantness and task arousing quality on desire to work, and (c) situational-task pleasantness and situation-task arousing quality on desire to work. Nie, *et al.* (1975) detailed the rationale and procedures for assessing interaction effects using multiple regression methods. For certain kinds of data all the information that is usually obtained from analyses of variance can be obtained using regression techniques without, however, the need to eliminate cases to achieve cell proportionality. The .01 level significant effects obtained from the three regression analyses are summarized in the following three equations which have been written for standardized variables.

1. Work = .36 Situational pleasantness − .11 Situation arousing quality
          + .08 Situational pleasantness × Situation arousing quality
2. Work = .10 Task Pleasantness + (.05 Task pleasantness × Task arousing quality)
3. Work = .37 Situation-task pleasantness − .10 Situation-task arousing quality
          + .09 Situation-task pleasantness × Situation-task arousing quality

The effect noted in parenthesis in Equation 2 only achieved the .05 level of significance but was included for comparison with the corresponding effects in Equations 1 and 3. The multiple regression coefficients for Equations 1, 2, and 3 were .37, .12, and .39, respectively. It is noted that the pleasantness of a situation, the pleasantness of a task, and the pleasantness of a situation-task combination contributed directly and significantly to the desire to work. Although the arousing quality of a situation in Equation 1 related inversely to desire to work, that is, detracted from the desire to work, no significant corresponding effect was found for the arousing quality of a task in Equation 2. Nevertheless, Equation 3 shows that the combined situation-task arousing quality did in fact significantly and inversely relate to desire to work. Finally all three equations show that, as predicted, pleasantness and arousing quality interact in determining desire to work. As already noted, the key determinant of desire to work in each experimental condition was the emotional impact of the situation-task combination. Thus cell means corresponding to the interaction effect of Equation 3 are theoretically the most relevant and are given in Fig. 2.1. The cell means in Fig. 2.1 were calculated by partitioning both the situation-task pleasantness and situation-task arousing quality variables at the 33 and 67 percentile levels.

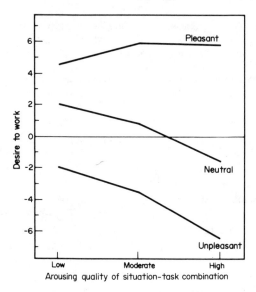

Figure 2.1 Desire to work as a function of pleasantness and arousing quality of situation-task combination. *Note:* Desire to work is a standardized variable with a mean of 0 and a standard deviation of 10. To compare simple effects of arousing quality at each level of pleasantness, note that *t* tests show cell mean differences exceeding 1.8 in absolute value to be significant at the .01 level.

For convenience, prior to calculation of regression equations and cell means reported in Fig. 2.1, the "desire to work" dependent measure was transformed into a standardized variable with a mean of 0 and a standard deviation of 10. To assess the simple effects of arousing quality, i.e., to compare cell means at each level of pleasantness, note that *t* tests indicate cell mean differences exceeding 1.8 in absolute value to be significant at the .01 level.

Regression analyses of the effects of the experimental conditions and stimulus screening. Having determined the effects of the experimental variables in the preceding section, the possible main and interactive effects of stimulus screening (the individual-difference measure) together with those due to pleasantness and arousing quality of task and situation were explored in a parallel set of three regression analyses.

Specifically, the three regression analyses explored the main and interactive effects of (a) situational pleasantness, situation arousing quality, and stimulus screening, (b) task pleasantness, task arousing quality, and stimulus screening, and (c) situation-task pleasantness, situation-task arousing quality, and stimulus screening on the desire to work. The .01 level significant effects obtained from the three regressions are summarized in the following three equations which have been written for standardized variables.

4. Work = 36 Situational pleasantness − .11 Situation arousing quality + .08 Stimulus screening + .08 Situational pleasantness × Situation arousing quality − .07 Situational pleasantness × Stimulus screening

5. Work = .09 Task pleasantness + (.05 Stimulus screening) + (.05 Task pleasantness × Task arousing quality)

6. Work = .37 Situation-task pleasantness − .10 Situation-task arousing quality + .06 Stimulus screening + .09 Situation-task pleasantness × Situation-task arousing quality − .09 Situation-task pleasantness × Stimulus screening

The effects in Equation 5 that are noted in parentheses only attained the .05 level of significance but are reported for comparison purposes. The multiple regression coefficients for Equations 4, 5, and 6 are .38, .11, and .41, respectively. It is seen that those with higher scores on stimulus screening, i.e., screeners as compared with nonscreeners, showed a greater desire to work, as evidenced by the positive relationship of stimulus screening to the dependent measure in all three equations. Equations 4 and 6 also show significance, in the same direction, for Pleasantness × Stimulus screening in determining desire to work. Once again, the theoretically most relevant variables are those characterizing the emotional impact of situation-task combinations. Thus cell means corresponding to the latter interaction are taken from the results reported in Equation 6 and are diagrammed in Fig. 2.2.

The cell means in Fig. 2.2 were calculated by partitioning both the situation-task pleasantness and the stimulus-screening variables at the 33 and 67 percentile levels. To assess the simple effects of stimulus screening, i.e., to compare cell means at each level of pleasantness, note that t tests indicate cell differences exceeding 1.8 in absolute value to be significant at the .01 level.

DISCUSSION

In the present framework desire to work is conceptualized as being a function of the pleasantness and arousing qualities of the task and of the situation in which work is performed. It was hypothesized that pleasantness of the work situation or task is a direct correlate of the desire to work. Further it was hypothesized that pleasantness of the work situation and/or task interacts with the arousing quality of work setting and/or task in determining the desire to work as follows: Desire to

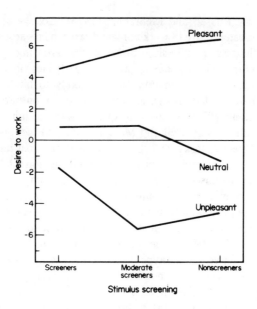

Figure 2.2.   Desire to work as a function of pleasantness of situation-task combination and stimulus screening level of the subject. *Note:* Desire to work is a standardized variable with a mean of 0 and a standard deviation of 10. To compare simple effects of stimulus screening at each level of pleasantness, note that *t* tests show cell mean differences exceeding 1.8 in absolute value to be significant at the .01 level.

work is directly correlated with arousing quality in pleasant situations and/or pleasant tasks, whereas the desire to work is inversely correlated with arousing quality in unpleasant work situations and/or unpleasant tasks.

Although separate analyses were performed to explore desire to work as functions of situational and task variables, it is the emotional impact of particular situation-task combinations which provides the most direct test of the proposed hypotheses. The corresponding results given in Equation 3 and Fig. 2.1 show that in fact both of the proposed hypotheses were supported. More pleasant situation-task combinations led to stronger expressions of desire to work among the subjects. This was the strongest and most consistent effect. Note the relative positions of the three lines corresponding to pleasant, neutral, and unpleasant situation-task combinations in Fig. 2.1. It is apparent that desire to work increases progressively with increases in the pleasantness of situation-task combinations.

To discuss the implications of the present findings for the hypothesized interaction of Pleasantness × Arousing quality, we must first consider the second main effect in Equation 3 which shows that desire to work was inversely related to the situation-task-arousing quality. This finding corroborates and supplements an earlier finding by Russell and Mehrabian (1975). College students in that study expressed a greater desire to work at mental tasks in less arousing settings.

The obtained inverse relationship between the arousing quality of the situation-task combination and desire to work indicates that tasks and/or situations that are high in information rate are likely to hinder performance relative to tasks and/or situations that are low in information rate.

This particular main effect of arousing quality was not hypothesized here, since the earlier finding by Russell and Mehrabian (1975) had been based on a limited sample of (mental) tasks, and it had been assumed that mental tasks are understandably hindered by highly arousing (high information rate) settings. The present results which are based on a very wide selection of physical, manual, and mental tasks show the earlier findings to have much general validity. That is, if information about the pleasantness of a task and/or its setting is not available, one is likely to be correct in predicting that performance will be lower when the tasks or the situations in which they are performed are higher in information rate.

The discrepancy between the hypothesized interaction of Pleasantness × Arousing quality and the corresponding results noted in Fig. 2.1 can now be understood in terms of the preceding main effect of arousing quality. It had been predicted that desire to work is (a) a direct correlate of arousing quality in pleasant settings and for pleasant tasks, whereas desire to work is (b) an inverse correlate of arousing quality in unpleasant settings and for unpleasant tasks. It is now seen that the inverse main effect of arousing quality served to attenuate the hypothesized simple effect (a) and magnify the hypothesized simple effect (b).

The findings in Fig. 2.1 show that, when the emotional impact of a situation-task combination is neither pleasant nor unpleasant, or when it is unpleasant, a worker's desire to perform (and we would infer, his level of performance) can be increased by *reducing* the information rate, e.g., complexity, changeable quality, or novelty, of the task itself or of the situation in which it is performed. In contrast, desire to work is not significantly influenced by the information rate of task and/or setting when the combined emotional impact of setting and task is strongly pleasant. Of course, the most reliable finding here is that one can increase a worker's desire to perform by modifying task or environmental qualities to increase their pleasantness.

Equation 6 provides the most direct test of the hypotheses for the effects of stimulus screening, since it is based on the over-all emotional impact of particular situation-task combinations. In proposing the hypotheses for stimulus screening, it was noted that nonscreening should produce a set of results analogous to those produced by arousing quality of situation-task combinations. Equation 6 shows this indeed to be the case. Thus, whereas situation-task-arousing quality related inversely to desire to work, screening related directly; that is, nonscreeners in general reported a lower desire to work than did screeners.

Once again, whereas the Situation-task pleasantness × Situation-task-arousing quality effect was significant and positive in Equation 6, the Situation-task pleasantness × Stimulus screening effect was significant and negative in that equation. The corresponding cell means were plotted in Fig. 2.2 with the abscissa ranging from high screeners on the left to low screeners (nonscreeners) on the right to facilitate comparison of the expected and parallel sets of results in Figs. 2.1 and 2.2. It is seen that for pleasant situation-task combinations, nonscreeners expressed a greater desire to work than screeners. However, the opposite is true when the situation-task combination is neutral or unpleasant in quality. These relationships in Fig. 2.2 are exactly as predicted when one compares the upper and lower thirds of subjects on the stimulus screening dimension, i.e., those referred to in the figure as screeners and nonscreeners. The only exception to the expected trends is the smaller cell mean (-5.63) for moderate screeners than nonscreeners (-4.66) in unpleasant situation-task combinations. A t test, however, does not show these two cell means differ significantly ($t = 1.18, p > .05$). Nevertheless, it is useful to note that the theoretically predicted relationships are more likely to be upheld for subjects with more extreme scores on the stimulus-screening dimension.

Practical implications of the findings summarized in Fig. 2.2 are simply summed up by noting that nonscreeners are more sensitive than screeners to the pleasant versus unpleasant quality of tasks and work settings. Thus, even though both nonscreeners' and screeners' desire to work (and we would expect, performance) can be improved by increasing the pleasantness of tasks and/or the environments in which they are performed, such improvement is expected to be even greater for the nonscreeners. Alternatively, when tasks and/or the situations in which they are to be performed are essentially unpleasant, e.g., hazardous, personnel administrators may selectively assign screeners to such tasks.

The present study relied on written descriptions of 36 situations and 36 tasks and on verbal reports of reactions to each of 16 replications of 81 experimental conditions. This method was employed because use of actual situations and tasks for a comprehensive test of the hypothesized general relationships would have been prohibitively expensive and time consuming. The findings with our method are admittedly preliminary; nevertheless, they highlight the consistency and importance of certain sets of relationships and should be of heuristic value for further experimentation with actual situations and tasks and experimental ratings of subjects' work performance.

REFERENCES

Bindra, D. *Motivation: a systematic reinterpretation.* New York: Ronald, 1959.
Boggs, D. H., & Simon, J. R. Differential effect of noise on tasks of varying complexity. *Journal of Applied Psychology,* 1968, 52, 148-153.

Broadbent, D. E. Some effects of noise on visual performance. *Quarterly Journal of Experimental Psychology*, 1954, 6, 1-5.

Duffy, E. *Activation and behavior*. New York: Wiley, 1962.

Hebb, D. O. Drives and the C.N.S. (conceptual nervous system). *Psychological Review*, 1955, 62, 243-254.

Kuder, G. F., & Richardson, M. W. The theory of estimation of test reliability. *Psychometrika*, 1937, 2, 151-160.

Malmo, R. B. Activation: a neuro-psychological dimension. *Psychological Review*, 1959, 66, 367-386.

Mehrabian, A. *Public places and private spaces: the psychology of work, play, and living environments*. New York: Basic Books, 1976. (a)

Mehrabian, A. Manual for the questionnaire measure of stimulus screening and arousability. UCLA, 1976. (b)

Mehrabian, A. A questionnaire measure of individual differences in stimulus screening and associated differences in arousability. *Environmental Psychology and Nonverbal Behavior*, 1977, 1, 89-103.

Mehrabian, A., & Russell, J. A. *An approach to environmental psychology*. Cambridge, Mass.: M.I.T. Press, 1974. (a)

Mehrabian, A., & Russell, J. A. A verbal measure of information rate for studies in environmental psychology. *Environment and Behavior*, 1974, 6, 233-252. (b)

Nie, N. H., Hull, C. H., Jenkins, J. G., Steinbrenner, K., & Bent, D. H. *Statistical package for the social sciences*. (2nd ed.) New York: McGraw-Hill, 1975.

Russell, J. A., & Mehrabian, A. Task, setting, and personality variables affecting the desire to work. *Journal of Applied Psychology*, 1975, 60, 518-520.

Russell, J. A., & Mehrabian, A. Evidence for a three-factory theory of emotions. *Journal of Research in Personality*, 1977, 11.

Schroder, H. M., Driver, M. J., & Streufert, S. *Human information processing*. New York: Holt, Rinehart & Winston, 1967.

Woodhead, M. M. An effect of noise on the distribution of attention. *Journal of Applied Psychology*, 1966, 50, 296-299.

Yerkes, R. M., & Dodson, J. D. The relation of strength of stimulus to rapidity of habit-formation. *Journal of Comparative and Neurological Psychology*, 1908, 18, 459-482.

3

Similar Situations—Similar Behaviors?*

A Study of the Intraindividual Congruence between Situation Perception and Situation Reactions

David Magnusson and Bo Ekehammar

A basic assumption in an interactional model of behavior is that individual behavior is more similar across situations which are perceived and interpreted as similar by the individual than across situations which are perceived as less similar or not similar at all. This proposition was investigated using a psychophysical scaling method for the study of perceived similarity between situations and measures of similarity between reaction profiles as expressions of cross-situational similarity in reactions. *Individual* data from 39 adolescents were analyzed. Hypothetical anxiety-evoking situations, and self-reported anxiety reactions, were used. The overall outcome of the comparison was in the predicted direction. For about 77% of the subjects the relationship was in the expected direction and for about 40% the relationship was statistically significant.

The obvious fact that situational factors influence behavior has been considered in most theoretical models of behavior. However, in empirical research, situational factors have been held constant but for one manipulated working factor, as in experimental psychology, or considered in a very limited way, as in the traditional trait measurement model (see Magnusson, 1974a, 1976a). A more elaborated role for situations in the process underlying actual behavior is advocated by the interactional model of behavior (for reviews see, e.g., Ekehammar, 1974; Endler & Magnusson, 1976; Magnusson & Endler, 1977; Magnusson, 1976a, 1976b). A crucial role in the process in which behavior

---

*Journal of Research in Personality, 1978, 12, 41-48. Copyright 1978 by Academic Press, Inc. Reprinted by permission.

develops is played by the individual's perception of the situations, how he interprets them, and what significance he assigns to them as wholes and to specific cues within them (Magnusson, 1976b).

The idiographic character of an individual's cross-situational pattern of stable and changing behaviors is determined by his specific interpretation of the situations in which he occurs. It can be explained by the fact that individuals construe (perceive, cognize, categorize, experience, interpret, etc.) the same situation differently. Expressed in a slightly modified way, this means that the same situation may have different meanings for different individuals (see Rotter, 1954) or that the psychological situation may differ among individuals also for the same physical situation (see Lewin, 1935).

One implication of the view summarized above is that behavior should be more similar across situations which are perceived as similar than across situations which are perceived as dissimilar, i.e., situation response data would then be congruent to situation perception data for single individuals. The problem is intimately connected with the proposition by some psychologists (e.g., Hartshorne & May, 1928; Mischel, 1968) that similar situations evoke similar behaviors. However, in contrast to these propositions, the view adopted here implies that similarity is not objectively determinable but must be defined by the perceiving individual (see e.g., Magnusson, 1976b). Thus if a person *perceives* Situations A and B as more similar than Situations C and D, we expect him to behave more similarly in the former situations than in the latter.

The view presented above is a crucial point in the interactionist interpretation of individual behavior. The existence of interindividual differences in the interpretation of the same situations has been empirically illustrated (see Magnusson, 1971, 1974b) but not much empirical research has been done on the congruence between how individuals perceive situations and how they behave in the same situations. In two earlier empirical studies on this question (Ekehammar, Schalling, & Magnusson, 1975; Magnusson & Ekehammar, 1975), data were obtained for a sample of individuals across a set of stressful situations. Situation perception data were obtained as similarity estimates of each successive pair of situations. Response data were obtained as the subjects' ratings of their reactions to each of the situations on a number of scales. The matrices of mean similarities across subjects were analyzed by a multidimensional scaling method, and the matrices of intersituational correlations across subjects were treated with factor analyses. The congruence in dimensional structure at group level between situation perception data and situation response data was considerable, although there were also some interesting discrepancies.

The potentialities of the results from these two studies—for determining whether a congruence exists between situation perceptions and situation reactions—are seriously limited by the fact that in both cases the analyses concerned group data. Since one of the basic assumptions, in an interactionist view, is that individuals may differ in their perceptions of one and the same situation, the proper way of investigating the problem is by using and analyzing data for single individuals.

With this background, the general aim of the present study was to analyze the congruence between how individuals perceive situations and how they actually react in the same situations. With the present approach, the problem could also be formulated as: Do situations that are perceived as similar by a person evoke behaviors that are more similar, as expressed in that person's reaction profiles, than those evoked by dissimilar situations? The situations across which behavior was studied were hypothetical situations verbally described, and the data for actual behavior (reactions) were inventory data. The set of individual data used for the analyses was taken from the earlier study by Magnusson and Ekehammar (1975), where the data collection is described in detail.

METHOD

Situation Reaction Data

Data from 39 (25 girls and 14 boys) of the original 42 subjects were suitable for analysis at the individual level. The subjects were pupils from two ninth-grade classes of the compulsory unselected school system and can be regarded as fairly representative of their age group (16 years).

The subjects answered the second version of an anxiety inventory entitled "The Inventory of Reactions to Stressful Situations" (IRS-2; Magnusson & Ekehammar, 1975). The 12 situations used in this version were chosen so as to cover four types of stressful situations (three situations for each type) tentatively denoted "Threat of punishment," "Ego threat," "Threat of pain," and "Inanimate threat." The 10 reactions were chosen so as to cover two types of anxiety reactions tentatively denoted "Psychic anxiety" and "Somatic anxiety."

The 12 verbally described situations of the inventory, grouped according to the a priori classification, were: (1) have just been caught pilfering, (2) called to the headmaster for doing something forbidden, (3) discovered by a teacher when playing truant ("Threat of punishment"), (4) going to have an injection that will hurt, (5) going to have a wound sewed up at the hospital, (6) waiting at the dentist to have a tooth pulled ("Threat of pain"), (7) alone at home hearing someone trying to get in, (8) lost in the woods at nightfall, (9) alone in a desert cottage during a violet thunderstorm ("Inanimate threat"), (10) give an oral report before the class, (11) starting a summer job for the first time, and (12) entering an athletics contest ("Ego threat").

For each situation, each subject was instructed to rate the degree of experienced intensity of each reaction. The ratings were given on a numerical 5-point scale ranging from 1, "not at all" to 5, "very much." The order of presentation of reaction scales was the same for each situation. The reactions assumed to indicate "Psychic anxiety" were: (1) become nervous, (4) get worried, (6) get feelings of insecurity, (8) get depressed, and (10) get feelings of panic. The reactions assumed to indicate "Somatic anxiety" were: (2) hands begin to shake, (3) swallowing difficulties, (5) heart beats faster, (7) get in a sweat, and (9) get stomach trouble.

The Situation × Reaction matrix was analyzed for each of the 39 subjects. The aim was to assess, for each subject, the similarity between reaction profiles for all pair-wise combinations of situations. This is a profile similarity problem, and a lot of numerical indexes have been proposed for describing the overall similarity between profiles (see, e.g., Cattell, 1949; Cohen, 1969; Cronbach & Gleser, 1953; Osgood & Suci, 1952; Sjöberg & Holley, 1967). The following similarity indexes which are discussed at greater length by Cronbach and Gleser (1953), were used in the present study:

$$D_x = \left| \sum_{j=1}^{n} (X_{ji} - X_{jk})^2 \right|^{1/2}, \tag{1}$$

$$D_{\bar{x}} = \left| n(\bar{X}_i - \bar{X}_k)^2 \right|^{1/2}, \tag{2}$$

$$D_E = \left| D_x^2 - D_{\bar{x}}^2 \right|^{1/2}, \tag{3}$$

$$D_S = \left| \frac{D_E^2 - (S_i - S_k)^2}{S_i S_k} \right|^{1/2} \tag{4}$$

where i and k are two out of N situations, j is one out of n reactions, and S_i and S_k denote the standard deviations for situations i and k across the n reactions. All indexes are distance measures (dis-similarities).

D_x, Eq. (1), gives the euclidean distance between situations i and k, taking into account differences in elevation, scatter, and shape of the reaction profiles for each pair of situations. Thus, this index takes into account differences in all of the three important aspects that characterize a profile.

$D_{\bar{x}}$, Eq. (2), is a distance measure for differences in elevation (here, anxiety level) between situations and ignores differences in scatter and shape. This index was computed in order to test whether perceptual similarity might be related to differences in anxiety level rather than in pattern.

D_E, Eq. (3), is a distance measure that ignores differences in elevation but takes scatter and shape into account. This means that it is not affected by differences in overall anxiety level among situations.

D_S, Eq. (4), is a distance measure that ignores differences both in elevation and in scatter but takes shape into account.

Situation Perception Data

Measures of perceived similarity between all pair-wise combinations of situations were obtained by similarity estimation. The usefulness of this technique in the present context has been demonstrated earlier (see Magnusson, 1971; Ekehammar & Magnusson, 1973; Magnusson & Ekehammar, 1973). The subjects and situations were the same as for the situation reaction approach.

The subjects were instructed to estimate the degree of perceived similarity for each pair of situations. The order of presentation of stimulus pairs was randomized among subjects. A numerical 5-point rating scale was used, ranging from 0, "not at all similar" to 4, "completely similar." This procedure yielded 66 similarity estimates, among all combinations of situations, for each subject.

Situation Perception versus Situation Reaction

For each subject, the correspondence between his estimates of perceived similarity among the situations (situation perception data) and the dissimilarity measures of reaction patterns in the same situations (situation reaction data) was investigated by computing product-moment correlations. For each subject one data vector of similarity estimates was compared with four vectors of different types of profile dissimilarity indexes. Thus, four correlation coefficients were computed for each of the 39 subjects. One would expect these intraindividual coefficients, or at least some of them, to be high in order to support the hypothesis about a congruence between situation perception and situational behavior, as discussed in the introduction.

RESULTS

Table 3.1 presents the 39 sets of intraindividual correlation coefficients between similarity estimates of situations, as expressions of perceived similarities between situations, and each of the four indexes of dissimilarity between reaction profiles for the same situations.

The coefficients in Table 3.1 were expected to be negative, since the data on the response side express dissimilarity between situational reaction profiles, whereas the perception data express perceived similarity between the situations. The relevant information from Table 3.1 is presented in condensed form in Table 3.2.

DISCUSSION

The overall outcome of the study, as summarized in Table 3.2, is clearly in the direction predicted from an interactional frame of reference, and so far the results are in accordance with an interactionist view. For the four different measures of relationship, 77, 79, 67, and 85%, respectively, were in the hypothesized direction and 44, 33, 38, and 44%, respectively, were statistically significant.

Table 3.1 Intraperson Correlation Coefficients for the Agreement between Similarity Estimates (Situation Perception Data) and Different Statistical Indexes of Situation Dissimilarity with Respect to Reaction Profiles (Situation Reaction Data)

Person	Index of profile dissimilarity			
	D_X	$D_{\bar{X}}$	D_E	D_S
1	−.30**	−.30*	.10	−.17
2	−.03	.02	−.12	−.15
3	.21	.28	.14	−.18
4	.04	.07	.01	.12
5	−.03	−.08	.01	−.25*
6	−.14	−.12	−.13	−.15
7	−.12	−.02	−.21*	−.20*
8	−.29**	.31**	−.08	−.24*
9	−.03	−.03	.03	−.07
10	−.31**	−.34**	−.26*	−.23*
11	.05	−.27*	.10	−.07
12	−.11	−.21*	−.06	.04
13	−.18	−.23*	−.09	−.16
14	−.12	−.13	.01	−.03
15	.12	.08	.14	−.01
16	−.41**	−.37**	−.37**	−.13
17	.19	.25	.05	−.13
18	−.26*	−.19	−.28**	−.28**
19	−.19	−.16	−.17	−.39**
20	−.15	−.01	−.37**	−.27*
21	−.32**	−.18	−.31**	−.43**
22	−.23*	−.11	−.23*	−.13
23	−.31**	−.33**	−.21*	−.41**
24	−.18	−.14	−.21*	−.23*
25	−.27*	−.05	−.39**	.00
26	.26	.24	.24	.09
27	−.19	−.17	−.15	−.13
28	−.24*	−.14	−.34*	−.27*
29	.02	.06	−.04	−.08
30	−.15	−.09	−.17	−.30**
31	−.25*	−.28**	−.04	−.15
32	−.25*	−.15	−.24*	−.26*
33	−.37**	−.44**	.07	−.05
34	.08	−.06	.23	.02
35	−.63**	−.60**	−.54**	−.59**
36	.01	.01	.07	.09
37	−.23*	−.10	−.21*	−.30**
38	−.25*	−.28**	−.12	−.22*
39	−.38**	−.31**	−.27*	−.42**

Note. The indexes of profile dissimilarity are explained in the text.

* $p \leq .05$, one-tailed text ($n = 66$).

** $p \leq .01$, one-tailed test ($n = 66$).

Table 3.2 Summary of Relevant Information from Table 3.1

Characteristic compared	D_X	$D_{\bar{X}}$	D_E	D_S
Mean correlation across subjects	−.15	−.13	−.11	−.17
Number/percentage of correlations in expected direction	30/77	31/79	26/67	33/85
Number/percentage of significant correlations in expected direction	17/44	13/33	15/38	17/44

Without referring to a strict statistical test of the significance between the different measures of congruence, only one tendency will be commented upon. According to an interactionist view, the characteristic of an individual is to be found in his specific cross-situational *pattern* of stable and changing behavior (see Magnusson, 1971, 1976a, 1976b; Magnusson & Endler, 1977; Pervin, 1977). Then it is interesting to note that the highest congruence between measures of situation perception data and situation reaction data is obtained when the reaction profile similarity measures take only shape into account, neglecting scatter and elevation.

When evaluating the results, one should be clear about the character of the situational factors that were taken into account in the data for the subjects' perceptions of the situations. A situation affects behavior in two main ways (see Magnusson, 1976b): (1) by providing, within each situation, a continuous stream of stimuli, some of which are selected by the individual and attended to as cues for his behavior, and (2) by providing, as a whole, a frame of reference for the choice of cues to attend to and for the interpretation of these cues. A formal committee meeting and a family dinner, for instance, may form quite different frames of reference for the interpretation of a certain behavior shown by one and the same person. It should be observed that our measure of perceived similarity between situations takes only the second kind of situational factors into account and leaves out similarities and dissimilarities in the interpretation of specific cues. One possible direction for further research would be to base the measure of similarities on more specific situational elements.

The appropriate study of the intraindividual congruence between situation perception and situation reaction should also involve a better matching with respect to *content* between the kind of perceived similarity, that the subjects are instructed to rate, and the kind of reactions, which are defined in the reaction scales. In the present case the instruction for the subjects, in the ratings of perceived similarity, did not direct them to base their ratings of the anxiety-provoking character of the situations, which would have been more adequate. The character of the data, *self-reports* referring to *hypothetical* situations, should also be taken into account when interpreting and evaluating the results. Each of the two data characteristics contributes to make the data weak for our purpose.

Against the background of the study's characteristics as discussed above, we regard the results as promising. The next step would be to investigate the congruence between situation perception and situation reaction using other types of data, which are better matched with respect to situation specificity as well as to content. A particular need here is objective measures of response in actual situations.

REFERENCES

Cattell, R. B. r_p and other coefficients of pattern similarity. *Psychometrika*, 1949, **14**, 279-298.

Cohen, J. r_c: A profile similarity coefficient invariant over variable reflection. *Psychological Bulletin*, 1969, **71**, 281-284.

Cronbach, L. J., & Gleser, G. C. Assessing similarities between profiles. *Psychological Bulletin*, 1953, **50**, 456-473.

Ekehammar, B. Interactionism in personality from a historical perspective. *Psychological Bulletin*, 1974, **81**, 1026-1048.

Ekehammar, B., & Magnusson, D. A method to study stressful situations. *Journal of Personality and Social Psychology*, 1973, **27**, 176-179.

Ekehammar, B., Schalling, D., & Magnusson, D. Dimensions of stressful situations: A comparison between a stimulus analytical and a response analytical approach. *Multivariate Behavioral Research*, 1975, **10**, 155-164.

Endler, N. S., & Magnusson, D. Toward an interactional psychology of personality. *Psychological Bulletin*, 1976, **83**, 956-974.

Hartshorne, H., & May, M. A. *Studies in the nature of character: Studies in deceit*. New York: Macmillan, 1928.

Lewin, K. *A dynamic theory of personality: Selected papers*. New York: McGraw-Hill, 1935.

Magnusson, D. An analysis of situational dimensions. *Perceptual and Motor Skills*, 1971, **32**, 851-867.

Magnusson, D. The individual and the situation in the traditional measurement model. *Reports from the Psychological Laboratories, University of Stockholm*, 1974, No. 426. (a)

Magnusson, D. The individual in the situation: Some studies on individuals' perception of situations. *Studia Psychologica*, 1974, **16**, 124-132. (b)

Magnusson, D. Consistency and coherence in personality: A discussion of lawfulness at different levels. *Reports from the Department of Psychology, the University of Stockholm*, 1976, No. 472. (b)

Magnusson, D. The person and the situation in an interactional model of behavior. *Scandinavian Journal of Psychology*, 1976, **17**, 253-271. (a)

Magnusson, D., & Ekehammar, B. An analysis of situational dimensions: A replication. *Multivariate Behavioral Research*, 1973, **8**, 331-339.

Magnusson, D., & Ekehammar, B. Perceptions of and reactions to stressful situations. *Journal of Personality and Social Psychology*, 1975, **31**, 1147-1154.

Magnusson, D., & Endler, N. S. Interactional psychology: Current issues and future prospects. In D. Magnusson & N. S. Endler (Eds.), *Personality at the crossroads: Current issues in interactional psychology.* Hillsdale, New Jersey: Erlbaum (Wiley), 1977.

Mischel, W. *Personality and assessment.* New York: Wiley, 1968.

Osgood, C. E., & Suci, G. J. A measure of relation determined by both mean difference and profile information. *Psychological Bulletin,* 1952, **49,** 251-262.

Pervin, L. A. The representative design of person-situation research. In D. Magnusson & N. S. Endler (Eds.), *Personality at the crossroads: Current issues in interactional psychology.* Hillsdale, New Jersey: Erlbaum (Wiley), 1977.

Rotter, J. B. *Social learning and clinical psychology.* New York: Prentice-Hall, 1954.

Sjöberg, L., & Holley, J. W. A measure of similarity between individuals when scoring directions of variables are arbitrary. *Multivariate Behavioral Research,* 1967, **2,** 377-384.

Stressful Situations:
Introduction

This group of studies is concerned with the classification and analysis of situations which are experienced as stressful.

Bryant and Trower (1974) carried out a survey of 10% of second year Oxford undergraduates, in which they were asked to rate the amount of difficulty they had with 30 everyday social situations. A surprisingly high rate of difficulty was found—9% reported great difficulty or avoidance for six or more situations, and 99% reported some difficulty. A principal components analysis produced two components: the first consisted of situations involving meeting new people, e.g. at parties, especially the opposite sex; the second factor contained situations where deeper and more intimate relationships are established. Greater difficulty was reported by students of lower social class origins, who perhaps found Oxford more difficult, and by those from smaller families, especially only children. Similar research has found that though neurotic mental patients have a lot of difficulty with social situations, they can be taught by social skills training to handle these situations in a more satisfactory manner (Trower, Bryant and Argyle, 1978).

Hodges and Felling (1970) tested Spielberger's theory that trait anxiety leads to heightened state anxiety in situations where there is a possibility of failure or loss of self-esteem. A large sample of students rated 40 anxiety-producing situations, which covered eight areas of university life. Factor analysis produced four factors—physical danger, pain and squeamishness; speaking in class; social and academic failure; and dating. Trait anxiety correlated with the last three factors, but not with the first, and females scored higher on the first factor but not on the others; thus the study supported Spielberger's hypothesis.

Kendall (1978) showed how different kinds of trait anxiety lead to anxiousness in different kinds of situations. Subjects completed questionnaires that measured trait anxiety over physical danger, evaluated social stress, and measured state-trait anxiety. Physical danger stress was produced by a film of car crashes; social evaluation stress was produced by a decoding test with ego-involving instructions; a scale for state anxiety showed that subjects high in physical danger trait anxiety were made anxious by the film, those high in evaluation anxiety by the test, but not vice versa. This is a realistic test of Spielberger's ideas on state and trait anxiety, and also of Endler's theories about different kinds of anxiety.

SUGGESTED ADDITIONAL REFERENCES

Alker, H. and Owen, D. Bibliography, trait, and behavioral sampling predictions of performance in a stressful life setting. *Journal of Personality and Social Psychology,* (in press).

Archer, R. and Stein, D. Personal control expectancies and state anxiety. *Psychological Reports,* 1978, *42,* 551-558.

Bergman, L., and Magnusson, D. Overachievement and catecholamine excretion in an achievement-demanding situation. *Psychosomatic Medicine,* 1979, *41,* 181-188.

Bernstein, L. Situational anxiety reduction in medical students. *Journal of Thanatology,* 1975, *3,* 187-190.

Bloom, L., Houston, B., Holmes, D., and Burish, T. The effectiveness of attentional diversion and situational redefinition for reducing stress due to a nonambiguous threat. *Journal of Research in Personality,* 1977, *11,* 83-94.

Bryant, B. and Trower, P. Social difficulty in a student population. *British Journal of Educational Psychology,* 1974, *44,* 73-91.

Cartwright, D. Trait and other sources of variance in the S-R Inventory of Anxiousness. *Journal of Personality and Social Psychology,* 1975, *32,* 408-414.

Coleman, S. and Halstead, H. A questionnaire study of situations and responses in anxiety: a pilot study. *British Journal of Social and Clinical Psychology,* 1973, *12,* 393-401.

Dohrenwend, B., and Dohrenwend, B. (Ed.). *Stressful Life Events: Their Nature and Effects.* New York: Wiley, 1974, pp 73-80.

Ekehammar, B., Schalling, D., and Magnusson, D. Dimensions of stressful situations. *Multidimensional Behavioral Research,* 1975, *10,* 155-164.

Endler, N., Hunt, J., and Rosenstein, A. An S-R Inventory of Anxiousness. *Psychological Monographs,* 1962, No. 17, 1-33.

Endler, N., and Okada, M. A multidimensional measure of trait anxiety: The S-R Inventory of General Trait-Anxiousness. *Journal of Consulting and Clinical Psychology,* 1975, *43,* 319-329.

Hagtvet, K. Components of test anxiety measured in and out of explicitly defined situational contents. *Psychological Reports,* 1978, *43,* 979-984.

Houston, B., Bloom, L., Burish, T., and Cummings, E. Positive evaluation of stressful experiences. *Journal of Personality,* 1978, *46,* 205-214.

Houston, B. and Hodges, W. Situational denial and performance under stress. *Journal of Personality and Social Psychology,* 1970, *16,* 726-730.

Hoy, E. and Endler, N. Reported anxiousness and two types of stimulus incongruity. *Canadian Journal of Behavioral Science,* 1970, *4,* 207-214.

Janisse, M., Goto, T., Usui, S., Ikegaya, K. and Tsuji, K. The frequency and intensity of anxiety situations reported by Japanese university students. *Psychologia,* 1978, *21,* 1-10.

Janisse, M. and Palys, T. Frequency and intensity of anxiety in university students. *Journal of Personality Assessment*, 1976, *40*, 502-515.

Jeger, A. and Goldfried, M. A comparison of situation tests of speech anxiety. *Behavior Therapy*, 1976, *7*, 252-255.

Jurich, A. and Jurich, J. Factor analysis of expression of anxiety. *Psychological Reports*, 1978, *42*, 1203-1210.

Lazarus, R. and Launier, R. Stress-related transactions between person and environment. In L. Pervin and M. Lewis (Eds.) *Perspectives in Interactional Psychology*, 1978, pp. 287-322.

Loo, R. The state-trait anxiety inventory A-Trait scales: dimensions and their generalization. *Journal of Personality Assessment*, 1979, *43*, 50-53.

Magnusson, D. and Ekehammar, B. Anxiety profile based on both situational and response factors. *Multidimensional Behavior Research*, 1975, *10*, 27-43.

Magnusson, D. and Stattin, H. A cross-cultural comparison of anxiety responses in an interactional frame of reference. *International Journal of Psychology*, 1978, *13*, 316-332.

Melamed, B., Yurcheson, R., Fleece, E., Hutcherson, S. and Hawes, R. Effects of film modeling on the reduction of anxiety-related behaviors in individuals varying in level of previous experience in the stress situation. *Journal of Consulting and Clinical Psychology*, 1978, *46*, 1357-1367.

Mellstrom, M. General vs. specific traits in the assessment of anxiety. *Journal of Consulting and Clinical Psychology*, 1978, *46*, 423-431.

Morelli, G. and Friedman, B. Cognitive correlates of multidimensional trait anxiety. *Psychological Reports*, 1978, *42*, 611-614.

Muller, A. Police service in psycho-social problem situations. *The Police Chief*, Sept., 1979.

Naylor, F. Success and failure experiences and the factor structure of the state-trait anxiety inventory. *Australian Journal of Psychology*, 1978, *30*, 217-222.

Richardson, F. and Tasto, D. Development and factor analysis of a social anxiety inventory. *Behavior Therapy*, 1976, *7*, 453-462.

Sanchez-Craig, B. Cognitive and behavioral coping strategies in the reappraisal of stressful social situations. *Journal of Counseling Psychology*, 1976, *23*, 7-12.

Saul, E. and Kass, J. Study of anticipated anxiety in a medical school setting. *Journal of Medical Education*, 1969, *44*, 526-532.

Selby, J. Situational correlates of death anxiety: reactions to funeral practices. *Omega*, 1977, *8*, 247-250.

Sharma, S. and Dang, R. A study of trait anxiety in relation to types of stressful situations among males and females. *Indian Journal of Psychology*, 1976, *51*, 49-54.

Smith, R. and Lay, C. State and trait anxiety: an annotated bibliography. *Psychological Reports*, 1974, *34*, 519-594.

Spielberger, C. The effects of anxiety on complex learning and academic achievement. In C. Spielberger (Ed.) *Anxiety and Behavior*, New York: Academic Press, 1966.

Spielberger, C. (Ed.) *Anxiety: Current Trends in Theory and Research*. (Vol. 1) New York: Academic Press, 1972.

Stringer, P., Crown, S., Lucas, C. and Supramaniam, S. Sex differences, personality, and study difficulty in university students. *Journal of Biosocial Science*, 1978, *10*, 221-229.

Whalen, C., Henker, B., Collins, B., Finck, D. and Dotemoto, S. A social ecology of hyperactive boys. *Journal of Applied Behavior Analysis,* 1979, *12,* 65-81.

Yamamoto, K. Children's ratings of the stresstulness of experience. *Developmental Psychology,* 1979, *15,* 581-582.

1

Social Difficulty in a Student Sample*

Bridget Bryant and P. E. Trower

Recent research shows a high prevalence of psycho-social disturbance in university students, and there is some evidence that inadequate social participation is associated with disturbance and with failure to complete courses. This study examines the extent, degree and type of difficulty in social situations reported by a random sample of Oxford University students. Nearly 10 per cent, mostly from lower social classes and small families, had great difficulty in, or tried to avoid, about six common social situations described in a questionnaire, and a principal components analysis discriminated different types of social difficulty.

INTRODUCTION

Recent studies indicate that, while there is little evidence to suggest that students are more at risk to serious psychiatric disturbance than other members of the population (Payne, 1969; Davidson and Hutt, 1964), there does seem to be a high prevalence of less serious problems which have been called 'psycho-social' (Lucas and Linken, 1970; Kidd and Caldbeck-Meenan, 1966; Kessel and

*Reprinted with permission of the authors and publisher from: British Journal of Educational Psychology, 1974, 44, 13-21. Copyright 1974 by Scottish Academic Press Ltd.

Shepherd, 1962). Attempts to identify the precipitating social factors in psycho-social disturbance and academic failure or drop-out have suggested that they were often associated with, amongst other things, few or unsuccessful attempts at social participation (Lucas, Kelvin and Ojha, 1966; Hopkins, Malleson and Sarnoff, 1958; Kidd, 1965; Summerskill, 1962).

The focus of interest in the present study was the extent and degree of difficulty reported by a random sample of students in social situations, and the sorts of situations which present most difficulty to them. This study forms part of a research programme concerned with the problem of social inadequacy and its treatment by social skills training (Argyle, Trower and Bryant, in press).

METHOD

The Sample

A 1 in 10 random sample of second year members of Oxford University, admitted in 1969, was drawn from the 1971 university register, and this procedure yielded the names of 312 individuals, 252 men and 60 women, to whom questionnaires were sent. Of these, 223 (71 per cent) returned completed questionnaires, 69 per cent of the men and 82 per cent of the women. No reply was received from 77 (25 per cent), 26 per cent of the men and 18 per cent of the women, even after two further attempts to contact them. Of the remaining men, five refused to participate, one had died and six were no longer members of the university.

Table 1.1 shows the distribution, on various social attributes, of the sample of respondents and the total population from which the sample was drawn. This confirms that the sample represents the universe within the limits of chance sampling error, in terms of age, marital status, nationality, student status and faculty.

The vast majority of the students were, as would be expected, single, under 21, British undergraduates. Three-quarters came from middle class homes, and 57 per cent had been educated in independent and direct grant schools. 13 per cent were only children.

The Questionnaire

The quesionnaire, administered by post in May, 1971, asked about the degree of difficulty felt in 30 specified situations which were selected on the basis of difficulties raised by a study of psychiatric patients. They ranged from encounters of the 'rubbing shoulders' variety, such as walking down the street or using public transport, to more intimate situations such as getting to know someone in

Table 1.1   Distribution of Men and Women in the Student Sample on Various Social Attributes and Comparison with the Total Population

		Sample			Total* Population (N=2,761) %
		Men (N=174) %	Women (N=49) %	Total (N=223) %	
Age	Under 21	84	83	84	81
	21+	16	16	16	19
Marital State	Single	94	96	94	94
	Married	6	4	6	6
Nationality	British	91	92	91	87
	Other	9	8	9	13
Student Status ...	Undergraduate ...	86	90	87	87
	Graduate	14	10	13	13
Faculty	Sciences	40	38	39	36
	Social Sciences ..	30	6	24	24
	Arts	30	56	36	40
No. of Children	One	13	14	13	
in family	Two	38	45	39	Not
(including	Three	27	24	26	available
subject)	Four+	21	16	20	
Social Class	I	26	37	29	
(Father's	II	44	45	45	
occupation) ...	III	23	12	21	Not
	IV	2	2	2	available
	V	4	2	3	
	Forces	0	1	1	
Composition of	Single Sex	88	88	88	Not
last school	Co-educational ..	12	12	12	available
					1965/66 Admissions †
Last School	Independent	38	31	37 (37)	40
Attended	Direct Grant	18	25	20 (21)	18
	Maintained	38	35	36 (40)	41
	Other	6	8	6 (2)	1

*Source: University Registry Statistical Unit.

†Source: Franks Commission, University of Oxford (1966). This data was for undergraduates only. The comparable figures for undergraduates in the sample are given in parentheses.

No significant differences were found between the sample and the total population. Test of significance: X^2 for finite universe compared with sample of universe (McNemar, 1949).

depth. Respondents were asked, for each situation, to rate themselves on a five point scale: 0—no difficulty, 1—slight difficulty, 2—moderate difficulty, 3—great difficulty, and 4—avoidance if possible. In the instructions difficulty was defined as follows: "The situation makes you feel anxious or uncomfortable, either because you don't know what to do or because it makes you feel frightened, embarrassed or self-conscious." The ratings covered two time periods, the present time and the equivalent time a year ago.

RESULTS

In the analysis each individual was given a score of difficulty by ascribing a numerical value to the ratings, so that rating 0 contributed zero to the score, and rating 4 contributed 4; the scores across all 30 situations were then summed. The mean scores for the present time and a year ago, and for men and women, are shown in Table 1.2. The scores for the present time were significantly lower than for a year ago. This difference recurred throughout the analysis, and is discussed later.

Table 1.2 Mean Scores of Difficulty for all Respondents and for Men and Women Separately

	Present time			A year ago			
	Mean	Range	S.D.	Mean	Range	S.D.	Sig. Level*
Total	17·48	0-48	11·69	24·21	0-66	13·96	.001
Men	16·97	0-48	11·48	23·59	0-59	13·41	.001
Women	19·31	0-44	12·23	26·44	0-66	15·56	.001

*Significance levels were calculated by means of the Wilcoxon matched pairs, signed-ranks test.

Almost everyone (99 per cent) rated themselves as having difficulty, although in many instances this was only slight. However it is probable that some degree of anxiety in social situations is normal and for this reason the ratings of slight difficulty were combined with the 'no difficulty' ratings for most of the analysis. Ratings of moderate difficulty or worse were made by three-quarters of the respondents in, on average, five to six situations at the present time. Ratings of great difficulty or avoidance were made by 40 per cent in an average of two to three situations. 21 students reported great difficulty or avoidance in as many as six or more situations in their first year and 19 did so in four or more situations in their second year; it is possible that these students, about 9 per cent of the sample, were suffering from quite serious social problems.

Individual Situations

(a) **Overall difficulty.** The 30 situations on the questionnaire are shown in Table 1.3, rank ordered according to the percentage of respondents who rated moderate difficulty or worse in them.

The situations should not be considered as representing equal forms of stress, since some are clearly less taxing than others, for instance, walking down the street compared with getting to know someone in depth. The order of difficulty

Table 1.3   Percentage of Respondents Scoring Moderate Difficulty or Worse (2, 3 or 4) in Each Situation.
(N = 223)

	Situation*	Present Time	Year Ago	P
21	Approaching others	36	51	.001
14	Going to dances/discotheques	35	45	.01
25	Taking initiative in conversation	26	44	.001
5	Going to parties	25	42	.001
19	People you don't know well	22	37	.001
8	Going out/opposite sex	21	38	.001
11	Being in a group/opposite sex	21	35	.001
24	Getting to know someone in depth	21	29	.001
29	Talking about self and feelings	19	26	.001
26	Looking at people in the eyes	18	26	.001
22	Making decisions affecting others	17	31	.001
17	Going into a room full of people	17	30	.001
30	People looking at you	16	26	.001
18	Meeting strangers	13	28	.001
16	Being with younger people	13	19	.01
7	Making friends of own age	11	20	.001
27	Disagreeing/putting forward views	9	23	.001
4	Going into pubs	9	17	.001
9	Being in a group/same sex	9	15	.01
28	People standing/sitting very close	9	14	.001
10	Being in a group/men and women	8	18	.001
6	Mixing with people at work	8	16	.001
12	Entertaining in your own home	7	19	.001
15	Being with older people	5	8	
23	Being with just one other person	4	9	.01
13	Going into restaurants/cafes	3	10	.001
2	Going into shops	1	5	.05
1	Walking down the street	1	4	
3	Using public transport	1	3	
20	Being with friends	1	1	

Test of significance: X^2, using McNemar's formula for correlated data. Yates's correction for continuity used where applicable.
*Some situations quoted in abbreviated form.

found was in this sense much what one would expect. Little difficulty was reported in situations requiring relatively superficial contact or where close bonds had already been established, such as being with close friends. More difficulty was reported in situations demanding a more complex level of interaction, often with people of the opposite sex, and where close bonds had not been established. The latter could be described as posing a greater personal risk in terms of acceptance or rejection.

Although the order was not unexpected, the proportions of students reporting difficulty was surprisingly high in some cases. For example, half of them reported moderate or worse difficulty in approaching others and making the first move in starting up a friendship in their first year, something which could be considered essential to their social well-being at university. Although this improved, a third were still reporting difficulty in doing this a year later.

At the other end of the scale there was a small cluster of students who reported difficulty in such apparently 'easy' situations as going into shops and restaurants, walking down the street and using public transport. This is typical of the pattern of difficulties reported by individuals suffering from social phobias, a psychiatric problem which has recently come under increasing investigation. Although numerically small in the student sample, it is a matter of concern that between 3 and 10 per cent reported such difficulties in their first year.

(b) Differences between the present time and a year ago. Table 1.3 also shows the proportions of people reporting difficulty now compared with a year ago. In all but four situations there was a significant change from difficulty a year ago to little or no difficulty now, and this trend held for all except one situation for both men and women.

This decrease in the amount of difficulty reported by students in their second year at the university may merely reflect a tendency to magnify problems in retrospect, or people's desire to believe or to report that they have increased in maturity and sophistication. On the other hand, it seems reasonable on common sense grounds to assume that moving into a totally new environment, particularly when in most instances this coincided with leaving school, is likely to be a stressful experience, and we would suggest that the greater difficulty reported in the first year does represent a genuine difference.

If this is so, it suggests that many difficulties in social situations resolve themselves with time and experience. This would appear to be supported by the fact that the proportions of ratings of 'avoidance of the situation' had not decreased by the second year, suggesting that without experience improvement is unlikely.

(c) Differences between men and women. There were some significant differences between the men and women in the situations they found difficult, and these are shown in Table 1.4.

Table 1.4 Differences Between Men and Women in the Percentage Who Scored Moderate
Difficulty or Worse in Various Situations

Q. no. Situation	Present time				A year ago			
	Men %	Wmn. %	X^2	P	Men %	Wmn. %	X^2	P
14 Going to dances, discos ...	31	46	4·2	·05				
5 Going to parties	22	35	3·6		39	53	3·1	
8 Going out/opposite sex	24	12	3·0					
19 People don't know well ...	20	33	4·2	·05				
11 Group/opposite sex	26	4	11·0	·001	39	21	5·7	·05
22 Decisions affecting others	15	24	3·6					
17 Room full of people	13	29	6·5	·05	27	42	4·1	·05
30 People looking at you	14	24	2·8					
27 Disagreeing	5	25	15·1	·001	18	40	10·5	·01
4 Going into pubs	4	28	24·0	·001	11	37	18·8	·001
6 Mixing at work	6	16	4·4	·05				

Apart from going into pubs, a traditionally male preserve, these differences do not seem to follow a pattern. For example, they would not seem particularly to support the finding of Argyle and Williams (1969) that adolescent females felt observed while males felt themselves observers during cross-sex social contacts. Nor, with the exception of disagreeing with others, would they seem to support the suggestion that women are expected to be dependent and accommodating towards the opposite sex (e.g., Danziger, 1971), in which case one would have expected them to report more difficulty in situations requiring assertive behaviour, for example, situations 21, 22 and 25.

One factor which should be taken into account in considering the differences between men and women is the overall preponderance of men at Oxford University, something in the order of four men to one woman. This may well create problems and anxieties for the men in cross-sexual encounters which would not arise in other groups.

Principal Components Analysis

A principal components analysis on the data from the present time was carried out in order to find out (a) if any items were correlated, and whether there were any general components of social difficulty, and (b) if any persons correlated on these general components could also be correlated on their personal characteristics. The calculations were made on the scores of all 223 respondents on all 30 situations, using the procedure described by Slater (1967). The analysis was applied to the variances and covariances of the scores of each student without normalisation, so differences in their variation were retained. This involved treating the differences as meaningful, in the hope that this would increase the questionnaire's sensitivity to variations in difficulty. The vectors show the correlation of the item with the component.

(a) The components: *Component 1.* The first component accounted for 25.5 per cent of the variance. Its positive pole refers to situations which involve actively seeking contact with relative strangers, particularly of the opposite sex.

Item	Vector	Content
14	.50	Going to dances.
21	.37	Approaching others.
5	.26	Going to parties.
25	.22	Taking the initiative in conversation.
19	.18	Being with people you don't know well.
8	.17	Going out with someone of opposite sex.

The contrasting pole refers to a more heterogeneous group of situations which are less socially involving or which involve less exposure to strangers:

23	−.17	Being with one other person.
13	−.17	Going into restaurants or cafes.
2	−.25	Going into shops.
20	−.26	Being with close friends.
3	−.27	Going on public transport.
1	−.28	Walking down the street.

It will be recalled that these situations are almost exactly those ranked at the extreme top and bottom of Table 1.3. It is clear, therefore, that the first component is also closely related to 'social difficulty,' and that there is a fairly general component of social difficulty roughly describable as actively seeking out relative strangers, particularly of the opposite sex.

Component 2. The second component accounts for 9.9 per cent of the variance. It selects from the situations found at the positive pole of the first component the ones which involve public social contact:

Item	Vector	Content
14	.56	Going to dances, discos.
5	.33	Going to parties.
4	.26	Going to pubs.
16	.14	Being with younger people.

This is in contrast to situations demanding more intimate contact:

26   −.16   Looking at people directly in the eyes.
29   −.18   Talking about yourself and your feelings.
21   −.30   Making the first move in starting a friendship.
25   −.30   Taking the initiative in keeping conversation going.
24   −.33   Getting to know people in depth.

From Table 1.3, it can be seen that this component cuts across the 'social difficulty' dimension, with situations ranked high in difficulty appearing at both poles. This means that the component does not discriminate individuals in terms of the amount, so much as the type of difficulty they report. Thus, difficulty for one group concerns the casual, public type of social contact, while another group finds more intimate contact difficult. This suggests there are two fairly substantial groups whose social experiences are quite distinct. The first may, for instance, be reticent in initial contacts but are then able to consolidate their friendships, while the second may be more socially outgoing but less able to make deeper acquaintances.

The remaining components accounted for very small proportions of the variance, 6.3 per cent or less, and are not reported since their interpretation can only be highly speculative.

(b) The persons: In order to examine whether there were any associations between social difficulty and background characteristics of the respondents, a group of 'high difficulty' and 'low difficulty' individuals were isolated. This was done by using the first component as an indicator of social difficulty, and selecting the 30 individuals who loaded highest and the 30 who loaded lowest on it. An alternative method was to select the respondents with the highest and lowest total scores of difficulty; this was also done, and yielded substantially the same results.

(i) Social class. There were significantly more respondents in social classes I and II in the low difficulty group, and in social classes III, IV and V in the high difficulty group ($X^2 = 4 \cdot 74$, df 1, P< $\cdot$ 05). One possible explanation for this association is that since the majority of the students were from social classes I and II (about three-quarters of the sample) the students from lower social classes experienced more social difficulty than they would in a milieu predominantly of their own social class.

(ii) Family size. Significantly more students who were only children or who had only one sibling in the high difficulty group than were those from larger families ($X^2 = 4 \cdot 56$, df 1, P< $\cdot$ 05). This may be in line with some other findings concerning only children and first borns. For example, Smith (1971) found that more students who were only children withdrew from Sussex University than

those from families of two or more children. Schachter (1964) found that only children and first borns tended to be more timid, dependent and influenceable, and he suggested that this would be likely to lead to more interpersonal problems.

(iii) Nationality. There was a trend which did not quite reach significance towards a disproportionate number of overseas students in the *low* difficulty group compared to the high difficulty group, and a further comparison between the low difficulty group and the rest of the sample produced a significant difference in this direction ($X^2 = 6 \cdot 81$, df 1, P$< \cdot 01$). This association is difficult to explain, and indeed one might well have expected students from abroad to have more difficulties rather than less. However, the overseas students in the low difficulty group did not, with one exception, come from the countries which, for example, Still (1961) found to be associated with a higher incidence of psychological symptoms (the Middle East, West Africa and India).

None of the other characteristics shown in Table 1.1 was significantly related to social difficulty.

DISCUSSION

One question raised by this study is the relationship between social difficulty and psychological disturbance. Precipitating social factors in 'psycho-social' disturbance has already been referred to in the introduction, and many writers claim a strong link between breakdown in social interaction and mental illness (Sullivan, 1953; Ryle and Breen, 1972; Argyle, 1969; Zigler and Phillips, 1960).

In the present study, taking only the most stringent estimate of difficulty, great difficulty in or avoidance of at least four situations, one in 11 students would appear to have been experiencing considerable stress. Almost all of this difficulty occurred in the situations found at the positive pole of the first component, which involved actively seeking contact with relative strangers, particularly of the opposite sex, situations of considerable importance for young, single men and women. On a 10 per cent sample, even assuming that all the non-respondents had no difficulties, this could mean as many as 190 second-year students in the university as a whole. The extent to which this degree of difficulty represents 'pathological' social inadequacy is not known, but we suspect these may be 'at risk' individuals.

Further information on this problem is being obtained from a more extensive study of a sample of psychiatric out-patients. One aim of this latter study is to examine the relationship firstly, between observed social inadequacy and reported social difficulty, and secondly, between these and clinical state. A second aim is to explore further the value of 'treating' socially inadequate patients by training in social interaction skills, a method with which we have already had some success, and which might be extended to other individuals with similar difficulties, such as students.

The work we have done so far with psychiatric patients has suggested that interpersonal difficulties may be of two kinds: firstly, a lack of basic social skills which makes people unrewarding to others and leads to unsuccessful attempts at meeting people, and, secondly, problems in establishing deep relationships with others which do not appear to be due to lack of skill. These two kinds of difficulty are very similar to the two patterns of difficulty which emerged on the second component of the principal components analysis. It is the first kind, the lack of skill, which we would call social inadequacy, and which is most likely to be helped by social skills training. If the psychiatric survey yields useful results, the method described in the student survey could possibly be used to identify socially inadequate individuals.

REFERENCES

Argyle, M. (1969). *Social Interaction*. London: Methuen.

Argyle, M., Trower, P., and Bryant, B. (in press). Explorations in the treatment of personality disorders and neuroses by social skills training. *Br. J. Med. Psychol.*

Argyle, M., and Williams, M. (1969). Observer or observed? A reversible perspective in person perception. *Sociometry, 32,* 396-412.

Danziger, K. (1971). *Socialization*. London: Penguin. (Science of Behaviour Series).

Davidson, M. A., and Hutt, C. (1964). A study of 500 Oxford student psychiatric patients. *Br. J. Soc. Clin. Psychol., 3,* 175-185.

Hopkins, J., Malleson, N., and Sarnoff, I. (1958). Non-intellectual correlates of success and failure among university students. *Br. J. Educ. Psychol., 28,* 23-35.

Kessel, W. I. N., and Shepherd, M. (1962). Neurosis in hospital and general practice. *J. Ment. Sci., 108,* 195-196.

Kidd, C. B. (1965). Psychiatric morbidity among students. *Br. J. Prev. Soc. Med., 19,* 143-150.

Kidd, C. B., and Caldbreck-Meenan, J. (1966). A comparative study of psychiatric morbidity among students at two different universities. *Br. J. Psychiat., 112,* 57-64.

Lucas, C. J., Kelvin, R. P., and Ojha, A. B. (1966). Mental health and student wastage. *Br. J. Psychiat., 112,* 277-284.

Lucas, C. J., and Linken, A. (1970). *Student Mental Health: A Survey of Developments in the United Kingdom*. Paper delivered to the Fifth National Conference on Health in the College Community, Boston, USA.

McNemar, Q. (1949). *Psychological Statistics*. New York: John Wiley and Sons.

Payne, J. (1969). *Research in Student Mental Health*. Monograph, Society for Research into Higher Education, London.

Ryle, A., and Breen, D. (1972). Some differences in the personal constructs of neurotic and normal subjects. *Br. J. Psychiat., 120,* 483-489.

Schachter, S. (1964). Birth order and sociometric choice. *J. Abnorm. Soc. Psychol., 68,* 453-456.

Slater, P. (1967). *Notes on Ingrid* 67. Institute of Psychiatry, London. (Unpublished.)

Smith, B. M. (1971). A preliminary report on the socio-educational research data. Sussex University. (Unpublished.)

Still, R. J. (1961). Mental health in overseas students. *Proc. Br. Student Health Ass. Conf.*, 59-67.

Sullivan, H. S. (1953). *The Interpersonal Theory of Psychiatry*. New York: Grune and Stratton.

Summerskill, J. (1962). Drop-outs from college. In Sanford, N. (Ed.), *The American College*. New York: J. Wiley and Sons.

University of Oxford (1966). *Report of Commission of Inquiry, II: Statistical Appendix*. Oxford: Clarendon Press.

Zigler, E., and Phillips, L. (1960). Social effectiveness and symptomatic behaviours. *J. Abnorm. Soc. Psychol.*, 61, 231-238.

2

Types of Stressful Situations and Their Relation to Trait Anxiety and Sex*

William F. Hodges and James P. Felling

Spielberger has proposed that trait anxiety scores reflect a predisposition to respond with heightened state anxiety to situations involving the possibility of failure or loss of self-esteem. Thus it was predicted that Ss who indicated that they were high in A-trait would report anticipating greater fears in these situations and not in situations involving physical pain or danger. The Ss rated 40 situations according to the degree of apprehension that they thought they might feel if in that situation. The 40 items were intercorrelated and factor analyzed. Of the four factors obtained, the three factors associated with failure correlated significantly with a measure of trait anxiety, while the fourth factor, involving pain and danger, did not, supporting Spielberger's hypothesis. Sex differences were found only for the pain-danger factor.

Spielberger (1966) has emphasized the importance of identifying stimuli which are perceived as stressful by those individuals who report that they are frequently anxious. Investigations of the effects of various stressful situations on anxiety have typically ignored the importance of the *type* of stress used, assuming that situations which are generally perceived as threatening will have the same effect on everyone. Lazarus (1966), however, has emphasized the importance of determining the cognitive appraisal of S in evaluating the presence of a threat. Furthermore, Spielberger (1966) has suggested that one reason why the identification of anxiety provoking stimuli has not been extensively investigated is the

*Journal of Consulting and Clinical Psychology, 1970, 34, 3, 333-337. Copyright 1970 by the American Psychological Association. Reprinted by permission.

conceptual ambiguity of the concept of anxiety. Developing further the ideas of Freud (1933, 1936) and Cattell and Scheier (1961), Speilberger has proposed a theoretical statement of the relationship between two aspects of anxiety, trait anxiety (A-trait) and state anxiety (A-state). He defined A-state as the "subjective, consciously perceived feelings of apprehension and tension" accompanied by autonomic nervous system arousal, and A-trait as anxiety proneness or the predisposition to appraise many situations as threatening (Spielberger, 1966). As Spielberger has indicated, most studies have been concerned with either A-state or A-trait and have not been concerned with the type of stimuli which produce differential A-state responses for individuals who differ in levels of A-trait.

Learning theory applications to clinical psychology have resulted in a great deal of interest in the type of stimuli leading to anxiety and fear. Endler, Hunt, and Rosenstein (1962) factor analyzed fearful situations and found three factors: interpersonal, inanimate, and ambiguous. The Fear Survey Schedule (FSS) was designed to measure fears in various areas, but in most studies using this questionnaire, the scales of fears were arbitrarily defined (Wolpe & Lang, 1964) rather than empirically determined. One exception was a study by Scherer and Nakamura (1968) who found 10 factors of fears on a children's form of the FSS. These factors ranged from fears involving physical danger to fears of criticism and failure. No correlations between individual factor scores and any measure of A-trait were presented. In fact, few of the studies have attempted to evaluate the relationship between A-trait measures and individual fear scales. Correlations of the *total* number of fears with such measures of A-trait as the Manifest Anxiety (*MA*) scale, Test Anxiety Questionnaire, Welsh Anxiety Scale, and Children's Manifest Anxiety Scale, have yielded correlations ranging from .27 to .66 (Geer, 1965; Grossberg & Wilson, 1965; Manosevitz & Lanyon, 1965; Scherer & Nakamura, 1968). Lang and Lazovik (1963) reported an exceptionally high correlation of .80, but this correlation was based on a sample of only 13 Ss. One study (Grossberg & Wilson, 1965) has evaluated the relationship between particular types of fears and A-trait. They reported correlations of .46 and .49 between the *MA* scale and their Social-Interpersonal and Miscellaneous scales, respectively, and found no correlation between the *MA* scale and the Tissue Damage scale. Thus, it is apparent that there is some relationship between fears of specific, perceived dangers and A-trait, but the above studies do not clearly define whether a particular *type* of fear is more likely to be related to A-trait.

Because of the difficulty of producing a relevant, realistic stress in the laboratory, research on anxiety has typically utilized stress involving phsyical danger, actual or implied, such as mutilative movies (Lazarus, Speisman, Mordkoff, & Davison, 1962), shock (Deane, 1961), pain (Malmo & Shagass, 1949), and danger (Ax, 1953). However, recent evidence by Hodges and Spielberger (1966) and Hodges (1968) indicates that reaction to such dangers as threat of shock may be related to individual differences in fear of shock, but unrelated to A-trait. Similarly Zuckerman, Schultz, and Hopkins (1967) found no relationship between the *MA* scale and their Sensation-Seeking Scale, a measure of the tendency to be involved in exciting or dangerous experiences. However, there is evidence of a relationship between A-trait level and responses in situations involving the possibility of loss of self-esteem. Differences in performance in learning and conditioning for *S*s who differ in level of A-trait has been found primarily under conditions of failure or ego-involvement (Hodges & Spielberger, 1969; Spence & Spence, 1966; Spielberger & Smith, 1966). These findings are consistent with Spielberger's (1966) proposal that A-trait involves fear of failure or loss of self-esteem.

The goal of the present study was to identify the type of situations which are perceived as differentially threatening by *S*s who differ in level of A-trait. In accordance with Spielberger's theoretical proposals, it was predicted that *S*s who indicated that they were high in levels of A-trait would report heightened fears only in situations involving the possibility of loss of self-esteem and that there would be no difference in the response of high and low A-trait *S*s to situations involving physical pain or danger.

METHOD

The *S*s were 228 undergraduates enrolled in the introductory psychology courses at the University of Colorado. They were given research participation credit for participating in the experiment. There were 141 males and 87 females in the sample. The *S*s were administered two questionnaires: the Stressful Situations Questionnaire and an early experimental form of the Spielberger, Lushene, and McAdoo (in press) Trait Anxiety scale of the State-Trait Anxiety Inventory.

The Stressful Situations Questionnaire was made up of 40 items which describe situations which might be considered stressful by some people. The *S*s were required to rate on a 5-point scale (none at all, slight, moderate, considerable, or extreme) the degree of apprehensiveness or concern he has felt or believes he would feel if in that situation. The items used are presented in Table 2.1. The 40 items[2] were selected to have some relevance for the life of the college student. Five items were selected to measure each of eight different areas of anxiety-provoking aspects of college life. The items constructed to measure fear or apprehension in situations involving the possibility of failure were: Dating (Items: 1, 2, 24, 35, 43); Classroom Participation (4, 21, 30, 38, 44); Speech (5, 23, 25, 28, 37); Social Failure (6, 16, 20, 34, 36); and Academic Failure (9, 11, 22, 26, 39). The three areas in which loss of self-esteem is not the anxiety-

---

[2]There were an additional five items testing another hypothesis and not relevant to the predictions of the present study. The item numbers therefore go to 45.

Table 2.1   Stressful Situations Questionnaire Items and Factor Loadings for Each Item

Item no.	Item	Factor loadings			
		I	II	III	IV
3	Seeing someone bleed profusely from a cut arm	57	10	16	−01
7	Putting iodine on an open cut	53	10	04	04
10	Seeing a dog run over by a car	49	−05	30	−12
12	Walking in a slum alone at night	57	14	23	05
13	Giving blood at the blood bank	44	25	07	05
14	Riding an airplane in a storm	45	07	15	30
15	Being present at an operation or watching one in a movie	57	23	09	12
17	Having a tooth cavity filled	32	22	08	12
18	Climbing too steep a mountain	38	06	26	32
19	Paying respects at the open coffin of an acquaintance	41	06	30	04
29	Riding in a car going 95 miles per hour	46	−03	14	27
33	Passing a very bad traffic accident	56	15	28	05
42	Participating in a psychology experiment in which you receive electric shock	44	05	04	22
4	Asking a teacher to clarify an assignment in class	10	61	13	03
5	Giving a speech in front of class	17	56	25	09
21	Asking a question in class	08	78	12	05
23	Reciting a poem in class	11	62	20	13
25	Reciting in language class	09	50	12	18
30	Asking a teacher to explain the grading of your test	23	50	16	33
38	Volunteering an answer to a question in class	12	72	10	15
44	Asking a teacher to explain a question during a test	14	55	08	38
6	Introducing a friend and forgetting his name	14	23	47	02
9	Taking a test that you expect to fail	12	−02	56	17
11	Being in a difficult course for which you have inadequate background	22	10	45	15
16	Belching aloud in class	30	21	46	−17
20	Being refused membership in a social club	16	16	49	−01
22	Doing poorly in a course which seems easy to others	11	08	61	00
24	Having your date leave a dance with someone else	09	02	53	07
26	Finding the questions on a test extremely difficult	24	08	50	26
28	Forgetting lines in a school play	17	10	57	10
34	Being the only person at a party not dressed up	10	29	59	11
36	Spilling your drink on yourself at a formal dinner party	05	22	57	16
39	Getting back a test you think you may have failed	26	12	46	20
1	Going on a blind date	−02	20	11	57
2	Asking someone for a date to a party	17	37	14	45
35	Introducing yourself to someone very attractive of the opposite sex	07	42	29	47
43	Kissing a date for the first time	07	20	02	54
31	Getting hurt in a fight	31	02	29	23
37	Having an interview for a job	32	35	21	37
40	Skiing out of control	35	06	22	40
Point-biserial correlation of sex with factor scores (High = Females)		49*	01	02	−08
Correlation of Trait Anxiety scale with factor scores		02	24*	24*	26*

Note.—Italicized numbers indicate high factor loadings for specific kinds of items.
*$p < .01$.

provoking aspect of the situation were: Physical Danger (12, 14, 18, 29, 40); Pain (7, 13, 17, 31, 42); and Squeamishness (3, 10, 15, 19, 33).

The early experimental form of the Trait Anxiety scale was made up of 20 items indicating anxiety or tension which the S rated on a 4-point scale from almost always to almost never, reporting how he generally felt. Thus, if the S indicated that he frequently felt tense and anxious and seldom felt calm and relaxed, he was given a high score on A-trait. Spielberger[3] has found that this scale correlated highly with the Taylor MA scale and has satisfactory reliability. The latest form of the scale (Spielberger et al., in press) may be considered an improved version of the scale used in this study, but highly correlated with it, since many of the items are the same.

RESULTS

In order to determine if the eight logically determined scales have empirical validity, all 40 items were intercorrelated and this matrix subjected to a minimum residual factor analysis (Comrey & Humada, 1964). A convergence limit of .005 was used and four factors were extracted. The four factors were then subjected to a Varimax rotation (Kaiser, 1950). The resulting factor structure is presented in Table 2.1. Items have been ordered so that items loading heavily on the same factor are grouped together. The first factor is made up of items associated with physical danger, pain, and squeamishness. The second factor is determined by items involving anxiety from classroom participation and speech. The third factor involves situations of social and academic failure, and the fourth factor, of only four items, involves dating. Three items at the end of the list did not load on any particular factor but tended to have low moderate loadings on at least three of the factors.

In order to determine the relationships between these factors, sex, and A-trait, factor scores for each S were obtained and the results correlated with these variables. These results are presented at the end of Table 2.1. The correlations of sex with the four factors indicate that females tend to be more apprehensive than males in situations involving physical danger or pain, but that males are just as likely as females to indicate anxiety in situations involving speech, social or academic failure, and dating. A-trait did not correlate with being anxious in situations involving physical danger, pain, or squeamishness, but demonstrated low moderate correlations with the other three factors.

While these correlations are low, it should be noted that only the factors involving threat to self-esteem correlate significantly with the Trait Anxiety scale. A multiple correlation of the three ego-involving factors (II, III, and IV)

---

[3]C. D. Spielberger, personal communication, August 1968.

on the Trait Anxiety scale was performed. The obtained R of .46 demonstrated a sharp increase in predictive power by including the anxiety reaction to all ego-involving situations.

DISCUSSION

The obtained factors are similar to those reported in other studies (Endler, Hunt, & Rosenstein, 1962; Scherer & Nakamura, 1968). Factor I, with its loadings on danger, pain, and squeamishness, is similar to Endler, Hunt, and Rosenstein's inanimate fear factor, while the other factors correspond more closely to their interpersonal fears factor. Factor II involves apprehension over speech and classroom participation, both tasks requiring talking in the presence of a large number of people. Factor III involves both social and academic failure. Dating apparently has some unique fear-provoking aspects, so that it forms a factor of its own.

Most studies have indicated that females tend to be more fearful than males (Geer, 1965; Manosevitz & Lanyon, 1965) and at least one has found sex differences on individual items (Manosevitz & Lanyon, 1965). The present data indicate that the sex differences occur primarily for physical danger and pain, but not for the other types of situations. It is interesting to note the failure to find sex differences in situations involving speech, social and academic failure, and dating. Apparently many of the stressful situations frequently found in college life are just as threatening for men as women.

The finding that the Trait Anxiety scale did not correlate with the physical danger or pain factor but did correlate with the factors involving speech and classroom participation, social and academic failure, and dating is consistent with Spielberger's (1966) contention that A-trait is a measure of the predisposition to respond with heightened A-state to situations involving failure or loss of self-esteem. These findings are also similar to those obtained by Grossberg and Wilson (1965), who found a moderate correlation of the *MA* scale with the social-interpersonal scale of the FSS, but now with fears of tissue damage. The magnitude of the correlations of A-trait with the three "self-esteem" factors was unexpectedly low. However, when all three of these factors were taken into account in predicting the level of A-trait, the obtained R of .46 is similar to the values obtained for the correlation of various A-trait scores with the total number of fears on the FSS (Geer, 1965; Grossberg & Wilson, 1965; Manosevitz & Lanyon, 1965; Scherer & Nakamura, 1968). Thus, knowledge of the anxiety reaction to several types of ego-involving situations is required before a moderately precise prediction of A-trait level can be made. It is apparent, however, that only situations involving the possibility of loss of self-esteem or failure will be differentially perceived as threatening by *S*s who differ in A-trait level.

These results also suggest important implications for the area of behavior therapy where it might be assumed that desensitization or other counterconditioning techniques of a specific fear would result in generalization to fears within the same factor but not to other factors. In addition, the present study indicates that when a college student reports that he is frequently anxious, he is probably indicating fears associated with situations involving speech, failure, and dating, rather than concern over physical danger.

REFERENCES

Ax, A. F. The physiological differentiation between fear and anger in humans. *Psychosomatic Medicine,* 1953, **15,** 433-442.

Cattell, R. B., & Scheier, I. H. *The Meaning and Measurement of Neuroticism and Anxiety.* New York: Ronald Press, 1961.

Comrey, A. L., & Humada, A. An improved procedure and program for minimum residual factor analysis. *Psychological Reports,* 1964, **15,** 91-96.

Deane, G. E. Human heart responses during experimentally induced anxiety. *Journal of Experimental Psychology,* 1961, **61,** 489-493.

Endler, N. S., Hunt, J. McV., & Rosenstein, A. J. An S-R inventory of anxiousness. *Psychological Monographs,* 1962, **76** (17, Whole No. 536).

Freud, S. *New Introductory Lectures on Psychoanalysis.* New York: Norton, 1933.

Freud, S. *The Problem of Anxiety.* New York: Norton, 1936.

Geer, J. The development of a scale to measure fear. *Behaviour Research and Therapy,* 1965, **3,** 45-53.

Grossberg, J., & Wilson, H. K. A correlational comparison of the Wolpe-Lang Fear Survey Schedule and Taylor Manifest Anxiety Scale. *Behaviour Research and Therapy,* 1965, **3,** 125-128.

Hodges, W. F. Effects of ego threat and threat of pain on state anxiety. *Journal of Personality and Social Psychology,* 1968, **8,** 364-372.

Hodges, W. F., & Spielberger, C. D. The effects of threat of shock on heart rate for subjects who differ in manifest anxiety and fear of shock. *Psychophysiology,* 1966, **2,** 287-294.

Hodges, W. F. & Spielberger, C. D. Digit span: An indicant of trait or state anxiety? *Journal of Consulting and Clinical Psychology,* 1969, **33,** 430-434.

Kaiser, H. F. Computer program for Varimax rotation in factor analysis. *Educational and Psychological Measurement,* 1959, **19,** 413-419.

Lang, P. J., & Lazovik, A. D. Experimental desensitization of a phobia. *Journal of Abnormal and Social Psychology,* 1963, **66,** 519-525.

Lazarus, R. S. *Psychological Stress and the Coping Process.* New York: McGraw-Hill, 1966.

Lazarus, R. S., Speisman, J. C., Mordkoff, A. M., & Davison, L. A. A laboratory study of psychological stress produced by a motion picture film. *Psychological Monographs,* 1962, **76** (34, Whole No. 553).

Malmo, R. B., & Schagass, C. Physiological studies of reaction to stress in anxiety and early schizophrenia. *Psychosomatic Medicine,* 1949, **11,** 9-24.

Manosevitz, M., & Lanyon, R. I. Fear Survey Schedule: A normative study. *Psychological Reports*, 1965, **17**, 699-703.

Scherer, M. W., & Nakamura, C. Y. A Fear Survey Schedule for Children (FSS-FC): A factor analytic comparison with manifest anxiety (CMAS). *Behaviour Research and Therapy*, 1968, **6**, 173-182.

Spence, J. T., & Spence, K. W. The motivational components of manifest anxiety: Drive and drive stimuli. In C. D. Spielberger (Ed.), *Anxiety and Behavior*. New York: Academic Press, 1966.

Spielberger, C. D. Theory and research on anxiety. In C. D. Spielberger (Ed.), *Anxiety and behavior*. New York: Academic Press, 1966.

Spielberger, C. D., Lushene, R. E., & McAdoo, W. G. Theory and measurement of anxiety states. In R. B. Cattell (Ed.), *Handbook of Modern Personality Theory*. Chicago: Aldine, in press.

Spielberger, C. D., & Smith, L. H. Anxiety (drive), stress, and serial position effects in serial-verbal learning. *Journal of Experimental Psychology*, 1966, **72**, 589-595.

Wolpe, J., & Lang, P. J. A fear survey schedule for use in behavior therapy. *Behaviour Research and Therapy*, 1964, **2**, 27-30.

Zuckerman, M., Schultz, D. P., & Hopkins, T. R. Sensation seeking and volunteering for sensory deprivation and hypnosis experiments. *Journal of Consulting Psychology*, 1967, **31**, 358-363.

3
Anxiety: States, Traits—Situations?*
Philip C. Kendall

The present study investigated the utility of situational assessments of trait anxiety in predicting state anxiety reactions. Ninety-six male subjects preselected at either high or low on three measures of trait anxiety—S-R Inventory of General Trait Anxiousness (S-R GTA) Physical Danger; S-R GTA Evaluation; State-Trait Anxiety Inventory (STAI A-Trait) Anxiety Trait scale—were exposed to two experimentally induced stresses (a physical danger stress and an evaluation stress). Results indicated that the STAI A-Trait and the S-R GTA Evaluation measures correlated significantly higher with each other than either did with the S-R GTA Physical Danger measure and that both stresses produced a significant increase in state anxiety. In addition, the triple interaction of type of stress, trait level, and trait measure was, as predicted, significant. This finding indicated that high-trait-anxious subjects responded with greater state reactions when the trait measure corresponded with the type of stress. The results are discussed as support for the interaction model of anxiety and for the need to measure situational components of trait anxiety.

The state-trait model of anxiety (Spielberger, 1972) is based on the conceptual framework of transitory anxiety states (A-State) and relatively stable predispositions or traits (A-Trait). The task of state-trait researchers, according to Spielberger (1972), is to "describe and specify the characteristics of stressor stimuli that evoke differential levels of A-State in persons who differ in A-Trait" (p. 39).

*Journal of Consulting and Clinical Psychology, 1978, 46, 2, 280-287. Copyright 1978 by the American Psychological Association. Reprinted by permission.

The central notion of the state-trait model is that persons high in A-Trait have a greater tendency to perceive situations as dangerous or threatening than persons who are low in A-Trait, and thus they are expected to respond to threatening situations with state anxiety elevations of greater intensity. Essentially, Spielberger views trait anxiety as the measure of anxiety proneness from which predictions of state reactions can be made.

The interaction model of anxiety (Endler, 1975) was basically derived from the rationale that had been used to develop the original S-R Inventory of Anxiousness (Endler, Hunt, & Rosenstein, 1962) and its revisions (Endler & Okada, 1975). The major point that Endler and his colleagues have made is that an appropriate assessment of anxiety must consider all sources of variability: individual differences, the responses that characterize anxiety, and the *situations* that are likely to arouse anxiety.

Recently, Endler (1975) viewed the situational component as vital for predicting state anxiety reactions. He made this position clear when he stated that

if one wants to examine the interaction of physical threat and A-Trait on state anxiety, it is necessary to assess physical danger A-Trait independent of other facets of A-Trait. (p. 161)

Within the interaction model the state-trait relationship is essentially similar to that of the state-trait model with the exception that trait anxiety is multidimensional and not unidimensional. The interaction model and the state-trait model agree that subjects high in trait anxiety will show greater state anxiety reactions under stress than will subjects low in trait anxiety, but the interaction model separates from state-trait theory in the specificity of the trait measure needed to make the differential state anxiety predictions.

The results of research using Spielberger, Gorsuch, and Lushene's (1970) State-Trait Anxiety Inventory (STAI) have indicated that individual differences in anxiety proneness (Trait Anxiety Scale—A-Trait) are relatively stable and impervious to stress (Auerbach, 1973a, 1973b; Spielberger, 1972; Spielberger, Auerbach, Wadsworth, Dunn, & Taulbee, 1973), whereas the State Anxiety scale (A-State) has been found to be sensitive to various stresses (Hodges & Spielberger, 1969; Kendall, Finch, Auerbach, Hooke, & Mikulka, 1976). In addition, stressful situations of an ego-threatening nature have been found to evoke greater increases in state anxiety for high-trait-anxious than for low-trait-anxious subjects (Auerbach, 1973a; Hodges & Spielberger, 1969; O'Neil, Spielberger, & Hansen, 1969; Rappaport & Katkin, 1972) except where subjects have equal requisite skills (Kendall et al., 1976). On the other hand, in situations involving physical danger, such as threat of electric shock (Hodges & Spielberger, 1966), imminent surgery (Auerbach, Kendall, Cuttler, & Levitt, 1976; Johnson, Dabbs, & Leventhal, 1970; Spielberger et al., 1973), or films depicting physically painful accidents (Kendall et al., 1976), state anxiety reactions have been found to be unrelated to level of trait anxiety.

The S-R Inventory of General Trait Anxiousness (S-R GTA; Endler & Okada, 1975) is a self-report inventory designed to measure trait anxiety and emphasizes the importance of measuring trait anxiety in specific situations. The S-R GTA has been reported to be both a reliable measure of situational trait anxiety and one that is insensitive to momentary stress (Endler & Okada, 1975). In addition, the authors reported that the situational scales were found to be relatively independent measures.

As yet, no known study has compared the efficacy of the S-R GTA situation-specific measures and the STAI for predicting differential state anxiety reactions. The purpose of the present study was to conduct a comparison of the models of anxiety by investigating differential state anxiety reactions in two stress situations—a physical danger stress and an evaluation stress. It was hypothesized that high-physical-danger/trait-anxious subjects (S-R GTA Physical Danger trait measure) would show greater state anxiety elevations than low-physical-danger/trait-anxious subjects for the physical danger stress, and that high-evaluation-trait (S-R GTA Evaluation trait measure) and high A-Trait (STAI) subjects would show greater state anxiety elevations than low evaluation trait and A-Trait anxious subjects for the evaluation stress. The basic hypothesis was that the trait anxiety measure corresponding to the situation would be the best predictor of the state anxiety aroused in that situation. For the S-R GTA each situational trait was expected to be predictive of that stress situation, whereas for the STAI A-Trait previous research in evaluation situations (see above), the unidimensionality of the scale (Kendall et al., 1976) and the anticipated relationship between the STAI A-Trait and S-R GTA Evaluation trait measure are indicative of accurate prediction only in evaluation stress situations. Confirmation of the hypothesis would provide support for the interaction model and would emphasize the importance of assessments of situational trait anxiety.

METHOD

Subjects

The subjects in the present experiment were 101 male college students selected from a pool of 173 male students (M age = 20.1) at an urban Virginia university. Only male subjects and a male experimenter participated to control for reactions characteristic of the Subject Sex × Experimenter Sex interaction. For example, it was felt that males might protect their masculine image with a female experimenter and would subsequently report less anxiety, whereas females might seek to appear in a feminine stereotyped role with a male experimenter.

Subjects were selected based on their scores on preexperimental measures of trait anxiety. The subject selection procedure was designed to gather subject groups of high and low trait anxiety on the three preexperimental trait measures. The criterion for inclusion in the subject groups required scores that were in the upper 40% for the high-trait-level group and the lower 40% for the low-trait-level group. Also, to control for the other trait measures, subjects selected as high (or low) on the physical danger trait measure (S-R GTA) were not in the upper (or lower) 40% of the evaluation trait and A-Trait (STAI) scores. Likewise, subjects selected for high (or low) evaluation trait (S-R GTA) or A-Trait (STAI) groups were not in the upper (or lower) 40% of the physical danger trait scores. The means, standard deviations, and ranges of the trait scores are presented in Table 3.1. Three subjects were eliminated because they had previously seen the stress film, and 2 subjects were randomly eliminated to achieve an equal number of subjects in each cell. The remaining 96 subjects, 56 whites and 40 blacks, were distributed comparably across the six subject groups (one high and low group for each trait measure).

Table 3.1 Means, Standard Deviations, and Range of Scores of
the Three Trait Measures

Trait measure	*M*	*SD*	Range
S-R GTA Physical Danger	54.09	12.19	18-75
S-R GTA Evaluation	44.34	12.32	18-73
STAI A-Trait	38.89	8.85	22-59

Note. S-R GTA = S-R Inventory of General Trait Anxiousness; STAI
A-Trait = Trait Anxiety scale of the State-Trait Anxiety Inventory.

Measure of State Anxiety

State anxiety was measured using the A-State portion of the STAI. This scale consists of 20 descriptive statements that require the subjects to individually endorse on a 4-point scale (not at all, somewhat, moderately so, very much so) the degree to which each statement characterized their feelings *at a particular moment in time*.

Measures of Trait Anxiety

STAI A-Trait. The STAI A-Trait scale consists of 20 items that require the subjects to individually describe how they generally feel. Subjects respond to each item (e.g., "Some unimportant thought runs through my mind and bothers me") by endorsing 1, 2, 3, or 4 representing "almost never," "sometimes," "often," or "almost always."

S-R GTA. This scale consists of 15 items for each of five situations in which trait anxiety is assessed.[1] The two situations used in this study were (a) "You are in situations where you are about to or may encounter physical danger" and (b) "You are in situations where you are being evaluated by other people." The 15 items for each of these situations required responses from 1 to 5 indicating "very much" to "not at all."

Types of Stress

A physical danger and an evaluation stress were arranged to induce anxiety within an experimental laboratory setting.

Physical danger stress. This stress was a 22-minute Harvest (1970) film entitled *In the Crash*. The film presents graphic scenes of automobile crash tests at both high and low speeds. These crash tests were filmed under experimental as well as real highway circumstances. *In the Crash* has been used in previous research and has been found to be an effective stressor (Kendall et al., 1976).

Evaluation stress. The evaluation stress was a decoding task in which a word problem had to be decoded into an arithmetic solution. The problem is as follows:

$$\begin{array}{r} \text{DONALD} \\ + \text{GERALD} \\ \hline \text{ROBERT} \end{array} \quad D = 5.$$

Subjects were instructed that letters had been substituted for numbers and that the task would be to decode the letters. One part of the solution, D= 5, was provided. Support for the stressful nature of the task is found in previous research using similar tasks (Finch, Kendall, Montgomery, & Morris, 1975). To maximize the stress, ego-involving instructions (Spence & Spence, 1966) and a brief failure instruction (Finch et al., 1975) were included. The exact instructions and time limit are presented in the Procedure section.

Procedure

Subjects participated in groups according to one of two sequences. The sequences pertained to the order of presentation of the stress situations (physical

---

[1] The S-R Inventory of General Trait Anxiousness, which was published in the *Journal of Consulting and Clinical Psychology*, 1975, *43*, 319-329, has only four situations. The revised version has five situations and 15 items per situation. The revised version is available from Norman S. Endler, York University, Toronto, Canada.

danger then evaluation and vice versa). The two sequences were included as a counterbalanced control for order and carryover effects. The stress sequence for a given evening was decided on a restricted random basis before subjects arrived.

As subjects arrived at the laboratory room for their 7:00 p.m. appointment, they were instructed to have a seat and get comfortable. The experiment began after a 5-10 minute late grace period. Subjects were then informed by the experimenter that

I am interested in the relationship between feelings and behavior, and in order to investigate this you will be asked to fill out the "How I feel questionnaire" at certain times and later to describe some behaviors.

Following a pause, the experimenter stated that

I will be instructing you throughout your participation, so listen and you will find your job easy. If you are uncertain at any time about what you are to do, please feel free to ask.

Once everyone appeared ready, the experimenter continued by saying "What I would like you to do first is to complete the How I feel questionnaire." The STAI A-State scale was distributed with pencils, the standard instructions were read from the top of the form, and the forms were collected when all subjects had completed them.

Subjects were then instructed that they would be watching a film. They were told to "pay attention and try to get into the film, but you should not try to remember facts or details about the movie because I will not be asking questions—just watch and get the feeling." Initially, and when necessary, subjects were instructed not to talk to any of the other people during the course of the study.[2]

Following the film, subjects were again asked to complete the How I feel questionnaire by reporting how they had felt during the film. Subjects were next informed that the experimenter would have to rewind the film and that there were magazines available to read. The experimenter provided numerous sports and entertainment magazines (prescreened to provide an absence of stressful material, e.g., car crash pictures) and suggested that the subjects stand, stretch, relax, and look through the magazines. Subjects were reminded not to converse with each other.

When the film was rewound (approximately 10 minutes), the experimenter announced, "Now I want each of you to do something else." A pencil and a sheet of blank white paper (8½ × 11 inches) was given to each subject at his desk, and he was told to write his name across the top of the page. The

---

[2]In my previous research, induced stress tended to increase the conversion level. To prevent intersubject comparisons, subjects were instructed not to talk to each other.

experimenter then wrote the evaluation stress task on the blackboard and provided the following instructions:

> This is an addition problem, only letters have been substituted for the numbers. For instance, D stands for 5. In each place where there is a D there is really a 5. Your task is to solve or decode the rest of the letters. There is a possible solution, I guarantee it. You must work on this individually, and you will be allowed a sufficient amount of time to work out the problem.

Questions were answered at this time, but no additional information was given. Finally, the experimenter provided an ego-involving comment. "This task will give me some information about your abilities that I can use to evaluate you." After 3 minutes subjects were told, "OK, everyone please stop and turn your paper over. Do not talk to your neighbors." The STAI A-State form was again distributed to the subjects while the experimenter commented:

> Fill this out according to how you felt during the task. You all should have gotten the solution or at least most of it, but if you didn't, I will show you the solution at the end of tonight's projects.[3]

No subject solved the task in the allotted time, and all subjects should have experienced some failure and thus maximized the evaluation stress. When all STAI A-State forms were completed and collected, subjects were told that "the project is almost over, and you should sit and relax for a few minutes while I get these papers straight." After a short break subjects were asked to fill out a questionnaire not related to the present study.

Debriefing

Although the present study was rather straightforward, the debriefing explained to the subjects the actual interests of the experimenter and a brief background for the study. Subjects were also told that the experimenter had never intended to ask them to describe behavior as he had stated originally. The answer to the decoding task was presented along with a clarification of its true difficulty and an explanation that most people should not have been able to solve the problem in the allotted time. Subjects were asked not to discuss the project with other students but were told that they could talk among themselves about it. When the questions and discussion were completed. subjects were dismissed.

Only one session was held on a given evening to prevent subjects just finishing the project from passing on information to subjects just arriving. This also prevented subjects from arriving early and overhearing the debriefing session.

---

[3]The procedural sequence in which the evaluation stress preceded the physical danger stress was identical to that just described with the following exception: The break between stressors was covered by the experimenter stating that he had to prepare the projector for the film.

RESULTS

Preexperimental Measures

Correlations of the trait measures using the original pool of 173 subjects resulted in a .38 correlation between the S-R GTA Physical Danger and Evaluation measures, a .19 correlation between the S-R GTA Physical Danger and STAI S-Trait measures, and a .52 correlation between the S-R GTA Evaluation and STAI A-Trait measures. Tests for significant differences between the correlations revealed that the S-R GTA Evaluation/STAI A-Trait correlation was significantly greater than the S-R GTA Physical Danger/STAI A-Trait correlation, $t(167) = 4.33, p < .001$, and that the S-R GTA Evaluation/STAI A-Trait correlation was also significantly greater than the S-R GTA Evaluation/Physical Danger correlation, $t(167) = 1.71, p < .05$. These analyses indicated that the STAI A-Trait and S-R GTA Evaluation measures correlated significantly higher with each other than either did with the S-R GTA Physical Danger measure.

The means and standard deviations of the initial (prestress) A-State scores for the subject groups are presented in Table 3.2. An analysis of variance of the prestress scores indicated that the groups did not differ significantly, $F(5, 90) = 1.62$.

Table 3.2 Means and Standard Deviations of the Initial (Pre-stress) A-State Scores for the Subject Groups

Trait measure and level	Initial prestress A-State	
	M	SD
S-R GTA Physical Danger		
High	33.00	5.69
Low	35.62	6.48
S-R GTA Evaluation		
High	34.37	8.41
Low	30.81	7.67
STAI A-Trait		
High	37.06	7.47
Low	32.56	6.43

Note. S-R GTA = S-R Inventory of General Trait Anxiousness; STAI A-Trait = Anxiety Trait scale of the State-Trait Anxiety Inventory.

Experimental Checks

Stress. The stressful nature of the film was demonstrated by a significant t test for differences between related means of the initial and stress assessment of A-State,

$t(95) = 6.08, p < .001$. Similarly, it was demonstrated, $t(95) = 5.50, p < .001$, that the evaluation task produced elevations in state anxiety. In addition, an inspection of the subjects' performance on the decoding evaluation task showed that all subjects performed at a poor level. Specifically, no one solved more than one of the letters beyond the information given.

Counterbalancing. To confirm the utility of counterbalancing the stress presentations, an analysis of variance of difference scores was conducted for subjects receiving the physical danger stress first and for those receiving it second. There was not a significant difference between the two, $F(1, 94) = 2.13$. Similarly, an analysis for the sequence of the evaluation stress revealed no significant difference, $F(1, 94) = 2.86$.

Experimental sessions. Two additional analyses were carried out to test whether there were meaningful variations in the state anxiety difference scores due to the experimental sessions. To this end, a single factor analysis of variance of A-State difference scores for the five experimental sessions was conducted. The results yielded no significant difference in physical danger of evaluation stress reactions for subjects participating in any of the sessions, $F(4, 91) = .75, p > .10; F(4, 91) = 2.45, p > .10$; respectively. This outcome indicated that different experimental sessions did not produce different results.

Major Hypothesis

The major hypothesis was that the change in A-State from an initial prestress period to a stress period would be greater for high-trait-level subjects than for low-trait-level subjects when the trait measure corresponded to the stressor. Thus, the A-State difference score (stress score minus initial prestress score) was the dependent measure. This hypothesis was examined via a $3 \times 2 \times 2$ analysis of variance in which type of stress was a within variable and trait level and trait measure were between variables (a three-factor mixed design with repeated measures on one factor; Winer, 1962, pp. 337-344).

The results of this analysis indicated that the main effect for trait level and the Type of Stress $\times$ Trait Level $\times$ Trait Measure triple interaction were significant, $F(1, 90) \times 7.81, p < .01$, and $F(2, 90) = 9.52, p < .001$, respectively. The main effects of trait measure and type of stress as well as the Trait Level $\times$ Trait Measure, Type of Stress $\times$ Trait Level, and Type of Stress $\times$ Trait Measure interactions were not significant. These results demonstrate that the change in state anxiety was greater for high- than for low-trait-level subjects but was not significantly different for groups based on the trait measure or for the type of stress.

The nature of the significant triple interaction is presented in Figure 3.1. This illustration shows how the state anxiety difference scores varied for the trait

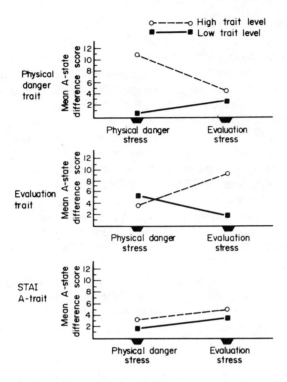

Figure 3.1. Mean A-State (State Anxiety scale) difference scores for the two types of stress and for subjects high and low on each of the trait measures. (A-Trait = STAI Trait Anxiety scale.)

measures, how they differed for the types of stress, and also how they varied for the high- and low-trait-level subjects. An analysis of the predicted simple effects (*t* tests) indicated that for physical danger, high-trait-level subjects were significantly greater than low-trait-level subjects on the A-State difference score under the physical danger stress, $t(30) = 3.87, p < .001$, but not significantly different under the evaluation task, $t(30) = .90, p > .10$. When high- and low-evaluation-trait subjects were compared, there was no significant difference under the physical danger stress, $t(30) = .64, p > .10$, but there was a significant difference in the evaluation task situation, $t(30) = 2.62, p < .01$, with the high-evaluation-trait subjects showing the greater A-State difference score. When high and low STAI A-Trait subjects were compared, there were no significant differences under either the physical danger stress, $t(30) = .47, p > .10$, or the evaluation stress, $t(30) = .56, p > .10$. These analyses indicated that the difference scores of the high-trait-level subjects were greater than those of the low-trait-level subjects when the situation trait measures were congruent with the stress but not when subjects were divided into high and low groups on the basis of the STAI A-Trait.

DISCUSSION

The present study demonstrated that the STAI A-Trait and the S-R GTA Evaluation measure correlated significantly higher with each other than either did with the S-R GTA Physical Danger measure. This outcome suggests that the STAI A-Trait measure is more like the S-R GTA Evaluation measure than like the S-R GTA Physical Danger measure and appears to support previous research, which found the STAI A-Trait to be related to state anxiety in evaluation stress situations (Auerbach, 1973a; Hodges & Spielberger, 1969). Also of interest from the correlational analyses is the relatively low relationship among the measures of trait anxiety (other than the STAI A-Trait/S-R GTA Evaluation correlation). These correlations support the notion of relatively separate anxiety traits.

The efficacy of using a situational anxiety trait measure that is congruent with the stress situation in the prediction of state anxiety reactions was demonstrated in the present study. The trait measures that were viable in the present study were two *situation-specific* measures of anxiety traits, physical danger and evaluation. When the subjects were grouped according to their physical danger trait, the high-trait-level subjects showed significant differential responsiveness to the physical danger stress but not to the evaluation stress. The opposite was true when subjects were grouped on the basis of their evaluation trait scores. On the other hand, the use of a nonsituational, unidimensional trait measure (STAI A-Trait) did not predict differential state anxiety reactions. Thus, the results of the present study support both the need for including situations in the measurement of trait anxiety and, correspondingly, the interaction model of anxiety.

The present results also support the utility of the state-trait distinction, a distinction that has already been supported in both manipulation studies and factor-analytic work (Kendall et al., 1976; Newmark, Faschingbauer, Finch, & Kendall, 1975). However, the present investigation of "states" and "traits" suggests a clarification of their relationship: Anxiety traits are predictive of anxiety states when the trait measure is congruent with the evocative situation. It appears that there is use for the inclusion of situational trait measures.

The lack of differential state anxiety responsiveness for high and low STAI A-Trait subjects under both stresses was unexpected. Since the STAI A-Trait measure correlated more with the S-R GTA Evaluation trait measure than with the physical danger measure, since previous research has reported greater state reactions for high STAI A-Trait subjects in evaluation stresses, and since the trait measure is unidimensional, the STAI A-Trait measure was viewed as indicative of a predisposition to become anxious in evaluation situations. Based on these findings, differential state reactions for high STAI A-Trait subjects were hypothesized under the evaluation stress. However, this hypothesis was not supported in the present study.

In speculating about the reasons for the insensitivity of the STAI A-Trait measure in the evaluation stress situation, the previous findings of Kendall et al.

(1976) are suggestive. In that study, in which subjects were shown to have performed equally under stress and thus were considered to have had relatively equal requisite skills, high and low A-Trait subjects reacted similarly to an examination stress. In the present experiment subjects indeed performed equally; no one decoded more than one letter beyond the given information. The present inability of the STAI A-Trait to predict differential responses in an evaluation stress could be due to the similar performance of all subjects. However, this possibility is directly contradicted by the results found when the S-R GTA Evaluation measure was used (i.e., high- and low-evaluation-trait anxious subjects *did* respond differentially).

A more parsimonious speculation about the unexpected results using the STAI A-Trait measure concerns the measure itself. That is, whereas the STAI A-Trait measure requires subjects to indicate how they generally feel, it does not specify a situation in its assessment of the anxiety trait. The ignoring of situational specificity by the STAI A-Trait measure could account for the present findings.

More importantly, the present study provides major construct validation for the Physical Danger and Evaluation portions of the S-R GTA. Since only two situations were directly investigated, the validity of the other situation traits is yet to be examined. But both the present study and the work of Endler and Okada (1975) suggest that it would be beneficial to further examine situational measures of trait anxiety.

The outcome of the present study has implications for future research in personality in general and anxiety in particular. The generality of this finding suggests that personality trait measures should be reexamined in light of the situational dimensionality of each particular trait. This reexamination would entail investigating all the situations related to the trait, organizing these situations into *classes,* and developing an instrument for the assessment of each *situational class.* Thus, instead of continuing to assess cross-situational traits or attempting to measure situation-specific responses, researchers would potentially profit from focusing on the assessment of traits in relation to *classes* of situations.

REFERENCES

Auerbach, S. M. Effects of orienting instructions, feedback-information, and trait-anxiety level on state anxiety. *Psychological Reports,* 1973, *33,* 779-786. (a)

Auerbach, S. M. Trait-state anxiety and adjustment to surgery. *Journal of Consulting and Clinical Psychology,* 1973, *40,* 264-271. (b)

Auerbach, S. M., Kendall, P. C., Cuttler, H. F. & Levitt, N. R. Anxiety, locus of control, type of preparatory information and adjustment to dental surgery. *Journal of Consulting and Clinical Psychology,* 1976, *44,* 809-818.

Endler, N. S. A person-situation interaction model for anxiety. In C. D. Spielberger & I. G. Sarason (Eds.), *Stress and Anxiety* (Vol. 1). Washington, D.C.: Hemisphere Publications, 1975.

Endler, N. S., Hunt, J. McV., & Rosenstein, A. J. An S-R Inventory of Anxiousness. *Psychological Monographs*, 1962, *76* (17, Whole No. 536).

Endler, N. S., & Okada, M. A multidimensional measure of trait anxiety: The S-R Inventory of General Trait Anxiousness. *Journal of Consulting and Clinical Psychology*, 1975, *43*, 319-329.

Finch, A. J., Jr., Kendall, P. C., Montgomery, L. E., & Morris, J. Effects of two types of failure on anxiety in emotionally disturbed children. *Journal of Abnormal Psychology*, 1975, *84*, 583-585.

Harvest. *In the Crash*. New York: Harvest Films, 1970. (Film)

Hodges, W. F., & Spielberger, C. D. The effects of threat of shock on heart rate for subjects who differ in manifest anxiety and fear of shock. *Psychophysiology*, 1966, *2*, 287-294.

Hodges, W. F., & Spielberger, C. D. Digit span: An indicant of trait or state anxiety? *Journal of Consulting and Clinical Psychology*, 1969, *33*, 430-434.

Johnson, J. E., Dabbs, J. M., & Leventhal, H. Psychological factors in the welfare of surgical patients. *Nursing Research*, 1970, *19*, 18-29.

Kendall, P. C., Finch, A. J., Jr., Auerbach, S. M., Hooke, J. F., & Mikulka, P. J. The State-Trait Anxiety Inventory: A systematic evaluation. *Journal of Consulting and Clinical Psychology*, 1976, *44*, 406-412.

Newmark, C. S., Faschingbauer, T. R., Finch, A. J., Jr., & Kendall, P. C. Factor analysis of the MMPI-STAI. *Journal of Clinical Psychology*, 1975, *31*, 449-452.

O'Neil, J. F., Spielberger, C. D., & Hansen, D. N. The effects of state anxiety and task difficulty on computer-assisted learning. *Journal of Educational Psychology*, 1969, *60*, 343-350.

Rappaport, H., & Katkin, E. S. Relationships among manifest anxiety, response to stress and the perception of autonomic activity. *Journal of Consulting and Clinical Psychology*, 1972, *38*, 219-224.

Spence, J. T., & Spence, K. W. The motivational components of manifest anxiety: Drive and drive stimuli. In C. D. Spielberger (Ed.), *Anxiety and Behavior*. New York: Academic Press, 1966.

Spielberger, C. D. Anxiety as an emotional state. In C. D. Spielberger (Ed.), *Anxiety: Current trends in theory and research* (Vol. 1). New York: Academic Press, 1972.

Spielberger, C. D., Auerbach, S. M., Wadsworth, A. P., Dunn, T. M., & Taulbee, E. S. Emotional reactions to surgery. *Journal of Consulting and Clinical Psychology*, 1973, *40*, 33-38.

Spielberger, C. D., Gorsuch, R. L., & Lushene, R. E. *STAI manual for the State-Trait Anxiety Inventory ("Self-Evaluation Questionnaire")*. Palo Alto, Calif.: Consulting Psychologists Press, 1970.

Winer, B. J. *Statistical Principles in Experimental Design*. New York: McGraw-Hill, 1962.

Interactional Psychology: Introduction

These three papers are important recent contributions to research on person-situation interaction. Other research is reported in Endler and Magnusson (1976) and Magnusson and Endler (1977).

Buss (1977) points out that a number of writers in this area have failed to distinguish between two uses of the term "interaction." The earlier use referred to *statistical interaction,* in analysis of variance designs, between the effects of personality and situation variables. The other sense is of *dynamic interaction* between persons and situations, wherein persons select and alter situations, and situations influence persons. This is seen as an "organic" and two-way process. Interactions in analysis of variance are not relevant to dynamic interaction.

Endler has been one of the most active contributors to the research on person-situation interaction. In his paper (1975) he reviews the main results of research in the field of analysis of person and situation variance, and other research procedures, including his own research on anxiety. He then argues that we should study how persons and situations interact dynamically, though he does not say how this should be done. One aspect of this dynamic situation that has been investigated by us is the selection of situations by persons; we have found that the situations a person enters are a function of his enduring traits and that he chooses different situations for family and friends, those he likes and dislikes, etc. (Argyle, Furnham and Graham, 1981). There have also been a number of studies of the long-term effects of certain situations on persons.

Mischel played an important role in the early days of person-situation research through his book *Personality and Assessment* (1968) which drew attention to the inconsistency of individual behaviour between situations. In his paper (1977) he discusses the question of personality assessment in the light of what is now known about the effects of situations. Like Endler, he favours a dynamic view of interaction. He argues that the most useful person variables are cognitive ones, such as category systems, expectancies of outcomes, and values; and he believes that these can be assessed by verbal reports. The interface with the environment can be handled by finding the scripts or grammars for situations and the grammars for individuals. The difficulty with this view is that there is evidence that people often have very poor insight into themselves (Nisbett and Wilson, 1977); there are aspects of persons which are not accessible to self-report—social skills, non-verbal communication, emotional and other physiological reactions, for example. Still, his paper, combined with those of Buss and Endler, sheds valuable insights on recent research on person-situation interaction.

SUGGESTED ADDITIONAL REFERENCES

Alker, H. Is personality situationally specific or intraphysically consistent. *Journal of Personality*, 1973, *40*, 1-16.

Allport, G. Trait revisited. *American Psychologist*, 1966, *21*, 1-10.

Alston, W. Traits, consistency, and conceptual alternatives for personality theory. In R. Harré (Ed.) *Personality*, Oxford: Blackwell, 1976.

Archer, R. Relationships between locus of control, trait anxiety, and state anxiety: an interactionist perspective. *Journal of Personality*, 1979, *47*, 305-316.

Archer, R., Foushee, H., and Davis, M. Emotional empathy in a courtroom simulation: a person-situation interaction. *Journal of Applied Social Psychology*, 1979, *9*, 275-291.

Argyle, M. Personality and Social Behaviour. In R. Harré (Ed.) *Personality*, Oxford: Blackwell, 1976.

Argyle, M. and Little, B. Do personality traits apply to social behaviour. *Journal for the Theory of Social Behaviour*, 1972, *2*, 1-35.

Argyle, M., Shimoda, K., and Little, B. Variance due to persons and situations in England and Japan. *British Journal of Social and Clinical Psychology*, 1978, *17*, 335-337.

Bearden, W., Woodside, A., and Jones, J. Beliefs and anticipated situations influencing intentions to use drugs. *Perceptual and Motor Skills*, 1979, *48*, 743-751.

Becherer, R., Morgan, F., and Richard, L. Person-situation interaction within a consumer behavior context. *Journal of Psychology*, 1979, *102*, 235-242.

Bem, D. Constructing cross-situational consistencies in behavior: some thoughts on Alker's critique of Mischel. *Journal of Personality*, 1972, *40*, 17-26.

Bem, D. and Allen, A. On predicting some of the people some of the time: the search for cross-situational consistency in behavior. *Psychological Review*, 1974, *81*, 506-520.

Bem, D. and Funder, D. Predicting more of the people more of the time: assessing the personality of situations. *Psychological Review*, 1978, *85*, 485-501.

Bishop, D. and Witt, P. Sources of behavioral variance during leisure time. *Journal of Personality and Social Psychology*, 1970, *16*, 352-360.

Block, J. Some reasons for apparent inconsistency of personality. *Psychological Bulletin*, 1968, *70*, 210-222.

Bourne, E. Can we describe an individual's personality. *Journal of Personality and Social Psychology*, 1977, *35*, 863-872.

Buss, A. The trait-situation controversy and the concept of interaction. *Personality and Social Psychology Bulletin*, 1977, *3*, 196-201.

Breen, L. P × S interaction in personality prediction. *Journal of Consulting and Clinical Psychology,* 1978, 567-568.

Bruno, F. The situational approach—a reaction to individualism. *Social Forces,* 1931, *9,* 482-483.

Burton, R. The generality of honesty reconsidered. *Psychological Review,* 1963, *70,* 481-499.

Buss, A. and Royce, J. Note on the temporality of trait constructs. *Journal for the Theory of Social Behaviour,* 1976, *6,* 171-176.

Campus, N. Transituational consistency as a dimension of personality. *Journal of Personality and Social Psychology,* 1974, *29,* 592-600.

Cantor, N., and Mischel, W. Traits as prototypes: effects on recognition memory. *Journal of Personality and Social Psychology,* 1977, *35,* 38-48.

Coie, J. An evaluation of the cross-situational stability of children's curiosity. *Journal of Personality,* 1974, *42,* 93-116.

Dornbusch, S., Hatdorf, A., Richardson, S., Muzzy, R., and Vreeland, R. The perceiver and the perceived. *Journal of Personality and Social Psychology,* 1964, *1,* 335-440.

Dworkin, R. Genetic and environmental influences on person-situation interactions. *Journal of Research in Personality,* 1979, *13,* 279-293.

Dworkin, R. and Kihlstrom, J. An S-R Inventory of dominance for research on the nature of person-situation interaction. *Journal of Personality,* 1978, *46,* 43-56.

Ekehammar, B., Magnusson, D., and Ricklander, L. An interactionist approach to the study of anxiety. *Scandinavian Journal of Psychology,* 1974, *15,* 4-14.

Ekehammar, D. Interactionism in personality from a historical perspective. *Psychological Bulletin,* 1974, *80,* 1026-1048.

Ellett, R., and Bersoff, D. An integrated approach to the psycho-situational assessment of behavior. *Professional Psychology,* 1976, *7,* 485-494.

Endler, N. A person-situation interaction model for anxiety. In C. Spielberger (Ed.) *Stress and Anxiety,* Vol. 1. Washington: Hemisphere, 1975.

Endler, N. Estimating variance components from mean squares for random and mixed effects, analysis variance model. *Perceptual and Motor Skills,* 1966, *2,* 559-570.

Endler, N. The person versus the situation—a pseudo issue? A response to Alker. *Journal of Personality,* 1973, *41,* 287-303.

Endler, N. Grand illusions: traits or interactions. *Canadian Psychological Review,* 1976, *17,* 174-179.

Endler, N. The role of the person by situation interactions in personality theory. In I. Uzgiris and D. Weizmann (Eds.) *The Structuring of Experience,* New York: Plenum, 1977.

Endler, N. and Hunt, J. Inventories of hostility and comparisons of the proportions of variance from persons, responses and situations for hostility and anxiousness. *Journal of Personality and Social Psychology,* 1968, *9,* 309-315.

Endler, N. and Hunt, J. Generalizability of contributions from sources of variance in the S-R Inventory of Anxiousness. *Journal of Personality,* 1969, *37,* 1-24.

Endler, N., Hunt, J., and Rosenstein, A. An S-R Inventory of Anxiousness. *Psychological Monographs,* 1962, *76,* 1-33.

Endler, N. and Magnusson, D. Toward an interactional psychology of personality. *Psychological Bulletin,* 1976, *83,* 956-974.

Endler, N. and Magnusson, D. Multidimensional aspects of state and trait anxiety: a cross-cultural study of Canadian and Swedish college students. In C. Speilberger and R. Diaz Guerrero (Eds.) *Cross-Cultural Research on anxiety,* Washington: Hemisphere, 1976.

Endler, N. and Magnusson, D. The interaction model of anxiety: an empirical test in an examination situation. *Canadian Journal of Behavioral Science,* 1977, *9,* 101-107.

Epstein, S. The stability of behavior: 1. On predicting most of the people much of the time. *Journal of Personality and Social Psychology,* 1979, *36,* 1097-1126.

Eysenck, M. & Eysenck, H. Mischel and the concept of personality. *British Journal of Psychology,* 1980, *71,* 191-204.

Fiske, D. The limits for the conventional science of personality. *Journal of Personality,* 1974, *42,* 1-14.

Fiske, S. and Cox, M. Person concepts: the effects of target familiarity and descriptive purpose on the process of describing others. *Journal of Personality,* 1979, *47,* 136-161.

Furnham, A. Personality and activity preference. *British Journal of Social Psychology,* 1981 (in press).

Goldberg, L. Some recent trends in personality assessment. *Journal of Personality Assessment,* 1972, *36,* 547-560.

Golding, S. Flies in the ointment: methodological problems in the analysis of variance due to persons and situations. *Psychological Bulletin,* 1975, *82,* 278-288.

Golding, S. Method variance, inadequate constructs, or things that go bump in the night. *Multivariate Behavioral Research,* 1977, *12,* 89-98.

Hayden, T. and Mischel, W. Maintaining trait consistency in the resolution of behavioral inconsistency: the wolf in sheep's clothing. *Journal of Personality,* 1976, *44,* 109-132.

Heffler, B. and Magnusson, D. Generality of behavioral data. IV. *Perceptual and Motor Skills,* 1979, *48,* 471-477.

Hogan, R., De Soto, C. and Solano, C. Traits, tests, and personality research. *American Psychologist,* 1977, *32,* 246-264.

Howard, J. Person-situation interaction models. *Personality and Social Psychology Bulletin,* 1979, *5,* 191-195.

Hunt, D. Person-environment interaction: a challenge found wanting before it was tried. *Review of Educational Research,* 1975, *45,* 209-230.

Hunt, J. Traditional personality theory in the light of recent evidence. *American Scientist,* 1965, *53,* 80-96.

Kassin, S. Physical continuity and trait inference: a test of Mischel's hypothesis. *Personality and Social Psychology Bulletin,* 1977, *3,* 633-640.

Kenrick, D., & Strongfield, D. Personality traits and the eye of the beholder: Crossing some traditional philosophical boundaries in the search for consistency in all of the people. *Psychological Review,* 1980, *87,* 88-104.

Knudson, R. and Golding, S. Comparative validity of traditional versus S-R format inventories on interpersonal behavior. *Journal of Research in Personality,* 1974, *8,* 111-127.

Krauskopf, C. Comments on Endler and Magnusson's attempt to redefine personality. *Psychological Bulletin,* 1978, *85,* 280-283.

Kuhl, J. Situations-, reaktiions- und personbezogene Konsistenz des Leistungsmot -ivs bei der Messung mittles des Hackhausen- TAT. *Archiv fur Psychologie*, 1978, *130*, 37-52.

Long, G., Calhoun, L., and Selby, J. Personality characteristics related to cross-situational consistency on interpersonal distance. *Journal of Personality Assessment*, 1977, *41*, 274-278.

Magnusson, D. An analysis of situational dimensions. *Perceptual and Motor Skills*, 1971, *32*, 851-867.

Magnusson, D. The individual in the situation. *Studia Psychologica*, 1974, *16*, 124-132.

Magnusson, D. The person and the situation in an interactional model of behaviour. *Scandinavian Journal of Psychology*, 1976, *17*, 253-271.

Magnusson, D. Consistency and coherence in personality. *University of Stockholm Reports, 1976, No. 472*.

Magnusson, D. and Ekehammar, B. An analysis of situational dimensions: a replication. *Journal of Personality and Social Psychology*, 1973, *8*, 331-339.

Magnusson, D., Gerzen, M., and Nyman, B. The generality of behavioral data I: generalisations from observations to one occasion. *Multidimensional Behavioral Research*, 1968, *3*, 370-395.

Magnusson, D., Heffler, B. and Nyman, B. The generality of behavioral data II: replication of an experiment on generalisation from observation on one occasion. *Multidimensional Behavioral Research*, 1968, *3*, 415-422.

Magnusson, D. and Heffler, B. The generalization of behavioral data III: generalisation potential as a function of the number of observation instances. *Multidimensional Behavioral Research*, 1969, *4*, 29-42.

Miller, K. and Ginter, J. An investigation of situational variance in brand choice behavior and attitude. *Journal of Marketing Research*, 1979, *16*, 111-123.

Mischel, W. Continuity and change in personality. *American Psychologist*, 1969, *24*, 1012-1018.

Mischel, W. Towards a cognitive social learning reconception of personality. *Psychological Review*, 1973, *80*, 252-283.

Mischel, W. On the future of personality measurement. *American Psychologist*, 1977, *32*, 246-254.

Mischel, W. On the interface of cognition and personality: beyond the person-situation debate. *American Psychologist*, 1979, *34*, 740-754.

Mischel, W. (1968) *Personality and Assessment*. New York: Wiley.

Moos, R. Sources of variance in response to questionnaire and behavior. *Journal of Abnormal Psychology*, 1969, *74*, 405-412.

Nelson, E., Grinder, R., and Mutterer, M. Sources of variance in behavioral measures of honesty in temptation situations: methodological analyses. *Developmental Psychology*, 1969, *1*, 265-279.

Nisbett, R.E. and Wilson, T.D. (1977) Telling more than we can know: verbal reports on mental processes. *Psychological Review*, *84*, 231-259.

Olweus, D. Personality and aggression. *Nebraska Symposium on Motivation*, 1972, *10*, 261-319.

Olweus, D. Stability of aggressive reaction patterns in males: a review. *Psychological Bulletin*, 1979, *86*, 852-875.

Ringuette, E. The stability of individual differences in behavior across experimental conflict situations. *Journal of Research into Personality*, 1976, *10*, 177-182.

Rushton, J. and Endler, N. Person by situation interaction in academic achievement. *Journal of Personality*, 1977, *45*, 297-304.

Sadava, S. and Forsyth, R. Person-environment interaction and college student drug use. *Genetic Psychology Monographs*, 1977, *96*, 211-245.

Sarason, I., Smith, R., and Diener, E. Personality research: components of variance attributable to the person and the situation. *Journal of Personality and Social Psychology*, 1975, *32*, 199-204.

Schweder, R. How relevant is an individual difference theory of personality. *Journal of Personality*, 1975, *43*, 455-484.

Shedletsky, R. and Endler, N. Trait vs. state anxiety, and authoritarianism: the interaction model. *Journal of Personality*, 1974, *42*, 511-527.

Shouval, R., Zakay, D., and Halfon, Y. Autonomy or the autonomies: trait consistency or situation specificity. *Multivariate Behavioral Research*, 1977, *12*, 143-158.

Silverstein, A. and Fisher, G. Estimated variance components in the S-R Inventory of Anxiousness. *Perceptual and Motor Skills*, 1968, *27*, 740-742.

Soloman, S. Measuring dispositional and situational attributions. *Personality and Social Psychology Bulletin*, 1978, *4*, 589-594.

Staats, A. 'Behavioural interaction' and 'interactional psychology' theories of personality: Similarities, differences and the need for unification. *British Journal of Psychology*, 1980, *71*, 205-220.

Turner, R. Consistency, self-consciousness and the predictive validity of typical and marginal personality measures. *Journal of Research in Personality*, 1978, *12*, 117-132.

Van Hech, G. and Van Der Leeuw, E. Situatie ed dispositie als variantie-komponenten in zelfbeoordeling en becordeling van de ander. *Gedrag tijdshrift voor Psychologie*, 1975, *4*, 202-214.

Wachtel, P. On fact, hunch and stereotype: a reply to Mischel. *Journal of Abnormal Psychology*, 1973, *82*, 537-540.

Wallace, J. What units shall we employ? Allport's question revisited. *Journal of Consulting Psychology*, 1967, *31*, 56-64.

Wallach, M. and Leggett, M. Testing the hypothesis that a person will be consistent. *Journal of Personality*, 1972, *40*, 309-330.

Zuckerman, M. Personality and situational factors in the process of inferring attitudes from behaviour. *Psychological Reports*, 1972, *31*, 386-389.

1

The Trait-Situation Controversy and the Concept of Interaction*

Allan R. Buss

The trait-situation issue has been reviewed, discussed, criticized, and "resolved" by several individuals within the last few years. Four recent contributors to this topic—Bowers, Ekehammar, Endler, and Mischel—all have in common recommending an interactionist position. That is where the similarities end, however, to the extent that some of these individuals have advanced relatively consistent but different interactionist views, while others have become tangled in a web of conceptual confusion over the concept of interaction. After determining the meaning of the term "interaction" as it has been used in major contributions to the trait-situation issue, it is concluded that intelligent debate on this topic requires more precise use of this term.

Within the last few years a number of major articles have examined the interrelationship of traits and situations in predicting and or understanding behavior (e.g., Bowers, 1973; Ekehammar, 1974; Endler, 1975; Endler & Magnusson, 1976; Mischel, 1973). While differing in their orientation, emphasis, and conclusions, these particular articles all attempt to resolve the trait "versus" situation controversy by resorting to some form of *interactionism*. A careful reading of the recent articles by Bowers, Ekehammar, Endler, and Mischel on the trait-situation issue reveals that, while each advocates an *interactionist* position, they do not all mean the same thing by this term. Moreover, in certain instances these authors advocate incompatible formulations in the same article. If the continuing debate surrounding the trait-situation

*Personality and Social Psychology Bulletin, 1977, 3, 21-29. Copyright 1977 by the Society for Personality and Social Psychology. Reprinted by persmission.

controversy is to proceed in a meaningful way, then it is extremely important that the term "interaction" be clearly understood in order to avoid using inappropriate empirical evidence to support a particular view, and, to avoid constructing what, upon closer inspection, turn out to be inherently contradictory arguments. Thus the purpose of the present article is to contribute to clearer thinking about the various interactionist solutions to the trait-situation controversy which have been proposed.

THE CONCEPTUAL STRUCTURE OF THE TERM "INTERACTION"

Psychologists tend to use the term "interaction" in at least two major and mutually contradictory ways. In order to develop an analytic basis for distinguishing between the two meanings of the term "interaction" within the context of the trait-situation controversy, it is first necessary to characterize what may be called four major subperspectives.

The "pure" *situationist position* may be characterized by $B=f(E)$, that is, behavior is a function of the environment. This view tends to be of the stimulus-response variety, where causality is considered in terms of the situational stimuli determining or evoking behavior. The "pure" *trait position* may be characterized by $B=f(P)$, that is, behavior is a function of the person, personality, or traits. In this view, it is the relatively permanent properties of people, that is, dispositions, which determine behavior. The "pure" *cognitive position* may be characterized by $E=f(P)$, that is, the environment or situation is constructed by the person via certain cognitive processes and structures. In this view, the focus is upon the means by which an individual cognizes his/her world, rather than upon behavior per se, where the meaning of a situation is determined by what is *in* the organism. The "pure" *social learning position* may be characterized by $P=f(E)$, that is, person or individual differences variables are a function of the environment or social learning history of the individual. Here it is the environmental contingencies which are considered to shape relatively enduring psychological structures.

Of the four sub-perspectives mentioned above, the first two specify *behavior* as a function of either the environment or the person. Taken together, $B=f(E)$ and $B=f(P)$ are the basic components of one interactionist model—a model which may be interpreted as specifying behavior as some joint function of both the environment and the person, or $B=f(E,P)$. In other words, the environment and the person interact in producing or determining behavior. While this concept of interaction leaves open the specific function through which the environment and the person *co*determine behavior, that which is not left open is the nature of the causal relationship—it is unidirectional. That is to say, causality is from the environment *and* person *to* behavior. Both environmental variables and person variables are independent variables, while behavior is the dependent variable.

Within the context of the trait-situation controversy, the B=f(E,P) type of interaction has been almost exclusively formuated in terms of the analysis of variance (ANOVA) model, where the variability in the behavioral dependent variable is partitioned into additive sources associated with environmental variables, person variables, and an interactional component. Thus, many authors have attempted to settle the trait "versus" situation controversy by reviewing those empirical researches which permit the evaluation of the relative proportion of variance associated with environmental variables, person variables, and their interaction (for recent reviews, see Argyle & Little, 1972; Bowers, 1973; Ekehammar, 1974; Endler and Magnusson, 1976). The general conclusion of these reviews has been that the interactional component accounts for the highest proportion of variance, thereby supporting an interactionist position. However, as noted by Overton and Reese (1973), the ANOVA model is a linear model, and by the term "interaction" within the ANOVA model, one *means* specifying the *nonreciprocal relationship* between environmental and person variables which best accounts for, predicts, or "explains" the behavioral variability.

The second major type of interaction is bound up in the remaining two major sub-perspectives previously characterized, that is, E=f(P) and P=f(E). In contrast to the first type of interaction, which makes use of a *common* dependent variable (i.e., behavior is a joint function of environmental and person variables), the second major type of interaction focuses upon the psychological environment and the person as these affect and are affected by each other. In other words, the *relationship* between environmental and person variables is one of *reciprocal* or bidirectional causation, where each is at the same time both a dependent and independent variable. This type of interaction, which is an interaction between cause and effect variables, rather than simply between two different kinds or classes of causal variables, can be loosely characterized by jointly considering E=f(P) and P=f(E), or more simply, E→P. A well known example of the use of this meaning of interaction from developmental psychology would be Piaget's notion of assimilation-accommodation.

Building upon the previous work of von Bertalanffy (1968) and Bunge (1963), Overton and Reese (1973) have developed the argument that the two types of interaction (as exemplified by ANOVA and by what might be termed a systems view) are *incompatible* in so far as they are embedded in two different metaphysical systems. Thus Overton and Reese have linked each of the above two concepts of interaction to the mechanistic model and organismic model respectively, thereby implying that each type of interaction carries along with it certain modal and ontological assumptions which are basically inconsistent with each other. Such inconsistency between basic concepts is thought to be unresolvable, where neither logical argument nor empirical studies of the "crucial experiment" type can be brought to bear in arbitration. In Kuhn's

(1962) terminology, each concept of interaction is embedded in a distinct paradigm, and each involves a commitment to a certain perspective through which to view reality.

INTERACTION IN THE TRAIT-SITUATION CONTROVERSY

In light of the above discussion, the question now arises as to how the concept of interaction has been employed by those writing on the trait-situation issue. One might well wonder if the discussion has recognized and kept separate the two distinct kinds of interaction, or, has there been a fundamental confusion undermining intelligent debate? Let us examine separately the major contributors who have recently advanced an interactionist position on this issue.

Bowers' Interactionism.

Bowers' (1973) scholarly article criticized what has been called here the "pure" situationalist view, or $B=f(E)$, and argued for an interactionist position. In so doing Bowers made an unjustifiable shift from the linear, unidirectional, codetermination notion of interaction, to the bidirectional, organismic conception. Thus, Bowers opened on the issue of interactionism by developing a persuasive argument for the $B=f(E,P)$ interaction model, and more specifically, the ANOVA version. After reviewing 11 articles published since 1959 which allow for the assessment of the relative importance of environmental variables, person variables, or their interaction in terms of accounting for behavioral variance, Bowers concluded that "interaction of persons and settings accounts for a higher percentage of variance than either main effect in 14 of 18 possible comparisons, and in 8 out of 18 comparisons the interaction term accounts for more variance than the sum of the main effects" (Bowers, 1973, p. 321). Thus it is apparent that Bowers was initially committed to the $B=f(E,P)$ type of interaction, stating that "Obviously, and to some considerable extent, the person and the situation are codeterminers of behavior, and they need to be specified simultaneously if predictive accuracy is desired" (Bowers, 1973, p. 322).

Towards the end of Bowers' article, however, it is not clear as to what type of interactionism is being advanced. Bowers (1973, p. 327) notes that "An interactionist or biocognitive view denies the primacy of either traits or situations in the determination of behavior." However, just two sentences later conceptual confusion over the concept of interaction becomes apparent when he emphatically states what in the end will undermine his endeavor, namely, "interactionism argues that *situations are as much a function of the person as the person's behavior is a function of the situation*" (Bowers, 1973, p. 327, original emphasis). In this statement there has been a definite shift from the previous kind of interactionism Bowers had outlined, namely from a linear and unidirectional model of codetermination of behavior, to an interactionism which emphasizes reciprocal causation between the environment and the person, that is, from $B=f(E,P)$ to the joint consideration of $E=f(P)$ and $P=f(E)$. Thus Bowers argues "that people do indeed foster consistent social environments, which then reciprocate by fostering behavioral consistency" (Bowers, 1973, p. 329).

As is evident in the above quote, Bowers has now fully embraced an organismic view of interactionism. In accepting the Overton and Reese (1973) view that the two types of interactionism are embedded in incompatible metaphysical systems, then it is true that Bowers has generated two incompatible answers while giving a semblance of unity to his article with the ambiguous term "interactionism." Bowers' article is confusing in so far as it advances an initial interactionist position which, by the very nature of its conceptual structure, cannot be used to bolster a second and incompatible interactionist position.

Endler's Interactionism

In contrast to Bowers, Endler (Endler, 1975; Endler & Magnusson, 1976) has kept separate the two interactionist positions. Thus in one place (Endler, 1975) he has stated that:

> a useful paradigm . . . for the trait versus situation issue is an interactionist one that assesses the relative variance contribution by situations and persons to behavior, and examines how situations and persons *interact* in evoking behavior. (Endler, 1975, p. 17, original emphasis)

At no point did Endler use the findings from ANOVA studies to support an organismic view of interaction, and he explicitly acknowledged (Endler, 1975; Endler & Magnusson, 1976) the two concepts of interaction as outlined by Overton and Reese (1973). In the more recent article, Endler and Magnusson (1976) seem to favor the bidirectional, organismic interpretation of "interaction." However Endler does, in the author's opinion, incorrectly characterize the organismic view of interaction when he states that it "would refer to the mutual interdependence of persons-situations and behavior so that the persons-situations influence behavior and vice versa" (Endler, 1975, p. 18). Thus, as previously set out, the organismic view of interaction focuses upon the reciprocal influence between persons and situations and *not* persons-situations and behavior. Contrary to Endler's view, in the organismic sense of interaction person and situation variables are different *kinds* of variables which interact with each other, rather than together interacting with behavior.

Mischel's Interactionism

Like Endler, Mischel (1973) puts forth a logically consistent interactionist position, although it falls within an organismic bidirectional perspective, Mischel's "cognitive social learning" view of interaction combines the two perspectives E=f(P) and P=f(E) into a unified E→P. Thus Mischel (1973) states his position clearly:

> The person continuously influences the "situations" of his life as well as being affected by them in a mutual, organic two-way interaction, (p. 278).
>
>   The person continuously selects, changes, and generates conditions just as much as he is affected by them. The mutual interaction between person and conditions . . . cannot be overlooked. (p. 278).

While Mischel (1973, pp. 255-258) does consider the value of the B=f(E,P) type of interaction in the form of ANOVA designs and "moderator variables," he largely dismisses the predictive utility of such interactions and ultimately dismisses the concept of interaction underlying *that* body of empirical research. This strategy is quite consistent with his later proposal for an organismic cognitive social learning theory of interaction. Mischel, then, has implicitly recognized the two kinds of interactionism in his article, and has been successful in keeping them conceptually separate.

Ekehammar's Interactionism

In a recent historical review of interactionism in personality theory and research, Ekehammar (1974) has argued that interactionist ideas were alive and well 40-50 years ago. Ekehammar also argued that such interactionist ideas have not been empirically tested until quite recently since they had to await the development and refinement of certain statistical models, namely, ANOVA. Unfortunately, Ekehammar, like Bowers, confuses the two major types of interaction previously outlined. While Bowers at one point clearly changes direction in going from one interactionist model to the other and never looks back, Ekehammar creates much more uneasiness in the reader by slipping back and forth from the linear, unidirectional, codetermination interactionist position, to the organismic, bidirectional, interactionist model.

   In his historical review of interactionism, Ekehammar cites Kantor, Lewin, Angyal, Murray, and others as specifically advancing an interactionist position in the organismic, bidirectional, systems sense of that term. From the discussion of that historical material, it would seem that Ekehammar was paving the way for looking at modern versions of a particular kind of interactionism. However, in reviewing modern interactionist positions, Ekehammar (1974, pp. 1032-1041) is almost exclusively concerned with ANOVA researches and the linear, unidirectional, codetermination model of interaction. This would be acceptable if one ignored the beginning section on the historical roots of the organismic systems view of interaction, and the Summary and Conclusion section in which Ekehammar attempts to glue the two incompatible interactionist concepts together. A paragraph in the last section of the article is telling, for here statistically significant person-situation interactions in ANOVA models are mentioned, along with a plurality of organismic and phenomenological concepts such as "man-world reciprocal implication" and "circular causality." Ekehammar's attempt to demonstrate that recent statistical studies, which assume a linear, unidirectional, co-determination of behavior, provide the empirical support for the "older" organismic, reciprocal causation type of interactionism, is a misguided adventure based upon a failure to appreciate that a particular term may stand for different, and in this case, contradictory, concepts. Although Ekehammar (1974, p. 1041) demonstrates an awareness of the Overton and Reese (1973) article, and recognizes certain "limitations" of ANOVA, he still fails to appreciate that he is dealing with two different *kinds* of interactionism which cannot speak to each other. Thus I believe Ekehammar (1974) is in error when he states that "analysis of variance components seems to be the best of the mentioned approaches for testing *the* interactionist hypothesis" (p. 1041, emphasis added). Contrary to Ekehammar's intention, he is not addressing a *single* hypothesis or concept of interactionism, but, rather, two different and contradictory types.

SUMMARY AND CONCLUSION

Recent debate on the trait-situtation issue has been plagued by a failure on the part of some of the contributors to distinguish between two radically different concepts of interaction. Such conceptual confusion has resulted in offering inappropriate empirical evidence generated within one framework as supporting what in fact is a very different position. If one does not accept the Kuhnian position that the two concepts of interaction are incompatible, then an argument must be made for using empirical evidence generated within one interactionist framework as supporting another. Neither Bowers or Ekehammar have done the latter.

Progress in an area is dependent upon the clarity of one's basic concepts. Those interested in advancing our knowledge about interactionism within personality theory would be wise to explicitly make the conceptual distinction between the two major and contradictory types of interactionism discussed in this article.

REFERENCES

Argyle, M., & Little, B. R. Do personality traits apply to social behavior? *Journal for the Theory of Social Behaviour,* 1972, *2,* 1-35.

Bertalanffy, L. von. *General systems theory.* New York: George Braziller, 1968.

Bowers, K. S. Situationism in psychology: An analysis and a critique. *Psychological Review,* 1973, *80,* 307-336.

Bunge, M. *Causality: The place of the causal principle in modern science.* New York: World Publishing, 1963.

Ekehammar, B. Interactionism in personality from a historical perspective. *Psychological Bulletin,* 1974, *81,* 1026-1048.

Endler, N. S. The case for person-situation interactions. *Canadian Psychological Review,* 1975, *16,* 12-21.

Endler, N. S. & Magnusson, D. Toward an interactional psychology of personality. *Psychological Bulletin,* 1976, *83,* 956-974.

Kuhn, T. S. *The structure of scientific revolutions.* Chicago: University of Chicago Press, 1962.

Mischel, W. Toward a cognitive social learning reconceptualization of personality. *Psychological Review,* 1973, *80,* 252-283.

Overton, W. F., & Reese, H. W. Models of development: Methodological implications. In J. R. Nesselroade and H. W. Reese (Eds.), *Lifespan developmental psychology: Methodological issues.* New York: Academic Press, 1973.

2
The Case for Person-Situation Interactions*
Norman S. Endler

The important and complex personality issue of cross-situational consistency (stability) versus situational specificity (change) was discussed.
Personologists and clinicians have assumed that personality traits are the
major source of behavioural variance, whereas social psychologists and
sociologists have assumed that situations are the major source. There is
little empirical evidence to support either the claim of the trait theorists or
that of the situationists. It was pointed out that not enough attention has
been paid to assessing the psychological significance of various types of
situations, and the person-situation issue has been inappropriately phrased.
Various research strategies were discussed, and the advantages of the
interactionist approach, and supporting empirical data, were presented.
Finally a person-situation interaction model for anxiety was proposed.

Cross-situational consistency (stability) versus situational specificity (change) is
an important and complex issue in personality theorizing and research. Are there
personality traits that are manifested in terms of response consistencies across a
wide variety of situations, or is behaviour situation specific? As Mischel (1968),
and Endler (1973) have indicated, personality research and theory have been
primarily dominated by trait theories and by psychodynamic theories. These
theories, which are response-response (R-R) theories, have assumed an underlying basic stability and continuity of personality, and have furthermore assumed
the existence of trans-situational consistency.

*Canadian Psychological Review 1975, 16, 1, 12-31. Reprinted by permission.

Clinicians (Rapaport, Gill and Schafer, 1945), as well as personologists (Alker, 1972; Cattell, 1946, 1950; Cattell and Scheier, 1961; Guilford, 1959; McClelland, 1951; Murray, 1938) have proclaimed that *traits* are the prime or basic personality constructs or variables, and are the major determinants of behaviour. Traits are inferred from cross-situational response consistencies. Unfortunately different trait theorists derive different *kinds* of traits and different *numbers* of traits. If traits were really basic, then at the very least one would expect that different theorists derive the same kinds of traits, or at least the same number of traits. Furthermore, although the evidence for the reliability of traits is relatively good, *validity* coefficients for measures of personality traits are typically about .30, i.e., they account for about nine percent of the variance.

Sociologists and social psychologists (Cooley, 1902; Cottrell, 1942a, 1942b; and George Herbert Mead, 1934) as well as social learning theorists (Bandura and Walters, 1963; Mischel, 1968, 1971; Rotter, 1954; Skinner, 1953, 1960) have proclaimed that *situations* are the prime determinants of behavioural variance. With respect to personality these theories are stimulus-response (S-R) theories, and many of these theorists have focused on the situations and the meanings these situations have for individuals in terms of cultural rules and roles. The assumption has been that S-R theories are more "scientific" than R-R theories of personality, because for the S-R theories it is possible to *control* the stimuli that evoke the responses, while no such control is possible for the R-R theories. However, as Bowers (1973) has pointed out, situationism has errone-ously assumed that the S-R approach is identical to the experimental method and has taken a very myopic viewpoint regarding causality and explanation. Furthermore, the developmental aspect of the psychoanalytic position is basically an S-R approach to personality because it examines the relationships between childhood experiences and adult personality responses (Hilgard, Atkinson, and Atkinson, 1971), and yet it minimizes situational factors and maximizes response consistencies (traits).

Vernon (1964) and Mischel (1968, 1969, 1971) have both evaluated the data regarding personality traits and have found that there is little empirical evidence to support the trait theorists regarding transituational response consistencies. In emphasizing the importance of situational factors, Mischel (1971) has stated "that a person will behave consistently across situations only to the extent that similar behavior leads, or is expected to lead, to similar consequences across these conditions" (p. 74). That is, if situations have the same meaning for subjects, response consistency will occur, if situations have different meanings then inconsistency of responses should be expected.

Bowers (1973) has recently provided an extensive critique of situationism in terms of its metaphysical, psychological, and methodological assumptions, and Wachtel (1973) has suggested that some of the apparent discrepancies between psychodynamic trait theories and situation specific behaviour therapy theories may be due to differing perspectives of these two approaches in terms of the subjects studied, the content or phenomena of central interest, and research strategies. In a sense these two critiques of the situational approach serve as an antidote to the extensive critiques of trait theories provided by Farber (1964), Mischel (1968, 1969, 1971, 1973), Peterson (1969), and Vernon (1964). Block (1968) has suggested some conceptual reasons for the apparent inconsistency of personality including "(a) the mixing of behavior of different levels of salience, (b) the failure to recognize the effect of environmental factors, (c) the comparison of behaviors mediated by different underlying variables, and (d) the failure to specify or to recognize the bounds within which the posited relationship may be expected to exist" (p. 210).

Complexity of Personality

The trait (consistency) versus the situational (specificity) controversy is a complex and important issue for the area of personality. Although no one would deny the presence of personality stability and continuity (e.g. Block, 1971), there is persuasive evidence (e.g. Mischel, 1968, 1969, 1971) to suggest that there are both cross-situational personality differences at any given time for a particular individual, and substantial longitudinal personality changes over time.

There are differences with respect to consistency both *between* conceptual personality domains (e.g. cognitive versus social) and *within* a single domain (e.g. anxiety versus hostility). There is some evidence for trans-situational consistency and stability over time with respect to *intellectual and cognitive* factors (Mischel, 1969), but even here Hunt (1966) has provided evidence to indicate that the belief in fixed intelligence may well be a myth. With respect to *noncognitive personality dimensions* and *social behaviour* there is strong evidence for behavioural specificity. Argyle and Little (1972) have provided evidence in favor of situational factors with respect to social behaviour, social response questionnaires, and person perception; Endler (1966a), and Endler and Hoy (1967) have shown the importance of situational factors in social conformity; and Mischel (1968) has reviewed the evidence in favor of *situational specificity* for such character traits as aggression, attitudes to authority, conformity, dependency, rigidity and many other noncognitive personality variables. Mischel (1969) has suggested that on both an empirical and theoretical basis "the observed inconsistency so regularly found in studies of noncognitive personality dimensions often reflect the state of nature and not merely the noise of measurement" (p. 1014). The evidence then indicates that there is more consistency for the cognitive personality domain than for the noncognitive domain.

Within the *noncognitive personality* domain, Endler and Hunt (1968, 1969) found that individual differences account for 15-20 percent of the total variation for hostility but only 4 .5 percent for the total variation for anxiety. Endler and Hunt suggest that the two traits may operate differently. Therefore, one cannot generalize from one trait to another with respect to consistency, and must pay attention not only to specific situations and various domains of personality but to the specific trait in question. We do not mean to deny the existence of traits, but merely to indicate the complexity of the human personality.

The complexity of the person versus the situation issue is also attested to by the phenomenon that *"there is a pervasive tendency for actors to attribute their actions to situational requirements, whereas observers tend to attribute the same actions to stable personal dispositions"* (Jones and Nisbett, 1971, p. 2). That is, when people explain their own behaviours they emphasize situational factors, but when they describe others they do so in terms of consistent dispositional personality constructs. Nisbett, Caputo, Legant and Marecek (1973), found that subjects describe *others* in terms of dispositional traits, but describe themselves in terms of "depends-on-the-situation" constructs. Lay, Ziegler, Hershfield and Miller (1973) using variations of the S-R inventories of Anxiousness (Endler, Hunt and Rosenstein, 1962) and Hostility (Endler and Hunt, 1968) found that predicted self-judgments produced less consistency over situations (i.e. less dispositional constructs) than judgments of others. Jones and Nisbitt (1971) state that "the observer, even when he is a professional psychologist, is apt to conceive of the personalities of others as a collection of broad dispositions or traits, despite the scant empirical evidence for their existence" (p. 13). They suggest that this may be due to both biases of observer *information,* and biases of *information processing* on the part of the observer. Schneider (1973) has questioned "whether traits are the most appropriate units of person cognition and whether perceivers see traits as distributed across situations as well as stimulus persons" (p. 294).

Validity of Traits

Endler (1973, 1974), Endler and Hunt (1969), Hunt (1965), and Mischel (1968, 1969) have all indicated that validity coefficients for measures of personality traits typically range from .20 to .50 and are usually about .30. Stagner (1973) has provided evidence for the internal consistency reliability of trait measures. But it is not the *reliability* of traits that is being questioned, but rather their validity. It is true that validity coefficients are attenuated by errors of measurement, primarily reliability coefficients, and that self-report measures present methodological and statistical problems. However, it is equally evident that response indicators of presumed stable personality traits are specific and are dependent both on the modes of response used to assess the behaviours, and the evocative situations.

Situations

Although the S-R social learning theorists have emphasized the importance of the situation as a determinant of behaviour, very little has been done about defining and determining the nature of situations. While it is true that there have been attempts to classify situations (e.g. Sells, 1963, 1966) there has been little effort expended towards studying situations psychologically. Gibson (1960) has pointed to the difficulties inherent in defining a stimulus, let alone situations. Arsenian and Arsenian (1948) have proposed a psychosocial model for examining "tough" and "easy" cultures in terms of needs (persons) and paths of goals (situations) and the interaction between the two, and Chein (1954) has suggested a schema for investigating the objective behavioural environment. There is no indication that any investigators have attempted to empirically investigate either of these models. Endler, Hunt and Rosenstein (1962) have factor analyzed situations with respect to anxiousness and hostility, Magnusson (1971), and Ekehammar and Magnusson (1973) have analyzed individuals' perceptions of situations, Frederiksen (1972) has proposed a taxonomy of situations, and recently Moos (1973, 1974) has reviewed "six major methods by which characteristics of environments have been related to indexes of human functioning . . ." (Moos, 1973, p. 652). However, there has been no *systematic* attempt to study the situation *psychologically*. Situations do not exist in a vacuum but have psychological meaning and significance for people. Wachtel (1973) has pointed out that people select, create, and construct their own environments, and even Mischel (1973) has conceded this point. Stagner (1973) has suggested that traits determine what situations a person selects, and how he perceives situations. Furthermore, Wachtel has suggested that when stimuli are ambiguous, individual differences resulting from past experience are more discernable. All this points to the interaction between persons and situations, which is an issue we now wish to explore in greater detail.

PERSON-SITUATION INTERACTIONS

Endler and Hunt (1969) have presented self-report anxiety data, based on their S-R Inventories of Anxiousness (Endler *et al.*, 1962, Endler and Hunt, 1969) for 22 samples of males and 21 samples of female subjects. The samples of subjects varied in age, education level, geographical location, social class and mental health. They found that on the average, persons (individual differences) accounted for 4.44 percent of the variance for males, and 4.56 percent of the variance for females. Before the situationists gleefully proclaim that situations are more important than traits, let me point out that situational variance accounted for 3.95 percent of the variance for males and 7.78 percent of the variance for females. The interactions seem to be more important than either persons or situations. *Each* of the two-way interactions (Person by Situations, Persons by Modes of Response, and Situations by Modes of Response) account for, on the average, about 10 percent of the variance.

Bowers (1973) has summarized the results of 11 articles, published since 1959, that deal directly with the situation versus person controversy. These studies include data based on (a) self-report measures which most people have experienced personally or vicariously (e.g. S-R self-report inventories of anxiousness and hostility); (b) self-ratings of real situations (measuring feelings of trust, affiliation, affect, etc.); and (c) actual behaviour or observed behaviour in specific situations (e.g. honesty, hyperaggressive behaviour, smoking, talking). He found that the person by situation *interaction* accounts for more variance than either the person *or* the situation in 14 out of 18 possible comparisons, and the interaction accounts for more variance than the *sum* of the main effects in eight out of the 18 comparisons. Bowers (1973) found, that for these studies, the average variance due to persons was 12.71 percent, that due to situations was 10.17 percent, but that due to the person by situation interaction was 20.77 percent. Argyle and Little (1972) in reviewing the evidence with respect to person perception studies, social behaviour studies, and social response questionnaire studies have concluded that the "Person X Situation Interaction accounts for more variance than either situations or persons alone. With the passage of time and in more adequately functioning groups, Situations are relatively more important sources of variation than are Persons" (Argyle and Little, 1972, p. 16). While it is true that many of these results are based on self-reports and it would be desirable to have more behavioural measures, and in addition some physiological measures, one cannot dismiss these results as inconclusive.

Furthermore, studies in leadership (Fiedler, 1971), aggressive behaviour (Berkowitz, 1973; Moyer, 1973; Feshbach, 1956) and on language performance (Moore, 1971) point to the importance of situational factors for these variables and to the relevance of a person by situation interaction in investigating personality. For example, Fiedler's (1971) contingency model of leadership indicates that the effectiveness of a leader is a function of the situation, the characteristics of the group and whether the leader is person oriented or task motivated. Berkowitz (1973) emphasizes the importance of cognitive and situational factors in aggression, and Moyer (1973) presents a physiological model of aggression which emphasizes the interaction of biological and learning factors in evoking violence. Moore (1971) reviews some literature that emphasizes "the interaction of characteristics of the speaker with characteristics of the situation in actual language performance" (pp. 18-19).

A Pseudo Issue

As Endler (1973) and Endler and Hunt (1966) have indicated "the question of whether individual differences or situations are the major source of behavioral variance, like many issues in the history of science, turns out to be a pseudo issue" (Endler and Hunt, 1966, p. 344). This does not mean to imply that persons and situations are unimportant sources of behavioural variance, nor does it deny that this is an important recurrent issue. "Rather it is the manner in which the question has been raised (e.g. which one, or how much is due to situations and how much to persons) that makes it a pseudo issue. Asking whether behavioral variance is due to either situations *or* to persons, or how much variation is contributed by persons and how much by situations (an additive approach) is analogous to asking whether air *or* blood is more essential to life or asking to define the area of a rectangle in terms of length *or* width" (Endler, 1973, p. 289). If we continue to ask inappropriate questions about this important personality issue, we will encounter the same difficulties as have been encountered with respect to intelligence and the nature-nurture issue. The appropriate and logical question is "*How* do individual differences and situations *interact* in evoking behavior?"

The notion of interaction is certainly nothing new. In the seventeenth century the physicist Robert Hooke proposed Hooke's law which stated that "within the elastic limit, strain is proportional to stress. For fluids and gases elasticity has a different meaning" (Bridgwater and Kurtz, 1963, p. 637). In other words, the elasticity of a substance is an interactive function of the nature of the material and the degree of situational stress. There is some evidence to suggest that there may be a Hooke's law for personality, in that anxiety reactions, for example, are an interactive function of personality traits (material) and situational stress (Endler and Shedletsky, 1973; Spielberger, 1972; Hodges, 1968).

However, as Mischel (1973) suggests it is insufficient to proclaim that interactions exist. One should be able to *predict* the nature of the interaction if the science of personality is to advance. Wallach and Leggett (1972) have made a similar point in their discussion of the failure to replicate interactions, and have also indicated their disenchantment with the moderator variable approach.

RESEARCH STRATEGIES FOR PERSONALITY RESEARCH

Let me briefly review some of the personality research strategies, and then suggest one approach to studying the nature of interactions. For a more extended presentation see Endler (1973).

Correlation measures

The usual strategy has been to correlate measures (e.g. responses to question-naires) that are presumed indicators of a personality trait. This strategy has usually yielded correlations of .30, and the "failure to obtain construct validation using this strategy has been used as support for the situational-specificity model" (Endler, 1973, p. 295). However, while the correlational approach does not support the trait position, it also does not offer direct support for situational specificity. Low correlations may be due to a number of factors (e.g. reliability, methodological and statistical problems, interactions, etc.) in addition to the effect of situational specificity.

Moderator variables

Situationists (e.g. Mischel, 1968, 1969; Bem, 1972) as well as trait theorists (Alker, 1972) have proclaimed that the "moderator" variable strategy (e.g. a variable affecting the relationship between two other variables) is very useful for seeking trans-situational consistency. Zedeck (1971) has suggested that there are inherent difficulties in identifying moderators, and that they present methodolog-ical and statistical problems. Wallach and Leggett (1972) do not believe that the moderator variable approach using selected subsamples, is any different than the correlational aproach using total samples. Both attempt to determine consistency by seeking evidence for dispositional traits. The interactions obtained in one study do not usually hold up in a replication of that study.

Behavioral measures

Wallach and Leggett (1972) suggest that one should look for consistency in behaviour and its products rather than looking for it in response indicators (test measures) of traits or constructs. The approach has merit since psychologists are ultimately interested in predicting actual behaviour. Wallach and Leggett (1972) compared childrens' drawings of a Santa Claus figure before, during, and after Christmas. Since they found no significant differences in size of drawings, as a function of the different occasions, but did find significant correlations (ranging from .47 to .68) of the size of the drawings across occasions, they suggest that this provides evidences for trans-situational consistency. However, it is our contention that their study neither proves nor disproves the consistency nor situational specificity hypothesis. One cannot prove the null hypothesis, and the lack of difference across situations may point to the ineffectiveness of their technique, but does not imply consistency. Similarly, the correlations may represent test-retest reliabilities of their behavioural measure rather than consistency. The Wallach and Leggett (1972) paradigmatic approach is not appropriate in that it treats consistency and specificity as either situations *or* persons propositions. An interactionist approach would be more appropriate.

An interactionist approach

As indicated earlier human personality is very complex and therefore it is our contention that a useful paradigm (Kuhn, 1962) for the trait versus situation issue is an interactionist one, that examines *how* situations and persons *interact* in evoking behaviour. Methodology influences observations and results, and evidence from research on the nature-nurture intelligence controversy suggests that those favoring a heredity position use the correlational approach and those favoring environment use a mean-difference approach. We would therefore suggest that one should be openminded in one's approach to this problem. Note that low correlations of different measures of personality traits neither proves nor disproves consistency, and differences across situations do not conclusively demonstrate the primacy of situational factors.

We need a paradigm that can examine the interaction of situational and personal factors within the same experimental design (e.g. Bowers, 1973; McGuire, 1968). There are a number of different ways of approaching this problem. One method is to assess via variance components, derived from analysis of variance (Endler, 1966b), the relative variance contributed by situations and persons to behaviour and especially the contributions of person-situation interactions to behaviour. Endler and Hunt (1968, 1969) have done this with respect to the variables of anxiousness and hostility. Another approach exemplified by Raush (1965) in his research on the social behaviour of children, is to use multivariate information analysis to account for the relative contribution (in percent) of persons, situations and person by situation interactions in reducing the uncertainty of subsequent behavioural acts. In both these cases we are referring to the interaction of two independent variables (persons and situations) in effecting behaviour (the dependent variable) and *not* to the interaction between independent and dependent variables.

McGuire (1973) in discussing social psychology research, has recently criticized the simple linear sequential (cause and effect) model, including analysis of variance, and Fiske (1974) has been critical of current models in personality research. Overton (1973) in discussing the nature-nurture issue has stated that the interaction terms in analysis of variance are linear functions of independent elements and fall within, what he calls, the additive paradigm. He proposes an interactive paradigm where events are due to interactions that "are not decomposable into individual components" (p. 83). Vale and Vale (1969) have also proposed a paradigm that attempts to discover variables that underlie interactions.

Overton and Reese (1973) have made a useful distinction between the reactive organism (mechanistic) model of man and the active organism (organismic) model of man. For the mechanistic model, which uses analyses of variance procedures, the interaction term is concerned with an interdependency of determinants of behaviour. The "interaction is not between cause and effect, but between causes" (p. 78). For the organismic model, interaction refers to reciprocal causation or reciprocal action between environmental events and behaviour. In the present context, mechanistic interaction (which is unidirectional) would simply refer to the interactions of persons and situations in influencing behaviour, whereas organismic interaction (which is bidirectional) would refer to the mutual interdependence of persons-situations and behaviour so that the persons-situations influence behaviour and vice versa.

Mischel (1973), and Wachtel (1973) have recently focused on this dynamic view of interaction and Bowers (1973) has stated "that situations are as much a function of the person as the person's behavior is a function of the situation" (p. 327). Nevertheless, while it is important to study dynamic interaction and to develop appropriate techniques for doing this, we have still not fully explored the nature of mechanistic interaction. (It should be noted that Overton, 1973, would suggest that these two approaches imply differing, and possibly mutually exclusive, philosophies regarding the nature of man.) Concurrent with an investigation of dynamic interaction we must also examine how persons and situations interact (mechanistic interation) in influencing behaviour. While Endler and Hunt (1968, 1969) have done this with respect to the variables of anxiousness and hostility (and Rausch, 1965 with respect to social behaviour of children) their approach has been primarily descriptive. The next step is to experimentally examine the joint effects (on behaviour) of situations and of persons and to study behavioural measures as well as self-report measures, and subsequently to examine the effects of behaviour on persons and situations. To have any value such an approach must have predictive power rather than merely provide post hoc explanations.

A PERSON-SITUATION INTERACTION MODEL FOR ANXIETY

Let me briefly summarize a person-situation (mechanistic) interaction model for anxiety which is presented more extensively in Endler (1974). Spielberger (1966, 1972) has made an important distinction between *trait* anxiety (A-trait) (a personality variable) and *state* or acute anxiety (A-state) a transitory situational response. However, this theory has certain limitations in that it assesses trait anxiety unidimensionally. A multidimensional measure of trait anxiousness was developed (Endler and Okada, 1975) which provides independent measures of interpersonal A-trait, physical danger A-trait, and ambiguous A-trait. One can then examine the joint or interactive effects of A-trait (personality) and situational stress on state anxiety. However, in order for this person by situation interaction to be effective in inducing A-state anxiety, it is necessary for the A-trait measure to be congruent to the threatening situation. We are now conducting experiments in our laboratory in which we are predicting that *interpersonal* A-trait will interact with an *interpersonal* threat situation to elicit A-state changes, but will not interact with a physical danger threat situation. However, physical danger A-trait will interact with a physical danger threat situation to elicit changes in A-state. This approach enables us to examine the interaction between personality and situational factors and examine trheir joint effects on behaviour. Ultimately we would have to extend this to deterine how behaviour influences persons and situations (dynamic interaction).

The search for traits as prime determinants of behaviour has led to much misguided research. Similarly, an approach that focuses on situational factors can lead us astray. Human behaviour is complex and psychologists have to be willing to tolerate ambiguity and complex approaches rather than looking for simple solutions in terms of either traits or situations. A specific consideration of interactions would improve personality description ''by emphasizing what kinds of responses individuals make with what intensity in various kinds of situations'' (Endler and Hunt, 1966, p. 336).

REFERENCES

Alker, H. A. Is personality situationally specific or intrapsychically consistent? *Journal of Personality,* 1972, *40,* 1-16.

Argyle, M. and Little, B. R. Do personality traits apply to social behaviour? *Journal for the Theory of Social Behaviour,* 1972, *2,* 1-35.

Arsenian, J. and Arsenian, J. M. Tough and easy cultures. *Psychiatry,* 1948, *11,* 377-385.

Bandura, A. and Walters, R. *Social Learning and Personality Development.* New York: Holt, Rinehart and Wilson, 1963.

Bem, D. J. Constructing cross-situational consistencies in behavior: Some thoughts on Alker's critique of Mischel. *Journal of Personality,* 1972, *40,* 17-26.

Berkowitz, L. The case for bottling up rage. *Psychology Today,* 1973, *7,* 24-31.

Block, J. Some reasons for the apparent inconsistency of personality. *Psychological Bulletin,* 1968, *70,* 210-212.

Block, J. *Lives through time.* Berkley, California: Bancroft, 1971.

Bowers, K. S. Situationism in psychology: An analysis and a critique. *Psychological Review,* 1973, *80,* 309-336.

Bridgwater, W. and Kurtz, S. *Columbia Encyclopedia (3rd Edition)*. New York: Columbia University Press, 1963.

Cattell, R. B. *The Description and Measurement of Personality*. New York: World Book 1946.

Cattell, R. B. *Personality: A Systematic Theoretical and Factual Study*. New York: McGraw-Hill, 1950.

Cattell, R. B. and Scheier, I. H. *The Meaning and Measurement of Neuroticism and Anxiety*. New York: Ronald, 1961.

Chein, I. The environment as a determinant of behavior. *The Journal of Social Psychology*, 1954, *39*, 115-127.

Cooley, C. H. *Human Nature and the Social Order*. New York: Scribner's, 1902.

Cottrell, L. S., Jr. The analysis of situational fields. *American Sociological Review*, 1942, *7*, 370-382(a).

Cottrell, L. S., Jr. The adjustment of the individual to his age and sex roles. *American Sociological Review*, 1942, *7*, 618-625(b).

Ekehammar, B. and Magnusson, D. A method to study stressful situations. *Journal of Personality and Social Psychology*, 1973, *27*, 176-179.

Endler, N. S. Conformity as a function of different reinforcement schedules. *Journal of Personality and Social Psychology*, 1966, *4*, 175-180(a).

Endler, N. S. Estimating variance components from mean squares for random and mixed effects analysis of variance models. *Perceptual and Motor Skills*, 1966, *22*, 559-570(b).

Endler, N. S. The person versus the situation—a pseudo issue? A response to Alker. *Journal of Personality*, 1973, *41*, 287-303.

Endler, N. S. A person-situation interaction model for anxiety. In C. D. Spielberger and I. G. Sarason (Eds.), *Stress & Anxiety* Vol. 1. Washington: Hemisphere Publications (J. Wiley), 1974 (in press).

Endler, N. S. and Hoy, Elizabeth. Conformity as related to reinforcement and social pressure. *Journal of Personality and Social Psychology*, 1967, *7*, 197-202.

Endler, N. S. and Hunt, J. McV. Sources of behavioral variance as measured by the S-R Inventory of Anxiousness. *Psychological Bulletin*, 1966, *65*, 336-346.

Endler, N. S. and Hunt, J. McV. S-R Inventories of Hostility and comparisons of the proportions of variance from persons, responses, and situations for hostility and anxiousness. *Journal of Personality and Social Psychology*, 1968, *9*, 309-315.

Endler, N. S. and Hunt, J. McV. Generalizability of contributions from sources of variance in the S-R Inventories of Anxiousness. *Journal of Personality*, 1969, *37*, 1-24.

Endler, N. S., Hunt, J. McV. and Rosenstein, A. J. An S-R Inventory of Anxiousness. *Psychological Monographs*, 1962, *76*, No. 17 (Whole No. 536), 1-33.

Endler, N. S. and Odaka, Marilyn. A multidimensional measure of Trait Anxiety: The S-R Inventory of General Trait Anxiousness. *Journal of Consulting and Clinical Psychology*, 1975 (in press).

Endler, N. S. and Shedletsky, R. Trait versus state anxiety, authoritarianism and ego threat versus physical threat. *Canadian Journal of Behavioural Science*, 1973, *5*, 347-361.

Farber, I. E. A framework for the study of personality as a behavioral science. In P. Worchel and D. Byrne (Eds.), *Personality change*. New York: Wiley and Sons, 1964.

Feshbach, S. The catharsis hypothesis and some consequences of interaction with aggressive and neutral play objects. *Journal of Personality,* 1956, *24,* 449-462.

Fiedler, F. E. Validation and extension of the contingency model of leadership effectiveness: A review of empirical findings. *Psychological Bulletin,* 1971, *76,* 128-148.

Fiske, D. The limits for the conventional science of personality. *Journal of Personality,* 1974, *42,* i-ii.

Frederiksen, N. Toward a taxonomy of situations. *American Psychologist,* 1972, *27,* 114-123.

Gibson, J. J. The concept of the stimulus in psychology. *American Psychologist,* 1960, *15,* 694-703.

Guilford, J. P. *Personality.* New York: McGraw-Hill, 1959.

Hilgard, E. R., Atkinson, R. C. and Atkinson, R. L. *Introduction to Psychology* (5th Edition). New York: Harcourt Brace Jovanovich Inc., 1971.

Hodges, W. F. Effects of ego threat and threat of pain on state anxiety. *Journal of Personality and Social Psychology,* 1968, *8,* 364-372.

Hunt, J. McV. Traditional personality theory in the light of recent evidence. *American Scientist,* 1965, *53,* 80-96.

Hunt, J. McV. The psychological basis for using pre-school enrichment as an antidote for cultural deprivation. In O. J. Harvey (Ed.) *Experience, Structure and Adaptability.* New York: Springer Publishing Co., 1966, 235-276.

Jones, E. E. and Nisbett, R. E. *The actor and observer: Divergent perceptions of the causes of behavior.* New York: General Learning Press, 1971.

Kuhn, T. S. *The structure of scientific revolutions.* Chicago: University of Chicago Press, 1962.

Lay, C., Ziegler, M., Hershfield, L., and Miller, D. The perception of situational consistency in behavior. Assessing the actor-observer bias. York University, Toronto, 1973 (Unpublished manuscript).

Magnusson, D. An analysis of situational dimensions. *Perception and Motor Skills,* 1971, *32,* 851-867.

McClelland, D. C. *Personality.* New York: Dryden, 1951.

McGuire, W. J. Personality and susceptibility to social influence. In E. F. Borgatta and W. W. Lambert (Eds.) *Handbook of Personality and Social Research.* Chicago: Rand McNally, 1968, 1130-1187.

McGuire, W. J. The yin and yang of progress in social psychology: Seven koan. *Journal of Personality and Social Psychology,* 1973, *26,* 446-456.

Mead, G. H. *Mind, self and society.* Chicago: University of Chicago Press, 1934.

Mischel, W. *Personality and assessment.* New York: Wiley, 1968.

Mischel, W. Continuity and change in personality: *American Psychologist,* 1969, *24,* 1012-1018.

Mischel, W. *Introduction to Personality.* New York: Holt, Rinehart and Winston, 1971.

Mischel, W. Towards a cognitive social learning reconceptualization of personality. *Psychological Review,* 1973, *80,* 252-283.

Moore, D. R. Language research and preschool language training. In C. Stendler Lavatelli (Ed.) *Language training in early childhood education.* Champaign-Urbana, Illinois: University of Illinois Press, 1971, 3-48.

Moos, R. Conceptualization of human environments. *American Psychologist*, 1973, *28*, 652-655.

Moos, R. Systems for the assessment and classification of human environments: An overview (Part 1, no. 1). In R. H. Moos and P. M. Insel (Eds.) *Issues in Social Ecology*. Palo Alto: National Press Books, 1974, 5-28.

Moyer, K. E. The physiology of violence. *Psychology Today*, 1973, *7*, 35-38.

Murray, H. A. *Explorations in Personality*. New York: Oxford University Press, 1938.

Nisbett, R. E., Caputo, C., Legant, P. and Marecek, J. Behavior as seen by the actor and as seen by the observer. *Journal of Personality and Social Psychology*, 1973, *27*, 154-164.

Overton, W. F. On the assumptive base of the nature-nurture controversy: Additive versus interactive conceptions. *Human Development*, 1973, *16*, 74-89.

Overton, W. F. and Reese, H. W. Models of development: Methodological implications. (Chapter 4.) In J. R. Nesselroade and H. W. Reese (Eds.), *Life-span developmental psychology: Methodological issues*. New York: Academic Press, 1973, 65-86.

Peterson, D. R. *The Clinical Study of Social Behavior*. New York: Appleton-Century-Crofts, 1968.

Rapaport, D., Gill, M. and Schafer, R. *Diagnostic Psychological Testing*. Chicago: Year Book, 1945, 2 Volumes.

Raush, H. S. Interaction sequences. *Journal of Personality and Social Psychology*, 1965, *2*, 487-499.

Rotter, J. B. *Social Learning and Clinical Psychology*. Englewood Cliffs, New Jersey: Prentice-Hall, 1954.

Schneider, D. J. Implicit personality theory: A review. *Psychological Bulletin*, 1973, *79*, 294-309.

Sells, S. B. (Ed.) *Stimulus Determinants of Behavior*. New York: The Ronald Press Co., 1963.

Sells, S. B. Ecology and the science of psychology. *Multivariate Behavioral Research*, 1966, *1*, 131-144.

Skinner, B. F. *Science and Human Behavior*. New York: Macmillan, 1953.

Skinner, B. F. Pigeons in a pelican. *American Psychologist*, 1960, *15*, 28-37.

Spielberger, C. D. The effects of anxiety on complex learning and academic achievement. In C. D. Spielberger (Ed.) *Anxiety and behavior*. New York: Academic Press, 1966.

Spielberger, C. D. Anxiety as an emotional state (Ch. 2) In C. D. Spielberger (Ed.) *Anxiety: Current trends in theory and research*. Volume I., New York: Academic Press, 1972, 23-49.

Stagner, R. Traits are relevant: logical and empirical analysis. Paper presented at a symposium on "Traits, Persons and Situations: Some Theoretical Issues" at the American Psychological Association annual convention in Montreal, August 29, 1973.

Vale, J. R. and Vale, C. A. Individual differences and general laws in psychology. *American Psychologist*, 1969, *24*, 1093-1108.

Vernon, P. E. *Personality Assessment*. London: Methuen, 1964.

Wachtel, P. Psychodynamics, behavior therapy and the implacable experimenter: An inquiry into the consistency of personality. *Journal of Abnormal Psychology*, 1973, *82*, 324-334.

Wallach, M. A. and Leggett, M. I. Testing the hypothesis that a person will be consistent: Stylistic consistency versus situational specificity in size of children's drawings. *Journal of Personality*, 1972, *40*, 309-330.

Zedeck, S. Problems with the use of "moderator" variables. *Psychological Bulletin*, 1971, *76*, 295-310.

3

On the Future of Personality Measurement*

Walter Mischel

This article examines a number of closely related issues in personality theory and assessment that have troubled the history of personality measurement and must be dealt with in its future. These issues include the multiple determinism of behavior, the role of context, the multiple goals of personality measurement, the "subject" as potential expert and colleague, the analysis of environments, and the role of person variables. Finally, some close parallels developing between personality psychology and cognitive psychology and the emergence in psychology of a new image of the human being are considered.

My look at the future of personality measurement begins by asking, What are some of the main lessons we have learned—or should have learned—from its past?

*American Psychologist, 1977, 32, 4, 246-254. Copyright 1977 by the American Psychological Association. Reprinted by permission.

MULTIPLE DETERMINISM OF BEHAVIOR AND "CONTEXTUALISM"

For me, one of the most impressive—and obvious—lessons from the history of personality measurement is the recognition that complex human behavior tends to be influenced by many determinants and reflects the almost inseparable and continuous interaction of a host of variables both in the person and in the situation. In the abstract, this recognition seems as bland and obvious as a cliché, and one wonders if a focus on "interactionism" and multiple determinism may not be little more than the substitution of new slogans for old varieties. But when examined more concretely, this recognition has deeper implications that I sense are being felt independently in many other areas of psychology and even in the social sciences more generally.

Namely, if human behavior is determined by many interacting variables—both in the person and in the environment—then a focus on any one of them is likely to lead to limited predictions and generalizations. This recognition of the limits of prediction is not confined to the area of personality psychology. The same conclusion has been reached in analyses of topics as diverse as the effects of interview styles in psychotherapy, the impact of teaching practices and classroom arrangements in education, and the role of instructions to aid recall in memory experiments (Mischel, 1976). For example, after a survey of research on memory, Jenkins (1974) cautioned:

> What is remembered in a given situation depends on the physical and psychological context in which the event was experienced, the knowledge and skills that the subject brings to the context, the situation in which we ask for evidence for remembering, and the relation of what the subject remembers to what the experimenter demands.

The sentence would be equally apt if we substituted action for memory: Thus, what is done (or thought, or felt) in a given situation depends on the physical and psychological context in which the event was experienced, the knowledge and skills that the subject brings to the context, the situation in which we ask for evidence, etc. Identical conclusions probably would be reached for the subject matter of any other subarea of psychology and perhaps throughout the social sciences. Hence it becomes difficult to achieve broad, sweeping generalizations about human behavior; many qualifiers (moderators) must be appended to our "laws" about cause-and-effect relations—almost without exception and perhaps with no exceptions at all (Cronbach, 1975).

Specificity (or *contextualism,* to use Jenkins's phrase) may occur because of the large range of different ways that different people may react to the "same" treatments and reinterpret them (e.g., Cronbach, 1975; Neisser, 1974) and because the impact of most situations can usually be changed easily by coexisting conditions (Mischel, 1974). Thus, even a relatively simple "stimulus" or "situation" may produce a variety of often unpredictable specific (and weak) effects depending on a large number of moderating variables and the many different ways in which the particular "subjects" may view them and transform them.

I want to underline that the fact that the details of context—or, if you will, of the situation—crucially affect behavior is as true when one wants to understand how a sentence is recognized or how a geometric pattern is identified as it is in the more global domain of our area of the field. Our colleagues in such areas as cognition, memory, and psycholinguistics are discovering, just as we have, the limits of the generalizations they can achieve and the necessity of taking full account of context in their theorizing (e.g., Bransford & Johnson, 1973). The problems of our area may be more dramatic, but they are not unique.

While the more modest, carefully circumscribed goals, and the predictive limitations, implied by these conclusions appear to depress and discourage some social scientists (e.g., Cronbach, 1975; Fiske, 1974), I do not share such gloom. On the contrary, more limited, specific, modest goals may be refreshing for a field in which hubris has often exceeded insight. The need to qualify generalizations about human behavior complicates life for the social scientist, but it does not prevent us from studying human affairs scientifically; it only dictates a respect for the complexity of the enterprise and alerts one to the dangers of oversimplifying the nature and causes of human behavior. It should be plain that this danger is equally great whether one is searching for generalized (global) person-free situational effects or for generalized (global) situation-free personality variables. In the context of personality measurement, a serious recognition of multiple determinism and interactions has many specific implications, and I want to consider a few of them now.

MULTIPLE GOALS FOR MEASUREMENT

An enduring source of confusion in the area of personality psychology is the failure to specify clearly the goals, purposes, or objectives of one's particular enterprise. It is perfectly legitimate, interesting, and appropriate to study what "people are like" (in general), if one is interested in such person perceptions; likewise, it is equally valid to study what "people will do" (in specific situations), if one is interested in that question. Each goal requires different strategies and provides somewhat different—albeit, hopefully, complementary—insights. But there is no reason to think that one will substitute for the other. The value of each depends in part at least on the investigator's purposes and the types of generalizations sought.

It is easy to forget that one may construe the study of persons alternatively from many complementary perspectives. Construed from the viewpoint of the psychologist seeking strategies to induce changes in performance, it may be most useful to focus on the environmental *conditions* or situations required to modify behavior, and therefore to speak of stimulus control, operant conditioning, classical conditioning, counterconditioning, reinforcement control, modeling, and the like. Construed from the perspective of the theorist interested in how these operations produce their effects in the individual who undergoes them, it may be more useful to focus on competencies, constructs, expectancies, subjective values, rules, and other theoretical *person variables* that mediate the effects of conditions upon behavior (Mischel, 1973). Construed from the viewpoint of the experiencing subject, it may be more useful to speak of the same events in terms of their *phenomenological impact* as affects, thoughts, wishes, and other subjective (but communicable) internal states of experience. Confusion arises when one fails to recognize that the same events (e.g., the desensitization of a client's anxieties) may be alternatively construed from each of these perspectives and that the choice of constructions and of measures depends on the construer's purpose. Ultimately, conceptualizations in the field of personality will have to be large enough to encompass the phenomena seen from such multiple perspectives.

In sum, different goals require different foci and measurement strategies, all of which may be legitimate routes for moving toward one's particular objectives. For a more concrete illustration, consider, for example, the old but often forgotten differences between norm-centered and person-centered measurement. Traditionally, most attention in personality measurement has been devoted to comparing differences *between* people on some norm or standard or dimension selected by the assessor. Such a norm-centered approach compares people against each other, usually on a trait or attribute continuum—for example, amount of introversion—extraversion. The results can help with gross screening decisions, can permit group comparisons, and can answer many research questions. But a norm-centered objective obviously requires a different strategy than one which is person-centered (Mischel, 1968).

With a person-centered focus, one tries to describe the particular individual in relation to the particular psychological conditions of his life. In my view, some especially interesting recent developments in personality measurement have been of this type, arising from clinical work with troubled individuals in the real-life setting in which the behaviors of interest unfold naturally. While there are many methodological variations, the essence of the approach is a functional analysis that investigates in vivo covariations between changes in the individual and changes in the conditions of his or her life. The interest here is not in how people compare to others, but in how they can move closer to their own goals and ideals if they change their behavior in specific ways as they interact with the significant people in their lives (e.g., Kelly, 1955; Mischel, 1968, 1976).

In this venture there are many challenges to measurement. Perhaps most important is the fact that clients—like other people—don't describe themselves with operational definitions. They invoke motives, traits, and other dispositions as ways of describing and explaining their experiences and themselves. Much of the assessor's task is to help clients in the search for clear referents for their own personal constructs, instead of forcing the assessor's favorite dispositional labels on them. Rather than leading clients to repackage their problems in our terms, with our constructs, we need to help them objectify *their* constructs into operational terms, so that the relevant behaviors can be changed by helping the clients achieve more judicious arrangements of the conditions in their lives.

In my crystal-ball gazing, the future of personality measurement hopefully will include increasingly imaginative and effective versions of such person-centered functional analyses. When done well, they can provide not only a helpful service to people who need it; they also simultaneously offer a testing ground for our theoretical notions about the basic rules that underly behavior. An increasing merging of personality measurement with therapeutic change programs strikes me as one of the more promising elements in the future of the field.

ACTIVE ORGANISMS INTERACTING IN ACTIVE ENVIRONMENTS

Both conceptually and methodologically, such therapeutic efforts are closely related to the broader problems of analyzing both behavioral stability and change under in vivo conditions. In the future, measurement hopefully will be directed increasingly at the analysis of naturally occurring behaviors observed in the interactions among people in real-life settings. Traditionally, trait-oriented personality research has studied individual differences in response to the "same" situation, usually in the form of a standard set of test questions. But some of the most striking differences between persons may be found not by studying their responses to the same situation but by analyzing their *selection* and construction of stimulus conditions. In the conditions of real life, the psychological "stimuli" that people encounter are neither questionnaire items, nor experimental instructions, nor inanimate events, but involve people and reciprocal relationships (e.g., with spouse, with boss, with children). We continuously influence the "situations" of our lives as well as being affected by them in a mutual, organic interaction (e.g., Raush, Barry, Hertel, & Swain, 1974). Such interactions reflect not only our reactions to conditions but also our active selection and modification of conditions through our own choices, cognitions, and actions (Wachtel, 1973). Different people select different settings for themselves; conversely, the settings that people select to be in may provide clues about their personal qualities (Eddy & Sinnett, 1973). The mutual interaction between person and conditions becomes evident when behavior is studied in the interpersonal contexts in which it is evoked, maintained, and modified.

The study of social interactions vividly reveals how each person continuously selects, changes, and generates conditions just as much as he or she is affected by them. The future of personality measurement will be brighter if we can move beyond our favorite pencil-and-paper and laboratory measures to include direct observation as well as unobtrusive nonreactive measures to study lives where they are really lived and not merely where the researcher finds it convenient to look at them. In such studies, striking individual differences in preferred situations—in the contexts, environments, and activities different people prefer and select—are sure to be found. Such findings might permit profiles of high- and low-frequency situations and high- and low-frequency behaviors somewhat like those supplied by interest inventories.

THE SUBJECT AS EXPERT AND COLLEAGUE

While direct observation is essential for the ecologically valid study of stability and change, I am equally impressed by another point that seems to be emerging from many different research directions: Namely, our "subjects" are much smarter than many of us thought they were. Hence, if we don't stop them by asking the wrong questions, and if we provide appropriate structure, they often can tell us much about themselves and, indeed, about psychology itself.

In some recent pilot work, for example, Harriet Nerlove Mischel and I have started to ask young children what they know about psychological principles—about how plans can be made and followed most effectively, how long-term work problems can be organized, how delay of gratification can be mastered. We also ask them to tell us about what helps them to learn and (stimulated by Flavell and his colleagues, e.g., Kreutzer, Leonard, & Flavell, 1975) to remember. Although our results are still very tentative, we are most impressed by how much even an 8-year-old knows about mental functioning. Indeed, one wonders how well such young children might perform on a final exam in introductory psychology (if the jargon and big words were stripped away. (I do not want to imply, incidentally, that psychology knows little; rather, I believe, people are good psychologists and know a lot. We professionals might be wise to enlist that knowledge in our enterprise.)

The moral, for me, is that it would be wise to allow our "subjects" to slip out of their roles as passive "assessees" or "testees" and to enroll them, at least sometimes, as active colleagues who are the best experts on themselves and are eminently qualified to participate in the development of descriptions and predictions—not to mention decisions—about themselves. Of course if we want individuals to tell us about themselves directly, we have to ask questions that they can answer. If we ask people to predict how they will behave on a future criterion (e.g., "job success," "adjustment") but do not inform them of the specific criterion measure that will constitute the assessment, we cannot expect them to be accurate. Similarly, it might be possible to use self-reports and self-predictions more extensively in decision making—for example, to help the person to "self-select" from a number of behavioral alternatives (e.g., different types of therapy, different job assignments). Such applications would require conditions in which peoples' accurate self-reports and honest choices could not be used against them. We might, for example, expect job candidates to predict correctly which job they will perform best, but only when all the alternatives available to them in their choice are structured as equally desirable. We cannot expect people to deny themselves options without appropriate alternatives.

Self-reports will always be constrained by the limits of the individual's own awareness. Too often, however, it has been assumed that people were unaware when in fact they were simply being asked the wrong questions. In the context of verbal conditioning, for example, more careful inquiries suggest that subjects may be far more aware than we thought (e.g., Spielberger & DeNike, 1966). Similarly, while a belief in the prevalence of distortions from unconscious defenses such as repression is the foundation of the commitment to an indirect-sign approach in assessment, the experimental evidence for the potency of such mechanisms remains remarkably tenuous (e.g., Mischel, 1976). And in laboratory research into unconscious responding (e.g., Eriksen, 1960), just as in the context of personality testing, what the person tells us directly generally turns out to be as valuable an index as any other more indirect sign (e.g., galvanic skin response).

One demonstration of the wisdom of enlisting the "subject's" self-knowledge to increase predictive power is the recent Bem and Allen (1974) study. Fully recognizing the "discriminativeness" that people so often display, Bem and Allen proposed that "consistency" may characterize *some* people at least in *some* areas of behavior. They suggested that while some people may be consistent (maintaining their position relative to others) on some traits, practically nobody is consistent on all traits; indeed, many traits that are studied by investigators may be completely irrelevant for many of the people who are studied. To get beyond this problem, they tried to identify those college students who would be consistent and those who would not be consistent on the traits of friendliness and conscientiousness. Their hypothesis was simply this: "Individuals who identify themselves as consistent on a particular trait dimension will in fact be more consistent cross-situationally than those who identify themselves as highly variable" (Bem & Allen, 1974, p. 512). On the whole, their results supported the hypothesis, demonstrating consistency for "some of the people some of the time." To me it is most interesting that it was the people themselves who predicted their own consistency, again providing support for the notion that each person knows his or her own behavior best.

The search for subtypes of people who display consistencies on some well-defined dimensions of behavior under some subtypes of conditions represents a more modest (and much more reasonable) search for personality typologies. Of course, the demonstration of such consistencies would not mean that the individuals did not discriminate among situations in their behavior, but it would indicate that they maintained their expected position relative to others with regard to certain types of behavior under certain types of conditions. "Consistency" in personality need not imply sameness, but it does imply a degree of predictability based on the individual's qualities. To the extent that such typologies are carefully qualified and take account of types of situations as well as types of people, they are likely to be more successful (albeit more limited) than their more global and ambitious ancestors.

THE ANALYSIS OF ENVIRONMENTS

In the future, many of us are sure to continue searching for cross-situationally consistent types of people, but others seem to be focusing increasingly on the social and psychological environments in which people live and function. The dramatic rise of interest in the environment as it relates to the person is documented easily; from 1968 to 1972 more books appeared on the topic of man-environment relations from an ecological perspective than had been published in the prior three decades (Jordan, 1972). As is true in most new fields, a first concern in the study of environments is to try to classify them into a taxonomy. Environments, like all other events, of course, can be classified in many ways, depending mainly on the purposes and imagination of the classifiers. One typical effort to describe some of the almost infinite dimensions of environments, proposed by Moos (1973, 1974), calls attention to the complex nature of environments and to the many variables that can characterize them. Those variables include the weather, the buildings and settings, the perceived social climates, and the reinforcements obtained for behaviors in that situation—to list just a few.

The classification alerts us to a fact that has been slighted by traditional trait-oriented approaches to personality: Much human behavior depends delicately on environmental considerations, such as the setting (e.g., Barker, 1968), and even on such specific physical and psychosocial variables as how hot and crowded the setting is, or how the room and furniture are arranged, or how the people in the setting are organized (e.g., Krasner & Ullmann, 1973; Moos & Insel, 1974). Many links betwen characteristics of the environment and behavior have been demonstrated. For example, measures of population density (such as the number of people in each room) may be related to certain forms of aggression (even when social class and ethnicity are controlled [Galle, Gove, & McPherson, 1972]). Likewise, interpersonal attraction and mood are negatively affected by extremely hot, crowded conditions (Griffitt & Veitch, 1971).

Depending on one's purpose, many different classifications are possible and useful (e.g., Magnusson & Ekehammar, 1973; Moos, 1973, 1974). To seek any single "basic" taxonomy of situations may be as futile as searching for a final or ultimate taxonomy of traits: We can label situations in at least as many different ways as we can label people. It will be important to avoid emerging simply with a trait psychology of situations, in which events and settings, rather than people, are merely given different labels. The task of naming situations cannot substitute for the job of analyzing *how* conditions and environments interact with the people in them.

Although person-condition interactions are never static, sometimes environmental variables can be identified which help to explain continuities in behavior and allow useful predictions. Of course, the psychology of personality cannot ignore the person; nevertheless, behavior sometimes may be predicted and influenced efficaciously from knowledge of powerful stimulus conditions (Mischel, 1968). The value of predictions based on knowledge of stimulus conditions is illustrated, for instance, in efforts to predict the posthospital adjustment of mental patients. Such investigations have shown that the type, as well as the severity, of psychiatric symptoms displayed depends significantly on environmental conditions, with little consistency in behavior across changing situations (Ellsworth, Foster, Childers, Arthur, & Kroeker, 1968). Accurate predictions of posthospital adjustment require knowledge of the environment in which the ex-patient will be living in the community—such as the availability of jobs and family support—rather than any measured person variables or in-hospital behavior (e.g., Fairweather, 1967; Fairweather, Sanders, Cressler, & Maynard, 1969). Likewise, to predict intellectual achievement, it also helps to take account of the degree to which the child's environment supports (models and reinforces) intellectual development (Wolf, 1966). And when powerful treatments are developed—such as modeling and desensitization therapies for phobias— predictions about outcomes are best when based on knowledge of the treatment to which the individual is assigned (e.g., Bandura, Blanchard, & Ritter, 1969). In the same vein, the significance of the psychological situation was vividly demonstrated in the simulated prison study conducted by Haney, Banks, and Zimbardo (1973).

PERSON VARIABLES

However, when relevant situational information is absent or minimal, when predictions are needed about individual differences in response to the same conditions, or when situational variables are weak, information about person variables becomes essential. Moreover, a psychological approach requires that we move from descriptions of the environment—of the climate, buildings, social settings, etc., in which we live—to the psychological processes through which environmental conditions and people influence each other reciprocally. For this purpose, it is necessary to study in depth how the environment influences behavior and how behavior and the people who generate it in turn shape the environment in an endless interaction. To understand the interaction of person and environment we must consider *person variables* as well as environmental variables.

The person variables that in my view demand more research in the future must subsume such cognitive work as information processing with all its many ramifications. They include selective attention and encoding, rehearsal and storage processes, cognitive transformations, and the active construction of cognitions and actions (Bandura, 1971; Mischel, 1973; Neisser, 1967). Elsewhere, I proposed a synthesis of seemingly promising constructs about persons developed in the areas of cognition and social learning (Mischel, 1973); hence, I called them "cognitive social learning person variables." The constructs I selected were intended to be suggestive and constantly open to progressive revisions. I did not expect these variables to provide ways to predict accurately broad cross-situational behavioral differences between persons. In my view, the "discriminativeness" of behavior and its unique organization within each person are facts of nature, not limitations specific to particular theories. But hopefully these variables may suggest useful ways of conceptualizing and studying specifically how the qualities of the person influence and even transform the effects of stimuli ("environments," "situations," "treatments") and how each person generates distinctive, complex behavior patterns in interaction with the conditions of his or her life.

To summarize very briefly—first, individuals differ in their cognitive and behavioral *construction competencies,* that is, in their competence or ability to generate desired cognitions and response patterns. Second, differences in behavior may also reflect differences in how individuals *categorize* a particular situation. Obviously, people differ in how they encode, group, and label events and in how they construe themselves and others. Performance differences in any situation depend on differences in *expectancies* and specifically on differences in the expected outcomes associated with particular response patterns and stimulus configurations. Third, differences in performance may also be due to differences in the subjective *values* of the expected outcomes. And finally, individual differences often may reflect differences in the *self-regulatory systems and plans* that each individual brings to the situation. The study of this latter person variable will require analyses of the rules people use to guide their own behavior; it will also require investigation of how people pursue their long-term goals and how they select and transform stimulus conditions.

THE INTERFACE OF PERSONALITY AND COGNITION: GRAMMARS FOR PEOPLE?

Hopefully, in the future there will be an increasing awareness, and fertile exploration, of the many close parallels between the study of personality and of cognitive psychology. I believe that personality measurement (and personality psychology more generally) can benefit directly from the methods being developed by cognitive psychologists and, in turn, can enrich their work. Earlier in this article I noted the parallel between the discovery (or rediscovery?) of "contextualism" in cognitive psychology and in personality psychology. That is only one of many common parallels, only one of many shared concerns and problems that are hopefully amenable to similar strategies of theoretical and empirical analysis. Let us consider a few of the others.

Ultimately, the study of individuality will have to deepen our understanding of how people abstract the "gist" of each other and themselves, of how they form schemata, expectations, or other cognitive representations that serve guiding and simplifying functions enabling them to distill essential features from the otherwise overwhelming flood of trivial behavioral tidbits that confront the "unprepared mind." While a recognition of the need for such constructs as schemata, expectancies, scripts, frames, etc., is hardly novel, there are now some exciting signs that they may serve psychologists as more than beguiling mental fictions. Some promising beginnings in the use of such cognitive constructs come, for example, from efforts to understand how people comprehend sentences, conversations, and stories (e.g., Bower, Note 1).

These and related undertakings (e.g., Abelson, 1975; Schank, 1975) suggest that an adequate approach to how people understand their world—including events, sentences, and people—will have to take account of how they organize information in meaningful, hierarchical, rule-guided ways. Even the understanding of simple stories, for example, may be guided by a kind of "grammar" that provides a framework of rules for organizing information so that it may be more easily comprehended and remembered. Likewise, an adequate approach to the understanding of a person may require the development of a grammar of the individual. Such a grammar, to be useful, would help to specify the organization and relations among diverse parts or components of the individual's actions and attributes, allowing one to understand his or her goal-directed patterns and transactions with the world in a coherent fashion. Ideally, an adequate grammar of the individual also would specify how person variables like those discussed in the preceding section are organized and interrelated.

Again, a search for such a structural approach to individuality is far from new: It has long been the enduring ambition of most serious personality theorists. But as one looks to the future, such a structural approach appears to have a better change of successful realization, guided by the methods for the analysis of human understanding that are beginning to be developed by our cognitive colleagues. Such an approach will somehow have to transform the fine-grained formal analyses of the sort modeled by the best psycholinguists and cognitive psychologists to fit the persistently complex, molar, multifaceted subject matter of the personality psychologist. To me that prospect looks difficult and full of hazards but highly challenging and well worth pursuing (e.g., Cantor & Mischel, 1977).

TOWARD A RESEARCH-BASED IMAGE OF THE INDIVIDUAL?

Traditionally, most theorists of personality have invoked a few concepts and stretched them to encompass all the phenomena of human individuality, including thought, feeling, and behavior. As a result, we have theories of personality built on a few body types, or on a handful of factors, or on simple conditioning and environmental contingencies, or on the vicissitudes of one or more favorite motives—sex, aggression, competence, achievement, dissonance, self-realization—or on a humanism that correctly emphasizes the humanity of people but too easily loses sight of (or perhaps interest in?) its antecedents. The list is long but the strategy is the same: Take a few concepts and stretch them as far as possible. This may be a valuable exercise for theorists interested in defending their favorite concepts. For the teacher, it may provide a handy set of controversies in which any one set of obviously incomplete, fragmentary ideas may be sharply contrasted against any other, with each sure to be found sorely lacking in at least some crucial ways. But for the psychologist who seeks a cumulative science of psychology based on the incremental empirical discoveries of the field rather than on the biases of theoreticians committed to defending their viewpoints, such a strategy leaves dreadful voids.

To help overcome these voids, a conception of personality is required that, at the least, is nourished broadly by the research of the field. The massiveness of available data and, of course, their frequent flaws make it possible to read them in many different ways. In my reading, however, a distinctive image of the human being does begin to emerge from empirical work on cognition and social behavior.

One strand of this research suggests that the individual generally is capable of being his or her own best assessor; that the person's own self-statements and self-predictions tend to be at least as good as the more indirect and costly appraisals of sophisticated tests and clinicians (e.g., reviewed in Mischel, 1968, 1972). A related theme is that the individual's awareness of the contingencies in the situation—his or her understanding (not the psychologist's) of what behavior leads to what outcome—is a crucial determinant of the resulting actions and choices, including behavior in the classical and instrumental conditioning paradigms (as discussed in Bandura, 1974; Mischel, 1973). In the same vein, any given, objective, stimulus condition may have a variety of effects, depending on how the individual construes and transforms it (e.g., Mischel, 1974).

While these research themes focus on the centrality of each individual's interpretations, there is also much evidence for the potency and regularity of the effects that may be achieved when the rules of behavior are applied—with the individual's full cooperation and by the individual—to achieve desired outcomes (e.g., Bandura, 1969). There is also considerable support, in my view, for the fact that while consistencies surely exist within each person, they tend to be idiosyncratically organized (e.g., Bem & Allen, 1974), a circumstance which makes nomothetic comparisons on common traits difficult and which highlights the uniqueness that Gordon Allport (1937) has so long emphasized.

Taken collectively, these and related research themes suggest an emerging image of the human being that seems to reflect a growing synthesis of several theoretical influences in current personality psychology. It is an image that seems compatible with many qualities of both the behavioral and the cognitive approaches to personality and yet one that departs from each in some respects.

This image is one of the human being as an active, aware problem-solver, capable of profiting from an enormous range of experiences and cognitive capacities, possessing great potential for good or ill, actively constructing his or her psychological world, and influencing the environment but also being influenced by it in lawful ways—even if the laws are difficult to discover and hard to generalize. It views the person as so complex and multifaceted as to defy easy classifications and comparisons on any single or simple common dimension, as multiply influenced by a host of interacting determinants, as uniquely organized on the basis of prior experiences and future expectations, and yet as rule-guided in systematic, potentially comprehensible ways that are open to study by the methods of science. It is an image that has moved a long way from the instinctual drive-reduction models, the static global traits, and the automatic stimulus-response bonds of traditional personality theories. It is an image that highlights the shortcomings of all simplistic theories that view behavior as the exclusive result of any narrow set of determinants, whether these are habits, traits, drives, reinforcers, constructs, instincts, or genes and whether they are exclusively inside or outside the person. It will be exciting to watch this image change as new research and theorizing alter our understanding of what it is to be a human being.

REFERENCE NOTE

Bower, G. H. *Comprehending and recalling stories.* Division 3 presidential address delivered at the meeting of the American Psychological Association, Washington, D.C., September 6, 1976.

REFERENCES

Abelson, R. P. Concepts for representing mundane reality in plans. In D. G. Bobrow & A. Collins (Eds.), *Representation and understanding*. New York: Academic Press, 1975.

Allport, G. W. *Personality: A Psychological Interpretation*. New York: Holt, Rinehart & Winston, 1937.

Bandura, A. *Principles of Behavior Modification*. New York: Holt, Rinehart & Winston, 1969.

Bandura, A. *Social Learning Theory*. Morristown, N.J.: General Learning Press, 1971.

Bandura, A. Behavior theory and the models of man. *American Psychologist*, 1974, *29*, 859-869.

Bandura, A., Blanchard, E. B., & Ritter, B. Relative efficacy of desensitization and modeling approaches for inducing behavioral, affective, and attitudinal changes. *Journal of Personality and Social Psychology*, 1969, *13*, 173-199.

Barker, R. G. *Ecological Psychology*. Stanford, Calif.: Stanford University Press, 1968.

Bem, D., & Allen, A. On predicting some of the people some of the time: The search for cross-situational consistencies in behavior. *Psychological Review*, 1974, *81*, 506-520.

Bransford, J. D., & Johnson, M. K. Considerations of some problems of comprehension. In W. Chase (Ed.), *Visual Information Processing*. New York: Academic Press, 1973.

Cantor, N., & Mischel, W. Traits as prototypes: Effects on recognition memory. *Journal of Personality and Social Psychology*, 1977, *35*, 38-48.

Cronbach, L. J. Beyond the two disciplines of scientific psychology. *American Psychologist*, 1975, *30*, 116-127.

Eddy, G. L., & Sinnett, R. E. Behavior setting utilization by emotionally disturbed college students. *Journal of Consulting and Clinical Psychology*, 1973, *40*, 210-216.

Ellsworth, R. B., Foster, L., Childers, B., Arthur, G., & Kroeker, D. Hospital and community adjustment as perceived by psychiatric patients, their families, and staff. *Journal of Consulting and Clinical Psychology Monograph*, 1968, *32* (5, Pt. 2).

Eriksen, C. W. Discrimination and learning without awareness: A methodological survey and evaluation. *Psychological Review*, 1960, *67*, 279-300.

Fairweather, G. W. *Methods in Experimental Social Innovation*. New York: Wiley, 1967.

Fairweather, G. W., Sanders, D. H., Cressler, D. L., & Maynard, H. *Community life for the mentally ill: An alternative to institutional care*. Chicago: Aldine, 1969.

Fiske, D. W. The limits of the conventional science of personality. *Journal of Personality*, 1974, *42*, 1-11.

Galle, O. R., Gove, W. R., & McPherson, J. M. Population density and pathology: What are the relations for man? *Science*, 1972, *176*, 23-30.

Griffitt, W., & Veitch, R. Hot and crowded: Influences of population density and temperature on interpersonal affective behavior. *Journal of Personality and Social Psychology*, 1971, *17*, 92-98.

Haney, C., Banks, C., & Zimbardo, P. Interpersonal dynamics in a simulated prison. *International Journal of Criminology and Penology*, 1973, *1*, 69-97.

Jenkins, J. J. Remember that old theory of memory? Well, forget it! *American Psychologist*, 1974, *29*, 785-795.

Jordan, P. A real predicament. *Science*, 1972, *175*, 977-978.

Kelly, G. A. *The Psychology of Personal Constructs* (2 vols.). New York: Norton, 1955.

Krasner, L., & Ullman, L. P. *Behavior Influence and Personality: The Social Matrix of Human Action*. New York: Holt, Rinehart & Winston, 1973.

Kreutzer, M., Leonard, C., & Flavell, J. An interview study of children's knowledge about memory. *Monographs of the Society for Research in Child Development*, 1975, *40* (1, Serial No. 159).

Magnusson, D., & Ekehammar, B. An analysis of situational dimensions: A replication. *Multivariate Behavioral Research*, 1973, *8*, 331-339.

Mischel, W. *Personality and assessment*. New York: Wiley, 1968.

Mischel, W. Direct versus indirect personality assessment: Evidence and implications. *Journal of Consulting and Clinical Psychology*, 1972, *38*, 319-324.

Mischel, W. Toward a cognitive social learning reconceptualization of personality. *Psychological Review*, 1973, *80*, 252-283.

Mischel, W. Processes in delay of gratification. In L. Berkowitz (Ed.), *Advances in Experimental Social Psychology* (Vol. 7). New York: Academic Press, 1974.

Mischel, W. *Introduction to Personality* (2nd ed.). New York: Holt, Rinehart & Winston, 1976.

Moos, R. H. Conceptualizations of human environments. *American Psychologist*, 1973, *28*, 652-665.

Moos, R. H. Systems for the assessment and classification of human environments. In R. H. Moos & P. M. Insel (Eds.), *Issues in Social Ecology*. Palo Alto, Calif.: National Press Books, 1974.

Moos, R. H., & Insel, P. M. *Issues in Social Ecology*. Palo Alto, Calif.: National Press Books, 1974.

Neisser, U. *Cognitive psychology*. New York: Appleton-Century-Crofts, 1967.

Neisser, U. Review of "Visual information processing." *Science*, 1974, *183*, 402-403.

Rausch, H. L., Barry, W. A., Hertel, R. K., & Swain, M. A. *Communication, conflict, and marriage*. San Francisco: Jossey-Bass, 1974.

Schank, R. C. The structure of episodes in memory. In D. G. Bobrow & A. Collins (Eds.), *Representation and Understanding*. New York: Academic Press, 1975.

Spielberger, D. C., & DeNike, L. D. Descriptive behaviorism versus cognitive theory in verbal operant conditioning. *Psychological Review*, 1966, *73*, 306-326.

Wachtel, P. Psychodynamics, behavior therapy, and the implacable experimenter: An inquiry into the consistency of personality. *Journal of Abnormal Psychology*, 1973, *82*, 324-334.

Wolf, R. The measurement of environment. In A. Anastasi (Ed.), *Testing problems in perspective*. Washington, D.C.: American Council on Education, 1966.

Part 3
The Approach of Other Areas in the Social Sciences

Environmental Psychology: Introduction

These papers are concerned with the perception of rooms, buildings, and other physical settings, and their effects on behaviour. Further literature on these topics can be found in Proshanksy, Abelson and Rivlin (1978).

Barker, together with Wright and others, has carried out an important series of field studies of social behaviour in natural settings. In this paper (1965) he defends the use of naturalistic observation, of what he calls T-data, and gives some of the findings of these studies. This work involved surveys of "behaviour settings," and of the behaviour episodes in some of these settings. One of the properties of the ecology studied was the extent to which settings were overmanned or undermanned, which was found to have important consequences. This line of work has proceeded independently of most other work on situations and the environment. The early work on behaviour settings focussed on the main aspects of situations—the pattern of behaviour and the physical setting, but did not deal with goals, rules, or other structural features. The episode sequences work was some of the first in this area, but did not discover any principles of sequence. The research on over- and undermanning is a very interesting example of research on the effects of ecology on behaviour in situations.

Clarke (1980) describes how modification of the physical environment can be used to prevent crime. Attempts to change people in this sphere have not been very successful; changing environmental settings may have better results. In fact considerable success has been obtained for several forms of crime: the suicide rate fell when different gas was supplied, car thefts fell when steering wheel locks were introduced in Germany, and theft from telephone boxes was stopped by the use of stronger coin boxes. Increased surveillance has also been found to be an effective factor towards the reduction of shop-lifting and vandalism. It is recognised that certain kinds of crime will probably not be affected much, e.g. professional crime and some impulsive offences. On the other hand crime is obviously greatly affected by situational factors, which have been shown capable of controlling crime rates in a number of specific settings.

The other two papers in this section concern reactions to different rooms, an important matter for architects. Canter, West and Wools (1974) studied the effect of rooms on the perception of other people in those rooms. They presented drawings and slides of rooms with blank outlines of people, or evidence of habitual use. They found that similar ratings were given to rooms and occupants on some scales, like friendliness, though not on others, like potency. When photographs of people in rooms were rated there was a room effect on both potency and activity. This is similar to the earlier study by Maslow and Mintz (1956) showing that faces were judged more favourably in a beautiful, compared with an ugly, room. It is possible however that this effect would be weaker if more information were available about the persons; Argyle and McHenry (1971) found that the effect of spectacles on judged intelligence disappeared if the target person was heard talking for 4 minutes.

Moos, Harris and Schonborn (1969) studied the perception of rooms by psychiatric patients and staff. Six rooms were judged by 100 subjects on 66 scales, and principal components analyses carried out. The dimensions that emerged were aesthetic appeal, physical organization, size and temperature-ventilation. Analyses of variance for each dimension confirmed earlier findings by Moos and colleagues to the effect that for patients more variance was due to persons and less to situations; in other words a patient's reaction to a room could be predicted better by knowing which patient rather than which room was involved. For staff most variance was due to judge-room interaction, i.e. some staff members appraised particular rooms as warmer, or more pleasing, others as less so. This study might have been improved by the inclusion of a larger sample of rooms, but the factors obtained are similar to those found in some other studies.

SUGGESTED ADDITIONAL REFERENCES

Altman, I. Environmental psychology and social psychology. *Personality and Social Psychology Bulletin*, 1976, *2*, 96-113.

Argyle, M. and McHenry, R. (1971) Do spectacles really affect judgements of intelligence? *British Journal of social and clinical Psychology*, *10*, 27-29.

Baird, J., Cassidy, B., and Kurr, J. Room preference as a function of architectural features and user activities. *Journal of Applied Psychology*, 1978, *63*, 719-727.

Bronfenbrenner, U. Toward an experimental ecology of human development. *American Psychologist*, 1977, *32*, 513-531.

Canter, D. Children in hospital: a facet theory approach to person/place synomorphy. *Journal of Architectural Research*, 1977, *6*, 20-32.

Canter, D. *The Psychology of Place*. Wallop, Hampshire: BAS, 1977.

Canter, D., and Lee, K. *Psychology and the Built Environment*. London: Architectural Press, 1974.

Chein, I. The environment as a determinant of behavior. *Journal of Social Psychology*, 1954, *39*, 115-127.

Dipboye, R. and Flanagan, M. Research settings in industrial and organizational psychology. *American Psychologist*, 1979, *34*, 141-150.

Falender, C. and Mehrabian, A. The effects of day care on young children: an environmental psychology approach. *Journal of Psychology*, 1979, *101*, 241-255.

Feshbach, S. The environment of personality. *American Psychologist*, 1978, *33*, 447-455.

Garling, T. A multidimensional scaling and semantic differential technique study of the perception of environmental settings. *Scandinavian Journal of Psychology*, 1976, *17*, 323-332.

Gibbs, J. The meaning of ecologically oriented inquiry in contemporary psychology. *American Psychologist*, 1979, *34*, 127-140.

Gump, P. and Adelberg, B. Urbanism from the perspective of ecological psychologists. *Environment and Behavior*, 1978, *10*, 171-191.

Herr, E. Different perceptions of environmental press by high school students. *Personnel and Guidance Journal*, 1965, *7*, 678-686.

Ittelson, W., Proshansky, H., Rivlin, L., and Winkel, G. *An Introduction to Environmental Psychology*. New York: Holt, Rinehart and Winston.

Lockhart, K., Abrahams, B., and Osherson, D. Children's understanding of uniformity in the environment. *Child Development*, 1977, *48*, 1521-1531.

Maslow, A.H. and Mintz, N.L. (1956) Effects of esthetic surroundings upon perceiving "energy" and "well-being" in faces. *Journal of Psychology*, *41*, 247-254.

Mehrabian, A. Characteristic individual reactions to preferred and unpreferred environments. *Journal of Personality* 1978, *13*, 317-332.

Mellenberg, G., Kelderman, H., Stijlen, J., and Zondag, E. Linear models for the analysis and construction of instruments in a facet design. *Psychological Bulletin*, 1979, *86*, 766-776.

Metzer, R., Boschee, P., Haugen, T., and Schnobrich, B. The classroom as learning context: changing rooms effects performance. *Journal of Educational Psychology*, 1979, *4*, 440-442.

Moos, R. Differential effects of psychiatric ward settings on patient change. *Journal of Nervous and Mental Diseases*, 1970, *151*, 316-321.

Moos, R. *The Human Context: Environmental Determinants of Behavior*. New York: Wiley, 1975.

Moos, R. and Gherst, M. Social ecology of university students' residences. *Journal of Educational Psychology*, 1972, *6*, 613-625.

Moos, R., Harris, R. and Schonborn, K. Psychiatric patients and staff reaction to their physical environment. *Journal of Clinical Psychology*, 1969, *25*, 322-324.

Moos, R. and Moos, B. A typology of family social environments. *Family Process*, 1976, *15*, 357-371.

Moos, R., Van Dort, B., Smail, P., and Deyoung, A. A typology of university student living groups. *Journal of Educational Psychology*, 1975, *67*, 359-367.

Murphy, K. Comments on Pugh's method and model for assessing environmental effects. *Organizational Behavior and Human Performance*, 1979, *23*, 56-59.

Nielson, D. and Moos, R. Exploration and adjustment in high school classrooms: a study of personal environment fit. *Journal of Educational Research*, 1978, *72*, 52-57.

Oostendorp, A., McMaster, S., Rosen, M., and Waino, P. Towards a taxonony of responses to the built environment. *International Review of Applied Psychology*, 1978, *27*, 9-16.

Pace, C. and Stern, G. An approach to the measurement of psychological characteristics of college environments. *Journal of Educational Psychology*, 1958, *11*, 377-385.

Patterson, G. and Bechtel, G. Formulating the situational environment in relation to states and traits. In R. Cattell and R. Dreger, (Eds.) *Handbook of Modern Personality Theory*. Washington: Hemisphere, 1977.

Payne, R. and Pugh, D. Organizational structure and climate. In W. Dunnette (Ed.) *Handbook of Industrial and Organizational Psychology*, Chicago: Rand McNally, 1976.

Pederson, D., Johnson, M., and West, J. Effects of room hue on ratings of self, other, and environment. *Perceptual and Motor Skills*, 1978, *46*, 403-410.

Price, R. The taxonomic classification of behaviors and situations and the behavior-environment congruence. *Human Relations*, 1975, *27*, 567-585.

Proshansky, H.M., Ittelson, W.H. and Rivlin, L.G. (eds.) (1976) *Environmental Psychology: People and their Physical Settings*. New York: Holt, Rinehart and Winston.

Pugh, W. Assessment of environmental effects: method or model. *Organizational Behaviour and Human Performance*, 1977, *18*, 175-187.

Rausch, H., Farbman, I., and Llewellyn, L. The interpersonal behavior of children in residential treatment. *Journal of Abnormal and Social Psychology*, 1959, *58*, 9-27.

Russell, J. and Mehrabian, A. Approach-avoidance and affiliation as functions of the emotion-eliciting quality of an environment. *Environment and Behavior*, 1978, *3*, 355-387.

Sewell, W. and Little, B. Specialists, laymen and the process of environmental appraisal. *Regional Studies*, 1973, *7*, 161-171.

Sherrod, D. and Downs, R. Environmental determinants of altruism: the effects of stimulus overload and perceived control on helping. *Journal of Experimental Social Psychology*, 1974, *10*, 468-479.

Sommer, R. *Personal Space: the Behavioral Basis of Design*. Englewood Cliffs: Prentice-Hall, 1969.

Stokols, D. Environmental psychology. *Annual Review of Psychology*, 1978, *29*, 253-295.

Wicker, A. Ecological psychology: some recent and prospective developments. *American Psychologist*, 1978, *34*, 755-765.

Wicker, A. Processes which mediate behavior-environment congruence. *Behavioral Science*, 1972, *17*, 265-277.

Zaralloni, M. and Louis-Guerin, C. Social psychology at the crossroads: its encounter with cognitive and ecological psychology, and the interactive perspective. *European Journal of Social Psychology*, 1979, *9*, 307-321.

1

Explorations in Ecological Psychology *

Roger G. Barker

Ecology is a wide-angle word which I shall not attempt to define here, and ecological psychology refers to a broad and poorly defined class of behavior phenomena. The explorations which I shall discuss this evening occurred within these ill-defined realms, but fortunately their locus can be identified with precision. Fortunately, too, the identification involves issues of general significance for psychology.

Many subdivisions of psychology can be described in terms of their place on the continuum of events that originates in distal objects in the preperceptual environment, and extends via proximal events at the sensory surfaces of organisms, through their afferent, central, and efferent systems, to molecular responses, finally terminating in the environment again via molar actions which alter the postbehavioral environment. The whole range of psychological phenomena is encompassed by this environment-organism-environment continuum (E-O-E arc, psychological unit, behaviour unit); and Brunswik (1955) convincingly demonstrated its value for the identification and appraisal of many facets of psychological science. Schools, specialties, and particular problems are concerned with differing sectors of this continuum; and theories set forth differing relations between the inputs, the outputs, and interior conditions of the sectors.[1] But psychologists know the phenomena along this continuum only via data, and important subdivisions of the science are associated with different kinds of data as well as with different sectors of the continuum. It is necessary,

---

[1] "Interior conditions," as used here, include the properties of the sector (state, operands), the laws governing their functioning (transfer functions, transformations), and changes in the laws (parameters). See Ashby (1956) and Grodins (1963).

therefore, to consider the relation between psychological phenomena and psychological data.

PHENOMENA AND DATA

The phenomena of psychology occur without benefit of psychologists, but the data of psychology are the joint product of psychologists and psychological phenomena coupled within specially contrived data-generating systems.[2] The characteristics of data-generating systems, including the details of the couplings between psychologists and phenomena, are almost limitless; they are the province of psychological methodology and cannot be considered here. However, the great diversity of couplings between psychologists and psychological phenomena can be divided into two types which produce data of crucially different significance for the science of psychology.

Psychologists as Transducers: T Data

The Type 1 data-generating system is shown in Figure 1.1. It is characterized by a single kind of transitive connection between phenomena and data, extending from psychological phenomena to psychologist and from psychologist to data.

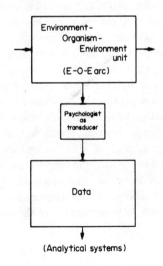

Fig. 1.1.   Data-generating system: Type 1, psychologist as transducer.

---

[2] See Coombs (1964) for a related discussion of the data of psychology.

Psychological phenomena are scanned by the psychologist who functions with respect to them as a transducer, transforming them in accordance with coding categories into data. This data-generating system is, in effect, a translating machine; it translates psychological phenomena into data. The data it generates are operative images of the phenomena, prepared in retrievable form for storage and further analysis. Here is an early example of this type of data, gathered by Susan Isaacs (1950) on July 19, 1926:

> When Mrs. I. lifted up the smouldering rubbish in the bonfire to put more paper under it and make it flame, Dan (5:2) said, "Oh you *are* brave!" Later on, Jessica used the word "brave" without appearing to understand it and Dan corrected her, telling her, " 'Brave' is when you stand close to something you don't like, and don't go away" [p. 112].

Psychological phenomena dominate this data-generating system: They are the operators; the psychologist is a docile receiver, coder, and transmitter of information about the input, interior conditions, and output of psychological units. The data as they issue from the system answer the question, "What goes on here?"; en masse, the data report the abundance and distribution of psychological phenomena with varying input, interior, and output attributes.[3] Here are examples:

> 1. (a) Two-thirds of the behavior units of children of the town of Midwest, Kansas, receive some input from persons or animals, i.e., they are social units; in three-fifths of these social units the person providing the input is an adult, and in two-thirds of the units, a female; animals are the source of 3% of the social input; (b) adults dominate children in about one-third of the units to which they supply input; children dominate children in one-sixth of the units to which they provide input; (c) the input to two-thirds of the social units is compatible with the child's behavior in the unit (Barker & Wright, 1955).
> 2. Disturbances, i.e., unpleasant disruptions in the child's experience as indicated by his expressive behavior, occur at a median rate of 5.4 disturbances per hour; half of these disturbances are evoked by adults, and 5% of them are occasioned by the loss of something the child values (Fawl, 1963).
> 3. The units of Midwest children are of shorter duration, on the average, than those of comparable Yoredale, Yorkshire, children (Schoggen, Barker, & Barker, 1963).
> 4. Yoredale adults provide children with devaluative social inputs four times as frequently as Midwest adults (Barker & Barker, 1963).

---

[3] Transducer and operator as used in this paragraph are defined in Ashby (1956, pp. 44ff., 143ff., 10ff.). T data can be translated back into psychological phenomena, and the agreement between the original phenomena and the reconstituted phenomena is the ultimate test of the adequacy of T data. In actual fact, psychological phenomena are infrequently completely reconstituted in psychological science, but often intermediate steps of the first translation are reconstituted in the course of.data analysis. This is the case when ratings of the content or quality of the original phenomena are made from T data. In court proceedings, behavior phenomena are sometimes reenacted from data supplied by witnesses; and most of the so-called performing arts are based upon the possibility of reconstituting behavior from coded records. See Wiener (1963, pp. 11ff.) and Ashby (1956, pp. 145ff.).

The Type 1 data-generating system provides information about psychological phenomena in terms of transformations made by a psychologist; the transformations constitute the psychologist's only contribution to the data of the system. By using the psychologist as a transducer only, and not as operator, this system produces data which denote a world the psychologist did not make in any respect; they signal behavior and its conditions, *in situ*.

Type 1 data-generating systems have no commonly accepted name, so we have called them, after the psychologist's role, *transducer data systems,* and, for short, T systems. We shall also use the terms transducer methods, or T methods, and transducer data, or T data.

Psychologists as Operators: O Data

In the Type 2 data-generating system there are two kinds of couplings between psychological phenomena and psychologist, as represented in Figure 1.2. In

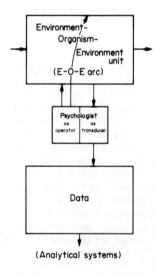

Fig. 1.2.   Data-generating system. Type 2, psychologist as operator and transducer.

addition to functioning as transducer, as in the first type, the psychologist, here, is coupled into the psychological unit as an operative part of it, regulating input, and/or influencing interior conditions, and/or constraining output. The psychologist dominates this system; as operator, he sends messages via the unit to himself as receiver and transducer. The data answer the question, "What goes on here, under the conditions of input, interior conditions, and output which I impose?'' Here is an example of this type of data from the Stanford-Binet test, 1937 revision (11-year level—Terman & Merrill, 1937):

> Psychologist as Operator: What do we mean by *courage?*
> Subject: Do something you don't want to do 'cause you're afraid of getting hurt [p. 269].

The crucial feature of this data generating system is that by becoming involved as an operator in the units he is investigating, the psychologist achieves control which allows him to focus upon segments and processes of particular concern to him, via data that refer to events which he, in part, contrives.

Type 2 data-generating systems may be appropriately called, after the psychologist's role, *operator data systems,* or O systems. We shall also use the terms O method and O data. Operator data-generating systems are, in essence, experimental methods. We have not used the term, however, because of its common restriction in psychology to operations carried out in laboratories, and hence its exclusion of clinical methods, a restriction and an exclusion that do not apply in any degree to O methods.

Locus of Our Explorations

The purpose of this methodological prologue is to identify the locus of our explorations, and this purpose can now be accomplished: We have explored, via transducer data, behavior units of the children of Midwest, Kansas, and of Yoredale, Yorkshire, on particular occasions since 1949.

USES OF DATA

When the difference between psychologists as operators and as transducers within data-generating systems is stated with precision, some questions are likely to arise: Why be satisfied with less than the most rigorously defined and controlled data-generating arrangements? Why bother with the role of transducer? To be specific, why, in the year 1964, should a cross-cultural, psychological study of children be based upon T data?

Similar questions have been asked in connection with a motley class of methods variously called field methods, naturalistic approaches, observational techniques. These methods have not infrequently been judged and found wanting. It is commonly said of them that almost anything they can do, experiments can do better. Their advantage is said to lie in their relative simplicity, which makes them useful as rough and ready methods for reconnoitering new problems, and especially, for identifying variables to be included in crucial experiments.[4] It is not easy to evaluate these judgments about the untidy

---

[4] This viewpoint is presented in Festinger, Schachter, and Back (1963), Cattell (1959), and Hinde (1959).

class of methods to which they refer. But it is clear that the judgments do not apply to transducer and operator methods.

The models show that T data refer to psychological phenomena which are explicitly excluded when the psychologist functions as operator. Indeed, the primary task of the psychologist as transducer is carefully to preserve phenomena that the psychologist as operator carefully alters, namely, psychologist-free units.[5] We have to say, therefore, that what T methods do, O methods cannot do at all: O methods cannot signal behavior and its conditions unaltered by the system that generates the data.

The models show, too, that O data refer to phenomena that psychologists as transducers explicitly exclude, namely, psychological units arranged in accordance with the curiosities of the psychologist. The primary task of the operator is to alter, in ways that are crucial to his interests, phenomena that the psychologist as transducer leaves intact. It should be noted, however, that an investigator can sometimes select T data which refer to psychological units with the particular attributes in which he is interested.[6] We have to say, therefore, that what O methods do, T methods usually cannot do at all, or can do less efficiently: T methods cannot focus so clearly upon the particular events within psychological units which interest the investigator.[7]

In short the data which psychologists produce as operators and as transducers refer to non-overlapping classes of psychological phenomena. That the two classes of phenomena differ in ways which are of fundamental significance for the science is obvious in concrete cases.

---

[5] O methods may be used to simulate the phenomena to which T data refer. When this can be done O methods facilitate T methods, for simulation may be easier technically than discovering the phenomena in sufficient amounts for efficient investigation. This has been the case with radiation phenomena, for example. However, simulation requires T data in the first place to guide experiments. Furthermore, the equivalence of the arranged phenomena and the T phenomena has to be clearly demonstrated; this may be difficult to do, as it was in the case of frustration to be cited in this paper. Gump and Kounin (1959-60) discuss this issue, and Reitman (1964) discusses some efforts at simulation of psychological phenomena.

[6] In other words, T data can sometimes serve the purposes that O data usually serve, i.e., to isolate particular variables of concern to the investigator. This is the counterpart of the simulation of the phenomena of T data by O methods (see Footnote 5). It is an important adaptation of T methods, for O methods cannot arrange some of the conditions in which an investigator may be interested, e.g., traumatic conditions, children without siblings.

[7] T data and O data may bear upon the same theoretical issue, e.g., upon the hypothetical processes within the organism sector of the E-O-E arc. In fact, hypotheses suggested by T data can sometimes be tested most effectively by O data; nevertheless, the phenomena in these cases differ, unless the test is merely a simulation of the phenomena of the T data. Data which refer to genotypic phenomena are of course more significant than data with only a phenotypic reference, and T data are sometimes criticized on this ground; but O methods are obviously no guarantee that the data refer to genotypic phenomena.

Take intelligence, for example. Millions of reliable and valid intelligence tests have been administered, scored, and reported, thus providing a vast store of O data, for psychologists are strong operators in test situations, supplying input ("What do we mean by courage?"), regulating interior conditions ("Work carefully; speed is not important"), and constraining output ("Underline the correct response"). These data provide basic information about intellectual functioning within test-score generating systems, and about intellectual processes and their constants: about IQ, about g, about verbal factors, etc. But this great and successful scientific assault upon the problem of intelligence has provided almost no information about the intellectual demands the environments of life make upon people, and how people respond to the "test items" with which they are confronted in the course of living.[8] The science of psychology provides virtually no information about the intelligence of people outside of data-generating systems operated by psychologists.

Or take frustration as another example. Some years ago, when I was a student of Kurt Lewin, he and Tamara Dembo and I carried out some experiments upon frustration (Barker, Dembo & Lewin, 1941). The findings of these experiments have been verified by others, and they have become part of the literature of scientific psychology. The experiments provided basic information about the consequences for children of frustration, as defined in the experiments, and about the processes that produce these consequences. Time passed. In due course I had a student, and he undertook to study frustration. So far, so good. All in the grand tradition! My student, Clifford L. Fawl, did not replicate the earlier study; he did not *contrive* frustration for his subjects; he pioneered, and extended the investigation from children *in vitro,* so to speak, to children *in situ.* He searched our specimen records of children's everyday behavior for instances of this allegedly important phenomenon without psychologists as operators. Here are the words of his report (Fawl, 1963),

The results . . . were surprising in two respects. First, even with a liberal interpretation of frustration fewer incidents were detected than we expected. . . . Second . . . meaningful

---

Figures 1 and 2 display only the distinguishing features of the two types of data-generating systems; they have many details and complications. In most investigations there are many replications of psychological units, and in many investigations only parts of the whole E-O-E arcs, and only some of the many events within them are involved; the data generating systems may be more or less automated, with the psychologist represented by instruments he has created; there may be a variety of feedback loops within the systems; in addition to the output of data, there are other outputs from the systems, e.g., test-wise subjects. In fact, data-generating systems vary on a continuum from O systems where the psychologist as operator intervenes in very many of the variables of E-O-E arcs to systems where he does not intervene at all. The discussion here deals with the *pure cases* at the ends of the continuum.

[8] Aside from Isaac's (1950) pioneering work, Ragle's (1957) research is one of the few investigations of intellectual development via T data.

relationships could not be found between frustration . . . and consequent behavior such as . . .
regression . . . and other theoretically meaningful behavioral manifestations [p. 99].

In other words, frustration was rare in the children's days, and when it did occur
it did not have the behavioral consequences observed in the laboratory. It appears
that the earlier experiments simulated frustration very well as we defined and
prescribed it for our subjects (in accordance with our theories); but the
experiments did not simulate frustration as life prescribes it for children.

Fawl's results made us wonder, and worry![9]

The conclusion is inescapable that psychologists as operators and as transducers are not analogous, and that the data they produce have fundamentally
different uses within the science. One may contend that the phenomena denoted
by T data are unimportant, or that they are not psychology. One may argue that O
data refer, potentially at least, to more fundamental, universal, invariant
psychological processes than T data. But, however the phenomena denoted by T
data are classified and evaluated, they comprise a realm of phenomena forever
inaccessible via O data. The data which psychologists produce as transducers are
not horse-and-buggy versions of the data they produce as operators; and a
cross-cultural study of children via T methods is not more primitive than one via
O methods: the phenomena, the methods, and the data are all different. If one
wishes to know, for example, such information as the duration of behavior units,
the sources of social input, or the frequency of disturbances only T data will
provide the answers.

A well-known fact about psychology takes on new significance in the light of
this analysis. From the earliest days of the science, psychologists have been
operators: in laboratories, in clinics, even in field studies. They have infrequently
functioned as transducers. This is documented for the 1960s in the report of our
Association's project, *Psychology: A Study of a Science* (Koch, 1959a, 1959b,
1959c, 1962, 1963a, 1963b). Surely everyone who reads the volumes of the
study which are now available will be impressed with the variety of methods,
facts, and theories it displays, and with the range of viewpoints it presents. There
is something in the study for everyone, or almost everyone. Psychologists of
every persuasion, or almost every persuasion, will find allies in it. Few need
leave the magnificent feast it offers without nourishment. But among these few
are psychologists concerned with behavior *in situ*. One has to look long, and
winnow carefully, to discover any discussion of non-experimental methods or

---

[9] Such wonders and worries are not infrequently expressed; here is a recent instance: George A.
Miller wrote in the introduction to a study of the spontaneous speech of an infant (Weir, 1962),
"After many years of reading . . . about the environmental events that strengthen or weaken various
stimulus-response associations, I was completely unprepared to encounter a two-year-old boy
who—all alone—corrected his own pronunciations, drilled himself on consonant clusters, and
practiced substituting his small vocabulary into fixed sentence frames [p. 15]."

data. Without a doubt *Psychology: A Study of a Science* presents, in this respect, a true picture of psychology today.[10]

This state of affairs is most surprising in view of the situation in the old, prestigeful sciences which psychology so admires and emulates in other respects. In these sciences, the quest for the phenomena of science as they occur unaltered by the techniques of search and discovery is a central, continuing task; and the development of techniques for identifying entities and signaling processes without altering them (within organisms, within cells, within physical systems, and within machines) is among the sciences' most valued achievements.[11] Handbooks and encyclopedias attest to the success of these efforts. I read, for example, that potassium (K) ranks seventh in order of abundance of elements, and constitutes about 2.59% of the igneous rocks of the earth's crust; that its compounds are widely distributed in the primary rocks, the oceans, the soil, plants, and animals; and that soluble potassium salts are present in all fertile soils (*Encyclopaedia Britannica,* 1962). The fact that there is no equivalent information in the literature of scientific psychology (about playing, about laughing, about talking, about being valued and devalued, about conflict, about failure) confronts psychologists with a monumental incompleted task.

STRUCTURE OF BEHAVIOR

It was in 1947 that Herbert F. Wright and I established a field station in Midwest, Kansas, for the purpose of finding out "What goes on here?" with respect to the behavior and living conditions of the children of the town. Midwest was reputed to be a simple country town where not much happened; and as there were only about 100 children among the 715 inhabitants, we seemed embarked upon a routine expedition. We are still on the expedition. One of the reasons is that we had much to learn about the nature of our science: about phenomena and data, and about T data and O data, for example. We also had much to unlearn about its methodology.

Very soon after we arrived in Midwest we were confronted with the practical problem of what to record, as transducers, and what to count as analysts of T data. What *is* a unit of a child's unbroken behavior stream? This question is

---

[10] This conclusion is verified by Berelson and Steiner (1964), and by textbooks of psychology.

[11] Exemplifying evidence of the importance attached to noninterfering techniques in science are: *(a)* a society of physical and engineering scientists concerned with nondestructive methods of examining and testing material (National Organizations, 1961); *(b)* an American Association for the Advancement of Science award for the development of techniques of recording heart functioning in animals without interfering with the heart's behavior (AAAS, 1959). See von Hippel (1956) and Weiskopf (1961) for discussion of aspects of this problem.

ordinarily settled very shortly: A unit is an answer to a questionnaire item (the investigator's item); it is a trial on a maze (the investigator's maze), it is the completion of a sentence (the investigator's sentence). But when an investigator does not impose *his* units on the stream of behavior, what are *its* units? We found that when observers approach subjects' behavior streams as sensors and transducers, signalling in literary language what they see, structural-dynamic units are always generated.[12] Here is an example of narrative data denoting two such units; these data refer to 5-year-old Maud Pintner in Clifford's Drugstore in Midwest. Maud sat at the fountain waiting to order the treat her mother had promised her. On the stool next to Maud was her 2-year-old brother, Fred; her mother sat beside Fred. The two units occurred successively and they occupied, together, less than ½ minute:

> 2:48 P.M. From her jeans' pocket Maud now took an orange crayon.
> She brushed it across her lips as if it were a lipstick.
> Maud then leaned over, sliding her arms along the counter, as she watched a man serve a strawberry soda to his blond, curly-headed, three-year-old girl.
> Maud seemed fascinated by the procedure; she took in every detail of the situation [Barker & Wright, 1951, p. 248].

The analyst titled these units: Pretending to Use Lipstick and Watching Girl Eat Soda.

Herbert Wright and others have studied these units, called behavior episodes, in great detail and have discovered some of their attributes (Barker & Wright, 1955). Altogether the evidence is convincing that behavior episodes are fundamental molar units of the behavior stream. It is impressive, I think, that the results of this empirical work should agree so well with Brunswik's independent, theoretical formulation of the unit of psychological phenomena. Two things which are absolutely clear about behavior episodes are (*a*) that they are inherent parts of the behavior stream, entirely free from impositions by psychologists, and (*b*) that they can be reliably identified.

Our studies revealed important differences between the behavior stream's own units, and the units psychologists impose upon them. Behavior episodes do not march along single file with their accompanying inputs as they do in psychophysics experiments, in intelligence tests, in polling interviews, for example, where the psychologist is operator. Rather, they go one, two or three abreast quite irregularly. In the upper row of Figure 1.3, the structure of Maud's behavior in the corner drugstore is represented in terms of episodes. During this 11-minute period Maud engaged in 25 episodes of behavior, including Pretending to Use Lipstick and Watching Girl Eat Soda. Ten of these episodes occurred

---

[12] See Dickman (1963) in this connection; Barker (1963b) identified other varieties of behavior units.

singly, but 15 of them occurred simultaneously with other episodes, and in one case there was a triple overlap, namely, Eating Ice Cream Cone, Watching Girl Eat Soda (on another occasion), and Trying to Get Her Mother's Attention. Two episodes were interrupted and later resumed. This segment of behavior is by no means atypical. We have episoded over 200 hours of children's specimen

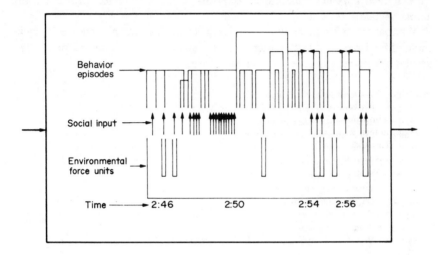

Fig. 1.3.   Behavior setting: Clifford's Drugstore, Maud is treated to ice-cream cone.

records, including 18 day-long records, and this picture always emerges: 73% (median) of Midwest children's episodes overlap simultaneously with one or more other episodes (Barker & Wright, 1955). So far as behavior structure is concerned, O systems are, indeed, great simplifiers; the question is: Are they also great destroyers of essential attributes of psychological phenomena? One wonders, for example, how the properties which behavior units possess when they are lined up Indian file by an operator are modified when they occur in overlapping formation, as they so often do in the phenomena reported by T data.

STRUCTURE OF THE ENVIRONMENT

We found the structure of the behavior stream on the level of episodes to be complicated, but definite; and on the basis of Brunswik's model we expected to find the structure of the environment to be, *pari passu*, complicated and definite, also. We expected to find this, too, on the basis of O data where a unit of an operator's input is almost always coupled with a unit of a subject's output:

stimulus with response, problem with attempted solution, question with answer. Furthermore, O data led us to expect conformity between the ecological and behavioral sides of psychological units; operators' inputs require that the subjects' outputs fall within limits set by operators. If a subject does not respond to the operator's inputs, or if he responds outside of the limits set by the operator, he is eliminated as a subject. This is an efficient arrangement; it avoids a number of analytical nuisances and embarrassments, and every subject provides a full quota of data.

We found that T data are not so obliging. Here, for example, are the 26 social inputs Maud received in the drugstore as they occurred in temporal order. The source of the input is given first in each case.

Mother: "We'll all go to the drugstore."
Mother: "Not now; you're not having a comic now."
Mother: "Leave things [Christmas cards] alone."
Mother: "Come on now, get your coat off."
Mother: "Maud, come back and sit down."
Mother: Pushes Maud toward the stool.
Mother: "Now you sit here."
Mother: "What do you want, Maud?"
Mother: "Oh, you don't want a *soda*."
Mother: "No, you don't get a soda."
Mother: "What do you want?"
Mother: "You don't want a soda. Besides you wouldn't drink it if you had it."
Mother: "Do you want a coke?"
Mother: "Do you want an ice cream cone?"
Mother: "*Do* you want an ice cream cone?"
Clerk: "What flavor, Maud?"
Clerk: "Vanilla, that's the white one."
Clerk: "Don't eat Fred's cone."
Mother: "Come on. Get your coat on, Maud."
Mother: Refuses Maud's whispered request.
Fred: Snatches Maud's coat.
Clerk: "Hi, Maud," as she ruffles Maud's hair.
Mother: "Come on."
Mother: Pushes Maud toward her coat.
Fred: Asks Maud for gum (from gum-machine).
Mother: Urges children from store with words and motions.

These 26 social inputs are represented on Figure 1.3 where it is apparent that there is no simple coupling of units of behavior with units of social input. In fact, Maud responded and conformed to about one-third of the social inputs she received in the drugstore. Maud was not extreme in this respect; in large samples we have found that there is responsiveness and conformity to about one-half of all social inputs (Barker & Wright, 1955).

These findings were disturbing. They were equivalent to finding half of a colony of rats refusing to run a maze, or to having half the items of a questionnaire returned unanswered. The T methods could not bypass this difficulty and assure responsiveness and conformity as O methods do: by forcing compliance via instructions or motivating conditions, by using only volunteer subjects, by omitting recalcitrant subjects, or by altering procedures to make them more acceptable. Our T methods had to deal with phenomena as they came, and this complicated immensely the problem of discovering lawful relations between environmental input and behavioral output. The findings were disturbing, also, because they were not in accord with the larger picture of the behavior stream and its environment. Although Maud did not respond or conform to most of the social inputs she received in the drugstore, the whole course of her drugstore behavior was actually harmonious with and appropriate to the drugstore setting: Maud had her treat and enjoyed it, she did *not* read the comics or handle the Christmas cards to an appreciable extent, she *did* sit on the stool, she did *not* have a soda, she *was* uncoated, recoated, and shepherded from the store in a generally agreeable way. Maud's relation to her environment was quite different in the large than in the small. If we look upon this as a test of Maud's drugstore behavior, we see that Maud failed most of the items, but she passed the test. And this was generally true of Midwest children, as I shall document with data below.

Despite the disharmonies between T data and O data, and between T data in the small and in the large, we were loath to abandon the precision of exactly identified, reliably rated, and correctly enumerated inputs and episodes; they satisfied the first requirement of good research, replicable data. They seemed to provide firm ground in an unfirm region. But the firm ground was small comfort when we found ourselves firmly stranded upon it in our search for lawful relations between input and output. So we engaged in considerable trial-and-error behavior, including turning against our own cherished dogmas and theories, and listening to scientifically unsophisticated lay experts. We even went so far as to remove our sensors from our subjects, the children of Midwest, and to attach them to the environment surrounding our subjects. When we did this, we discovered something that is spread out for all to see, namely, that the structure of the environment of children is not usually isomorphic with the structure of their behavior; the two do not usually occur in coupled units. In fact it was immediately obvious that the discrete inputs upon which we had been fixated were very often not environmental units at all, but fragments of units, environmental tesserae.

After this painful confrontation with reality we had no difficulty in discriminating units of the environment. Schoggen identified an environmental unit, which he called an environmental force unit(s) (EFU), that is an action by an environmental agent toward a recognizable end state for a person (Schoggen, 1963). The unity of an EFU comes from its constancy of direction with respect to the person upon whom it bears. The EFU often involve series, or programs, of discrete inputs. The EFU acting upon Maud in the drugstore are presented in the third row of Figure 1.3; her 25 behavior episodes and the 26 social inputs she received in the drugstore are encompassed by these eight EFU. They all included at least one social input, and the large, inclusive EFU (Maud to Have Treat at Drugstore) had 18 social inputs. Schoggen discovered many interesting facts about EFU, but for us, the most interesting finding was that a person's behavior is more frequently responsive and conforming to intact EFU than to separate components of EFU. Simmons and Schoggen (1963) found that half of the EFU, whose initial inputs elicited unresponsive or unconforming behavior, elicited responsive and conforming behavior at the terminal input. Here was documentation of what we observed in general, namely, that isomorphism between the environment and behavior is more frequent over long than over short segments of the behavior stream. It was evident, however, that duration, itself, is not the crucial variable. Schoggen's data show that environmental units (EFU) usually endure longer than psychological units (episodes). This means that when behavior episodes are used to mark off units of the environment, the resulting environmental segments are usually not unitary parts of the environment, or multiples thereof, but random fragments of the environment. To use these fragments in an investigation of the relation between environmental input and behavioral output is analogous to studying the relation between the slope of 4-foot sectors of a roadway (the circumference of a wheel) and the speed of vehicles over them.

ENVIRONMENT AND BEHAVIOR: SEPARATE AND INTERDEPENDENT

According to these findings, the environmental component of a psychological unit, the input, is often not the environment of the unit. This paradox is not peculiar to psychology. It occurs whenever independent self-governing systems become coupled. The common parts, the points of contact of the coupled systems, do not define either system; yet the total systems interact.[13]

One side of this relationship is well established in psychology, where it is recognized that the distal, environmental event at the origin of an E-O-E arc does not identify the *psychological* unit of which it is a part. In Maud's case, the

---

[13] Other examples of this paradox are abundant. For instance, when my car (a transportation system) and the petroleum industry (an economic system) are joined at the service station pump, the gasoline which is common to both does not define and describe either system. Furthermore, the petroleum industry and my car are each a unitary system and their properties are incommensurate. Nevertheless, they are linked. The petroleum industry is the environing fuel-supply system of my car, and my car is a component element of the industry. The two are mutually, causally related. See Barker (1963a.)

environmental event "What do you want, Maud?" is singularly uninformative about the behavior episode it initiated in Maud, namely, Asking for Ice-cream Soda. It is also well established that psychological units interact with the environment via feedback from the environment regarding the fate of the units' outputs in the ecological world. Proprioceptive, visual, and auditory feedback inform behavior units that targets have or have not been reached, and in the latter case instigate adjusting reactions.[14] In Maud's case, her efforts to be treated to a soda were progressively modified as her mother's feedback signalled that Maud's efforts had failed. Early in our explorations, we saw the necessity of identifying complete behavior units and of studying them in relation to environmental inputs.

The other side of the coupling of behavioral and environmental phenomena is less well established in psychology. It is not so generally recognized that the same distal event at the origin of a psychological unit does not identify the *environmental* unit of which it is simultaneously a part. In Maud's case, again, the event, "What do you want, Maud?" is singularly uninformative about the environmental unit (EFU) of which it is a part, namely, Maud Not to Have a Soda. It is also less well recognized that the environment interacts with behavior via feedback. In the drugstore, the mother's no-soda policy was modified when Maud's feedback to her signalled its failure.

We failed to see for a long time that behavior and the environment are mutually causally related systems. We know some of the reasons for this failure. Independent, self-organized, but coupled systems present great conceptual and analytical difficulties, and one way to simplify the difficulties is to treat one system (the behavior unit in this case) as a unitary system and the other system (the environment unit) as a series of discrete, unrelated events which happen to converge upon the unitary system. When we did this, the environmental system was, of course, destroyed and its events became parts of the apparently ineffective inputs we discovered surrounding the behavior stream.

There was another reason for our failure to accept our own findings. Narrative T data indicated that more is involved on the environmental side of a psychological unit than relations with associates, i.e., than EFU. The environment is more than diadic, or triadic; it is more than social. Maud in the drugstore was incorporated into and she contributed to an ongoing program of events in which not only her mother and the clerk had a part, but all the staff, the customers, the equipment, the merchandise, the spatial and temporal arrangements, and the rules of the store as well. Such extrabehavioral phenomena seemed just too much to cope with.

Yet there was systematic evidence that situations *in toto* influence behavior; that more than people are involved in the mutual causal relations between the

---

[14] The feedback loop and its place in psychology are excellently presented by Miller, Galanter, and Pribram (1960).

environment and behavior. Gump, Schoggen, and Redl (1963), Gump and Sutton-Smith (1955), Raush, Dittman, and Taylor (1959), and Ashton (1964) have found that different categories of situations such as drugstores, arithmetic lessons, streets and sidewalks, and mealtimes, have differential effects upon behavior even when the same persons are involved as subjects. This was something we could see directly: The relations between Maud and her mother were quite different in the drugstore than they were at home. But how does one deal with background conditions in the situation at large?

We received most help with this task from practical men and technologists, on the one hand, and from cybernetic theorists on the other. In the experience of practitioners, mongrel, ecobehavioral entities are the common coin of those who cope with communities and institutions. Here is one such entity as identified and described by a journalist in a recent issue of the local Yorkshire newspaper:

> Members and friends of the Women's Bright Hour [a church women's society] held their annual outing on Thursday of last week when Newcastle and Whitby Bay were visited. The weather was not too favorable but the day's pleasure was enjoyed [*Darlington and Stockton Times*, 1964].

You will note that both behavior (annual outing, the day's pleasure) and environment (Newcastle, not too favorable weather) are included as components of the entity Bright Hour Annual Outing, and that it is described without reference to particular persons. This and other ecobehavioral entities, which we have called behavior settings, are preperceptual units; they exist independently of anyone's perception of them, qua units. They can be exactly identified, reliably described, and correctly enumerated. When we turned to them, we were on firm ground again; in fact, we were on firmer ground than in the case of social input, EFU, and behavior episodes. Behavior settings have spatial and temporal indices, and they have human-size durations and extents; they can be entered by investigators are inspected and re-inspected; they are stable; they are as substantial as people.

We identified, described, and catalogued the behavior settings of Midwest and Yoredale (Barker & Barker, 1961; Barker & Wright, 1955); but we were most concerned with the relations between their ecological properties and the behavior of their human components. We were particularly interested in discovering how independent persons with their own plans[15] are accommodated within behavior settings with their particular programs of events.

One property of behavior settings which varies widely and is widely believed to have important consequences for the functioning of settings and for the behavior of persons within them is number of human components. In fact, we had long been intrigued by sandlot baseball games in Midwest with varying

---

[15] "Plans" is here used as by Miller et al. (1960).

numbers of players: A game with four players on a side has manifestly different consequences for the players than a game with nine players on a side; it makes no difference who the players are, once a boy becomes part of a four-man team he plays four-man baseball, with all of its privileges (of frequent batting, for example) and all of its burdens (such as a wide, fatiguing field to cover). These observations and some pilot data provided the basis for a theory of behavior-setting differentiation, with special reference to the number of human components.

I shall not present the theory here; instead, I shall report some results of research which was guided by the theory, for the results will outlive the theory, and shape the more adequate theories we shall surely have.[16] The burden of our findings, for which theories must account, is that one ecological property of behavior settings, number of inhabitants, has univocal (and predictable) consequences for the behavior and experiences of the inhabitants even when this property has no direct, univocal representation at the sensory surfaces of the individuals who inhabit the settings.

Gump and Friesen, and Willems compared the behavior and experiences of high school students in voluntary, nonacademic behavior settings of small schools having relatively few students per setting (median number in attendance, 11), and of a large school having relatively many students per setting (median number in attendance, 36). The behavior settings were comparable in all respects except that the large school had a greater variety of better equipped settings. The findings were in some respects surprising, even paradoxical.

1. Different kinds of satisfactions were reported. In comparison with the students of the large school, the students of the small schools reported having *more* satisfactions related (*a*) to the development of competence, (*b*) to being challenged, (*c*) to engaging in important actions, (*d*) to being involved in group activities, (*e*) to being valued, and (*f*) to gaining moral and cultural values. In their own words, students reported having more experiences of these kinds in the small schools: "It gave me confidence"; "It gave me a chance to see how good I am"; "I got the speakers for all of these meetings"; "The class worked together"; "It also gave me recognition"; "I feel it makes a better man of me." The same students reported some other satisfactions *less* frequently than their counterparts in the large school. They reported fewer satisfactions referring (*a*) to vicarious enjoyment, (*b*) to affiliation with a large entity, (*c*) to learning about the school's persons and affairs, and (*d*) to gaining "points" via participation. In the students' own words, again, *fewer* experiences of these kinds came from the small school students: "I enjoyed watching the game"; "I like the companionship of mingling with the rest of the crowd"; "I enjoyed this because I learned

---

[16] The theory is presented in papers by Barker and Barker (1961), Barker (1960, 1963a), Barker and Gump (1964, pp. 1-28).

who was on the team''; ''You get to build up points for honors'' (Gump & Friesen, 1964b). We were confronted with this surprise: Students in the schools with the less consequential behavior settings had more frequent satisfactions relating to themselves as persons of consequence, i.e., as competent, important, valued, and good, than students in the school with more consequential behavior settings.

2. Different degrees of participation occurred. Students of the small schools performed in 2.5 times as many important and responsible positions, on the average, as students of the large school; and for crucial, central positions, such as team members or chairmen of meetings, they performed in 6 times as many positions. Two percent of them filled no important and responsible positions, while 29% of their counterparts in the large school were nonperformers. Furthermore, the students in the small schools filled important and responsible positions in twice as many *varieties* of behavior settings as their counterparts (Gump & Friesen, 1964a). We were confronted with this paradox: The schools with the smaller and less varied settings were, for their students, functionally larger and more varied than the schools with the more populous and more varied settings.

3. There were differences in pressures to take part in the programs of behavior settings. In the small schools, where students had relatively few associates within behavior settings they reported twice as many pressures upon them to take part in the programs of the settings, as did students in the large school with relatively many associates within settings. In their own words small school students reported more frequently ''I had to march in the band''; ''My family urged me to take part''; ''Everyone else was going.'' Surprisingly, these pressures were neither uniformly nor randomly distributed among the students; they occurred selectively, and the basis of the selection differed in the two types of schools. In the small schools, marginal students (students without the abilities and backgrounds which facilitate school success) reported almost as many pressures to participate as did regular students (students with the abilities and backgrounds for school achievement). But within the large school, the marginal students reported about one-fourth as many pressures to participate as did the regular students. Not even one of the marginal students in the small schools reported no pressures to participate in school settings, while about one-third of the marginal students in the large school reported no pressures (Willems, 1964). We were confronted with another surprise: The small behavior settings with modest activity programs generated more forces toward participation than the large settings with ambitious programs.

According to this evidence, behavior settings are not regions within which people play their parts with greater or less support or resistance from the setting. They are, rather, entities that regulate some aspects of the behavior of their human components. The data just presented reveal two of the ways in which this was done in the schools; they are opposite ways, in important respects, and the two types of schools differed in the frequency with which each was used.

In the small schools, with the meagerly populated settings, regulation occurred by means of negative feedback to all students, i.e., pressures against deviation from the programs of settings. Here, for example, are reports of negative feedback by students of the small schools: "My teacher talked me into it"; "They needed girls in the cast"; "Everyone was supposed to be there"; "I was assigned to work there." We have seen that such pressures occurred twice as frequently in the small schools as in the large school, and that all students of the small schools, even marginal ones, received them. This control system contributed to the harmony between the plans of individual inhabitants and the programs of the settings by regulating behavior (all behavior), and therefore incorporating all students within behavior settings.

In the school with the populous settings, on the other hand, regulation was in two stages: (a) discrimination of students with the more and the less promising behavior and (b) provision of negative feedback to the behavior of the more promising (regular) students and no feedback at all to the behavior of most of the less promising (marginal) students. We have seen that in the large school most of the pressures to participate in the behavior settings were applied to regular students, that many marginal students received no pressures against failure to participate, and that, in fact, an appreciable percentage of them were nonperformers. This control system contributed to the harmony between individual plans and behavior-setting programs by selecting the behavior (and the students) requiring least regulation and discarding the behavior (and the students) requiring most regulation. The latter was accomplished by allowing marginal students to disqualify themselves via unregulated deviancy.

The control of behavior by behavior settings was not only by means of negative feedback and selection, but also by way of rewards. The behavior settings of the small and large schools did not differ greatly in the number of satisfactions they provided students, but as we have seen they differed greatly in the content of the satisfaction they provided. The students of the small schools achieved satisfactions more frequently by being competent, by accepting challenges, by doing important things, by engaging in group activities, and by engaging in valued actions, all of which could be gained only by serious participation in the programs of the settings. The students of the large school achieved satisfactions more frequently by watching others participate, by mingling with the crowd, by learning about the school, and by gaining points, none of which required serious participation in the schools' settings; the participation rewards went only to the students who had not been allowed to count themselves out of the programs of the settings.

These different kinds of control systems had wide significance for the students. Behavior settings with negative feedback to the deviant behavior and rewards for the appropriate participation of all inhabitants provided quite a different environment with respect to interpersonal relations, values, and achievement possibilities from settings where control was achieved by restricting feedback and rewards to the promising students only and allowing the marginal ones to withdraw from the programs of the settings.

These data indicate that the environment is sometimes much more than a source of inputs to behavior arranged in particular array and flow patterns. They indicate, rather, that the environment provides programs of inputs with controls that regulate the inputs in accordance with the systemic requirements of the environment, on the one hand, and in accordance with the behavior attributes of its human components, on the other. This means that the same environmental unit provides different inputs to different persons, and different inputs to the same person if his behavior changes; and it means, further, that the whole program of the environment's inputs changes if its own ecological properties change, if it becomes more or less populous, for example.

This presents quite a different problem to an investigator from the analysis of stable patterns of input. If an investigator wants to discover not only the gross, residual consequences of environments for people, but the processes as well, the processes have to be studied intact—in process, in fact—and this is only possible when the investigator functions as a transducer.

A central problem of our science is the relation between ecological events (the distal stimuli) at the origin of E-O-E arcs and the succeeding events along these arcs. To solve this problem psychologists will have to become transducers vis-à-vis the phenomena of psychology. The problem here is not "What behavior occurs when I, as operator, introduce Input X?" but rather "What inputs do I, as transducer, sense under ecological Condition Y?" An operator, by undertaking to regulate the input to the psychological phenomena he studies, deprives himself of the possibility of investigating the unregulated input.

But there are a number of reasons for avoiding the role of transducer in psychological research: The resulting T data do not fit easily into the hardware, the bureaucracies, the research designs, or the concepts of psychology's establishment which has been shaped by prevailing operator data-generating systems. The skills and personality attributes required of a successful transducer are different from those of a successful operator, and they are doubtless not congenial to many persons. The techniques of the transducer are in many respects more difficult than those of the operator. And, most important, perhaps, the transducer has less easy access to the organism sector of psychological units, i.e., to psychology's challenging "black box."

However, there are grounds for believing that despite these reasons for voiding the transducer role, it will become more important in the years ahead. In relatively uniform and stable environments, people are the source of behavior variance and the dominant scientific problem concerns the nature of the black box where the secrets of individual differences are stored. The persistent query from the applied fields and from the sciences to which psychology is propaedeutic is: What are *people* like? How can people be selected and sorted into the pockets provided by bureaucracies, schools, business, armies, etc.? What are the needs and capacities of people to which highways, curricula, and laws must be adapted? These questions can only be answered by psychologists functioning as operators using standard inputs.

But in varied and changing environments, the contribution of environmental input to the variance of behavior is enhanced. In a restless world, the nature of the environment is the intriguing scientific problem. And the applied fields and neighboring sciences ask: What are environments like? What programs of inputs do underdeveloped countries, windowless office buildings, and integrated schools provide for people? These questions can only be answered by psychologists functioning as transducers.

We know which of these worlds we live in today, and it does not seem likely that our own curiosities and the demands of engineers, economists, educators, and political leaders will allow us to be content with a psychology of people to the neglect of a psychology of the environment of people.

REFERENCES

American Association for the Advancement of Science. Annual meeting awards. *Science,* 1959, *129,* 138.

Ashby, W. R. *An Introduction to Cybernetics.* New York: Wiley, 1956.

Ashton, Margaret. An ecological study of the stream of behavior. Unpublished master's thesis, University of Kansas, 1964.

Barker, R. G. Ecology and motivation. In M. R. Jones (Ed.), *Nebraska Symposium on Motivation: 1960.* Lincoln: Univer. Nebraska Press, 1960. Pp. 1-49.

Barker, R. G. On the nature of the environment. *Journal of Social Issues,* 1963, *19*(4), 17-38. (a)

Barker, R. G. The stream of behavior as an empirical problem. In R. G. Barker (Ed.), *The Stream of Behavior.* New York: Appleton-Century-Crofts, 1963. Pp. 1-22. (b)

Barker, R. G., & Barker, Louise S. Behavior units for the comparative study of cultures. In B. Kaplan (Ed.), *Studying Personality Cross-Culturally.* New York: Harper & Row, 1961. Pp. 457-476.

Barker, R. G., & Barker, Louise S. Social actions in the behavior streams of American and English children. In R. G. Barker (Ed.), *The Stream of Behavior.* New York: Appleton-Century-Crofts, 1963. Pp. 127-159.

Barker, R. G., Dembo, Tamara, & Lewin, K. Frustration and regression: A study of young children. *University of Iowa Studies in Child Welfare,* 1941, *18,* No. 1.

Barker, R. G., & Gump, P. *Big School, Small School.* Stanford: Stanford Univer. Press, 1964.

Barker, R. G., & Wright, H. F. Maud Pintner: A full day study. Unpublished manuscript, University of Kansas, Midwest Psychological Field Station, 1951.

Barker, R. G., & Wright, H. F. *Midwest and its Children.* New York: Harper & Row, 1955.

Berelson, B., & Steiner, G. A. *Human Behavior: An Inventory of Scientific Findings.* New York: Harcourt, Brace & World, 1964.

Brunswik, E. The conceptual framework of psychology. *International Encyclopedia of unified science.* Vol. 1, Part 2. Chicago: Univer. Chicago Press, 1955. Pp. 656-750.

Cattell, R. B. Personality theory growing from multivariate quantitative research. In S. Koch (Ed.), *Psychology: A study of a science.* Vol. 3. *Formulations of the person and the social context.* New York: McGraw-Hill, 1959. Pp. 257-327.

Coombs, C. H. *A Theory of Data.* New York: Wiley, 1964.

Darlington and Stockton Times. (Darlington, England) 1964, July 13.

Dickman, H. R. The perception of behavioral units. In R. G. Barker (Ed.), *The Stream of Behavior.* New York: Appleton-Century-Crofts, 1963. Pp. 23-41.

Encyclopaedia Britannica. Vol. 18. Chicago: William Benton, 1962. P. 32.

Fawl, C. L. Disturbances experienced by children in their natural habitats. In R. G. Barker (Ed.), *The Stream of Behavior.* New York: Appleton-Century-Crofts, 1963. Pp. 99-126.

Festinger, L., Schachter, S., & Back, K. *Social Pressures in Informal Groups.* Stanford: Stanford Univer. Press, 1963.

Grodins, F. S. *Control Theory and Biological Systems.* New York: Columbia Univer. Press, 1963.

Gump, P., & Friesen, W. Participation in nonclass settings. In R. G. Barker & P. Gump, *Big School, Small School.* Stanford: Stanford Univer, Press, 1964. Pp. 75-93. (a)

Gump, P., & Friesen, W. Satisfactions derived from nonclass settings. In R. G. Barker & P. Gump, *Big School, Small School.* Stanford: Stanford Univer. Press, 1964. Pp. 94-114. (b)

Gump, P., & Kounin, J. S. Issues raised by ecological and "classical" research efforts. *Merrill-Palmer Quarterly of Behavior and Development,* 1959-60, *6,* 145-152.

Gump, P., Schoggen, P., & Redl, F. The behavior of the same child in different milieus. In R. G. Barker (Ed.), *The Stream of Behavior.* New York: Appleton-Century-Crofts, 1963. Pp. 169-202.

Gump, P., & Sutton-Smith, B. Activity-setting and social interaction: A field study. *American Journal of Orthopsychiatry,* 1955, Oct., 755-760.

Hinde, R. A. Some recent trends in ethology. In S. Koch (Ed.), *Psychology: A study of a science.* Vol. 2. *General systematic formulations, learning, and special processes.* New York: McGraw-Hill, 1959. Pp. 561-610.

Isaacs, Susan. *Intellectual Growth in Young Children.* London: Routledge & Kegan Paul, 1950.

Koch, S. (Ed.) *Psychology: A study of a science.* Vol. 1. *Sensory, perceptual, and physiological formulations.* New York: McGraw-Hill, 1959. (a)

Koch, S. (Ed.) *Psychology: A study of a science.* Vol. 2. *General systematic formulations, learning, and special processes.* New York: McGraw-Hill, 1959. (b)

Koch, S. (Ed.) *Psychology: A study of a science.* Vol. 3. *Formulations of the person and the social context.* New York: McGraw-Hill, 1959. (c)

Koch, S. (Ed.) *Psychology: A study of a science.* Vol. 4. *Biologically oriented fields: Their place in psychology and in biological science.* New York: McGraw-Hill, 1962.

Koch, S. (Ed.) *Psychology: A study of a science.* Vol. 5. *The process areas, the person, and some applied fields: Their place in psychology and in science.* New York: McGraw-Hill, 1963. (a)

Koch, S. (Ed.) *Psychology: A study of a science.* Vol. 6. *Investigations of man as socius: Their place in psychology and the social sciences.* New York: McGraw-Hill, 1963. (b)

Miller, G. A., Galanter, E., & Pribram, K. H. *Plans and the Structure of Behavior.* New York: Holt, Rinehart & Winston, 1960.

National organizations of the United States. *Encyclopedia of Associations.* Vol. 1. (3rd ed.) Detroit: Research Company, 1961. Pp. 315.

Ragle, D. D. M. Children's problems and problem solving behavior. Unpublished doctoral thesis, University of Kansas, 1957.

Raush, H. L., Dittmann, A. T., & Taylor, T. J. Person, setting and change in social interaction. *Human Relations.* 1959, *12,* 361-378.

Raush, H. L., Dittmann, A. T., & Taylor, T. J. Person, setting and change in social interaction: II. A normal control study. *Human Relations,* 1960, *13,* 305-332.

Reitman, W. R. Information-processing models in psychology. *Science,* 1964, *144,* 1192-1198.

Schoggen, P. Environmental forces in the everyday lives of children. In R. G. Barker (Ed.), *The Stream of Behavior.* New York: Appleton-Century-Crofts, 1963. Pp. 42-69.

Schoggen, Maxine, Barker, Louise S., & Barker, R. G. Structure of the behavior of American and English children. In R. G. Barker (Ed.), *The Stream of Behavior.* New York: Appleton-Century-Crofts, 1963. Pp. 160-168

Simmons, Helen, & Schoggen, P. Mothers and fathers as sources of environmental pressure on children. In R. G. Barker (Ed.), *The Stream of Behavior.* Appleton-Century-Crofts, 1963. Pp. 70-77.

Terman, L. M., & Merrill, Maud A. *Measuring intelligence.* New York: Houghton Mifflin, 1937.

Von Hippel, A. Molecular engineering. *Science,* 1956, *123,* 315-317.

Weir, Ruth H. *Language in the crib.* The Hague: Mouton, 1962.

Weiskopf, V. F. Quality and quantity in quantum physics. In D. Lerner (Ed.), *Quantity and quality.* New York: Macmillan, 1961. Pp. 53-67.

Wiener, N. The mathematics of self-organizing systems. In R. E. Machol & P. Gray (Eds.), *Recent developments in information and decision processes.* New York: Macmillan, 1963. Pp. 1-21.

Willems, E. P. Forces toward participation in behavior settings. In R. G. Barker & P. Gump, *Big school, small school.* Stanford: Stanford Univer. Press, 1964. Pp. 115-135.

2

'Situational' Crime Prevention: Theory and Practice*

by R.V.G. Clarke

Conventional wisdom holds that crime prevention needs to be based on a thorough understanding of the causes of crime. Though it may be conceded that preventive measures (such as humps in the road to stop speeding) can sometimes be found without invoking sophisticated causal theory, 'physical' measures which reduce opportunities for crime are often thought to be of limited value. They are said merely to suppress the impulse to offend which will then manifest itself on some other occasion and perhaps in even more harmful form. Much more effective are seen to be 'social' measures (such as the revitalisation of communities, the creation of job opportunities for unemployed youth, and the provision of sports and leisure facilities) since these attempt to remove the root motivational causes of offending.

These ideas about prevention are not necessarily shared by the man-in-the-street or even by policemen and magistrates, but they have prevailed among academics, administrators and others who contribute to the formulation of criminal policy. They are also consistent with a pre-occupation of criminological theory with criminal 'dispositions' (cf. Ohlin, 1970; Gibbons, 1971; Jeffery, 1971), and the purpose of this paper is to argue that an alternative theoretical emphasis on choices and decisions made by the offender leads to a broader and perhaps more realistic approach to crime prevention.

*Home Office Research Unit, London.
British Journal of Criminology, 1980.

'DISPOSITIONAL' THEORIES AND THEIR PREVENTIVE IMPLICATIONS

With some exceptions noted below, criminological theories have been little concerned with the situational determinants of crime. Instead, the main object of these theories (whether biological, psychological, or sociological in orientation) has been to show how some people are born with, or come to acquire, a 'disposition' to behave in a consistently criminal manner. This 'dispositional' bias of theory has been identified as a defining characteristic of 'positivist' criminology, but it is also to be found in 'interactionist' or deviancy theories of crime developed in response to the perceived inadequacies of positivism: perhaps the best known tenet of at least the early interactionist theories, which arises out of a concern with the social definition of deviancy and the role of law enforcement agencies, is that people who are 'labelled' as ciminal are thereby prone to continue in delinquent conduct (see especially Becker, 1962). In fact, as Tizard (1976) and Ross (1977) have pointed out, a dispositional bias is prevalent throughout the social sciences.

The more extreme forms of dispositional theory have moulded thought about crime prevention in two unfortunate ways. First, they have paid little attention to the phenomenological differences between crimes of different kinds, which has meant that preventive measures have been insufficiently tailored to different kinds of offence and of offender, and second, they have tended to reinforce the view of crime as being largely the work of a small number of criminally-disposed individuals. But many criminologists are now increasingly agreed that a 'theory of crime' would be almost as crude as a general 'theory of disease'. Many now also believe, on the evidence of self-report studies (see Hood and Sparks, 1970), that the bulk of crime—vandalism, autocrime, shoplifting, theft by employees— is committed by people who would not ordinarily be thought of as criminal at all.

Nevertheless, the dispositional bias remains and renders criminological theory unproductive in terms of the preventive measures which it generates. People are led to propose methods of preventive intervention precisely where it is most difficult to achieve any effects, i.e. in relation to the psychological events or the social and economic conditions that are supposed to generate criminal dispositions. As James Q. Wilson (1975) has argued, there seem to be no acceptable ways of modifying temperament and other biological variables, and it is difficult to know what can be done to make parents more inclined to love their children or exercise consistent discipline. Eradicating poverty may be no real solution either, in that crime rates have continued to rise since the war despite great improvements in economic conditions. And even if it were possible to provide people with the kinds of jobs and leisure facilities they might want, there is still no guarantee that crime would drop: few crimes require much time or effort and work and leisure in themselves provide a whole range of criminal opportunities. As for violent crime, there would have to be a much clearer link between this and media portrayals of violence before those who cater to popular taste would be persuaded to change their material. Finally, given public attitudes to offending, which judging by some opinion surveys can be quite punitive, there may not be a great deal of additional scope for policies of diversion and decriminalisation which are favoured by those who fear the consequences of 'labelling'.

These difficulties are primarily practical, but they also reflect the uncertainties and inconsistencies of treating distant psychological events and social processes as the 'causes' of crime. Given that each event is in turn caused by others, at what point in the infinitely regressive chain should one stop in the search for effective points of intervention? This is an especially pertinent question in that it is invariably found that the majority of individuals exposed to this or that criminogenic influence do not develop into persistent criminals. Moreover, dispositions change so that most 'official' delinquents cease to come to the attention of the police in their late teens or early twenties (presumably because their life changes in ways incompatible with their earlier pursuits, cf. Trasler, 1979). Finally, it is worth pointing out that even the most persistently criminal people are probably law-abiding for most of their potentially available time, and this behaviour, too, must equally have been caused by the events and experiences of their past.

CRIME AS THE OUTCOME OF CHOICE

Some of the above theoretical difficulties could be avoided by conceiving of crime not in dispositional terms, but as being the outcome of immediate choices and decisions made by the offender. This would also have the effect of throwing a different light on preventive options.

An obvious problem is that some impulsive offences and those committed under the influence of alcohol or strong emotion may not easily be seen as the result of choices or decisions. Another difficulty is that the notion of 'choice' seems to fit uncomfortably with the fact that criminal behaviour is to some extent predictable from knowledge of a person's history. This difficulty is not properly resolved by the 'soft' determinism of Matza (1963) under which people retain some freedom of action albeit within a range of options constrained by their history and environment. A better formulation would seem to be that recently expounded by Glaser (1977): "both free will and determinism are socially derived linguistic representations of reality" brought into play for different explanatory purposes at different levels of analysis and they may usefully co-exist in the scientific enterprise.

Whatever the resolution of these difficulties—and this is not the place to discuss them more fully—commensense as well as the evidence of ethnographic studies of delinquency (e.g. Parker, 1974) strongly suggest that people are usually aware of consciously choosing to commit offences. This does not mean that they are fully aware of all the reasons for their behaviour nor that their own account would necessarily satisfy a criminologically-sophisticated observer, who might require information at least about: (i) the offender's motives; (ii) his mood; (iii) his moral judgments concerning the act in question and the 'techniques of moral neutralisation' open to him (cf. Matza, 1963); (iv) the extent of his criminal knowledge and his perception of criminal opportunities; (v) his assessment of the risks of being caught as well as the likely consequences; and finally, as well as of a different order, (vi) whether he has been drinking.

These separate components of subjective state and thought processes, which play a part in the decision to commit a crime, will be influenced by immediate situational variables and by highly specific features of the individual's history and present life circumstances in ways that are so varied and countervailing as to render unproductive the notion of a generalised behavioural disposition to offend. Moreover, as will be argued below, the specificity of the influences upon different criminal behaviours gives much less credence to the 'displacement' hypothesis; the idea that reducing opportunities merely results in crime being displaced to some other time or place has been the major argument against situational crime prevention.

In so far as an individual's social and physical environments remain relatively constant and his decisions are much influenced by past experience, this scheme gives ample scope to account not only for occasional offending but also for recidivism: people acquire a repertoire of different responses to meet particular situations and if the circumstances are right they are likely to repeat those responses that have previously been rewarding. The scheme also provides a much richer source of hypotheses than 'dispositional' views of crime for the sex differences in rates of offending: for example, shoplifting may be a 'female' crime simply because women are greater users of shops (Mayhew, 1977). In view of the complexity of the behaviours in question, a further advantage (Atkinson, 1974) is that the scheme accords some place in explanation to the variables thought to be important in most existing theories of crime, including those centred on dispositions. It is perhaps closest to a social learning theory of behaviour (Mischel, 1968; Bandura, 1973) though it owes something to the sociological model of crime proposed by the 'new criminologists' (Taylor et al., 1973). There are three features, however, which are particularly worth drawing out for the sake of the ensuing discussion about crime prevention: first, explanation is focussed more directly on the criminal event; second, the need to develop explanations for separate categories of crime is made explicit; and, third, the individual's current circumstances and the immediate features of the setting are given considerably more explanatory significance than in 'dispositional' theories.

PREVENTIVE IMPLICATIONS OF A 'CHOICE' MODEL

In fact, just as an understanding of past influences on behaviour may have little preventive pay-off, so too may there be limited benefits in according greater explanatory importance to the individual's current life circumstances. For example, the instrumental attractions of delinquency may always be greater for certain groups of individuals such as young males living in inner-city areas. And nothing can be done about a vast range of misfortunes which continually befall people and which may raise the probability of their behaving criminally while depressed or angry.

Some practicable options for prevention do arise, however, from the greater emphasis upon situational features, especially from the direct and immediate relationship between these and criminal behaviour. By studying the spatial and temporal distribution of specific offences and relating these to measurable aspects of the situation, criminologists have recently begun to concern themselves much more closely with the possibilities of manipulating criminogenic situations in the interests of prevention. To date studies have been undertaken of residential burglary (Scarr, 1973; Reppetto, 1974; Brantingham and Brantingham, 1975; Waller and Okhiro, 1978), shoplifting (Walsh, 1978), and some forms of vandalism (Ley and Cybrinwsky, 1974; Clarke, 1978), and it is easy to foresee an expansion of research along these lines. Since offenders' perceptions of the risk and rewards attaching to different forms of crime cannot safely be inferred from studies of the distribution of offences, there may be additional preventive benefits if research of this kind were more frequently complemented by interviews with offenders (cf. Tuck, 1979; Walker, 1979).

The suggestions for prevention arising out of the 'situational' research that has been done can be conveniently divided into measures which (i) reduce the physical opportunities for offending or, (ii) increase the chances of an offender being caught. These categories are discussed separately below though there is some overlap between them, for example, better locks which take longer to overcome also increase the risks of being caught. The division also leaves out some other 'situational' crime prevention measures such as housing allocation policies which avoid high concentrations of children in certain estates or which place families in accommodation that makes it easier for parents to supervise their children's play and leisure activities. Both these measures make it less likely that children will become involved in vandalism and other offences (cf. Wilson, 1978).

Reducing Physical Opportunities for Crime and the Problem of Displacement

Variations in physical opportunities for crime have sometimes been invoked to explain differences in crime rates within particular cities (e.g. Boggs, 1965;

Baldwin and Bottoms, 1975), or temporal variations in crime—for example Wilkins (1964) and Gould and his associates (Gould, 1969; Mansfield et al., 1974) have related levels of car theft to variations in the number of vehicles on the road. But these studies have not generally provided practicable preventive ideas—for example, the number of cars on the road cannot be reduced simply to prevent their theft—and it is only recently that there has been a concerted effort on the part of criminologists to find viable ways of blocking the opportunities for particular crimes.

The potential for controlling behaviour by manipulating opportunities is illustrated vividly by a study of suicide in Birmingham (Hassal and Trethowan, 1972). This showed that a marked drop in the rates of suicide between 1962 and 1970 was the result of a reduction in the poisonous content of the gas supplied to householders for cooking and heating so that it became much more difficult for people to kill themselves by turning on the gas taps. Like many kinds of crime, suicide is generally regarded as being dictated by strong internal motivation, and the fact that its incidence was greatly reduced by a simple (though unintentional) reduction in the opportunities to commit it suggests that it may be possible to achieve similar reductions in crime by 'physical' means.

Though suicide by other methods did not increase in Birmingham, the study also leads to direct consideration of the fundamental theoretical problem of 'displacement' which, as Reppetto (1976) has pointed out, can occur in four different ways: time, place, method, and type of offence. In other words, does reducing opportunities or increasing the risks result merely in the offender choosing his moment more carefully or in seeking some other, perhaps more harmful method of gaining his ends? Or, alternatively, will he shift his attention to a similar but unprotected target, for example, another house, car, or shop? Or, finally, will he turn instead to some other form of crime?

For those who see crime as the outcome of criminal disposition, the answers to these questions would tend to be in the affirmative ("bad will out"), but under the alternative view of crime represented above, matters are less straightforward. Answers would depend on the nature of the crime, the offender's strength of motivation, knowledge of alternatives, willingness to entertain them, and so forth. In the case of opportunistic crimes (i.e. ones apparently elicited by their very ease of accomplishment such as some forms of shoplifting or vandalism) it would seem that the probability of offending could be reduced markedly by making it more difficult to act. For crimes such as bank robbery, however, which often seem to be the province of those who make a living from crime, reducing opportunities may be less effective. (This may be less true of increasing the risks of being caught except that for many offences the risks may be so low at present that any increase would have to be very marked.) Providing effective protection for a particular bank would almost certainly displace the attention of potential robbers to other ones, and if all banks were given increased protection many robbers would no doubt consider alternative means of gaining their ends. It is by no means implausible, however, that others, for example, those who do not have the ability to develop more sophisticated methods or who may not be willing to use more violence, may accept their reduced circumstances and may even take legitimate employment.

It is the bulk of offences, however, which are neither 'opportunistic' nor 'professional' that pose the greatest theoretical dilemmas. These offences include many burglaries and instances of auto-crime where the offender, who may merely supplement his normal income through the proceeds of crime, has gone out with the deliberate intention of committing the offence and has sought out the opportunity to do so. The difficulty posed for opportunity-reducing measures is one of the vast number of potential targets combined with the generally low overall level of security. Within easy reach of every house with a burglar alarm, or car with an anti-theft device, are many others without such protection.

In some cases, however, it may be possible to protect a whole class of property as the Post Office did when they virtually eliminated theft from telephone kiosks by replacing the vulnerable aluminum coin boxes with much stronger steel ones (cf. Mayhew et al., 1976). A further example is provided by the recent law in this country which requires all motorcyclists to wear a crash helmet. This measure was introduced to save lives, but it has also had the unintended effect of reducing thefts of motorcycles (Mayhew et al., 1976). This is because people are unlikely to take someone else's motorbike on the spur of the moment unless they happen to have a crash helmet with them—otherwise they could easily be spotted by the police. But perhaps the best example comes from West Germany where, in 1963, steering column locks were made compulsory on *all* cars, old and new, with a consequent reduction of more than 60% in levels of taking and driving away (Mayhew et al., 1976). (When steering column locks were introduced in this country in 1971 it was only to new cars and although these are now at much less risk of being taken, overall levels of car taking have not yet diminished because the risk to older cars has increased as a result of displacement.)

Instances where criminal opportunities can be reduced for a whole class of property are comparatively few, but this need not always be a fatal difficulty. There must be geographical and temporal limits to displacement so that a town or city may be able to protect itself from some crime without displacing it elsewhere. The less determined the offender, the easier this will be and a simple example is provided by Decker's (1972) evidence that the use of 'slugs' in parking meters in a New York district was greatly reduced by replacing the meters with ones which incorporated a slug-rejecter device and in which the last coin inserted was visible in a plastic window. For most drivers there would be little advantage in parking their cars in some other district just because they could continue to use slugs there.

The question of whether, stopped from committing a particular offence, people would turn instead to some other quite different form of crime is much more difficult to settle empirically, but many of the same points about motivation, knowledge of alternatives, and so forth still apply. Commonsense also suggests, for example, that few of those Germans prevented by steering column locks from taking cars to get home at night are likely to have turned instead to hijacking taxis or to mugging passers-by for the money to get home. More likely, they may have decided that next time they will make sure of catching the last bus home, or that it is time to save up for their own car.

Increasing the Risks of Being Caught

In practice, increasing the chances of being caught usually means attempting to raise the chances of an offender being seen by someone who is likely to take action. The police are the most obvious group likely to intervene effectively, but studies of the effectiveness of this aspect of their deterrent role are not especially encouraging (Kelling et al., 1974; Manning, 1977; Clarke and Hough; 1980). The reason seems to be that when set against the vast number of opportunities for offending, represented by the activities of a huge population of citizens for the 24 hours of the day, crime is a relatively rare event. The police cannot be everywhere at once and, moreover, much crime takes place in private.

Nor is much to be expected from the general public (Mayhew et al., 1979). People in their daily round rarely see crime in progress; if they do they are likely to place some innocent interpretation on what they see; they may be afraid to intervene or they may feel the victims would resent interference; and they may encounter practical difficulties of summoning the police or other help in time. They are much more likely to take effective action to protect their own homes or immediate neighbourhood, but they are often away from these for substantial periods of the day and, moreover, the risks of crime in residential settings, at least in many areas of this country, are not so great as to encourage much vigilance. For instance, assuming that about 50% of burglaries are reported to the police (cf. Home Office, 1979), a house in this country will on average be burgled once every thirty years. Even so, there is evidence (Department of the Environment, 1977; Wilson, 1978) that 'defensible space' designs on housing estates confer some protection from vandalism if not as much as might have been expected from the results of Newman's (1973) research into crime on public housing projects in the United States (cf. Clarke, 1979; Mayhew, 1979).

A recent Home Office Research report (Mayhew et al., 1979) has argued, however, that there is probably a good deal of unrealised potential for making more deliberate use of the surveillance role of employees who come into regular and frequent contact with the public in a semi-official capacity. Research in the United States (Newman, 1973: Reppetto, 1974) and Canada (Waller and Okhiro, 1978) has shown that apartment blocks with doormen are less vulnerable to burglary while research in this country has shown that vandalism is much less of a problem on buses with conductors (Mayhew et al., 1976) and on estates with resident caretakers (Department of the Environment, 1977). There is also evidence (in Post Office records) that public telephones in places such as pubs or launderettes, which are given some supervision by staff, suffer almost no vandalism in comparison with those in kiosks; that car parks with attendants in control have lower rates of autocrime (Sunday Times, 9 April 1978); that football hooliganism on trains has been reduced by a variety of measures including permission for club stewards to travel free of charge; and that shoplifting is discouraged by the presence of assistants who are there to serve the customers (Walsh, 1978). Not everybody employed in a service capacity would be suited to or would be willing to take on additional security duties, but much of their deterrent role may result simply from their being around. Employing more of them, for greater parts of the day, may therefore be all that is needed in most cases. In other cases, it may be necessary to employ people more suited to a surveillance role, train them better to carry it out, or even provide them with surveillance aids. Providing the staff at four London Underground stations with closed circuit television has been shown in a recent Home Office Research Unit study (Mayhew et al., 1979) to have substantially reduced theft and robbery offences at those stations.

SOME OBJECTIONS

Apart from the theoretical and practical difficulties of the approach advocated in this paper, it is in apparent conflict with the 'nothing works' school of criminological thought as given recent expression by Wolfgang (1977): ". . . the weight of empirical evidence indicates that no current preventative, deterrent, or rehabilitative intervention scheme has the desired effect of reducing crime". But perhaps a panacea is being sought when all it may be possible to achieve is reductions in particular forms of crime as a result of specific and sometimes localised measures. Examples of such reductions are given above and while most of these relate to rather commonplace offences of theft and vandalism there is no reason why similar measures cannot be successfully applied to other quite different forms of crime. It has been argued by many people (Rhodes, 1977, provides a recent example) that reducing the availability of handguns through gun control legislation would reduce crimes of violence in the United States and elsewhere. Speeding and drunken driving could probably be reduced by fitting motor vehicles with devices which are now at an experimental stage (Ekblom, 1979). And there is no doubt (Wilkinson, 1977) that the rigorous passenger and baggage screening measures introduced at airports, particularly in the United States, has greatly reduced the incidence of airline hijackings. There are many crimes, however, where either the offender is so determined or so emotionally aroused, that seem to be beyond the scope of this approach. A further constraint will be costs: many shops for example, which could reduce shoplifting by giving up self-service methods and by employing more assistants or even store detectives, have calculated that this would not be worth the expense either in direct costs or in a reduction of turnover. Morally dubious as this policy might at first sight appear, these shops may simply have learned a lesson of more general application, i.e. a certain level of crime may be the inevitable consequence of practices and institutions which we cherish or find convenient and the 'cost' of reducing crime below this level may be unacceptable.

The gradualist approach to crime prevention advocated here might also attract criticism from some social reformers, as well as some deviancy theorists, for being unduly conservative. The former group, imbued with dispositional theory, would see the only effective way of dealing with crime as being to attack its roots through the reduction of inequalities of wealth, class, and education—a solution which, as indicated above, has numerous practical and theoretical difficulties. The latter group would criticise the approach, not for its lack of effectiveness but—on the grounds that there is insufficient consensus in society about what behaviour should be treated as crime—for helping to preserve an undesirable status quo. Incremental change, however, may be the most realistic way of achieving consensus as well as a more equitable society. Most criminologists would probably also agree that it would be better for the burden of crime reduction to be gradually shifted away from the criminal justice system, which may be inherently selective and punitive in its operation, to preventive measures whose social costs may be more equitably distributed across all members of society. The danger to be guarded against would be that the attention of offenders might be displaced away from those who can afford to purchase protection to those who cannot. This probably happens already to some extent and perhaps the best way of dealing with the problem would be through codes of security which would be binding on car manufacturers, builders, local transport operators and so forth. Another danger is that those who have purchased protection might become less willing to see additional public expenditure on the law enforcement and criminal justice services—and this is a problem that might only be dealt with through political leadership and public education.

Many members of the general public might also find it objectionable that crime was being stopped, not by punishing wrong-doers, but by inconveniencing the law-abiding. The fact that opportunity-reducing and risk-increasing measures are too readily identified with their more unattractive aspects (barbed wire, heavy padlocks, guard dogs, and private security forces) adds fuel to the fire. And in some of their more sophisticated forms (closed circuit television surveillance and electronic intruder alarms) they provoke fears, on the one hand, of 'big brother' forms of state control and on the other, of a 'fortress society' in which citizens in perpetual fear of their fellows scuttle from one fortified environment to another.

Expressing these anxieties has a value in checking potential abuses of power, and questioning the means of dealing with crime can also help to keep the problem of crime in perspective. But it should also be said that the kind of measures discussed above need not always be obtrusive (except where it is important to maximise their deterrent effects) and need not in any material way infringe individual liberties or the quality of life. Steel cash compartments in telephone kiosks are indistinguishable from aluminum ones, and vandal-resistant polycarbonate looks just like glass. Steering column locks are automatically brought into operation on removing the ignition key, and many people are quite unaware that their cars are fitted with them. 'Defensible space' designs in housing estates have the additional advantage of promoting feelings of neighbourliness and safety, though perhaps too little attention has been paid to some of their less desirable effects such as possible encroachments on privacy as a result of overlooking. And having more bus conductors, housing estate caretakers, swimming bath attendants, and shop assistants means that people benefit from improved services—even if they have to pay for them either directly or through the rates.

Finally, the idea that crime might be most effectively prevented by reducing opportunities and increasing the risks is seen by many as, at best, representing an over-simplified mechanistic view of human behaviour and, at worst, a ''slur on human nature'' (cf. Radzinowicz and King, 1977). (When the contents of *Crime as Opportunity* (Mayhew et al., 1976) were reported in the press in advance of publication an irate psychiatrist wrote to the Home Secretary demanding that he should suppress the publication of such manifest nonsense.) As shown above, however, it is entirely compatible with a view of criminal behaviour as predominantly rational and autonomous and as being capable of adjusting and responding to adverse consequences, anticipated or experienced. And as for being a pessimistic view of human behaviour, it might indeed be better if greater compliance with the law could come about simply as a result of people's free moral choice. But apart from being perilously close to the rather unhelpful dispositional view of crime, it is difficult to see this happening. We may therefore be left for the present with the approach advocated in this paper, time-consuming, laborious, and limited as it may be.

SUMMARY

It is argued that the 'dispositional' bias of most current criminological theory has resulted in 'social' crime prevention measures being given undue prominence and 'situational' measures being devalued. An alternative theoretical emphasis on decisions and choices made by the offender (which in turn allows more weight to the circumstances of offending) results in more support for a situational approach to prevention. Examples of the effectiveness of such an approach are provided and some of the criticisms that have been made of it on social and ethical grounds are discussed.

REFERENCES

Atkinson, M. (1974) "Versions of deviance". Extended review in *Sociological Review*, 22, 616-624.

Baldwin, J. and Bottoms, A. E. (1975). *The Urban Criminal*. London: Tavistock.

Bandura, A. (1973) *Aggression: A Social Learning Analysis*. London: Prentice Hall.

Becker, H. S. (1962) *Outsiders: Studies in the Sociology of Deviance*. Glencoe: The Free Press.

Boggs, S. L. (1965) "Urban crime patterns". *American Sociological Review, 30*, 899-908.

Brantingham, P. J., and Brantingham, P. L. (1975) 'The spatial patterning of burglary'. *Howard Journal of Penology and Crime Prevention, 14*, 11-24.

Clarke, R. V. G. (Ed.) (1978) *Tackling vandalism*. Home Office Research Study No. 47. London: HMSO.

Clarke, R. V. G. (1979) Defensible space and vandalism: the lessons from some recent British research". *Stadtebau und Kriminalamt (Urban planning and crime)*. Papers of an international symposium, Bundeskriminalamt, Federal Republic of Germany, December, 1978.

Clarke, R. V. G., and Hough, J. M. (Eds.) (1980) *The Effectiveness of Policing*. Farnborough, Hants: Saxon House.

Decker, J. F. (1972) Curbside deterrence: an analysis of the effect of a slug-rejector device, coin view window and warning labels on slug usage in New York City parking meters. *Criminology, August*, 127-142.

Department of the Environment (1977) *Housing Management and Design*. (Lambeth Inner Area Study). IAS/IA/18. London: Department of the Environment.

Ekblom, P. (1979) "A crime-free car?" *Research Bulletin No. 7*. Home Office Research Unit, London: Home Office.

Gibbons, D. C. (1971) Observations on the study of crime causation. *American Journal of Sociology, 77*, 262-278.

Glaser, D. (1977) "The compatibility of free will and determinism in criminology: comments on an alleged problem". *Journal of Criminal Law and Criminology, 67*, 486-490.

Gould, L. C. (1969) "The changing structure of property crime in an affluent society." *Social Forces, 48*, 50-59.

Hassal, C., and Trethowan, W. H. (1972) "Suicide in Birmingham". *British Medical Journal, 1*, 717-718.

Hirschi, T. (1970) *Causes of Delinquency*. California: University of California Press.

Home Office. (1979) *Criminal Statistics: England and Wales 1978*. London: HMSO.

Hood, R., and Sparks, R. (1970) *Key Issues in Criminology*. London: Weidenfeld and Nicolson.

Jeffery, C. R. (1971) *Crime Prevention Through Environmental Design*. Beverly Hills: Sage Publications.

Kelling, G. L., Pate, T., Dieckman, D., and Brown, C. E. (1974) *The Kansas City Preventive Patrol Experiment*. Washington: Police Foundation.

Ley, D., and Cybrinwsky, R. (1974) "The spatial ecology of stripped cars". *Environment and Behaviour, 6*, 53-67.

Manning, P. (1977) *Police Work: The Social Organisation of Policing.* London: Massachusetts Institute of Technology Press.

Mansfield, R., Gould, L. C., and Namenwirth, J. Z. (1974) "A socioeconomic model for the prediction of societal rates of property theft". *Social Forces, 52,* 462-472.

Matza, D. (1964) *Delinquency and Drift.* New York: John Wiley and Sons.

Mahew, P. (1977) "Crime in a man's world". *New Society,* 16 June, 1977.

Mayhew, P. (1979) "Defensible space: the current status of a crime prevention theory". *The Howard Journal of Penology and Crime Prevention,* (in press).

Mayhew, P., Clarke, R. V. G., Burrows, J. N., Hough, J. M., And Winchester, S. W. C. (1979) *Crime in Public View.* Home Office Research Study No. 49, London: HMSO.

Mayhew, P., Clarke, R. V. G., Sturman, A., And Hough, J. M. (1976) *Crime as Opportunity.* Home Office Research Study No. 34. London: HMSO.

Mischel, W. (1968) *Personality and Assessment.* New York, John Wiley and Sons.

Newman, O. (1973) *Defensible Space: People and Design in the Violent City.* London, Architectural Press.

Ohlin, L. E. (1970) *A Situational Approach to Delinquency Prevention.* Youth Development and Delinquency Prevention Administration. U. S. Department of Health, Education and Welfare.

Parker, H. (1974) *View from the Boys.* Newton Abbott: David and Charles.

Radzinowicz, L., and King, J. (1977) *The Growth of Crime.* London, Hamish Hamilton.

Reppetto, T. A. (1974) *Residential Crime.* Cambridge, Mass.: Ballinger.

Reppetto, T. A. (1976) "Crime prevention and the displacement phenomenon". *Crime and Delinquency,* April, 166-177.

Rhodes, R. P. (1977) *The Insoluble Problems of Crime.* New York: John Wiley and Sons.

Ross, L. (1977) "The intuitive psychologist and his shortcomings: distortions in the attribution process". In: Berkowitz, L. (Ed.) *Advances in Experimental Social Psychology (Vol. 10).* New York: Academic Press.

Scarr, H. A. (1973) *Patterns of burglary.* U. S. Department of Justice, Washington DC: Government Printing Office.

Taylor, I., Walton, P., and Young, J. (1973) *The New Criminology.* London: Routledge and Kegan Paul.

Tizard, J. (1976) "Psychology and social policy". *Bulletin of the British Psychological Society, 29,* 225-233.

Trasler, G. B. (1979) "Delinquency, recidivism, and desistance". *British Journal of Criminology, 19,* 314-322.

Tuck, M. (1979) "Consumer behaviour theory and the criminal justice system: towards a new strategy of research". *Journal of the Market Research Society, 21,* 44-58.

Walker, N. D. (1979) "The efficacy and morality of deterrents". *Criminal Law Review,* 129-144.

Waller, I., and Okihiro, N. (1978) *Burglary: The Victim and the Public.* Toronto: University of Toronto Press.

Walsh, D. P. (1978) *Shoplifting: Controlling a Major Crime.* London: MacMillan.

Wilkins, L. T. (1964) *Social Deviance.* London: Tavistock.

Wilkinson, P. (1977) *Terrorism and the Liberal State.* London: MacMillan.

Wilson, J. Q. (1975) *Thinking About Crime.* New York: Basic Books.

Wilson, S. (1978) "Vandalism and 'defensible space' on London Housing estates". In: Clarke, R. V. G. (Ed.). *Tackling Vandalism*. Home Office Research Study No. 47. London: HMSO.

Wolfgang, M. E. (1977) Real and perceived changes in crime. In Landau, S. F., and Sebba, L. (Eds.) *Criminology in Perspective*. Lexington, Mass.: Lexington Books.

3

Judgements of People and Their Rooms*

D. Canter, S. West and R. Wools

It is hypothesized that inference rules operate which assume similarity between people and their physical surroundings. The first experiment described used line drawings of rooms containing seated figures. Ratings of the rooms and separate ratings of the people who it was assumed used those rooms were made. The second experiment used colour slides of actual rooms and ratings were made both by architecture and by non-architecture students. The third experiment used head and shoulder photographs of people superimposed upon a variety of room backgrounds. In all three experiments significant relationships were found between rooms and judgements of the people associated with them, thus supporting the general hypothesis.

INTRODUCTION

Many studies have indicated that a wide variety of peripheral attributes of people influence judgements made of them. For instance, glasses (Thornton 1944) or lipstick (McKeachie 1952) or the type of clothes worn (Gibbins, 1969) all relate to judged attributes of the wearer. Indeed early studies in person perception (e.g. Thorndike 1920, Asch 1946) showed that seemingly independent judgements did in fact relate to one another. More recently sociological studies (Laumann and House, 1970) have shown that living room furnishings can predict the social attributes of their owners. It might be expected, then, that the physical

*British Journal of Social and Clinical Psychology, 1974, 13, 113-118. Reprinted by permission of the publisher, the British Psychological Society.

environment also plays a role in person perception.

The surrounding environment forms an enduring and central part of the impression of a person (considerable effort and money is frequently used to create the right "atmosphere" or best "image", whether in private rooms or directors' offices). In dramaturgical terms the architectural setting forms part of a front; the expressive equipment used by the performer during his performance (Goffman, 1959).

A number of studies have indicated that rooms act as a context for judgements made within them. Rosenthal (1966) found relationships between judgements of people and their surroundings; the experimenter was perceived as more 'statusful' in an untidy laboratory. Kasmar (1968), however, found no effect of different room furnishings on judgements of psychiatrists by patients. The Maslow & Mintz (1956) study of the effect of room context on perceptual judgements showed faces were judged differently in a "beautiful" room from the way they were judged in an "ugly" room. Wools and Canter (1970) showed a similar effect when subjects judged drawings of rooms.

The above considerations gave rise to the general hypothesis that relationships will be obtained between ratings of people and the rooms with which they are associated. The most parsimonious inference rule which might underline these relationships was assumed to be the one of similarity between a person and their room. The hypothesis was investigated using increasingly complex stimuli.

EXPERIMENT I

In this experiment line drawings of rooms containing outlined seated figures were used in order to produce a wide range of standardised room variations. As factor analytic studies of environmental stimuli (Vielhauer, 1965, Hershberger 1969, Canter, 1969, Canter & Wools 1970) had indicated the four commonly occurring major dimensions of friendliness, harmony, activity and formality; these were used to rate the rooms in this experiment.

Method

a) Sixty-seven students from many disciplines, but none from architecture or design, rated 15 monochromatic line drawings of rooms. The drawings were selected to give a wide range on the four dimensions above. Ratings were made from one to seven on four bipolar adjectival pairs for each dimension, e.g. for Friendliness, friendly—unfriendly, unwelcoming—welcoming; for Harmony, unstable—stable, discordant—harmonious; Activity, calm—lively, active—passive; and Formality, statusless—statusful, formal—informal.

b) A further 24 non-architecture students assessed the same 15 line drawings rating the person shown in outline from one to seven on four item scales representing Osgood's dimensions, Evaluation, e.g. good—bad, pleasant—

unpleasant; Potency, strong—weak, brave—cowardly; and Activity, active—passive, tense—relaxed.

For scoring each set of items was formed into a Guttman scale by dichotomisation (cf. Wools, 1971). Summing the ratings over the four bipolar scales gave scores for each dimension. Means were calculated from the scores for each drawing on the seven dimensions for all subjects in each group. It was thus possible to compare judgements of the rooms with judgements of the person in the room by intercorrelating the two sets of mean scores.

Table 3.1 Product—moment correlations between mean "room" judgements and mean "person" judgements in Experiment I.

	Room:	Friendliness	Harmony	Activity	Formality
Person:	Evaluation	0.90*	0.84*	0.55	0.89*
	Potency	0.61*	0.63	0.23	0.62*
	Activity	0.02	0.13	0.05	0.05
		df = 13	*p < .01		

Results

These correlations lend support to the general hypothesis of a similarity relation between ratings of rooms and people associated with them. The activity dimensions are the only ones which do not give significant correlations although three of the four bipolar adjectives were the same for the two groups of subjects.

The lack of correlation for the activity dimensions implies that the subject groups were actually making different ratings and not ignoring instructions by making similar judgements in both cases. If the activity rating of rooms had simply been unreliable or random it would have been impossible to isolate an activity dimension or from it produce a Guttman scale with an acceptable level of reproducibility. If activity ratings of the people in the drawings had been unreliable or random the scores would not have correlated significantly (0.66) with the potency dimension, as they did.

A further implication is that these rooms give little indication of the "activity" of their occupier and *vice versa*. These results show that the general similarity hypothesis is not supported for all dimensions.

EXPERIMENT II

To test the above findings with more realistic architectural stimuli colour slides of real rooms were used. The slides were of offices in Edinburgh University and although there were no people in them there was considerable evidence of habitual use by one individual, e.g. coffee mugs, briefcases etc. In order to examine the possible effects of training and professional orientation on judgements 41 architecture and 32 psychology students were used as subjects. They were presented with 24 colour slides of rooms unfamiliar to them. All slides were rated for both room and user using a split half design such that each subject viewed and rated each one only once. The users of the rooms were rated on five bipolar adjectival scales representing the dimensions of evaluation, e.g. kind—cruel; potency, bold—timid; and activity, e.g. fast—slow. For the rating of the rooms two sets of 10 adjectives were used; one set e.g. friendly—unfriendly, happy—sad, being a development of the ''friendliness'' dimension used in Experiment I (Canter & Wools, 1970). The second set were drawn from the main dimension, ''adequacy'' e.g. comfortable—uncomfortable, adequate—inadequate, found by Canter (1971) in his study of school buildings. Both sets had been found highly reliable in ratings of buildings and formed Guttman scales with high coefficients of reproducibility.

Table 3.2   Product-moment correlations between mean room judgements and mean user judgement for the two subject groups in Experiment II.

Rooms:	Architects Users:			Psychologists Users:		
	Evaluation	Potency	Activity	Evaluation	Potency	Activity
Friendliness	0.70*	0.07	0.47	0.66*	−0.36	0.39
Adequacy	0.78*	−0.10	0.50*	0.63*	−0.31	0.35
	df = 22			*p < .01		

Results

No significant differences were found between the means for the two groups using t tests, variances of the two groups using F tests or between the correlation coefficients using $\bar{z}$ the normally distributed difference between standardised correlation coefficients.

As with the line drawings there is a significant correlation between ratings of evaluation of the users and friendliness of the rooms. However potency of the user shows no significant correlation with the room ratings. Activity does show some small but significant correlations. These two studies together indicate that the central evaluation dimension correlates in either mode but that the correlations of other variables are more specific.

EXPERIMENT III

As Experiments I and II showed that ratings of central dimensions of rooms and people were associated it was decided to examine the effects of the room background on judgements of people in photographs. Besides enabling us to examine the contribution of an actual photograph of a person to the general room effect this experiment also has everyday relevance in that the mass media frequently show certain people against particular backgrounds. As these visual representations may help influence public opinion the environmental context may also be important. A further point is that frequent association of certain people and environments is possibly one way in which attitudes develop towards these environments. Experiment III was a first attempt to study these problems experimentally.

Method

Through the assistance of a local newspaper nine photographs were prepared from three head and shoulder photographs of people and three of rooms such that each person appeared in the same position in each room. The three people were all smiling well dressed men wearing glasses, two in their 40's, the other looking rather older. Room A was a Victorian window overlooking an industrial scene; Room B was the library of the Q.E.2 and Room C a large I.B.M. office with filing cabinets and luminous ceiling. Thirty architecture students rated the person in each of the composite photographs on the three five item evaluation, potency and activity scales used in Experiment II.

As the photographic superimposition became clear to the subjects at the latest upon seeing the fourth photograph, the presentation order was varied for each of three groups of ten subjects. This ensured all nine photographs were seen by ten ''naive'' subjects, and provided a three variable factorially designed experiment: each of the variables of order of presentation, person and room existing at three levels. The photographs were converted into black and white slides for presentation.

Results

To see if any room effect existed t tests were carried out between the means for each combination of backgrounds for each person. As shown in Table 3.3 nine of a possible twenty-seven t tests were significant. An analysis of variance showed that although the people were rated differently at the .01 per cent level for all three dimensions, the room effect was only present on the potency dimension at the five per cent level. The effect of order was present on the activity dimension also at the five per cent level. There was also a significant person x order interaction on all three dimensions.

The picture presented by these analyses and by further analyses dealing only with first, second or third ratings for each subject is a very complex one. They indicate that the room effect is marked by interactions between person and order effects. However it does appear that there is a room effect and that this is most marked for person 3. Furthermore the library/office comparison produced the most consistent results on all three dimensions.

GENERAL DISCUSSION

The three experiments taken together strongly support the general hypothesis of relationships existing between judgements of people and their rooms. There is also an indication that the inference rule of similarity between room and user underlies these relationships. Experiment III suggests that this inference rule can lead to what may be regarded as a ''room effect'', whereby judgements of people are modified by the room in which the person is seen to be.

Table 3.3 Semantic Differential means showing significance of difference between means.

| | Means for rooms A and B | | | | | |
| | Person 1 | | Person 2 | | Person 3 | |
	A	B	A	B	A	B
E	18.6	16.7	19.1	22.2	19.0	21.8*
A	21.1	19.9	19.9	16.6*	21.2	20.0
P	22.0	20.1	16.7	16.2	21.5	21.5

| | Means for rooms A and C | | | | | |
| | Person 1 | | Person 2 | | Person 3 | |
	A	C	A	C	A	C
E	18.6	17.4	19.1	19.1	19.0	18.1
A	21.1	20.8	19.9	16.7*	21.2	15.9***
P	22.0	23.0	16.7	18.1	21.5	18.1*

| | Means for rooms B and C | | | | | |
| | Person 1 | | Person 2 | | Person 3 | |
	B	C	B	C	B	C
E	16.7	17.4	22.2	19.1*	21.8	18.1*
A	19.9	20.8	16.6	16.7	20.0	15.9***
P	20.1	23.0	16.2	18.1	21.5	18.1*

* $p < .05$
** $p < .01$
*** $p < .001$

ACKNOWLEDGEMENTS:

The preparation of this paper was partly assisted by an award from the Architects Registration Council of the United Kingdom.

REFERENCES

Asch, S. (1946) "Forming impressions of personality," *Journal of Abnormal and Social Psychology*, 41, 258-290.

B.P.R.U., (1970) "Building Appraisal, St. Michael's Academy, Kilwinning", *A.J., 151*, pp. 4-50.

Canter, D. V. (1969) "An Inter-group Comparison of Connotative Dimensions in Architecture", *Environment and Behaviour 1* (i) pp. 38-48.

Canter, D. V. (1970) *"Architectural Psychology"*, London: RIBA Publications.

Canter, D. V. (1971) *"Scales for the Evaluation of Buildings"*, Glasgow: Strathclyde University (mimeo.)

Canter, D. V. and Wools, R. (1970) "A Technique for the Subjective Appraisal of Buildings", *Building Science,* 5 (3 and 4) pp. 187-198.

Cook, M. (1971) "Interpersonal Perception" *Penguin Books*

Gibbins, K. (1969) "Communication Aspects of Women's Clothes and Their Relation to Fashionability", *Brit J. Soc., Clin. Psych., 8,* pp. 301-312.

Goffman, E. (1959) "The Presentation of Self in Everyday Life", New York: Doubleday Anchor Books.

Hershberger, R. (1969) *"A Study of the Meaning of Architecture"* Environmental Design Research Association, 1st Annual Conference: Chapel Hill, N. Carolina.

Kasmar, J. V., Griffin, W. V. & Mauritzen, J. H. (1968). Effect of environmental surroundings on outpatients' mood and perception of psychiatrists.   *consult. clin. Psychol.* 32, 223-226.

Laumann, E. O. & House, J. S. (1970). Livingroom styles and social attributes: the patterning of material artifacts in a modern urban community. *Sociol. soc. Res.* 54, 321-342.

McKeachie, W. J. (1952). Lipstick as a determiner of first impressions of personality: an experiment for the general psychology course.   *soc. Psychol.* 36, 241-244.

Maslow, A. H. & Mintz, N. L. (1956). Effects of aesthetic surroundings. I. Initial effects of three aesthetic conditions upon perceiving 'energy' and 'well-being' in faces.   *Psychol.* 41, 247-254.

Rosenthal, R. (1966). *Experimenter Effects in Behavioural Research*. New York: Appleton-Century-Crofts.

Thorndike, E. L. (1920). A constant error in psychological rating.   *appl. Psychol.* 4, 25-29.

Thornton, G. R. (1944). The effect of wearing glasses upon judgements of personality traits of persons seen briefly.   *appl. Psychol.* 28, 203-207.

Vielhauer, J. A. (1966). The development of a semantic scale for the description of the physical environment. *Dissert. Abstr.* 26, 4821.

Wools, R. M. (1971). The subjective appraisal of buildings. (Unpublished Ph.D. thesis, University of Strathclyde.)

4

Psychiatric Patients and Staff Reaction to Their Physical Environment

Rudolf H. Moos, Robert Harris, Karl Schonborn

PROBLEM

There has recently been rapidly growing research interest in man's response to his physical environment.[1,4,5,7] The problems of the description and measurement of both behavior and environment are paramount in these studies. Wohlwill[10] states that one must resort to "indirect methods based on ratings of other subjective scaling methods." Sommer[8] calls for the use of techniques such as Osgood's Semantic Differential in exploring "connotations of environment". Vielhauer[9] has developed an Environmental Description Scale (EDS), initially consisting of 66 adjective scales, which was used by 500 persons in describing three rooms. The resulting descriptions were factor analyzed and five factors were found: esthetic appeal, physical organization, size, temperature-ventilation, and lighting.

The three major aims of this study were (a) to replicate the five factor dimensions found on the EDS; (b) to investigate the differences between psychiatric patients and staff in their perceptions of rooms; and (c) to provide information on the extent to which the perception of a room is determined by the actual physical stimulus characteristics of the room, by the S doing the perceiving, and by the interaction between the S and the room.

Journal of Clinical Psychology, 1969, 25, 3, 322-324. Reprinted by permission of the authors and the Clinical Psychology Publishing Co., Inc.

Methods

The Ss were 64 psychiatric patients (51 male, 13 female) and 36 staff (14 male, 22 female) in a Veterans Administration Hospital. The average age of the patients was 38.8 years (SD = 9.6), and their average length of time on the ward was 21.3 weeks (SD = 32.0). For the staff, the respective figures were 27.4 years (SD = 9.0) and 28.2 weeks (S.D = 37.5).

Each S was asked to describe each of six rooms on each of 66 seven-point bipolar adjective scales taken from Vielhauer's original list. The rooms included a dayroom, a dining room, a lecture room, a bedroom, a bathroom, and a meeting room. The questionnaire also elicited information about the number of previous times the S had been in each of the six rooms.

RESULTS

The data from the 100 Ss were intercorrelated and factor analyzed (principal components factor analysis and varimax rotation) separately for each of the six rooms. The first three of Vielhauer's five factors (esthetic appeal, physical organization, and size) appeared as the first three factors in each of the six rooms. Vielhauer's fourth factor (temperature-ventilation) appeared in five of the six rooms; it tended to merge with the physical organization factor in the lecture room. Her fifth factor (lighting) appeared much less consistently, being relatively clear in only one of the rooms (meeting room) and tended to merge either with esthetic appeal or with temperature-ventilation in the other five rooms. Thus, four of Vielhauer's five environmental description factors were essentially replicated, whereas the fifth was not.

Each S was given four factor scores by adding up his scores for each of the adjective scales on each of the four factors. In general, staff tended to perceive these six rooms differently from patients; e.g., staff perceived the dayroom as having less esthetic appeal, less physical organization, and as being less adequate in temperature-ventilation than did the patients. The differences between patients and staff for the other five rooms were relatively similar, although somewhat smaller, than the differences shown in the dayroom.

There also were differences among the rooms; e.g., the lecture room was perceived as having greater esthetic appeal by both patients and staff than either the bedroom or the bathroom, and the dining room was perceived as having greater physical organization by both patients and staff than either the dayroom or the meeting room. The important point is that the environmental description factors do significantly differentiate between rooms; i.e., different rooms are perceived differently. Patients and staff who had been in the rooms most frequently tended to perceive them less positively (less esthetic appeal, less physical organization, smaller, poorer temperature-ventilation).

An analysis of variance was calculated, separately for patients and staff, for each of the four factor scales. The results showed significant between Ss and significant between room variance for all four factor scales in both the patient and the staff analyses. There was also a significant Ss × rooms interaction effect for three of the scales in the patient analyses and for all four of the scales in the staff analyses. Table 1 shows the percentage of variance accounted for by each effect.[2]

Table 4.1 Percentages of Variance Accounted for by Subjects, Rooms, and Subject × Room Interactions

Factors	Subjects	Rooms	Subjects × Rooms	Residual
Patients				
Esthetic Appeal	31.1	7.2	19.1	42.7
Physical Organization	28.8	6.8	18.0	46.4
Size	26.1	8.0	19.4	46.5
Temperature-Ventilation	27.2	2.2	1.8	68.8
Staff				
Esthetic Appeal	12.6	11.7	31.8	43.9
Physical Organization	17.8	12.5	26.0	43.8
Size	17.2	14.0	23.5	48.4
Temperature-Ventilation	11.4	2.4	18.5	67.8

These results indicate that: (1) Ss tend to react consistently to the physical environment, regardless of the room in which they happen to be. Our patients reacted more consistently than staff. (2) An average of less than 10% of the total variance was related to the rooms effect, indicating that these rooms had only a small tendency to elicit consistently different reactions. This indicates that one can predict an S's reaction to a room better by knowing who the S is than by knowing which room he is rating. Many architects and building designers operate on the assumption that the physical characteristics of the room by themselves determine Ss' reactions to the room; the present results suggest that this may not be the case. (3) The proportion of variance attributable to the Ss × rooms interaction is high in both groups. For example, whereas some Ss feel that one room (e.g., dayroom is more appealing than another (e.g., lecture room, other Ss feel just the reverse. This substantiates that no one building design will satisfy

[2]The percentages of variance accounted for by each source of variance were calculated for this random-effects analysis of variance model utilizing the rationale given by Edwards (3, pp. 306-309).

all people, and that the architect and designer must take into account the reactions of those specific groups of individuals for whom the particular environment is being designed.

SUMMARY

A 22 item, four subscale questionnaire was derived from the reactions of patients and staff to six different hospital rooms. The results, which essentially replicate Vielhauer's, indicate that reactions to rooms may be described on four recurring dimensions: esthetic appeal, physical organization, size, and temperature-ventilation.

Analyses of variance indicated that Ss, rooms, and Ss × rooms interactions each accounted for important proportions of the variance in the perceptions of the rooms. In general, the proportions of variance attributable to consistent differences between Ss and to Ss × rooms interactions were each greater than the proportions attributable to consistent differences between rooms. Thus, it was possible to predict only a very small proportion of the reaction of an S to a room by knowing about the physical dimensions, color, lighting, and other characteristics of the room. However, the selection of a wider range of rooms would probably substantially increase the proportion of variance in perceptions attributable to consistent differences between rooms.

Individual differences in reactions to the same physical environment may shed some light on the increasing number of findings relating building designs to important psychological variables. For example, Myrick and Marx[6] have discussed the relationships between the architecture of school buildings and student informal interaction. Standard assessment tools to measure reactions to the physical environment should facilitate the increase of dependable knowledge about how man reacts to all facets of his environment. In this connection, Craik[2] has programmatically outlined research directions geared toward "the comprehension of the everyday physical environment."

REFERENCES

Baker, A., Davies, R. L. and Sivadon, P. *Psychiatric Servies and Architecture*. Geneva: World Health Organization Public Health Papers, 1959.

Craik, K. The comprehension of the everyday physical environment. *Amer. Inst. Planning J.*, 1968, 29-37.

Edwards, A. *Experimental Design in Psychological Research*. New York: Holt, Rinehart and Winston, 1960.

Good, L., Siegel, S. and Bay, A. *Therapy by Design*. Springfield, Ill.: C. C. Thomas, 1965.

Mintz, N. Effects of esthetic surroundings: II. Prolonged and repeated experience in a "beautiful" and an "ugly" room. *J. Psychol.*, 1956, *41*, 459-466.

Myrick, R. and Marx, B. Informal conversations and learning among dental students: Influence of school design. *J. Dent. Educ.*, 1967, *31*, 488-492.

Searles, H. *The Nonhuman Environment in Normal Development and in Schizophrenia.* New York: International Universities Press, 1960.

Sommer, R. Man's proximate environment. *J. Soc. Issues,* 1966, *22*, 59-70.

Vielhauer, J. The development of a semantic scale for the description of the physical environment. Doctoral Dissertation, Louisiana State University, 1965.

Wohlwill, J. The physical environment: A problem for a psychology of stimulation. *J. Soc. Issues,* 1966, *22*, 29-38.

Symbolic Interactionism and Ethnomethodology: Introduction

Perinbanayagam (1974) discusses different views that have been taken about the definition of the situation. How do individuals come to agree on such definitions, he asks, and how do they learn them from society, since communication is impossible without shared meanings? Is there an objective situation apart from individuals to give it meaning? The ethnomethodologists, he writes, argue that individuals establish the meaning of a situation by a process of psychological construction and inference, by asking questions, and doing their best to make sense of stimuli. The symbolic interactionists, the author argues, offer a better account—people cooperate to negotiate and create shared meanings of situations by dramatic performances that create identities; dramatization is genuine communication that induces others to cooperate in sustaining certain meanings. It would be useful to relate this rather abstract debate to the empirical study of interaction. For example how do infants learn definitions of situations; what is the difference between fantasy play in children and non-play behaviour; and how far does social behaviour involve pretence and deception?

Stebbins (1967) offers a conceptual analysis of the definition of the situation. He deals first with the objective situation, which consists of the actor's immediate physical and social surroundings and his or her physiological and psychological state. The subjective situation is defined as any aspect of the objective situation that the actor perceives as relevant to his or her behaviour, and which must therefore be given meaning. It includes the temporal and physical boundaries, and is affected by the individual's personality traits and by cultural factors. The actor interprets and gives meaning to the situation, especially a new situation, by a process of conscious reflection, which enables the actor to engage in goal-directed action. Situations involving habitual behaviour require almost no reflection, and it is possible for the definition of a situation to change, which would affect the pursuit of goals. This analysis suggests new lines of research to test the ideas about definitions affecting goal-directed action, and about the effect of new and unusual situations on conscious reflection.

Harré (1979) describes a structural approach to the understanding of physical settings and situations. He takes a ''dramaturgical'' perspective—an ''ironic stance'' that looks on others as actors in a play, mainly concerned with expressive display, following rules, and collaborating in the generation of meaning, but only partly aware of what is going on. Settings are bounded in time by openings and closings, and in space by visible and invisible boundaries. Different parts of space have different social meanings, for example different social status. Physical structures can convey social meaning; the arrangement of a Berber house reflects cosmology. In situations people are related to the setting in ways like ''ownership,'' and to each other by various relationships established by rituals like introductions. This approach does not look for empirical laws or verification, but rather for interpretations of phenomena in terms of structural concepts. The research methods are not clear, but include both the observation and collection of accounts.

SUGGESTED ADDITIONAL REFERENCES

Bertocci, P. The person, his personality and environment. *Review of Metaphysics,* 1979, *32,* 605-621.

Brittain, *Meanings and situations.* Boston: Routledge & Kegan Paul, 1973.

Clough, F. The validation of meaning in illness-treatment situations. In D. Hall and M-Stacey (Eds.) *Beyond Separation—Further studies of children in hospital,* London: Routledge & Kegan Paul, 1979.

Dakin, R. Cultural occasions and group structures: a photographic analysis of American social situations. *American Sociological Review,* 1960, *25,* 66-74.

Deseran, F. Community satisfaction as definition of the situation: some conceptual issues. *Rural Sociology,* 1978, *43,* 235-249.

Deutscher, I. The quality of postparental life: definition of the situation. *Journal of Marriage and the Family,* 1964, *Feb.,* 52-59.

Douglas, J. *Understanding everyday life.* London: Routledge & Kegan Paul, 1974.

Farr, R. On the varieties of social psychology: an essay on the relationships between psychology and other social sciences. *Social Science Information,* 1978, *17,* 503-525.

Glasner, B. and Strauss, A. Awareness contexts and social interaction. *American Sociological Review,* 1967, *29,* 660-678.

Goffman, E. Studying the neglected situation. In R. Lauer and W. Handel (Eds.) *Social Psychology: the theory and application of symbolic Interaction,* London: Houghton, Mifflin, 1977.

Gonos, G. Situation versus frame. *American Sociological Review,* 1977, *42,* 854-867.

Gordon, R. Interaction between attitudes and the definition of the situation in the expression of opinion. *American Sociological Review,* 1952, *17,* 50-58.

Green, A. The social situation in personality theory. *American Sociological Review,* 1942, *5,* 388-393.

Hewitt, J. and Hall, P. Social problems, problematic situations and quasi theories. *American Sociological Review,* 1973, *38,* 367-374.

Icheiser, G. Misinterpretation of personality in everyday life and the psychologist's frame of reference. *Character and Personality,* 1943, *12,* 145-160.

Kohn, M. and Williams, R. Situational patterning in intergroup relations. *American Sociological Review,* 1956, *21,* 164-174.

Lerner, M. and Becker, S. Interpersonal choice as a function of ascribed similarity and definition of the situation. *Human Relations,* 1962, *15,* 27-34.

Manis, J. and Meltzer, B. (Eds.) *Symbolic Interaction.* Boston: Allyn & Bacon, 1967.

McSweeney, B. Meaning, content and situation. *European Journal of Sociology,* 1973, *16,* 137-153.

Miller, D. The study of social relationships: situation, identity and social interaction. In S. Koch (Ed.) *Psychology: A Study of a Science* vol. 5, New York: McGraw Hill, 1963.

Miyamoto, S. The social act: re-examination of a concept. *The Pacific Sociological Review,* 1959, *Fall,* 50-56.

O'Keefe, D. Ethnomethology. *Journal for the Theory of Social Behaviour.* 1979, *9,* 187-219.

Reinhardt, J. Personality traits and the situation. *American Sociological Review,* 1937, *2,* 492-500.

Stone, G. and Farberman, H. *Social Psychology through Symbolic Interaction.* Waltham: Lynn-Blarsdell, 1976.

Stebbins, R. Studying the definition of the situation. *The Canadian Review of Sociology and Anthropology,* 1969, *6,* 193-211.

Stebbins, R. *Teachers and Meanings: Definitions of Classroom Situations.* Leiden, Holland: E. J. Brill, 1975.

Waller, R. The definition of the situation. In his *The Sociology of Teaching,* New York: Wiley, 1961.

Ward, P. The doctrine of the situation and the method of social science. *Social Forces,* 1930, *9,* 49-54.

Weber, M. Subjective meaning in the social situation. In his *The Theory of Social and Economic Organisation,* Edited by A. Henderson and T. Parsons, New York: Free Press, 1947.

Wolff, K. and Barbu, Z. Definition of the situation. In J. Gould and W. Kolb (Eds.) *Dictionary of the Social Sciences,* London: Tavistock, 1964.

Znaniecki, F. Subjective meaning in the social situations. *Social Action,* New York: Rinehart, 1936, pp. 11-17.

1

The Definition of the Situation: an Analysis of the Ethnomethodological and Dramaturgical View*

R.S. Perinbanayagam

The dramaturgical and the ethnomethodological positions of the definition of the situation is discussed, after a brief history of the concept. The ethnomethodologists claim to take their cues from Wittgenstein and Schutz, whereas the dramaturgists take theirs from G. H. Mead; these positions are examined in terms of their relative power to explain the problem of the definition of the situation, concluding that the Meadian position is the more powerful one. It is then argued that the essential sociological ontology—that given expression by Weber and Durkheim—is best realized by adopting *some form of the dramaturgical argument*.

The concept of the definition of the situation has been with us a long time now. First given expression in recent years by W. I. Thomas, it has since achieved the status of a sociological axiom due to the efforts of the many who expanded on it. Merton, making an early effort at explicating it and naming it a theorem, brought it to the attention of many sociologists. Since then, whole monographs and essays have been published utilizing the concept (See Stebbins (1967); McHugh (1968); Britten (1973)). So much has been written recently that Goffman's earlier lament about "the neglected situation" (1964) seems outdated. Herein he stated:

*The Sociological Quarterly, 1974, 15, 521-541. Reprinted by permission.

At present, the idea of the social situation is handled in the most happy-go-lucky way. . . . I do not think this opportunistic approach to social situations is always valid. It can be argued that social situations, at least in our society, constitute a reality sui generis, as He used to say and, therefore, need and warrant analysis in their own right, much like that accorded other basic forms of social organization (1964: 133).

While the qualification, "at least in our society" is rather unnecessary, Goffman's essential contention that situations have Durkheimian properties seems indisputable, and no one has made that more evident by his own research and thought than Goffman himself. In doing this, of course, he was influenced to a considerable extent by the thought of Cooley, Mead, Blumer, and Burke, not to speak of others, such as Evreinoff, the Russian dramaturgist, and Ichheiser.

In recent years, a new perspective calling itself ethnomethodology has arrived on the scene, and addresses itself to problems similar to those tackled by the interactionists. Denzin, in an effort to analyze the positions of ethnomethodology and symbolic interactionism, concludes that "a degree of convergence between the two" exists and that such convergence "should permit an expanded treatment of how individuals are linked to, shaped by, and in turn create social structure" (1970: 259). Such a convergence has been denied by Zimmerman and Wieder (1970: 295), who insist that ethnomethodology has "claims to be a radical departure from traditional sociological thinking." Nothing less than a total clearing of the decks is demanded and despite Denzin's heroic effort, even symbolic interactionism is to be swept away.

Since the ethnomethodologists and symbolic interactionists claim to deal at least with similar problems, one can compare and contrast the way in which they handle these problems and examine which one is the more sociological and more powerful in explaining these problems. I propose to take one such problem to which both interactionists and ethnomethodologists have made contributions and assess the assumptions and solutions that have come from their respective works. The problem to which such common contributions have been made is that of the definition of the situation. The works from the interactionists that attempt to explicate the problem are those of Goffman and other dramaturgists, while the contributions from the ethnomethodologists are a monograph by McHugh (1968) and a paper by Garfinkel (1967): the works of the latter two are, in fact, accounts and explanations of the same experiment that the authors undertook together, though they were reported separately.

It is, of course, well known that these two schools of thought derive their intellectual support from different sources: the dramaturgist derives his from the pragmatic philosophers, whereas the ethnomethodologists derive theirs from the phenomenology of Schultz and to some extent from the later Wittgenstein. In confronting these schools of thought (and their disciples) which discuss at length the problem of meaning and, by implication, the definition of the situation, one runs the risk of obscuring their fundamental differences and focusing on their superficial similarities. That Thomas and Mead on the one hand, and Wittgenstein and Schutz on the other, concerned themselves with the problem of meaning and arrived at brilliant solutions is well known. Were their solutions similar enough, however, to be merged and made the basis of a study in sociology and social psychology? This is what McHugh (1968) claims to be doing and his work is, in fact, entitled "Defining the Situation," and is claimed "as a solution of the problem of the organizing of meaning in social interaction" (1968). Garfinkel, using the same data, claims to come to conclusions about the "Commonsense Knowledge of Social Structures"; that is to say, how people in situations of everyday life come to conclusions about the basis of their actions. Let us then examine these two different approaches to this problem, after a discussion of the concept of the definition of the situation before dramaturgists and ethnomethodologists took possession of it.

THE DEFINITION OF THE SITUATION

Thomas said, "If men define situations as real, they are real in their consequences," and sociologists and social psychologists have ever since taken the proposition seriously. But, Thomas also said, "There is always a rivalry between the spontaneous definitions of the situation made by the member of an organized society and the definitions which his society has provided for him" (1923: 42). Definitions that ultimately determine conduct are a result of attending to certain features of a situation, and then resolving at times a major tussle, and at others a minor tussle, between cues provided by "society" and the spontaneous definitions made by the actor. Thomas speaks of cues provided by "society," but does not tell us how these cues are, in fact, made available; nor does he give any clear delineation of what constitutes a situation. Though society is said to provide cues, there is a suggestion in these sentences of an actor who is defining situations all alone: there is no conception of an interaction, of an "other." In short, Thomas, even in the initial articulation of the problem, left many questions unanswered and did not specify the processes by which situations are in fact defined—the systematics by which meanings are created. Merton tried his hand at unravelling some of these problems, after detailing a history of the usage of the concept in the works of earlier writers.

> The first part of the Thomas Theorem provides an increasing reminder that men respond not only to the objective features of a situation, but also and at times, primarily to the meaning this situation has for them. Once they have assigned some meaning to the situation, their consequent behavior and some of those consequences are determined by the ascribed meanings. (Merton, 1968: 475-476).

Merton seems to be saying that men respond to some mysterious "objective situation" and sometimes to the meaning this situation has for them. In other words, there are two dimensions to human conduct—one a series of responses to objective situations and another to a series of responses to meanings. Such a distinction between objects and meaning is an untenable and indefensible one in terms of human conduct. Mead spent his entire scholarly life refuting such a position and insisted that the distinction between objects in nature and meanings is quite false *insofar as the task at hand is the accounting of human perception and conduct*. It is possible to quote extensively from Mead here, but his view is lucidly presented by the foremost Meadian as follows:

> The concept of object is another pillar in Mead's scheme of analyses. Human beings live in a world or environment of objects and their activities are formed around objects. This bland statement becomes very significant when it is realized that for Mead, objects are *human constructs* and not self-existing entities with intrinsic natures (Blumer, 1969:68. Italics mine.)

From such a stance, it follows that whether one is responding to an objective feature in nature, abstract features in nature, or to other selves as well as to one's own self, one is responding to meanings. In other words, one is always defining situations and responding to such situations—one is condemned, so to speak, to a world of meanings.

Stebbins, whose paper is boldly entitled "A Theory of the Definition of the Situation," makes a similar error of separating a "subjective" and an "objective" situation. Following this separation, Stebbins goes on to discuss a "party" and a "railway station" as objective situations to which a subject brings a disposition and then proceeds to define the situation, presumably as a party and a railway station.

> A basic feature of the situation for any individual is how it will effect his action orientations, for it is in these terms that certain situational elements become meaningful. These elements are selected out of the objective situation to become part of the subjective situation (Stebbins 1967:149).

But what is the objective situation? Who set that up? In other words, parties and railway stations did not just happen to be there: *they were established as ways of eliciting a particular definition from whoever may come along*. Railway stations of course can be redefined, for example, as a place to sleep, but defining a railway station as a place to sleep and then using it as such is indeed different from defining a bedroom as a place to sleep and then using it as such. The railway station, in other words, permits redefinition in certain ways and constrains and limits these definitions as well: there are factors outside the constitutive capacities of the ego, factors which contribute a certain obduracy to the acts and arenas that others have constructed for us.

The two approaches to the definition of the situation, both of them embodying in some form the pre-Goffman and Garfinkel approaches,[1] do have something very fundamental in common: they both treat the problem of the definition of the situation as apart and different from the work of other interactionist thinkers and try to explicate it within very narrow limits. This is an error—both philosophically and biographically. Thomas' work must be considered along with that of Mead and must, in fact, be read as a continuing explication of certain intellectual problems that confronted Thomas and Mead, and before them, Cooley.[2] In other words, the best way of explicating the full range of the concept of definition of the situation is to consider it in association with Mead's concept of the *social act:*

> The social process relates the responses of one individual to the gestures of another, as the meanings of the latter, and is thus responsible for the rise of and existence of new objects in the social situation, objects depending upon or constituted by these meanings. Meaning is thus not to be conceived fundamentally as a state of consciousness or as a set of organized relations existing or subsisting mentally outside the field of experience into which they enter; on the contrary, it should be conceived objectively as having its existence entirely within the field itself. The response of one organism to the gesture of another in any given *social act* is the meaning of that gesture (Mead 1932:78).

Meaning is then *established;* it is created in responsive discourse between actors, between participants in a social act. Each party to such a transaction anticipates the responses that he wants and elicits it by one strategy or another. For example, a railway station is itself a situation that has already been defined and those who enter it are constrained to define it as indeed a railway station at the risk of dire consequences to themselves. A social act is this kind of transaction between actors and such an act is possible because actors are capable of manipulating the same symbolic system—what Mead called a "significant symbol." He defined a significant symbol, not very elegantly however, as "the gesture, the sign, the word which is addressed to another, in form, to all other individuals when addressed to the self" (1922, reprinted 1964:246).

Mead's position is also different from Wittgenstein and Schutz in these dimensions. The myths concerning Wittgenstein's career suggest that as a result of two or three events that could only be described as eye-opening ones, he arrived at two different theories of meaning that were later discovered to have many similarities. The first such event was in the trenches during World War I, when he discovered the "picture" theory of meaning, only to change it later to a theory of meaning by usage. "For a large class of cases—though not for all—in which we employ the word meaning, it can be defined thus: the meaning of a

---

[1]Though Stebbins' paper was published in 1967, he does take his cues from many previous papers on the subject that he cites.

[2]See Miller (1973) for a discussion of the friendship between Mead and Thomas at Chicago.

word is its use in the language'' (1963:20). Such a view is indeed a distinct improvement insofar as it is no longer atomistic in its implications. Meaning is no longer conceived of as being somehow contained in the pictures created by words or objects, but is defined by their usage in a grammatical system, and even grammar is defined broadly to signify that usage is really what works in a social context. Those who employ a language are essentially engaged in, or participating in a ''game''—a language game. As Quinton puts it: ''He sums up his theory of meaning by saying that the language games, within which alone words have meaning are forms of life, modes of activity, governed by systems of rules. A form of life involves attitudes, interests and behavior; it is far more comprehensive than the manipulation of a clearly specified calculus (Quinton, 1966:13).

For Wittgenstein, the philosopher, as well as for other philosophers, the mere assertion that meaning arises out of the social process, out of ''life forms,'' is perhaps adequate. But, it is important to specify the nature of the process and demonstrate how a mutuality of perspectives is possible and how *common usages* begin to occur. Merely to say meaning is created by usage is to leave unanswered questions that are at least fundamental to sociology and social psychology. The clear implication in Wittgenstein's theory is that meanings are, in fact, easily and effortlessly created: everyone knows the relevant usages and hence participates in the creation of meaning. But, if that is really the case, there is no sociological, perhaps not even a philosophical problem, to be investigated and solved: if the rules of usage are commonly and unproblematically held by all members of a society, then there is no problem of discrepancy, variance, conflict, ambiguity, and no issue to be unravelled. But of course there are these issues of ambiguity, discrepancy, and conflict to be solved in social life and they constitute in fact the social psychological and sociological problem: there are a variety of usages, definitions, and meanings available, and actors must agree, however tentatively, to one. How these differences can be reconciled—how the question *whose usage* shall be accepted is answered, and a common definition arrived at or negotiated—constitute the central problem of the field. Wittgenstein and his followers have explored this problem under the rubric of ''knowledge of other minds,'' and have concluded that one's knowledge of other minds depends on a conceptual connection between the observed behavior of the others and the linguistic forms available to describe it (Malcolm, 1966:381). But is the behavior, circumstance, or utterance of the other not purposive, not controlled, not intentional? Don't they, in other words seek to *show,* or dramatize a particular state of mind and even to insist that a particular usage be accepted, rather than another, and thereby seek to control the meaning that will in fact arise?

Schutz's work, in spite of its considerable quota of insights, similarly fails to come to grips with the problem of interaction—the problem that meanings and definitions are *negotiated* between participants and not merely constituted by the self, or ego, as Schutz calls him. He gives expression to the issues of relevance here in terms of three central concepts:

a) The general thesis of the alter-ego
b) The reciprocity of perspectives.
c) The thesis of intersubjectivity.

Among these notions, the last one is the most germane to the problem of meaning and interaction and is defined as follows:

> If we retain the natural attitude as men among other men, the existence of others is no more questionable to us than the existence of an outer world. We are simply born into a world of others and as long as we stick to the natural attitude we have no doubt that intelligent fellow-men do exist (Schutz 1967a:168).

This thesis is the strongest statement in Schutz's work on the subject of an interactional relationship with an other: but, nevertheless, it is incomplete insofar as it does not give substance or control to the recipient of the communication. He is viewed as a passive subject, with no capacity or voluntariness left to participate in the definition of the situation and the creation of meaning. Schutz's "other" is incapable of negotiating a situation, of actively refusing to complete a preferred definition, and is merely a victim of the "ego's" constitutive capacities.

This becomes clear when he turns to a discussion of the "foundations of a theory of intersubjective understanding." Here, after asserting that the subjective experience of one "is essentially inaccessible to every other individual" (1967b:99), he goes on to show how, nevertheless, such experiences become a part of the ego's constitution of the other.

The full implications of this are not followed through, however, in the rest of the work. Witness for example Schutz's treatment of an actual instance of such a constitution:

> An an example of "the understanding of a human act," without any communicative intent, let us look at the activity of a woodcutter.
> Understanding that wood is being cut can mean any of three things:
> 1. That we are noticing only the "external event," the axe slicing the tree and the wood splitting into bits which ensues.
> 2. That changes in another's body are perceived, which changes are interpreted as indications that he is alive and conscious.
> 3. That the center of attention is the woodcutter's own lived experience as actor. . . .
> Is this man acting spontaneously according to a project he had previously formulated? If so, what is this project? What is his in-order-to motive? In what meaning context does the action stand for him?
> These questions are neither concerned with the facticity of the situation, nor the bodily movements as such. Rather the outward facts and bodily movements are understood as indications of the lived experience of the person being observed. The attention of the observer is focused, not on the indications, but what lies behind them. *This is genuine understanding of the other person* [Italics in original (1967b:110-111)].

In the first place, there is no such thing as an action without any communicative *value,* and it is impossible to conceive of anyone not being aware of the communicative value of his own actions: to live and participate in a live-world is to know and recognize the communicative value of one's actions and words. Further, there is no such thing as a mere woodcutter cutting wood in the woods. He is always a woodcutter and he is always cutting somebody's wood. In other words, his actions are *situated*. He is usually visible and presents himself—and intends to do so presumably—as a man cutting wood belonging to him by right, and doing a good job of it. (Conversely, he may be stealing the wood and presenting himself accordingly—wanting to deceive the observer and hence, acting confidently, or not being aware of an observer and presenting himself surreptitiously.) Genuine understanding of the other person is achieved by responding to the situation that the other seeks to create, and to ask him questions—but that, it seems, is forbidden. Here Schutz displays an aversion to responsive discourse that is to plague his followers:

> Let us take actions performed without any communicative intent. We are watching a man in the act of cutting wood and wondering what is going on in his mind. Questioning him is ruled out, because that would require entering into a social relationship with him, which in turn would involve the use of signs. (1967b:114).

Why questioning should be ruled out is never made clear, and surely such a method only leads to a kind of mind reading.

In other words, Schutz retreats to a position where a subjective intelligence is seen as perceiving and defining the world; a close perusal of the rest of Schutz's writings reveals this (1967a; 1964; 1967b). The people in Schutz's world are alone and isolated in their personal facticity; they are strangers barely interested in even asking directions from the others in the situation, or *finding out* how the others are, by asking them, or listening to them, and certainly, according to all appearances, capable of taking care of themselves, of constituting the world all by themselves with never a moment of self-doubt or suspicion. A paper by Zaner, a follower of Schutz, unwittingly highlights this issue:

> How is it possible that although I cannot live in your seeing of things, cannot feel your love and hatred, cannot have an immediate and direct perception of your mental life, as it is to you—how is it possible that I can nevertheless share your thoughts, feelings, attitudes? For Schutz, the problem of intersubjectivity is here encountered in its full force (1961:76).

But the answer to these questions, according to Zaner, for all their rhetorical vigor is not that the "other" takes the trouble to tell the self or ego what his own mental life is like and what his loves, hates, thoughts, feelings, and attitudes are: the self, or ego, merely assumes the other's existence and assumes the state of his feelings, etc. In other words, there is no intercommunication or interaction. The actions in Schutz's world are all one sided: one assumes a state of intersubjectivity, one assumes a reciprocity of perspectives, and one assumes the existence of the other or the alter-ego. The self is said to constitute the world and not *participate in its constitution with other people*. As Schutz puts it:

> The experience of the other's stream of consciousness in vivid simultaneity, I propose to call the *general thesis of the alter-ego*. It implies that this stream of thought which is not mine, shows the same fundamental structure as my own consciousness. This means that the other is like me, capable of acting and thinking . . . (1967:174. Italics in original.)

The other is merely known to exist and known to have similar attitudes: he is not invited in, nor does he show any inclination to force himself in! This handicaps the phenomenologists and their followers so much in their work that whenever they are confronted with having to analyze the real world, they have to invoke some other sociological theory to be able to complete their work or lapse into an unmitigated psychologism. Zaner himself accepts aid from Mead to rescue Schutz's theory of intersubjectivity from being less inter and more subjective than was considered proper (1961), though the most celebrated example in this context is the work of Peter Berger and Thomas Luckmann: Schutz gives them the initial insights and a framework, but its completion depends on considerable assistance from Mead, Durkheim, etc. (1967).

These, then, are the solutions to the problem of meaning and definition of the situation proposed on the conceptual level by several scholars. How have their separate disciples realized these solutions in their own work?

THE ETHNOMETHODOLOGICAL SOLUTION

How have McHugh and Garfinkel set about fulfilling the programs of their respective mentors—Wittgenstein and Schutz? At the outset it could be said they have remained faithful to them. However, let us take them separately. McHugh devotes a whole monograph to advance his thesis about the definition of the situation. He accepts Wittgenstein's philosophical solution in toto and programs an experiment to put it to the test. Before that, however, he undertakes an expansion of the content of the concept of the definition of the situation that is certainly very enlightening: the definition of the situation becomes *problematic* and presents a *choice* to an actor rather than eliciting an automatic response, because it is characterized by the twin properties of "emergence" and "relativity." Emergence is defined as "the temporal dimension of activity wherein past, present, and future are analytically distinct and at the same time inextricable for they are not correspondingly distinct in their influence upon concrete behavior" (McHugh, 1968:24). Relativity is defined "as emergence is temporal and involves an event in both the old and the new, relativity is spatial and characterizes an event in its relationship to other events across the boundaries of space'' (McHugh, 1968:28). He then describes an experiment where these ideas, derived from Wittgenstein presumably, are put to the test. He brings some subjects into the laboratory and tells them that he is doing a study of the efficiency of certain psychotherapeutic methods. On arriving for the experiment, the S is told to think over his problems, relate some background to them, and then ask questions about them that can be answered only by Yes or No. The experimenter meanwhile has gone to another room and gives his ''answer'' through an intercom; but ''his answer has been predecided by consulting a table of random numbers and *would be the same regardless of the questions asked''* (McHugh, 1968:66, our italics). In other words, McHugh programs his research in such a way that by giving random Yes or No answers, a definition of the situation is prevented from arising and anomie is created. In Wittgensteinian terms, the rules have been violated deliberately; and from the responses the subjects make to this ''anomie,'' McHugh is able to conclude:

> Emergence predominates during orderly interactions. On the other hand, relativity predominates when order is challenged. An orderly interaction always contains pre-existing assumptions which the participants document through the emergent course of interaction. As discrepancies arise, however, these assumptions are thrown into doubt and rise to the surface. Actors resolve the doubt by assessing them against the immediate environment (1968:124).

These statements are unexceptionable ones, but it is a great mystery how McHugh was able to come to these conclusions on the basis of his experiments. However that may be, surely the relevant observation on McHugh's experiment was that the only definition of the situation which could possibly have occurred was that of someone doing an experiment about therapeutic practices, and that occurred in spite of the experimental procedures used. What transpired between McHugh and his subjects was a mechanical series of responses given by one to the statements of another, and hence it is incorrect to talk of the ''emergent course of the interaction''—at least in reference to the matter that McHugh takes up for analysis. The subjects are said to have come to conclusions regarding therapeutic practices as a result of the ''answers'' given by McHugh: but does this constitute a definition of the situation? It certainly does not. The situation that was, in fact, sustained by McHugh and his subjects was that of an experiment which was eliciting some bizarre responses from the experimenter. There is really little warrant to come to any other conclusion. In other words, a traditionally determined usage of certain words by *one* actor in an artificial situation is *only a part* of the process by which meaning is created; the natural interactional process is what Blumer calls ''joint action'': ''it refers to the larger collective form of action that is constituted by the fitting together of the lines of behavior of the separate participants'' (Blumer, 1969:70). McHugh's work seems to have missed the heart of the problem: the mutual exchange of cues, gestures, signs, and symbols, the anticipating tentativeness of all normal interactions, the responsive adjustment of the participants in a transaction. The "usages" imposed on the "situation" by one actor do not define it; they merely thwart a definition from arising.[3]

The definition of situation can arise only when the parties in a transaction are even minimally familiar with the usages current in a group, and draw on such knowledge to interpret a situation that is being proferred, and indeed to profer a situation to be accepted. There must be basic "agreement" on the use of symbols, basic capacities to operate in one among many coding systems available, elaborate or restricted, or in between, as Bernstein might put it (1964:55-69).

Examining the work of Garfinkel on the question of definition of the situation reveals more clearly the inadequacies of the ethnomethodological position in coming to grips with the problem. His interpretation of the results of the same study that McHugh wrote up leads him to different realms, though seeking to solve the same problem. He claims:

> This paper is concerned with common-sense knowledge of social structures as an object of theoretical sociological interest. It is concerned with descriptions of a society that its members, sociologists included, as a condition of their enforceable right to manage and communicate decisions of meaning, fact, method and causal texture without interference, use and treat as known in common with other members and which other members take for granted (1967:77).
>
> How do they—laymen, sociologists, etc., do this? They follow the documentary method of interpretation and it consists of "treating an actual appearance as the 'document of,' 'as pointing to,' 'as standing on behalf of,' a presupposed underlying pattern." Not only is the underlying pattern derived from its individual documentary evidences, but the individual documentary evidences in their turn are interpreted on the basis of "what is known" about the underlying pattern. Each is used to interpret the other (1967:77).

This, it seems, is an unexceptionable statement, up to a point which will be taken up later. To demonstrate this method, an experiment designed to exaggerate its features is undertaken. As described earlier, the subjects come in under the impression that they are testing alternative therapeutic methods, and are given Yes or No answers on a random basis to their questions concerning their personal problems, after which the subjects record their observations. From these, Garfinkel is able to conclude that the subjects were able to construct a meaningful structure out of the arbitrary answers that the experimenter gave to their questions. In addition, Garfinkel concluded that the subjects continued to make sense of the words provided by the experimenter on the basis of the "retrospective-prospective possibilities of the present situation," that "the subjects assigned a scenic source to answers that lacked one," and that the

---

[3]The exception to this situation is the one where one actor has total and overwhelming power that he or she imposes his definition of the situation or his rules of usage on the others. But even this survives only when the others accept the definition and the "usages," and in effect participate actively in the transaction.

subjects referred to "institutionalised features" as an aid to interpretation (1967:89-94). It is not clear however, what is gained by not providing them with intelligible answers as an aid to defining the situation; what is achieved by again creating an occasion where actors are exposed to solitary cogitations. Surely the situations that humans are asked to define are those that already have received (or receive at the crucial moment) cooperative attentions from others that function to elicit rhetorically the needed constructions.

Notice that the subjects listened to a random series of affirmative and negative responses and managed to do all those things. But, these procedures have very little to do with the way humans—including presumably ethnomethodologists— and sociologists—come to conclusions. The "documents" they interpret are rather more cooperative than Garfinkel's documents: they talk, argue, fight, define, correct, and redefine as aids to arriving at proper conclusions. Not to put too fine a point, they engage in social acts and jointly participate in the construction of meaning. They, in fact, cooperate and conspire with each other to create at least a modicum of meaning in any transaction and nothing about interactions and meaning can be learned by creating a situation where meaning could not possibly emerge (except, of course, that we could learn that meaning could not emerge under these circumstances). The common-sense knowledge of social structure, as well as the routine grounds of everyday action are constructed on these bases; or else there will not be too much ground or too much action in the human sphere. To use an illustration used earlier, the railway station, as a routine ground (in every sense of that term) of everyday action, or as an item of commonsense knowledge, is not available to a subject for any kind of action, except insofar as the others put up the grounds of the railway station for such a definition and constitution to be made by the subject. And so it is with conversations and exchanges of all sorts in the human world. That is to say, definitions of situations are serialled and mutually sensitive acts of negotiations and not *psychologistically* constructed inferences arrived at alone and unaided.[4] In short, McHugh, taking off from Wittgenstein, and Garfinkel, taking off from Schutz, have in our view not very surprisingly trapped themselves into a psychologistic epistemology.[5] This, of course, makes it easier to do tests, research, etc., but certainly the evidence that such procedures advance knowledge of the human world is still very slight.

---

[4]This of course does not apply to decipherment of codes and languages that are strange and unfamiliar to decoders. For example, the decipherment of Linear B was accomplished in exactly the one-sided process that McHugh and Garfinkel made their subjects utilize. Everyday communications are accomplished by other processes. On the decipherment of Linear B, see Chadwick (1970).

[5]See Day's (1969) papers on the question of the psychologism in Wittgenstein and phenomenology. Though Wittgenstein managed to escape from the obvious psychologism of the Tractatus— Philosophicus Logicus, and its subjectivistic principle of verification, he apparently did not go far enough away; the fly was still partially in the bottle!

THE DRAMATURGICAL SOLUTION

The dramaturgical solution to the problem of meaning has been hinted at in the preceding pages and I shall bring it into relief here. Interactions and definitions of the situations are not what S believes is true of the situation, but are syntactical activities engaged in by two or more persons. People in each others' presence, as well as people who anticipate eliciting certain responses from others, take steps to ensure that the different parties in a transaction are properly informed about their intentions. They cooperate, sometimes in moods of desperation, and always with a certain tentativeness, to create a definition or to prevent one from dissolving into disorder or nonsense. How is this achieved? The dramaturgists—in particular Goffman and Stone—have answered this question very effectively. Let us take Stone's surprisingly neglected paper on ''appearance'' for analysis first. He studied the meaning of appearance in interpersonal relations, and concluded that appearance, as manifest in clothing, constitutes an important dimension of interpersonal discourse. As he puts it:

> The meaning of appearance can be studied by examining the responses mobilized by clothes. Such responses take on at least four forms: Identities are placed, values appraised, moods appreciated and attitudes anticipated. Appearance provides the identities, values, moods and attitudes of the person in communication since it arouses in others the assignment of words embodying these dimensions to the one who appears. . . . By appearing, the person announces his identity, shows his value, expresses his mood and proposes his attitude (Stone 1962:10).

In other words, both parties in a transaction are involved in the definition of the situation: for example, a person dresses himself in the ''appearance'' of the identity, value, mood, and attitude that he wants his audience to take to be his identity, etc.; he cooperates, thus making interaction, communication, and hence society possible. Typically, he does not hide his identity, etc., to confuse his co-actors—unless professional and situational demands make it imperative to do for the ongoing interaction to proceed.[6] In Stone's words:

> As the self is dressed, it is simultaneously addressed for whenever we clothe ourselves, we dress ''toward'' or address some audience whose validating responses are essential to the establishment of our self (101-102).

Even if he conceals his identity and his ''true intentions,'' the ensuing interactions will be based on *whatever it is that the respondent takes to be the other's identity, etc.,* until such time as he finds the evidence to repudiate the

---

[6]Naturally, confidence tricksters and professionals in charge of terminal patients have to play a different game, in which case the recipients of their attention—if not immediately, after some time develop special techniques of arriving at the proper definition of the situation. See Glaser and Straus (1965) for a study of terminal patients.

earlier identity, etc., and substitute a new one. But, in any given interaction, subjects take steps to find out the identity, etc., of the other. Whatever it is, the doing produces the being, until a new doing is taken to constitute a new being. In a different vocabulary, it could be said that we dramatize our identities, values, moods, and whatever else we think may be relevant to the sustenance of a relationship and a situation.

Goffman's work uses the vocabulary of the theatre explicitly, and thereby brings into sharper focus the dramaturgical approaches to definition of the situation. However, when one removes these words from the theatre—Goffman calls them scaffolding—we are still left with the observation that people in social life perform to immediate or anticipated audiences, and that in order to do this, they use all the resources available: the manipulation of objects, and space, and even time. Furthermore, people also use the arts of both concealment and strategic revelation to create the sort of impression that they do want to create to certain audiences, and the audiences presumably cooperate by being impressed in the ways in which they are required to be impressed. For Goffman then, an interaction is a management of impression *between* actors, where one proposes a certain definition of the situation by using whatever objects and words are necessary, and the others accept this preferred definition and thereby create a smooth interaction and a consensual definition of the situation. But, the others also can reject the preferred definition and suggest their own version, in which case the initiator now has the choice of refusing it and thereby terminating the interaction, or demanding a new definition altogether, or accepting the one preferred by the others and thereby saving the situation. Whichever of these steps are accepted by self and other, the paramount consideration is that they must be announced, articulated, and dramatized (Goffman, 1959; 1965; 1967). To dramatize, then, is to invite or profer a particular situation to another, and the other in return dramatizes his intentions and an interaction is established. Goffman puts this very felicitiously as follows:

> I assume that the proper study of interaction is not the individual and his psychology, but rather the syntactical relations among the acts of different persons mutually present to one another...Not then men and their moments. Rather moments and their men (1967:3).

Dramatization is not a ploy to manipulate others, nor to exploit them, but a genuine act of communication, an invitation to view the self and its material circumstances in a certain way. In fact, many critics of the dramaturgical perspective are unable to distinguish between drama and dramaturgy: the former is, of course, make-believe, whereas the latter is a technique of communication. It is also a more powerful and sociologically acceptable solution to the problem of the creation of meaningful interaction. It avoids the traps of both a psychologistic epistemology and a solipsistic theory of knowledge, and indeed stands at the very heart of the sociological argument.

DRAMATISM AND SOCIOLOGY

How is this achieved? Or, in other words, what is the basis of the power of dramaturgical analyses? Messinger et al., in a paper published soon after Goffman's first book (1959) appeared, argue that Goffman's work is interesting and acceptable because it is, after all, an argument by analogy: life is, at times, like a theatre and social reality can be profitably and easily analyzed with drama as a framework (Messinger et al., 1962). This is indeed not the case, though some cautionary statements in Goffman's first book may have encouraged Messinger et al. to conclude this. It is not that social reality is *like drama,* but that it *is drama,* insofar as social reality is drawn out of a communicational and symbolic matrix in which socially constructed persons engage in the processes of articulation, definition, and interaction. Drama is not something that is drawn out of life and put on stage for some people to watch and obtain cathartic delight. The drama on a stage is rather a microcosmic representation of life for those who find the drama of everyday life tiresome or boring, and the activities on stage *recreate* the action that takes place in the authentic arenas of our life.[7] And the work of the dramaturgical sociologists is based on this assumption—the assumption of a *dramatistic ontology.* The finest contemporary statement on a dramatistic ontology is that given by Burke, though unfortunately he gives nowhere a succinct definition that can be cited here: his entire opus is such a contribution (Burke, 1935; 1945; 1950; 1966). He asks in the opening sentence of one of his works "what is involved when we say what people are doing and why they are doing it?" (1962:xvii). He offers the whole book (and later books as well) in answer to that question. In any case, the point of the question is that people themselves are always asking the two questions contained in the statement, to borrow a phrase, in "everyday life," and providing answers by some means or other. These means, Burke argues, can be summarized in the concept of dramatism. As people experience the world, they have to come to conclusions on those aforementioned questions and are, in fact, made to come to conclusions by the employment of the principles of drama.

> It is a principle of drama that the nature of acts and agents should be consistent with the nature of the scene. . . . The nature of the scene may be conveyed primarily by suggestions built into the lines of the verbal action itself . . . or it may be conveyed by non-linguistic properties as with the materials of naturalistic stage sets. In any case, examining first the relation between scene and act, all we need to note here is the principle whereby the scene is a fit "container" for the act, expressing in fixed properties the same quality that action expresses in terms of development (Burke, 1945:3).

In other words, in dramatic constructions, acts, and scenes in which acts occur, must bear a particular congruent relation, and one may add here, so it is in

---

[7]See Duncan (1962) for a discussion of dramatism and sociology.

real life. Churches are constructed to *promote* pious sentiments, and streets are constructed so as to drive or walk on them, just as railway stations are built to *elicit* congruent acts in them. In other words, these "objects" that constitute the scene are utilized *rhetorically* to create an interaction, establish a meaningful transaction or define a situation. These properties of human relations are basic to the human condition; Burke expresses it as follows:

> For rhetoric as such is not rooted in any past conditions of the human society. It is rooted in an essential function of language itself, a function that is wholly realistic and is continually born anew; the use of language as a symbolic means of inducing cooperation in beings that by nature respond to symbols (1962:567).

Words and objects are utilized by "human agents" to persuade others, to induce their cooperation in sustaining the definition of a situation; and this is a characteristic human activity and constitutes, or should constitute, the ontologistical basis of the human sciences. In the work of the symbolic interactionists and the dramaturgists, this particular ontology finds its analytical expression. Critics of the dramaturgical perspective err in supposing that the drama of social life is a mere metaphor (whatever that may be); it is rather the stuff and fibre of social relations, and the very substance of the sociological perspective invites consideration in dramatistic terms.[8] An examination of Weber and Durkheim, as well as Mead and Cooley, will reveal both the utility and the inescapability of a dramatistic ontology, if one is still committed to maintaining sociology as an enterprise that is fundamentally different from other perspectives in the human sciences.[9]

Weber's methodological position is well known. According to him, the task of sociology is to understand and interpret "social action," which is defined thus:

> In action is included all human behavior when and insofar the acting individual attaches a subjective meaning to it. Action in this sense may be either overt or purely inward or subjective: it may consist of positive intervention in a situation of deliberately refraining from such intervention, or passively acquiescing in the situation. (Action is) social insofar as by virtue of the subjective meaning attached to it by the acting individual (or individuals) it takes account of the behavior of others and is thereby oriented in its course (1947:88).

Action is oriented by the account the actor takes of the other: the actor is aware of the other and trims and contours his conduct accordingly. But what does this

---

[8] A folk aphorism of the sixties had it, "reality is a crutch." I would amend it to "Reality is also a crutch," or a metaphor. Compare the position advanced above to that of Arendt (1958:175-247).

[9] We will forebear to include Marx in our analyses here. However, it may be pointed out that the Danish sociologist, Joachim (1971) has referred to the "Marx-Mead-Cooley paradigm of interaction" and a recent study of the Frankfurt school refers to Mead's thought as supportive of the assumptions of Marx and his followers (Jay, 1973:289).

awareness of the other, the "taking account of the behavior of the others" consist of? Weber was not particularly interested in addressing himself to this issue: the problem of *how* a subject comes to orient his conduct to that of others, and what part the others play in consummating this process. Nevertheless, it is important to raise the issue since a whole array of problems are dependent on it. Is it a reference to the "subjective" experience of the other, or is it a reference to the overt behavior of the other?[10] Whichever it is, and even if it is both, the "acting individual" must be made to *become aware of the other's* "subjective" and "objective" experience by the other taking the necessary steps to publicize these experiences: in fact, whatever the other publicizes becomes the behavior that the acting individual "can take account of." In other words, the actor becomes aware of the other, as well as the other's subjective "experiences" *only to the extent that these experiences are dramaturgically available*. Interaction proceeds on the basis of *whatever it is that one takes to be the other's* subjective experience and to the extent that neither the other nor "brute facts" challenge what one takes to be the case, an ongoing definition of the situation has been negotiated. In a very fundamental sense, there is a presumption on the part of both actors that if one shows such an activity or speaks such words, they will lead to such a definition of the situation and the interaction will be based on these definitions. Hence, each actor in a social situation must take the necessary pains to dramatize his subjective experiences, his "intentions" as he wants them to be defined or "taken account of." As a result, the actors in a situation fuse their "subjectivities" and arrive at an objective working definition of the situation by dramatistic means.

Durkheim was perhaps the sociologist who challenged the validity of the psychologistic epistemology most deliberately. Kemper has recently stated this view forcefully:

> With compelling logic, Durkheim demolished the claims of the psychological atomists on the origins of society. He argued for the existential priority of society over the individual and, as far as can be judged from the history of ideas, won the debate (1972:739).

Durkheim asserted these claims about the individual and society, not only in his theories on the division of labor, but also in everything else that he wrote. The Durkheimian work of particular relevance to us here is his contribution to a sociological epistemology. Herein he asked, "What is a social fact?" and proceeded to give an answer:

---

[10]Schutz himself raises this question; but the solution proposed here is, of course, different from that proposed by him (1967:15-20).

Here then is a category of facts with very distinctive characteristics: it consists of ways of acting, thinking and feeling, external to the individual and endowed with the power of coercion by reasons of which they control him (1939:3).[11]

These facts have an independent existence; they are external to the individual and coerce him as well. However, the manner and method by which these facts accomplish these remarkable actions must be examined closely. One certainly cannot accept the mystical notion that these facts, independent and coercive as they are, exist independently and outside of human actions and interactions. Social facts then, in their exteriority and constraint, exist and function in the meanings and actions of individuals: social facts have become incorporated into the persons of the society's members, and it is their actions that give them reality and substance. My socialized actions (or societalized actions, if one prefers) constrain the socialized actions of others; one may add that my socialized actions elicit the socialized actions of others as well, and vice-versa. And how is this achieved? My actions and the actions of others interact, and we each know and understand each other's actions because each of us has to *act them out* or dramatize them, so that they can have exteriority and contribute to the constraining of the actions of each other. The existential and causal priority of society, unless we want to get entrapped in the quicksands of reification, cannot mean anything more than the priority and facticity of social interactions, social relationships, and that pattern of interactions called social institutions.

My argument certainly is not that Durkheim (and Weber) were developing a dramatistic ontology. It is that the ontological goals that they, Durkheim and Weber, tried to reach are best served by the assumptions and arguments of dramatism. Indeed, a sociological argument is possible only with *at least* a weak form of the dramatistic argument: but for drama, there will not be any communication, and without communication there cannot be interaction; and without interaction there can be no social fact or social structure; and without social facts and social structure, there is no such thing as the sociological argument.

An examination of the work of the interactionist social psychologists will show the congruence between their work and that of other sociologists. Cooley, in fact, gives a more forthright basis for our statement on dramatism:

If we are to understand social life, then we must have insight into the minds of people, for it is there that we can perceive the influence of others upon them. A's idea of B is what is chiefly important as far as A's conduct is concerned. . . . The images which people have of each other

---

[11]It has been argued that Durkheim in later life was less commited to this view (Lukes, 1973). However, he never really abandoned it, and his best sociological work was done when he was under the constraining influence of these premises. It seems however that the rise of ethnomethodology belies Kemper's claim that Durkheim won the debate!

then are the solid social facts and the sociologist must make it his business to observe and
interpret them (1933:47).

In other words, Cooley is saying that we respond to the other essentially in
terms of what we think he is, how we constitute our *image* of him. But what is
this image of the other that a self has, and how is it created? If the other has an
image, it is an object over which he has some control and interest, so much so
that we can talk of it being constructed or assembled by him. And the reasonable
presumption is that he would assemble it in accordance with what he wants others
to take his image to be. In short, he will dramatize his self through the process of
assembling an "image." A self can, and indeed must, constitute the world and
the other, but such constitution is of a world and an other that has already been
assembled for the self to constitute—or at least participate with others in
assembling and constituting.

It is Mead's thought, however, that develops the dramatistic lines of argument
more clearly, and Burke himself is clearly indebted to Mead. As we argued
earlier, Mead's theory of meaning was derived from what he termed the
processes of the social act:

The response of one organism to the gesture of another in any given social act is the meaning of
that gesture and is also in a sense responsible for the appearance or coming into being of the
new object—or a new content of an old object—to which that gesture refers through the
outcome of the given social act (1932:78).

That is to say, actors have to respond to each other for meaning to emerge and
they are able to respond to each other because each of them takes the necessary
steps to ensure that they announce their intentions—verbally and gesturally—so
that the announcement would elicit the needed responses: they dramatize their
meanings and create a social act.

Dramatism as an ontology takes off from the premise that humans cannot
help but communicate, and cannot help but be aware that the others around us are
interpreting the world around them, which world includes us as well as the
others. The world consists of communication-worthy social facts or social
objects that dramatistically develop and present a theme. As Artaud, one of the
authentic geniuses of the world of contemporary dramaturgical theory, puts it:

The theatre is nothing but (that it) makes use of everything—gestures, sounds, words, screams,
light, darkness—rediscovers itself at precisely the point where the mind requires a language to
express its manifestations (1959:12).

Dramatism gains its standing as an ontology when we examine ritual as
theatre. Such a version was, of course, known to Durkheim (1915:417), though
he did not think it fit to develop it fully. In recent years, Young (1965) has shown
the crosscultural validity of the thesis that initiation ceremonies are dramatiza-

tions of sexual roles and identities and the changes thereof. But even he does not press the ontological implications of his data and conclusions.[12] It is indeed an old theory in theatre studies that the theatre as a form originated in ritual: humans perform rituals to the sun, the moon, the seasons, and spirits, forces, and powers, and then personify them and establish contexts and situations where they come alive and act. Then the humans impersonate these personifications, and act their careers out, and theatre is born—initially of course as religious representation, and then as secular ones. As Harrison puts it ". . . in Athens, ritual became art, a *dromenon* became the drama and . . . the shift is symbolized by the addition of the *theatre* on spectator-space to the orchestra or dancing-place" (1948:135. Italics in original).[13] This perhaps may explain how a particular theatrical form emerged from ritual, but leaves the question of why ritual emerged in the first place unanswered. And in our view, to trace the theatrical form to ritual is to reverse the process: theatre emerged before ritual and ritual is merely the continuation of the theatrical impulse that humans first gained with their capacity for meaning. Meaning, of course, exists as a public phenomenon: it must receive articulation and validation in a public enterprise, and there are no such things as private languages (that is, private to the individual). And theatricality or dramaturgy is the method—the efficient, efficacious, and parsimonious method of articulating it.

Ritual then is theatre: an assured way of communicating important significations that are necessary for the community or society that is supporting it. Religious ritual is the drama of personifying impersonal forces and establishing a relationship with them; weddings are dramas of personal transformations, and funerals are dramas of death and living with death—they involve transformations of identity for the living and the dead, and the public and private recognition of same (Gennep, 1960). Theatre is prior to special forms of theatre called ritual. To quote Artaud again, "This perspective leads to rejection of the usual limitations of man and man's powers and infinitely extends the frontiers of what is called reality" (1958:13). It is not that reality is theatrical or dramatic; rather what is considered reality by society, or a part thereof, is theatrically or dramatistically realized and constructed, so much so that we can say that reality is a drama, a theatre, that the order of things is inherently dramatic. Evereinoff puts it this way:

> Theatre, as I understand it, is infinitely wider than the stage. It is more valuable and necessary to man than even the highest blessings of modern civilization. We can live without those and

---

[12]See also Peacock (1968) for a study of the ritual aspects of drama in Indonesia.

[13]See also Harrison's (1912) study of the social origins of Greek religion, including her discussion of the work of "M. Durkheim," for other developments of this theme. Murray also contributes an interesting essay on this theme in the same volume.

we actually did for thousands of years as is known from the history of primitive man. But no man has been able to get along without the theatre . . . (1927:8).

There are, however, special problems with actors who are unable to engage in a continued responsive discourse, who are unable either to engage in immediate dramatizations or to respond to those of others. Some are too far apart from each other or are dead and are unable to participate in the ongoing transactions. Goffman was quoted earlier referring to "persons mutually present to one another." Needless to say, such *mutual presence* need not necessarily involve *proximate physical* presence, though all of Goffman's work is concerned with such occasions: written documents, for example, can be interactional statements that readers have to interpret and respond to, in order to establish a meaning. Ricouer, in a recent paper, argues that the human sciences are fundamentally concerned with the interpretation of the spoken or written "documents" of a culture. He suggests that the following two hypotheses could be examined as a consequence:

1) To what extent may we consider the notion of text as a good paradigm for the object of the social sciences?

2) To what extent may we use the methodology of text interpretation as a paradigm for interpretation in general in the field of the human sciences? (Ricouer, 1971:529)

Indeed we may fruitfully treat all human communicated material as "texts" (spoken, written, and I may add, carved, sculpted, painted, hieroglyphed, symbolized, emblemized, dramatized, filmed) and apply the same methods of interpretation and understanding. Conversely, we can treat written materials as an instance of an interaction between an actor and a text: the actor responds to the written text as if to another actor, and attempts a plausible definition of the situation. If meaningful action can be considered as a text, as Ricouer states, then texts can be considered as meaningful actions. But, it does not rest there. The reader submits the interpretation, the definition of the text to another—the author, if he is available, or to "experts"—for a searching scrutiny and validation of his own interpretations. In fact, whole scholarly industries arise out of this seeking to find out what exactly the author was trying to say. Once such an interpretation is made, someone else will want to check the interpretation out . . . and so it becomes another interaction, another situation to be explored and negotiated, between the actors.[14]

---

[14]This is different, of course, from not telling the subjects or readers what one is about, or giving them misleading cues and then wondering how they came to conclusions.

CONCLUSION

The contrast between the dramaturgical and the ethnomethodological positions is striking. In McHugh's and Garfinkel's work, the notion of responsive discourse, of the mutuality of actions is absent. In ordinary interactions, when a subject receives foolish, contradictory, meaningless, abnormal, vague, etc., answers, he immediately—or at least sooner or later—asks, "What do you mean?" He challenges the other and asks him to explain himself, to extrapolate on his obscure and recalcitrent responses. And woe unto those who cannot and are also powerless—they may get carted off to an asylum. Thus, situations are not defined and social structures are not constructed on the basis of mute and/or intransigent responses by co-actors; quite the contrary. Even the search for pattern, the assignment of scenic background, the filling-in of blank spaces in ongoing interpersonal transactions are conducted in terms of questions and answers. In fact, the epistemological significance of Chicken Little's experience is that he did not check with others about the veracity of his conclusions regarding the scenic properties of the sky: had he done so, he would have found out, just as Garfinkel's subjects would have, the true nature of the case. Such knowledge is neither static nor is it available to the subject in an immanent form: they have to be actively sought and constructed. Knowledge, even of social structures, is not acquired by passively participating in what one of Garfinkel's subjects himself called "a one-sided" event, but conjointly, by dramatistically constructing it.

REFERENCES

Arendt, Hannah. *The Human Condition*. Chicago: University of Chicago Press, 1958.

Artaud, Antonin. *The Theatre and Its Double*. New York: The Grove Press, 1958.

Berger, Peter and Thomas Luckmann, *The Social Construction of Reality*. New York: Doubleday and Co., Inc., 1967.

Bernstein, Basil. "Elaborated and restricted codes: their social origins and some consequences." *American Anthropologist*, 1964, 66, 6 part 2 (December): 55-69.

Blumer, Herbert. "The sociological implications of the thought of G. H. Mead". Pp. 61-77 in Herbert Blumer, *Symbolic Interactionism, Perspective and Method*. Englewood Cliffs: Prentice-Hall, 1969.

Britten, Arthur. *Meanings and Situations*. London: Routledge, Kegan, Paul and Trench, 1973.

Burke, Kenneth. *Language as Symbolic Action*. Berkeley: University of California Press, 1966; A Rhetoric of Motives. New York: Prentice-Hall, 1950. Republished with (1945) 1962, New York: World Publishing Company; A Grammar of Motives. New York: Prentice-Hall, 1945; Permanence and Change, 1935. Republished 1966, Indianapolis: Bobbs-Merrill.

Chadwick, John. *The Decipherment of Linear B*. Cambridge: The University Press, 1970.

Cooley, C. H. *Introductory Sociology*. New York: Charles Scribner's Sons, 1933.

Day, W. F. "Radical behaviorism in reconciliation with phenomenology." *Journal of the Experimental Analysis of Behavior* 12, 1969a (March): 315-328; "On certain similarities between the philosophical investigations of Ludwig Wittgenstein and the operationism of B. F. Skinner." *Journal of the Experimental Analysis of Behavior* 12, 1969b (May): 489-506.

Denzin, Norman. "Symbolic interactionisms and ethnomethodology." Pp. 281-286 in Jack Douglas (Ed), *Understanding Everyday Life*. Chicago: Aldine Publishing Co., 1970.

Duncan, Hugh D. *Communication and the Social Order*. New York: Oxford University Press, 1962.

Durkheim, Emile. *The Rules of Sociological Method*. New York: Free Press, 1938, Reprinted 1965.

Evreinoff, Nikolai. *The Theatre in Life*. Reissued (1970). New York: Benjamin Blom, 1927.

Garfinkel, Harold. *Studies in Ethnomethodology*. Englewood Cliffs: Prentice-Hall, 1967.

Gennep, Arnold van. *The Rites of Passage*. Chicago: University of Chicago Press, 1960.

Glaser, Barney and Anselm Straus. *Awareness of Dying*. Chicago: Aldine Publishing Company, 1965.

Goffman, Erving. *Interaction Ritual*. New York: Doubleday and Company, Inc., 1967; "The neglected situation". *American Anthropologist* 66 No. 6 Part 2: 133-136., 1964; *Stigma*. Englewood Cliffs: Prentice-Hall, 1963; *Presentation of Self in Everyday Life*. New York: Doubleday and Co., Inc., 1959.

Harrison, Jane. *Ancient Art and Ritual*. London: Williams and Norgate, 1948. (First published in 1913); *Themis–A Study of the Social Origins of Greek Religion*, Cambridge: Cambridge University Press, 1912.

Ichheiser, Gustav. *Appearances and Realities*. San Francisco: Josey-Bass Inc. 1970. First published in the American Journal of Sociology 55, No. 2 (Part 2) (September) Special Supplement, 1949.

Jay, Martin. *The Dialectical Imagination*. Boston: Little Brown and Company, 1973.

Joachim, Israel. *Alienation: From Marx to Modern Sociology*. Boston: Allyn and Bacon, Inc., 1971.

Kemper, T. "The division of labor: a post Durkheimian analytical view." *American Sociological Review* 37, 1972 (December) :739-753.

Lukes, Steven. *Emile Durkheim: His Life and Works*. London: Allen Lane and Penguin Press, 1973.

McHugh, Peter. *Defining the Situation*. New York: Bobbs-Merrill Company, Inc., 1968.

Malcolm, Norman. "Knowledge of other minds." Pp. 371-383 in George Pitcher (Ed.), *Philosophical Investigation: A Collection of Critical Essays*. New York: Doubleday and Co., Inc., 1966.

Mead, George H. *Mind, Self and Society*. Chicago: University of Chicago Press, 1932.

Merton, Robert K. *Theory and Social Structure*. New York: The Free Press, 1968.

Messinger, S., H. Sampson, and R. Towne. "Life as theatre: some notes on the dramaturgic approach to social reality". *Sociometry* 25, 1962 (September) :98-110.

Miller, David. *George Herbert Mead: Self, Language and the World*. Austin: University of Texas Press, 1973.

Murray, Gilbert. "An excursus on ritual forms preserved in Greek tragedy". Pp. 341-363 in Jane Harrison. *Themis–A study of the Social Origins of Greek Religion.* Cambridge: Cambridge University Press, 1912.

Peacock, James. *Rites of Modernization: Symbolic and Social Aspects of Proletarian Drama.* Chicago: University of Chicago Press, 1968.

Quinton, A. M. "Contemporary British philosophy." Pp. 1-22 in George Pitcher (ed). *The Philosophical Investigations: A Collection of Critical Essays.* New York: Doubleday and Company, Inc., 1966.

Ricour, Paul. "The model of the text: meaningful action considered as a text." *Social Research* 38, 1971 (Autumn) :528-562.

Schutz, Alfred. *Collected Papers* Vol. II. The Hague: Martinus Nijhoff, 1964; Collected Papers Vol. I. The Hague: Martinus Nijhoff, 1967a; *ThePhenomenology of the Social World.* Evanston: Northwestern University Press, 1967b.

Stebbins, R. "A theory of the definition of the situation." *The Canadian Review of Sociology and Anthropology,* 1967 (Winter) :148-164.

Stone, Gregory P. "Appearance and the self." Pp. 86-117 in Arnold Rose (Ed.), *Human Behavior and Social Process.* Boston: Houghton Mifflin, 1962.

Thomas, W. I. *The Unadjusted Girl.* Boston: Little Brown and Company, 1923.

Weber, Max. *The Theory of Economic and Social Organization.* Talcott Parsons (Trans.). Republished in paperback (1964) New York: The Free Press, 1947.

Wittgenstein, Ludwig. *The Philosophical Investigations.* G. E. M. Anscombe (Trans.). Oxford: Basil Blackwell, 1963.

Young, Frank W. *Initiation Ceremonies: A Cross-Cultural Study of Status Dramatization.* New York: Bobbs-Merrill Co., Inc., 1965.

Zaner, Richard. "The theory of intersubjectivity: Alfred Schutz." *Social Research* 29, 1961 (Spring) : 71-94.

Zimmerman, Don H. and Lawrence Weider. "Ethnomethodology and the problem of order: comment on Denzin." Pp. 287-302 in Jack Douglas (Ed.), *Understanding Everyday Life.* Chicago: Aldine Publishing Co., 1970.

2

A Theory of the Definition of the Situation

Robert A. Stebbins

Since John Dewey, the pragmatic sociologists, and especially W. I. Thomas, the terms 'situation' and 'definition of the situation' have become much used in the textbooks, monographs, and articles of modern sociology, and even in the conversation of social scientists. There is a reason for this popularity. A powerful group of decisive social science traditions analyze social behaviour as a product of the situation and the actor's definition of it. The influence of these traditions prompted Professor Cottrell to state in his Presidential Address at the 1950 meeting of the American Sociological Society that "indeed sociology can be thought of as a discipline devoted to the analysis of social situations."[1] The Sherifs have defined social psychology as "the scientific study of the experience and behaviour of individuals in relation to social stimulus situations."[2]

Yet, conceptually, sociology finds itself in an awkward position, for the popularity of the term 'situation' is equalled by its vagueness. Both Volkart and Cottrell have complained of the indefiniteness of this term.[3] Even W.I. Thomas, who is usually given credit for having done the most work with the situational approach, occasionally used the term as a synonym for such varied concepts as social institution, neighbourhood, group, individual experience, and even a

---

The Canadian Review of Sociology and Anthropology, 1967, 4, 148-164, Reprinted by permission of the publisher, Fitzhenry and Whiteside Limited.

[1]Leonard S. Cottrell, Jr., "Some Neglected Problems in Social Psychology," *American Sociological Review,* XV, 711 (1950).

[2]Muzafer and Carolyn W. Sherif, *An Outline of Social Psychology,* rev. ed. (New York, 1956), 4.

[3]Edmund H. Volkart, "Introduction: Social Behavior and the Defined Situation," in William I. Thomas, *Social Behavior and Personality: Contributions of W. I. Thomas to Theory and Social Research* (New York, 1951), 29; Cottrell, "Some Neglected Problems in Social Psychology," 711.

complete illusion.[4] And Cottrell himself in an earlier article defined a social situation as "the system of self-other patterns comprising a given act," which is at bottom social interaction.[5] This confusion may be appreciated as a sign of the complexity of the idea of situation, a fact which most contemporary sociologists have apparently grasped, for they only occasionally attempt to define it. Even less frequently do they discuss, in general terms, what constitutes a situation.

Discussions of the definition of the situation are only slightly more prevalent than definitions of the concept of situation. Texts in social psychology have given only scattered attention to it and in most cases they have given no attention at all.[6] In fact, there is no adequate presentation of the full sequence of relevant activities, processes, and conditions which occur between the time a person enters a situation and when he finally begins to act with reference to it.[7]

It is this latter problem which this paper proposed to take up. We will be concerned with how one arrives at a definition of the situation and the relationship between this definition and behaviour in the situation. To answer these questions, a theory of the definition of the situation will be presented in the framework of a chronology from the time the actor enters the situation until he defines it and begins the relevant action. Additionally, because the idea of situation is a fundamental concept in this theory, it will be carefully defined and described.

THE OBJECTIVE AND SUBJECTIVE SITUATIONS

While for any individual a situation has observable social, physical, and physiological characteristics, it is fundamentally a mental construction the

---

[4] Volkart, "Introduction: Social Behavior and the Defined Situation," 29; Arnold Green, "The Social Situation in Personality Theory," *American Sociological Review,* VII, 388-93 (1942).

[5] Leonard S. Cottrell, Jr., "The Analysis of Situational Fields in Social Psychology," *American Sociological Review,* VII, 377 (1942).

[6] There are exceptions to this statement. See Theodore M. Newcomb, Ralph H. Turner, and Philip E. Converse, *Social Psychology: The Study of Human Relations* (New York, 1965), 67-71. One introductory text in sociology has recently devoted an entire chapter to the definition of the situation. See Glenn M. Vernon, *Human Interaction: An Introduction to Sociology* (New York, 1965), chap. 11.

[7] There are several discussions of the process of defining the situation, the most adequate being that by Florian Znaniecki, *Cultural Sciences* (Urbana, Ill., 1952), 242-60. Others include the following: Lowell J. Carr, *Situational Analysis* (New York, 1948), 19-25; Robert M. MacIver, *Social Causation* (New York, 1942), 291-300; Newcomb, *et al, Social Psychology: The Study of Human Relations,* Thomas, *Social Behavior and Personality, passim.;* W. I. Thomas and Florian Znaniecki, *The Polish Peasant,* Vols. I & II (New York, 1927), *passim.;* Vernon, *Human Interaction: An Introduction to Sociology.*

elements of which have been taken from a larger whole. This mental construction is partly realized through the process of selective perception: a sensitization to those elements of the environment which are of direct interest to the individual. It is also realized through the occasional infusion into the situation of values which are not objectively there or the exaggeration of the importance of certain elements actually present. Any rigorous effort to define situation must inevitably start here, for the vast array of potentially situational elements is greatly reduced by the actor through selective perception.

Many who have written about definition of the situation have acknowledged the effects of selective perception. However, most scholars have concentrated only on the selection of the social elements.[8] There can be little doubt of the importance of the physiological, psychological, and environmental circumstances in which the individual finds himself, and it is only reasonable that these be included as part of his mental construction of the situation. Moreover, since situations as perceived by the participant are selectively constructed, it is well to distinguish, as some scholars have done, between the "objective" and "subjective" situations. Thus, we shall define the objective situation as the immediate social and physical surroundings and the current physiological and psychological state of the actor. It is, as MacIver put it, "the situation as it might appear to some omniscient and disinterested eye, viewing all its complex interdependencies and all its endless contingencies."[9] The subjective situation shall be defined as those components of the objective situation which are *seen by the actor* to affect any one of his action orientations and therefore must be given meaning before he can act.[10] The term "action orientation" as used here refers to any purpose which the actor has as he enters the objective situation. This purpose may be one of relative unimportance such as going into the kitchen for a sandwich, or it may be a lifetime goal, such as striving to become president of the firm for which he works. The point is that action orientations guide behaviour at the time when the individual enters the objective situation.

The epistemological question raised here of whether or not a truly "objective" view is possible is being sidestepped. The objective situation is to be seen simply

---

[8] See Thomas and Znaniecki, *The Polish Peasant,* Vol. I, 68; Znaniecki, *Cultural Sciences,* 243. Thomas explicitly states that he is not interested in the "spatial-material" situation but in the situation of social relationships. See Thomas, *Social Behavior and Personality,* 87.

[9] MacIver, *Social Causation,* 295.

[10] There are definitions which are similar to the ones given here in that they incorporate the nonsocial as well as the social aspects of the setting. The basic difference is that these do not distinguish between objective and subjective situations. See H. J. Friedsam, "Social Situations," in Julius Gould and William L. Kolb, eds., *A. Dictionary of the Social Sciences* (New York, 1964), 667-68; Talcott Parsons and Edward A. Shils, "Values, Motives, and Systems of Action," in Parsons and Shils, eds., *Toward a General Theory of Action* (Cambridge, Mass., 1951), 56-57. Erving Goffman makes a twofold distinction between the physical "situation" and the more social "gathering" in *Behavior in Public Places* (New York, 1963), 18.

as the total collection of situational elements and their interrelationships from which the actor constructs his subjective situation. How we may get a view of the objective situation, if we can get such a view, is a philosophical issue of long standing and quite beyond the scope of this paper. For research purposes, however, one can operationalize it in at least two ways: (1) the social scientist's picture of the objective situation in which the actor finds himself; (2) the aggregate view of the objective situation as constructed from the individual views of a number of actors in the same situation. A combination of both definitions would appear to be the most adequate.

A basic feature of the situation for any individual is how it will affect his action orientations, for it is in these terms that certain situational elements become meaningful. These elements are selected out of the objective situation to become part of the subjective situation. It is this latter construction of the person's world that is of concern to sociologists. In this paper the term situation will refer to the subjective kind unless stated otherwise.

The Personal Structuring of the Subjective Situation

It has been asserted that action orientations guide the selection of elements from the objective situation for the construction of the subjective situation. While some sociologists seem to have been aware of the importance or purpose in this regard (especially MacIver), none of them have carried the matter to its logical next step: a description of these constructions from the standpoint of the actor's action orientation. A start toward such a description will be made here by

---

[11]Probably the point of greatest similarity between a related approach in psychology, ecological psychology, and the theory of the definition of the situation being developed here, is this attempt to distinguish situational boundaries and thereby to be able to separate one situation from another. However, ecological psychology differs in several critical ways from our approach. Foremost among these differences is that of theoretical background: ecological psychology is linked with the theories of Kurt Lewin while definition of the situation theory originated in the interactionist theories of W. I. Thomas and Florian Znaniecki, and the social action theories of Robert MacIver. Furthermore, the major theoretical concepts of ecological psychology, the "behaviour setting" and the "standing behaviour pattern," are limited to institutionalized situations, whereas the notion of "situation" as it is being developed here, and as it is used in sociology, can also be applied to noninstitutionalized circumstances. There is also a much greater concern with the definition of the situation here. Finally, the ecological psychologists appear to have little interest in the subjective situation. For an overview of ecological psychology see Roger G. Barker and Herbert Wright, *Midwest and Its Children* (Evanston, Ill., 1955), chap. 1; Roger G. Barker and Louise S. Barker, "Behavior Units for the Comparative Study of Cultures," in Bert Kaplan, ed., *Studying Personality Cross-Culturally* (New York, 1961), 457-76; Roger G. Barker, "Explorations in Ecological Psychology," *American Psychologist*, XX, 1-14 (January, 1965). For a discussion of the theoretical differences between Kurt Lewin and the founders of definition of the situation theory, see Don Martindale, *Nature and Types of Sociological Theory* (Boston, 1960), chaps. 14, 15, 19.

presenting some hypotheses about the delineation of temporal, social, and physical boundaries of subjective situations.

Temporal boundaries. One can do more than simply point out that subjective situations have time limits; that they do not go on forever. The action orientations of the person play a crucial role in time calculations, for situations exist as long as it takes him to manipulate them in terms of these ends. The simplest case is where a person has a single action orientation, say, to have a good time at a party. One's subjective situation is constructed around this orientation, and it will last as long as it takes to manipulate the relevant situational elements toward this end. When he becomes bored with the party and begins to entertain the idea of leaving it, a new subjective consideration arises initiating a new situation composed of partially new elements. For instance, the person in question begins to notice where the door is, how many others have already left, where his host and hostess are so that he may express his final gratitude for the party, and so forth.

Often the temporal relevance of situational elements for the actor is more complicated than this. Sometimes it is possible to pursue more than one action orientation at a time, or perhaps, situational elements may affect action orientations which are not salient at the moment, but which become so because of these situational circumstances. When this is the case the situation can be said to last as long as it takes an individual to manipulate it in terms of the end which he is *immediately* pursuing, that is, the end he was pursuing when he entered the objective situation. To return to the party example, let us say that the elements of this situation affect more than our actor's desire to have a good time. Perhaps he also sees a person there whom he has been trying to contact about the sale of his boat, or someone learns in conversation with him that he is interested in buying a boat and gives him the name of someone selling one. The subjective situation is now temporally structured in terms of two action orientations: having a good time and buying a boat. This situation will persist as long as it takes this person to manipulate it in terms of the goal which he is immediately pursuing, namely, that of having a good time. Manipulation is simply getting out of the situation all that one can in relation to one's purpose. When our actor has enjoyed himself as much as he desires or finds that he cannot enjoy himself at all, then another orientation takes over, in this case leaving the party. The subsidiary orientation of buying the boat may be present in both situations (he gives the boat seller a ride home), but the situation has changed because his principal action orientation has been realized or dropped and another has taken its place.

There are also types of time limits to subjective situations which usually are somewhat independent of the action orientations of an individual. One such class of time limits is the daily routines, either individually or culturally imposed, in which the person stops one activity in order to start another. Eating periods and work schedules are two of the most universal examples. Another class of time limits is referred to by Moore in a different context as *physiological* time demands.[12] He points out that, although such wants as sleep, food, and elimination are greatly elaborated and modified by society, the organism must ultimately attend to them. The satisfaction of these wants becomes an action orientation itself which eventually modifies other purposes of the actor.[13] And this new orientation signals the entry into a new subjective situation. These physiological time demands illustrate the necessity of including this component of the actor's experience as part of the subjective situation.

Social and physical boundaries. The social limits of the subjective situation are set by the interaction requirements of the individual's action orientation. In our party example these would involve all the people at the party who in some way affect the goal of having a good time, although some will be more directly concerned with the actor than others and at different times during the course of the situation. If he has more than one action orientation affected by the situation, then the social limits are expanded to include those persons affecting each.

In small closed situations where no one enters during the duration of the person's action orientation, the social boundaries are readily identified by the people present. In objective situations which involve a large, shifting number of individuals, such as a department store or railway station, subjective situations can be identified only by reference to the action orientations salient at that time. Arrivals and departures of individuals, where they are noticed, will be assessed for their relevance for the purposes at hand.

The subjective situation ranges as far spatially as the person can pick up meaningful stimuli: those elements which are seen to affect in some way his action orientations. In some situations barriers like doors, walls, distance, noise, darkness, physically limit situations. In others these barriers are not effective or simply do not exist, in which case the physical boundaries of the situation are set by the combined limits of sense perception.

Social convention plays a rôle in the subjective limiting of the physical situation as seen in Goffman's notion of the "conventional situational closure." Even though there is almost always the possibility of some communication across physical boundaries, social arrangements lead persons both inside and outside to act as if the barriers have cut off more than they actually have.[14] Similar conventions can also be observed with respect to physically unbounded social encounters within a larger collection of people.[15]

---

[12]Wilbert E. Moore, *Man, Time and Society* (New York, 1963), 15.

[13]The reader is no doubt aware of the exceptions to this statement, such as fasting to death.

[14]Goffman, *Behavior in Public Places,* 151-52.

[15]*Ibid.,* 156; Erving Goffman, *The Presentation of Self in Everyday Life* (Garden City, N.Y., 1959), 230.

In summary, a person temporally, socially, and physically structures his subjective situations in terms of his immediate action orientation. That subjective situations have these limits should not be taken to mean that we are always aware of them. It is probably true that most of the time we are not aware of or are only dimly aware of such boundaries. Much depends, no doubt, on the nature of the situation and the nature of one's action orientation.[16] The degree of awareness in any subjective situation should be established by empirical investigation. This discussion about awareness is limited to the boundaries of the subjective situation. The actor, as we shall see in a later section, is well aware of many of those elements of the situation which influence his action orientation.[17]

We have already noted that subsidiary orientations may be called out by the situated stimuli. Such an event is made possible by the fact that the temporal, social, and physical boundaries are not rigid but fluctuate within the subjective situation as a result of stimuli which are extraneous to the action orientation but occasionally attract attention for other reasons. These subsidiary orientations do not, however, delimit the situation unless they replace the orientation which the actor had when he entered that particular set of circumstances. If this happens then the actor has entered a new subjective situation. There is always this possibility that more than one subjective situation can occur within a single objective situation.

Uniqueness of the Objective and Subjective Situations

Objective situations are unique. In the words of W. I. Thomas "social situations never spontaneously repeat themselves, every situation is more or less new, for every one includes new human activities differently combined."[18] Moreover, converging definitions of similar subjective situations by many different actors

---

[16]The objective situation itself can influence this subjective boundary awareness of being closed or open. One is certainly more aware of the physical and social boundaries of the subjective situation when they are embodied in the limits of a small and relatively soundproof room than when they are, as at a public picnic grounds, based on quite nebulous and shifting stimuli. In the latter case the person's attention is constantly barraged by new stimuli, making him less certain where the boundaries of the subjective situation actually lie. Additionally, the individual's action orientation may be one of great importance to him so that he is less likely, than when it is of a more personally superficial nature, to be disturbed by extraneous stimuli. Thus, the action orientation of a person can influence boundary awareness.

[17]The fact that the actor is aware of the salient elements of the situation makes it possible to do research on the boundaries of the subjective situation. It is true that the actor is often not aware of what his action orientation leads him to overlook in the objective situation; thus, he is often not aware of a boundary. However, as researchers we may discover this boundary by determining what in the situation is of recognized importance to him, information which we can get directly from the individual.

[18]Thomas, *Social Behavior and Personality,* 158.

can change the objective situation.[19] We could also add that subjective situations are unique because of the disparate array of personal orientations which the different actors bring to a given setting, leading them to perceive different elements and form different temporal, social, and physical boundaries. Such an observation is based on the uniqueness of background and personality of each individual, a condition which makes itself felt even where the immediate action orientations of those present are the same.

Still, we should not let observations such as those made in the last paragraph deter us from carrying out generalizing sociological research simply because it is on unique phenomena. As Kaplan has stated in his rebuttal to the argument that behavioural science focuses on particulars and therefore can have no laws: "uniqueness does not imply that *nothing* is shared with other individuals, only that *not everything* is common to them."[20] And it is easy to find common features in the subjective situations of quite different people. For example, they share immediate action orientations such as watching a football game, shopping, or driving home from work. Some of these same people have similar backgrounds and attitudes which lead them, as we shall soon see, to structure and define their subjective situations in a similar way. In the same vein the objective situations of the football game, the shopping setting, and the setting of driving home from work have many common aspects. Uniqueness is a quality of situations, but it cannot be cited as a barrier to the scientific study of them.

Research on the Subjective Situation

These hypotheses about the temporal, social, and physical structuring of situations not only provide a start toward more accurate description but also facilitate research on the process of defining the situation and on the definition of the situation itself. In investigating objective situations which have not been examined before, as Goffman and Barker and Wright are doing, one of the crucial questions has been how do people react to them? In attempting to answer this question these scholars have spent considerable time describing the *objective* situation and the ongoing behaviour of the people in it. They are studying the situation *after* the actors have defined it.

---

[19]MacIver in his discussion of "group assessments" points out that separate definitions of the situation may eventually come together to form various sorts of group definitions, *Social Causation*, 300-313. Robert Merton, in effect, utilizes MacIver's idea in formulating his hypothesis of the "self-fulfilling prophecy." Under certain conditions if a group of people believe in a collective definition of the situation long enough it will come to influence behaviour and eventually change the objective situation. See Robert K. Merton, *Social Theory and Social Structure*, rev. ed. (New York, 1957), 421-36.

[20]Abraham Kaplan, *The Conduct of Inquiry* (San Francisco, 1964), 117.

One of the major themes of this paper is that there is much to be learned about situational behaviour by studying *what* it is that they are reacting to: that is, by studying their subjective situations and the process in which they are defined. What do they expect to get out of the objective situation? Which elements in it are important and which are not? How do the answers to these questions vary from one class of actors to another? To do this, we must be able to describe and delimit the subjective situation and the hypotheses about its boundaries can be highly useful for this purpose.

Research on subjective situations would necessarily be of the exploratory variety, because there has been so little of it. Thus we would want to rely, as did Thomas and Znaniecki, on techniques such as the life record, in-depth interviews, participant observation, and so forth.[21] In this sort of study we are ultimately looking for the common features of the subjective situations of classes of people. But, in order to discover that which is common, we must *first* examine everything, the common and the unique. Exploratory devices are well suited for this purpose.

Having defined and described the subjective situation, we turn now to a discussion of the definition of it. Here the situation as the individual perceives it and his personal background are combined to provide an interpretation of that situation.

Defining the Subjective Situation

Once the subjective situation has been identified by the actor he must interpret it or give it meaning in terms of his own background. This interpretation, which we shall discuss shortly, is the definition of the situation, and its final formulation is affected by a great many factors. These can be grouped into two categories: personality-cultural and situational.

The personality-cultural factors affecting the definition of the situation may be summarized as an organized set of predispositions which one brings to any situation.[22] Included among these are the individual's predispositions stemming from past definitions of situations, from his former and future plans of action, from his past and present action orientations, from his set of values and

---

[21]Thomas and Znaniecki in the *Polish Peasant* and Thomas in his later works emphasized the importance of personal records of all kinds in learning how a person defines a situation.

[22]This use of predisposition follows that of Newcomb, *et al., Social Psychology; The Study of Human Relations,* 40-46, 67-73.

attitudes,[23] and from his set of social and personal identities.[24] Thomas and Znaniecki's notion of the Four Wishes and Thomas' philistine and Bohemian types of personality also predispose the individual to act in certain ways under specified conditions.[25] Consequently, they help form this organized set of predispositions. Many of these have their origin in the society and its groups to which the actor belongs, in its moral and legal codes, in its special definers of situations (such as prophets, lawgivers, politicians, scientists, and judges).[26] And as these change so do the individual predispositions in which they are manifested. However, vague cultural definitions, because of rapid change, contribute to an absence of predispositions.

Some of these predispositions are not so social in origin. They are what Gordon Allport called *traits:* "a generalized and focalized neuropsychic system (peculiar to the individual), with the capacity to render many stimuli functionally equivalent, and to initiate and guide consistent (equivalent) forms of adaptive and expressive behaviour."[27]Utilizing Allport's idea, Yinger develops an important distinction in the set of predispositions. Predispositions are not all alike, but instead they vary from strong ones or "traits" (activated by many functionally equivalent stimuli) to weak ones or "attitudes" (activated by a specific stimulus).[28]

In addition to these predispositional factors there is the matter of the availability to the person of adequate linguistic symbols for describing the

---

[23]Some authors have grouped values and attitudes and past experience in general in the concept of "perspective." See Tamotsu Shibutani, "Reference Groups as Perspectives," *American Journal of Sociology,* LX, 562-69 (1955); Leon H. Warshay, "Breadth of Perspective," in Arnold M. Rose, ed., *Human Behavior and Social Processes* (Boston, 1962), 148-76.

[24]The concept of predisposition includes the dispositions to respond which are related to one's social identities as discussed in Nelson N. Foote, "Identification as the Basis for a Theory of Motivation," *American Sociological Review,* XVI, 18 (February, 1951). This point is suggested by Reinhard Bendix in the "discussion" which follows, 22. It also includes the idea of "role-identity" or an individual's imaginative view of himself as he likes to think of himself being and acting as an occupant of a particular position. George J. McCall and J. L. Simmons, *Identities and Interactions* (New York, 1966), chap. 4. The distinction between social and personal identity is clearly presented in Erving Goffman, *Stigma* (Englewood Cliffs, N.J., 1963), 55-65.

[25]Thomas and Znaniecki, *The Polish Peasant,* 1847; Thomas, *Social Behavior and Personality,* 159-60, 175.

[26]Thomas, *Social Behavior and Personality,* 108. It is in this connection that Znaniecki draws his distinction between "realistic attitudes" or definitions of the situation developed by agents in the course of action and "idealistic attitudes" or definitions of the situation presented by speakers and writers. See Znaniecki, *Cultural Sciences,* 260.

[27]Gordon Allport, *Personality* (New York, 1937), 295.

[28]J. Milton Yinger, *Toward a Field Theory of Behavior* (New York, 1965), 40.

subjective situation. Reflection, the process involved in structuring the situation and in defining it, demands the use of symbols of some kind.[29]

Of course, no situation is related to the entire set of predispositions of an individual, rather the elements of the subjective situation call out in him only the appropriate tendencies towards them. To repeat, these elements include all aspects of the objective situation which are seen by the actor to affect his action orientation. In this connection traits are activated in many more situations than are attitudes because they render many stimuli functionally equivalent.

While these elements are all factors which affect the definition of the situation, the social components are often the most important and the most complicated. There is the question of who are the others in the situation and their predispositions towards him and that situation. Certain relationships among the elements of the objective situation will be important and will come to be included in the subjective situation. Additionally, certain sequences of events, numbers of people and objects, and spatial relationships will be of significance. Finally, the degree of order among the elements will affect the definition of the situation.[30]

The Definition of the Situation

The definition of the situation is a more or less conscious synthesis and personal interpretation of the interrelation of the set of predispositions and the elements of the subjective situation. As Kurt Wolff has observed we may distinguish this, the actor's personal definition, from "cultural definitions" of the situation: "culturally formulated, embodied, and shared perceptions and interpretations of situations considered identical or similar".[31] Cultural definitions are collective representations which have developed from the interrelationship of many similar

---

[29]When one is reasoning he is indicating to himself the characters of the situation which call out certain responses. The gesture including language, among human beings serves to indicate these characters so that they may be brought into the field of our attention. George H. Mead, *Mind, Self, and Society* (Chicago, 1934), 93-95.

[30]For a further discussion of the various factors in the situation, see Sherif and Sherif, *An Outline of Social Psychology*, 121-24.

[31]Kurt Wolff, "Definition of the Situation," in Gould and Kolb, *A Dictionary of the Social Sciences*, 182. Cultural definitions, of course, become part of one's set of predispositions and influence the actor's definition of the situation. Wolff goes on to mention the fact that Znaniecki's "humanistic coefficient," Parson's "orientation," Weber's "meaning," and MacIver's "dynamic assessment" can be taken as synonyms of the concept of definition of the situation. It must be emphasized that the first three of these are synonyms for the notion of cultural definition only; MacIver's formulation is the sole synonym for the actors definition. This point is not always grasped in the literature. See, for example, the section entitled "Definition of the Situation" in Lewis A. Coser and Bernard Rosenberg, eds., *Sociological Theory: A Book of Readings*, 2nd ed. (New York, 1964), 231-58; or Jack L. Roach, "A Theory of Lower-Class Behavior," in Llewellyn Gross, ed., *Sociological Theory: Inquiries and Paradigms* (New York, 1967), 297.

personal definitions. Personal definitions, on the other hand, are more idiosyncratic (though in degree only), usually designed to interpret some situation for which there is no sufficient cultural definition. Chronologically, the definition of the situation immediately precedes the behaviour which manipulates or reacts to the subjective situation. It is important to note that this definition is arrived at only after a certain amount of conscious reflection, a point which Newcomb and his associates seem to miss in their formulation. Goal-oriented behaviour (or behaviour based on one's action orientation) is delayed long enough to allow the actor to define the situation and to formulate a plan of action or inaction or select an already formulated plan, whatever the definition suggests. Such plans are generally accompanied by justifications based on anticipated consummations and consequences.[32] The selection and formulation of a plan of action is part of the process of defining the situation and the definition of the situation includes such a strategy for action.

Between the time the actor enters the objective situation and the time he delineates and defines a subjective version of it, he is likely to behave either in a trial-and-error fashion or engage in little overt action at all. This period is predominantly one of reflection, and, until the situation can be defined and a plan of action selected, the individual is in a real sense immobilized; *goal-directed* action becomes possible only after the situation has been given meaning in terms of the current action orientation.

This process of reflection includes a number of different activities. It has already been indicated earlier that reasoning involves the presentation to oneself of the salient characteristics of the situation. The various predispositions to behave which these characteristics call out must be assessed from the standpoint of one's past experience with them and their future consequences. Thus, reflection requires the utilization of images, memory images of past acts and images of the completion of one's action orientation.[33] Moreover, reflection includes implicit testing of the alternatives, and possibly a recombining of the various elements of the situation to elicit still more predispositions. Here Mead calls our attention to the usefulness of the hands as one way of bringing new elements into our awareness.

Definitions of situations in general demand varying amounts of reflection. There is a class of situations which call for habitual behaviour and therefore are characterized by *almost* no reflection because there are no recognized new elements in the subjective situation to define. Starting one's car (on a normal day), or getting dressed in the morning, can be cited as examples. Nevertheless, these habitual and routine situations can be seen as calling for a defining of the situation, even though it is generally nothing more than a recognizing of the fact

---

[32]Anselm L. Strauss, *Mirrors and Masks: The Search for Identity* (New York, 1959), 51.
[33]Mead, *Mind, Self and Society,* 99, 337-46.

that they are like many other situations for which the individual and/or society have established personal or cultural definitions.[34] The observation made earlier in this paper on the uniqueness of objective situations forces us to conclude that, to the extent in which the novel elements are perceived in the subjective version of these situations, there will be a small but definite amount of reflection required.

A second class of situations are those which are sufficiently unusual to cause the actor to pause long enough to place them in a familiar category. A person driving at night may wonder about the identity of the car behind him; is it a police car or an ambulance or simply a taxicab? The final definition of the situation will make a difference in how fast he drives. Definitions of this sort are generally conventional ones for the individual and/or the community, definitions which he has used before or recognizes that others use. This class of situations differs from the first in that the situations, while familiar, are not habitual or routine. Consequently, they require more reflection before they can be defined.

The greatest amount of reflection is demanded when the subjective situation is so unusual that a relatively new definition of the situation is called for. Crisis situations, such as the sudden death of a significant other or a natural calamity, are examples. Less dramatic, but still requiring considerable reflection, are the unexpected events connected with everyday living; for instance, an unexpected encounter with an old friend, or happening upon an automobile accident. However, it should be noted that regardless of the amount of reflection no definition is completely new. It is always drawn in part from preceding experiences and predispositions and also, as Schutz has suggested, from the general style in which members of the community are accustomed to dealing with extraordinary events.[35] It can be hypothesized here that the degree of novelty in the actor's definition of the situation is directly related to the degree of novelty for him in the subjective situation.

---

[34]Thomas, *Social Behavior and Personality,* 158. Znaniecki in *Cultural Sciences* missed this point that definitions of the situation (cultural definitions) may be brought to the situation. For a critique on this point and others in Znaniecki's work, see William L. Kolb, "The Changing Prominence of Values in Modern Sociological Theory," in Howard Becker and Alvin Boskoff, eds., *Modern Sociological Theory: In Continuity and Change* (New York, 1957), 104-105.

[35]Alfred Schutz, *Collected Papers: Studies in Social Theory,* Vol. II, Arvid Brodersen, ed. (The Hague, 1964), 109.

Vastly new situations seem to elicit emotional reactions but demand rational consideration.[36] They are vague and unsettling, and yet if one is going to pursue his action orientation effectively he must be rational in defining them. Where crisis situations bring on extreme emotional reactions, we can expect intelligent judgments and skilful activities to suffer from the resulting overmotivation.[37] This throws into doubt Znaniecki's assertion that "whenever considerable reflection is involved, intellectual processes predominate."[38]

Types of Definitions of the Situation

It is probably true that most of the time the individual is defining a concrete or ongoing situation in which he finds himself at a particular moment. However, as Znaniecki observes, there are also definitions which are prospective, which refer to situations which the definer believes he will or may face in the future.[39] And one can define situations in the opposite direction; retrospective definitions refer to situations which were faced in the past. In this case the individual has redefined that situation after the benefit of intervening experience. Finally, definitions can be vicarious. These refer to other's situations whether they be present, past, or future. In all of these instances one first imaginatively constructs

---

[36]By the phrase "rational consideration" is meant *reasoned* consideration as opposed to unreasoned and emotional consideration. The reader should be careful not to confuse the defining of the situation with the total rational social act as discussed by Weber and Mead. The difference lies in the fact that the definition of the situation is only the subjective and reflective part of the larger rational act; in Mead's theory it would be the "perception" phase of the act. See George H. Mead, *The Philosophy of the Act* (Chicago, 1938), 3-25. In Weber's classification of types of action the definition of the situation would be found in varying degrees of reflection in all of them, the greatest amount of reflection being exhibited generally in the rational and evaluative kinds, the least amount in affectual and traditional forms. See Max Weber, *The Theory of Social and Economic Organization*, trans., Talcott Parsons (New York, 1947), 115-18.

[37]Laurance F. Shaffer and Edward J. Shoben, Jr., *The Psychology of Adjustment*, 2nd ed. (Boston, 1956), 57. In many nonsocial tasks the efficiency of performance seems initially to increase with increasing arousal and then to decline. This varies, however, with the complexity of the task and learned patterns of response inhibition and control. Richard H. Walters and Ross D. Parke, "Social Motivation, Dependency, and Susceptibility to Social Influence," in Leonard Berkowitz, ed., *Advances in Experimental Social Psychology*, Vol. I (New York, 1964), 235.

[38]Znaniecki, *Cultural Sciences*, 247. It is also doubtful that Znaniecki's further comment on this matter is entirely valid. He states that "whenever relatively little reflection is involved, the definition of the situation is predominantly influenced by emotions and/or volitions of the agent." There is very little reflection involved in habitual behaviour or in reaction to situations which merely require recognition as being familiar. At the same time reflection here is not particularly influenced by emotions or volitions, for the definition of the situation mostly involves selecting a suitable pattern of behaviour learned in the past. Znaniecki's difficulty lies in the fact that he did not specify which kinds of situation are characterized by emotion or intellect.

[39]*Ibid.*, 251.

or reconstructs a subjective situation in the manner previously described and, after a degree of reflection, defines it.

This suggests that an individual's definition of a situation may change from one situation to another. It may change retrospectively after similar and now familiar situations are faced or just after the action orientation is completed. It may change subsequently as when one actually finds himself in the situation which he prospectively defined and now discovers it to be vastly different from what he expected. Vicarious definitions can also be seen to change with experience and knowledge.

Further, it should be noted that any definition can eventually influence a person's future action orientations. For instance, a college student may abandon his goal of a college degree after a retrospective definition of a number of negative examination situations or a series of financial situations where he has just barely had enough money to stay in school. These retrospective definitions (perhaps accompanied by other types of definitions as well) become part of one's set of predispositions at some future point in time, and play a part in transforming related action orientations. In short, while it is common knowledge that people's goals change, it is not so widely known that such changes are rooted in definitions of situations. The hypothesis being advanced here is that such goal changes require *interpreted* information or experience or both; goal transformation is, in the last analysis, rooted in *definitions* of situations, whether retrospective, ongoing, prospective, or vicarious. It is not rooted in the experience or information per se.

Although past theorists have paid little attention to this fact, it is evident that definitions of the situation change while the situation is in progress. Situations are structured by the immediate action orientation of the person, and as new elements which pertain to it enter his awareness or leave it new predispositions may be called out and incorporated in a new assessment. Thus, definitions of the situation may be retrospective *within* the situation as well as between situations. It seems, too, that they could also be prospective, in that as a person manipulates the situation with respect to his action orientation he comes to realize that, for example, he will be able to do a better job when so-and-so arrives or when certain tools are made available. And certainly definitions of the same situation could be *conditional,* as when one could do a better job *if only* he had better tools or if so-and-so *would only* come by. Changing definitions of the situation should not be construed as a change in the subjective situation, unless, of course, the immediate action orientation changes.

SUMMARY AND CONCLUSIONS

This paper has attempted to answer two questions: how does a person arrive at a definition of the situation and what is the relationship between this definition and behaviour in the situation? To answer these questions, a theory of the definition of the situation was presented in the framework of a chronology from the time the actor enters the situation until he defines it and begins the relevant action. In this theory the distinction between objective and subjective situation was emphasized, the objective situation being defined as the immediate social and physical surroundings and the current physiological and psychological state of the actor. The subjective situation was defined as those components of the objective situation which are seen by the actor to affect any one of his action orientations and therefore must be given meaning before he can act. By means of the action orientation or immediate purpose of the individual, a framework for delimiting the temporal, social, and physical boundaries of the subjective situation was presented.

Factors affecting the defining of the subjective situation were grouped into two categories: personality-cultural and situational. The personality-cultural factors were summarized under the idea of the set of organized predispositions. Certain predispositions to behave are called out by the elements of the subjective situation. However, the actual behaviour manipulating or reacting to the situation is preceded by the definition of the situation, the more or less conscious synthesis and interpretation of the interrelation of the set of predispositions and the subjective situation. The process of reflection and the definition of the situation were discussed, and this was followed by an examination of types of definitions of the situation.

One of the important assumptions in social science is the idea that human beings interpret or give meaning to the vast array of stimuli perceived in everyday life. Certainly, the actor's definition of the situation is one significant category of such interpretations, and it provides, within the situation itself, an important backdrop for other kinds of interpretations (e.g., interpretation of specific situational stimuli as they relate to the action orientation and the definition of the situation).

The fact that this is a major social science assumption (and not a testable, or at least testworthy, proposition) should not be allowed to obscure the importance of the total theory presented in this paper. This theory, along with the proper confirmatory evidence, tells us something which we *cannot* afford to assume: namely, *how* one defines a situation. It is, in brief, much more than another example of methodological individualism or even a basic social scientific postulate. Knowledge about how the situation is defined and what the definition of the situation is composed of can, as was suggested earlier, answer pertinent questions. This knowledge can tell us what people in situations are reacting to. It enables us to determine, from the "humanistic perspective," which elements of the situation are important for the actor and eventually for classes of actors.

The most urgent task at present is to put these formulations to empirical test, for scarcely any research has been conducted on them.[40] True, sociologists and social psychologists have talked about the definition of the situation for several decades, and they have used it in countless *post factum* explanations of any number of phenomena. However, this does not constitute an empirical testing of theoretical propositions, nor does it, given the current state of verification of the theory, make for strong explanation.[41] What is needed is a series of direct empirical tests of the propositions; the kind which Merton informs us is so rare in sociology and which is especially hard to find in the symbolic interactionist school of thought, the birth place of these theoretical ideas on definition of the situation.

Investigations should be carried out directly on the process of defining the situation and on the resulting definition, using initially, as we have already proposed, exploratory techniques. Gorden's experiment suggests that laboratory procedures might also be useful in this connection. Finally, we have seen that the definition of the situation, both as a process and as an individual state of information about a setting, is a complex affair, and it is on these grounds that the researcher is cautioned against studies which infer the definition from behaviour without directly studying it.

The problem is that too many social scientists willingly assume they know the definitions of the situation of their subjects or respondents simply because they are members of the same culture. (Many anthropologists must be exempted from this indictment.) But how do we know that this is an assumption we can afford to make? After all, modern Western societies are highly complex social systems, and there are many aspects of them which social scientists readily admit that they know little about. Indeed, it is much easier to be impressed with how little we know about life in these societies, than with how much. Some of this unknown complexity is manifested in the definitions of situations of the many subcultural groups. Some of it, too, may well be manifested in the definitions of situations of middle-class people about which we think we know so much. Whatever the case, the canons of science do not allow us to assume that we have the knowledge, at least until we have carried out much more research on the matter. When we do this we will likely discover that we have been missing out on some important data about human behaviour.

---

[40]The author could uncover only one study outside of the works by Thomas and Znaniecki which explicitly tested hypotheses about the definition of the situation. See Raymond L. Gorden, "Interaction between Attitude and the Definition of the Situation in the Expression of Opinion," *American Sociological Review*, XVII, 50-58 (1952). Given the confused state of the theory, it is little wonder that so little research has been carried out on this subject.

[41]Merton, *op. cit.*, 93-95.

3

The Dramaturgical Model*

Rom Harré

This is perhaps the oldest analytical model of all. We see and hear a simulacrum of life on the stage. Perhaps the way that simulacrum is created and the illusion sustained can be a guide to our understanding of how real life is created. There are obvious differences between real life and stage drama, and it would be as well, to prevent misunderstanding, to notice them now. Stage drama selects from, simplifies and heightens the act/action sequences and personal presentations of real life. Time is foreshortened. Only a few of the many threads of everyday life are followed. Resolutions are frequently achieved in contrast to the endless postponements of the daily round. Issues are faced rather than dodged; lies are discovered and so on. Furthermore a more clearly developed and fully articulated aesthetic frame controls the presentations of the people and the unfolding of their affairs. Life, too, is partly managed in accordance with aesthetic standards, which parallel those of the stage quite closely, but they are rarely dominant.

Despite all the differences the likenesses are worth exploiting. At the very least, as Goffman has observed, the way an actor shows he is a certain kind of person must parallel the way anyone would show, in a certain social milieu, that they are that kind of person.[1] Without some such matching the actor's performance would not 'work' and the audience would not know what he was doing or what kind of person he was supposed to be. The parallel is not perfect since actors and audiences may share certain conventions about the expression of these matters that once reflected everyday life but have long since ceased to do so. For instance we have no trouble recognizing the villain in a melodrama despite the fact that no one behaves that way any longer, if indeed they ever did carry on quite like that.

What then can we draw from the model? Primarily it is an analytical scheme, coupled with a specially watchful kind of consciousness—at once the conscious-

*R. Harré: Social Being (1979), 190-206. Reprinted by permission of the publisher, Blackwell Scientific Publishers Ltd.

ness of the actor, the producer, the audience and the critic. To adopt the model is to take a certain kind of stance to the unfolding of everyday life and to the performances of the people who live it. It could be described as an ironic stance, a viewpoint from which life goes forward, becomes visible. For the means of action are not usually attended to, so much do we concentrate on the aims and outcomes of our activities.

As a source-model for developing analyses of everyday activities the dramaturgical model leads to two interlocking conceptual systems. Looking ironically at the performance we can begin to analyse it according to the scheme proposed by Burke.[2] We can look for the way the kind of scene we are to be in is indicated. Scenes are complex objects including both the setting, the physical surrounding, stage props, and so on; and the situation, the human predicament which the unfolding of the drama will, we hope, resolve. The drama unfolds through the performances of the actors, playing parts, in styles we must be able to recognize. The action of the play is usually determined by a script, though actors and producers place their own interpretations on it. In improvised and experimental theatre the script may be reduced to a bare scenario, suggesting the predicament, the persons and the resolution, but leaving the performance and sometimes even the resolution to be created in the course of the action.[3]

Interlocking with all this is the interpretative activity of the producer. He proposes a reading, though his success depends on how far the audience can be persuaded to share it. By taking something of the position of both audience and producer, critics provide informed commentary upon the action, upon the players and their performance, upon the scene and the scenario. And this too can be looked at dramaturgically. It is a performance by people playing the parts of critics in the unfolding of yet another scenario.

As people living our own lives we are among the actors performing our parts in well or ill-defined scenes, sometimes fully scripted, sometimes improvising. As producers, audience and critics, we appear as social scientists commenting upon the drama. But as people playing the parts of social scientists in appropriate scenes we are performers in yet another drama.

A. SCENE ANALYSIS

1. Setting

(a) **Introduction.** All our actions are carried out against a structured background. The physical settings are not neutral. They contribute to the action. Settings broadcast messages of reassurance and threat. Until recently the messages from the background, social musak so to speak, were taken for granted as part of the common-sense world. However, the structure of settings and their manner of working on human social feelings was much discussed in the past. In the Renaissance various general theories were proposed: from Albertus Magnus to Kepler a variety of theories were broached.[4] But it is only very recently that sociologists and social psychologists have turned their attention to analysing and understanding settings. The environment of action, as meaningful to the actors, Burke called the 'scene'. It has several components. The physical scene can be considered first as to its overall spatio-temporal structure, and then as to the meaning of the various things with which it is furnished, including smells, colours, the state of the weather, and so on. In this section I shall be concerned only with the former, and shall speak of it, with a small measure of license, as the *Umwelt*. Just as each species of animal has its own spatial environment, in every given area each category of people, professions and sexes, families and age groups, have different spaces within which they freely move, all, for example, within the one city. Each has some spaces proper to itself alone.

We must first take a stand on the central matter of the nature of the environment of social action, whether we should follow Skinner or Kant; whether we should regard the environment as external to the action, or identify at least some of the properties of the environment of action as human products. I have argued in an earlier section for a generally Kantian outlook, which seems to me so utterly indisputable that I can find little to debate about with the other side. That a traffic light is what it is as part of the environment of social action by a social endowment of 'red', 'green', etc. with meanings, and those meanings embedded and maintained within a system of rules, seems to me so obvious that the idea that it is redness as a physical stimulus that brings me to brake can scarcely be taken seriously. Furthermore, it is also clear that the Skinnerian view must be wrong if applied to the institutional environment since that is clearly a product of knowledge and understanding. I hope that as our analysis of the *Umwelt* unfolds we shall see that much the same is true of the 'physical' environment.

The socially significant environment includes many nonstructural features. In countries with very variable weather the moods of the inhabitants can be much influenced by these changes. The significance of such moods may be great and read back into nature as a kind of social meteorology. I shall not be concerned with a detailed analysis of these features of the environment in this section, but only with the interrelated structures we impose on space and time, and the structures we build with things and events within space and time.

The socially meaningful physical environment within which we live seems to have two degrees of structure, two levels of granularity. The course-grained structure consists of distinct and separated areas in space and periods in time, distinguished as the places and times of socially distinct activities. For instance, the social activities of the street are quite distinct from those inside a bank adjoining that street, and opening off it. This is one of those obvious truths that should yet surprise us. How do I know that I am in the counting hall of a bank and that I should behave reverently therein? Part of the answers to these questions are to be found by *looking* at the décor of the banking hall. Our first task will be to examine some of the ways in which socially distinct areas and volumes of space and periods of time are demarcated and maintained. In this way the coarse-grained structure of the *Umwelt* will be revealed.

But each area and volume, and each period of time, and each thing within an area and each pattern of action within a time, has a structure which differentiates it from other things and makes it thereby a potential vehicle of significance or meaning. These are the fine-grained structures of the *Umwelt*. How are these structures socially significant? I shall try to establish, with a wide range of examples, that we create and maintain such structures and endow them with meaning as a kind of permanent or semi-permanent bill-board or hoarding upon which certain socially important messages can be 'written'. The very fact of order, when recognized by human beings, is, *in itself,* the source of a message that all is well. Orderliness of the physical environment broadcasts a kind of continuous social musak whose message is reassurance. But, as we shall see, the fine structuring of the *Umwelt* allows us to give and receive much more specific messages, public statements of how we wish to be taken as social beings. I will try to show, in broad outline, how these more specific messages are achieved.

If we define the *Umwelt* of a human being as he or she is a person of a certain social category, we could express this in a formula:

Umwelt = Physical Environment × Social Meanings.

This formula could be taken literally as a Boolean product. Thus if someone were to be found to be using two interpretative schemata, A and B, then $U = P \times (A \vee B)$ leads to $U = (P \times A) \vee (P \times B)$; in short that person lives in two *Umwelten*.

The Structure of an Umwelt: Boundaries in Space and Time Creating and Demarcating Socially Distinct Regions. As we pass through space and time we are continually adjusting ourselves to a complex social topography. Some regions are closed to us, some open. For some various keys or magic passwords are required, such as 'Oh yes, I'm a member here'. Looking at this ethogenically we must ask how these barriers are established and promulgated, how they are maintained, how legitimately crossed, how their accidental violation is remedied. This will reveal what the social structure of the topography thus established might be.

As an introductory illustration, consider the time barrier that separates the period before a school lesson from the lesson itself. It may be created by the ringing of a bell which separates two socially distinct regions. In the period before the lesson the social structure of the class is a complex network of microsocial groupings, one of which, usually the most socially powerful, may include the teacher. The whole interaction pattern is organized as 'chat'. After the lesson starts the social order simplifies into a one-many hierarchy, with the children oriented to the teacher, and an almost complete disappearance of the 'chatting' style of speech which characterized the previous period.

Spatial boundaries, like fences or white lines on the ground, demarcate socially distinct areas. Such social topographies may reflect the polarity between a safe and a dangerous area. But the boundaries may be invisible. Urban Americans are all too familiar with the feeling of relief and relaxation as one passes beyond Such and Such Street, into a 'safe' area.

The structures created by boundaries and associated barriers, the physical markers of boundaries, like fences in space and silences in time, can be very differently related to deliberate human effort. The English Channel is *there,* as is the moment of death, and both have to be coped with, whereas taking a stick and scratching a line on the sand, 'That's your team's home base' or beginning by 'O.K. let's get started', are more or less free creations. They can be challenged and are subject to negotiation in ways that death and geography cannot be. But some human constructions are geographical features, such as permanent architectural or agricultural arrangements. Time is structured permanently by such artifacts as clocks and calendars. Just as our only social response to such entities as the English Channel or the coming of spring can be semantic attributes of meaning, expressed in such famous aphorisms as 'Wogs start at Calais', or 'Oh to be in England now that Spring is here', so we may negotiate the meaning of an hour or of the Great Pyramid. Finally, in contrast to these permanent structurings are the wholly ephemeral, such as the lane changes in 'tidal flow' traffic schemes, and the agreement on the structure of times by which the order of speakers at a meeting is decided by the chairman. Most of the boundaries and barriers we will be examining in detail are neither so unresponsive to human renegotiation as the solar year of the Atlantic Ocean, nor as ephemeral as the chalked grid for street hop-scotch, or the intervention, 'I wish you'd shut up and let A have a chance to say something'.

Time structure and its marking. I shall call the boundaries of conventionally marked, socially distinct time-periods, 'openings' and 'closings' following Schegloff and Sacks.[5] A prime social differentium is whether opening and closing is done for one or achieved by the participant himself. We must also ask whether the openings and closings are natural or contrived.

Close observation of the way beginnings and ends of activities were managed in a kindergarten shows that the initial and final moves in the sequence of an activity are separated from the rest of the activity by being performed in a particularly flamboyant and exaggerated way. Their natural role as beginnings and endings is stylistically enhanced to demarcate the boundaries of distinctive times.

Social closings are notoriously more difficult to achieve than openings. One can, in desperation, just start. However, as a general rule things do not just start, they are opened by the recital of a ritual formula or the performance of a symbolic action: 'Oyez, Oyez, Oyez, as it pleases the Queen, Her Gracious Majesty . . .', cutting the ribbon to open the road, and so on. The variety and sources of such formulae would no doubt repay close sociological study.

The closing of conversations as socially distinct intervals of time has been much illuminated by the studies of Sacks and Schegloff. The problem is created by the fact that the normal ending of an utterance is not a sign of the ending of a conversation, rather it is the signal for next speaker. How is this transition relevance suspended?

Schegloff and Sacks found that there are two ways of generating a terminal section. A speaker can insert a preclosing phrase such as 'Well, O.K. . . .' to mark the end of a topic in such a way that a terminal sequence can politely be introduced. Alternatively one can pick up a topic at the beginning of an interaction to allow for a warrantable lead in the closing section.

The problem of natural openings and closings arises as a separate issue. We have already noticed the technique by which natural initial and terminal parts of a sequence can be stylistically elevated to become openings and closings. Some natural events could find no other place in the sequence than as beginnings and endings. Such for example, are spring and autumn, birth and death. They are not, therefore, available for stylistic heightening *as* openings and closings, they *are* openings and closings. But their importance is too great for them to merely pass by, unattended and unstressed. They become surrounded by ceremony. In general this network of natural openings and closings forms a closed system of metaphors, each binary opposition serving as a metaphor for the others.

Spatial structure and its marking. The boundaries of spaces may be marked by relatively insurmountable barriers, such as high walls, or wide waterways. Such barriers enter social reality only when they are given a meaning by a participant. Does the prison wall keep the prisoner in, or the unpredictable and threatening forces of society out? Is a prison a cage or a refuge? Does its wall show its sheer fact inwards or outwards? Clearly the sense of the wall, its vectorial significance, is a function of the way the areas within and without are socially conceived.

Other boundaries are marked by physically surmountable barriers, visible like low walls and white lines, invisible like the high and low status areas of a schoolroom, or the volume of private space around a person. Most boundaries tend to close up on themselves, enclosing areas. Social areas have portals, visible or invisible. These portals are generally valve-like. Passage out is easier than passage in, so that while not all who aspire are admitted, all who have been admitted eventually come out. In public buildings there is often a ceremonial performance involved in achieving entry but a mere valedictory nod marks acceptable leaving of the enclosed volume or area.

Invisible boundaries must be maintained through shared knowledge. They are usually generated by some potent or sanctified dangerous object at their centre. Goffman and others have noticed that the area around a 'with', a group who are bound together by social ties and who let it be seen that they are so, moves with the 'with'. Contrary walkers skirt around it. Similarly a person may leave a potent trace such as a pair of sunglasses and a towel upon a crowded beach, creating an unencroachable boundary. A participant has reported that around the door of a school staff-room there is an arc of inviolability, beyond which the pupils will not normally go. If forced to do so they exhibit signs of considerable uneasiness and distress.

The social texture of space and time. The original idea of a social texture to space and time comes from Lewin[6] who proposed a kind of vector analysis to represent the power of attributions of meaning to different features of an environment. This is particularly easy to illustrate in the behaviour of men involved in the trench warfare of the war of 1914-1918, where the terrain was textured by its potential as a source of danger and of protection from hostile action.

So far we have taken the physical topography as a datum, and seen how it can be endowed with meaning. But the microstructure of the *Umwelt* may be organized as a social topography. A concept like 'social distance' could be introduced to express the rarity and difficulty of a transition from one socially marked space to another.

Goffman's analysis of the texture of threat[7] in an urban *Umwelt* illustrates a space organized along one dimension of social meaning. In a dangerous section of a city the grid pattern of streets is replaced by a modulating structure of clear and dubious areas, areas in which someone might be lurking, the possibility constituting the threat. The boundary between the space that can be seen to be empty and the space that is obscured Goffman calls a 'lurk line'. The threat texture of a grid pattern of streets, from a momentary vantage point in the passage of O, our man on Michigan Avenue, as he passes through the street corner, would look something like Fig. 3.1.

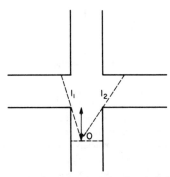

Figure 3.1 L_1 and L_2 are 'lurk lines' and the shaded and unshaded areas represent the structure of the texture of threat. As O moves forward the structural properties of the space change.

A pleasanter illustration of social topography can be found in the social map of a kindergarten. The map is plotted in two dimensions, staff sanctity v. child sanctity and comfort v. threat. The geographical map of the kindergarten (including play area) looks like Fig. 3.2:

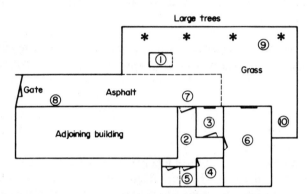

Figure 3.2   *Key* (1) Wendy house, (2) Lobby, (3) Staffroom, (4) Kitchen, (5) Lavatories, (6) Play room, (7) Near play area, (8)Far play area, (9) Distant grass, (10) Unobserved areas. Observation shows that children do not play in the areas marked (9) and (10).

Plotting these areas on the social map we get a topography such as in Fig. 3.3:

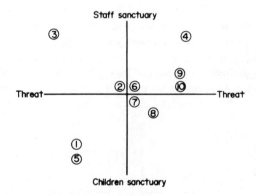

Figure 3.3   (5) and (4), though geographically adjacent, and from a spatial point of view therefore easy of mutual access, are socially very distant, and passage from one to the other is very difficult for a child. Entry to (4) is a special occasion and under close supervision, occurring only for those whose job it is to wash the cups, or for a 'cooking' group who prepare something for a playmate's birthday. (2), (6) and (7) are completely mutually open and the children and staff pass freely from one to the other, without social portals, that is rituals of passage like knocking or asking. But there are portals to be passed in making the passage from (2), (6) and (7) into (3), the teachers' room, whose door is ordinarily closed. The staff assert that the toilets are a child sanctuary which they do not enter, but observation shows that their sanctity is seldom taken seriously.[8]

Message-specific structures. The procedures and rituals we have examined so far serve to divide or bound socially distinct spaces and times. Within those areas and periods there are spatial and temporal structures, the arrangement of furniture in a room, or the complex orderliness of a meal. Viewed dramaturgically, these entities are the props which further define the scene, and which together with the *Umwelt* make up the setting. Such structures have a social meaning. But before examining some examples in detail we must ask how a physically structured feature of an environment can have meaning. Social meanings are also given to and read off qualitative properties, such as colours, for example red flags, brown shirts, black skins and so on. These do occur in the *Umwelt,* but as separable items, so I shall not pursue the question of their semantics here, but deal only with entities differentiated by their structural properties. A semantic unit is a structure and is embedded within a structure or structures. The internal structure presents no particular problems provided we recognize that the structure of the unit may be extended in space, in which case we shall look for its synchronic form, or extended in time, in which case we shall look for its diachronic layout. Provided entities are structurally differentiated they can bear distinctive meanings. In the traffic code a triangle has one meaning and a circle another, while in dog-handling the melodic differences between one whistle and another, structurally differentiated in time, are distinct signals. In general the semantic field of an item includes relations of exclusion, such as that between a circle and a triangle, whose meanings exclude each other; and inclusive relations such as that between a triangle and its red colour, relations that range from synomyny through metaphor to metonymy. To express a meaning, then, we must lay out as much of the semantic field as is required to distinguish this entity as meaningful from other items within their possible common contexts.

Furniture arrangements. If we examine a permanent arrangement of furniture in an office we are studying a structure that is physical, laid out in space. Each distinct layout can be assigned a social meaning. Studies have shown that the way furniture is arranged in an office is not just a matter of convenience but is a symbolic representation of the standing of the occupant.[9]

In general the principles seem to be the following:

(i)   the desk parallel to a wall is of lower status than at an angle to a wall;
(ii) the desk against a wall is of lower status than freestanding;
(iii) sitting on the side exposed to the door is of lower status than sitting on the side away from the door.

Applying these rules together we find that the person whose desk is freestanding, at an angle to the wall, and who sits behind the desk facing the door, is of the highest category admitted by that organization, a fact expressed in his furniture for all to see. He whose desk is up against the wall, who works with his back to the door on the exposed side, is the lowest. Whatever airs he may give himself his furniture shows his position for all to see. How far this code is general among bureaucratic man is uncertain, but the study reported covered both English Civil Servants and Swedish Executives, so it has some measure of generality as a sign system. An explanation of the etymology of the semantics is readily forthcoming from Goffman's theory of front and backstage divisions of personal territory. The person of low status is totally exposed, he or she has hardly any backstage area. His whole official life is enacted frontstage. He is under perpetual threat of supervision. But a simple visualizing of the plan of the office of the highest grade shows that tucked away behind his angled desk, he has the greatest amount of private space (of backstage) of any of the possible arrangements. Equally, and probably complementarily, the topology would admit of a Durkheimian account in terms of the protection of and at the same time the exhibition of the sanctity or inviolability of the highest status person, whose body is surrounded by a large protective area, freeing him from the possibility of profanation. There must surely be an element of truth in both accounts, and further study could probably elicit their balance in the way the furniture arrangement is read by the various individuals who act within it as their *Umwelt*.

The structure of food and drink episodes. A meal is a sequential eating of dishes which has a diachronic structure, while each dish, consisting of a variety of objects, is a synchronic structure. Dishes will be differentiated according to the salt/sweet dichotomy, as well as more finely by their ingredients. Along the diachronic dimension we shall ask whether one dish is served before or after another. I will be using a generally syntactical model for the analysis, though its applicability to the analysis of meals derives from their formal properties rather than their function as the vehicles of social meaning. As a part of the setting a meal may be orderly or disorderly. As an orderly event it contributes a general air of stability and rightness to the day.

There are two sets of distinctions to elucidate, those between cuisines and those between meals within a cuisine. Both the rules of cuisine and the rules for meals generate menus, plans for meals, which are concretely realized as actual structures in time, the elements of which are dishes. The rules ensure that despite the great variety of specific food items, repetition of structurally isomorphic sequences occurs day after day, week after week, at a fairly high level of perception, which are 'proper' meals. Since structure is, by itself, a source of intelligibility, the setting is stabilized at that point, and needs no further referent.[10]

The high degree of structural differentiation of meals not only serves to stabilize the setting but allows social meaning to be given to food items and drinks, as the differentiated elements in a simple symbolic system. A meal or meal-like social event, such as 'drinks', can convey a message concerning the relations among the people attending. The elements may have a more specific semantic loading. Perhaps this is part of the explanation of the alleged but quite mythological aphrodisiac properties of certain foods, such as oysters and champagne. They may have come to be sexually meaningful objects (the sea shell and the bottle with liquid foaming out as female and male symbols respectively). Though they have no special biochemical properties and are not causal agents in the ordinary sense, they may nevertheless be effective agents of sexuality through metonymy.

Interaction between the Structure of the Setting and Social Theory. The structure of a setting may be an icon of the social theory, that is the physical structure of a setting may function as a meaning-bearing entity, that is as a significant icon of the content of certain propositions within the cosmology of a people. A detailed and well documented example is P. Bourdieu's analysis of the microcosmic organization and meaning of the Berber house.[11] One might also cite Levi-Strauss's analysis of the meaning of the siting of an Amerindian village.[12] I will not discuss those individual items which have a social or cosmological significance in themselves, but only the way messages are conveyed by various structural properties of the house. According to Bourdieu, these properties match and hence represent some central structural properties of the Berber cosmology, that is of the content of certain of their important beliefs, expressed in proverbs and sayings.

Once again we find the two dimensions of *Umwelt* analysis, the structure of the entity, in this case the house, and the structure of the larger entity into which the house fits. And, of course, certain differentiated elements within the structure of the house are themselves structurally differentiated, and some qualitatively, as, for example, light and dark, or fresh and preserved. The appearance of both structurally differentiated elements, for example forked and straight, shows that we are dealing with basic semantic units, the higher-order structure having the character of syntax.

Our problem is *how* does the house as a structure, as a social or cosmological microcosm, express the macrocosm. There seem to be two distinct ways. In one the representation is established by isomorphism of structure, in the other by conventional assignment of meaning to generate a symbol. An etymology for the symbol can be reconstructed from the folk sayings, in terms of which the particular assignment of meaning makes sense. It is as a symbol, not as structured isomorph, that the fire is conceived by the Berber as the representation of the female principle in the house.

It seems from Bourdieu's account that structural properties of the house represent at two levels of sophistication. The ridge pole rests in the fork of the central wooden pillar, and this is read as an icon of the male/female relationship. Here the structural isomorphism is exceedingly simple. A considerable amount of social meaning is taken to be vested in this conjunction, and a good many of the rituals associated with procreation are related to it. Furthermore, the ridge pole and supporting pillar are the central metaphors in a large number of sayings and expressions by which the Berber social organization of the male/female dichotomy is described (and no doubt promulgated as rules and norms).

But Bourdieu has shown that the structure of the house is a microcosm in much more subtle ways. The division of the house into a light part and a dark part matches the division of social time into night and day. The openness of the light part is in contrast to the closedness of the dark part, matching the division between public (male) life and private (female) life. But these simple homologies are only the basis for more elaborate structures. 'The opposition between the world of female life and the world of the city of man is based upon the same principles as the two systems of opposition that it opposes.' In short, private life is not just female life, but as the procreative part of life is female/male. So the fact that the light part is in some sense the preserve of the women, where cooking and weaving are done, leads to the inner homology that the light part: dark part *as* public: private *as* male; female *as* female/female; female/male. Thus in general

$$a: b \; as \; b1 \; ; b2$$

Finally, the house can be considered in its geographical isomorphisms. The door is related to the compass points of geographical space. Going out one faces the East, the direction of worship, with the warm South on one's right. But the door is also related to a kind of inner geography. Coming in one faces the wall of the loom, which being illuminated by the door is treated as bright, honourable and so on, in short as the 'East' of the inner space. On one's right on entry is the wall with the fire, the 'South' of the interior. Thus the door is the point of logical inversion through which one passes from macrocosm and back, always in the same relation to the social and cosmological significance of these structured spaces.

Situations

My basic thesis is that in most times and most historical conditions expressive motivations dominate practical. Practical aspects of activities will usually have some part to play, but from the dramaturgical perspective they fade into relative unimportance. Situations will arise mostly from expressive contradictions.

In a general way one can see that there can be only two kinds of situations— those in which people are related to the setting, and those in which they are related to each other. I shall try to show how each naturally provides the opportunity for expressive tensions. There are many, many ways in which expressive tension can be created, and the cases I shall describe are meant only to illustrate the kind of thing I have in mind and not to masquerade as an exhaustive catalogue.

People in Relation to Setting. The simplest relation a person can have to a setting is to be occupying some part of its space and/or its time. And that occupancy seems to create in most people a sense of proprietorship. It would be very unwise, however, to follow Ardrey[13] and others in claiming a biological origin for this sense, or genetic inheritance as an explanation for its widespread appearance in the human race. But the sense of possession does seem to be close to universal. Mary Douglas has amplified our understanding of the sense of proprietorship or 'ownership' of spaces and times with the idea that we invest those for which we feel this relation with some measure of sanctity.[14] In consequence we tend to treat the intrusion of others as a profanation, a defilement of some *thing* close enough to us to be almost part of ourselves. Lyman has remarked on the way people will decorate whatever space they take to be theirs, emphasizing their proprietorship, even if the last territory for the dispossessed is their own bodies. If all this is in some measure sound, then one's dignity and worth would be seriously threatened by other people making free with those regions of space and time one felt proprietorial towards. And this provides our first source of social tension. It arises in the situation created by an actual, immanent or virtual violation of one's personal spaces and times. We shall see how this tension is dealt with in the section on action.

People in Relation to One Another. Of the innumerable variety of possible cases I shall sketch only two, as illustrative of rather different forms of tension:

(i) Social tension can arise, and what I have called a situation come into being, when it is apparent to two or more people that a relationship already exists between them, but it has not been publicly proclaimed or ritually ratified. A couple may have reached the point of establishing a very formal and apparently stable relationship which has to be transformed into a socially ratified bonding, either into the informal 'They are going out together' or the formal 'They are engaged'. This is the tension of the implicit about to be transformed into the explicit, the potential about to become actual. The scenes to be discussed in detail below concern the ritual transformation of a privately or personally experienced mutual liking into a publicly acknowledged friendship.

(ii) But social tensions can also arise in cases which it is uncertain what relation is going to come to exist between people. A perennial problem is posed by the appearance of a stranger, whose place in our network of social relations and reputations has yet to be determined. We shall look at introduction ceremonials as minor dramatic resolutions of this kind of problem.

There are a huge number of such tension-situations, which life dramas resolve. There is the discovery that someone is not what they seem. There is the realization that a relation which has been certified officially has no further foundation in personal feeling—how is it to be terminated? There is the challenge to established reputation for one who aspires to the mantle. There is the sudden realization that one is getting old and the bitter discovery of the uselessness of one's life in the eyes of others, and so on, and so on. The expressive aspect of action, the dominant aspect, I claim, can be understood from the partial point of view provided by the dramaturgical model as a resolution of these and other 'dramatic' situations.

REFERENCES

1. E. Goffman, *The Presentation of Self in Everyday Life,* Allen Lane, The Penguin Press, London, 1969.
2. E. Burke, *A Grammar of Motives,* Prentice Hall, Englewood Cliffs, N. J. 1945.
3. An interesting study of improvised theatre and its relation to ethogenic psychology has been undertaken by F. Coppieters, of, his doctorial dissertation. University of Antwerp, 1976.
4. Cf. Frances Yates' discussion in her *The Art of Memory,* Routledge and Kegan Paul, London, 1966, and *Giordano Bruno and the Hermetic Tradition,* Routledge and Kegan Paul, London, 1964.
5. E. Schegloff and H. Sacks, 'Opening up closings', in R. Turner, *Ethnomethodology,* Penguin, London, 1974, pp. 233-264.
6. K. Lewin, *Principles of Topological Psychology,* trans. F. and G. M. Heinder, McGraw-Hill, New York, 1935.
7. E. Goffman, *Relations in Public,* Allen Lane, The Penguin Press, London, 1971.
8. Comparison should be made with the traces of the passage of children through this miniature social world. A graphical representation of actual transitions does not match perfectly with a projection of ideal transitions from the social topography. This point helps to make clear the psychological character of the treat/comfort representation. It is a representation of the children's meanings for and attitudes to the various elements of their *Umwelt.* This should not be surprising since the graph is constructed from their accounts. A full social psychological theory of actual movements through the space would involve complementing the graph as a shared theory of the kindergarten, with the individual and occasional contingencies that were pertinent to the following of defiant paths. Jos Jaspars has suggested to me that both plots could be compared with a more conventional 'mental map' of that world.
9. D. Joiner, 'Social ritual and architectural space', *Architectural Research and Teaching, 1* (1971), 48 ff.
10. Mary Douglas has proposed an analytical scheme upon the main dish principal with stressed/unstressed elements as the main dichotomy. For a more detailed analysis see my 'Architectonic man' in R. H. Brown and S. M. Lyman (eds.), *Structure, Consciousness and History.* Cambridge University Press, Cambridge, etc. 1978, ch. 5.
11. P. Bourdieu, 'The Berber house', reprinted in M. Douglas (ed.), *Rules and Meanings,* Penguin, Harmondsworth, 1973, ch. 18.
12. C. Levi-Strauss, *The Savage Mind,* Weidenfeld and Nicholson, London, 1966.
13. R. Ardrey, *The Territorial Imperative,* Collins, London, 1967.
14. M. Douglas, *Purity and Danger,* Routledge and Kegan Paul, London, 1966.

Socio- and Psycholinguistics:

Introduction

Language varies between situations in a number of ways—the actual language itself may vary, as may its fluency, complexity, accent, and its sequence of utterances. Cazden (1970) reviews research on variations in childrens' speech in school as a function of (1) the topic discussed—where greater affect or involvement leads to greater complexity, and (2) what the subject is asked to do—working class children produce more formal, elaborated speech when carrying out a more abstract task, or when adults require more detailed information. Children also modify their speech according to the age of listeners. Test situations contain cognitive demands of the task and show the effects of formality and power. These findings extend the early findings by Labov about accent shifts in different situations, and provide some criticism of Bernstein's findings about class differences. The results provide at least a partial explanation of how class difference affects children's speech, since working class children who may have been more constrained by the test situation, shifted from their normal speech style.

Goffman (1964) points out that speech cannot be understood in terms of the activity of the speaker alone. For example the latter would speak more loudly to someone who is further away, differently in a more formal situation, so that his speech behaviour must be considered in relation to such features of the situation. However situations have so far been studied in a very haphazard way and this is the sense in which they have been "neglected". Goffman points out that the act of speaking is always part of an intricately organized social system, in which those present in the situation cooperate, for example in turn-taking. In a later book, Goffman (1971) produced a very interesting account of some of the sequences which occur in different situations such as the "remedial sequence" and embedded sequences, following a linguistic model. Goffman has made a number of important contributions to the study of social behaviour, through his sensitive observation of phenomena, and his ideas have sometimes led to more rigorous investigation by others. Personnel at five levels in the hierarchy of a department store were interviewed. More formal forms of address were used (title and last name) in the shop in front of customers, less formal in the canteen, and least formal at a staff dance, in the street or in a pub. There was little asymmetrical use of names in the formal situation (12%), but more in the informal situations (50%). These unreciprocated exchanges were based on differences in rank, and terms of address depended on relative rather than absolute rank. This study shows the complexity of the phenomenon by taking into account the effects of situational variables.

SUGGESTED ADDITIONAL REFERENCES

Bell, R. *Sociolinguistics*. London: Batsford, 1976.

Berger, C. and Perkins, J. Studies in interpersonal epistemology 1: Situational attributes in observation context selection. *Communication Yearbook*, 1979.

Bernstein, B. *Class, codes and control*. Vols. 1, 2, 3, (1971, 73, 75), London: Routledge.

Boggs, S. and Watson-Gegeo, K. Interweaving routines: strategies for encompassing a social situation. *Language in Society*, 1978, *7*, 375-392.

Brown, P. and Fraser, C. Speech as a marker of situation. In Scherer, K., and Giles, H. *Social Markers in Speech*, Cambridge: Cambridge University Press, 1979, 33-55.

Cole, M., Dore, J., and Hall, W. Situational variability in the speech of preschool children. *Annals of the New York Academy of Sciences*, 1978, *318*, 65-105.

Conboy, J. Social situation, age and gender assignment to English nouns: a study of sociology of language. *Mid-American Review of Sociology*, 1978, 17-37.

Coulthard, M. *An Introduction to Discourse Analysis*. London: Longman, 1977.

Dittman, N. *Sociolinguistics*. London: Arnold, 197.

Freedle, R. and Lewis, M. Prelinguistic conversations. In M. Lewis and L. Rosenblum (Eds.) *Interaction, Conversation and the Development of Language*, New York: Wiley, 1977.

Gak, V. Situational designations in 'Glossoethnographic' perspectives. *Soviet Psychology*, 1976, *7*, 70-84.

Gigioli, P. *Language and Social Context*. Harmondsworth: Penguin, 1972.

Giles, H. and St. Clair, R. *Language and Social Psychology*. Oxford: Blackwell, 1979.

Goffman, E. (1971) *Relations in Public*. London: Allen Lane.

Gregory, M. and Carroll, S. *Language and Situation*. London: Routledge & Kegan Paul, 1978.

Halliday, M. *Language as social semiotic*. London: Edward Arnold, 1978.

Hewes, D., and Hought, L. The cross-situational consistency of communicative behaviours: a preliminary investigation. *Communication Research*, 1979, *6*, 243-270.

Hymes, D. Models of the interaction of language and social setting. In J. Gumperz and D. Hymes (Eds.) *Directions in Sociolinguistics: The Ethnography of Communication*, New York: Holt, Rinehart & Winston, 1972.

Kirk, L. and Burton, M. Meaning and context: a study of contextual shifts in meaning of Maasai personality descriptors. *American Ethnologist*, 1977, *4*, 734-761.

Labov, W. *Sociolinguistic patterns*, University of Pennsylvania Press. Philadelphia, 1972.

Lindenfeld, J. The Social conditions of syntactic variation in French. *American Anthropologist,* 1969, 71, 890-898.

Liska, J. Situational and topical variations in credibility criteria. *Communication Monographs,* 1978, *45,* 85-92.

Newcomb, T. An approach to the study of communicative acts. *Psychological Review,* 1953, *60,* 393-404.

Rodgon, M. Situation and meaning in one- and two-word utterances. *Journal of Child Language,* 1976, *4,* 111-114.

Scherer, K. and Giles, H. *Social Markers in Speech.* Cambridge: Cambridge University Press, 1979.

1

The Neglected Situation*

E. Goffman

It hardly seems possible to name a social variable that doesn't show up and have its little systematic effect upon speech behavior: age, sex, class, caste, country of origin, generation, region, schooling; cultural cognitive assumptions; bilingualism, and so forth. Each year new social determinants of speech behavior are reported. (It should be said that each year new psychological variables are also tied in with speech.)

Alongside this correlational drive to bring in ever new social attributes as determinants of speech behavior, there has been another drive, just as active, to add to the range of properties discoverable in speech behavior itself, these additions having varied relations to the now classic phonetic, phonemic, morphemic and syntactical structuring of language. It is thus that new semantic, expressive, paralinguistic and kinesic features of behavior involving speech have been isolated, providing us with a new bagful of indicators to do something correlational with.

I'm sure these two currents of analysis—the correlational and the indicative—could churn on forever (and probably will), a case of scholarly

*Reprinted by permission of the American Anthropological Association from the American Anthropologist, 1964, 66, 6, 2, 133-136.

coexistence, However, a possible source of trouble might be pointed out. At certain points these two modes of analysis seem to get unpleasantly close together, forcing us to examine the land that separates them—and this in turn may lead us to feel that something important has been neglected.

Take the second-mentioned current of analysis first—the uncovering of new properties or indicators in speech behavior. That aspect of a discourse that can be clearly transferred through writing to paper has been long dealt with; it is the greasy parts of speech that are now increasingly considered. A wagging tongue (at certain levels of analysis) proves to be only one part of a complex human act whose meaning must also be sought in the movement of the eyebrows and hand. However, once we are willing to consider these gestural, nonwritable behaviors associated with speaking, two grave embarrassments face us. First, while the substratum of a gesture derives from the maker's body, the form of the gesture can be intimately determined by the microecological orbit in which the speaker finds himself. To describe the gesture, let alone uncover its meaning, we might then have to introduce the human and material setting in which the gesture is made. For example, there must be a sense in which the loudness of a statement can only be assessed by knowing first how distant the speaker is from his recipient. The individual gestures with the immediate environment, not only with his body, and so we must introduce this environment in some systematic way. Secondly, the gestures the individual employs as part of speaking are much like the ones he employs when he wants to make it perfectly clear that he certainly isn't going to be drawn into a conversation at this juncture. At certain levels of analysis, then, the study of behavior while speaking and the study of behavior of those who are present to each other but not engaged in talk cannot be analytically separated. The study of one teasingly draws us into the study of the other. Persons like Ray Birdwhistell and Edward Hall have built a bridge from speaking to social conduct, and once you cross the bridge, you become too busy to turn back.

Turn now from the study of newly uncovered properties or indicators in speech to the first-mentioned study of newly uncovered social correlates of speech. Here we will find even greater embarrassment. For increasingly there is work on a particularly subversive type of social correlate of speech that is called 'situational'. Is the speaker talking to same or opposite sex, subordinate or superordinate, one listener or many, someone right there or on the phone; is he reading a script or talking spontaneously; is the occasion formal or informal, routine or emergency? Note that it is not the attributes of social structure that are here considered, such as age and sex, but rather the value placed on these attributes as they are acknowledged in the situation current and at hand.

And so we have the following problem: a student interested in the properties of speech may find himself having to look at the physical setting in which the speaker performs his gestures, simply because you cannot describe a gesture fully without reference to the extra-bodily environment in which it occurs. And someone interested in the linguistic correlates of social structure may find that he must attend to the social occasion when someone of given social attributes makes his appearance before others. Both kinds of student must therefore look at what we vaguely call the social situation. And that is what has been neglected.

At present the idea of the social situation is handled in the most happy-go-lucky way. For example, if one is dealing with the language of respect, then social situations become occasions when persons of relevant status relationships are present before each other, and a typology of social situations is drawn directly and simply from chi-squaredom: high-low, low-high and equals. And the same could be said for other attributes of the social structure. An implication is that social situations do not have properties and a structure of their own, but merely mark, as it were, the geometric intersection of actors making talk and actors bearing particular social attributes.

I do not think this opportunistic approach to social situations is always valid. Your social situation is not your country cousin. It can be argued that social situations, at least in our society, constitute a reality *sui generis* as He used to say, and therefore need and warrant analysis in their own right, much like that accorded other basic forms of social organization. And it can be further argued that this sphere of activity is of special importance for those interested in the ethnography of speaking, for where but in social situations does speaking go on?

So let us face what we have been offhand about: social situations. I would define a social situation as an environment of mutual monitoring possibilities, anywhere within which an individual will find himself accessible to the naked senses of all others who are 'present', and similarly find them accessible to him. According to this definition, a social situation arises whenever two or more individuals find themselves in one another's immediate presence, and it lasts until the next-to-last person leaves. Those in a given situation may be referred to aggregatively as a *gathering,* however divided, or mute and distant, or only momentarily present, the participants in the gathering appear to be. Cultural rules establish how individuals are to conduct themselves by virtue of being in a gathering, and these rules for commingling, when adhered to, socially organize the behavior of those in the situation.[1]

Although participation in a gathering always entails constraint and organization, there are special social arrangements of all or some of those present which entail additional and greater structuring of conduct. For it is possible for two or more persons in a social situation to jointly ratify one another as authorized co-sustainers of a single, albeit moving, focus of visual and cognitive attention. These ventures in joint orientation might be called *encounters* or face engagements. A preferential mutual openness to all manner of communication is involved. A physical coming together is typically also involved, an ecological

---

[1] I have attempted to present this argument in detail in *Behavior in Public Places,* Free Press, 1963.

huddle wherein participants orient to one another and away from those who are present in the situation but not officially in the encounter. There are clear rules for the initiation and termination of encounters, the entrance and departure of particular participants, and demands that an encounter can make upon its sustainers, and the decorum of space and sound it must observe relative to excluded participants in the situation. A given social gathering of course may contain no encounter, merely unengaged participants bound by unfocused interaction; it may contain one encounter which itself contains all the persons in the situation—a favored arrangement for sexual interaction; it may contain an accessible encounter, one that must proceed in the presence of unengaged participants or other encounters.

Card games, ball-room couplings, surgical teams in operation and fist fights provide examples of encounters; all illustrate the social organization of shared current orientation, and all involve an organized interplay of acts of some kind. I want to suggest that when speaking occurs it does so within this kind of social arrangement; of course what is organized therein is not plays or steps or procedures or blows, but turns at talking. Note then that the natural home of speech is one in which speech is not always present.

I am suggesting that the act of speaking must always be referred to the state of talk that is sustained through the particular turn at talking, and that this state of talk involves a circle of others ratified as coparticipants. (Such a phenomenon as talking to oneself, or talking to unratified recipients as in the case of collusive communication, or telephone talk, must first be seen as a departure from the norm, else its structure and significance will be lost.) Talk is socially organized, not merely in terms of who speaks to whom in what language, but as a little system of mutually ratified and ritually governed face-to-face action, a social encounter. Once a state of talk has been ratified, cues must be available for requesting the floor and giving it up, for informing the speaker as to the stability of the focus of attention he is receiving. Intimate collaboration must be sustained to ensure that one turn at talking neither overlaps the previous one too much, nor wants for inoffensive conversational supply, for someone's turn must always and exclusively be in progress. If persons are present in the social situation but not ratified as participants in the encounter, then sound level and physical spacing will have to be managed to show respect for these accessible others while not showing suspicion of them.

Utterances do of course submit to linguistic constraints (as do meanings), but at each moment they must do a further job, and it is this job that keeps talk participants busy. Utterances must be presented with an overlay of functional gestures—gestures which prop up states of talk, police them, and keep these little systems of activity going. Sounds are used in this gestural work because sounds, in spoken encounters, happen to be handy; but everything else at hand is systematically used too. Thus many of the properties of talk will have to be seen as alternatives to, or functional equivalents of, extra-linguistic acts, as when, for example, a participant signals his imminent departure from a conversational encounter by changing his posture, or redirecting his perceivable attention, or altering the intonation contour of his last statement.

At one level of analysis, then, the study of writable statements and the study of speaking are different things. At one level of analysis the study of turns at talking and things said during one's turn are part of the study of face-to-face interaction. Face-to-face interaction has its own regulations; it has its own processes and its own structure, and these don't seem to be intrinsically linguistic in character, however often expressed through a linguistic medium.

2

The Situation: A Neglected Source of Social Class Differences in Language Use*

Courtney B. Cazden

Study of the acquisition of language has been based on the assumption that what had to be described and explained was the acquisition of a repertoire of responses (in the terminology of behaviorism) or the acquisition of a finite set of rules for constructing utterances (in the terminology of developmental psycholinguistics). On this assumption, the school language problems of lower-class (LC) children can have two explanations: either they have acquired less language than

*Journal of Social Issues, 1970, 26, 2, 35-59. Copyright 1970 by the Society for the Psychological Study of Social Issues. Reprinted by permission.

middle-class (MC) children or they have acquired a different language. The "less language" explanation has been given various names—cultural deprivation, deficit hypothesis, vacuum ideology—all with the same connotation of a non-verbal child somehow emptier of language than his more socially fortunate age-mates. The "different language" explanation is forcefully argued by William Stewart and Joan Baratz (Baratz, 1969a; Baratz, 1969b; Aarons, Gordon, & Stewart, 1970). It states that all children acquire language but that many children, especially LC black children, acquire a dialect of English so different in structural (grammatical) features that communication in school, both oral and written, is seriously impaired by that fact alone.[1]

THE "LESS LANGUAGE" EXPLANATION

Grammatical Competence. For different reasons neither of these explanations is adequate. Consider first the "less language" explanation. There is growing evidence that if we are referring to what is called "grammatical competence," the child's implicit knowledge of language structure, then social-class differences are simply not great enough to explain the language problems which teachers report from the classroom. Three pieces of evidence can be offered.

First, LaCivita, Kean, & Yamamoto (1966) report a study in which lower-middle and upper-class elementary school children from three schools in Youngstown, Ohio were asked to give the meaning of nonsense words in sentences such as the following:

Ungubily the mittler *gimmled*. (grammatical signal *-ed* only cue)
A twener *baikels* meedily. (grammatical signal plus position cue)

They hypothesized that lower-class children would have less understanding of grammatical structure and thus be less able to give a word that was the same part of speech as the underlined nonsense word (in the above instance, a verb). This hypothesis was not confirmed. Older children were better than younger children, and position cues aided comprehension, but the lower-class children were at no disadvantage.

Second, Slobin reports beginning returns from a cross-cultural study of the acquisition of language in Mexico, India, Samoa, Kenya, and the Negro ghetto in Oakland, California:

---

[1] See also the article preceding in this issue, "Implicit Assumptions Underlying Preschool Intervention Programs," by Marion Blank. [General Editor]

Though we have not yet analyzed the language development of the children studied in these diverse groups, it is the impression of the field workers that they all appear to acquire language at a normal rate and are clearly not "linguistically deprived." This is certainly true of the Oakland children whom we have begun to study in some detail [1968, p. 13].

Finally, when the mean length of utterance (in morphemes, see Slobin, 1967) of LC Negro children in a Boston day-care center (Cazden, 1965) is compared with the mean length of utterance of MC white children (Brown, Cazden, & Bellugi, 1969; Bloom, 1970), there is some evidence that the LC Negro children who were studied achieved grammatical development at a similar rate. Figure 2.1 gives this comparison. Dotted lines are for the three Cambridge children studied by Brown et al.—two children of graduate students on the left and a lower-middle class child on the right. Broken lines are for Bloom's three New York City children, all from MC families. Solid lines are for Cazden's twelve Negro children in Boston whose development was followed for only four months.

The speech of one of the Negro children studied is particularly interesting. Gerald is the boy whose mean length of utterance is above 5 morphemes, almost off the top of the graph. His first speech sample was taken when he was 33

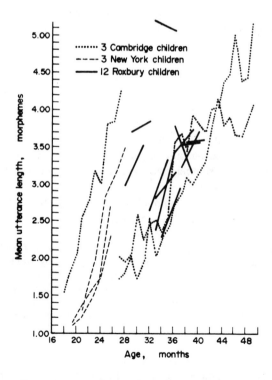

Figure 2.1 Mean Utterance Length and Age in 18 Children.

months old. Following are all his utterances of 7 or more morphemes in the first
200 utterances of that speech sample (unpublished speech samples from Cazden,
1965):

    29. I'm looking for a cup (7)
    36. I waiting for a other cup. (7)
    63. You put it up on there like dis. (8)
    69. I gon' put dis one in 'nere. (7)
   109. Look at what I made with dis one. (8)
   122. Den gon' put dis one back in here cause it fell out (12)
   155. I'm gonna knock dese things in. (8)
   171. Soon I get finish I gon' do dat way. (9)
   197. Can I take it off and put it on? (9)

Whatever Gerald's communication problems may be in any particular situation,
and I will suggest later that a problem could arise, they are not caused by
deficiencies in grammatical competence.

Admittedly, the fact that the grammatical development of these particular
twelve black children is comparable in rate to children the same age from MC
families does not prove that all LC children would do as well. But it does raise
questions about inferences made about children's language from test scores alone
or from less adequate samples of spontaneous speech (see Moore, in press, for
further arguments).

Vocabulary. So far I have been talking about the structure of the child's
language, his grammar, and have argued that the characterization of "less
language" does not fit LC children. Language also has a set of words—or
lexicon. Do LC children have "less language" in the sense of fewer words in
their mental dictionary? Here the characterization seems to fit better. All
vocabulary studies report wide social-class differences. (See Lesser et al., 1965,
for one study designed with exemplary care in respect to choice of test words and
conditions of test administration.)

However, nagging questions remain about the interpretation of such test
results. In an article published in 1966, I wrote:

> Tyler says that "lower-class children use a great many words, and a number of them use these
> words with a high degree of precision; but facility with words commonly used by the lower
> classes is not correlated with success in school" (Eels, Davis, Havighurst, Herrick, and Tyler,
> 1951, p. 40). Does Tyler mean that children from different status groups know and use
> different words? . . . How does this relate to Nida's (1958, p. 283) suggestion that
> "subcultures have proportionately more extensive vocabularies in the area of their distinctive-
> ness?" Can one speak of the vocabulary of a . . . dialect as structured?

While we have made real progress in understanding the structure of language in
the intervening years, comparable progress in the conceptual or semantic area is
yet to come. Our understanding of social class differences will gain from that

basic research. Note that research on "applied" questions about the nature of social-class differences can itself contribute to our understanding of "basic" questions about the nature of language, as Hymes (in press) argues. An outstanding example is the work of Labov et al. (1968) on the phonology and grammar of non-standard Negro English (NNE), which both uses and extends the linguistic descriptions of Chomsky's transformational grammar.

Lexical Representations. One new question about social class differences in word knowledge also derives from Chomsky's work (Chomsky & Halle, 1968). It is the relation between a person's understanding of the sound system of English and his knowledge of a particular part of the English lexicon, i.e., learn-ed or Latin-ate words. Briefly, if our knowledge of the sound system of English were limited to the sounds present in words as spoken, we would not understand morphemic relations such as: histor -y, histor -ical, histor -ian, anxi -ous, anxi-ety; courage, courage -ous; tele -graph, tele -graph -ic, tele -graph -y. The only way to account for this system of sound relationships is to postulate an underlying structure which consists of a single and highly abstract "lexical representation" of each morpheme (a unit of meaning, whether free like *courage* or bound like *-ous*). This underlying representation is related to the surface representation of the morpheme—its sound as spoken—by a complex set of phonological rules which somehow become part of the implicit linguistic knowledge of the native speaker.

> Much of the evidence that determines, for the phonologist, the exact form of this underlying system is based on consideration of learned words and complex derivational patterns. This is clear from examples presented earlier. . . . It is by no means obvious that a child of six has mastered this phonological system in full. He may not yet have been presented with the evidence that determines the general structure of this system. A similar question arises in the case of an adult who is not immersed in the literary culture [Chomsky, in press].

According to Chomsky & Halle (1968) the underlying system of lexical representations conforms extremely well to standard English spelling, contrary to popular notions of chaotic irregularities. But only someone who had acquired this full system, by familiarity with Latinate words, could take full advantage of that regularity in learning to read. This is one very specific but very important aspect of language where lower-class speakers may be at a disadvantage.

THE "DIFFERENT LANGUAGE" EXPLANATION

The "different language" explanation is clearly true, but also inadequate. Dialects do differ in structural features which must be taken into account in planning curriculum materials and instructional techniques. Labov's research is now providing analyses of one dialect, NNE, that will make such planning possible. (See Labov et al., 1968, Vol. 1, for a full report of the research on phonology and grammar, and Labov, 1969, for a brief and less technical summary with educational implications suggested.) According to Labov, the structural differences between NNE and standard English (SE) are few in number. Furthermore, a person's grammatical competence in speaking and understanding are not necessarily identical, and there is considerable evidence that speakers of the NNE understand some, though not all, of the features of SE they do not themselves produce. Repetition tests are one source of such evidence.

> In repetition tests with fourteen-year-old Negro boys, members of peer group we have known for several years, we find that many unhesitatingly repeat *ask Albert if he knows how to play baseball* as *axe Albert do he know how to play baseball*. On the other hand, if the test sentence *was ask Albert whether he knows how to play baseball*, most of the subjects had far more trouble [Labov, 1969, p. 46].

Correct translation of a SE sentence into the speaker's NNE dialect presupposes correct understanding of the original. While NNE speakers ask questions in the *do he know* form, they understand the SE use of *if* but not *whether*.

INADEQUACY OF BOTH EXPLANATIONS

The inadequacy of both the "less language" and the "different language" characterizations is two-fold. First, both refer only to patterns of structural form and ignore patterns of use in actual speech events. Second, they assume that the child learns only one way to speak which is reflected in the same fashion and to the same extent at all times. On both theoretical and practical grounds, we can no longer accept such limitations. We must attend not only to the abilities of individuals and how they develop, but to qualities of the situation, or temporary environment, in which those abilities are activated. Such attention to the interaction of abilities and environments is increasing in psychology, linguistics, and education.

The Power of Environments. Barker has coined the name "ecological psychology" and argues for its importance:

> When environments are relatively uniform and stable, *people* are an obvious source of behavior variance, and the dominant scientific problem and the persistent queries from the applied fields are: What are people like? What is the nature and what are the sources of individual differences? . . . But today *environments* are more varied and unstable than heretofore and their contribution to the variance of behavior is enhanced. Both science and society ask with greater urgency than previously: What are environments like? . . . How do environments select and shape the people who inhabit them? . . . These are questions for ecological psychology [1968, p. 3].

When Kagan (1967) issued a call for "relativism" in psychology which would include the context or situation in descriptions of behavior, Psathas answered:

> When Kagan uses the term "relativistic," he says that it "refers to a definition in which context and state of the individual are part of the defining statement." The "neglected situation" as Goffman (1964) has called it and the state of the individual, particularly his internal symbol manipulating state, need to be considered. They would involve Kagan in sociology and anthropology much more than he recognizes. The "context" that he refers to is one that has *socially* defined stimulus value. The social definitions for a situation are pregiven, i.e., exist before the psychologist or experimenter enters on the scene. He must, therefore, understand what these are and how they are perceived by the subject before he can claim to understand why the subject behaves the way he does. The "state of the individual" includes not only his biological and physiological state but his interpretive structuring of the world as he experiences it, based on his previous socialization experiences as a member of the culture [1968, p. 136].

While Barker seeks an objective description of the environment—analogous to the characteristics of light or sound in the study of perception, Psathas calls for study of the environment as socially defined and perceived by individuals.

Communicative Competence. Applied to language this means that we have to describe more than the child's grammatical competence; we have to describe what Hymes (in press) calls "communicative competence," which is how the child perceives and categorizes the social situations of his world and differentiates his ways of speaking accordingly. The important point here is not a contrast between competence or knowledge on the one hand, and performance or behavior on the other hand, though many people—including myself in an earlier paper (Cazden, 1967)—have formulated the question in this way. A child's manifest verbal behavior, or performance, has both grammatical and pragmatic aspects. And it is a reflection of implicit knowledge or competence, both of grammar and of use.

> The acquisition of competence for use, indeed, can be stated in the same terms as acquisition of competence for grammar. Within the developmental matrix in which knowledge of the sentences of a language is acquired, children also acquire knowledge of a set of ways in which sentences are used. From a finite experience of speech acts and their interdependence with socio-cultural features they develop a general theory of the speaking appropriate in their community, which they employ, like other forms of tacit cultural knowledge (competence) in conducting and interpreting social life [Hymes, in press].

Social Class Differences in the Explicit Expression of Meaning. We are a long way from understanding the range of communicative competences that different children have or how they develop. In fact, research on this enlarged question about the child's acquisition of language has only begun. Basil Bernstein (in press) has been a pioneer here. Unfortunately, although Bernstein himself has repeatedly said that he is describing patterns of use in actual speech performance, his work is frequently cited in support of "less language" assertions about grammatical competence. The unpublished research of Joan Tough at the University of Leeds replicates some of Bernstein's findings with preschool-age children who are matched on Stanford-Binet IQ but differ in social class background (see Cazden, in press). Both Bernstein and Tough find social class differences in the degree to which meaning is expressed explicitly, or independent of context. Explicitness is probably also related to what Labov calls "attention paid to the monitoring of [one's own] speech [1969, p. 32]."

The Speech Situation as an Independent Variable. Our eventual goal is to understand how a person's previous experience (of which his social class is simply a rough and composite index) interacts with factors in the momentary situation to affect his behavior. At any one moment, a child decides to speak or be silent, to adopt communicative intent a or communicative intent b, to express idea x or idea y, in form 1 or form 2. The options the child selects will be a function of characteristics of the situation as he perceives it on the basis of past experience. We observe that a particular child in a particular situation either makes or fails to make a particular utterance. Traditionally, we have related that utterance only to characteristics of the child, such as his social class, while ignoring characteristics of the situation. As Robinson points out, the tendency in child language research has been to ignore situational or contextual variables, or to combine speech data from several contexts. Instead, Robinson suggests, "it may be wiser methodologically to accumulate the (social class) differences within contexts and to see what higher order generalizations can be made about them [1968, p. 6]."

The next section is a survey of research on child language which includes aspects of the speech situation as independent variables, regardless of the social class of the subjects. The purpose is to illustrate the idea of situational relativity and to suggest significant variables which would be explored more systematically. While the research to be reported is all about monolingual children, the notion of a diversified speech repertoire applies even more obviously to bilinguals (Herman, 1961, and McNamara, 1967, especially the chapter by Hymes).

The final section of the paper raises questions about other necessary ingredients of a theory of oral language education.

THE EFFECTS OF SITUATIONS

Relevant studies are listed in Table 2.1. Columns represent a very gross categorization of situational differences (the independent variables in the research): topic, task, listener(s), interaction, and situations with mixed charac-

Table 2.1 Effects of the Situation on Child Language
(Classification of Relevant Studies)

Language Characteristics	Characteristics of the Situation				
	Topic	Task	Listener(s)	Interaction	Mixed
Fluency/ Spontaneity	Strandberg Strandberg & Griffith Williams & Naremore (a, b) Berlyne & Frommer	Heider et al. Brent & Katz	Labov et al.	Cooperman (personal communication)	Cowan et al. Cazden (1965) Labov et al. Pasamanick & Knobloch Resnick, Weld, & Lally (1969) Kagan (1969) Jensen
Length/ Complexity	Strandberg & Griffith Cowan et al. Moffett Williams & Naremore (a, b) Labov et al. Mackay & Thompson	Brent & Katz Cazden (1967) Lawton Robinson (1965) Williams & Naremore (a, b)	Cazden (1967) Smith	Plumer	Cowan et al.
Content or Style	Labov et al.	Lawton			
Approximation of Standard English		Labov et al.			

Note—Dates are cited here only where the Reference list contains more than one item by the same author(s).

teristics; rows represent more easily definable characteristics of language (the dependent variables): fluency and/or spontaneity, length and/or complexity, some characteristic of speech content such as abstractness, and degree of approximation to Standard English. Unless otherwise specified, all differences to be discussed below are differences in the way the same child, or group of children, speaks in different situations; occasionally, differences between similar groups of children are reported. All but two (Moffett, 1968, and Robinson, 1965) deal with oral language.

Topic

Picture. Four studies used different kinds of pictures. Strandberg (1969) found that four- and five-year-old children above average in intelligence (with different children in each stimulus group) talked more about either a toy or a twenty-second silent film of that toy than they did about a still color photograph of it. There was no difference, however, in either average length or complexity of the responses. Strandberg and Griffith (1968) gave four- and five-year-old children in a university laboratory school Kodak Instamatic cameras loaded with color film and then elicited conversation about the remarkably successful pictures the children took. The children talked more spontaneously (i.e., required fewer adult probes) and talked in longer and more complex utterances about the pictures they took at home of personally significant objects (like a favorite climbing tree or a closeup of Mother's mouth) than they did about pictures taken under adult direction during the period of orientation to the camera. Since the pictures taken at home were also frequently of only one object, the authors conclude that the difference lies in the degree of personal involvement. Although topic is compounded with order since all children told stories about the preselected objects first, it seems unlikely that this accounts for all the difference. Following are examples of one five-year-old's stories, first about an assigned picture and then about one of his choices:

> That's a horse. You can ride it. I don't know any more about it. It's brown, black and red. I don't know my story about the horse.

> There's a picture of my tree that I climb in. There's—there's where it grows at and there's where I climb up—and sit up there—down there and that's where I look out at. First I get on this one and then I get on that other one. And then I put my foot under that big branch that are strong. And then I pull my face up and then I get ahold of a branch up at that place—and then I look around [Strandberg & Griffith, personal communication, 1969].

Cowan et al. (1967) presented elementary school children of mixed socio-economic status with ten colored pictures from magazine covers. The effect of the particular picture on the mean length of response (MLR) was strong across all age, sex, socio-economic class, and Experimenter categories. One picture of a group standing around a new car elicited significantly shorter MLR's and one picture of a birthday party elicited significantly longer MLR's, while the other eight pictures were undifferentiated between the two extremes. Although the authors cannot specify the source of the stimulus effect, they conclude that "the implicit assumption that magnitude of MLR is a property of the subject independent of his setting should be permanently discarded (Cowan et al., 1967, p. 202)."

Finally, Berlyne and Frommer (1966) studied the properties of different pictures and stories in eliciting one particular form of speech—questions. They presented children from kindergarten and grades 3, 5, and 6 at a university laboratory school with stories, pictures, and stories accompanied by pictures, and then invited the children to ask questions about them. Novel, surprising, and incongruous items elicited more questions than others, but provision of answers (an interaction characteristic) had little effect.

TV Narratives. Two studies compared narratives about TV programs with other topics. Williams and Naremore (1969, a and b) analyzed forty interviews with Negro and white fourth through sixth graders who were selected from the extremes of the socio-economic distribution of a larger group of 200 interviewees in a Detroit dialect study (Shuy et al., 1967). All informants had responded to three topics: games ("What kinds of games do you play around here?"); television ("What are your favorite TV programs?"); and aspirations ("What do you want to be when you finish school?"). Social class differences in number of words spoken—on an elaboration index (the proportion of utterances which went beyond a simple yes-no answer or a label to a description or explanation), on a ranking of the degree of connectedness of the utterances in a response, and on verbal indices of specific grammatical features—appeared only for the topic of TV.

> Although it is at best a subjective interpretation, the concentration of status differences in three of the clause indices on the TV topic seem to be a reflection of the tendency of the H.S. (high status) children to engage in story-telling or narrative while the L.S. (low status) children tended to itemize instances of what they had seen or preferred. The language used by the child in an interview is as much a reflection of his engagement within the constraints of a communication situation as it is a reflection of his linguistic capabilities [Williams & Naremore, 1969 b].

Labov has collected narratives of TV programs and personal experience from pre-adolescent boys attending vacation day camps (VDC) in Central Harlem. Following are two such narratives by two different 11-year-old boys—the first about "The Man From Uncle" and the second about a personal fight.

a This kid—Napoleon got shot
b and he had to go on a mission
c And so this kid, he went with Solo.
d So they went

e And this guy—they went through this window.
f and they caught him.
g And then he beat up them other people
h And they went

i and then he said
    that this old lady was his mother

j and then he—and at the end he say that he
    was the guy's friend.

        (Carl, 11, VDC, #386)

a When I was in fourth grade—
    no it was in third grade—
b This boy he stole my glove.
c He took my glove
d and said that his father found it downtown on
    the ground.
    (And you fight him?)
e I told him that it was impossible for him
    to find downtown cause all those
    people were walking by and just
    his father was the only one that
    found it?
f So he got all (mad).
g So then I fought him.

h I knocked him all out in the street.

i So he say he give.
j and I kept on hitting him.
k Then he started crying

l and ran home to his father

m And the father told him
n that he didn't find no glove.

    (Norris, W., VDC, 11, #378)
    [Labov et al., 1968, Vol. 2, pp. 298-299.]

Labov finds that the main difference between the two sets of narratives is the absence of evaluation in the TV narratives: "the means used by the narrator to indicate the point of the narrative, its *raison d'être,* why it was told, and what the narrator is getting at (Labov et al., 1968, Vol. 2, p. 297)." Absence of evaluation from accounts of vicarious experience reduces structural complexity. "The syntax of the narrative clause itself is one of the simplest structures that may be found even in colloquial language (Labov et al., 1968, Vol. 2, p. 308)." But explanations, one of the devices for evaluation, may be exceedingly complex. Following is the diagram for one section of the personal experience narrative; the symbol S indicates that one sentence has been embedded in another (Labov et al., 1968, Vol. 2, p. 332):

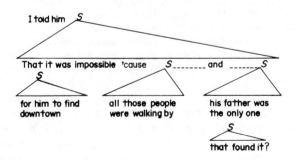

It does not seem far-fetched to suggest a common element in those findings: the greater the degree of affect or personal involvement in the topic of conversation, the greater the likelihood of structural complexity.

Some final examples of the effect of topic on linguistic structure are, first, Moffett:

> While watching some third-graders write down their observations of candle-flames—deliberately this time, not merely in note form—I noticed that sentences beginning with if-and-when clauses were appearing frequently on their papers. Since such a construction is not common in third-grade writing, I became curious and then realized that these introductory subordinate clauses resulted directly from the children's *manipulation of what* they were observing. Thus: "If I place a glass over the candle, the flame turns blue." Here we have a fine example of a physical operation being reflected in a cognitive operation and hence in a linguistic structure. . . . The cognitive task entailed in the candle tests *created a need* for subordinate clauses, because the pupils were not asked merely to describe a static object but to describe changes in the object brought about by changing conditions (*if* and *when*), [1968, p. 180].

My last example comes from my observations of the written compositions by five-year-old children in two English Infant Schools, both in neighborhoods of mixed socio-economic status (Cazden, in press). In the first school, all the children were given their first writing books (blank with unlined pages for pictures and related stories), asked to draw a picture and then dictate a story for the teacher to write. All the resulting stories were simple sentences and all but one was of the form *This is a ----------*. The exception was the sentence *This boy is dead*. In the second school, children were using experimental beginning reading materials developed by Mackay & Thomson (1968). Each child had a word folder with a preselected store of basic words plus some blanks for his personal collection. He also had a stand on which words from the folder could be set up as a text. These children composed sentences very different from each other, including the following:

My Mum takes me to school.
Is my sister at school and is my baby at home?
My cousin is skinny.
I like Siam she gave me one of David's doggies.
On Tuesday the movie camera man is coming.
I ask Helen to come to my birthday.

Whereas the presence of the pictures somehow constrained the first children to the simplest and most routine labels, absence of a picture seemed to free the second child to work with far more of their linguistic knowledge.

Task

In some studies, differences are found which seem to relate more to what the subject is asked to do with the topic than to the topic itself. For instance, Brent & Katz (1967) asked white Headstart children to tell stories about pictures from the WISC picture arrangement task, then removed the pictures and asked the children to tell the stories again. They found that the stories told without the pictures were superior. The children produced longer stories without prompting, and ideas were related more logically and explicitly. Brent & Katz suggest that "the actual presence of the pictures, which constitute a *spatially distributed* series of *perceptually discrete events,* may in fact interfere with our younger subjects' ability to form a *temporally distributed* and *logically continuous* story, a task which required a conceptual and linguistic "bridging-the-gap' between discrete frames" (1967, pp. 4—5). "We cannot tell from this study whether first telling the stories with the pictures present contributes to the more successful attempt when they are removed.

Lawton (1968), a student and then colleague of Basil Bernstein's in London, gave a series of language tasks to boys aged 12-15 years. In an interview he elicited both descriptive and more abstract speech: e.g., describe your school and then answer "what do you think is the real purpose of education?" All the boys used more subordinate clauses and complex constructions on the abstraction task than on the description task.

The Structure of Directions

Four studies report differences which result from different degrees of structure or constraint in the directions. With the same boys, Lawton also conducted a discussion of capital punishment, replicating an earlier study by Bernstein (1962), and gave assignments to write on four topics such as "My life in ten years time." In the more open unstructured discussions, middle-class boys used more abstract arguments and hypothetical examples, while the working-class boys used more concrete examples and clichés or anecdotes. But in the abstract sections of the interviews, social class differences were much smaller.

> The inference I would draw is that in an "open" situation the working-class boys tend to move towards concrete, narrative/descriptive language, but in a "structured" situation where they have little or no choice about making an abstract response, they will respond to the demand made upon them. They may have found the task extremely difficult, but it was not impossible for them [Lawton, 1968, p. 138].

Comparable results were obtained by Williams and Naremore (1969 b) and Heider et al. (1968). One way in which Williams and Naremore scored the interviews on games, aspirations, and TV was by the type of questions asked by the interviewer and the corresponding type of child response. There were three types of probe constraints: (1) simple (Do you play baseball?), (2) naming (What television programs do you watch?), and (3) elaboration (How do you play kick-the-can?). Response-style was categorized as follows: (1) simple (Yeah.), (2) naming (Baseball.), (3) qualified naming (I usually watch the Avengers and lots of cartoons.), and (4) elaboration (Last night the Penguin had Batman trapped on top of his tower. . . .).

Results show that in response to the first two probes, "The lower status children had more of a tendency to supply the minimally acceptable response, whereas their higher status counterparts had a greater tendency to elaborate their remarks (Williams & Naremore, 1969 a)." Following the probe for elaboration, however, these differences disappeared. "The mark of a lower-status child was that he had some tendency to provide the type of response which would minimally fulfill the fieldworker's probe, [but] not go on to assume a more active role in the speech situations including elaboration of more of his own experience (Williams & Naremore, 1969 a)."

Heider et al. (1968) report an experiment in which lower- and middle-class white 10-year-old boys were asked to describe a picture of one animal out of a large array. Criterial or essential attributes were the name of the animal and three others: number of spots, standing or lying down, and position of the head. The density of criterial attributes named by the children was almost identical for the two groups: MC children mentioned 67 attributes of which 18 were criterial, while LC children mentioned 69 attributes of which 16 were criterial. But there was a significant social class difference in the number of requests the listener had to make for more information before the picture was adequately specified: LC mean = 6.11 requests; MC mean = 3.56 requests. Thus the lower-class children's performance was far superior to what it would have been if the amount of probing or feedback had been standardized for the two groups as it usually is in both experimental situations and classrooms.

Robinson (1965), another colleague of Basil Bernstein, gave two writing assignments to 120 middle-class and working-class twelve and thirteen year old boys and girls in a comprehensive school. One assignment, to tell a good friend news of the past fortnight, presumably elicited informal or restricted codes from all subjects. The other assignment, advising a governor of the school how some money he had donated might be spent, presumably elicited a formal or elaborated code from anyone who could use one. Contrary to expectations, there were no significant differences between the middle-class and working-class formal letters, and differences only in lexical diversity (number of different nouns, adjectives, etc.) between the informal letters where the topic was less constrained.

While the results of Lawton, Williams and Naremore, Heider et al., and Robinson have indicated that working-class children display greater abstraction, elaboration, or informational analysis when it is demanded by an adult, analyses by Anita R. Olds and myself (Cazden, 1967) of the speech of two first-grade children in eight situations showed different results when the dependent variable is simply mean length of utterance in morphemes (utterance defined as an independent clause and any syntactically related dependent clauses). Martin, a middle-class white boy, spoke longer utterances on the average in the three structured task situations: retelling *Whistle for Willie*—7.09; describing an object hidden in a cloth bag—6.52; and describing five pictures about school—6.44. By contrast Rita, a lower-class Negro girl, spoke longer utterances on the average in three more informal interviews: 7.94, 7.53, and 6.20. While this study of two children must be considered only a pilot venture, it does provide an example of interaction between a child's background and the situations which elicit the longest utterances. Presumably, there are more such interactions to be discovered if we knew where and how to look for them.

Formality of the Situation. Speech situations can also be differentiated on an informal-formal continuum, according to the amount of attention paid to language itself. Labov (1968, vol. 1) has collected speech samples at several points along such a continuum from the least self-conscious and most excited speech in peer group sessions, through accounts of fights in individual interviews and other interview speech, to reading a connected sentence, and finally to reading a list of unconnected words. All speakers speak more standard English in their most formal and careful speech.

Listener(s)

One important characteristic of the listener is age in relation to the speaker. In an early study, Smith (1935) found that children 18 to 70 months old spoke longer sentences at home with adults than at play with other children, presumably because at home they gave fewer answers to questions and fewer imperatives, and had greater opportunity for more connected discourse with less active play and less frequent interruptions. We also found (Cazden, 1967) that both Rita and Martin spoke their shortest sentences, on the average, in two experimental situations with their peers: an arithmetic game where Rita averaged 4.50 and Martin 4.78, and a telephone conversation where Rita scored 5.60 and Martin 3.58.

Two students at Harvard found that children modified their speech when speaking to younger children. Yurchak (1969) analyzed the language of her three-year-old daughter, Kathleen, as she talked to herself, her mother, and her 18-month-old baby sister. Kathleen's longest utterances were spoken to her mother, her shortest utterances to her sister, while speech to herself was somewhere inbetween. Bernat (1969) taped the speech of three girls, 9 and 11 and 13 years old, when talking to younger boys ages 18, 30, and 29 months. The extent to which the girls adapted their speech to their young listener depended not on his age, but on evidence of his capacity to talk and understand. Their average sentence length with the first child was 4.06 morphemes, with the second 5.23 morphemes; with the third—a very verbal child with excellent comprehension—they talked in normal, mature sentences. On replaying the tape, Bernat found to her surprise that she herself did too.

Younger listeners aren't the only restraining influence. Power relations between older and younger children can also influence speech:

Stevie: He gon' getchyou with 'Is li's . . . he got li-' he got leg like di - like -
Stevie is ordinarily very fast and fluent with words, but he finds it very difficult to say what he means to these sixteen-year-olds—another example of how power relations can determine verbal ability available at the moment [Labov et al., 1968, Vol. 2, p. 117].

Interaction of Speakers

Here we have only one report from a pilot study and one hypothesis now being tested. But both are worth consideration by others. Oliver Cooperman, a student at Harvard Medical School on leave to work with Barbara Tizard at the University of London on the effects of various conditions of residential care on preschool age children, conducted a pilot study of various aspects of conversation. He found that "conversation is more likely to occur and include a greater number of exchanges back and forth when initiated by the child" and "a child almost never responds verbally to an adult command 'Stop doing X' except rarely, to say 'no'; on the other hand, commands to initiate action, to 'do X', frequently provoked verbal reply [personal communication, 1969]."

A student at Harvard, Davenport Plumer, is conducting his doctoral research on dialogue strategies among twelve families with children seven or eight years old, six with sons of high verbal ability (as measured on the Stanford-Binet and a combination of WISC-ITPA), and six with sons of average verbal ability. Recording equipment is given to each family in turn, and dialogue is recorded from a wireless microphone worn by the focal child. Each family records a total of seven hours during one week, including twenty-minute sessions at breakfast, supper, and bedtime. One measure used will be the length of a dialogue—the number of verbal exchanges between the initiation and termination of a topic; one analysis undertaken will be the relation of length of dialogue to complexity of the child's utterances.

A major assumption underlying this study is that the longer the dialogue the more likely the child is to hear and use a wide range of the resources and strategies of his language. The ability to elaborate and qualify—or to follow elaboration and qualification—is most likely to be learned in an extended dialogue after an initial exchange has set up the need for clarification and elaboration [Plumer, 1969, pp. 7-8].

If either Cooperman's or Plumer's hypothesis is borne out in further research, it would have important implications for planning classrooms for maximally productive conversation. For instance, initiation of conversation probably takes place more often in a classroom where children carry major responsibility for planning their activities. But this may only be productive for language usage if involvement, and thereby conversation on a topic, is sustained over some period of time.

Mixed Aspects of Situations

Classrooms. Two kinds of situations which seem to contain a mixture of relevant aspects are the various activities in any classroom and the testing situations. Cowe (1967) has recorded the conversations of kindergarten children in nine activities. In both amount and maturity of speech, housekeeping play and group discussion held the greatest potential for language, while play with blocks, dance, and woodworking held least. She suggests that factors influencing speech are adult participation, something concrete to talk about, physical arrangements, and noise. I made similar observations when selecting play materials for the tutorial language program from which the data in Figure 2.1 are taken (Cazden, 1965).

Tests. Testing situations contain the effects of interpersonal formality and power relationship mixed with the cognitive demands of particular tasks. Pasamanick & Knobloch (1955) and Resnick, Weld, and Lally (1969) report evidence that the verbal expressiveness of working-class Negro two-year-olds is artificially depressed in testing situations. Even Jensen, arguing that social-class differences in intelligence are largely inherited, reports from his own clinical experience that he regularly raised IQ scores on the Stanford-Binet (largely a test of verbal performance) eight to ten points by having children from an impoverished background come in for two to four play sessions in his office so that the child could get acquainted and feel more at ease (Jensen, 1969).

Kagan, in answer to Jensen, reports the experience of Francis Palmer in New York City:

> Dr. Palmer administered mental tests to middle and lower class black children from Harlem. However, each examiner was instructed not to begin testing with any child until she felt that the child was completely relaxed, and understood what was required of him. Many children had five, six, and even seven hours of rapport sessions with the examiner before any questions were administered. Few psychological studies have ever devoted this much care to establishing rapport with the child. Dr. Palmer found few significant differences in mental ability between the lower and middle class populations. This is one of the first times such a finding has been reported and it seems due, in part, to the great care taken to insure that the child comprehended the nature of the test questions and felt at ease with the examiner [1969, p. 276].

Labov provides a dramatic example of the effect of the test situation on an older child. Attacking the conditions under which much of the data on ''verbal deprivation'' is collected, he quotes an entire interview with a pre-adolescent boy in a New York City school and contrasts it with his own methods and findings:

> The child is alone in a school room with the investigator, a young, friendly white man, who is instructed to place a toy on the table and say ''Tell me everything you can about this.'' The interviewer's remarks are in parentheses.

(Tell me everything you can about *this*.) [Plunk]
    [12 seconds of silence]
(What would you say it looks like?)
    [8 seconds of silence]
A space ship.
(Hmmmm.)
    [13 seconds of silence]
Like a je-et
    [12 seconds of silence]
Like a plane.
    [20 seconds of silence]
(What color is it?)
Orange. [seconds] An' whi-ite. [seconds] An' green.
    [6 seconds of silence]
(And what could you use it for?)
    [8 seconds of silence]
A jet.
    [6 seconds of silence]
(If you had two of them, what would you do with them?)
    [6 seconds of silence]
Give one to some-body
(Hmmm. Who do you think would like to have it?)
    [10 seconds of silence]
Clarence.
(Mm. Where do you think we could get another one of these?)
At the store.
(O-Ka-ay!)

The social situation which produces such defensive behavior is that of an adult asking a lone child questions to which he obviously knows the answers, where anything the child says may well be held against him. It is, in fact, a paradigm of the school situation which prevails as reading is being taught (but not learned).

We can obtain such results in our own research, and have done so in our work with younger brothers of the "Thunderbirds" in 1390 Fifth Avenue. But when we change the social situation by altering the height and power relations, introducing a close friend of the subject, and talking about things we know he is interested in, we obtain a level of excited and rapid speech [Labov et al., 1968, Vol. 2, pp. 340-341].

The Situation as a Source of Social Class Differences

Because all the above examples illustrate how the same children respond in different situations, it may not be clear how the situation can be considered a neglected source of social class differences. Two ways are possible. Differential responses according to aspects of the situation may be intensified for lower-class speakers (an ordinal interaction). So for example, all children may be constrained in a testing situation and lower-class children especially so. Labov found this kind of interaction between style shifting and social stratification in his study of phonological and grammatical features:

> The same variables which are used in style shifting also distinguish cultural or social levels of English. This is so for stable phonological variables such as *-th* and *-ing,* for such incoming prestige forms as *-r;* for the grammatical variables such as pronominal opposition, double negative, or even the use of *ain't* [1969, p. 17].

For instance, all speakers shift from *workin'* to *working* as they shift from casual speech to reading style. But the shift is much greater for lower-class speakers.

Alternatively, there may be interactions between language and situation in which the relationships are reversed (a disordinal interaction) rather than varying in intensity for the different social class groups. Middle-class children may be more fluent in one set of situations, while lower-class children talk more fluently in another. Such a finding was suggested for our research subjects, Martin and Rita, above. Only further research can sort these possibilities out.

TOWARDS A THEORY OF ORAL LANGUAGE EDUCATION

Even if we had the kind of understanding of communicative competence among diverse groups of children which Hymes calls for, we would still be far from a theory of oral language education. That requires, in addition, decisions about which goals are important, what communicative competence we seek. Sociolinguistic interference from contrasting communicative demands outside and in school are almost certainly more important than grammatical interference (Hymes, in press; Labov et al., 1968). To reduce this interference, we have to know both what capabilities the child brings and what we want him to be able to do.

Language Use Rather Than Language Form Is Important

Discussions of the goals of education, like analyses of child language, too often focus on language form when they should be concerned with language use. In arguing against oral language programs for teaching standard English to speakers of a nonstandard dialect, Kochman says:

> My first quarrel with such a program is that it does not develop the ability of a person to use language, which I would further define as performance capability in a variety of social contexts on a variety of subject matter. . . . Underlying this approach seems to be a misapplication of Basil Bernstein's terms which falsely equate *restrictive code* and *elaborated code* with, respectively, non-standard dialect and standard dialect. It ought to be noted, as Bernstein uses the term, code is not to be equated with *langue,* but *parole,* not with *competence* but *performance.* What is restrictive or elaborated is not in fact the *code* as sociolinguists use the term, but the message [1969, p. 2].

To reject attempts to teach a single, socially prestigious language form is not to reject all attempts at change. Cultural differences in language use can result in deficiencies when children confront the demands of particular communicative situations.

Cultural relativism, inferred from an enormous variety of existing cultures, remains a prerequisite of objective analysis. . . . But the moral corollary of cultural relativism—moral relativism—has been quietly discarded except as a form of intellectual indulgence among those who claim the privilege of non-involvement [Wolf, 1964, pp. 21-22].

Educators certainly cannot claim any privilege of non-involvement, and they must decide what goals they seek. Taking as his goal the education of a person who knows enough not to remain a victim, Olson says, "A teacher must possess extraordinary knowledge and humanity if he is to distinguish what the school demands of children simply to symbolize its capacity for authority over them from what it legitimately 'demands' or 'woos out of them' to equip them for a niche in a technological society (1967, p. 13)."

Pieces of an answer can be suggested. On the basis of his experience as a teacher in a village school for Kwakiutl Indian children on Vancouver Island, Wolcott (1969) suggests teaching specific skills rather than trying to make over the child into one's own image. In an article in this volume, Marion Blank argues for education in the use of language for abstract thinking. Kochman (personal communication, 1969) recommends opportunity for the use of language in "low-context" situations where speaker and listener do not share a common referent and where a greater burden of communication falls on the words alone; this requires a skill that 33-month-old Gerald (Cazden, 1965) needs help in acquiring. Cazden & John (1969) argue for coordinate education for cultural pluralism in which patterns of language form and use (and beliefs and values as well) in the child's home community are maintained and valued alongside the introduction of forms of behavior required in a technological society.

In the end the goals of education are in large part matters of value, and decisions about them must be shared by educators and spokesmen for the child and his community. Such decisions, combined with knowledge of communicative competence and how it develops, will enable us to design more productive situations for oral language education in school.

REFERENCES

Aarons, A. C., Gordon, B. Y., & Stewart, W. A. (Eds.) Linguistic-cultural differences and American education. *Florida FL Reporter*, 1970, 7, No. 1.

Baratz, J. C. A bi-dialectal task for determining language proficiency in economically disadvantaged Negro children. *Child Development*, 1969, 889-901. (a)

Baratz, J. C. Language and cognitive assessment of Negro children. *ASHA*, 1969, *11*, 87-91. (b)

Barker, R. G. *Ecological psychology*. Stanford Cal.: Stanford University Press, 1968.

Berlyne, D. E., & Frommer, F. D. Some determinants of the incidence and content of children's questions. *Child Development*, 1966, *37*, 177-189.

Bernat, E. How speakers of different ages alter their speech when conversing with small children. Unpublished term paper, Harvard Graduate School of Education, 1969.

Bernstein, B. Social class, linguistic codes and grammatical elements. *Language and Speech*, 1962, *5*, 221-240.

Bernstein, B. A critique of the concept "compensatory education." Introduction to Gahagan, D. M., & Gahagan, G. A. *Talk reform: Explorations in language for infant school children*. London: Routledge & Kegan Paul, in press. Also in Cazden, C. B., Hymes, D., & John, V. (Eds.), *Functions of language in the classroom*. New York: Teachers College Press, in press.

Bloom, L. M. *Language development: Form and function in emerging grammars*. Cambridge: M.I.T. Press, 1970.

Brent, S. B., & Katz, E. W. A study of language deviations and cognitive processes. Progress Report No. 3, OEO Job Corps contract 1209, Wayne State University, 1967.

Brown, R., Cazden, C. B., & Bellugi, U. The child's grammar from I to III. In J. P. Hill (Ed.), *1967 Minnesota Symposium on Child Psychology*. Minneapolis: University of Minn. Press, 1969.

Cazden, C. B. Environmental assistance to the child's acquisition of grammar. Unpublished doctoral dissertation, Harvard Univ., 1965.

Cazden, C. B. Subcultural differences in child language. *Merrill-Palmer Quarterly*, 1966, *12*, 185-219.

Cazden, C. B. On individual differences in language competence and performance. *Journal of Special Education*, 1967, *1*, 135-150.

Cazden, C. B. Language programs for young children: Views from England. In C. B. Lavatelli (Ed.), *Preschool Language Training*. Urbana: Univer. of Illinois Press, in press.

Cazden, C. B., & John, V. P. Learning in American Indian children. In S. Ohannessian (Ed.), *Styles of learning among American Indians: An outline for research*. Washington, D.C.: Center for Applied Linguistics, 1969.

Chomsky, N. Phonology and reading. In H. Levin and J. Williams (Eds.), *Basic Studies on Reading*. New York: Harper & Row, in press.

Chomsky, N., & Halle, M. *The sound patterns of English*. New York: Harper & Row, 1968.

Cowan, P. A., Weber, J., Hoddinott, B. A., & Klein, J. Mean length of spoken response as a function of stimulus, experimenter, and subject. *Child Development*, 1967, *38*, 199-203.

Cowe, E. G. A study of kindergarten activities for language development. Unpublished doctoral dissertation, Columbia Univer., 1967.

Eels, D., Davis, A., Havighurst, R. J., Herrick, V. E., & Tyler, R. W. *Intelligence and Cultural Differences*. Chicago: Univer. of Chicago Press, 1951.

Goffman, E. The neglected situation. *American Anthropologist*, 1964, *66* (Part 2), 133-136.

Heider, E. R., Cazden, C. B., & Brown, R. Social class differences in the effectiveness and style of children's coding ability. Project Literacy Reports, No. 9. Ithaca, N.Y.: Cornell Univer., 1968.

Herman, S. R. Explorations in the social psychology of language choice. *Human Relations,* 1961, *14,* 149-164.

Hymes, D. On communicative competence. In R. Huxley & E. Ingram (Eds.), *The Mechanism of Language Development.* London: CIBA Foundation, in press.

Jensen, A. R. How much can we boost IQ and scholastic achievement? *Harvard Educational Review,* 1969, *39,* 1-123.

Kagan, J. On the need for relativism. *American Psychologist,* 1967, *22,* 131-142.

Kagan, J. Inadequate evidence and illogical conclusions, *Harvard Educational Review.* 1969, *39,* 274-277.

Kochman, T. Special factors in the consideration of teaching standard English. Paper read at convention of Teachers of English to Speakers of other Languages (TESOL), Chicago, March 1969.

Labov, W. *The Study of Non-Standard English.* Washington, D.C.: Clearinghouse for Linguistics, Center for Applied Linguistics, 1969. (Available from ERIC Document Reproduction Service.)

Labov, W., Cohen, P., Robins, C., & Lewis, J. *A study of the non-standard English of Negro and Puerto Rican speakers in New York City.* Final report of Cooperative Research Project No. 3288, Columbia University, 1968. 2 vols. (Available from ERIC Document Reproduction Service.)

LaCivita, A. F., Kean, J. M., & Yamamoto, K. Socio-economic status of children and acquisition of grammar. *Journal of Educational Research,* 1966, *60,* 71-74.

Lawton, D. *Social Class, Language and Education.* New York: Schocken, 1968.

Lesser, G. S., Fifer, G., & Clark, D. H. Mental abilities of children in different social and cultural groups. *Monographs of the Society for Research in Child Development,* 1965, *30,* No. 4 (Serial No. 102).

Mackay, D., & Thompson, B. *The Initial Teaching of Reading and Writing: Some Notes toward a Theory of Literacy.* Program in linguistics and English teaching, Paper No. 3. London: University College and Longmans Green, 1968.

McNamara, J. (Ed.) Problems of bilingualism. *Journal of Social Issues,* 1967, *23* (2).

Moffett, J. *Teaching the universe of discourse.* Boston: Houghton Mifflin, 1968.

Moore, D. R. Research on children's language as it relates to a language program for lower class preschool children. In C. B. Lavatelli (Ed.), *Preschool Language Training.* Urbana, Ill.: University of Illinois Press, in press.

Nida, E. A. Analysis of meaning and dictionary making. *International Journal of American Linguistics,* 1958, *24,* 279-292.

Olson, P. A. Introduction: The craft of teaching and the school of teachers. Report of the first national conference, U.S. Office of Education Tri-University Project in Elementary Education, Denver, Sept. 1967.

Pasamanick, B., & Knobloch, H. Early language behavior in Negro children and the testing of intelligence. *Journal of Abnormal and Social Psychology,* 1955, *50,* 401-402.

Plumer, D. Parent-child verbal interaction: A naturalistic study of dialogue strategies. Interim report, Harvard Graduate School of Education, 1969.

Psathas, G. Comment. *American Psychologist,* 1968, *23,* 135-137.

Resnick, M. B., Weld, G. L. & Lally, J. R. Verbalizations of environmentally deprived two-year olds as a function of the presence of a tester in a standardized test situation.

Paper presented at the meeting of the American Educational Research Association, Los Angeles, February 1969.

Robinson, W. P. The elaborated code in working-class language. *Language and Speech,* 1965, *8,* 243-252.

Robinson, W. P. Restricted codes in socio-linguistics and the sociology of education. Paper presented at Ninth International Seminar, University College, Dar es Salaam, December 1968.

Shuy, R. W., Wolfram, W. A., & Riley, W. K. *Linguistic Correlates of Social Stratification in Detroit Speech.* Final report of Cooperative Research Project No. 6-1347, Wayne State University, 1967. (Available from ERIC Document Reproduction Service.)

Slobin, D. I. (Ed.) *A Field Manual for Cross-Cultural Study of the Acquisition of Communicative competence* (second draft). Berkeley, Cal.: University of California, 1967.

Slobin, D. I. Questions of language development in cross-cultural perspective. Paper prepared for symposium on "Language learning in cross-cultural perspective," Michigan State University, Sept. 1968.

Smith, M. E. A study of some factors influencing the development of the sentence in preschool children. *Journal of Genetic Psychology,* 1935, *46,* 182-212.

Strandberg, T. E. An evaluation of three stimulus media for evoking verablizations from preschool children. Unpublished Master's thesis, Eastern Illinois Univer., 1969.

Strandberg, T. E., & Griffith, J. A study of the effects of training in visual literacy on verbal language behavior. Unpublished manuscript, Eastern Illinois University, 1968.

Williams, F., & Naremore, R. C. On the functional analysis of social class differences in modes of speech. *Speech Monographs,* 1969, *36,* 77-102. (a)

Williams, F., & Naremore, R. C. Social class differences in children's syntactic performance: A quantitative analysis of field study data. *Journal of Speech and Hearing Research,* 1969, *12,* 777-793. (b)

Wolcott, H. F. The teacher as an enemy. Unpublished manuscript, Univer. of Oregon, 1969.

3

Address Forms Used by Members of a Department Store*

L. Staples and W. Robinson

Address forms are one readily observed index of the nature of social relationships among participants in face-to-face interactions. Previous work has related asymmetry of forms to differences in power and status, and symmetrical use of 'informal' forms to solidarity and friendship. In this study address forms given to and received from members of the same and different ranks in an hierarchically ordered department store are shown to vary as a function of situation and the relative rather than absolute status of participants. Asymmetry of address forms appears to be mainly a matter of rank rather than age. Discrepancies between expected and received forms are interpreted as a result of high status persons maximising differentials and of low status persons minimising them.

INTRODUCTION

Forms of address have provided social psychologists with easily collected data of relevance to the role relationships existing between participants in any interaction involving a verbal exchange. Brown and Gilman (1960) capitalized on the T/V distinction in the second person pronouns of many Standard Average European languages and, by means of analyses of literary products and not overly systematic studies of modern usage, were able to construct an explanation of how the distinctions came to be made and how they operate now. Brown and Ford (1961) collected contemporary data on proper name usage in English speaking

*British Journal of Social and Clinical Psychology, 1974, 13, 1-11. Reprinted by permission of the British Psychological Society.

communities, referred to severally as 'a usage in modern American plays', 'actual usage in a Boston business firm', 'reported usage of business executives' and 'recorded usage in Midwest'—and a final category which included comparison group of 56 children from Yoredale, England (the results of this comparative study have not yet been published). Variants used have been extracted (Fig. 3.1), and the significance of two main reciprocal and one non-reciprocal patterns of address interpreted against a two-dimensional grid.

Elaborated by Brown (1965), the system postulates a status norm and a solidarity norm. Inequality of status is marked by a system of non-reciprocal address; typically high status persons give T pronouns and First Names (FN), but receive V pronouns and Title Last Name (TLN). Equality of status, without solidarity, is marked by the mutual use of V and TLN forms; equality of status, with solidarity, by T and FN forms. In English there are five main forms: T, Title, Madam; TLN, Title Last Name, Miss Jones; LN, Last Name, Jones; FN, First Name, Marion; MN, Multiple Names, Marion, Cuddles, Thingy, and other terms, usually affectionate. The forms are arranged on the staircase in the manner and order portrayed for two reasons. Increases along the solidarity dimension are marked by a progression from left to right. Although steps can be omitted and developing relationships may not proceed all the way to multiple naming, the order chosen gives the best fit to data collected. Further, inequalities of status are commonly marked by non-reciprocal forms only one step apart, and if this criterion is applied to the data, the steps take the form illustrated. The status steps can be superimposed upon the solidarity progression with no conflicts. Hence, this particular ordering gives the simplest diagrammatic representation of the associations between naming and relationships.

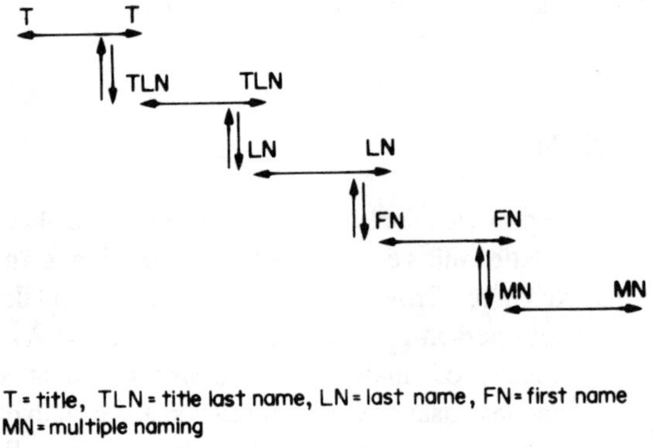

T = title, TLN = title last name, LN = last name, FN = first name
MN = multiple naming

Figure 3.1   Address Forms for Proper Names in English (after Brown and Ford, *op. cit.*)

Brown (*op. cit.*) has extended the details of this analysis in respect of other address form variants, problems of conflict between the norms, behaviours other than forms of address, and he has inquired into possible determinants of both status differentials, *e.g.* power, age, *etc.*, and bases of solidarity, *e.g.* kinship ties, friendship, group membership.

Slobin, Miller and Porter (1968) investigated reported address forms used to other employees at four organizational levels in an American insurance firm. FN was used between equals and in addressing subordinates. A higher proportion of non-reciprocal FN/TLN combinations characterized status differentials. Age, time in firm, and measures of status striving and self assurance were unrelated to address patterns. (Interestingly enough, evidence was found of a propensity to make more personal self-disclosures to immediate superiors than to immediate subordinates with TLN retained as a form of address. This is in apparent conflict with Brown and Ford's suggestion that increased intimacy has to be initiated from above.)

Of the many questions that remain unanswered or even unposed (see Robinson, 1972), we are interested in tackling four:

1. *Situation as a determinant of address forms.* Hymes (1967) has attempted to list a number of 'variables' which may co-vary with speech forms selected when alternatives are available (Setting, Participants, Ends, Art characteristics, Key, Instrumentalities, Norms, and Genre). 'Setting' and 'Participants' are self-explanatory. By 'Ends' is intended both the purposes of the participants and the outcome of the speaking which of course may be different. One may use flattering forms of address in order to ingratiate oneself with powerful persons, but the outcome may be a contemptuous dismissal. 'Art characteristics' likewise has a double component: message form and topic, both of which are used in their everyday sense. 'Key' refers to manner. 'Hail, King of the Jews' was sarcastic rather than sincere. With 'Instrumentalities', it is again two aspects that are covered, channel and code. 'Channel' distinguishes among media of communication. To start a letter 'Dear John' may be commonly appropriate, but it is not the most common form of oral greeting. 'Code' refers to the language employed, while 'sub-code' is reserved for dialects and other variants. The Latin form of names of graduands distinguishes the Oxford degree ceremony from some others. 'Norms' refers both to norms of interaction (like not interrupting) and norms of interpretation. 'Genre' means types of speech event such as conversation, lecture or prayer.

    Research on address forms has been concentrated upon Participants and their relationships. Situation (Hymes' setting) will also be relevant. In 'The Admirable Crichton' the master/servant relationships are reversed as a consequence of an aristocratic family being shipwrecked—and the address forms switch too. One can conceive of a society where situational variation might be irrelevant to address forms, *e.g.* a caste system where caste differentials formed the major stratifying variable for all interactions. One can also conceive of the possibility of a pair of people switching address forms across a variety of situations as their role relationships change. If we ignore institutionalized roles associated with explicitly role-related address forms (Madam Chairman), we might imagine that our society would operate with a formal-informal dimension such as that postulated by Joos (1952) and elegantly exposed by Labov (1966) in his study of phonemic pronunciation shifts from careful to casual speech. For personnel in an hierarchically ordered organization in a society such as ours, rank has been shown to be associated with the use of particular non-reciprocated address forms within the confines of the organization. What happens when such people meet in other contexts? We might expect that the further one moves away (psychologically) from situations which directly emphasise the occupational role and into more informal situations, the smaller the incidence of unreciprocated forms and the greater the incidence of those associated with solidarity. This possibility was the primary focus of the present study.

2. *Relative status differentials and absolute status as determinants of address forms received.* In any two-person interaction, there are three components related to the status of the participants: the absolute status of each and the status differential between them. Slobin *et al.* claimed that the differential is important, but did not explicitly test the relative importance of each of the three, and their reported results do not permit calculations that could isolate the operation of the variables.

3. *Reliability of data.* Are forms of address reported as being used by persons reliable and valid? There are no estimates of either. Observed forms were used in some of Brown's analyses, but most data have been based on reported usage. While we might expect subjects to be able to report reliably and validly on such a matter and in general to have no reasons for lying, it might be helpful to meet the logically-based criticism with empirical data. We therefore collected answers to questions about forms expected from others and used by others, and noted the incidence of discrepancies between the two. This provides for an estimation of reliability. While it would have been additionally helpful to have checked these results against observed behaviour, the administrative difficulties would have been too great.

4. *Regularities in discrepancies between expected and received address forms.* Where statuses are in fact different, but address forms used are reciprocated, it is supposed that it is the person of higher status whose position is diminished and the lower status person's position that is enhanced. We would therefore expect that, where discrepancies obtain between received and expected forms, higher status persons will expect to receive more 'formal' forms than they do from lower status persons, but lower status persons expect to receive less 'formal' forms than they in fact do from persons of higher status—assuming a general aspiration to increase status, and that reception of FN is indicative of status equality rather than of condescension.*

METHOD

Subjects

Thirty personnel were selected from seven departments of a large department store. One person from each of these was chosen from the four lower ranks in the hierarchy. Two divisional managers supervised the seven departments and they were included to provide subjects for a fifth rank, but since their data were

---

*There is an ambiguity in the meaning of address forms that this study fails to resolve. While it should be possible to distinguish the FN of condescension from the FN of cohesiveness by the existence of asymmetry and symmetry respectively, once we move into the regions in which persons disagree about what happens, it is no longer possible to distinguish between different possibilities. Our interpretation favours the dominance of status differentials over cohesiveness, but a reviewer of the article preferred to adopt the reverse view and I do not think our evidence enables us to discriminate between these accounts. Probing interviews could. (WPR).

excluded from the main analysis, they are hardly mentioned further. The intention to include only male staff could not be fully implemented, and six of the 14 sales staff were female. The known characteristics of the subjects are given in Table 3.1.

Table 3.1   Characteristics of Subjects

Rank	Number	Age		Years of Service	
		Mean	Range	Mean	Range
1. Divisional Manager	2	41.5	25-58	22.0	6-38
2. Department Manager	7	40.4	22-58	12.4	1.21
3. Dep. Asst. Manager	7	34.1	21-62	5.1	.5-16
4. Senior Sales Staff	7	49.4	19-58	4.2	.5-.9
5. Junior Sales Staff	7	17.1	16-23	.7	.3-.1

In the second section, the first set of questions was repeated, but subjects were asked by what name the other people addressed them in each of the five situations or would address them by if the occasion arose.

Situations.   A   In the store in front of a customer
B   In the staff canteen at stocktaking
C   At a staff dance
D   In the street
E   In a pub (restaurant for teetotallers and spinsters!)

Materials—Questionnaire

In the first section, each *S.* from ranks 2-5 was asked by what name he would address a specified person of his own rank in his department, three other named members of his department but of different ranks—and the divisional manager. Divisional managers were asked about all included personnel from ranks 2-5 and about each other. The five questions were repeated for each of the five situation contexts.

Procedure

E. interviewed each *S.* individually. She stated that she was interested in what names people used to address each other in different situations, outlined the form of the interview questionnaire, and mentioned she was unconnected with the store. Confirmation of understanding was established. *S.* was asked to mention all names, if he might use more than one in any situation, and he was asked to imagine that only he and the other were immediately involved in the encounter. On the first series presented, *E.* referred to everyone by status and TLN, but shortened this to TLN on the subsequent ones. The order of presentation was Situation A first for all ranks in the order 1-5, then Situation B. *etc*. Completion took between 10 and 20 minutes.

Treatment of Results

All varieties of naming mentioned in the Introduction occurred, including one additional form—Title First Name (TFN), *e.g.* Mr. Charles. The vast majority of responses were TLN and FN, and as far as possible, the other variants were incorporated under whichever of these was more appropriate. T alone (Sir) was almost wholly confined to addressing Divisional Managers in Situation A. TFN was accorded to one person in Situation A only. Both these were re-scored as TLN. LN appeared to substitute for FN (surprisingly?) as ascertained on the basis of further questioning, and hence was categorised there. Where MN occurred, *S*. was asked whether particular names varied with topics of conversation or affective states, and if any claim of this nature were asserted, MN was scored. The three forms were scored: TLN + 1, FN 0, and MN − 1, for both Address Form Expected and Address Form Received. Scores for each of these were entered into a four-way analysis of variance.

1. Address Form Expected and Received (G): 2 sets of 3 values each: TLN, FN, MN.
2. Situation (S): 5 values: Shop serving, Shop canteen, Staff dance, Street, Pub.
3. Rank of Addresser (A): 4 values: Ranks 2-5.
4. Rank of Receiver (R): 4 values: Ranks 2-5.

Subsidiary analyses of variance were conducted to resolve problems thrown up by the results of the main analysis and to answer questions outside its coverage.

RESULTS

Address Form Expected was not differentiated from Address Form Received, which testifies to the reliability of data. Both Situation and Receiver rank had significant associations with Address Forms used, but Addresser rank did not (Table 3.2). Of the interactions, Receiver/Addresser rank and Receiver/Address Forms Expected and Received were significant.

1. *Situation as a determinant of address forms*. Since Situation was not represented in any significant interactions, we could proceed to examine its manner of operation directly. Ten tests for simple effects of Situation showed that Situation A (in shop in front of a customer) evoked more formal address than each of the others (p < .001 in every case), Situation B (in staff canteen) more than C, D, or E (p < .001, p < .1, p < .01), but C, D, and E were not

Table 3.2. Analysis of Variance for Formality of Address Forms as a Function of Expectation/Actual Receipt, Situation, Rank of Addresser and Rank of Receiver.

Source	df	F	p value
Received vs. Expected (G)	1	<1	-
Situation (S)	4	97.42	<.001
Rank of Addresser (A)	3	<1	-
Rank of Receiver (R)	3	50.64	<.001
G × S	4	<1	-
G × A	3	<1	-
G × R	3	3.01	<.05
S × A	12	1.61	-
S × R	12	<1	-
A × R	9	16.40	<.001
G × S × A	12	<1	-
G × S × R	12	<1	-
G × A × R	9	2.15	-
S × A × R	36	<1	-
Residual	336		

differentiated. For these respondents, there would appear to be no grounds for having more than a three-point scale of formality of situation.

2. *Relative and absolute status as determinants of address forms.* Although Receiver rank appeared as a main effect, since it was also involved as a significant interaction term, one has to ask whether or not there is a significant F ratio when the interaction variance estimate is used as the error term for it to be useful to make comments about its independent relevance. This value is not significant. For the Receiver/Addresser interaction, the most obvious differences were for Receivers at Ranks 2 and 5; while there was a steep rise in formality for Receivers of Rank 2 as Addresser rank declined, there was a mirror image reduction for Receivers at Rank 5 (Figs. 3.2 and 3.3). This may be construed as a propensity for low ranking Addressers to make more marked discrimination by rank while high ranking Addressers shift but little. High ranking Addressers are, if anything, most formal with the lowest ranks which appears to be a different pattern from that reported by Slobin *et al.* (1968). It is also noteworthy that Rank 4 (Senior Sales Staff) were accorded more formal address than Rank 3 (Assistant Managers). This reversal was associated with an age difference of 15 years and a confounding sex factor of four women at Rank 4. That sex has a relevance is suggested by the differential proportion of TLN offered to men and women of Grade 4. As shown in Table 3.3; 8% of address forms received by men at Rank 4 in situations B, C, D, E were TLN as opposed to 35% by women; in Situation A

the figures were 92% and 93%. It was also the case that women in Rank 4 were more likely to expect TLN in Situations B, C, D, and E (69% against 17%).

The Address Form Expected and Received/Receiver rank interaction showed quite different pattern. While formality increases with reductions in Receiver rank for Addressers at rank 2, it decreased with a reduction in Receiver rank for Addressers at rank 5.

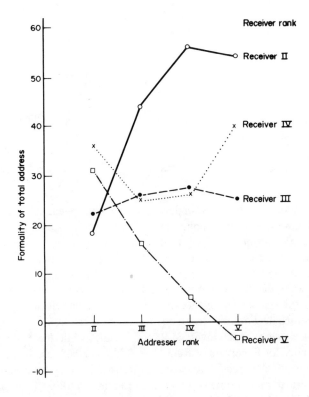

Figure 3.2 Total formality of address forms given to each receiver rank by each addresser rank.

The Receiver/Addresser interaction shows that status differentials rather than absolute rank were relevant. That Receiver, but not Addresser, rank was significant is taken up in the discussion.

3. *Reliability of data.* There was no difference between Address Forms Expected and Received, so that, in the context of the other significant differences, we may claim that the data obtained are reliable.

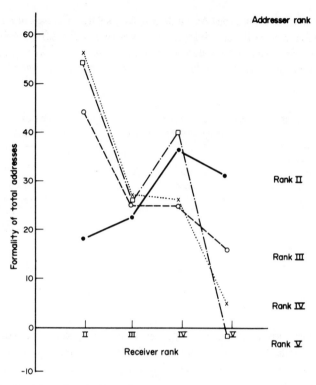

Figure 3.3   Total formality of address forms received by each receiver rank from each addresser rank.

4. *Non-reciprocal address patterns and discrepancies in expected and received forms.* With a reasonable incidence of non-reciprocated address patterns in the data, it was possible to ask how these distributed by rank (absolute and

Table 3.3.   Proportions of TLN among Address Forms Received and Expected by Men and Women of Grade 4 across Situations.

	Situation				
	A	B	C	D	E
Received by men	.92	.15	.08	.08	0
Received by women	.93	.40	.33	.33	.33
Expected by men	.83	.25	.08	.17	.17
Expected by women	.94	.69	.69	.69	.69

relative), age, and situation. As Table 3.4 shows 94% of these unreciprocated forms were correctly anticipated, and whereas only 7% fitted an age differential criterion, 97% fitted a status differential one. How degrees of inequality of rank related to non-reciprocity was exposed by an analysis

Table 3.4. Non-reciprocal Address Patterns among Unequals explicable in terms of Status and Age Differentials.

Situation	Number of non-reciprocal patterns	Number explicable in terms of (a) Status	(b) Age	%Correct anticipation
A	5	4	1	100
B	19	15	2	89
C	23	20	1	91
D	21	19	1	95
E	20	18	1	94
Total	88	76 (87%)	6 (7%)	94

showing proportions of non-reciprocal patterns for 1, 2 and 3 rank differences in status (Table 3.5). While reciprocity obtained generally in Situation A, all other situations revealed a similar distribution of incremental increases with rank difference.

Table 3.5. Proportions of Non-reciprocal Address Forms as a Function of Status Differential and Situation.

	Situation				
	A	B	C	D	E
Between equals	.04	.07	0	.04	0
Between unequals	.12	.45	.55	.50	.48
Inequality of 1 rank	0	.33	.48	.33	.38
Inequality of 2 ranks	.14	.43	.57	.64	.50
Inequality of 3 ranks	.21	.86	.86	.71	.86

One final question posed about non-reciprocal forms was whether forms expected were more or less formal than those received. As the data of Table 3.6 indicate, high ranking personnel expected more formality than low ranking personnel were inclined to give, low ranking personnel expected less.

Table 3.6.   Proportions of Non-reciprocal Address Patterns where Forms Received by Subjects are More Formal than Expected by Rank and Situation.

	Situation				
	A	B	C	D	E
Rank					
2	-	0	0	.17	0
3	.50	.32	.60	.33	.33
4	.67	.60	.76	.67	.67
5	.72	.80	1.00	1.00	.80

DISCUSSION

Both the failure to find differences between reported given and received address forms and 94% congruence of unreciprocated forms testify to the reliability of the data—and by extension to other data collected by similar means.

Situation proved to be a strong determinant of forms used. Although the staff dance, the street and the pub were not discriminated, the staff canteen evoked more formal exchanges than these and in the store in front of customers the most formal of all. The difference between the predominating mutual TLN of an English department store and the FN of Slobin et al's American insurance firm may be less indicative of British reserve than the difference in situations. Their results were probably derived from only two-person encounters, whereas in our Situation A, the department store was presenting its image to the public.

While the results suggest only a three-category division of 'at work on display', 'at work', 'at leisure', the similarity of the leisure situations may be an artefact of inexperience. Encounters in these three may be relatively rare or even non-existent, but at least respondents are prepared for such with their more informal address forms.

If we attempt to return to the status/solidarity framework proposed by Brown, we may first of all note that the power differential in our most formal situation is not characterised by the use of unreciprocated forms of address—only 12% of exchanges between unequals were so marked. What is presumably a norm for mutual TLN is dominant. In the other situations, there is considerable similarity in the proportion of unreciprocated exchanges between unequals, amounting on average to 50% of the possible (Table 3.5). 87% of these are explicable on the basis of differences in rank, 7% in terms of age, both status variables. Hence, in so far as differentials are maintained, it is in the informal settings that status superiors switch to FN while inferiors do not. Equals do tend to switch to address forms allegedly more indicative of solidarity, although again these might be better understood in terms of an FN norm in informal settings. If these interpretations are valid, the address form variants across situations are a function of more general social norms, with considerations of status and solidarity entering as second-order factors.

In the examination of whether absolute and relative status were determinants of address forms used, we found that Addresser rank was irrelevant, Receiver rank and Addresser/Receiver interaction were significant. The details of the interaction from the point of view of addressers help to clarify what appears to be happening (Fig. 3.2). Taking speakers of rank 2 it may be seen that they tend to give more informal speech to those of ranks 2 and 3, than to those of ranks 4 and 5. With the addition that they give more formal forms to rank 2, members of levels 3 and 4 have an identical pattern, mutatis mutandis. Members of grade 5 gave significantly more formal speech the greater the 'distance' between them and the addressee. Thus all ranks except grade 5 treat one other group in the same way they treat their equals. For ranks 2 and 3, it is the rank below, but for rank 4 it is the grade above.

These differences are perhaps related to the organisation. In treating another rank as equals, rank 2 can only choose a subordinate rank, if at all. That they do, probably reflects the fact that both have managerial status. Whilst members of rank 3 have greater occupational status than those of rank 4, the latter are on average 15 years older, and the treatment of each other as equals may represent the achievement of an equilibrium when these two sources of status are in opposition. In all cases, where distance between members of the dyad is two ranks or more, speech terms are significantly different from those given to those of the same rank.

In no case, however, can the absolute scores be taken on their own. They must be considered in terms of whether the forms given or received are relatively more or less formal than those given to or received by other ranks. Members of rank 2 receive more formal speech from ranks 3, 4, and 5, than from equals (Fig. 3.3). Members of level 3 received similar speech from all ranks, but they receive from rank 2 the same speech as rank 2 afford to equals, which is less formal than that given to ranks 2 and 4. Thus, although members of rank 3 are given the same total speech forms by all other ranks, they have been perceived in different ways by the addressers of different ranks. They have been treated by equals, not only by actual equals, but also by ranks 2 and 4, and as seniors by grade 5. Members of level 4 have received the same speech from those of ranks 2 and 5, although 2 considers them as subordinates, and rank 5 as superiors. They have received less formal speech from those of ranks 2 and 3, both of whom treated them as equals.

Members of rank 5 receive increasingly formal speech as the distance between Receiver and Addresser increases. They are treated as subordinates by all ranks except equals. This is interesting, in that while members of rank 2 are superior to all other ranks, they do not receive greater formality as the status inequality increases, whilst those of rank 5, who are subordinate to all other ranks, do receive great formality as status inequality increases. Thus, grade 2 receives no more formal speech from grade 4 than from grade 3, whilst grade 5 do. This may reflect the fact that in an interaction it is the inferior who is enhanced by the relationship, and thus the desire to minimise status inequality upward, but maximise it downward. At the same time, this formality between extremes may also signify a mutual denial of solidarity. With address forms we can reject solidarity as well as accept it.

It may be seen then from the study of the Addresser/Receiver interaction why the rank of the Addresser did not emerge as a significant factor. In each case, the manner in which personnel addressed the members of a particular rank was only of significance when related to the ways in which they addressed other ranks. This is particularly clear in the case of grade 3.

Power in the status of the Receiver was also involved in a significant interaction between Receiver and Address Form Given and Received. Whilst members of grades 3 and 4 do not differ in the amount of formal speech which they receive, members of grade 3 expect more formal speech than those of grade 4. Members of grade 2 receive and expect significantly more formal speech than any other grade, and members of grade 5 receive and expect significantly less.

This may help to explain why Receiver but not Addresser rank is significant. It is as though the Receiver Scale is stretched at its extremes. By the forms selected, an Addresser can attempt to enhance or deflate the Receiver's status, but cannot immediately affect his own. In one sense the Addresser has no discretion to choose what he will be called, only what he will call other people. In another sense, of course, he can make his expectations clear and can exert an influence.

The data on individual non-reciprocal address patterns illuminate the relationships further. These data showed that non-reciprocity was most common in Situations other than A, and when the question is posed as to whether forms are more or less formal than expected, high ranking personnel expect more formality than others given them and low ranking personnel expected less. This is consistent with the interpretation of the results of the main analysis of variance showing the extension of the Receiver scale.

Our data seem therefore to exhibit a subtlety of detail beyond what might be expected from a simple application of Brown's two-factor grid. Shifts of address forms across situations and ranks are statistical trends not uniform switches; the system has a looseness in it—which gives it adaptability in the face of change?

This investigation like all others, poses the problem of what next and so what? More detailed analyses could have been made of the data collected, *e.g.* multiple naming, an apparent tendency for the youngest people to be more likely to use FN across situations and ranks, isolation of discrepancies between address forms given and received where these occurred, but to pursue these problems it is probably more useful to select situations and participants where these phenomena are likely to be writ large. These would seem to be next steps in elaborating and probing Brown's general theoretical framework (*op. cit.*). Another possibility is to investigate patterns of change of address forms between participants through time. Slobin *et al.* (*op. cit.*) have suggested that inferiors can take steps, of unknown utility, to diminish differences between ranks with the implication that these, if successful, might lead to changes from non-reciprocal to reciprocal address patterns. The behaviour of younger personnel indicate the converse possibility that a utilization of FN address forms to superiors might diminish status differentials.

A final methodological note might also be made. If the interpretations of the reasons why Receiver but not Addresser rank is significant and how the Receiver/Address Form interaction functions are valid, the results merit comparison with studies in other areas where apparently 'objective' scales become phenomenologically distorted. In this case the characteristics of the rank scale change according to whether one looks at it from the Addresser or the Receiver perspective and in the latter case also has its extreme intervals extended. This is reminiscent of Tajfel's (1959) work of valued attributes and the properties of judgements about attitude scales (Sherif, Sherif and Nebergall, 1965).

REFERENCES

Brown, R. *Social Psychology*. New York: Free Press, 1965.

Brown, R. and Ford, M. Address in American English. *J. Abnorm. Soc. Psychol.* 1961, *62*, 375-385.

Brown, R. and Gilman, A. The pronouns of power and solidarity. In T. Sebeok (Ed.), *Style in Language*. New York: Wiley, 1960.

Hymes, D. Models of the interaction of languages and social setting. *J. Soc. Issues*, 1967, *23*, 8-28.

Joos, M. The five clocks. *Internat. J. Amer. Linguistics*, 1962, *28*, Part 5.

Labov, W. *The Social Stratification of English in New York City*. Washington: Center Applied Linguistics, 1966.

Robinson, W. P. *Language and Social Behaviour*. Harmondsworth, Middlesex: Penguin, 1972.

Sherif, C. W., Sherif, M. and Nebergall, R. E. *Attitude and Attitude Change: the Social Judgement-Involvement Approach*. Philadelphia: Saunders, 1965.

Slobin, D. I., Miller, S. H. and Porter, L. W. Forms of address and social relations in a business organisation. *J. Pers. Soc. Psychol.*, 1968, *8*, 289-293.

Staples, L. M. *A Study of Address Forms used in a Hierarchical Organisation*. Unpub. mss. Dept. Psychology: Univ. Southampton, 1971.

Tajfel, H. Quantitative judgement in social perception. *Br. J. Psychol.*, 1959, *50*, 16-29.

Clinical Psychology: Introduction

Research on the effect of situations on behaviour is very important in clinical psychology. Holmes and Huston (1974) showed that it is possible to reduce the effects of stressful situations by altering the definition of the situation. Subjects who were told they would receive "painful electric shocks" for 30 seconds showed less physical traces of anxiety when instructed to change their psychological definition of the stressful situation. In one experimental condition they were instructed to remain calm and relaxed, and to adopt an unemotional and detached attitude, thus "isolating" the shocks. In another condition subjects were instructed to think of the shocks as an interesting new physiological sensation, a kind of vibration. Physiological measures were taken of heart rate and skin conductance: both the isolation and redefinition groups showed lower levels of anxiety than a threat group, though not as low as in a non-threat control group.

Eisler, Hersen, Miller and Blanchard (1975) extended the earlier work by this group on situational factors in assertiveness. Sixty patients role-played 32 varied assertiveness situations, and their performances were videotaped. Verbal and non-verbal components of assertiveness in individuals were found to vary between positive and negative assertiveness situations, according to sex and familiarity of the other person. This confirms previous findings that assertiveness is greatly affected by the nature of the situation. High-and low-assertiveness subjects were identified from overall ratings and self-ratings; on average the assertive subjects produced longer utterances, spoke louder, made more requests etc., though there was interaction with situational variables for some of these modes of response. That it is necessary to train individuals for assertiveness in the type of situation they find most difficult, and that this training involves learning the appropriate behavior for each situation, is a relevant finding for the practice of assertiveness training and clinical psychology.

In their article on the situational factors that influence smoking behavior, Best and Hakstian (1978) report the valuable results of a study involving more than 300 subjects who rated their urge to smoke in 50 different moods and situations. The ratings were factor analysed, yielding 12 factors for males and 11 for females; then the factor scores were subjected to cluster analysis, yielding 4 male and 5 female clusters. The male smokers were divided into two clusters of heavy smokers who smoked in most situations, and two clusters of light smokers who smoked in few situations. Both clusters responded differentially to various situations that induced smoking. This study shows that smoking is based on a number of different motivational processes, and adds that these processes vary between situations. The findings of this study, which suggest that alternative ways should be found of meeting the same needs in different situations, are not only relevant to the designing of procedures for helping people give up smoking, but also support the findings of other situation research.

SUGGESTED ADDITIONAL REFERENCES

Alonzo, A. Everyday illness behavior: a situational approach to health status deviations. *Social Science and Medicine,* 1979, *13,* 397-404.

Bauer, R. and Craighead, W. Psychophysiological responses to the imagination of fearful and neutral situations. *Behavior Therapy,* 1979, *10,* 389-403.

Bearden, W., Woodside, A. and Jones, J. Beliefs and anticipated situations influencing intention to use drugs. *Perceptual and Motor Skills,* 1979, *48,* 743-751.

Calhoun, L., Selby, J. and Wroten, J. Situational constraint and type of causal explanation: the effects on perceived 'mental illness' and social rejection. *Journal of Research into Personality,* 1977, *11,* 95-100.

Chang, B. Perceived situational control of daily activities: a new tool. *Research in Nursing and Health,* 1978, *1,* 181-188.

Chapman, S. and Jeffrey, D. Situational management, standard setting, and self-reward in a behavior modification weight loss program. *Journal of Consulting and Clinical Psychology,* 1980, *46,* 1588-1589.

Coleman, R., Whitman, T. and Johnson, M. Suppression of self-stimulatory behavior of a profoundly retarded boy across staff and settings: an assessment of situational generalization. *Behavior Therapy,* 1979, *10,* 266-280.

Coyne, J. Toward an interactional description of depression. *Psychiatry,* 1976, *39,* 28-40.

Coyne, J. Depression and the response of others. *Journal of Abnormal Psychology,* 1976, *85,* 186-193.

Deutscher, I. The quality of post parental life: definitions of the situation. *Journal of Marriage and the Family,* 1964, *26,* 52-59.

Edinger, J. and Auerbach, S. Development and validation of a multivariate model for accounting for infractions in a correctional setting. *Journal of Personality and Social Psychology,* 1978, *36,* 1472-1489.

Ferguson, J. *Learning to eat: Behavior modification for weight control.* New York: Hawthorn Books, 1975.

Garcia, L. and Griffitt, W. Authoritarianism-situation interactions in the determination of punitiveness: engaging authoritarian ideology. *Journal of Research in Personality,* 1978, *12,* 469-478.

Geroes, E. Automatic arousal as a cognitive cue in stressful situations. *Journal of Personality*, 1979, *47*, 678-711.

Goldsmith, J. and McFall, R. Development and evaluation of an interpersonal skill—training program for psychiatric patients. *Journal of Abnormal Psychology*, 1975, *84*, 51-58.

Hart, R. Therapeutic effectiveness of setting and monitoring goals. *Journal of Consulting and Clinical Psychology*, 1978, *46*, 1242-1245.

Janda, L. and Rimm, D. Type of situation and sex of counselor in assertive training. *Journal of Counseling Psychology*, 1977, *24*, 444-447.

Kazdin, A. Situational specificity: The two-edged sword of behavioural assessment. *Behavioral Assessment*, 1979, *1*, 57-76.

Knapp, T., Crosby, H. and O'Boyle, M. Using the natural environment in counselling for therapeutic change: a case study. *Psychological Reports*, 1978, *42*, 1048-1050.

Larson, L. The influence of parents and peers during adolescence: the situation hypothesis revisited. *Journal of Marriage and the Family*, 1972, *Feb.*, 67-74.

Levenson, R. and Gottman, J. Toward the assessment of social competence. *Journal of Consulting and Clinical Psychology*, 1978, *46*, 453-462.

Lippa, R. Expressive control, expressive consistency, and the correspondence between expressive behavior and personality. *Journal of Personality*, 1978, *46*, 438-461.

Mariotto, M. and Paul, G. Persons versus situations in real-life functioning of chronically institutionalised mental patients. *Journal of Abnormal Psychology*, 1975, *84*, 483-493.

Matheny, A. and Dolan, A. Persons, situations, and time: a genetic view of behavioral change in children. *Journal of Personality and Social Psychology*, 1975, *32*, 1106-1110.

Meier, E. Interaction between the person and his operational situation. *Social Casework*, 1965, *65*, 43-58.

Mellstrom, M., Zuckerman, M. and Cicala, G. General versus specific traits in the assessment of anxiety. *Journal of Consulting and Clinical Psychology*, 1978, *46*, 423-431.

Moos, R. Differential effects of psychiatric ward settings of patient change. *Journal of Nervous and Mental Disease*, 1970, *151*, 316-321.

Moos, R. Situational analysis of a therapeutic community milieu. *Journal of Abnormal Psychology*, 1968, *73*, 49-61.

Moos, R. Changing the social milieu of psychiatric treatment settings. *The Journal of Applied Behavioural Science*, 1973, *9*, 575-593.

Moos, R. Determinants of physiological responses to symbolic stimuli: the role of the social environment. *International Journal of Psychiatry in Medicine*, 1974, *5*, 389-399.

Moos, R. and Otto, J. The community-oriented programme environment scale. *Journal of Psychology*, 1972, *8*, 28-37.

Moos, R. and Schwartz, J. Treatment environment and treatment outcomes. *Journal of Nervous and Mental Diseases*, 1973, *154*, 264-275.

Orcutt, J. Deviance as a situated phenomenon: variations in the social interpretation of marijuana and alcohol use. *Social Problems*, 1975, *23*, 346-356.

Pace, R. Situational therapy. *Journal of Personality*, 1957, *25*, 578-589.

Perri, M., and Richards, C. An investigation on naturally occurring episodes of self-controlled behaviour. *Journal of Counseling Psychology*, 1971, *24*, 178-183.

Price, R. and Moos, R. Toward a taxonomy of inpatient treatment environments. *Journal of Abnormal Psychology*, 1975, *84*, 181-187.

Rappaport, E. General vs situation-specific trait anxiety in prediction of state anxiety during group therapy. *Psychological Reports*, 1979, *44*, 715-718.

Rime, B., Bouvy, H., Leborgne, B., and Rouillon, F. Psychopathy and nonverbal behavior in an interpersonal situation. *Journal of Abnormal Psychology*, 1978, *87*, 636-643.

Schiedt, R. and Schaie, K. A taxonomy of situations for an elderly population: generating situational criteria. *Journal of Gerontology*, 1978, *33*, 848-857.

Siporin, M. Situational assessment and interaction. *Social Casework*, 1972, *68*, 91-109.

Sheffield, A. The situation as a unit of family case study. *Social Forces*, 1931, *9*, 465-474.

Trower, P., Bryant, B., and Argyle, M. *Social skills and mental health*. London: Methuen, 1978.

Twentyman, G., and McFall, R. Behavioral training of social skills in shy males. *Journal of Consulting and Clinical Psychology*, 1975, *43*, 384-395.

Wachtel, P. Psychodynamics, behavior therapy and the implacable experiment: an inquiry into the consistency of personality. *Journal of Abnormal Psychology*, 1974, *82*, 324-334.

Wertheim, E. Person-environment interaction: the epigenesis of autonomy and competence. *British Journal of Medical Psychology*, 1975, *48*, 1-8, 95-111, 237-256, 391-402.

Wodarski, J. A comparison of behavioral consistency of anti-social and pro-socialy children in different contexts. *Journal of Behavior Therapy and Experimental Psychiatry*, 1977, *8*, 275-280.

Yamamoto, K. Children's ratings of the stressfulness of experiences. *Developmental Psychology*, 1979, *15*, 581-582.

Zieliniski, J. Situational determinants of assertive behavior in depressed alcoholics. *Journal of Behaviour Therapy and Experimental Psychology*, 1978, *6*, 103-107.

1

Effectiveness of Situation Redefinition and Affective Isolation in Coping with Stress*

David S. Holmes and B. Kent Houston

Subjects in three threat conditions were told that they would receive a series of painful electric shocks, while the subjects in a no-threat condition were not told about shocks. In one threat condition (threat redefinition), the subjects were told to reduce stress by thinking of the shocks as interesting new physiological sensations. In another threat condition (threat isolation), the subjects were told to reduce stress by remaining detached and uninvolved. Data from self-report of anxiety, pulse rate, and skin resistance indicated that the threat of shock increased stress and that subjects using redefinition and isolation showed smaller increases in stress than subjects who were not told to use those coping strategies.

Probably the most prominent experimental research to date on the effectiveness of cognitive coping strategies is the series of investigations reported by Lazarus and his colleagues (e.g., Lazarus & Alfert, 1964; Lazarus, Opton, Nomikos, & Rankin, 1965; Speisman, Lazarus, Mordkoff, & Davison, 1964). These investigations generally took the following form: To induce arousal, subjects were

*Journal of Personality and Social Psychology, 1974, 29, 212-215. Copyright 1974 by the American Psychological Association. Reprinted by permission.

shown a stressful film dealing with subincision (a ritual in which the penis and scrotum of male adolescents are cut deeply with sharpened stone). Attempts were made to manipulate cognitive coping strategies by varying the descriptions which accompanied, or in some experiments preceded, the film. The sound track used to induce denial as a cognitive coping strategy asserted that

> the adolescent participants in the genital operation were not mutilated or harmed by it or in significant pain. . . . It was emphasized that they [the boys in the film] viewed the ritual positively and happily [Lazarus & Opton, 1966, p. 244].

In a sound track used to encourage intellectualization as a coping strategy,

> an anthropological view of the affair was presented in intellectualized and emotionally detached words and style. . . . The operation procedures were described, but as one might in a technical manual, so as to encourage remoteness from the feelings of the boys who were exposed to the procedure [Lazarus & Opton, 1966, p. 244].

For purposes of comparison, two other sound tracks were employed; one emphasized the horror of the situation while the other was silent. The results indicated that both the denial and intellectualization orientations reduced the stress reaction as measured by physiological measures. It was concluded that the reduction in stress in the subjects who were provided with the coping strategies was due to the fact that they were able to appraise the situation as less threatening than those not provided with these orientations.

Unfortunately, the work described above suffered from two methodological problems. First and most important, it should be noted that rather than acknowledging (explicitly or implicitly) to the subjects in the denial condition that the situation was stressful (as was done in the comparison groups) and then instructing the subjects to reduce their stress by using denial (i.e., instructing the subjects to reappraise the situation for themselves), the experimenter explicitly told the subjects that the situation was not stressful (i.e., that the boys in the film enjoyed the ritual and were happy). In other words, rather than presenting the subjects in the denial condition with a stressful situation and determining whether by reappraising the situation the subjects could reduce stress, the investigators merely presented the subjects in the denial condition with a less stressful situation. A similar criticism can be offered for the intellectualization condition. Although in that condition the experimenters did not explicitly present the situation as benign, the suggestion was made implicitly through the experimenters' approach, and again—in this case through modeling—the experimenters rather than the subjects defined the situation. In view of these criticisms, the experiments seem to have been more tests of the experimenters' credibility and the effects of modeling than of the subjects' ability to use denial and intellectualization.

The second problem with these investigations revolves around the question of whether the stressful film was an adequate analogue of "real life" stress. Although it must be acknowledged that the film did result in vicarious involvement and stress, the fact that the subjects were not directly threatened undoubtedly made the situation and the subjects' responses to it somewhat different from the more typical situation in which a person is directly involved and threatened. For example, in the film situation the subjects might effectively cope by saying to themselves, "This is just a movie—it's not really happening to me or anyone else." Consistent with this speculation in a recent experiment (Koriat, Melkman, Averill, & Lazarus, 1972) it was found that subjects who were shown a stressful film but instructed to remain unemotional most frequently coped with the stress by reminding themselves that the stress was only "a film rather than a real occurrence." It seems clear that results concerning coping strategies generated in film-induced stress situations have limited generalizability; that is, the experiments have limited *external validity* (Campbell & Stanley, 1963).

Independent of the research discussed thus far, however, there does seem to be evidence for the effectiveness of denial as a means of reducing stress. For example, it has been reported that subjects who characteristically used denial showed less performance decrement when faced with threat to self-esteem (Houston, 1971) and showed less performance decrement and less physiological arousal when faced with threat of electric shock (Houston, 1972) than subjects who did not characteristically use denial. Although these results indicated that some subjects can effectively reduce stress, they did not indicate which of the variety of strategies subsumed under the term denial are actually used or are effective in reducing the stress.

The present research was carried out in an attempt to answer questions concerning the nature and effectiveness of specific strategies for handling stress. In this experiment, the subjects were exposed or were not exposed to a direct threat (painful electric shocks). Subjects in two groups which were threatened were reminded of the threat and were instructed to use one of the two strategies to reduce their stress. One of these groups was instructed to redefine the aversive stimuli (i.e., think of the shocks as interesting vibrating sensations) and the other group was instructed to use isolation (i.e., remain unemotional, uninvolved, and detached). Response to stress was measured by changes in pulse rate, skin resistance, and self-report of anxiety. It was predicted that subjects who were instructed to use the coping strategies (redefinition and isolation) would evidence less response to stress than subjects who were not instructed to use the strategies.

METHOD

Subjects

Subjects in this experiment were 32 male and 32 female students from introductory psychology classes at the University of Kansas. Male and female subjects were randomly assigned in equal numbers to four conditions: threat, threat isolation, threat redefinition, and no threat.

Procedure

When a subject arrived for his appointment, he was taken into the experimental room and seated at a desk on which there was a control panel containing buttons labeled yes and no and a large red signal light. The experimenter then attached two silver galvanic skin response (GSR) electrodes to the third and fourth fingers of the subject's nondominant hand, a Beckman plethysmographic finger transducer to the index finger of that hand, and a large electrode with heavy red wires strapped above the wrist of that hand. While these were being attached, the experimenter gave the subject a general explanation of the devices used to measure his skin resistance and pulse rate, but nothing was said about the function of the large electrode which had been placed on the arm. After the devices had been attached to the subject, the experimenter explained that the experiment involved "studying the relationship between stimulation, physiological responses, and emotion" and that all of the instructions for the experiment would be given through the speaker which was mounted on the wall in front of the subject. The experimenter then went to an adjoining room and started a tape recorder which gave the instructions.

For all four conditions the tape-recorded instructions first asked the subject to indicate how he was feeling at that moment by pushing either the yes or the no button on the panel in front of him after hearing each of 21 adjectives (e.g., calm, tense, relaxed, thoughtful) from the Affect Adjective Check List (Zuckerman, 1960). The subject's response to each adjective was recorded in the adjoining room by the experimenter. After this point, the procedures differed for subjects in the four groups.

Threat condition. For this condition, the tape-recorded instructions went on to point out that the stimulation which was being studied in the experiment was "painful electric shocks" and that although "students do find them to be quite painful," the shocks "are not physically dangerous or harmful." It was explained that he would receive between two and eight shocks at random times and that they would be administered through the large electrode which had been strapped to the subject's arm. It was also explained that the shocks would only come during the time that the red signal light was on. The subject was then informed that if he wished, he could withdraw from the experiment at any time and still receive credit for participation in the entire experiment. He was then asked to sign a consent form indicating his willingness to continue in the experiment but cautioned to tell the experimenter if he had ever had any heart trouble, in which case the experiment would be terminated immediately. If the subject agreed to continue and signed the form, the tape-recorded instructions were resumed.[3]

The next set of instructions informed the subject that it was important to know how he was feeling while "waiting for, or actually receiving, the shocks" and therefore, as soon as the light which signaled the possibility of shock came on, the list of adjectives would again be read to him. The subject was asked to indicate how he felt at that time by using the buttons on the response panel as before. After that, the red signal light came on and the 21 adjectives were read again. When this was completed, the experimenter entered the experimental room, interviewed the subject to determine whether he believed that he would be shocked, and completely debriefed the subject concerning the procedure and the purpose of the experiment.[4]

Threat-isolation condition. The procedures for the threat-isolation condition were exactly the same as those for the threat condition except that immediately after the subject completed the first Affect Adjective Check List (i.e., before he was given the instructions concerning the shocks), the experimenter entered the experimental room and gave the instructions to elicit the use of isolation. In these instructions it was pointed out that (a) in this experiment it was extremely important that the subject remain calm and relaxed; (b) the subject would receive some electrical shocks, about which he would be told more later; (c) although the shocks were painful, it was important that the subject not be afraid; (d) one way to eliminate fear and to relax is to maintain a completely unemotional and totally detached attitude toward the shocks; (e) over 100 students had already participated in the experiment and almost everyone was able to remain relaxed by maintaining an attitude of detachment and uninvolvement; (f) for the success of the experiment, it was important that the subject not become nervous; and finally, (g) the experimenter did not want the subject to stop thinking about the shocks; rather, the experimenter wanted him not to be afraid of the shocks. After giving these instructions and clarifying any points on which the subject had any

---

[3]Across conditions, two subjects elected not to continue and one subject reported a history of heart murmur. These subjects were immediately debriefed and dismissed, and additional subjects were run to replace them.

[4]Across conditions, three subjects did not believe what they had been told, and consequently additional subjects were run to replace them.

questions, the experimenter left the room and the experiment was completed as it was with the threat group.

Threat-redefinition condition. The procedures for the threat-redefinition condition were exactly the same as those for the threat condition except that immediately after the subject completed the first Affect Adjective Check List (i.e., before he was given the instructions concerning the shocks), the experimenter entered the experimental room and gave the instructions to encourage the subject to reinterpret the aversive stimuli. These instructions were similar to those for the threat-isolation condition except that rather than being told to be detached and uninvolved, the subjects were told to think of the shocks as an interesting new type of physiological sensation. It was suggested that the shocks could be thought of as a "vibrating sensation" and that the subjects could say to themselves, "These aren't shocks; they are vibrations." The subjects were told that over 100 students had already participated in the experiment and that almost everyone had been able to remain relaxed by thinking of the shocks as interesting sensations rather than shocks. Finally, it was pointed out that the experimenter did not want the subject to stop thinking about the shocks; rather, the experimenter wanted the subject to reinterpret the shocks. After giving these instructions and clarifying any points on which the subject had any questions, the experimenter left the room and the experiment was completed exactly as it was for the threat condition.

With regard to the instructions given to subjects in the threat-isolation and threat-redefinition conditions, it is important to recognize that at no time did the experimenter directly or indirectly indicate that the shocks would not be painful. Instead, the experimenter asked the subjects to remain calm and suggested ways in which this might be accomplished despite the forthcoming "painful shocks." This distinction is critical to the interpretation of the previous work in this area.

No-threat condition. After a subject in this condition completed the first Affect Adjective Check List, the tape-recorded instructions went on to point out that the stimulation which was being studied in the experiment was "simple visual stimulation" and that the visual stimulation would be provided by the red light in front of him. After this instruction, the procedures were similar to those used with the threat condition except that visual stimulation rather than electric shocks was discussed and when the subject was asked to sign the consent form, no mention was made of terminating the experiment if the subject had a history of heart trouble.

RESULTS

Physiological Measures

There were three periods in this experiment during which physiological measures were recorded: (a) the initial period, which was the 30-second period during which the subjects responded to the first Affect Adjective Check List; (b) the anticipation period, which was the last 30 seconds of the period during which the subjects were told they would receive electric shocks or visual stimulation; and (c) the stimulation period, which was the second 30-second period after the red light came on (signaling the beginning of either a period of shocks or visual stimulation) and during which the subjects responded to the second Affect Adjective Check List. To eliminate the effects of the "law of initial values" (Wilder, 1962), the pulse rate and skin resistance scores for the anticipation and stimulation periods were adjusted for differences during the initial period by means of a covariance technique (McNemar, 1962). The adjusted pulse rate and skin resistance scores were then analyzed in 4 (Conditions) × 2 (Sex) × 2 (Periods, i.e., anticipation and stimulation) analyses of variance.

Pulse rate. The pulse rate data are presented graphically in Figure 1.1. The analysis of these data revealed a significant sex effect ($F = 5.02, df = 1/56, p <$

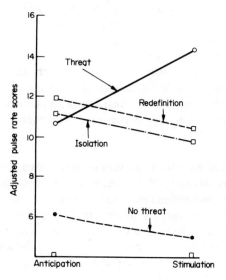

Figure 1.1   Mean pulse rate score (adjusted for initial period) for subjects in each condition during the anticipation period (when subjects were told they would receive electric shocks or visual stimulation) and the stimulation period (when the signal light came on indicating beginning of the shock period or the visual stimulation).

.01), reflecting the fact that in general, males had higher pulse rates than females. The analysis also revealed a significant conditions effect ($F = 8.03$, $df = 3/56$, $p < .001$) and a significant Conditions $\times$ Periods interaction ($F = 4.13$, $df = 3/56$, $p < .025$).[5] Inspection of Figure 1.1 and subsequent analyses indicated that during the anticipation period, subjects who had been threatened showed higher levels of stress (i.e., higher pulse rates) than subjects who had not been threatened and more important, that between the anticipation and stimulation periods, subjects in the threat condition showed an increase in stress ($F = 5.19$, $df = 1/14$, $p < .05$), while there were decreases in stress between the anticipation and stimulation periods for the subjects in the threat-redefinition ($F = 6.21$, $df = 1/14$, $p < .05$), threat-isolation ($F = 1.43$, $df = 1/14$), and no-threat ($F = 2.49$, $df = 1/14$, $p < .20$) conditions. To determine whether the predicted ordering of means accounted for a significant amount of the variance within each period, the sum of squares for conditions within each period was partitioned into two components (Winer, 1962). The first component reflected the amount of variance accounted for by the predicted ordering (i.e., that the subjects in the threat condition would show higher pulse rates than the subjects in the threat-redefinition and threat-isolation conditions, who would show higher pulse rates than subjects in the no-threat condition), while the second component reflected the amount of residual variance not accounted for by the predicted ordering. As might be expected from inspection of Figure 1.1, for the anticipation period the predicted ordering of the means was not significant ($F = 1.68$, $df = 1/56$) and the residual component was significant ($F = 5.99$, $df = 2/56$, $pf < .01$). On the other hand, for the stress period the predicted ordering of means was significant ($F = 28.58$, $df = 1/56$, $p < .001$) and the residual component was not significant ($F = .13$, $df = 2/56$). From the pulse rate it appears that the defensive strategies of redefinition and isolation were not effective in reducing stress during the period preceding the shocks but that the strategies were effective in reducing stress during the period in which the subjects expected the shocks. This difference in effectiveness between periods is discussed later.

Skin resistance. The analysis of the skin resistance data indicated a significant conditions effect ($F = 3.61$, $df = 3/56$, $p < .05$). Inspection of the adjusted means for both the anticipation and stimulation periods revealed that the highest level of stress (i.e., the lowest skin resistance) was shown by subjects in the threat condition, intermediate levels of stress were shown by subjects in the threat-redefinition and threat-isolation conditions, and the lowest level of stress was shown by subjects in the no-threat condition. The amount of between-

---

[5]Main and interaction effects not reported for this and subsequent analyses were neither statistically significant nor approached statistical significance.

conditions variance accounted for by this ordering of means approached statistical significance during the anticipation period ($F = 2.80$, $df = 1/56$, $p < .10$) and reached statistical significance during the stress period ($F = 11.82$, $df = 1/56$, $p < .01$), while in neither period was there a significant amount of residual variance (Fs of .00 and .20, respectively, $df = 2/56$). These results indicated that the defensive strategies of redefinition and isolation were effective in reducing stress both during the period preceding the shocks and during the period in which the subjects expected the shocks.

In considering the results provided by the two physiological measures of stress, it should be noted that there is one inconsistency: The pulse rate measure indicated that the coping strategies were not effective during the anticipation period but were effective during the stimulation period, while the skin resistance measure indicated that the coping strategies were effective during both the anticipation and stimulation periods. This inconsistency can probably be accounted for by the fact that the latency of change is generally much shorter for measures of skin resistance than pulse rate. In other words, it may be that the pulse rate measure did not reflect the effectiveness of the strategies in the anticipation period because the amount of time which elapsed between the introduction of the threat and the measurement period was not sufficient for the coping strategies to influence the pulse rate. Although a definite explanation cannot be offered for the inconsistency between the two measures during the anticipation period, because of the relatively minor nature of the inconsistency it does not seem to be a source of serious concern.

Self-Report Measure

The Affect Adjective Check List scores reflecting the subjects' level of subjective stress during the stimulation period were adjusted for differences during the initial period as had been done with the physiological measures. A 4 (Conditions) × 2 (Sex) analysis of variance carried out on the adjusted Affect Adjective Check List scores revealed a significant conditions effect ($F = 7.49$, $df = 3/56$, $p < .001$). Inspection of the adjusted means indicated that as expected, the highest level of stress was reported by the subjects in the threat condition ($\overline{X} = 12.87$), intermediate levels of stress were reported by subjects in the threat-redefinition ($\overline{X} = 10.70$) and threat-isolation ($\overline{X} = 10.22$) conditions, and the lowest level of stress was reported by subjects in the no-threat condition ($\overline{X} = 6.21$). A partitioning of the sum of squares associated with the conditions effect indicated that this expected ordering of means accounted for a significant amount of the between-conditions variance ($F = 21.56$, $df = 1/56$, $p < .001$), while the remaining variance not accounted for was not significant ($F = .93$, $df = 2/56$). These results were consistent with the results obtained with the physiological measures and indicated that as expected, the coping strategies of redefinition and isolation were effective in reducing stress. It should be noted, however, that these strategies did not eliminate stress; that is, they did not reduce stress to the level of subjects who had not been stressed; rather, the strategies enabled the subjects to maintain a level of stress intermediate between those of subjects who were and were not threatened.

DISCUSSION

Before attempting to draw any conclusions or implications from the data presented in this article, it must first be asked whether the reductions in stress observed in the threat-isolation and threat-redefinition conditions were due to the use of the coping strategies or whether the subjects were simply responding to the demand characteristics of the experiment and role playing the reduced stress. With regard to this question, it should be noted that Houston and Holmes (1973) recently found that subjects who were stressed with a threat of shock like that of the present experiment but who were instructed to role play being calm were able to simulate the self-reports (viz., the Affect Adjective Check Lists) but not the physiological responses (viz., pulse rates and skin resistances) of subjects who were not stressed. Rather than simulating the responses of nonthreatened subjects, the physiological responses of subjects attempting to role play being calm were like those of threatened subjects. In view of those findings, it does not appear that the results of the present experiment could be attributed to the demand characteristics of the experiment.

In reviewing the results of this experiment, it is clear that when subjects were faced with a threat (i.e., during the stimulation period), the instructions to redefine the threat so as to reduce its stressful quality and the instructions to isolate the feelings of stress were effective in reducing stress. It should be noted, however, that although the subjects in the threat-isolation and threat-redefinition conditions evidenced less arousal than the subjects in the threat condition, their arousal was greater than that of the subjects in the no-threat condition. In other words, the coping strategies were not completely effective in reducing stress. In many stressful situations, however, a minimal increase in arousal may be very adaptive.

The results of this experiment are important for at least two reasons. First, the results provide strong experimental support for the effectiveness of redefinition and isolation as coping strategies. Verification of strategies which increase the psychological comfort of people caught in unavoidable stress situations is noteworthy. Second, since the effective experimental manipulation of the coping strategies was relatively simple, the findings suggest that persons could be taught to use these strategies where appropriate. More work employing different types of stress is neded, but the present findings with their theoretical and practical implications can provide the basis for such work.

REFERENCES

Campbell, D., & Stanley, J. *Experimental and Quasi-Experimental Designs for Research*. Chicago: Rand McNally, 1963.

Houston, B. K. Trait and situational denial and performance under stress. *Journal of Personality and Social Psychology*, 1971, *18*, 289-293.

Houston, B. K. Viability of coping strategies, denial, and response to stress. *Journal of Personality*, 1972, *41*, 50-58.

Houston, B. K., & Holmes, D. Role playing versus deception: The ability of subjects to simulate self-report and physiological responses. *Journal of Social Psychology*, 1973, in press.

Koriat, A., Melkman, R., Averill, J., & Lazarus, R. The self-control of emotional reactions to a stressful film. *Journal of Personality*, 1972, *40*, 601-619.

Lazarus, R., & Alfert, E. Short-circuiting of threat by experimentally altering cognitive appraisal. *Journal of Abnormal and Social Psychology*, 1964, *69*, 195-205.

Lazarus, R., & Option, E. The study of psychological stress: A summary of theoretical formulations and experimental findings. In C. Spielberger (Ed.), *Anxiety and Behavior*. New York: Academic Press, 1966.

Lazarus, R., Opton, E., Nomikos, M., & Rankin, N. The principle of short-circuiting of threat: Further evidence. *Journal of Personality*, 1965, *33*, 622-635.

McNemar, Q. *Psychological statistics*. (3rd ed.) New York: Wiley, 1962.

Speisman, J., Lazarus, R., Mordkoff, A., & Davision, L. Experimental reduction of stress based on ego-defense theory. *Journal of Abnormal and Social Psychology*, 1964, *68*, 367-380.

Wilder, J. Basimetric approach (law of initial value) to biological rhythms. *Annals of the New York Academy of Science*, 1962, *98*, 1211-1220.

Winer, B. *Statistical principles in Experimental Design*. New York: McGraw-Hill, 1962.

Zuckerman, M. The development of an affect adjective check list for the measurement of anxiety. *Journal of Consulting Psychology*, 1960, *24*, 457-462.

2

Situational Determinants of Assertive Behaviors*

Richard M. Eisler, Michel Hersen, Peter M. Miller and Edward B. Blanchard

Thirty-two assertive situations that varied in social-interpersonal context were administered to 60 hospitalized psychiatric patients via role playing. Half of the role-played situations required the expression of negative (hostile) assertiveness, and the other half required positive (commendatory) assertive expression. Situational context was varied by having the subjects respond to male and female interpersonal partners who were either familiar or unfamiliar to patients. Responses were videotaped and rated on five measures of speech content and seven measures of nonverbal behavior. Additionally, groups of high- and low-assertive patients were identified from the total sample using a behavioral measure of global assertiveness and a self-report instrument. Results indicated that interpersonal behavior in assertive situations varied as a function of social context. Further, high- and low-assertive subjects were differentiated on the basis of 9 of the 12 measures of interpersonal behavior. Support for a stimulus specific theory of assertive behaviors and implications for assertive training are discussed.

Assertive training (Wolpe, 1958, 1969; Wolpe & Lazarus, 1966), originally developed as a treatment for individuals with a passive or inhibited life style, has reportedly been successful in the treatment of various clinical problems including sexual deviation (Edwards, 1972; Stevenson & Wolpe, 1960), depression (Piaget & Lazarus, 1969), and marital conflict (Eisler, Miller, Hersen, & Alford, 1974; Fensterheim, 1972). Assertive training has also been used to improve the

---

*Journal of Consulting and Clinical Psychology, 1975, 43, 3, 330-340 Copyright 1975 by the American Psychological Association. Reprinted by permission.

interpersonal functions of schizophrenics (Weinman, Gelbart, Wallace, & Post, 1972). Recently there has been an increased interest in identifying the most effective treatment ingredients comprising assertive training. McFall and his colleagues (McFall & Lillesand, 1971; McFall & Marston, 1970) have shown that behavior rehearsal both with and without performance feedback was superior to control procedures. Studies examining acquisition of assertive responses with modeling and therapeutic instructions have also yielded positive results (Eisler, Hersen, & Miller, 1973; Goldstein, Martens, Hubben, Van Belle, Shaaf, Wiersma, & Goedhart, 1973; Hersen, Eisler, Miller, Johnson, & Pinkston, 1973; Kazdin, 1974).

Although a number of well-controlled studies attest to the efficacy of various assertive training procedures, several important issues require clarification. With respect to the scope of behaviors considered "assertive," Lazarus (1971) has pointed out that most definitions of assertiveness do not include the expression of positive emotions such as affection, empathy, admiration, and appreciation. Wolpe (1969) has also differentiated between "hostile" assertive responses such as "I insist that you come to work on time" or "Please don't stand in front of me," compared with "commendatory" remarks such as "I admire your tenacity" or "You look lovely, terrific, ravishing, glamorous, etc." Most studies to date have been concerned primarily with assertion in the narrow sense, or what Wolpe would call hostile assertion, and have failed to consider the positive aspects of assertive expression.

A second unexplored issue is delineating the role of the social-interpersonal context in determining whether or not a response is "assertive." Behaviors that are socially appropriate in one circumstance may not be so in another. For example, if one is waiting in line to purchase a ticket at a movie theater and someone cuts in front of them, the response socially sanctioned will differ depending on whether the person is a middle-aged man, a young child, or an old woman. Similarly, the assertive response required will differ depending on whether one is relatively familiar with the other person as compared with one's response to a total stranger.

Finally, development of valid measures of assertive behavior has been difficult. This is partly due to the fact that (a) assertive behavior involves many simultaneously occurring verbal and nonverbal responses; (b) there has been a confusing array of behavioral, physiological, and self-report indices used as dependent measures of assertiveness; and (c) it is not clear how these indices relate to global judgments of assertiveness. In a preliminary study, Eisler, Miller, and Hersen (1973) attempted to delineate specific behaviors related to judgments of assertive expression. These authors extended the use of McFall and Marston's (1970) role-playing technique by developing 14 standard interpersonal situations requiring negative (hostile) assertive responses. The role-playing situations were administered to 30 male psychiatric inpatients. A female assistant prompted subjects' responses to a role-played wife, waitress, saleslady, etc. These role-played interactions were videotaped and rated on various verbal and nonverbal behaviors. Global judgments of overall assertiveness were also made independently of the behavioral ratings. Subjects were then dichotomized at the median into high- and low-assertive groups. *t* tests performed on ratings of behavior showed that the more highly assertive patients evidenced lengthier responses, louder speech with shorter latencies, and more pronounced affect than low-assertive subjects. Additionally, the speech content of patients in the high-assertive groups exhibited less compliance and more requests for the interpersonal partner to change her behavior.

One purpose of the present investigation was to extend the previous Eisler, Miller, and Hersen (1973) study, which identified some of the behavioral components of negative assertion while adding situations that typically elicit positive (commendatory) responses. A second purpose was to examine more systematically the effects of social context on interpersonal behavior in assertive situations. In one instance the effects of responding assertively to a male was contrasted with assertive responding to a female. A second aspect of social context was varied depending on whether or not the subject had recurrent interactions with the interpersonal partner (familiarity). For example, it was presumed that a subject's responses to a person he interacted with on a day-to-day basis such as his wife or employer would differ from his responses to a less familiar person such as a waitress or the mechanic who repaired his car. Finally, an additional objective was to delineate behaviors that would differentiate high- from low-assertive patients in each of the aforementioned contexts of assertion.

METHOD

Subjects

Sixty male psychiatric patients hospitalized at the Veterans Administration Center (Jackson, Mississippi) served as subjects. While no attempt was made to select subjects on the basis of diagnosis, patients who were acutely psychotic or with evidence of organic brain syndrome were excluded. With respect to diagnostic classification, the group selected included 30 character disorders, 25 neurotics, 3 schizophrenics, and 2 with adult situational reactions. The patients ranged in age from 21 to 67 years, with a mean age of 43.4 years. Educational level ranged from 3 to 18 years, with a mean of 11.2 years.

Thirty-seven of the subjects were currently married, while the remaining 23 were either divorced, separated, or widowed. Patients who had never married were excluded since some of the scenes required assertive responding to a role-played wife.

Role-Played Assertive Situations

Thirty-two role-played situations that required assertive responding in simulated real-life encounters were used. Some of the role-played scenes that required responses to familiar and unfamiliar females were adapted from previous research on hostile assertion (Eisler, Miller, & Hersen, 1973). Additional scenes that would elicit both positive and negative assertive expressions to familiar and unfamiliar individuals of both sexes were constructed by the authors.

Sixteen of the 32 scenes required the subject to express "positive" feelings such as praise, appreciation, or liking for his interpersonal partner, while the remaining 16 required the subject to express "negative" feelings such as anger, displeasure, or disappointment toward the role-played partner. In half of the scenes the role-playing partner was male while in the other half the partner was female. Finally one half of the scenes required the patient to respond to a person with whom he was presumed to have had a good deal of interactive experience, e.g., wife or employer (familiar). In the other 16 scenes, the patient was required to interact with a person with whom it was presumed he had little interactive experience, e.g., cashier or waitress (unfamiliar).

All three situational variables contained two levels (i.e., positive and negative, male and female, familiar and unfamiliar) that were nested. Thus, there were eight categories of stimulus scenes with four scenes in each category. The following are sample scenes from each category as narrated to the patients.[1]

1. *Male-Positive-Familiar*
   Narrator: "You have been working on a difficult job all week, your boss comes over with a smile on his face." *Your boss says:* "That's a very good job you have done; I'm going to give you a raise next week."

2. *Male-Positive-Unfamiliar*
   Narrator: You are the leader of the company bowling team. Your team is slightly behind when one of the men on your team makes three strikes in a row to even up the score. You are really proud of him." *He says:* "How did you like that one?"

3. *Male-Negative-Familiar*
   Narrator: "You have had a very busy day at work and are tired. Your boss comes in and asks you to stay late for the third time this week. You really feel you would like to go home on time tonight." *Your boss says:* "I'm leaving now; would you mind staying late again tonight and finishing this work for me?"

4. *Male-Negative-Unfamiliar*
   Narrator: "You go to a ballgame with reserved seat tickets. When you arrive you find that someone has put his coat in the seat for which you have reserved tickets. You ask him to remove his coat and he tells you that he is saving that seat for a friend." *He says:* "I'm sorry, this seat is saved."

---

[1]Complete descriptions of the 32 role-played scenes may be obtained free of charge from the first author.

5. *Female-Positive-Familiar*
   Narrator: "Your wife has just bought a new outfit and is trying it on. You really like it and think that she looks very nice in it." *Your wife says:* "Well, how do I look in this outfit?"

6. *Female-Positive-Unfamiliar*
   Narrator: "You are in a restaurant and the waitress had just served you an excellent meal cooked just the way you like it. You are pleased with her prompt, efficient service." *She comes by and says:* "I hope you enjoyed your dinner, sir."

7. *Female-Negative Familiar*
   Narrator: "You are in the middle of watching an exciting football game on television. Your wife walks in and changes the channel as she does every time you are watching a good game." *Your wife says:* "Let's watch the movie instead; it's really supposed to be good."

8. *Female-Negative-Unfamiliar*
   Narrator: "You are in a crowded grocery store and are in a hurry because you are already late for an appointment. You pick up one small item and get in line to pay for it. Then a woman with a shopping cart full of groceries cuts in line right in front of you." *She says:* "You don't mind if I cut in here, do you?"

Procedure

The Wolpe-Lazarus (1966) self-report inventory of assertiveness was administered to all subjects. The 32 assertive situations were then presented via role playing in a furnished room containing a portable television camera and a two-way intercom system. An adjoining control room contained recording equipment and a television monitor for observing subjects' responses. (See Eisler, Hersen, & Agras, 1973, for details.) All instructions to the subjects were given by the experimenter in the control room through the intercom. A female research assistant was used to role play all scenes involving a woman interpersonal partner, and a male research assistant role played all interactions involving a male interpersonal partner.

One half of the subjects were presented with all scenes involving a female interpersonal partner first, and then responded to all scenes involving a male. The remaining 30 subjects responded to all male-related scenes first and then were administered for female-related scenes. Scenes within sex of partner were presented in different random order for all 60 subjects.

Each patient was escorted into the experimental videotape studio and seated next to either the male or female interpersonal partner, both of whom had been trained to deliver a predetermined prompt to the patient following narration of each scene from the control room. Following the patient's reply the interpersonal partner made no further response until narration of the next scene when a new prompt was delivered. Instructions were given to the subjects by the experimenter as follows:

The purpose of today's procedure is to find out how you react to some everyday situations that might occur outside the hospital. The idea is for you to respond just as if you were in that situation at home, at work, at a store, or in a restaurant. I will describe various situations that you might find yourself in with your wife, your boss, or some other person such as a waitress or salesclerk. When each situation is described to you, try and imagine that you really are there. In order to make these situations seem more real life, Miss Jones will play the part of your wife or another woman who is in the scene. Mr. Smith will play the part of your boss or another man who is in the scene. For example, after I have described a situation, Miss Jones will say something to you. After she speaks, I want you to say what you would say if she had said this to you in the situation that was described. *This is important.* Some of the scenes will be such that you would feel irritated or annoyed if you were actually in that situation.

At this point the experimenter narrated a practice scene that required expression of "negative" feelings:

"You have just put together a new shelf which you have hung up in the kitchen. You are proud of the shelf, but your wife makes some comments to the effect that you are a poor carpenter." *Your wife says:* "That shelf looks awful."

Once it appeared that the patient understood the instructions and gave an appropriate response, the experimenter gave additional instructions for the positive scenes: "In other scenes you might feel appreciative or friendly toward the other person." The experimenter then narrated the following practice scene: "You are just coming in the house after cutting the grass on a hot afternoon. Your wife meets you at the door with a glass of ice cold lemonade." *Your wife says:* "You looked so hot, I thought you'd enjoy something cold to drink." The experimenter then said, "Remember, try to express your true feelings whatever they might be. Also, be sure to express yourself as fully as possible." (Responses to the practice scenes were not included in the analysis.)

Videotape Ratings

All ratings of the patients' responses were made independently by two judges who observed replays of the videotaped situations. The raters had over a year of experience in rating patient behaviors that were found to be related to negative (hostile) assertiveness in previous research (Eisler, Miller, & Hersen, 1973; Hersen et al., 1973). Ratings of interactive behaviors from videotape have been shown to be highly reliable and equivalent to rating the same behaviors from live observation (Eisler, Hersen, & Agras, 1973). Additional measures of speech content that have been described in the literature as related to positive or commendatory assertion were further elaborated and rated in a similar manner (Lazarus, 1971; Wolpe, 1969).

Components of social interactive behavior were broadly categorized in terms of (a) nonverbal behaviors, (b) positive content, (c) negative content, and (d) overall assertiveness. They were defined as follows:

Nonverbal behaviors. (a) *Duration of eye contact:* Length of time that a subject looked at his interpersonal partner from delivery of prompt to termination of response (in sec) was recorded for each scene. (b) *Smiles:* Smiles were recorded on a dichotomous occurrence or nonoccurrence basis for each scene from delivery of prompt to termination of response. (c) *Duration of reply:* Length of time (in seconds) that the subject spoke to his partner was recorded for each scene. Speech pauses of greater than 3 sec terminated timing until the subject began speaking again. (d) *Latency of response:* The subject's latency of response from the time that the partner delivered his prompt to the beginning of the subject's speech was recorded for each scene. (e) *Loudness of speech:* Loudness of the subject's speech for each scene was rated on a 5-point scale from 1 (very low) to 5 (very loud). (f) *Appropriate affect:* Subject's affect was scored on a 5-point scale with 1 indicating a very flat, unemotional tone of voice and 5 indicating a full and lively intonation appropriate to each situation. (g) *Ratio of speech disturbances to duration of speech:* Frequency of speech disturbances categorized by Mahl (1956) including pauses, stutters, and expletives such as "ah," "oh," "um," etc., were recorded for each scene. The ratio was computed by dividing the number of speech disturbances by the total duration of speech (in seconds).

Negative content. (a) *Compliance:* Verbal content indicating compliance was rated on a dichotomous occurrence or nonoccurrence basis for each scene. Compliance was scored if the subject did not resist his partner's position (e.g., if he agreed to stay and work late for the boss or let his wife change the television channel). (b) *Request for new behavior:* Verbal content requesting new behavior from the interpersonal partner was scored on an occurrence or nonoccurrence basis for each scene. Responses scored in this category required more than mere noncompliance. The subject had to show evidence that he wanted his partner to change his behavior (e.g., he had to request the person at the ballgame to remove his coat or ask the woman who cut in front of him at the grocery store to step to the end of the line).

Positive content. (a) *Praise:* This consisted of verbal content indicating that the subject expressed approval, admiration, or was complimentary toward the partner's behavior (e.g., if the subject told his wife she looked very good, terrific, etc., in the new outfit.) Praise was scored on an occurrence or nonoccurrence basis for each scene. (b) *Appreciation:* This was verbal content indicating that the subject expressed gratitude or thankfulness for the partner's behavior (e.g., if the subject thanked his boss for the raise). Appreciation was scored on an occurrence or nonoccurrence basis for each scene. (c) *Spontaneous positive behavior:* This was verbal content indicating that the subject has volunteered to perform some act for the partner (e.g., if the subject offered to buy a beer for his teammate who just bowled three strikes in a row). Positive behavior was scored on the basis of occurrence or nonoccurrence for each scene.

Overall assertiveness. After all previous behaviors were rated, two additional raters who were not familiar with the purposes of the study were asked to rate the subjects' behavior on overall assertiveness, using a 5-point scale, with 1 indicating "very unassertive" and 5 indicating "very assertive." The ratings were performed independently after the raters had familiarized themselves with Wolpe's (1959) definition of "hostile" and "commendatory" assertiveness.

Scoring

For all content measures and smiles, *presence of* the behavior in each category, i.e., compliance, appreciation, request for new behavior, praise, spontaneous positive behavior, was tallied for each subject for each of the eight categories of scenes (e.g., male-positive-familiar, female-negative-unfamiliar). For all other measures the subject's score was obtained by taking the mean value averaged over the four scenes in each of the eight categories. In analyzing the data for differences between high- and low-assertive subjects, scores were combined across all categories of scenes for each subject.

Reliability of Behavioral Measures

Two judges were used to assess interrater reliability. One judge rated the 60 subjects on all behavioral measures across all scenes while the second judge rated the behavior of 20 subjects selected at random. For the five measures of speech content, number of speech disturbances, and frequency of smiles, interjudge agreement was computed by dividing the total number of agreements by the total number of judgments (agreements plus disagreements) for each context. For these measures, percentage of agreement was over 95% across all situational contexts. For the remaining continuous measures, Pearson product-moment correlations were computed between the two sets of ratings. Correlation coefficients were all greater than .94. The exceptionally high reliabilities obtained appear to be related to the specificity of criteria outlined for each measure, the fact that only one measure was rated for each videotape playback, and the fact that the raters had several years of experience making similar ratings.

RESULTS

Separate three-factor analyses of variance with repeated measures were used to assess the effects of situational context on each response measure. The levels of each factor were (a) positive versus negative expression, (b) male versus female interpersonal partner, and (c) unfamiliar versus familiar interpersonal partner. The results of these analyses are summarized in Table 2.1, which shows significance levels for situational contexts and their interactions. There were no instances of positive content occurring in any scene requiring negative assertion and no instances of negative content occuring in any scene requiring positive assertion. This was assurance that scenes structured for positive assertive expression did in fact elicit only positive comments and scenes structured for negative assertive expression elicited only negative comments. Therefore, *content* measures were not analyzed with respect to positive or negative expression.

Effects of Situational Context

The results indicated that negative scenes elicited significantly different interpersonal behavior on all nonverbal response measures (see Table 2.1). In comparison to positive scenes, the responses to negative scenes could be characterized by generally longer replies, increased eye contact, greater affect, more speech volume, and increased latency of response. As expected, positive scenes elicited a greater number of smiles than did negative scenes. Finally, subjects tended to obtain higher ratings on overall assertiveness when expressing positive than negative feelings, $F(1, 59) = 6.71, p < .05$.

With respect to sex of interpersonal partner, subjects tended to talk longer to other men than to women. They also evidenced a greater ratio of speech disturbances, relative to total speech, when the interpersonal partner was male as compared to female. However, subjects smiled more at women than men.

In expressing negative content, subjects complied with the wishes of men more frequently than those of female partners. They were also more likely to request that a female partner change her behavior rather than verbalize such assertions to another male. Thus, in situations requiring negative (hostile) assertion, these subjects were significantly more assertive with women than men. Similarly, in situations requiring positive assertion, subjects were more likely to deliver praise and appreciation to females than to males. However, they were more likely to offer to perform a favor (spontaneous positive behavior) to another male as opposed to a female.

In comparing responses to familiar versus unfamiliar persons, subjects were rated higher in overall assertiveness when their expressions were directed toward unfamiliar persons when compared to familiar persons $F(1, 59) = 8.56, p < .01$. In situations requiring positive expression, subjects were more likely to offer praise, appreciation, or to do a favor for a person they did not know well as compared with persons with whom they were more familiar. When in situations requiring negative expression, there were no differences due to familiarity of interpersonal partner. With respect to noncontent measures, few significant

Table 2.1 Effects of Situational Context on Measures of Interpersonal Behavior

Dependent variable	Situational context			Interaction effects			
	Positive vs. negative expression	Male vs. female	Unfamiliar vs. familiar	Expression × sex	Sex × Familiarity	Familiarity × expression	Expression × Sex × Familiarity
Nonverbal measure							
Duration of eye contact	13.89***	2.81	<1.00	<1.00	1.41	<1.00	1.17
No. smiles	9.25***	27.04***	11.71**	<1.00	23.05***	4.89*	<1.00
Affect	8.90**	1.00	<1.00	<1.00	24.66***	<1.00	<1.00
Duration of reply	92.08***	46.73***	<1.00	8.92**	2.51	<1.00	2.20
Latency of response	8.66**	<1.00	<1.00	12.29***	8.53**	2.36	<1.00
Loudness of speech	6.63*	<1.00	1.35	2.22	1.81	5.10*	<1.00
Speech disturbance ratio	2.53	6.43*	<1.00	6.25*	4.05*	1.29	<1.00
Content measure							
Compliance content	—	4.51*	<1.00	—	2.51	—	—
Request for new behavior	—	9.86*	<1.00	—	<1.00	—	—
Praise	—	118.06***	29.86***	—	292.69***	—	—
Appreciation	—	15.67***	28.27***	—	93.72***	—	—
Spontaneous positive behavior	—	122.02***	12.45***	—	26.54***	—	—

*$p < .05$.
**$p < .01$.
***$p < .001$.

differences emerged with respect to familiarity. However, as might be expected, subjects smiled more when talking with familiar than with unfamiliar partners.

Interaction Effects

Significant two-way interactions obtained between the independent variables (see Table 2.1) were further analyzed by Newman-Keuls tests, summarized in Table 2.2. No higher order interactions attained significance.

Expression × Sex. With respect to interactions between sex of interpersonal partner and type of assertive expression required (positive versus negative), it was found that significant differences emerged between all possible social context combinations for "duration of reply." Subjects generally tended to talk longer in negative contexts as compared with positive contexts. Also, irrespective of whether positive or negative expression was required, subjects spoke longer to males than to females. Latency of response was significantly longer to a male in a negative context than when initiating responses to females or to males in a positive context. There were no differences in latency of response to females, irrespective of type of expression, or between males and females when the expression was positive. Finally, there was a significantly greater ratio of speech disturbances per unit of time when speaking to males in a negative context than when speaking to females, in either positive or negative contexts, or to males in a positive context.

Sex × Familiarity. Interactions between sex of partner and familiarity of partner attained significance on 7 of the 12 dependent measures. Significantly more smiles were directed toward females in a positive context than to males in either context or females in a negative context. Also significantly more affect was expressed toward familiar males and unfamiliar females (who did not differ from each other) than to familiar females and unfamiliar males (who also did not differ from each other). Latency of response was greater to familiar males than to either unfamiliar males or familiar females. No other differences were significant with respect to latency. In general, there were fewer speech disturbances to unfamiliar females than to familiar females or familiar or unfamiliar males.

Significant interactions were obtained between sex of partner and familiarity of partner in situations requiring positive but not negative expression. Familiar females elicited praise almost three times as often as familiar males. Also, familiar females received more praise than unfamiliar females, and unfamiliar males received more praise than familiar males. Both unfamiliar females and familiar males elicited significantly more appreciation than either familiar females and unfamiliar males. Unfamiliar males did not differ from familiar females in receiving appreciation. Finally, males, irrespective of familiarity, elicited more spontaneous offers for a subject to return a favor than did females.

Table 2.2 Newman-Keuls Comparisons of Situational Context Interactions

Interaction

Expression × Sex

Measure				
Duration of reply	Female positive	Male positive	Female negative	Male negative
Latency	Male positive$_a$	Female positive$_{a,b}$	Female negative$_b$	Male negative
Speech disturbances	Female negative$_a$	Female positive$_a$	Male positive$_a$	Male negative

Sex × Familiarity

Measure				
Smiles	Male familiar$_a$	Female unfamiliar$_a$	Male unfamiliar$_a$	Female familiar$_b$
Affect	Male familiar$_a$	Female unfamiliar$_a$	Male unfamiliar$_b$	Female familiar$_b$
Latency	Female familiar$_a$	Male unfamiliar	Female unfamiliar$_{a,b}$	Male familiar$_b$
Speech disturbances	Female unfamiliar	Female familiar$_a$	Male unfamiliar$_a$	Male familiar$_a$
Appreciation	Male unfamiliar$_a$	Male familiar	Male unfamiliar$_a$	Female unfamiliar
Spontaneous positive	Female familiar$_a$	Male unfamiliar$_a$	Male familiar$_a$	Male familiar
Praise	Male familiar	Female unfamiliar	Male unfamiliar	Female familiar

Familiarity × Expression

Measure				
Smiles	Unfamiliar negative	Familiar negative$_a$	Unfamiliar positive	Familiar positive
Loudness	Familiar positive$_a$	Unfamiliar positive$_a$	Unfamiliar negative	Familiar negative

Note. Any two means with the same subscript are not significantly different, whereas any two means with different subscripts are significantly different. All differences are at $p < .05$. Means are presented in increasing order from left to right.

However, an unfamiliar female was more likely to elicit a favor than a familiar female.

Familiarity × Expression. There were two significant interactions between familiarity of partner and positive versus negative context. The significant interaction with respect to smiles was due to the fact that more smiles were delivered to familiar persons in a positive context than to unfamiliar persons in either context, or to familiar persons in a negative context. Additionally, unfamiliar persons in a negative context elicited fewer smiles than familiar persons in a negative context or unfamiliar persons in a positive context.

With respect to loudness, greater volume of speech was directed toward familiar persons in a negative context than to either unfamiliar persons in a negative context or to individuals in a positive context, irrespective of familiarity. Familiarity did not elicit differences in speech volume when the context was positive.

Comparisons Between High- and Low-Assertive Subjects

High- and low-assertive subjects were identified from the group used in the previous analysis. Subjects whose mean rating on ''overall assertiveness'' (across all scenes) fell in the top third of the distribution ($n = 20$) were designated as high assertive. Those subjects whose mean rating fell in the lower third of the distribution ($n = 20$) were designated as low assertive. A t test performed between the means of these groups indicated a highly significant difference in ratings of assertiveness, $t(38) = 8.95$, $p < .001$. Additionally, subjects in the high-assertive and low-assertive groups differed in the expected direction on the Wolpe-Lazarus Assertiveness Questionnaire, $t(38) = 2.11, p < .05$.

Separate four-way analyses of variance with high-assertive and low-assertive subjects as levels of one factor and situational contexts as three separate factors were performed on all dependent measures. Since the effects of situational contexts on measures of interpersonal behavior were previously presented on the full sample of 60 subjects, only the effects of subject differences in assertiveness and their interactions with situational context are presented here.

Table 2.3 depicts mean ratings and significant differences between high- and low-assertive subjects on all dependent measures. Also shown are interactions between levels of assertiveness and situational contexts. Significant interactions were further analyzed by means of Newman-Keuls tests.

Nonverbal Behavior

The results indicate that over all contexts, high-assertive subjects gave much lengthier replies than low-assertive subjects, $f(1, 38) = 15.8$, $p < .001$.

Table 2.3 Means, Significant Levels, and Interactions with Situational Contexts for High- and Low-Assertive Groups

Dependent variable	High$\bar{X}$[a]	Low $\bar{X}$[a]	F	Expression	Sex	Familiarity
Duration of eye contact	30.2	22.52	<1.00	<1.00	<1.00	<1.00
No. smiles	.30	.84	5.24*	<1.00	1.16	<1.00
Affect	13.91	12.25	23.4***	3.02	1.43	1.36
Duration of reply	244.85	120.43	15.8***	4.75	1.08	<1.00
Latency of response	53.52	58.36	<1.00	6.26*	1.10	<1.00
Loudness of speech	12.20	10.33	9.60**	5.15*	<1.00	6.75*
Speech disturbance ratio	.142	.073	6.93*	<1.00	<1.00	<1.00
Compliance content	.89	1.57	9.85***	—	<1.00	<1.00
Requests for new behavior	2.10	.98	31.9***	—	3.41	4.64*
Praise	1.56	1.13	10.80**	—	4.58*	3.70
Appreciation	2.03	1.80	1.40	—	1.00	<1.00
Spontaneous positive behavior	1.66	1.19	14.0**	—	<1.00	<1.00

[a]$n = 20$.
*$p < .05$.
**$p < .01$.
***$p < .001$.

449

However, both high-assertive ($p < .01$) and low-assertive subjects ($p < .01$) responded longer in situations that required negative rather than positive assertions. While there were no differences in latency of response between high- and low-assertive subjects across all contexts ($F < 1.00$), a significant interaction was obtained with type of expression. This resulted from the fact that latency of response was longer for low-assertive subjects than high-assertive subjects when the situation required negative assertion ($p < .05$). There were no differences between groups in the context of positive assertion.

In general, high-assertive subjects spoke significantly louder than low-assertive subjects, $F(1, 38) = 9.60, p < .01$. This was true irrespective of whether the interpersonal partner was familiar ($p < .01$) or unfamiliar ($p < .01$), or whether the interactional context was negative ($p < .01$) or positive ($p < .01$). However, when the context was negative, high-assertive subjects increased their volume of speech compared to when the context was positive ($p < .01$). There was no difference in speech volume for low-assertive subjects irrespective of whether the context was negative or positive. Irrespective of situational context, highly assertive subjects spoke with greater affect more appropriate to the situation than did low-assertive subjects, $F(1, 38) = 23.5, p < .001$, although frequency of smiles was greater for low-assertive than high-assertive subjects, $F(1, 38) = 5.24, p < .05$. Finally, with respect to nonverbal expression, high-assertive subjects evidenced a higher ration of speech disturbances per length of speech than did low-assertive subjects, $F(1, 38) = 6.93, p < .05$.

Speech Content

With respect to speech content in situations requiring negative assertion, it was found that, as expected, low-assertive subjects were more compliant than high-assertive subjects, $F(1, 38) = 9.85, p < .001$. Additionally high-assertive subjects requested more often that their interpersonal partner change their behavior in all situation contexts, $F(1, 38) = 31.9, p < .001$. This was true whether their partner was familiar ($p < .01$) or unfamiliar ($p < .01$).

With respect to situational contexts requiring the expression of positive assertion, it was found that subjects in the high-assertive group delivered more praise to their interpersonal partners than did low-assertive subjects, $F(1, 38) = 10.8, p < .01$. The significant interaction with sex of partner on this variable was due to the fact that low-assertive subjects delivered more praise to females than to males ($p < .01$), whereas high-assertive subjects praised males and females equally. Finally, with respect to content on positive situations, highly assertive subjects offered to spontaneously do a favor for an interpersonal partner more frequently than did less assertive subjects, $F(1, 38) = 14.0, p < .01$.

DISCUSSION

The results of this study substantiated the hypothesis that in situations requiring assertive expression an individual's behavior is functionally related to the social context of the interpersonal interaction. Obviously, content of speech, or *what* one says, will differ in relation to whether the situation requires positive or negative assertion. However, the present results demonstrated significant differences on six of the seven *nonverbal* interactional variables when comparing responses to negative and positive assertive situations. Additionally, males elicited different responses than females across situations on all measures of speech content. In negative situations requiring an individual to "stand up for his rights," male subjects evidenced greater assertion toward women than other men. Similarly, in situations requiring positive assertive expression, subjects were more likely to offer praise and appreciation to female than to male partners. The greater expression of positive assertion to women than men appears to be consistent with sociocultural norms in this country where it is permissible for males to be more effusive toward women than toward other men. Lack of deference on the part of male subjects to women in situations requiring negative assertion was more difficult to explain, and may be specific to the clinical or sociocultural characteristics of the present population. Similarly, the finding that unfamiliar individuals, particularly in positive contexts, elicited greater assertiveness than familiar persons may in part be a function of the sociocultural characteristics of these patients.

In general, the results support a stimulus-specific theory of assertiveness. That is, an individual who is assertive in one interpersonal context may not be assertive in a different interpersonal environment. Further, some individuals may have no difficulty responding with negative assertions, but may be unable to respond when the situation requires positive expression. This is consistent with the classic study of Hartshorne and May (1928) who demonstrated that "moral" behaviors in children were not consistent across various situations, and Mischel's (1968) argument against the utility of "trait" theories of personality. While Mischel (1968) did not deny the fact that some stable predispositions to respond in certain ways exist, he concluded:

> While trait and state theories have searched for broad, consistent dispositions, a considerable amount of experimental research has focused, instead, on the determinants of changes in behavior and on the stimulus conditions that seem to control these alterations. The principles that emerge from studies of the variables that control behavior in turn become the bases for developing theory, not about global traits and states, but about the manner in which behavior develops and changes in response to environmental stimulus changes. (p. 10)

In addition to showing the stimulus-specific nature of assertive responding, the results of the present study demonstrated the behavioral complexity of what is commonly referred to as "assertiveness." On the majority of verbal and nonverbal measures employed in this study, significant differences emerged between subjects who evidenced high versus low assertion on the global measure of assertiveness. Apparently, assertive responding requires the coordinated delivery of numerous verbal and nonverbal responses.

In general, high-assertive subjects tended to talk longer, with greater affect and speech volume, while smiling less frequently than low-assertive subjects. The fact that there were no significant differences between high- and low-assertive subjects on measures of speech duration and latency of response could, in part, have been a function of the short duration of the experimental interaction. Since subjects were permitted only one response to the role-played partner, who did not respond to the patients' assertions, differences that might have emerged on longer exchanges could have been artificially obscured. The finding that high-assertive subjects evidenced more speech disturbances per unit of time than the lows was an unexpected result. Mahl (1956), in studying the speech disfluencies of patients in psychotherapy, concluded that disruptions were related to judgments of the client's anxiety level although no objective measures of anxiety were used. It may be that assertive individuals take greater "risks" in expressing themselves than unassertive individuals, with concomitant emotional arousal being reflected in increased speech disruptions.

The significant differences obtained in this study between high- and low-assertive subjects on component behaviors related to negative assertion replicate previous findings by Eisler, Miller, and Hersen (1973). Additionally, there appear to be numerous behavioral components to positive assertion as well. In addition to differences in speech content between expression of positive compared with negative assertiveness, differences in nonverbal behaviors were also observed. For example, it was found that subjects tended to give lengthier replies with greater speech volume in negative contexts than in positive contexts. Also, when situations require negative assertion, the low-assertive subjects took longer to reply than the high-assertive subjects.

The generality of the specific effects of context on assertive behavior found here is, of course, limited to the characteristics of the present patient population, including their sociocultural background, and the assertive situations sampled in this study. Additional research is needed to determine the effects of additional interpersonal context variables with different populations. For example, further investigations are necessary to determine what constitutes *appropriate* assertive behavior for women, for individuals in different socioeconomic groups, and for individuals who live in different geographic regions. Nevertheless, this study has important implications for the treatment of patients who are deemed to have behavioral deficits in assertion. Positive assertive expression, or what Wolpe (1969) has termed "commendatory" behavior, appears to be a real phenomenon that should broaden the scope of assertive training. To date there appear to be few experimentally validated procedures for training individuals to increase their expression of affection, appreciation, satisfaction, etc. In summary, training individuals to be more reinforcing to others would appear to be indicated in a variety of clinical situations. Further, it is not likely that therapists can train clients to be ''more assertive'' in a general sense. Instead, clinicians should identify classes of interpersonal situations in which deficits can be identified. Training will then consist of increasing assertive responding to specific types of interactions with different individuals.

REFERENCES

Edwards, N. B. Case conference: Assertive training in a case of homosexual pedophilia. *Journal of Behavior Therapy and Experimental Psychiatry, 1972, 3,* 55-63.

Eisler, R. M., Hersen, M., & Agras, W. S. Videotape: A method for the controlled observation of nonverbal interpersonal behavior. *Behavior Therapy, 1973, 4,* 420-425.

Eisler, R. M., Hersen, M., & Miller, P. M. Effects of modeling on components of assertive behavior. *Journal of Behavior Therapy and Experimental Psychiatry, 1973, 4,* 1-6.

Eisler, R. M., Miller, P. M., & Hersen, M. Components of assertive behavior. *Journal of Clinical Psychology, 1973, 29,* 295-299.

Eisler, R. M., Miller, P. M., Hersen, M., & Alford, H. Effects of assertive training on marital interaction. *Archives of General Psychiatry, 1974, 30,* 643-649.

Fensterheim, H. Assertive methods of marital problems. In R. D. Rubin, H. Fensterheim, J. D. Henderson, & L. P. Ullmann (Eds.), *Advances in Behavior Therapy.* New York: Academic Press, 1972.

Goldstein, A. P., Martens, J., Hubben, J., Van Belle, H. A., Schaaf, W., Wiersma, H., & Goedhart, A. The use of modeling to increase independent behaviour. *Behaviour Research and Therapy, 1973, 11,* 31-42.

Hersen, M., Eisler, R. M., Miller, P. M., Johnson, M. B., & Pinkston, S. G. Effects of practice, instructions and modeling on components of assertive behaviour. *Behaviour Research and Therapy, 1973, 11,* 443-451.

Hartshorne, H., & May, M. A. *Studies in the Nature of Character* (Vol. 1). *Studies in Deceit.* New York: Macmillan, 1928.

Kazdin, A. E. Effects of covert modeling and model reinforcement on assertive behaviour. *Journal of Abnormal Psychology, 1974, 83,* 240-252.

Lazarus, A. A. *Behavior Therapy and Beyond.* New York: McGraw-Hill, 1971.

Mahl, G. F. Disturbances and silences in the patient's speech in psychotherapy. *Journal of Abnormal and Social Psychology, 1956, 53,* 1-15.

McFall, R. M., & Lillesand, D. B. Behavior rehearsal with modeling and coaching in assertion training. *Journal of Abnormal Psychology, 1971, 77,* 313-323.

McFall, R. M., & Marston, A. R. An experimental investigation of behavior rehearsal in assertive training. *Journal of Abnormal Psychology, 1970, 76,* 295-303.

Mischel, W. *Personality and Assessment.* New York: Wiley, 1968.

Piaget, G. W., & Lazarus, A. A. The use of rehearsal-desensitization. *Psychotherapy: Theory, Research, and Practice, 1969, 6,* 264-266.

Stevenson, I., & Wolpe, J. Recovery from sexual deviations through overcoming non-sexual neurotic responses. *American Journal of Psychiatry, 1960, 116,* 737-742.

Weinman, B., Gelbart, P., Wallace, M., & Post, M. Inducing assertive behavior in chronic schizophrenics. A comparison of socio-environmental, desensitization, and relaxation therapies. *Journal of Consulting and Clinical Psychology*, 1972, *39*, 246-252.

Wolpe, J. *Psychotherapy by reciprocal inhibition*. Stanford, Calif.: Stanford University Press, 1958.

Wolpe, J. *The Practice of Behavior Therapy*. New York: Pergamon Press, 1969.

Wolpe, J., & Lazarus, A. A. *Behavior Therapy Techniques*. New York: Pergamon Press, 1966.

3

A Situation-Specific Model for Smoking Behavior

J. Allan Best and A. Ralph Hakstian

Ratings of common cigarette smoking situations were analyzed to develop a model of smoking behavior consistent with behavioral intervention techniques. Mean intensity of urge was rated for each of 63 smoking situations by 177 males and 154 females drawn from the general population. Multivariate analyses of the data revealed distinct response patterns for males and females. Factor analyses for each sex yielded a relatively large number of homogeneous factors. In general, the results suggest a more varied and differentiated pattern of smoking than has been suggested previously. It is argued that this model of smoking behavior may be able to provide a basis for tailoring smoking modification procedures to individual reasons for smoking.

First published by Pergamon Press in Addictive Behaviors, 1978, 3, 79-92.

A SITUATION-SPECIFIC MODEL FOR SMOKING BEHAVIOR

Researchers in smoking modification are increasingly cognizant of the need to consider individual differences in smoking behavior when formulating treatment programs. Determinants of smoking behavior vary considerably from one individual to another and, within an individual, across situations. Treatment ought to prove more effective if individual reasons for smoking are understood and alternative, nonsmoking behaviors are developed (Bernstein, 1974; Best, Owen & Trentadue, in press; Mausner, 1971). This is especially likely to the extent that smoking is not solely respondent behavior conditioned to antecedent stimuli but also an operant used to cope with tension, boredom, and other motivational states.

Direct evidence for these premises is currently lacking. However, the recent success of cessation programs emphasizing self-management skills and alternative responses in the maintenance of change does lend support (e.g. Best, Owen, & Trentadue, in press; Brengelmann & Sedlmayr, 1975; Chapman, Smith & Layden, 1971; Morrow, Sachs, Gmeinder, & Burgess, 1973; Pomerleau & Ciccone, 1974).

Tailoring treatment techniques to individual reasons for smoking requires both an appropriate conceptual model and valid clinical assessment procedures. One of the more influential psychosocial models proposed is Tomkins' (1966, 1968). Smoking behavior is seen as motivated by affective states. Innate reinforcing properties combine with learning so that smoking becomes capable of relieving any negative affective state or evoking any positive affect. Tomkins posited smoker types corresponding to the affective significance of the smoking behavior. Thus there are positive affect smokers, negative affect smokers and "habitual" smokers from whom the affective involvement is minimal. He further described the "addictive" smoker who is characterized by a learned dependence on smoking such that awareness of not smoking per se elicits negative affects and thus further smoking.

Factor analysis of items reflecting these motives has been consistent with the hypotheses (Ikard, Green & Horn, 1969), stimulation and sensorimotor manipulation motives being added to the model. Others have further stressed the additional role played by social factors (Mausner & Platt, 1971; McKennell, 1970, 1973; Russell, Peto, & Patel, 1974).

In these psychosocial models, relatively little attention is paid to the physiological consequences of smoking, although effects are marked and likely of major reinforcing value (e.g., Dunn, 1973). The exception is Eysenck's (1973) case for the central role of physiological arousal factors. He has noted that the effect of smoking is dose-related and may be either stimulatory or sedative. The individual's response may be mediated by his current arousal level which will vary in large part as a function of introversion-extraversion propensity. Smoking is then seen as a mechanism for regulating arousal to maintain an optimal level.

Eysenck has drawn on the considerable literature relating smoking to arousal and introversion-extraversion factors to support his position.

Thus, smoking behavior has been variously conceptualized as determined by affective or arousal states, addiction, and social and related needs. These views are not inconsistent with one another but rather vary in relative emphasis. Similarly, they are not at odds with a habit conception of smoking which stresses the importance of learning (Hunt & Matarazzo, 1970, 1973). Yet there are limitations to the models' utility for the behavior modifier. This is unfortunate since the large majority of smoking modification programs are behaviorally oriented.

First, the models focus on *internal* determinants of smoking behavior. In contrast, most treatment programs adopt a habit conception of smoking which stresses observable *environmental* determinants. In fact, these are not polar positions. For example, McKennell's (1973) ''inner need'' and ''social need'' factors derive from data describing smoking frequency by smoking occasion. Furthermore, behavior modification programs increasingly do consider internal, especially cognitive, determinants. Nevertheless, the models are couched in terms not readily applied to common treatment methods.

Second, existing models have been unduly biased by theoretical rather than empirical considerations. Items for questionnaires often sample only those domains of a priori theoretical interest such that subsequent factor analysis becomes a self-fulfilling prophesy. Similarly, factor analysts have preferred solutions reflecting relatively few, broad factors in their models. Such solutions are inconsistent with the behavior modifier's expectation that smoking behavior is likely to show considerable situational variability and that factors should be relatively homogeneous and situation-specific.

In short, behavior modifiers rarely have utilized existing models describing individual differences in smoking behavior. Yet there is increasing recognition that such discrimination might promote more effective treatment. The present study was designed to examine variation in smoking behavior across a systematically derived domain of smoking situations and to develop a model of smoking behavior which would be comprehensive, empirically-derived, and consistent with current approaches to smoking modification.

METHOD

Smoking Situations

The domain of smoking situations was defined by two means. First, pretreatment records were reviewed of smoking behavior for 50 clients enrolled in a smoking cessation program (Best, Owen, & Trentadue, in press). The recording required clients to note time, place, activity, and perceived reason for cigarettes during normal smoking for seven days before treatment began. A list of all distinct, specific occasions for smoking was derived. Second, distinct situations defined in previous work (Horn, 1969; Mausner & Platt, 1971; McKennell, 1973; Russell et al., 1974) were added to this list. A total of 63 situations resulted.

Questionnaire Format

A questionnaire was constructed so that for each situation respondants were asked to rate on a seven point scale the typical strength of their urge to smoke, relative to their average urge. The questionnaire was administered to 50 subjects to ensure adequate item comprehension and variability in endorsement. No difficulty was reported with the instructions or items; range of response was at least five of a possible seven points for all items and the mean rating for most items was between 3 and 5 on a scale of 1 to 7.

Subjects and Administration Procedure

The questionnaire and a demographic information sheet were completed by 177 male and 154 female smokers, approached when they were waiting for a ferry between Vancouver and Vancouver Island, British Columbia. There are major concentrations of population at either end of the ferry and, since most residents do use the service on occasion, it was presumed that the sample would prove similar to the general population of smokers in the province. The sample had a mean age of 30.49, had smoked for 14.06 years, and reported smoking 21.75 cigarettes daily. Occupation was coded using the Canadian Census procedures, converted to socioeconomic status with Blishen & McRoberts (1976) procedure, and grouped to result in five levels of socioeconomic class. Comparisons with the 1971 provincial census data indicated that the sample was significantly biased towards over-representation of higher socioeconomic status status smokers [$X^2(4) = 17.70, p < .01$ and $X^2(4) = 20.03, p < .01$ for males and females respectively].

Analysis Procedures

The original pool of 63 items was reduced to 50 by eliminating some redundant items, along with others which displayed very low communalities in preliminary factor analyses. The resulting 50×50 covariance matrices for the sexes were then compared for equality, using the Barlett-Box procedure. The results showed that the two covariance matrices differed significantly, thus necessitating separate-sex factor analyses of the data, since the underlying covariance structures were demonstrably different.

Three factoring procedures were employed with the results for each sex. First, a principal components analysis was performed in order to examine the eigenvalues of the correlation matrices for indications of the correct number of factors. Both the Kaiser-Guttman rule (eigenvalues greater than unity) and Cattell's (1966) screen test suggested 12 factors for the male sample and 11 for the female. Next, a maximum likelihood common-factor analysis was performed, with the resulting likelihood ratio test for the number of factors suggesting 14 for the males and 11 for the females. Thus, all three rules for deciding the number of factors agreed for the female data. For the male data, the results were close, and the decision of 12 factors was made, since two of the three rules suggested this number and also because it was considered desirable to keep the number of factors as close as possible for the two sexes. Finally, an unweighted least squares (or minimum residuals) common-factor analysis was performed in which 12 factors were extracted for the male data, and 11 for the female.

The unrotated factor patterns were then transformed to oblique simple structure resolutions by means of the Harris-Kaiser (1964) procedure. The resulting primary-factor patterns (oblique primary-factor loading matrices) were of unusually clear quality for variables as inherently complex as reasons for smoking. If we use, as a rough indication of the quality of simple structure, the percentage of coefficients falling in the factor hyperplanes—typically operationalized as the percentage of coefficients in the $0 \pm .10$ region—the resulting figures were 62% overall for the male sample and 60% for the female. In addition, the factor intercorrelations which were low in both cases, indicating that extreme obliquity was not necessary to achieve clear simple structures. Factor scores were then calculated—for the 12 factors in the male sample, and 11 in the female sample—by the regression method. Following this, the 177 male and 154 female subjects were taxonomized by means of a cluster analysis (Ward, 1963). With this procedure, subgroups of males and females were identified in terms of their profile similarities over the 12 or 11 factor scores. Those subjects whose profiles were relatively similar were grouped together as a "cluster". The optimal number of such subgroupings was: for the males, *four* clusters, and for the females, *five*.

With "cluster-membership", or subgroup classification, the dependent variable (with, respectively, four and five levels for males and females), discriminant analyses were next performed for each sex. The predictor variables in these analyses were the 12 (males) or 11 (females) factor scores.

Finally, with "cluster-membership" the independent variable, one-way analyses of variance (ANOVAs) was performed, separately by sex, for several continuous dependent variables: age, length of time smoking, and amount smoked. These analyses were performed to ascertain whether the empirically-derived subgroups differed in these apparently relevant variables.

RESULTS

The results of the factor analyses of the 50 retained items are presented for males and females in Tables 3.1 and 3.2 respectively. The coefficients reported in these tables are the oblique primary-factor pattern coefficients (or "factor loadings" for an oblique solution). In addition, the mean ratings for each item are reported. Only the factor loadings judged large enough to mark each factor are given in Tables 3.1 and 3.2.[2] Factor congruence coefficients (Tucker, 1951) were computed between the factors for the male sample and those corresponding most closely in the female sample. Of these congruence coefficients, those for Factors 1 through 5 were large enough, i.e., .75 or greater, to warrant common descriptions for the two samples. The coefficient for Factor 6 was less satisfactory (0.68) but, given the item similarity, was judged of sufficient magnitude to justify the same description.

Table 3.1   Factor Pattern Coefficients from the Oblique Common-Factor Solution, and Mean Ratings, of Male Respondants (N = 177)

	Coefficient	Mean Rating
Factor 1: Nervous Tension		
20. When you feel nervous	.75	4.93
18. When you are worried	.71	4.88
15. When you feel tense	.70	4.89
19. When you are waiting for someone or something	.50	4.85
21. When you feel impatient	.42	4.59
40. When you are drinking an alcoholic beverage	.34	5.98
Factor 2: Self-Image		
38. When you want to feel more attractive	.79	1.99
48. When you are in a situation in which you feel smoking is a part of your self-image	.58	2.82
29. When you feel you need more energy	.55	2.50
12. When you want to feel more mature and sophisticated	.53	2.28
32. When you want to relax	.52	4.24
49. When you want to avoid eating sweets	.49	2.32
50. When you feel oversensitive	.32	3.40
Factor 3: Frustration		
37. When you feel annoyed	.78	4.10
35. When you feel angry	.77	4.14
41. When you feel frustrated	.66	4.39
45. When you feel upset	.57	4.32

---

[2]Because of journal space limitations, the complete primary-factor patterns for each sex are not given in Tables 3.1 and 3.2. The complete matrices are available from the authors upon request.

Table 3.1 continued

	Coefficient	Mean Rating
9. When you feel depressed	.36	4.49
28. When you are angry with yourself	.30	3.69
Factor 4: Relaxation		
32. When you want to relax	.65	4.24
39. When you feel tired	.49	3.24
8. When you are resting	.47	3.41
10. When you want to cheer up	.37	2.90
3. When you feel really happy	.36	3.29
Factor 5: Automatic		
5. When you simply become aware of the fact that you are not smoking	.61	3.27
14. When you realize you are lighting a cigarette even though you just put one out	.60	2.74
7. When you find a cigarette in your mouth and don't remember having lit it	.58	2.55
25. When you realize you have run out of cigarettes	.55	4.88
17. When you realize that you won't be able to smoke for a while	.33	4.50
Factor 6: Social		
46. When you see others smoking	.67	4.03
42. When someone offers you a cigarette	.63	4.23
Factor 7: Discomfort		
27. When you feel uncomfortable	.54	4.00
16. When you feel embarrassed	.44	3.48
10. When you want to cheer up	.32	2.90
31. When you want to fill a pause in a conversation	.31	3.33
13. When you light up a cigarette to go along with some activity you are doing (for example, while fixing a bicycle, writing a letter, doing housework)	.31	3.55
Factor 8: Inactive		
23. When you feel bored	.55	4.15
24. When you are drinking coffee or tea	.50	5.06
1. When you want to sit back and enjoy a cigarette	.45	4.59
33. When you want to keep slim	.34	2.09
Factor 9: Time Structuring		
26. When you want to have time to think in a conversation	.59	3.77
31. When you want to fill a pause in a conversation	.56	3.33
17. When you realize that you won't be able to smoke for a while	.33	4.50
24. When you are drinking coffee or tea	.30	5.06
Factor 10: Restlessness		
43. When you feel restless	.54	4.34
21. When you feel impatient	.38	4.59

Table 3.1 continued

	Coefficient	Mean Rating
47. When you are overly excited	.34	3.90
11. When you want to take a break from work or some other activity	.30	4.87
Factor 11: Sensory Stimulation		
4. When you want something to do with your hands	.66	4.29
6. When you want to reward yourself for something you've done or tell yourself that you can have a cigarette if you complete some task	.35	3.44
2. When you feel anxious	.35	4.66
Factor 12: Concentration		
30. When you want to concentrate	.49	3.50

Factors in the Male Sample

The factors for male smokers can be described as follows. The Nervous Tension (#1), Frustration (#3), Discomfort (#7), and Restlessness (#10) factors taken together account for 33% of the common-factor variance in the ratings. All reflect some aspect of the negative affect stressed in other models (e.g., Ikard et al., 1973; McKennell, 1973). However, the correlations between pairs of the factors are not high ($.10 \le r \le .23$), suggesting that response to affective situations is differentiated and relatively specific. Nervous Tension and Frustration are both relatively homogeneous factors which, although here distinct, are in combination quite similar to McKennell's (1973) Nervous Irritation and Horn's (1969) Tension Reduction. The Discomfort and Restlessness factors have not appeared in previous solutions. However, inspection of McKennell and Horn's item pools reveals that the present items were not included in their analyses but rather were generated by our recording procedure.

The Social-Image factor (#2) includes a greater variety of items than the four negative affect factors. The factor seems conceptually similar to Mausner and Platt's (1971) Self-Image and to McKennell's (1973) Social Confidence—but in fact the item overlap is negligible. The majority of the items dropped in reducing the number from 63 to 50 items loaded on a similar factor. These included sensorimotor items related to enjoying the smell of cigarettes, watching the cigarette burn, flicking ashes and feeling smoke in the lungs. All had low mean ratings, suggesting that sensorimotor effects of smoking may not be as important generally as suggested by previous work. It may be noted that the retained self-image items and dropped sensorimotor items together may define an "adolescent smoker" factor for whom sensorimotor effects might be particularly salient.

The Relaxation (#4), Inactive (#8), Sensory Stimulation (#11), and Concentration (#12) factors all may relate to the arousal function stressed by Eysenck (1973) and supported by Frith (1971). Together they account for 25% of the common-factor variance. The Relaxation factor is realtively homogeneous and quite similar to McKennell's (1973) Relaxation Smoking. Inactive, Sensory Stimulation, and Concentration do not seem closely related to other investigators' factors.

The Automatic (#5) factor is homogeneous and similar to the habitual smoking hypothesized by Tomkins (1966) and corresponding factors found by Ikard et al. (1969) and Mausner and Platt (1971). It is also consistent with the automaticity of smoking stressed by Hunt and Matarazzo (1973) and Hunt, Matarazzo, and Weiss (1976).

Social (#6) factors are also commonly proposed (Mausner & Platt, 1971; McKennell, 1973; Russell et al., 1974), although here the factor is defined by relatively few, specifically social influence items whereas other items previously related to social smoking (e.g. "when you are drinking an alcoholic beverage") loaded more highly on other factors.

The Time Structuring (#9) factor seems to be unique to our analysis. The items vary considerably but may be related by an hypothesized time structuring function. The concept is not dissimilar to the "need for motor expression," suggested as one motivator of smoking behavior by Hunt, Matarazzo, & Weiss (1976).

Table 3.2 Factor Pattern Coefficients from the Oblique Common-Factor Solution, and Mean Ratings, of Female Respondants (N = 154)

	Coefficient	Mean Rating
Factor 1: Nervous Tension		
18. When you are worried	.69	4.79
20. When you feel nervous	.67	5.01
15. When you feel tense	.60	4.90
9. When you feel depressed	.55	4.56
45. When you feel upset	.50	4.60
2. When you feel anxious	.49	4.55
16. When you feel embarrassed	.36	3.68
37. When you feel annoyed	.31	4.36
35. When you feel angry	.31	4.48
Factor 2: Self-Image		
38. When you want to feel more attractive	.75	2.05
12. When you want to feel more mature and sophisticated	.70	2.50
48. When you are in a situation in which you feel smoking is a part of your self-image	.65	2.69
16. When you feel embarrassed	.30	3.68

Table 3.2 continued

	Coefficient	Mean Rating
Factor 3: Frustration		
41. When you feel frustrated	.75	4.51
43. When you feel restless	.50	4.24
37. When you feel annoyed	.43	4.36
30. When you want to concentrate	.37	3.54
35. When you feel angry	.37	4.48
50. When you feel oversensitive	.33	3.96
Factor 4: Relaxation		
32. When you want to relax	.58	4.08
8. When you are resting	.54	2.65
11. When you take a break from work or some other activity	.49	4.66
1. When you want to sit back and enjoy a cigarette	.43	4.13
39. When you feel tired	.33	2.67
Factor 5: Automatic		
14. When you realize that you are lighting a cigarette even though you just put one out	.58	2.70
7. When you find a cigarette in your mouth and don't remember having lit it	.57	2.32
5. When you simply become aware of the fact that you are not smoking	.46	3.22
Factor 6: Social		
42. When someone offers you a cigarette	.56	3.86
46. When you see others smoking	.54	4.27
40. When you are drinking an alcoholic beverage	.45	5.57
Factor 7: Uneasy		
27. When you feel uncomfortable	.52	4.18
26. When you want to have time to think in a conversation	.50	3.69
21. When you feel impatient	.50	4.47
24. When you are drinking coffee or tea	.44	5.03
28. When you are angry with yourself	.43	3.88
35. When you feel angry	.39	4.48
31. When you want to fill a pause in a conversation	.35	3.53
22. When you want to keep yourself busy	.31	3.19
19. When you are waiting for someone or something	.31	4.75
Factor 8: Boredom		
23. When you feel bored	.72	4.03
34. When you are trying to pass time	.50	4.10
36. When you want something in your mouth	.36	3.12
4. When you want something to do with your hands	.31	3.99
22. When you want to keep yourself busy	.31	3.19
Factor 9: Food Avoidance		
49. When you want to avoid eating sweets	.79	3.36
33. When you want to keep slim	.78	3.51

Table 3.2 continued

	Coefficient	Mean Rating
Factor 10: Habit		
44. When you have finished a meal or snack	.56	5.25
24. When you are drinking coffee or tea	.43	5.03
13. When you light up a cigarette to go along with some other activity you are doing (for example, while fixing a bicycle, writing a letter, doing housework)	.40	3.84
17. When you realize that you won't be able to smoke for a while	.40	4.33
25. When you realize you have run out of cigarettes	.39	4.94
11. When you take a break from work or some other activity	.35	4.66
4. When you want something to do with your hands	.35	3.99
Factor 11: Stimulant		
29. When you feel you need more energy	.65	2.36
3. When you feel really happy	.55	3.10
39. When you feel tired	.46	2.67
47. When you are overly excited	.31	3.97
22. When you want to keep yourself busy	.31	3.19

Factors in the Female Sample

Considerations for the first six factors of the female solution are comparable to those outlined for the parallel male factors. Furthermore, Uneasy (#7), Boredom (#8) and Stimulant (#11), are conceptually similar to the males' Discomfort, Inactive and Sensory Stimulation respectively, although the congruence coefficients were not high.

Food Avoidance (#9) is similar to the Food Substitution reported by McKennell (1970, 1973) for samples of British males and females. McKennell did find the factor for both sexes although it is evident only here only for the females.

The Habit (#10) factor is an interesting one. Hunt et al. (1976) have recently argued that much smoking is maintained as the result of associative learning rather than reinforcement. Certainly many smoking cessation programs focus on stimulus control procedures consistent with this assumption. The situations represented in this factor seem of this kind. It is noteworthy that the factor is not found for males, perhaps suggesting that their smoking patterns tend to be less directly under the control of environmental cues.

Cluster Analyses and Smoker Types

The results of the cluster analyses, performed separately for males and females, are depicted—in profile form—in Figures 3.1 and 3.2. In the *overall* male and female groups, the factor scores were scaled to have a mean of 50 and standard deviation of 10.

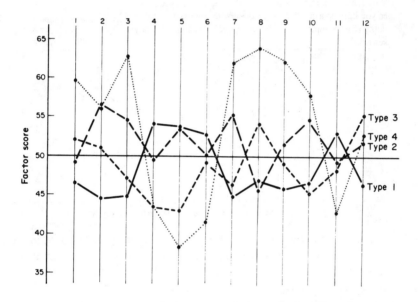

Figure 3.1. Mean Factor Scores for Male Cluster Types.

The profiles may be summarized as follows:

Male Group 1 smokers are relatively high on Relaxation, Automatic, Stimulation, and Social factors, low on Self-Image, Frustration, and Discomfort. In comparison, Group 2 are high on Self-Image, Discomfort, and Restlessness, low on Inactive. Group 3 males score high on Concentration and Inactive while scoring low on Automatic, Relaxation, and Restlessness. Finally, male Group 4 smokers are relatively high on a large number of factors including Inactive, Frustration, Time Structuring, Discomfort, Nervous Tension, and Restlessness. They are low on Automatic, Social, Sensory Stimulation, and Relaxation.

There are five cluster types for females. Group 1 smokers are high on Automatic and Social, low on Stimulation, Uneasy, Food Avoidance, and Self-Image. Group 2 is high on Uneasy, Self-Image, Frustration, and Nervous Tension while low on Social and Automatic. Group 3 is somewhat similar, being

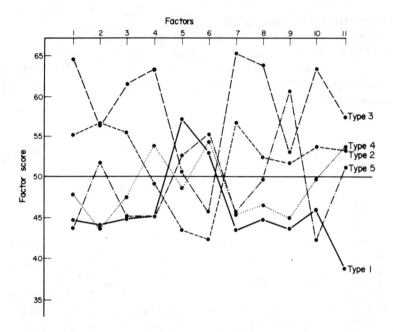

Figure 3.2. Mean Factor Scores for Female Cluster Types.

high on Uneasy, Nervous Tension, Boredom, Relaxation and Habit, low on Social. The Group 4 smoker scores high on Social, Relaxation, and Stimulation. She scores low on Self-Image and Habit. Female Group 5 smokers are high on Food Avoidance and Social, low on Habit, Frustration, and Relaxation.

From the discriminant analyses performed, the first two functions accounted for 94% and 84% of the discrimination for males and females respectively. Means on the first two discriminant functions are plotted by group in Figures 3.3 and 3.4.

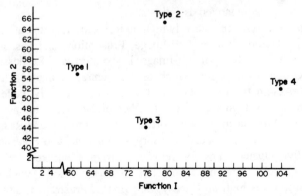

Figure 3.3. Means of the First Two Discriminant Functions for Male Cluster Types.

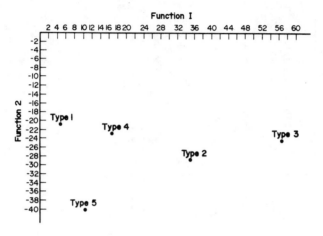

Figure 3.4.   Means of the First Two Discriminant Functions for Female Cluster Types.

Results of the ANOVAs using cluster group as the independent variable and age, daily smoking rate, years of smoking, mean factor score, and standard deviation of factor scores—are presented in Table 3.3.

Results from the cluster analyses, discriminant analyses, and these ANOVAs can now be summarized for male smokers. Group 1 is typified by a relatively low average urge, little variability across situations, and a relatively high daily rate. In contrast, Group 4 subjects have a relatively high mean urge rating, considerable variability across situations, and a low daily rate. Furthermore, the first discriminate function seems to reflect in large part differences between these two groups.

We view these differences as reflecting the situational specificity versus nonspecificity, or automaticity, of smoking behavior. That is, Group 4 smokers are light smokers for whom smoking occurs in relatively few situations. On the other hand, in those situations the associative links seem strong and the individual experiences quite a strong urge to smoke. Group 1 is composed of heavy smokers who do not respond differentially to their current situation. They may correspond to Tomkins' (1968) addictive type, and smoke automatically such that the possible reinforcing value of cigarettes is not a major causal factor (Hunt et al., 1976).

Alternatively, heavy smokers may report lower mean urges because they have learned to anticipate the aversity of an increasing urge by smoking before urge intensity reaches a very high level.[3]

---

[3]The authors are grateful to Edward Lichtenstein for this suggestion.

Table 3.3 Results of Analyses of Variance of Age, Rate, Years of Smoking, and Mean and Standard Deviation of Factor Scores, for the Cluster Groups

Males	Group Means (n's in parentheses)*						Significant Pairwise Differences** (p < .05)
	1	2	3	4	F	p	
Age	31.44(82)	30.1(44)	31.44(27)	28.96(23)	0.45	>.50	
Daily Rate	28.06(82)	23.8(44)	19.35(26)	13.92(23)	11.73	<.0001	1vs.3, 1vs.4, 2vs.4
Years of Smoking	15.78(82)	14.43(44)	13.93(11)	13.92(24)	0.36	>.50	
Mean Factor Score	48.43(82)	51.77(44)	48.72(22)	53.54(24)	36.19	<.00001	1vs.2, 1vs.4, 2vs.4, 3vs.4
Standard Deviation of Factor Scores	9.50(82)	10.77(44)	9.27(22)	14.93(24)	28.67	<.00001	1vs.4, 2vs.4, 3vs.4

Females	Group Means (n's in parentheses)							Significant Pairwise Differences*
	1	2	3	4	5	F	p	
Age	29.83(36)	35.95(41)	31.00(15)	23.60(35)	29.77(26)	5.68	<.0001	2vs.4
Daily Rate	23.47(36)	17.44(41)	14.08(13)	17.26(35)	21.85(26)	4.75	<.001	1vs.2, 1vs.3, 1vs.4
Years of Smoking	19.19(36)	16.81(42)	10.82(15)	7.91(33)	13.32(25)	4.29	<.005	2vs.4
Mean Factor Score	45.94(36)	51.82(42)	58.55(15)	48.70(35)	49.49(26)	79.46	<.0001	1vs.2, 1vs.3, 1vs.4 1vs.5, 2 vs.3, 2vs.4, 2vs.5, 3vs.4, 3vs.5
Standard Deviation of Factor Scores	7.91(36)	9.84(42)	11.54(15)	7.88(35)	9.29(26)	6.96	<.00001	1vs.2, 1vs.3 2vs.4, 3vs.4

*The tabled n's vary slightly as a function of missing values for the different dependent variables.
**By Scheffe's method.

468

Groups 2 and 3 are not as easily characterized. Their patterns, like those of Group 1, show relatively little variability. Group 2 is the second largest group and may be distinguished from 1 and 3 by the relatively high mean urge (51.77). Furthermore, the highest factor scores seem consistent with a negative affect hypothesis like Tomkins' (1966) or Eysenck's (1973) neurotic smoking.

Group 3 individuals are moderate smokers with relatively low urges (mean of 48.72). We might speculate that stimulation functions are important, since the Concentration and Inactive factors are the highest in the Group 3 profile, but the relationship is not a clear one. It is noteworthy that the Automatic factor is the lowest, distinguishing the group from Group 1.

Five female groups were identified by the cluster analysis. Group 1 seems relatively similar to the male Group 1 in that members tend to be heavy smokers who report a low mean urge (45.94), which is relatively constant across situations. The Automatic factor score is highest, again suggesting that smoking tends not to vary with situational antecedents.

Group 2 and 3 together bear some resemblance to the male Group 2 for which negative affect cues seemed salient. There are differences however. The patterning of factor scores is very similar for the two groups. Group 2 is higher on Self-Image and Group 3 on Relaxation but in other respects the profile differences seem small. We may speculate that negative affect is a major determinant for both groups but that the particular affective situations salient differ. Turning to the ANOVAs (Table 3.3), we see that Group 3 appears to be a relatively atypical group of smokers. They smoke fewer cigarettes per day (mean of 14.08) and, as was true for the low smoking male group, report a stronger mean urge overall (58.55). Their smoking also varies the most across situations, suggesting that they may be situation specific smokers like male Group 4, although for the females it is particularly negative affect situations which are associated with smoking. It is noted that Eysenck (1973) suggested that females will be more likely to smoke in an attempt to cope with negative affect. Finally, the average Group 3 member seems to have begun smoking later, at about age 20, than others for whom age 16 is typical.

In contrast to Groups 2 and 3, Group 4 and 5 are distinguished by the relatively low values for negative affect factors. Both groups also report relatively low mean urges. Group 2 is a young group for whom Social, Relaxation, and Stimulant determinants are high. In contrast, Relaxation is not an important function for Group 5 but both Food Avoidance and Self-Image are. In sum, both groups seem to smoke for reasons unrelated to negative affect but the particular determinants vary.

DISCUSSION

The patterns of smoking behavior which emerged in the present study both support the importance of factors previously proposed and call attention to the limitations of earlier models. Affective, social, and arousal needs may all elicit smoking. Habitual factors are also operative. We cannot assume that every kind of determinant is of equal importance. Indeed, some may be weak or infrequent in their influence on smoking behavior. The low ratings in our sample for the sensorimotor items identified by others may illustrate this point. Nevertheless, given our relatively primitive understanding of what *does* actually influence a smoker's everyday consumption, we would do well to consider all possibilities.

Two further features of the data are particularly noteworthy. First, the results are consistent with the behaviorist's assumption that smoking will be relatively specific to environmental circumstances. We find a relatively large number of factors, most of which are quite homogeneous. In a similar vein, we note a greater differentiation of response to affective cues than has been assumed. Second, most factors can be viewed as defining circumstances in which smoking serves a function. For the individual smoker, the functions may be complex and varied, supporting the need in smoking modification programs for multiple techniques, provision of functionally equivalent, alternative nonsmoking behaviors, and a concern with tailoring treatment to the individual's pattern of reasons for smoking.

An alternative view is that the majority of smoking behavior is not functional, but rather habitual or automatic. Retrospective self-report data such as ours may tend to underestimate the significance of these automatic factors while unduly emphasizing the role of affective determinants (Best & Best, 1975; Hunt & Matarazzo, 1973). It is also clear that the majority of our sample did indeed evidence smoking patterns which varied little by type of situation. The largest group for both sexes is one which we characterize as comprised of situation nonspecific or automatic smokers.

Tomkins (1966, 1968) proposes smoker types corresponding to the affective function of smoking. While affective factors may be important determinants of smoking behavior, our cluster analyses do not suggest affective or any other smoker type corresponding to broad individual differences. Rather, the data are consistent with the notion that a wide variety of specific environmental, cognitive, affective, pharmacological, and sensorimotor events may serve as discriminative cues for smoking. Each smoker is presumably conditioned to many such cues, although the association is stronger to some cues than others and hence the specificity of rated urges for at least some of the smokers studied here.

What are the implications for treatment? First note that there seems to be an inverse relationship between variability and strong urges on the one hand and smoking rate on the other. Many behavior modifiers have noted that as smokers reduce their rate, the remaining cigarettes both come to be smoked on specific occasions and to have a greater perceived value. Thus, a habitual smoking pattern may be distinguished from a withdrawal smoking pattern such that the functionality of smoking comes to be of increased importance at the time of behavior change. On the other hand, we cannot assume that all clients in a modification program will require functional alternatives. For many, a more appropriate course will be the practice of those general self-control strategies characterized as "nonsmoking behaviors".

One limitation of retrospective self-report data has been noted. The current findings do need to be replicated with dependent measures more likely to reliably reflect situational determinants of smoking. One option is to use self-monitoring data, requiring smokers to continuously record their smoking and relevant concomitants. A second method would be to employ independent observers, although the fact that many of the situations used in the present analyses are subjectively defined creates problems for such an approach.

There also needs to be a more thorough consideration of the parameters of smoking behavior to be studied. Our analyses are of the rated intensity of smoking urges. Other investigators have used rated frequency of urges. Most behavior modifiers would prefer an analysis of actual smoking behavior, and, as noted, the method variance associated with self-report data may lead to underestimation of habit factors (Hunt & Matarazzo, 1973).

Ideally, for a modification program we would like to be able to predict the degree of difficulty to be encountered in substituting nonsmoking for smoking behavior in each class of smoking situations. "Degree of difficulty" will potentially be a function of various factors including habit strength, availability of alternative behaviors, etc. With a view to predicting specific problems to be encountered by an individual quitting smoking, all these parameters may deserve consideration.

The model for smoking behavior presented here may contribute to the development of behavioral treatment programs which take cognizance of individual determinants of smoking. Such development will be facilitated by intermediary research. It would be instructive to view the smoking habit with an interest in determining factors influencing therapeutic change rather than variables governing continuing smoking. The concern then is "What situations are likely to prove problematic in treatment and why?" rather than "When do people normally smoke and why?" Analysis of changes in the determinants of smoking over treatment would be useful in this regard. We also need research designed to identify and inculcate good alternative behaviors. Behavior modifiers may agree that relaxation training might prove effective when nervous tension is a reason for smoking or that stimulus control is to be recommended for food substitution. There would be considerably less than consensus on alternatives for "frustration," "boredom," or "time structuring."

Smoking modification programs have met with increasing success in recent years (Bernstein & McAlister, 1976; Best & Bloch, in press; Lichtenstein &

Danaher, 1976). Consideration of individual determinants of smoking behaviors may provide a basis for the demonstration of specific treatment effects which to date have proved elusive.

REFERENCES

Bernstein, D. A. The modification of smoking behavior: some suggestions for programmed "symptom substitution." Paper presented to the annual meetings of the Association for the Advancement of Behavior Therapy, Chicago, 1974.

Bernstein, D. A. & McAlister, A. The modification of smoking behavior: Progress and problems. *Addictive Behaviors*, 1976, *1*, 89-102.

Best, J. A. & Best, H. Client self-monitoring in clinical decision making. *Canada's Mental Health*, 1975, *23*, 9-11.

Best, J. A. & Bloch, M. On improving compliance: Cigarette smoking. In R. B. Haynes & D. L. Sackett (Eds.) *Compliance*, Baltimore: Johns Hopkins Press, in press.

Best, J. A. Owen, L. E., & Trentadue, B. L. Comparison of satiation and rapid smoking in self-managed smoking cessation. *Addictive Behaviors,* in press.

Blishen, B. R. & McRoberts, H. A. A revised socioeconomic index for occupations in Canada. *Canadian Review of Sociology and Anthropology*, 1976, *13*, 71-79.

Brengelmann, J. C. & Sedlmayr, E. Experiments in the reduction of smoking behavior. Paper presented to the Third World Conference on Smoking and Health, New York, June 3, 1975.

Cattell, R. B. The scree test for the number of factors. *Multivariate Behavioral Research*, 1966, *1*, 245-276.

Chapman, R. F., Smith, J. W., & Layden, T. A. Elimination of cigarette smoking by punishment and self-management training. *Behavior Research and Therapy*, 1971, *9*, 255-264.

Dunn, W. L. Jr. Methods and models applied to motivation in cigarette smoking. In W. L. Dunn, Jr. (Ed.) *Smoking Behavior: Motives and Incentives*, Washington, D.C.: Winston and Sons, 1973.

Eysenck, H. J. Personality and the maintenance of the smoking habit. In W. L. Dunn, Jr. (Ed.) *Smoking Behavior: Motives and Incentives*, Washington, D.C.: Winston and Sons, 1973.

Frith, C. D. Smoking behavior and its relation to the smoker's immediate experience. *British Journal of Social and Clinical Psychology*, 1971, *10*, 73-78.

Harris, C. W. & Kaiser, H. F. Oblique factor analytic solutions by orthogonal transformations. *Psychometrika*, 1964, *29*, 347-362.

Hunt, W. A. & Matarazzo, J. D. Habit mechanisms in smoking. In W. A. Hunt (Ed.) *Learning Mechanisms in Smoking*. Chicago: Aldine, 1970.

Hunt, W. A. & Matarazzo, J. D. Three years later: Recent developments in the experimental modification of smoking behavior. *Journal of Abnormal Psychology*, 1973, *81*, 107-114.

Hunt, W. A., Matarazzo, J. D., & Weiss, S. M. Habit and the maintenance of behavior: implications for compliance behavior in medical regimens. Unpublished manuscript, Loyola University, 1976.

Ikard, F. F., Green, D. E., & Horne, D. A scale to differentiate between types of smoking as related to the management of affect. *International Journal of the Addictions,* 1969, *4,* 649-659.

Lichtenstein, E., & Danaher, B. G. Modification of smoking behavior: A critical analysis of theory, research and practice. In M. Hersen, R. M. Eisler, & P. M. Miller (Eds.) *Progress in Behavior Modification: Volume 3,* New York: Academic Press, 1976.

Mausner, B. Some comments on the failure of behavior therapy as a technique for modifying cigarette smoking. *Journal of Consulting and Clinical Psychology,* 1971, *36,* 167-170.

Mausner, B. & Platt, E. S. *Smoking: a behavioral analysis.* Toronto: Pergamon Press, 1971.

McKennell, A. C. Smoking motivation factors. *British Journal of Social and Clinical Psychology,* 1970, *9,* 8-22.

McKennell, A. C. *A Comparison of Two Smoking Typologies.* London: Tobacco Research Council, 1973.

Morrow, J. E., Sachs, L. B., Gmeinder, S., & Burgess, H. Elimination of cigarette smoking behavior by stimulus satiation, self-control techniques, and group therapy. Paper presented at the meetings of the Western Psychological Association, Anaheim, Calif., 1973.

Pomerleau, O. F. & Ciccone, P. Preliminary results of a treatment program for smoking cessation using multiple behavior modification techniques. Paper presented at the annual meetings of the Association for the Advancement of Behavior Therapy, Chicago, 1974.

Russell, M. A. H., Peto, J., & Patel, U. A. The classification of smoking by factorial structure of motives. *Journal of the Royal Statistical Society, Series A,* 1974, *137,* 313-346.

Tomkins, S. S. Psychological model for smoking behavior. *American Journal of Public Health,* 1966, *56,* 17-20.

Tomkins, S. A modified model of smoking behavior. In E. F. Borgatta and R. R. Evans (Eds.) *Smoking, Health and Behavior,* Chicago: Aldine, 1968.

Tucker, L. R. A method for synthesis of factor analysis studies. Personnel Research Section Report No. 984. Washington, D.C.: Department of the Army, 1951.

Ward, J. H. Hierarchical grouping to optimize an objective function. *Journal of the American Statistical Association,* 1963, *58,* 236-244.

Author Index

Subject Index